THE PETER NORTON
PC
Programmer's
Bible

The Ultimate Reference

to the IBM® PC and

Compatible Hardware

and Systems Software

Microsoft
P R E S S

PETER NORTON   **PETER AITKEN**   **RICHARD WILTON**

PUBLISHED BY
Microsoft Press
A Division of Microsoft Corporation
One Microsoft Way
Redmond, Washington 98052-6399

Library of Congress Cataloging-in-Publication Data
Norton, Peter, 1943–
    The Peter Norton PC programmer's bible / Peter Norton, Peter
Aitken, Richard Wilton. -- 3rd ed.
        p.   cm.
    Includes bibliographical references and index.
    ISBN 1-55615-555-7
    1. Microcomputers--Programming.   I. Aitken, Peter G.   II. Wilton,
Richard, 1953–   .   III. Title.
QA76.6.N686   1993
005.265--dc20   93-19424
                                                                 CIP

Printed and bound in the United States of America.

1 2 3 4 5 6 7 8 9   8 7 6 5 4 3

Distributed to the book trade in Canada by Macmillan of Canada, a division of Canada Publishing Corporation.

Distributed to the book trade outside the United States and Canada by Penguin Books Ltd.

Penguin Books Ltd., Harmondsworth, Middlesex, England
Penguin Books Australia Ltd., Ringwood, Victoria, Australia
Penguin Books N.Z. Ltd., 182-190 Wairau Road, Auckland 10, New Zealand

British Cataloging-in-Publication Data available.

Acquisitions Editor: Mike Halvorson
Manuscript Editor: Laura Sackerman
Project Editor: Mary Ann Jones
Technical Editors: James Johnson and Jim Fuchs

Critical acclaim for the previous editions of
PETER NORTON'S PC PROGRAMMER'S BIBLE

"Norton takes the fear out of bytes and bits and chips and FATs and tracks and leaves you not only understanding what's going on but also in control....For the professional programmer, [this book] will be a handy desk reference. However, intermediate programmers should view this book as a tutorial and read it like a novel from cover to cover....A must for every serious PC user's technical library."

PC Magazine

"If you plan on some serious programming using an IBM Personal Computer, this book will be a good companion to ease you through the rough spots....I recommend this guide to PC programmers and to those people who need the technical information."

BYTE

"This book belongs on the shelf of serious programmers of the IBM PC and its compatibles. It is a valuable reference for anyone, including non-programmers, who wants to know what happens in the PC, its software systems, and its peripherals."

Online Today

"Along with Microsoft Press, [Peter Norton] has presented us with another gem. [This book] provides intermediate and advanced users with the information needed to develop programs that can be ported from one member of the IBM PC family to another."

Computer Book Review

"Peter Norton's reputation as one of the foremost authorities on the IBM PC is founded on his clearheaded approach to programming the IBM PC series....[This book] shows how intermediate and advanced programmers can create effective business and professional programs for the entire family of IBM microcomputers....For every IBM PC programmer, [this] is the one reference to have closest to your computer."

Library of Computer and
Information Sciences

"Whether for advanced programmers involved in developing professional software or for those simply curious about how the PC really works, [this book] is mandatory reading."

Popular Computing

THE PETER NORTON

PC

Programmer's
Bible

CONTENTS

INTRODUCTION

Ten years ago, in September 1983, Peter Norton started work on the first edition of *The Peter Norton Programmer's Guide to the IBM PC*. The world of personal computers has certainly changed a lot since that first edition was started. A circa-1983 IBM PC/XT sported an 8088 microprocessor, a 10-MB hard disk, 512 KB of RAM, a CGA adapter card and monitor, and—if you were lucky—a speedy dot-matrix printer. Today, for roughly the same price, you can purchase a high-end IBM PC or compatible computer complete with an 80486 microprocessor, a 300-MB or larger hard drive, 8 MB or more of RAM, a Super VGA adapter and monitor, and perhaps even a laser printer.

Unfortunately, the task of the PC programmer has changed almost as much as the hardware since those early days. In the early 1980s, a PC applications programmer was concerned primarily with writing single-purpose applications for MS-DOS that supported a handful of computer models and peripherals. Today a PC programmer must be concerned with several graphical operating systems in addition to MS-DOS, as well as a wide variety of new devices and peripherals, including 32-bit microprocessors and support chips, EISA and Micro Channel bus architectures, advanced graphics adapters, and a variety of network adapters, memory chips, modems, pointing devices, and printers—all assembled by any number of PC clone manufacturers.

Although PC systems have clearly changed since the first edition of this book, our goal remains a simple but ambitious one: to help you master the principles of programming the entire family of IBM personal computers and compatibles. This book is about the knowledge, skills, and *concepts* that are needed to create programs for the PC family—not only for one member of the family (although you might perhaps cater to the peculiarities and quirks of one member) but for the family as a whole—in a way that is universal enough to allow your programs to work not only on all the current family members but on future members as well.

This book is for anyone involved in the development of programs for the PC family. It is for programmers, but not *only* for programmers. It is for anyone who is involved in or needs to understand the technical details and working ideas that are the basis for PC program development, including anyone who manages programmers, anyone who plans or designs PC programs, and anyone who uses PC programs and wants to understand the details behind them.

Some Comments on Philosophy

One of the most important elements of this book is the discussion of *programming philosophy*. You will find throughout this book explanations of the ideas underlying IBM's design of the PC family and of the principles of sound PC programming, viewed from experience.

If this book were to provide only facts—tabulations of technical information—it would not serve you well. That's why we've interwoven with the technical discussion an explanation of what the PC family is all about, of the principles that tie the various family members together, and of the techniques and methods that can help you produce programs that will endure and prosper as the PC family grows.

How to Use This Book

This book is both for reading and for reference, so you can approach it in at least two ways. You might want to read it from front to back, digging in where the discussion is immediately useful and quickly glancing through the material you don't yet need. This approach provides a grand overview of the workings (and the ideas behind the workings) of PC programs. You can also use this book purely as a reference, dipping into specific chapters for specific information. We've provided a table of contents at the beginning of each chapter and an extensive index to help you find what you need.

When you use this book as a random-access reference to the details of PC programming, you'll find that much of the material is intricately interrelated. To help you understand the interrelationships, we have repeated some details when it was practical to do so and have referred you to other sections when such repetition was less practical.

What's New in This Edition

As you might guess, this edition of "the Norton book" has been brought up-to-date for the new generation of PC hardware, system software, and programming tools. We've broadened the discussion of IBM-specific hardware and software in previous editions to include valuable information about compatible hardware and software from other companies. We've also included detailed discussions of Microsoft Windows, Microsoft Windows NT, and IBM OS/2, to give you an overview of what it takes to write applications for today's graphical user interfaces.

Here are some of the changes you'll find in this new edition:

New information about PC hardware. The last edition of this book stopped at the 80386 microprocessor and the base components included in an IBM PC system unit. This new edition covers the 80486 and the Intel Pentium microprocessors, EISA and Micro Channel bus architecture, new types of memory, and several important PC peripherals including modems, network adapters, multimedia hardware, and printers.

Up-to-date information about MS-DOS 6. MS-DOS 6 is a robust operating system, complete with several powerful tools and utilities and a rich programming environment. The fundamentals of MS-DOS programming are introduced in Chapter 9, and the essential MS-DOS and BIOS services are covered in detail in Chapters 10 through 13.

The fundamentals of programming for graphical operating systems. In addition to developing powerful MS-DOS applications, PC programmers are being asked to create full-featured applications that take advantage of graphical operating systems: Microsoft Windows, Microsoft Windows NT, and IBM OS/2. Chapters 14 and 15 will help you learn the basics of these operating systems and plan your graphical applications. You'll find that you can leverage much of your existing MS-DOS code in these graphical environments and that you will be able to port from one graphical environment to the next with relative ease.

Powerful new development tools and techniques. PC development tools have come a long way since the last edition of this book. In Chapters 16 and 17, we discuss several new tools and techniques for developing applications for both MS-DOS and Microsoft Windows.

The book concludes with a reference section containing four appendixes. Appendixes A and B contain summary information for all the BIOS and MS-DOS functions listed in the book. Appendix C offers some useful information about hexadecimal arithmetic and segment notation. And finally, Appendix D lists the complete ASCII and IBM extended character sets and provides information about common file formats.

We hope you enjoy this revised edition of *The Peter Norton PC Programmer's Bible,* and we look forward to seeing all the interesting applications that come out of the next 10 years of PC development.

PART I:

PC HARDWARE

Chapter 1

Anatomy
of the PC

From the programmer's point of view, all computers in the PC family consist of a microprocessor, memory chips, and several programmable circuit chips. In most PCs, all of the main circuit components are located on the system board (sometimes also called the motherboard); other important parts are located on expansion boards, which can be plugged into the system board. In some recent designs, the microprocessor itself is located on a plug-in board, which permits the user to upgrade the microprocessor without changing the system board.

Examples of PC system boards are shown in Figures 1-1 through 1-4. Each system board contains the microprocessor and at least 64 KB of random access memory (RAM). (Only older PCs have as little as 64 KB of RAM; modern PCs almost always have a minimum of 1 MB of RAM.) The system board also holds one or more read only memory (ROM) chips that contain the ROM BIOS (basic input/output system) and several very important support chips. (In IBM-manufactured PCs, the ROM also contains a version of the Basic programming language.) Some of the support chips control external devices, such as the disk drives or the display screen, and others help the microprocessor perform its tasks.

In this section, we describe the function of each major chip and give a few important technical specifications. You should be aware that these chips are frequently known by more than one name. For example, some peripheral input/output hardware is supervised by a chip known as the 8255. You might see this chip called the 8255A or the 8255A-5. The suffixes A and 5 refer to revision numbers and to parts rated for operation at different speeds. For programming purposes, any Intel chip part number that starts with 8255 is identical to any other chip whose part number starts with 8255, regardless of the suffix. However, when you replace one of these chips on a circuit board, use a chip with the same suffix. If the suffixes are different, the part might not operate at the proper speed.

The Microprocessor

The heart of all PCs is the *microprocessor,* also known as the central processing unit, or CPU. The CPU is the chip that actually runs programs. Modern CPUs can carry out a wide variety of tasks, including arithmetic calculations, numeric comparisons, and data transfers. Please note, however, that the CPU can do nothing by itself. It operates only when given the proper instructions that tell it exactly what actions to take. These instructions are provided by a program, or software, that is stored in memory. The software may be the operating system that was supplied with the computer, a commercial program that you purchased, or a program that you wrote yourself.

Expansion slots

8259A
interrupt
controller

ROM

RAM

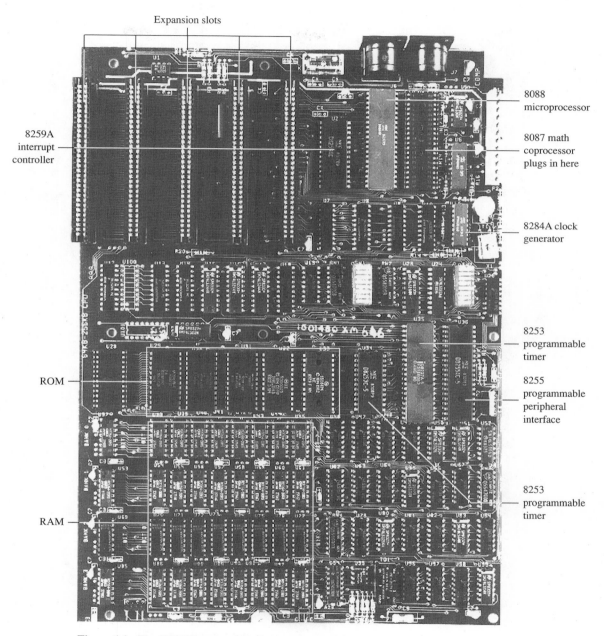

8088
microprocessor

8087 math
coprocessor
plugs in here

8284A clock
generator

8253
programmable
timer

8255
programmable
peripheral
interface

8253
programmable
timer

Figure 1-1. *The IBM PC system board.*

5

Expansion slots

80287 math
coprocessor
plugs in here

8259A
interrupt
controllers

8254-2
programmable
timer

80286
microprocessor

8284A clock
generator
(under shield)

ROM

RAM

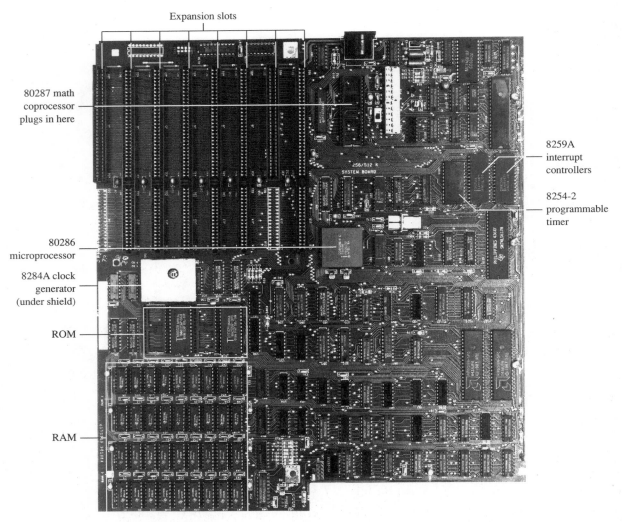

Figure 1-2. *The PC/AT system board.*

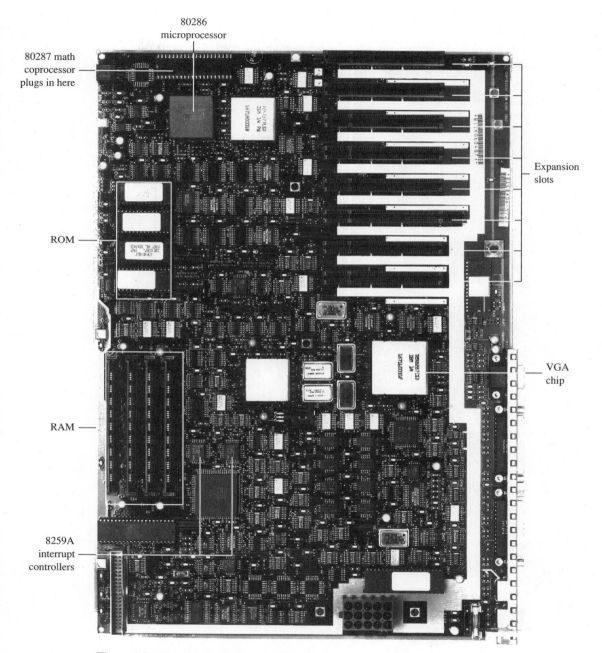

Figure 1-3. *The PS/2 Model 60 system board.*

Expansion slots

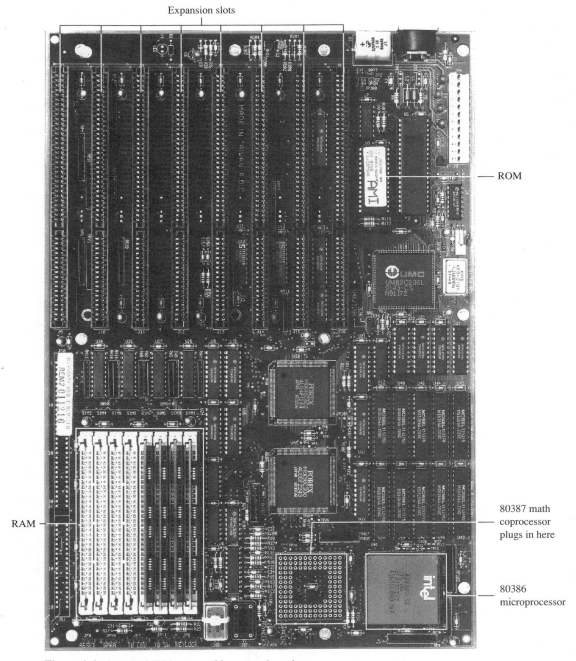

ROM

80387 math
coprocessor
plugs in here

RAM

80386
microprocessor

Figure 1-4. *A typical IBM-compatible system board.*

The CPU controls the computer's operation by sending control signals, memory addresses, and data from one part of the computer to another via a group of interconnecting electronic pathways called a *bus*. Located along the bus are input and output (I/O) ports that connect the various memory and support chips to the bus. Data passes through these I/O ports while it travels to and from the CPU and the other parts of the computer. Components that are located on the system board are connected directly to the bus. Other components can be connected to the bus by plugging them into an *expansion slot*. An expansion slot is a standardized electrical connector in which you can install adapters for any of a wide variety of peripheral devices, such as tape drives, hard disks, and displays. Most PCs have from three to eight expansion slots.

Every member of the PC family uses one of the Intel 8086 family of microprocessors or a clone of an Intel microprocessor. From oldest to youngest, this family contains the 8086, 8088, 80286, 80386, and 80486 microprocessors. (The 80186 followed the 8088 but was followed so quickly by the 80286 that the 80186 never was used in a significant number of systems.) Each new member of the family retained a basic compatibility with the earlier members and added features and speed. We'll point out the similarities and differences among the different microprocessors as we describe them.

The 8088 Microprocessor

The original IBM PC uses the 8088 microprocessor; this CPU is also used in the PC/XT, the Portable PC, and the PC*jr*. The 8088 is a 16-bit processor, which means that it processes data 16 bits, or 2 bytes, at a time. Inside the 8088 there are 14 registers that provide a working area for data transfer and processing. Each of the 14 registers can hold 16 bits of data. These internal registers are used for temporary storage of the data, memory addresses, program instruction pointers, and status and control flags that the processor is working with. The 8088 can access 1 MB, or more than 1 million bytes, of memory. Even though the 8088 uses 16 bits internally, it communicates with the rest of the system via an 8-bit data bus. The 8088 contains 29,000 transistors; at a clock rate of 4.77 MHz (megahertz, or million cycles per second), it has a rating of 0.33 MIPS (million instructions per second, a measure of CPU speed).

The 8086 Microprocessor

The 8086 is used in the early IBM PS/2 models 25 and 30 and in many IBM PC clones. The 8086 differs from the 8088 in only one respect: It uses a full 16-bit data bus instead of the 8-bit bus that the 8088 uses. (The difference between 8-bit and 16-bit buses is discussed on pages 19–20.) Virtually anything that you read about the 8088 also applies to the 8086; for programming purposes, consider them identical.

The 80286 Microprocessor

The 80286 first appeared in the IBM PC/AT; it is also used in several models in the IBM PS/2 line and in many clones. With 134,000 transistors, the 80286 has a rating of 2 MIPS (at 8 MHz). The 80286 is fully compatible with the 8086, which means that any program written for the 8086 will run without modification on the 80286. In addition, the 80286 executes programs more quickly and with more flexibility than the 8086. The increased speed is due in part to a faster clock rate; the 80286 operates at a minimum of 6 MHz, compared with the 8088's 4.77 MHz.

Perhaps the most important enhancement to the 80286 is its support for *multitasking*. Multitasking is the ability of a CPU to perform several tasks at a time—such as printing a document and calculating a spreadsheet—by quickly switching its attention among the controlling programs. Of course, at any instant only one task is being performed and the other task or tasks are "on hold." But because the CPU switches among tasks so quickly, it appears to the user that two or more tasks are being performed simultaneously.

The 8088 used in a PC or a PC/XT can support multitasking with the help of sophisticated control software. However, an 80286 can do a much better job of multitasking for several reasons: It executes programs more quickly, it can address much more memory than the 8088, and it has some special features that prevent tasks from interfering with each other.

The 80286 can run in either of two operating modes: *real mode* or *protected mode*. In real mode, the 80286 is programmed exactly like an 8086 and can access the same 1-MB range of memory addresses as the 8086. In protected mode, however, the 80286 can address up to 16 MB of memory and can reserve a predetermined amount of memory for each executing program, preventing that memory from being used by any other program. This means that several programs can execute concurrently (that is, multitask) without the risk of one program accidentally changing the contents of another program's memory area. An operating system using 80286 protected mode can allocate memory among several tasks much more effectively than can an 8086-based operating system.

The 80386 Microprocessor

The next member of the family is the 80386 microprocessor, used in the IBM PS/2 Model 80 and in many clone machines. The 80386 supports the same basic functions as does the 8086 and offers the same protected-mode memory management as does the 80286. It's a lot faster though, with clock speeds ranging from 16 MHz through 33 MHz and even higher in some systems. With 275,000 transistors, the 80386 has a MIPS rating of 11 (at 33 MHz). Beyond its increased speed, the 80386 offers two important advantages over its predecessors:

- The 80386 is a 32-bit microprocessor with 32-bit registers. It can perform computations and address memory 32 bits at a time instead of 16 bits at a time.

- The 80386 offers more flexible memory management than the 80286 and 8086 and, in the case of the 80386DX, can directly access as much as 2^{32} bytes of memory—well over 4000 MB.

The 80386 comes in two versions. The 80386DX has a 32-bit external data path and a 32-bit address bus width, whereas the 80386SX has a 16-bit external data path and a 24-bit address bus width. Otherwise, the two versions are identical, using 32 bits internally. We'll say more about the 80386 in Chapter 2.

The 80486 Microprocessor

As of this writing, the most advanced microprocessor used in PCs is the 80486. This CPU offers faster clock speeds than does the 80386, a built-in math coprocessor (in the 80486DX variants), and an integral cache. The 80486 sports 1,200,000 transistors and a MIPS rating of 41 (at 50 MHz). These features give the 80486 a significant speed advantage over other CPUs in the family.

A *cache* is used because the operating speed of today's CPUs is much faster than that of standard RAM chips. If a fast CPU tries to read data from RAM, it will have to pause while the slower RAM returns the data. These pauses, or *wait states,* can significantly slow down the system throughput. A cache consists of a small amount of special high-speed RAM, fast enough to return data to the CPU without wait states (but too expensive to use for main system RAM). The cache controller keeps a copy of the data and code that the CPU is working with in the cache. When the CPU needs data, it looks first in the cache, from which data can be retrieved without delay. Only if the needed data is not in the cache does the CPU go to the slower main RAM.

Many 80386 systems provide a cache that is implemented externally to the CPU on the system board. The 80486's internal cache can operate more efficiently than an external cache because the internal cache is more closely integrated with the CPU.

The Pentium Microprocessor

Intel has recently released the next member of the 8086 processor family. This new chip is called the Pentium, even though the logical next step in the CPU naming progression would have been "80586." The new chip is not only significantly faster than the 80486 but includes some new features designed specifically for file server applications. Among the new features are a 64-bit external data bus, additional memory addressing capability, improved performance with floating-point numbers, and a larger and more flexible internal cache. With more than 3,000,000 transistors, the Pentium can deliver 100+ MIPS (at 66 MHz).

The Math Coprocessor

The 8086, 80286, and 80386 CPUs can work only with integers; this is also true of the 80486SX CPU. To perform floating-point computations on one of these microprocessors, you must use special programming techniques that use integers to store and manipulate floating-point values. Even a relatively simple floating-point calculation can require a large number of integer operations. Thus, "number-crunching" programs can run very slowly; if you have a large number of calculations to perform, you'll spend a lot of time twiddling your thumbs.

Intel's solution to this problem was to create a separate math coprocessor chip that is specialized to perform floating-point operations. Each member of the 80x86 microprocessor family through the 80486SX has an accompanying math coprocessor: An 8087 math coprocessor is used with an 8086 or 8088; an 80287 math coprocessor is used with an 80286; an 80387 math coprocessor is used with an 80386; and an 80487SX math coprocessor is used with the 80486SX. (See Figure 1-5.) Most PCs and PS/2s designed for these CPUs are built with an empty socket on the motherboard into which you can plug a math coprocessor chip. (Many laptop and notebook systems do not have this empty socket.) Note that the clock-speed rating of a math coprocessor chip must meet or exceed the speed of the CPU it is being mated with.

Data Type	Approximate Range (From)	(To)	Significant Digits Bits	(Decimal)
Word integer	−32,768	+32,767	16	4
Short integer	−2 × 10E9	+2 × 10E9	32	9
Long integer	−9 × 10E18	+9 × 10E18	64	18
Packed decimal	−99...99	+99...99	80	18
Short real	8.43 × 10E−37	3.37 × 10E38	32	6–7
Long real	4.19 × 10E−307	1.67 × 10E308	64	15–16
Temporary real	3.4 × 10E−4932	1.2 × 10E4932	80	19

Figure 1-5. *The range of numeric data types supported by math coprocessors.*

From a programmer's point of view, the 8087, 80287, 80387, and 80487SX math coprocessors are fundamentally the same: They all perform floating-point arithmetic with much greater speed, and sometimes with a higher degree of precision, than can be achieved with software emulation. Programs that perform many trigonometric and logarithmic operations run up to 10 times faster with a math coprocessor than without.

Writing programs in assembly language that use these math coprocessors can be an exacting process. These techniques are too specialized to cover in this book. Fortunately, almost all high-level language compilers automatically take care of generating machine-level code for math coprocessors. The code produced by the compiler will make use of a coprocessor if one is installed and will revert to software emulation if a coprocessor is not installed. This enables programs to run on any machine regardless of whether a math coprocessor is installed.

Starting with the 80486DX CPU, Intel has integrated the specialized floating-point circuitry into the CPU, so a separate math coprocessor chip is not needed. The exception is the Intel 80486SX CPU, which was originally a standard 80486 CPU that had its floating-point capabilities intentionally disabled and which is now manufactured without floating-point capabilities.

CPU Summary

You can see that the Intel 80x86 CPU family is a large and complex one. To make things even more confusing, a number of other companies have developed and marketed clone chips that are functionally identical to the Intel CPUs and that sometimes offer slightly superior performance at lower cost. Figure 1-6 provides a summary of the Intel 80x86 CPU family and clones.

Type	Speed Range (MHz)	Internal Data Width (Bits)	Data Bus Width (Bits)	Address Bus Width (Bits)	Internal Cache	Notes
Intel 8088	4.7–10	16	8	20	No	Used in IBM PC and IBM PC/XT.
Intel 8086	4.7–10	16	16	20	No	
Intel 80286	6–20	16	16	24	No	Used in IBM PC/AT.
Intel 386DX	16–33	32	32	32	No	First 32-bit CPU to include memory management.
Intel 386SX	16–25	32	16	24	No	Identical to 386DX except for data and address bus widths.
Intel 386SL	20,25[1]	32	16	24	No	Designed for notebook computers.
AMD[2] 386SXLV	20,25[1]	32	16	24	No	Clone of Intel 386SX. Uses 3.3 volts rather than the standard 5 volts.
AMD[2] 386DXLV	20,25[1]	32	32	32	No	Clone of Intel 386DX. Uses 3.3 volts rather than the standard 5 volts.
AMD[2] 386SX	25,33[1]	32	16	24	No	Clone of Intel 386SX.
AMD[2] 386DX	25,33,40[1]	32	32	32	No	Clone of Intel 386DX.
C & T[3] 38600DX	16–40	32	32	32	No	Replacement for Intel 386DX.
C & T[3] 38605DX	16–40	32	32	32	.5 KB	Replacement for Intel 386DX. Internal cache increases speed.
IBM 386SLC	20	32	16	24	8 KB	Replacement for Intel 386SX. Internal cache increases speed.
Intel 486DX	25–50	32	32	32	8 KB	Has internal floating-point unit.
Intel 486DX2	40–66	32	32	32	8 KB	Has internal floating-point unit. Uses clock doubling to run internally at double the bus speed for improved performance.

[1]Chip is produced in different versions, each of which runs at only one speed.
[2]AMD = Advanced Micro Devices
[3]C & T = Chips and Technologies

Figure 1-6. *A summary of the Intel 80x86 CPU family and clones.* (continued)

Figure 1-6. *continued*

Type	Speed Range (MHz)	Internal Data Width (Bits)	Data Bus Width (Bits)	Address Bus Width (Bits)	Internal Cache	Notes
Intel 486SX	16–25	32	32	32	8 KB	Identical to Intel 486DX but lacks internal floating-point unit.
Cyrix 486SLC	20–33	32	16	24	1 KB	Like the Intel 486SX but pin-compatible with Intel 386SX. 2.5 times as fast as the 386SX.
Cyrix 486DLC	25–40	32	32	32	1 KB	Like Cyrix 486SLC, with 32-bit address and data buses.
Intel Pentium	66	32	64	32	16 KB	The "80586," the fastest CPU in the family.

Clones and Compatibles

No sooner had the success of the original IBM PC become evident than other manufacturers wanted to get in on the act. Very quickly a number of *clones*, or compatibles, appeared on the market. A clone is a non-IBM computer that is designed to be completely compatible with the real IBM item (and usually sells at a lower price). A clone uses the same CPU, the same bus design, and a functionally identical ROM BIOS so that it can run the same programs and use the same adapter cards and peripherals as an IBM PC.

Some early clones had compatibility problems because it was difficult to write a ROM BIOS that did the same job as the IBM ROM BIOS without infringing on IBM's copyright. These problems were quickly solved, however, and today the PC market is dominated by clones from dozens of manufacturers. In discussing different models of PCs, the important question is not who made them. Rather, you need to know the type of CPU, its clock speed, the type of video system, and the like. For the remainder of this book we will use the term *PC* generically to refer to any microcomputer that uses one of the Intel 80x86 family of CPU chips. This includes the original IBM PC, the IBM PC/AT, the IBM PS/2 line, and all compatible clone systems. If we are referring to a specific model or a specific CPU type, we will say so.

The Support Chips

The microprocessor cannot control the entire computer without some help—nor should it. By delegating certain control functions to other chips, the CPU is free to attend to its own work. These support chips are responsible for such processes as controlling the flow of information throughout the internal circuitry (as the interrupt controller and the DMA controller are) and controlling the flow of information to or from a particular device (such as a video display or a disk drive) attached to the computer. These so-called *device controllers* are often mounted on a separate board that plugs into one of the PC's expansion slots.

Many of the support chips in the PC are *programmable,* which means that their operation can be controlled by software. Direct programming of these chips is rarely necessary and is generally not a good idea unless you are sure of what you are doing. These advanced techniques are beyond the scope of this book, but the following descriptions will point out which chips are safe to program directly and which aren't. If you want to obtain additional information about directly programming the support chips, you should look in the IBM technical reference manuals and the chip manufacturers' technical literature for details about programming individual chips.

The Programmable Interrupt Controller

In a PC, one of the CPU's essential tasks is to respond to *hardware interrupts.* A hardware interrupt is a signal generated by a component of the computer, indicating that component's need for CPU attention. For example, when you press a key on the keyboard, a hardware interrupt signals the CPU that a key has been pressed. The system timer and the disk-drive controllers also generate hardware interrupts at various times. The CPU responds to an interrupt by temporarily suspending its current task and executing a special software routine called an *interrupt handler.* The code in the interrupt handler carries out the appropriate hardware-specific activity, such as incrementing a time-of-day counter or processing a keystroke. When the interrupt handler is finished, the CPU resumes its original task.

Each PC has an 8259 *programmable interrupt controller* (PIC) circuit that monitors interrupts and presents them one at a time to the CPU. Because each hardware interrupt has its own interrupt handler in the ROM BIOS or in MS-DOS, the CPU can recognize and respond specifically to the hardware that generates each interrupt. In systems with 8088 or 8086 CPUs (for example, the PC, PC/XT, and early PS/2 models 25 and 30), the PIC can handle 8 different hardware interrupts. In systems with an 80286 or higher CPU (for example, the PC/AT and PS/2 models 35 and higher, as well as later models 25 and 30), two 8259 PICs are chained together to allow a total of 15 different hardware interrupts to be processed.

Although the PIC is indeed programmable, hardware interrupt management is not a concern in most programs. The ROM BIOS and MS-DOS provide nearly all of the services you'll need for managing hardware interrupts. If you do plan to work directly with the PIC, we suggest you examine the ROM BIOS listings in the IBM technical reference manuals for samples of actual PIC programming.

The DMA Controller

DMA stands for *direct memory access*, a technique by which some peripheral components can transfer data to and from the computer's memory without passing the data through the CPU. DMA is handled by a chip known as the *DMA controller*. In the original IBM PC, the main purpose of the DMA controller was to speed up disk-drive read and write operations because the DMA circuit could transfer data faster than the relatively slow 8088 CPU. Most modern systems, which have faster CPUs, don't benefit from DMA data transfer. In these systems, the DMA controller is still present, but it is not used for its original purpose of transferring data between memory and disk drives. Instead, the DMA controller is used to perform RAM refresh. (Unlike static RAM, the dynamic RAM used in PCs must be periodically "recharged," or refreshed, for it to retain its information.)

The Clock Generator

The *clock generator* supplies the multiphase clock signals that coordinate the microprocessor and the peripherals. The clock generator produces a high-frequency oscillating signal. For example, in the original IBM PC, this frequency was 14.31818 MHz; in the newer machines, the frequency is higher. Other chips that require a regular timing signal obtain it from the system clock generator by dividing the base frequency by a constant to obtain the frequency they need to accomplish their tasks. For example, the IBM PC's 8088 is driven at 4.77 MHz, one-third of the base frequency. The PC's internal bus and the programmable interval timer (discussed shortly) use a frequency of 1.193 MHz, running at one-fourth of the 8088's rate and one-twelfth of the base rate.

The Programmable Interval Timer

The *programmable interval timer* generates timing signals at regular intervals controlled by software. The chip can generate timing signals on three different channels at once (four channels in some PS/2 models). The timer's signals are used for various system tasks. One essential timer function is to generate a clock-tick signal that keeps track of the current time of day. Another of the timer's output signals can be used to control the frequency of tones produced with the computer's speaker. See Chapter 7 for more information about programming the system timer.

Video Controllers

The *video controller* provides an interface between the CPU and the system's display monitor. It converts information sent to it by the CPU into the appropriate control signals to drive the display. Many different video subsystems are available for use with PCs, and each different subsystem has its own programmable control interface. Fortunately the programmer rarely has to deal directly with the video hardware because basic video control routines are provided in the ROM BIOS or in an installable device driver. We'll describe these routines in Chapter 11.

Input/Output Controllers

PCs have several input/output subsystems with specialized control circuitry that provides an interface between the CPU and the actual I/O hardware. For example, the keyboard has a dedicated controller chip that transforms the electrical signals generated by keystrokes into 8-bit codes that represent the individual keys. All disk drives have separate controller circuitry that directly controls the drive; the CPU communicates with the controller through a consistent interface. The serial and parallel communications ports also have dedicated input/output controllers.

You rarely need to worry about programming these hardware controllers directly because the ROM BIOS and DOS provide services that take care of these low-level functions. If you need to know the details of the interface between the CPU and a hardware I/O controller, see the IBM technical reference manuals and examine the ROM BIOS listings in the PC and PC/AT versions of those manuals.

Linking the Parts: The Bus

As we have mentioned, in all PCs the various internal components are linked by means of an electrical circuit known as a bus. A bus is simply a set of parallel connections, several dozen in all, that is located on the main system board. All of the controlling parts of the computer—the CPU, every control chip, and every byte of memory—are connected directly or indirectly to the bus. When data is transferred from one component to another, it travels along this common path from source to destination. When a new adapter is plugged into one of the expansion slots, it is actually plugged directly into the bus, making it an equal partner in the operation of the entire unit.

All information that the computer uses is temporarily stored in at least one location along the bus. The primary data storage is in main memory, or RAM. In PCs, main memory consists of thousands or millions of individual memory cells, each of which can hold 8 bits, or 1 byte, of data. Some data might be stored in an I/O port or a CPU register for a short time while it waits for the CPU to send it to its proper location. Generally, ports and registers hold only 1 or 2 bytes of information at a time, and they are usually used as stopover sites for data being sent from one place to another. (Ports and registers are described in Chapter 2.)

Whenever data is sent to or read from a memory cell or I/O port, the cell's or port's location is specified by a numerical value, or address, that uniquely identifies it. When data is transferred, its address is first transmitted along a part of the bus called the *address bus*. Once the address has been specified, the data is transmitted on a separate part of the bus called the *data bus*. The bus also has a section called the *control bus* that carries control information, such as timing signals (from the system clock) and interrupt signals. The final section of the bus, the *power lines*, carries electrical power. We're going to discuss address and data buses in greater detail because they move information in a way that helps to explain some of the unique properties of the PC family.

The Address Bus

PCs that use the 8088 or 8086 CPU have a 20-bit address bus, meaning that the bus consists of 20 separate address lines. Each of these lines can have two possible values: on (represented by 1) or off (represented by 0). The entire address bus can therefore specify 2^{20}, or 1,048,576, different addresses. This value, known as 1 MB, is the total memory addressing capability of the 8088 and 8086 CPUs.

The 80286 and 80386SX CPUs have these 24 address lines, so systems that use chips have a 24-line address bus and can address 2^{24} bytes, or 16 MB, of memory. Systems based on the 80386DX and 80486 CPUs have a 32-bit address bus and can address over 4000 MB of memory.

The Data Bus

The data bus works with the address bus to carry data throughout the computer. The PC's 8088-based system uses a data bus that has eight signal lines, each of which carries a single binary digit (bit). This means that data is transmitted along the bus 1 byte at a time. Remember that internally the 8088 is a 16-bit CPU and uses 8 bits only when communicating with the data bus. This has led some people to comment that the 8088 is not a true 16-bit microprocessor. Rest assured that it is, even though the 8-bit data bus results in slower data transfers than the 16-bit data bus used by the otherwise identical 8086 CPU.

You might be wondering why IBM chose to use the slower 8088 in the original PC. The reason was simple economics. A wide variety of 8-bit circuitry elements was available in large quantities at low prices. When the PC was being designed, 16-bit circuitry was more expensive and less readily available. The use of the 8088 rather than the 8086 was important not only to hold down the cost of the PC but also to avoid a shortage of parts.

The IBM PC/AT was the first system based on the 80286 CPU, and it sports a 16-bit data bus that can transfer data 2 bytes at a time. This bus offers flexible expansion slots that can accept either 8-bit or 16-bit expansion cards. The bus circuitry automatically senses whether a given card is 8 or 16 bits. For 8-bit cards, data is transferred using only 8 of the 16 data lines (mimicking the operation of the original 8-bit PC bus). For 16-bit cards, the full 16-bit data bus is used. This flexibility permitted 8-bit expansion cards designed for the PC to be used in newer systems, but higher-performance 16-bit expansion cards could be used if necessary.

The so-called AT bus soon became a standard and was used in many systems manufactured by IBM and others. This bus, officially known as the ISA (Industry Standard Architecture) bus, is also used in many more modern machines that use the 80386 or 80486 CPU. Since these more advanced CPUs have the ability to transfer data 32 bits at a time, their data input and output must be split into 16-bit chunks for transfer on the ISA bus.

With the early 80286-class machines, the bus signals operated at the same clock speed as the CPU: 6 or 8 MHz. As CPU clock speeds increased, it was not possible to increase the bus speed to match because the components on expansion cards cannot operate at the higher speeds. Thus, even with today's 25-MHz, 33-MHz, and 50-MHz machines, the ISA bus operates at a much slower speed. This speed difference and the 16-bit data transfer limitation discussed earlier place serious constraints on the overall performance of PC systems. For this reason, several new bus designs have been introduced.

Micro Channel Architecture

With the PS/2 models 50, 60, and 80, IBM introduced a new bus hardware design called *Micro Channel Architecture* (MCA). The MCA bus is used in many IBM systems and has also been licensed for use by some clone manufacturers. The MCA bus performs the same basic tasks as the ISA bus: communicating addresses, data, and control signals to plug-in adapters. Except for accessing RAM or supporting bus-master controllers, the MCA bus functions as a 16-bit data bus like the ISA bus, but it is designed to run at higher speeds and it provides additional control signals that allow for more flexible adapter hardware designs. The MCA bus differs from the ISA bus design both in its physical layout and in its signal specifications, so an adapter that can be used with one bus is incompatible with the other.

Enhanced Industry Standard Architecture

After IBM introduced the Micro Channel Architecture bus, other manufacturers saw the need for a high-performance bus design but did not want to use Micro Channel Architecture. A group of these companies collaborated to develop the EISA (Enhanced Industry Standard Architecture) bus. The EISA bus offers a 32-bit data bus, faster operating speeds, and other features that make it much superior to the ISA bus. In terms of performance, the EISA bus and the MCA bus are roughly equivalent. Electrically and mechanically, however, the two are quite different, and expansion cards designed for one type of bus cannot be used in the other. (The EISA bus is designed to accept ISA expansion cards as well as EISA-specific cards.)

Local Bus Architecture

When 80386 systems were introduced, designers saw the need for a high-speed connection between the CPU and system RAM. If data were transferred between RAM and the CPU via the expansion bus (whether ISA, MCA, or EISA), performance would suffer. To avoid this problem, RAM was connected directly to the CPU via a *local bus* that operated at the full clock speed and data bus width of the CPU. RAM chips were either wired directly on the system board or were mounted on a plug-in card that was inserted in a special local bus connector on the system board. (In early PCs, RAM chips were usually wired directly on the system board. Electrically, however, they were connected to the bus.) In either case, RAM access bypassed the performance bottleneck of the standard expansion bus.

More recently, some manufacturers have started using the local bus for the video adapter as well. When the rate of data transfer from the CPU to the video adapter is increased, the speed of the screen display can be increased significantly. At present, however, there are no industrywide standards for local bus architecture, so each implementation is specific to a single manufacturer.

Bus Architecture and Programming

The differences among the ISA bus, the MCA bus, and the EISA bus are important in operating system software but not in application programs. Although all programs rely implicitly on the proper functioning of the address and data buses, very few programs are concerned with programming the bus directly. We'll come back to Micro Channel Architecture only when we describe PS/2 ROM BIOS services that work specifically with it.

Memory

So far, we've discussed the CPU, the support chips, and the bus, but we've only touched on memory. We've saved the discussion of memory for the end of this chapter because memory chips, unlike the other chips we've discussed, don't control or direct the flow of information through a computer system; they merely store information until it is needed.

The number of memory chips installed in a computer and the storage capacity of each chip determine the amount of memory that is available for storage of programs and data. Installed memory varies from one computer to another, but all PCs come with at least 40 KB of ROM and between 16 KB and 8 MB of RAM. Some system boards provide empty sockets for installing additional ROM chips, although it's extremely uncommon to do so. Of more importance, a system's RAM can be increased by installing additional chips in empty sockets on the system board or on an adapter card.

But this is only the physical view of memory. More important is the logical view—the way memory is seen and used by a program. A program sees memory not as a collection of individual chips but as a set of thousands or millions of 8-bit (1-byte) storage cells, each with a unique address. Programmers must also think of memory in this way—not in terms of how much physical memory there is, but in terms of how much *addressable* memory there is. The 8086 and the 8088 can address up to 1 MB (1024 KB, or exactly 1,048,576 bytes) of memory. That's the maximum number of addresses, and therefore the maximum number of individual bytes of information, the processors can refer to. Memory addressing is discussed in more detail in Chapter 2.

CPU Address Space

A CPU's *address space* is the total range of memory addresses that it can access. Addresses are almost always given in hexadecimal (base-16) notation; if you have trouble understanding hex notation, you might want to take a quick look at Appendix C.

Each byte in the address space is referred to by a numeric address. The size of the address space is determined by the number of bits that the CPU can use to specify an address. In systems that use the 8086 or 8088 CPU, addresses are 20 bits wide. Thus the 8086 and 8088 have an address space with address values that range from 00000H through FFFFFH (0 through 1,048,575 in decimal notation).

The 24-bit addressing scheme of the 80286 and 80386SX lets them use address values in the range 000000H through FFFFFFH, for a total 16-MB address space. Similarly, the 80386DX can use 32-bit addresses, so its address space ranges from 00000000H to FFFFFFFFH; that is, the 80386DX and the 80486 can directly address up to 4,294,967,296 bytes, or 4 gigabytes (GB), of memory. This is enough memory for most practical purposes, even for the most prolific programmer. In systems with 80286 and higher CPUs, the memory above address FFFFFH is referred to as *extended memory*.

Although the 80286, 80386, and 80486 can address more than 1 MB of memory, any program compatible with the 8086 and with MS-DOS must limit itself to addresses that lie in the 1-MB range available to the 8086. When the IBM PC first appeared in 1981, 1 MB seemed like a lot of memory, but large business-application programs, memory-resident utility programs, and system software required for communications and networking can easily fill up the entire 8086 address space.

One way to work around the 1-MB limit is with the LIM (Lotus-Intel-Microsoft) Expanded Memory Specification (EMS). The EMS is based on special hardware and software that map additional RAM into the 8086 address space in 16-KB blocks. The EMS hardware can map a number of different 16-KB blocks into the same 16-KB range of 8086 addresses. Although the blocks must be accessed separately, the EMS lets up to 2048 different 16-KB blocks map to the same range of 8086 addresses. That's up to 32 MB of expanded memory.

> NOTE: *Don't confuse EMS expanded memory with the extended memory located above the first megabyte of 80286, 80386, or 80486 memory. Although many memory expansion adapters can be configured to serve as either expanded or extended memory (or both), these two memory configurations are very different in terms of both hardware and software considerations.*

The System Memory Map

On the original IBM PC, the 1-MB address space of the 8088 was split into several functional areas. (See Figure 1-7.) This memory map has been carried forward for compatibility in all subsequent PC and PS/2 models.

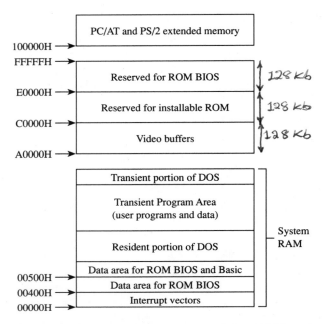

Figure 1-7. *An outline of memory usage in PCs and PS/2s.*

Some of the layout of the PC and PS/2 memory map is a consequence of the design of the 8086 microprocessor. For example, the 8086 always maintains a list of *interrupt vectors* (addresses of interrupt-handling routines) in the first 1024 bytes of RAM. Similarly, all 8086-based microcomputers have ROM at the high end of the 1-MB address space because the 8086, when first powered up, executes the program that starts at address FFFF0H.

The rest of the memory map follows this general division between RAM at the bottom of the address space and ROM at the top. A maximum of 640 KB of RAM can exist between addresses 00000H and 9FFFFH. (This is the memory area described by the DOS CHKDSK program.) Subsequent memory blocks are reserved for video RAM (A0000H through BFFFFH), installable ROM modules (C0000H through DFFFFH), and permanent ROM (E0000H through FFFFFH). We'll explore each of these memory areas in greater detail in the chapters that follow.

Design Philosophy

Before leaping into the following chapters, we should discuss the design philosophy behind the PC family. This will help you understand what is (and what isn't) important or useful to you.

Part of the design philosophy of the IBM personal computer family centers around a set of ROM BIOS interrupt service routines (see Chapters 10 through 13). These service routines provide essentially all the control functions and operations that are necessary for a program to interact with the system hardware. The basic philosophy of the PC family is this: Let the ROM BIOS do it; don't mess with direct hardware control. In our judgment, this is a sound idea and has several beneficial results. Using the ROM BIOS routines encourages good programming practices, and it avoids some of the kludgy tricks that have been the curse of many other computers. It also increases the chances of your programs working on every member of the PC family. In addition, it gives manufacturers more flexibility in making improvements and additions to the line of PCs. However, it would be naive of us to simply say to you, "Don't mess with direct control of the hardware." For good reasons or bad, you might want or need to have your programs work as directly as possible with the computer hardware and might choose to do what is colorfully called "programming down to the bare metal."

Still, as the PC family has evolved, programmers have had the opportunity to work with increasingly powerful hardware and system software. The newer members of the PC family provide faster hardware and better system software, so direct programming of the hardware does not necessarily result in significantly faster programs. For example, with an IBM PC running MS-DOS, the fastest way to display text on the video display is to use assembly language routines that bypass MS-DOS and to directly program the video hardware. Video screen output is many times slower if you route it through MS-DOS. Contrast this with a PC/AT or PS/2 running OS/2, where the best way to put text on the screen is to use the operating system output functions. The faster hardware and the efficient video output services in OS/2 make direct programming unnecessary.

As you read the programming details we present in this book, keep in mind that you can often obtain a result or accomplish a programming task through several means, including direct hardware programming, calling the ROM BIOS, or using an MS-DOS service. You must always balance portability, convenience, and performance as you weigh the alternatives. The more you know about what the hardware, the ROM BIOS, and the operating system can do, the better your programs can use them.

Chapter 2

The Ins and Outs

Generally speaking, the more you know about how your computer works, the more effective you'll be at writing programs for it. High-level programming languages, such as Basic and Pascal, are not designed to include every possible function that you might need while programming—although admittedly some languages are better than others. At some point, you will want to go deeper into your system and use some of the routines provided by the operating system or the ROM BIOS or perhaps go even deeper and program the hardware directly.

Most high-level languages provide limited means to directly manipulate memory (as with PEEK and POKE in Basic) or to communicate directly with support chips (as with Basic's INP and OUT statements). Even so, many programmers eventually resort to assembly language, the basic language from which many other languages and operating systems are built, for maximum speed and flexibility. The 8086 assembly language, like all other assembly languages, is composed of a set of symbolic instructions, as shown in Figure 2-1. Each instruction tells the CPU to perform a single, relatively simple operation, such as adding two numbers or transferring a byte of data to a specific memory location. Of course, your CPU cannot understand these symbolic instructions. An assembler translates the instructions and the data associated with them into a binary form, called *machine language,* which can reside in memory and can be directly processed by the CPU to accomplish specific tasks.

Mnemonic	Full Name	Mnemonic	Full Name
Instructions recognized by all 8086-family microprocessors:			
AAA	ASCII Adjust after Addition	CMP	CoMPare
AAD	ASCII Adjust before Division	CMPS	CoMPare String
AAM	ASCII Adjust after Multiplication	CMPSB	CoMPare String (Byte)
AAS	ASCII Adjust after Subtraction	CMPSW	CoMPare String (Word)
ADC	ADd with Carry	CWD	Convert Word to Doubleword
ADD	ADD	DAA	Decimal Adjust after Addition
AND	AND	DAS	Decimal Adjust after Subtraction
CALL	CALL	DEC	DECrement
CBW	Convert Byte to Word	DIV	unsigned DIVide
CLC	CLear Carry flag	ESC	ESCape
CLD	CLear Direction flag	HLT	HaLT
CLI	CLear Interrupt flag	IDIV	Integer DIVide
CMC	CoMplement Carry flag	IMUL	Integer MULtiply

Figure 2-1. *The instruction set used with the 8086, 80286, 80386, and 80486.*   (continued)

Figure 2-1. *continued*

Mnemonic	Full Name	Mnemonic	Full Name
Instructions recognized by all 8086-family microprocessors: (continued)			
IN	INput from I/O port	JS	Jump if Sign
INC	INCrement	JZ	Jump if Zero
INT	INTerrupt	LAHF	Load AH with Flags
INTO	INTerrupt on Overflow	LDS	Load pointer using DS
IRET	Interrupt RETurn	LEA	Load Effective Address
JA	Jump if Above	LES	Load pointer using ES
JAE	Jump if Above or Equal	LOCK	LOCK bus
JB	Jump if Below	LODS	LOaD String
JBE	Jump if Below or Equal	LODSB	LOaD String (Byte)
JC	Jump if Carry	LODSW	LOaD String (Word)
JCXZ	Jump if CX Zero	LOOP	LOOP
JE	Jump if Equal	LOOPE	LOOP while Equal
JG	Jump if Greater than	LOOPNE	LOOP while Not Equal
JGE	Jump if Greater than or Equal	LOOPNZ	LOOP while Not Zero
JL	Jump if Less than	LOOPZ	LOOP while Zero
JLE	Jump if Less than or Equal	MOV	MOVe data
JMP	JuMP	MOVS	MOVe String
JNA	Jump if Not Above	MOVSB	MOVe String (Byte)
JNAE	Jump if Not Above or Equal	MOVSW	MOVe String (Word)
JNB	Jump if Not Below	MUL	MULtiply
JNBE	Jump if Not Below or Equal	NEG	NEGate
JNC	Jump if No Carry	NOP	No OPeration
JNE	Jump if Not Equal	NOT	NOT
JNG	Jump if Not Greater than	OR	OR
JNGE	Jump if Not Greater than or Equal	OUT	OUTput to I/O port
JNL	Jump if Not Less than	POP	POP
JNLE	Jump if Not Less than or Equal	POPF	POP Flags
JNO	Jump if Not Overflow	PUSH	PUSH
JNP	Jump if Not Parity	PUSHF	Push Flags
JNS	Jump if Not Sign	RCL	Rotate through Carry Left
JNZ	Jump if Not Zero	RCR	Rotate through Carry Right
JO	Jump if Overflow	REP	REPeat
JP	Jump if Parity	REPE	REPeat while Equal
JPE	Jump if Parity Even	REPNE	REPeat while Not Equal
JPO	Jump if Parity Odd	REPNZ	REPeat while Not Zero

(continued)

Figure 2-1. *continued*

Mnemonic	Full Name	Mnemonic	Full Name
Instructions recognized by all 8086-family microprocessors: (continued)			
REPZ	REPeat while Zero	STC	SeT Carry flag
RET	RETurn	STD	SeT Direction flag
ROL	ROtate Left	STI	SeT Interrupt flag
ROR	ROtate Right	STOS	STOre String
SAHF	Store AH into Flags	STOSB	STOre String (Byte)
SAL	Shift Arithmetic Left	STOSW	STOre String (Word)
SAR	Shift Arithmetic Right	SUB	SUBtract
SBB	SuBtract with Borrow	TEST	TEST
SCAS	SCAn String	WAIT	WAIT
SCASB	SCAn String (Byte)	XCHG	eXCHanGe
SCASW	SCAn String (Word)	XLAT	transLATe
SHL	SHift Left	XOR	eXclusive OR
SHR	SHift Right		
Instructions recognized by the 80286, 80386, and 80486 only:			
ARPL	Adjust RPL field of selector	OUTS	OUTput String to I/O port
BOUND	Check array index against BOUNDs	POPA	POP All general registers
CLTS	CLear Task-Switched flag	PUSHA	PUSH All general registers
ENTER	Establish stack frame	SGDT	Store Global Descriptor Table register
INS	INput String from I/O port		
LAR	Load Access Rights	SIDT	Store Interrupt Descriptor Table register
LEAVE	Discard stack frame		
LGDT	Load Global Descriptor Table register	SLDT	Store Local Descriptor Table register
LIDT	Load Interrupt Descriptor Table register		
		SMSW	Store Machine Status Word
LLDT	Load Local Descriptor Table register	STR	Store Task Register
		VERR	VERify a segment selector for Reading
LMSW	Load Machine Status Word		
LSL	Load Segment Limit	VERW	VERify a segment selector for Writing
LTR	Load Task Register		

(continued)

Figure 2-1. *continued*

Mnemonic	Full Name	Mnemonic	Full Name
Instructions recognized by the 80386 and 80486 only:			
BSF	Bit Scan Forward	SETL	SET byte if Less
BSR	Bit Scan Reverse	SETLE	SET byte if Less or Equal
BT	Bit Test	SETNA	SET byte if Not Above
BTC	Bit Test and Complement	SETNAE	SET byte if Not Above or Equal
BTR	Bit Test and Reset	SETNB	SET byte if Not Below
BTS	Bit Test and Set	SETNBE	SET byte if Not Below or Equal
CDQ	Convert Doubleword to Quadword	SETNC	SET byte if No Carry
CMPSD	CoMPare String (Doubleword)	SETNE	SET byte if Not Equal
CWDE	Convert Word to Doubleword in EAX	SETNG	SET byte if Not Greater
JECXZ	Jump if ECX Zero	SETNGE	SET byte if Not Greater or Equal
LFS	Load pointer using FS	SETNL	SET byte if Not Less
LGS	Load pointer using GS	SETNLE	SET byte if Not Less or Equal
LSS	Load pointer using SS	SETNO	SET byte if Not Overflow
LODSD	LOaD String (Doubleword)	SETNP	SET byte if Not Parity
MOVSD	MOVe String (Doubleword)	SETNS	SET byte if Not Sign
MOVSX	MOVe with Sign-eXtend	SETNZ	SET byte if Not Zero
MOVZX	MOVe with Zero-eXtend	SETO	SET byte if Overflow
SCASD	SCAn String (Doubleword)	SETP	SET byte if Parity
SETA	SET byte if Above	SETPE	SET byte if Parity Even
SETAE	SET byte if Above or Equal	SETPO	SET byte if Parity Odd
SETB	SET byte if Below	SETS	SET byte if Sign
SETBE	SET byte if Below or Equal	SETZ	SET byte if Zero
SETC	SET byte if Carry	SHLD	SHift Left (Doubleword)
SETE	SET byte if Equal	SHRD	SHift Right (Doubleword)
SETG	SET byte if Greater	STOSD	STOre String (Doubleword)
SETGE	SET byte if Greater or Equal		
Instructions recognized by the 80486 only:			
BSWAP	Byte SWAP	INVLPG	INValidate TLB (for PaGe)
CMPXCHG	CoMPare and eXCHanGe	WBINVD	Write Back and INValidate Data cache
INVD	INValidate Data cache	XADD	eXchange and Add

NOTE: *Although this chapter discusses the details of 8086 programming, remember that we're implicitly talking about the 8088, 80286,
80386, and 80486 as well. Information pertaining exclusively to the
80286, 80386, or 80486 will be noted.*

The specific operations that the 8086 can perform fall into only a few
categories. It can do simple, four-function integer arithmetic and can move
data among RAM, I/O ports, and the CPU registers. It can, using only slightly
clumsy methods, manipulate the individual bits in a byte, and it can test
values and take action based on the result. Last but not least, the 8086 can interact with the circuitry around it.

Assembly language programming can be carried out on one of two
levels: You can create *interface routines* that will tie code written in a high-
level language to the lower-level MS-DOS and BIOS routines; or you can
create programs written entirely in assembly language. You might want to
create a program entirely in assembly language because an assembly language program usually runs faster and is smaller than an equivalent high-
level program. Assembly language can also be used to perform exotic tasks
at the hardware level—tasks that would be difficult or impossible to perform with a high-level language. Either way, to understand how to use
assembly language, you must understand how 8086-family microprocessors
process information and how they work with the rest of the computer. The
rest of this chapter describes how the microprocessor and the computer's
other parts communicate.

How the 8086 Communicates

The 8086 interacts with other system components in three ways: through
direct and indirect memory access, through input/output (I/O) ports, and with
signals called *interrupts*.

The microprocessor uses **memory** by reading data from, or writing
data to, memory locations that are identified by unique numeric addresses.
Memory can be accessed in one of two ways: through the direct memory access (DMA) controller or through the CPU's internal registers. The disk-drive
controller and the serial communications ports can also directly access
memory through the DMA controller (although in modern systems the DMA
controller is not used for these tasks). All other devices transfer data to and
from memory via the microprocessor's registers.

Input/Output (I/O) ports are the microprocessor's primary means of
communicating with any computer circuitry other than memory. Like
memory locations, I/O ports are identified by a numerical address, and data

can be read from or written to any port. The assignment of I/O ports to specific hardware devices is largely, but not completely, standardized. Generally, all members of the PC family use the same port assignments, with only a few variations among the different models. (See pages 48–49.)

Interrupts are the means by which the circuitry outside the CPU reports the occurrence of an event (such as a keystroke) that requires the microprocessor's attention. Although interrupts are essential to the microprocessor's interaction with the hardware around it, the concept of an interrupt is useful for other purposes as well. For example, a program can use the INT instruction to generate a software interrupt that requests a service from MS-DOS or from the system ROM BIOS. Interrupts are quite important in programming the PC family, so we devote a special section to them at the end of this chapter.

The 8086 Data Formats

The 8086 and 80286 are able to work with only four simple **numeric data** formats, all of which are integer values. The formats are founded on two building blocks: the 8-bit byte and the 16-bit (2-byte) word. Both of these basic units are related to the 16-bit processing capacity of the 8086. The byte is the fundamental unit; when the 8086 and 80286 access memory, each unique address refers to 1 byte of storage. In a single byte, these microprocessors can work with unsigned positive numbers ranging in value from 0 through 255 (that is, 2^8 possibilities). If the number is a signed value, 1 of the 8 bits represents the sign, so only 7 bits represent the value. Thus a signed byte can represent values ranging from –128 through +127. (See Figure 2-2.)

		Range	
Size	Signed?	Dec	Hex
8	No	0 through 255	00H through FFH
8	Yes	–128 through 0 through +127	80H through 00H through 7FH
16	No	0 through 65,535	0000H through FFFFH
16	Yes	–32,768 through 0 through +32,767	8000H through 0000H through 7FFFH
32	No	0 through 4,294,967,295	00000000H through FFFFFFFFH
32	Yes	–2,147,483,648 through 0 through +2,147,483,647	80000000H through 00000000H through 7FFFFFFFH

Figure 2-2. *The six data formats used in the 8086 family. (Only the 80386 and 80486 support the 32-bit formats.)*

The 8086 and 80286 can also operate on 16-bit signed and unsigned values, or words. Words are stored in memory in two adjacent bytes, with the low-order byte preceding the high-order byte. (See the discussion of back-words storage below.)

A word interpreted as an unsigned, positive number can have 2^{16} different values ranging from 0 through 65,535. As a signed number, the value can range from −32,768 through +32,767.

The 80386 and 80486 differ from their predecessors in that they can also work with 32-bit integer values, or *doublewords*. A doubleword represents a signed or unsigned 4-byte integer with any of 2^{32} (or 4,294,967,296) different values.

Character data (letters, numerals, punctuation marks, and other symbols) is stored using the standard ASCII code, with each character occupying 1 byte. The 8086 family knows nothing about ASCII characters and treats them as arbitrary bytes, with one exception: The instruction set accommo-

Back-Words Storage

Although the PC's memory is addressed in units of individual 8-bit bytes, many operations involve 16-bit words. In memory, a 16-bit word is stored in any two adjacent 8-bit bytes. The least significant byte of the word is stored in the lower memory location, and the most significant byte is stored in the higher memory location. From some points of view, storing a word this way is the opposite of what you might expect. Due to the backward appearance of this storage scheme, it is sometimes whimsically called "back-words" storage.

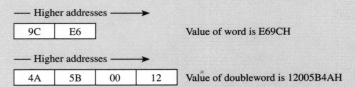

If you are working with bytes and words in memory, you should take care not to be confused by back-words storage. The source of the confusion has mostly to do with how you write data. For example, if you are writing a word value in hex, you write it like this: ABCD. The order of significance is the same as if you were writing a decimal number: The most significant digit is written first. But a word is stored in memory with the lowest address location first. Thus, in memory, the number ABCD appears as CDAB, with the bytes switched.

dates decimal addition and subtraction performed on binary-coded decimal (BCD) characters. The actual arithmetic is done in binary, but the combination of the AF flag (see page 43) and a few special instructions makes it practical to work on decimal characters and get decimal results, which can easily be converted to ASCII.

See Appendix D for more information on ASCII and the PC family's extended ASCII character set.

How the 8086 Addresses Memory

The 8086 is a 16-bit microprocessor and cannot therefore work directly with numbers larger than 16 bits. Theoretically, this means that the 8086 should be able to access only 2^{16}, or 64, KB of memory. But, as we noted in the previous chapter, it can in fact access much more than that—1024 KB, to be exact. This is possible because of the 20-bit addressing scheme used with the 8086, which expands the full range of memory locations that the 8086 can work with from 2^{16} (65,536) to 2^{20} (1,048,576). But the 8086 is still limited by its 16-bit processing capacity. To access the 20-bit addresses, it must use an addressing method that fits into the 16-bit format.

Segmented Addresses

The 8086 divides the addressable memory space into *segments*, each of which contains 64 KB of memory. Each segment begins at a *paragraph address*, a byte location that is evenly divisible by 16. To access individual bytes or words, you use an *offset* that points to an exact byte location within a particular segment. Because offsets are always measured relative to the beginning of a segment, they are also called *relative addresses* or *relative offsets*.

Together, a segment and an offset form a *segmented address* that can designate any byte in the 8086's 1-MB address space. The 8086 converts a given 32-bit segmented address into a 20-bit physical address by using the 16-bit segment value as a paragraph number and adding the 16-bit offset value to it. In effect, the 8086 shifts the segment value left by 4 bits and then adds the offset value to create a 20-bit address.

Figure 2-3 shows how this is done for a segment value of 1234H and an offset of 4321H. The segmented address is written as 1234:4321H, with 4-digit hexadecimal values and with a colon separating the segment and offset.

On the 8086, there's obviously a great deal of overlap in the range of values that can be expressed as segmented addresses. Any given physical address can be represented by up to 2^{12} different segmented addresses. For example, the physical address 16661H could be represented not only as 1234:4321H, but also as 1666:0001H, 1665:0011H, 1664:0021H, and so on.

Figure 2-3. *Decoding an 8086 segmented address. The segment value 1234H is shifted left 4 bits (1 hex digit) and added to the offset 4321H to give the 20-bit physical address 16661H.*

80286, 80386, and 80486 Protected-Mode Addresses

The 80286 also uses segmented addresses, but when the 80286 runs in protected mode, the addresses are decoded differently than on an 8086 or in 80286 real mode. The 80286 decodes protected-mode segmented addresses by using a table of segment descriptors. The "segment" part of a segmented address is not a paragraph value but a "selector" that represents an index into a segment descriptor table. (See Figure 2-4.) Each descriptor in the table contains a 24-bit base address that indicates the actual start of a segment in memory. The resulting address is the sum of the 24-bit base address and the 16-bit offset specified in the segmented address. Thus, in protected mode the 80286 can access up to 2^{24} bytes of memory; that is, physical addresses are 24 bits in size.

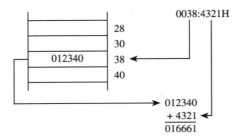

Figure 2-4. *Decoding an 80286 protected-mode segmented address. The segment selector 38H indicates an entry in a segment descriptor table. The segment descriptor contains a 24-bit segment base address, which is added to the offset 4321H to give the 24-bit physical address 016661H.*

This table-driven addressing scheme gives the 80286 a great deal of control over memory usage. In addition to a 24-bit base address, each segment descriptor specifies a segment's attributes (executable code, program data, read-only, and so on) as well as a privilege level that lets an operating system restrict access to the segment. This ability to specify segment attributes and access privileges is of great use to a multitasking operating system such as OS/2.

The 80386 and 80486 support both real-mode addressing and protected-mode addressing. These CPUs enhance the protected-mode addressing scheme by allowing 32-bit segment base addresses and 32-bit offsets. Thus, a single segmented address, consisting of a 16-bit selector and a 32-bit offset, can specify any of 2^{32} different physical addresses.

The 80386 and 80486 also provide a "virtual 8086" addressing mode, in which addressing is the same as the usual 8086 20-bit real-mode addressing, but with the physical addresses corresponding to the 1-MB 8086 address space mapped anywhere in the 4-gigabyte (GB) 80386/80486 address space. This lets an operating system execute several different 8086 programs, each in its own independent 1-MB, 8086-compatible address space.

Address Compatibility

The different addressing schemes used by the 80286, 80386, and 80486 are generally compatible (except, of course, for 32-bit addressing on the 80386 and 80486). However, if you are writing an 8086 program that you intend to convert for use in protected mode, be careful to use segments in an orderly fashion. Although it's possible to specify a physical 8086 address with many different segment-offset combinations, you will find it easier to convert 8086 programs to protected-mode addressing if you keep your segment values as constant as possible.

For example, imagine that your program needs to access an array of 160-byte strings of characters, starting at physical address B8000H. A poor way to access each string would be to exploit the fact that the strings are each 10 paragraphs long by using a different segment value to locate the start of each string:

    B800:0000H (physical address B8000H)
    B80A:0000H (physical address B80A0H)
    B814:0000H (physical address B8140H)
    B81E:0000H (physical address B81E0H)

A better way to accomplish the same addressing would be to keep a constant segment value and change the offset value:

    B800:0000H (physical address B8000H)
    B800:00A0H (physical address B80A0H)
    B800:0140H (physical address B8140H)
    B800:01E0H (physical address B81E0H)

Although the result is the same on an 8086 and in real mode on an 80286, you'll find that the second method is much better suited to protected mode, in which each different segment selector designates a different segment descriptor.

The 8086 Registers

The 8086 was designed to retrieve instructions from memory and execute them, to perform arithmetic and logical operations on data, and to pass data to and from memory. To perform these tasks, it uses a number of 16-bit *registers,* temporary data storage locations within the CPU itself. There are 14 registers in all, each with a special use. Four *scratch-pad registers* are used by programs to temporarily hold the operands and the intermediate results of arithmetic and logical operations. Four *segment registers* hold address segment values. Five *offset registers* hold the offsets used with the segment-register values to form the physical addresses that specify memory locations. Finally, one *flags register* contains nine 1-bit flags used to record 8086 status information and control 8086 operations. (See Figure 2-5.)

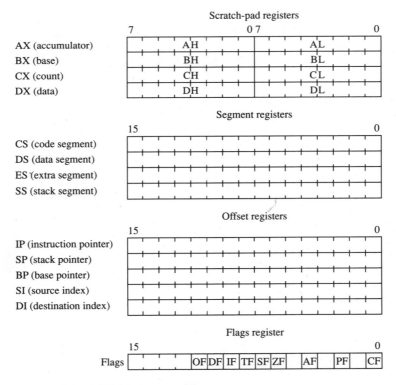

Figure 2-5. *The 8086 registers and flags.*

The Scratch-Pad Registers

When a computer is processing data, a great deal of the microprocessor's time is spent transferring data to and from memory. This access time can be greatly reduced by keeping frequently used operands and results inside the 8086. Four 16-bit registers, usually called the *scratch-pad* or *data registers,* are designed for this purpose.

The scratch-pad registers are known as AX, BX, CX, and DX. Each of these 16-bit registers can also be accessed as two separate 8-bit registers. The high-order 8-bit registers are known as AH, BH, CH, and DH, and the low-order 8-bit registers are known as AL, BL, CL, and DL.

The scratch-pad registers are used mostly as convenient temporary working areas, particularly for arithmetic operations. Addition and subtraction can be done in memory without using the registers, but the registers are faster.

Although these registers are available for any kind of scratch-pad work, each also has some special uses:

- The AX (accumulator) register is the main register used to perform arithmetic operations. (Although addition and subtraction can be performed in any of the scratch-pad or offset registers, multiplication and division must be done in AX or AL.)

- The BX (base) register can be used to point to the beginning of a translation table in memory. It can also be used to hold the offset part of a segmented address.

- The CX (count) register is used as a repetition counter for loop control and repeated data moves. For example, the LOOP instruction in assembly language uses CX to count the number of loop iterations.

- The DX (data) register is used to store data for general purposes, although it, too, has certain specialized functions. For example, DX contains the remainder of division operations performed in AX.

The Segment Registers

As we discussed earlier, the complete address of a memory location consists of a 16-bit segment value and a 16-bit offset within the segment. Four registers, called CS, DS, ES, and SS, are used to identify four specific segments of memory. Five offset registers, which we'll discuss shortly, can be used to store the relative offsets of the data within each of the four segments.

Each segment register is used for a specific type of addressing, as outlined on the following page.

- The CS register identifies the code segment—the memory region that contains the set of instructions, or program, that is being executed.

- The DS and ES registers identify data segments where data used by a program is stored.

- The SS register identifies the stack segment. (See page 42 for more information about stacks.)

Programs rarely use four separate segments to address four different 64-KB areas of memory. Instead, the four segments specified in CS, DS, ES, and SS usually refer to overlapping or identical areas in memory. In effect, the different segment registers identify areas of memory used for different purposes.

For example, Figure 2-6 shows how the values in the segment registers correspond to the memory used in a hypothetical MS-DOS program. The values in the segment registers are chosen to correspond to the start of each logically different area of memory, even though the 64-KB areas of memory identified by each segment overlap each other. (See Chapter 16 for more about segments and the memory layout of MS-DOS programs.)

All 8086 instructions that access memory will automatically use a particular segment register unless the programmer specifies otherwise. For example, the MOV instruction, which moves data to or from memory, uses the DS register as its default. Similarly, the JMP instruction, which affects the flow of a program's execution, automatically uses the CS register.

This means that you can address any 64-KB segment in memory by placing its paragraph address in the appropriate segment register. For example, to access data in the video buffer used by IBM's Color Graphics Adapter, you place the paragraph address of the start of the buffer in a segment register and then use the MOV instruction to transfer data to or from the buffer, as shown on the opposite page.

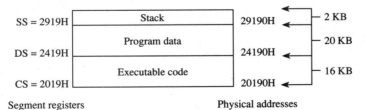

Figure 2-6. *Segment usage in a typical MS-DOS program. Each segment register contains the starting paragraph of a different area of memory.*

```
mov ax,0B800h            ; load the segment value into AX
mov ds,ax                ; move the segment value into DS
mov al,[0000]            ; copy the byte at B800:0000
                         ; into AL
```

In interpreted Basic, you can use this method with the DEF SEG statement:

```
DEF SEG = &HB800         ' move the segment value into DS
X = PEEK(0000)           ' copy the byte at B800:0000 into X
```

The Offset Registers

Five offset registers are used with the segment registers to contain segmented addresses. One register, called the *instruction pointer,* contains the offset of the current instruction in the code segment; two registers, called the *stack registers,* are used to manipulate the stack; and the remaining two registers, called the *index registers,* are used to address data in RAM.

The **instruction pointer** (IP), also called the *program counter* (PC), contains the offset within the code segment where the current program is executing. The IP register is used with the CS register to track the location of the next instruction to be executed.

Programs do not have direct access to the IP register, but a number of assembly language instructions, such as JMP and CALL, change the IP value implicitly.

The **stack registers,** called the *stack pointer* (SP) and the *base pointer* (BP), provide offsets into the stack segment. SP gives the location of the current top of the stack. Programs rarely change the value in SP directly. Instead, they rely on PUSH and POP instructions to update SP implicitly. BP is the register generally used to access the stack segment directly. You'll see BP used quite often in the assembly language examples that appear in Chapters 9 through 17.

The **index registers,** called the *source index* (SI) and the *destination index* (DI), can be used for general-purpose addressing of data. Also, all string move and comparison instructions use SI and DI to address data strings.

The Flags Register

The fourteenth and last register, called the *flags register,* is really a collection of individual status and control bits called *flags*. The flags are maintained in a register so that they can be either saved and restored as a coordinated set or inspected as ordinary data. Normally, however, the flags are set and tested as independent bits, not as a set.

There are nine 1-bit flags in the 8086's 16-bit flags register, leaving 7 bits unused. (The 80286, 80386, and 80486 use some of these "unused" bits to support protected-mode operation.) The flags can be logically divided into two groups: six *status flags,* which record processor status information (usually indicating what happened with a comparison or arithmetic operation); and three *control flags,* which control certain 8086 operations. A flag is said to be set, on, or true if its value is 1; it is said to be clear, off, or false if its value is 0. Figures 2-7 and 2-8 give the two-letter codes, full names, and functions of the status and control flags.

The Stack

Support for the *stack* is a built-in feature of the 8086. It provides programs with a place to store and keep track of work in progress. The most important use of the stack is to keep a record of where subroutines were invoked from and of what arguments were passed to them. The stack can also be used for temporary working storage, although this is less fundamental and less common. Note that the stack itself is part of the regular system RAM; the CPU simply provides special features for accessing and keeping track of this space.

The stack gets its name from an analogy to a spring-loaded stack of plates in a cafeteria: New data is "pushed" on the top of the stack, and old data is "popped" off. A stack always operates in last-in-first-out (LIFO) order: When you pop an item off the stack, you get the item that was most recently pushed on the stack. This LIFO organization is ideal when the stack is used to keep track of where to return to in a program because the most recent calling program is returned to first. In this way, a stack maintains the orderly workings of programs, subroutines, and interrupt handlers, no matter how complex their operation.

A stack is used from the bottom (highest address) to the top (lowest address) so that when data is pushed on the top of the stack, it is stored at the memory addresses just below the current top of the stack. The stack grows downward so that, as data is added, the location of the top of the stack moves to lower and lower addresses, decreasing the value of SP each time. You need to keep this in mind when you access the stack, which you are likely to do in assembly language interface routines.

Code	Name	Use
CF	Carry flag	Indicates an arithmetic carry
OF	Overflow flag	Indicates a signed arithmetic overflow
ZF	Zero flag	Indicates a zero result or an equal comparison
SF	Sign flag	Indicates a negative result or comparison
PF	Parity flag	Indicates an even number of 1 bits
AF	Auxiliary carry flag	Indicates an adjustment is needed in binary-coded decimal (BCD) arithmetic operations

Figure 2-7. *The six status flags in the 8086's flags register.*

Any part of any program can create a new stack space at any time, but this is not usually done. Normally, when a program is run, a single stack is created for it and used throughout the operation of the program.

There is no simple way to estimate the size of the stack that a program might need, and the 8086's design does not provide any automatic way to detect when stack space is in short supply or exhausted. This can make programmers nervous about the amount of space that should be set aside for a stack. A conservative estimate of how much stack space to maintain is about 2 KB (2048 bytes), the default amount that is automatically allocated by many high-level–language compilers.

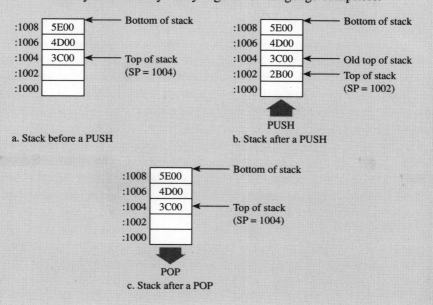

Code	Name	Use
DF	Direction flag	Controls increment direction in string operations (CMPS, LODS, MOVS, SCAS, STOS)
IF	Interrupt flag	Controls whether interrupts are enabled
TF	Trap flag	Controls single-step operation (used by DEBUG) by generating an interrupt at the end of every instruction

Figure 2-8. *The three control flags in the 8086's flags register.*

Addressing Memory Through Registers

You've seen that memory is always addressed by a combination of a segment value and a relative offset value. The segment value always comes from one of the four segment registers.

In contrast, the relative offset can be specified in many different ways. (See Figure 2-9.) For each machine instruction that accesses memory, the 8086 computes an effective address by combining one, two, or three of the following:

- The value in BX or BP

- The value in SI or DI

- A relative offset value, called a *displacement,* which is part of the instruction itself

Each of the various ways to form an effective address has its uses. You can use the Immediate and Direct methods when you know the offset of a particular memory location in advance. You must use one of the remaining methods when you can't tell what an address will be until your program executes. In the chapters ahead, you'll see examples of most of the 8086 addressing modes.

The notation used in specifying 8086 addresses is straightforward. Brackets, [ ], are used to indicate that the enclosed item specifies a relative offset. This is a key element of memory addressing; without brackets, the actual value stored in the register is used in whatever operation is specified.

Name	*Effective Address*	*Example*	*Comments*
Immediate	Value ''addressed'' is part of the 8086 instruction	mov ax,1234h	Stores 1234H in AX.
Direct	Specified as part of the 8086 instruction	mov ax,[1234h]	Copies the value at offset 1234H into AX. The default segment register is DS.
Register indirect	Contained in BX, SI, DI, or BP	mov ax,[bx]	Copies the value at the offset specified by BX into AX. The default segment register for [BX], [SI], and [DI] is DS; for [BP] the default is SS.
Based	The sum of a displacement (part of the instruction) and the value in BX or BP	mov ax,[bx+2] *or* mov ax,2[bx]	Copies the value 2 bytes past the offset specified by BX into AX. The default segment register for [BX] is DS; for [BP] the default is SS.
Indexed	The sum of a displacement and the value in SI or DI	mov ax,[si+2] *or* mov ax,2[si]	Copies the value 2 bytes past the offset specified by SI into AX. The default segment register is DS.
Based indexed	The sum of a displacement, the value in SI or DI, and the value in BX or BP	mov ax,[bp+si+2] *or* mov ax,2[bp+si] *or* mov ax,2[bp][si]	The offset is the sum of the values in BP and SI, plus 2. When BX is used, the default segment register is DS; when BP is used, the default is SS.
String addressing	Source string: register indirect using SI Destination string: register indirect using DI	movsb	Copies the string from memory at DS:[SI] to ES:[DI].

Figure 2-9. *8086 addressing modes. In assembly language, some instructions can be specified in several different ways.*

Rules for Using Registers

It is important to know that various rules apply to the use of registers, and it is essential to be aware of these rules in writing assembly language interface routines. Because the rules and conventions of usage vary by circumstance and by programming language, it's not possible to provide a list of exact rules here, but the general rules that follow apply in most cases. (You will find additional guidance, and working models to copy, in the examples in Chapters 9 through 17.) Keep in mind, though, that the following rules are general, not absolute.

Probably the most useful rule for using registers is simply to use them for their intended purpose. The idea that each of the 8086 registers has certain special uses may seem somewhat quirky, particularly to a programmer who is accustomed to working with CPUs that have a less specialized set of registers (the 68000 series, for example). On the 8086, using the registers for their natural functions leads to cleaner, more efficient source code and ultimately to more reliable programs.

For example, the segment registers are designed to contain segment values, and they shouldn't be used for anything else. (In protected mode, you can't use them for anything else anyway without generating an error condition.) The BP register is intended for stack addressing; if you use it for anything else, you'll have to do some fancy footwork when you need to address values in the stack segment.

Particular rules apply to the four segment registers (CS, DS, ES, and SS). The CS register should be changed only through intersegment jumps and subroutine calls.

Most programmers use the DS register to point to a default data segment that contains the data most frequently used by a program. This usually means that the value in the DS register is initialized at the beginning of program execution and then left alone. Should it be necessary to use DS to address a different segment, its original value must be saved, the new segment value placed in the register, and the original value restored. In contrast, the ES (extra segment) register has no default use and is typically used as needed to access arbitrary segments in memory.

The stack segment (SS) and stack pointer (SP) registers should usually be updated implicitly, either by PUSH and POP instructions or by CALL and RET instructions, which save subroutine return addresses on the stack. When MS-DOS loads a program into memory to be executed, it initializes SS and SP to usable values. In .COM programs, SS:SP points to the end of the program's default segment; in .EXE programs, SS:SP is determined by the size and location of the program's stack segment as specified by the compiler. In either case, you rarely need to change SS or SP explicitly.

If you need to discard a number of values from the stack or to reserve temporary storage space on top of the stack, you can increment or decrement SP directly:

```
add sp,8                    ; discard four words (8 bytes)
                            ; from stack
sub sp,6                    ; add three words (6 bytes)
                            ; to top of stack
```

If you need to move the stack to a different location in memory, you generally must update both SS and SP at the same time:

```
cli                         ; disable interrupts
mov ss,NewStackSeg          ; update SS from a memory variable
mov sp,NewStackPtr          ; update SP from a memory variable
sti                         ; reenable interrupts
```

Be careful when you change SS and SP explicitly. If you modify SS but fail to update SP, SS will specify a new stack segment while SP points somewhere inside another stack segment—and that's asking for trouble the next time you use the stack.

There are no hard-and-fast rules about the use of the other registers. In general, most programmers try to minimize memory accesses by keeping the intermediate results of lengthy computations in registers. This is because it takes longer to perform a computation on a value stored in memory than on a value stored in a register. Of course, the 8086 has only so many registers to work with, so you might find yourself running out of registers before you run out of variables.

How the 8086 Uses I/O Ports

The 8086-family microprocessors communicate with many parts of the computer by using input and output (I/O) ports. The I/O ports can be thought of as doorways through which information passes as it travels to or from an I/O device, such as a keyboard or a printer. Most of the support chips we described in Chapter 1 are accessed through I/O ports; in fact, each chip might use several port addresses for different purposes.

Each port is identified by a unique 16-bit port number, or address, that can range from 00H through FFFFH (65,535). The CPU identifies a particular port by its address.

As it does when accessing memory, the CPU uses the data and address buses as conduits for communication with the ports. To access a port, the CPU first sends a signal on the system bus to notify all I/O devices that the next address on the bus is a port address, not a RAM address. The CPU then sends the port address, and the device having the matching port address responds.

The port address specifies a storage location that is associated with an I/O device rather than being part of main memory. In other words, an I/O port address is not the same as a memory address. For example, I/O port 3D8H has nothing to do with memory address 003D8H. To access an I/O port, you don't use data transfer instructions such as MOV and STOS. Instead, you use the instructions IN and OUT, which are specifically for I/O port access.

NOTE: *Many high-level programming languages provide functions that access I/O ports. The Basic functions* INP *and* OUT *and the C functions* inp *and* outp *are typical examples.*

The functions of specific I/O ports are determined by the hardware designers. Programs that make use of I/O ports need to be aware of the port addresses, as well as their use and meaning. Port address assignments differ slightly among the PC family members, but in general, all PCs use the same ranges of I/O port addresses for the same input/output devices. (See Figure 2-10.) For details on how each I/O port is used, see the descriptions of the various input/output devices in the IBM technical reference manuals.

Description	I/O Port Numbers	Comments
DMA controller 1	00H–1FH	
Programmable interrupt controller (master)	20H–3FH	
System timer	40H–5FH	
Keyboard controller	60H–6FH	On PS/2 Model 30, ports 60H–6FH are reserved for system board control and status.
System control port B	61H	
Real-time clock, NMI mask	70H–7FH	On PC, PC/XT, and PS/2 Model 30, NMI mask is at port A0H.
DMA page register	80H–8FH	
System control port A	92H	PS/2 models with MCA and clones.
Programmable interrupt controller (slave)	A0H–BFH	On PS/2 Model 30, A0H–AFH.
Real-time clock	B0H–BFH, E0H–EFH	PS/2 Model 30 only.
DMA controller 2	C0H–DFH	
Clear math coprocessor busy	F0H	
Reset math coprocessor	F1H	

Figure 2-10. *PC input/output port assignments. This table lists the most frequently used I/O ports. (continued) For a complete list, see the IBM technical reference manuals.*

Figure 2-10. *continued*

Description	I/O Port Numbers	Comments
Math coprocessor	F8H–FFH	
Hard disk controller	1F0H–1F8H	
Game control adapter	200H–207H	
Parallel printer 3	278H–27BH	Parallel printer 2 on PC, PC/XT, and PC/AT.
Serial communications 2	2F8H–2FFH	
Hard disk controller	320H–32FH	PC/XT and PS/2 Model 30.
PC network	360H–363H, 368H–36BH	
Parallel printer 2	378H–37BH	Parallel printer 1 on PC, PC/XT, and PC/AT.
Monochrome Display Adapter	3B0H–3BBH	Also used by EGA and VGA in monochrome video modes.
Parallel printer 1	3BCH–3BFH	Monochrome display and printer adapter on PC, PC/XT, and PC/AT.
Enhanced Graphics Adapter (EGA), Video Graphics Array (VGA)	3C0H–3CFH	
Color Graphics Adapter (CGA), Multi-Color Graphics Array (MCGA)	3D0H–3DFH	Also used by EGA and VGA in color graphics video modes.
Floppy disk controller	3F0H–3F7H	
Serial communications 1	3F8H–3FFH	

How the 8086 Uses Interrupts

An interrupt is a signal to the microprocessor that its immediate attention is needed. The 8086-family microprocessors respond to interrupts generated by both hardware and software. An interrupt signal generated by a hardware device is first processed by the programmable interrupt controller (PIC) and then passed to the microprocessor. In software, a program can use a specific instruction to generate a software interrupt. In both cases, the microprocessor stops whatever it's doing and executes a memory-resident subroutine called an *interrupt handler* or *interrupt service routine*. After the interrupt handler has performed its task, the microprocessor resumes processing where it left off when the interrupt occurred.

The 8086 supports 256 different interrupts, each identified by a number from 00H through FFH (decimal 255). The segmented addresses of the 256 interrupt handlers are stored in an interrupt vector table that starts at 0000:0000H (that is, at the beginning of available memory). Each interrupt vector is 4 bytes in size, so you can locate the address of any interrupt handler by multiplying the interrupt number by 4. You can also replace an existing interrupt handler with a new one by storing the new handler's segmented address in the appropriate interrupt vector.

Software Interrupts

In assembly language, software interrupts are generated by the INT instruction. Consider what happens when the CPU executes the following INT instruction:

```
INT 12H
```

The CPU first saves information about what it's doing by pushing the contents of the flags register, the CS (code segment) register, and the IP (instruction pointer) register on the stack. Then it transfers control to the interrupt handler that corresponds to interrupt number 12H, using the segmented address stored in the interrupt vector table at 0000:0048H. The CPU executes the instructions in the interrupt 12H handler, which perform the appropriate actions for interrupt 12H. The final instruction in the interrupt handler is always an IRET instruction, which pops the original values of CS, IP, and the flags back into the registers, thus transferring control back to the interrupted task.

Hardware Interrupts

The microprocessor responds to a hardware interrupt in much the same way it responds to a software interrupt: by transferring control to an interrupt handler. The important difference lies in the way the interrupt is signaled.

Devices such as the system timer, the hard disk, the keyboard, and the serial communications ports can generate interrupt signals on a set of reserved interrupt request (IRQ) lines. These lines are monitored by the PIC circuit, which assigns interrupt numbers to them. When a particular hardware interrupt occurs, the PIC places the corresponding interrupt number on the system data bus, where the microprocessor can find it.

The PIC also assigns priorities to the various interrupt requests. For example, the highest-priority PIC interrupt in all PCs is the timer-tick interrupt, which is signaled on interrupt request line 0 (IRQ0) and is assigned interrupt number 08H by the PIC. When a system timer generates a timer-tick interrupt, it does so by signaling on IRQ0; the PIC responds by signaling the CPU to execute interrupt 08H. If a lower-priority hardware interrupt request occurs while the timer-tick interrupt is being processed, the PIC delays the lower-priority interrupt until the timer interrupt handler signals that it has finished its processing.

When you coldboot the computer, the system start-up routines assign interrupt numbers and priorities to the hardware interrupts by initializing the PIC. In 8088-based and 8086-based machines, interrupt numbers 08H through 0FH are assigned to interrupt request levels 0 through 7 (IRQ0 through IRQ7). In systems with 80286 or higher CPUs, an additional eight interrupt lines (IRQ8 through IRQ15) are assigned interrupt numbers 70H through 77H.

One hardware interrupt bypasses the PIC altogether. This is the *non-maskable interrupt* (NMI), which is assigned interrupt number 02H in the 8086 family. The NMI is used by devices that require absolute, "now-or-never" priority over all other CPU functions. In particular, when a hardware memory error occurs, the computer's RAM subsystem generates an NMI. This causes the CPU to pass control to the interrupt 02H handler; the default handler in the PC family resides in ROM and issues the "PARITY CHECK" message you see when a memory error occurs.

When you debug a program on any member of the PC family, remember that hardware interrupts are occurring all the time. For example, the system timer-tick interrupt (interrupt 08H) occurs roughly 18.2 times per second. The keyboard and disk-drive controllers also generate interrupts. Each time these hardware interrupts occur, the 8086 uses the current stack to save CS:IP and the flags register. If your stack is too small or if you are manipulating SS and SP when a hardware interrupt occurs, the 8086 may damage valuable data when it saves CS:IP and the flags.

If you look back at our example of updating SS and SP on page 47, you'll see that we explicitly disable hardware interrupts by executing the CLI instruction prior to updating SS. This prevents a hardware interrupt from occurring between the two MOV instructions while SS:SP is pointing nowhere. (Actually, this is a problem only in very early releases of the 8088; the chip was later redesigned to prevent this problem by disabling interrupts during the instruction that follows a data move into SS.)

We'll talk in more detail about how PCs use interrupts in Chapters 3 and 9.

Chapter 3

The ROM Software

It takes software to make a computer go. And getting a computer going and keeping it going are much easier if some of that software is permanently built into the computer. That's what the ROM programs are all about. ROM stands for *read only memory*—memory permanently recorded in the circuitry of the computer's ROM chips, ensuring that the information stored there cannot be changed, erased, or lost.

PCs come with a substantial amount of ROM, which contains the software routines and data needed to start the computer when it's first turned on and to operate the computer's various peripheral devices. The advantage of having these routines stored in ROM is that they are right there—built into the computer—and there is no need to load them into memory from disk the way that MS-DOS must be loaded. In addition, the ROM routines provide the basic capabilities on which most other programs are based, and building them into the system ensures that they will always be available.

In the PC family, ROM is made up of three main elements: the *start-up routines,* which get the computer started; the *ROM BIOS,* which is a collection of machine-language routines that provide support services for operating the computer's peripheral devices; and the *ROM extensions,* which are routines that are added to the main ROM when certain optional equipment is added to the computer. In IBM PCs, ROM also contains *ROM Basic,* which is a simple version of the Basic programming language. We'll examine each of these ROM components in this chapter.

The ROM routines occupy addresses F000:0000H through F000:FFFFH in the PC/XT/AT family and the 8086 versions of the PS/2 models 25 and 30, and they occupy E000:0000H through F000:FFFFH in the other PS/2s. However, the routines themselves are not located at any specific addresses in ROM as they are in other computers. The address of a particular ROM routine varies among the different members of the PC/XT/AT and PS/2 families.

Although the exact addresses of the ROM routines vary, IBM provides a consistent interface to the ROM software via interrupts. In Chapter 4 we'll show you exactly how to use interrupts to execute the ROM routines.

The Start-Up ROM

The first job the ROM programs have is to supervise the start-up of the computer. Unlike other elements of ROM, the start-up routines have little to do with programming the PC family, but it is still worthwhile to understand what they do.

The start-up routines perform several tasks:

- They run a quick reliability test of the computer (and the ROM programs) to ensure that everything is in working order.

- They initialize the chips and the standard equipment attached to the computer.

- They set up the interrupt vector table.

- They check to see what optional equipment is attached to the computer.

- They load the operating system from disk.

The *reliability test,* part of a process known as the Power On Self Test (POST), is an important first step in making sure the computer is ready to run. All POST routines are brief except for the memory tests, which can be annoyingly lengthy in computers that contain a large amount of memory.

The *initialization process* is slightly more complex. One initialization routine sets the default values for interrupt vectors. These default values either point to the standard interrupt handlers located inside the ROM BIOS or point to do-nothing routines in the ROM BIOS that might later be superseded by the operating system or by your own interrupt handlers. Another initialization routine determines what equipment is attached to the computer and then places a record of it at standard locations in low memory. (We'll discuss this equipment list in more detail later in the chapter.) How this information is acquired varies from model to model. For example, in the PC, it is taken mostly from the settings of two banks of switches located on the computer's system board; in systems with 80286 and higher CPUs, the ROM BIOS reads configuration information from a special nonvolatile memory area whose contents are initialized by special setup programs supplied by the system manufacturer. The POST routines learn about the computer's hardware by a logical inspection and test. In effect, the initialization program shouts to each configured option, ''Are you there?'' and listens for a response.

No matter how it is acquired, the status information is recorded and stored in the same way for all systems so that your programs can examine it. The initialization routines also check for new equipment and extensions to ROM. If they find any, they turn control momentarily over to the ROM extensions so that the extensions can initialize themselves. The initialization routines then execute the remaining start-up routines. (We will discuss this in more detail later in the chapter.)

The final part of the start-up procedure, occurring after the POST routines, the initialization process, and the incorporation of ROM extensions, is called the *bootstrap loader*, which is a short routine that loads a program

(or ROM)

from disk. In essence, the ROM bootstrap loader attempts to read a disk boot program from a disk (floppy disk drive A or, if no disk is inserted, the first hard disk). If the boot program is successfully read into memory, the ROM loader passes control of the computer to it. The disk boot program is responsible for loading another, larger disk program, which is usually a disk operating system such as MS-DOS, but which can be a self-contained and self-loading program. If the ROM bootstrap loader cannot read a disk's boot program, it either activates the built-in ROM Basic (on IBM systems) or displays an error message.

The ROM BIOS

The ROM BIOS is the part of ROM that is in active use whenever the computer is at work. The role of the ROM BIOS is to provide a consistent set of the fundamental services that are needed for the operation of the computer and its peripheral components. For the most part, the ROM BIOS controls the computer's peripheral devices, such as the display screen, keyboard, and disk drives. When we use the term *BIOS* in its narrowest sense, we are referring to the device control programs—the programs that translate a simple command, such as "read something from the disk," into all the steps needed to actually perform the command, including error detection and correction. In the broadest sense, the BIOS includes not only routines needed to control the PC's peripheral devices but also routines that contain information or perform tasks that are fundamental to other aspects of the computer's operation, such as keeping track of the time of day.

Conceptually, the ROM BIOS programs lie between the programs that are executing in RAM (including MS-DOS) and the hardware. In effect, this means that the BIOS works in two directions in a two-sided process. One side receives requests from programs to perform the standard ROM BIOS input/output services. A program invokes such services by calling a software interrupt. The exact service desired is specified by the interrupt number (which indicates the subject of the service request, such as printer services) and by a service number (which indicates the specific service to be performed). The other side of the ROM BIOS communicates with the computer's hardware devices (display screen, disk drives, and so on), using whatever detailed command codes each device requires. This side of the ROM BIOS also handles any hardware interrupts that a device generates to get attention. For example, whenever you press a key, the keyboard generates an interrupt to let the ROM BIOS know.

Of all the ROM software, the BIOS services are the most interesting and useful to programmers; we cover them in detail in four chapters (Chapters

10 through 13) and an appendix (Appendix A). Because we deal with them so thoroughly later on, we'll skip any specific discussion of what the BIOS services do and instead focus on how the BIOS as a whole keeps track of the computer's input and output processes.

Interrupt Vectors

All members of the IBM PC family are controlled largely through the use of interrupts, which can be generated by hardware or by software. The BIOS service routines are no exception; each BIOS service routine is, in fact, an interrupt service routine. To call a BIOS routine, a program must issue the corresponding software interrupt.

You learned in Chapter 2 that when an interrupt occurs, control of the computer is turned over to an interrupt-handling subroutine that is stored in the system's memory (either RAM or ROM). The interrupt handler is called by loading its segment and offset addresses into registers that control program flow—the CS (code segment) register and the IP (instruction pointer) register, together known as the CS:IP register pair. The segmented addresses that specify the locations of interrupt handlers are called *interrupt vectors*. Interrupt vectors are stored in the interrupt vector table, which is located at the beginning of RAM, starting at address 0000:0000H.

During the system start-up process, a start-up BIOS routine sets certain interrupt vectors to point to certain BIOS interrupt handlers in ROM. Each entry in the interrupt vector table is stored as a pair of words, with the offset portion first and the segment portion second. An interrupt vector can be changed to point to a new interrupt handler simply by locating the vector and changing its value.

As a general rule, PC-family interrupts can be divided into five categories: microprocessor, hardware, software, MS-DOS, and general use. A sixth category, Basic interrupts, exists on IBM systems.

Microprocessor interrupts, often called *logical interrupts,* are designed into the microprocessor. Four of them (interrupts 00H, 01H, 03H, and 04H) are generated by the microprocessor itself, and another (interrupt 02H, the nonmaskable interrupt) is activated by a signal generated by certain hardware devices, such as the math coprocessor and system RAM circuits.

Hardware interrupts are built into the PC hardware. In 8088 and 8086 systems, interrupt numbers 08H through 0FH are used for hardware interrupts; in 80286 and higher systems, interrupt numbers 08H through 0FH (decimal 8 through 15) and 70H through 77H (decimal 112 through 119) are reserved for hardware interrupts. (See Chapter 2 for more about hardware interrupts.)

Software interrupts incorporated into the PC design are part of the ROM BIOS programs. ROM BIOS routines invoked by these interrupts cannot be changed, but the vectors that point to them can be changed to point to different routines. Reserved interrupt numbers are 10H through 1FH (decimal 16 through 31) and 40H through 5FH (decimal 64 through 95).

The Part MS-DOS Plays

The ROM bootstrap loader's only functions are to read a bootstrap program from a disk and to transfer control of the computer to it. On a bootable MS-DOS disk, the disk bootstrap program verifies that MS-DOS is stored on the disk by looking for two hidden files named IO.SYS and MSDOS.SYS. (On IBM systems and some clones, these files are named IBMBIO.COM and IBMDOS.COM.) If it finds the hidden files, it loads them into memory along with the MS-DOS command interpreter, COMMAND.COM. During the boot process, optional parts of MS-DOS, such as installable device drivers, can also be loaded.

The IO.SYS (or IBMBIO.COM) file contains extensions to the ROM BIOS. These extensions can be changes or additions to the routines in the ROM BIOS; they can include corrections to the existing ROM BIOS, routines for new peripheral equipment, and customized changes to the standard ROM BIOS routines. Because they are part of disk software and can be easily changed and updated, the IO.SYS routines provide a convenient way to modify the ROM BIOS. All that is necessary, in addition to the new routine, is that the interrupt vectors for the previous ROM BIOS routines be changed to point to the location in memory where the new disk BIOS routines are placed. Whenever new devices are added to the computer, their support programs can be included in the IO.SYS file or as installable device drivers, eliminating the need to replace ROM chips. See Chapter 8 for more on device drivers.

You can think of the ROM BIOS routines as the lowest-level component of the system software. These routines interact directly with the hardware, performing the most fundamental and primitive I/O operations. The IO.SYS routines, being extensions of the ROM BIOS and providing basic I/O functions, are essentially on the same level. By comparison, the MSDOS.SYS routines are more sophisticated; think of them as occupying the next level up, sitting between the ROM BIOS routines and the application programs.

The MSDOS.SYS file contains the MS-DOS service routines. The MS-DOS services, like the BIOS services, can be called by programs

MS-DOS interrupts are always available when MS-DOS is in use. The MS-DOS interrupt routines are loaded into memory from disk during the boot process. Many programs and programming languages use the services provided by MS-DOS through the MS-DOS interrupts to handle basic

through a set of interrupts whose vectors are placed in the interrupt vector table in low memory. One of the MS-DOS interrupts, interrupt 21H (decimal 33), is particularly important because it gives you access to a rather large group of MS-DOS functions. The MS-DOS functions provide more sophisticated control over I/O operations than do the BIOS routines, especially with regard to disk-file operations. All standard disk processes (formatting disks; reading and writing data; opening, closing, and deleting files; and performing directory searches) are included in the MS-DOS functions. These functions provide the foundation for many of the higher-level MS-DOS utility programs, such as FORMAT, COPY, and DIR. Your own programs can use the MS-DOS services when they need more control of I/O operations than is provided by programming languages and when you are reluctant to dig all the way down to the BIOS level. The MS-DOS services are very important; we cover them in Chapters 10 through 13 and in Appendix B.

The COMMAND.COM file is the third major part of MS-DOS and is the part that all PC users deal with on a regular basis. COMMAND.COM is called the *command interpreter* because it interprets and executes the commands you type in at the MS-DOS prompt. Some of these commands, such as RENAME and ERASE, are internal to the COMMAND.COM file. Others are external, meaning they are separate programs located in separate disk files; examples include FORMAT and CHKDSK. When you enter a command, COMMAND.COM compares your input to a table of internal command names. If a match is found, the command is executed. If the command is not found, COMMAND.COM searches for the requested program on disk, loads it into memory, and executes it. If the program is not found, the message "Bad command or filename" is displayed. The whole subject of the COMMAND.COM file and how it works is intriguing and well worth investigating, as are the other MS-DOS programs. We recommend that you read the *DOS Technical Reference Manual* (for the older releases of DOS), *Inside the IBM PC*, or *The MS-DOS Encyclopedia* for additional information.

operations, especially disk I/O. MS-DOS interrupt numbers are 20H through 3FH (decimal 32 through 63).

Basic interrupts (available only on IBM systems that have Basic in ROM) are assigned by Basic itself and are always available when Basic is in use. The reserved interrupt numbers are 80H through F0H (decimal 128 through 240).

General-use interrupts are unused by the ROM BIOS, MS-DOS, or Basic and are available for temporary use in your programs. The reserved interrupt numbers are 60H through 66H (decimal 96 through 102).

Most of the interrupt vectors used by the ROM BIOS, MS-DOS, and Basic contain the addresses of interrupt handlers. A few interrupt vectors, however, point to tables of useful information. For example, interrupt 1EH contains the address of a table of floppy disk–drive initialization parameters; interrupt 1FH points to a table of bit patterns used by the ROM BIOS to display text characters; and interrupts 41H and 46H point to tables of hard disk parameters. These interrupt vectors are used as convenient places to store addresses, not for interrupts. If you tried to execute interrupt 1EH, for instance, you'd probably crash the system because the interrupt 1EH vector points to data, not to executable code.

The interrupt vectors are stored at the lowest memory locations; the first location in memory contains the vector for interrupt number 00H, and so on. Because each vector is two words in length, you can find a particular interrupt's location in memory by multiplying its interrupt number by 4. For example, the vector for interrupt 05H, the print-screen service interrupt, is at byte offset 20 ($5 \times 4 = 20$)—that is, at address 0000:0014H. You can examine the interrupt vectors by using DEBUG. For example, you can look at the interrupt 05H vector with DEBUG in the following way:

```
DEBUG
D 0000:0014 L 4
```

DEBUG will show 4 bytes, in hex, like this:

```
54 FF 00 F0
```

Converted to a segment and offset address and allowing for backwords storage, the interrupt vector for the entry point in ROM of the print-screen service routine (interrupt 05H) is F000:FF54H. (Of course, this address might be different for different members of the PC family.) The same DEBUG instruction finds any other interrupt vector just as easily.

Figure 3-1 lists the main interrupts and their vector locations. These are the interrupts that programmers will probably find most useful. Details about most of these interrupts are available in Chapters 10 through 13. Interrupts that are not mentioned in this list are, for the most part, reserved for future development.

Interrupt		Offset in Segment 0000		Interrupt		Offset in Segment 0000	
Hex	*Dec*	*0000*	*Use*	*Hex*	*Dec*	*0000*	*Use*
00H	0	0000H	Generated by CPU when division by zero is attempted	13H	19	004CH	Invokes disk services in ROM BIOS
01H	1	0004H	Used to single-step through programs (as with DEBUG)	14H	20	0050H	Invokes communications services in ROM BIOS
02H	2	0008H	Nonmaskable interrupt (NMI)	15H	21	0054H	Invokes system services in ROM BIOS
03H	3	000CH	Used to set break-points in programs (as with DEBUG)	16H	22	0058H	Invokes standard keyboard services in ROM BIOS
04H	4	0010H	Generated when arithmetic result overflows	17H	23	005CH	Invokes printer service in ROM BIOS
05H	5	0014H	Invokes print-screen service routine in ROM BIOS	18H	24	0060H	Activates ROM Basic language
08H	8	0020H	Generated by hardware clock tick	19H	25	0064H	Invokes bootstrap start-up routine in ROM BIOS
09H	9	0024H	Generated by keyboard action	1AH	26	0068H	Invokes time and date services in ROM BIOS
0EH	14	0038H	Signals floppy disk attention (e.g., to signal completion)	1BH	27	006CH	Interrupt by ROM BIOS for Ctrl-Break
0FH	15	003CH	Used in printer control	1CH	28	0070H	Generated at each clock tick
10H	16	0040H	Invokes video display services in ROM BIOS	1DH	29	0074H	Points to table of video control parameters
11H	17	0044H	Invokes equipment-list service in ROM BIOS	1EH	30	0078H	Points to floppy disk–drive parameter table
12H	18	0048H	Invokes memory-size service in ROM BIOS	1FH	31	007CH	Points to video graphics characters (CGA)

Figure 3-1. *Important interrupts used in the PC family.*

(continued)

Figure 3-1. *continued*

Interrupt		Offset in Segment		Interrupt		Offset in Segment	
Hex	Dec	0000	Use	Hex	Dec	0000	Use
20H	32	0080H	Invokes program-terminate service in MS-DOS	27H	39	009CH	Ends program but keeps it in memory under MS-DOS
21H	33	0084H	Invokes all function-call services in MS-DOS	2FH	47	00BCH	MS-DOS Multiplex interrupt
22H	34	0088H	Address of MS-DOS program-terminate routine	41H	65	0104H	Points to parameter table for first hard disk drive
23H	35	008CH	Address of MS-DOS keyboard-break handler	43H	67	010CH	Points to video graphics characters (EGA, PS/2s)
24H	36	0090H	Address of MS-DOS critical-error handler	46H	70	0118H	Points to parameter table for second hard disk drive
25H	37	0094H	Invokes absolute disk-read service in MS-DOS	67H	103	019CH	Invokes LIM Expanded Memory Manager
26H	38	0098H	Invokes absolute disk-write service in MS-DOS				

Changing interrupt vectors

Programmers are usually interested in interrupt vectors not to read them, but to change them so that they point to a new interrupt-handling routine. To do this, you must write a routine that performs the desired task, store the routine in RAM, and then load the routine's address into an existing interrupt vector in the table.

A vector can be changed byte by byte on an assembly language level or by using a programming-language instruction such as the POKE statement in Basic. One potential danger is that an interrupt might occur in the middle of the process of changing the vector. If you are not concerned about this, go ahead and use the POKE method. Otherwise, there are two ways to change a vector while minimizing the likelihood of interrupts: by suspending interrupts during the process or by using an MS-DOS interrupt service routine specially designed to change vectors.

The first method requires that you use assembly language to suspend interrupts while you change the interrupt vector. You can use the clear interrupts instruction (CLI), which suspends all interrupts until a subsequent set interrupts instruction (STI) is executed. By temporarily disabling interrupts with CLI, you ensure that no interrupts can occur while you are updating an interrupt vector.

> NOTE: *CLI does not disable the nonmaskable interrupt (NMI). If your application is one of the rare ones that needs to supply its own NMI handler, the program should temporarily disable the NMI while changing the NMI vector. (See your PC or PS/2 technical reference manuals for details.)*

The following example demonstrates how to update an interrupt vector with interrupts temporarily disabled. This example uses two MOV instructions to copy the segment and offset address of an interrupt handler from DS:DX into interrupt vector 60H:

```
xor     ax,ax
mov     es,ax               ; zero segment register ES
cli                         ; disable interrupts
mov     word ptr es:[180h],dx  ; update vector offset
mov     word ptr es:[182h],ds  ; update vector segment
sti                         ; enable interrupts
```

The second method of updating an interrupt vector is to let MS-DOS do it for you using MS-DOS interrupt 21H, service 25H (decimal 37), which was designed specifically for this purpose. There are two very important advantages to letting MS-DOS set interrupts for you. One advantage is that MS-DOS takes on the task of putting the vector into place in the safest possible way. The other advantage is more far-reaching. When you use MS-DOS service 25H to change an interrupt vector, you allow MS-DOS to track changes to any interrupt vectors it may itself be using. This is particularly important for programs that might run in the DOS compatibility box in Microsoft Windows or OS/2. Using an MS-DOS service to set an interrupt vector instead of setting it yourself is only one of many ways that you can reduce the risk that a program will be incompatible with new machines or with new operating system environments.

The example on the following page demonstrates how to use interrupt 21H, service 25H, to update the vector for interrupt 60H from values stored in a memory variable.

```
mov        dx,seg Int60Handler        ; store segment address in DX
mov        ds,dx                      ; copy new segment to DS
mov        dx,offset Int60Handler     ; store offset address in DX
mov        al,60h                     ; interrupt number
mov        ah,25h                     ; MS-DOS set-interrupt function number
int        21h                        ; MS-DOS function-call interrupt
```

This example shows, in the simplest possible way, how to use the MS-DOS service. However, it glosses over an important and subtle difficulty: You have to load one of the addresses that you're passing to MS-DOS into the data segment (DS) register, a process that effectively blocks normal access to data through the DS register. Getting around that problem requires you to preserve the contents of the DS register. Here is one way this can be done. In this example, taken from the Norton Utilities programs, the interrupt 09H vector is updated with the address of a special interrupt handler:

```
push       ds                         ; save current data segment
mov        dx,offset PGROUP:XXX       ; store handler's offset in DX
push       cs                         ; move handler's code segment...
pop        ds                         ; ...into DS
mov        ah,25h                     ; request set-interrupt function
mov        al,9h                      ; change interrupt number 9
int        21h                        ; MS-DOS function-call interrupt
pop        ds                         ; restore original data segment
```

Key Low-Memory Addresses

Many aspects of PC operation are controlled by data stored in low-memory locations, particularly in the two adjacent 256-byte areas beginning at segments 40H and 50H (addresses 0040:0000H and 0050:0000H). The ROM BIOS uses the 256 bytes from 0040:0000H through 0040:00FFH as a data area for its keyboard, video, disk, printer, and communications routines. The 256 bytes between 0050:0000H and 0050:00FFH are used primarily by Basic, although a few ROM BIOS status variables are located there as well.

Data is loaded into these areas by the BIOS during the start-up process. Although the control data is supposed to be the private reserve of the BIOS, MS-DOS, and Basic, your programs are allowed to inspect or even change it. Even if you do not intend to use the information in these control areas, it is worth studying because it reveals a great deal about what makes the PC family tick.

The ROM BIOS data area

Some memory locations in the BIOS data area are particularly interesting. Most of them contain data vital to the operation of various ROM BIOS and MS-DOS service routines. In many instances, your programs can obtain information stored in these locations by invoking a ROM BIOS interrupt; in all cases, however, they can access the information directly. You can easily check out the values stored at these locations on your own computer, using either DEBUG or Basic.

To use DEBUG, type a command of this form:

```
DEBUG
D XXXX:YYYY L 1
```

XXXX represents the segment part of the address you want to examine. (This would be either 0040H or 0050H, depending on the data area that interests you.) *YYYY* represents the offset part of the address. The L 1 tells DEBUG to display 1 byte. To see 2 or more bytes, type the number of bytes (in hex) after the L parameter. For example, the BIOS keeps track of the current video-mode number in the byte at 0040:0049H. To inspect this byte with DEBUG, you would type

```
DEBUG
D 0040:0049 L 1
```

To display the data with Basic, use a program of the following form, making the necessary substitutions for *segment* (&H0040 or &H0050), *number.of.bytes*, and *offset* (the offset part of the address you want to inspect):

```
10 DEF SEG = segment
20 FOR I = 0 TO number.of.bytes - 1
30   VALUE = PEEK(offset + I)
40   IF VALUE < 16 THEN PRINT "0";      ' needed for leading zero
50   PRINT HEX$ (VALUE);" ";
60 NEXT I
```

The following pages describe the most useful low-memory addresses.

0040:0010H (a 2-byte word). This word holds the equipment-list data that is reported by the equipment-list service, interrupt 11H (decimal 17). The format of this word, shown in Figure 3-2, was established for the PC and PC/XT; certain parts may appear in a different format in later models.

Bit F E D C B A 9 8 7 6 5 4 3 2 1 0	Meaning
X X	Number of printers installed
. . X	(Reserved)
. . . X	1 if game adapter installed
. . . . X X X	Number of RS-232 serial ports
. . . . X	(Reserved)
. . . . X X	+1 = number of floppy disk drives: 00 = 1 drive; 01 = 2 drives; 10 = 3 drives; 11 = 4 drives (see bit 0)
. . . . X X	Initial video mode: 01 = 40-column color; 10 = 80-column color; 11 = 80-column monochrome; 00 = none of the above
. . . . X X . .	For PC with 64-KB motherboard: Amount of system board RAM (11 = 64 KB; 10 = 48 KB; 01 = 32 KB; 00 = 16 KB) For PC/AT: Not used For PS/2s: Bit 3: Not used; Bit 2: 1 = pointing device installed
. . . . X .	1 if math coprocessor installed
. . . . X	1 if any floppy disk drives present (if so, see bits 7 and 6)

Figure 3-2. *The coding of the equipment-list word at address 0040:0010H.*

0040:0013H (a 2-byte word). This word contains the usable memory size in kilobytes. BIOS interrupt service 12H (decimal 18) can be used to report the value in this word.

0040:0017H (2 bytes of keyboard status bits). These bytes are actively used to control the interpretation of keyboard actions by the ROM BIOS routines. Changing these bytes actually changes the meaning of keystrokes. You can freely change the first byte, at address 0040:0017H, but it is not a good idea to change the second byte. See pages 155 and 156 for the bit settings of these 2 bytes.

0040:001AH (a 2-byte word). This word points to the current head of the BIOS keyboard buffer at 0040:001EH, where keystrokes are stored until they are used.

0040:001CH (a 2-byte word). This word points to the current tail of the BIOS keyboard buffer.

0040:001EH (32 bytes, used as sixteen 2-byte entries). This keyboard buffer holds up to 16 keystrokes until they are read via the BIOS services through interrupt 16H (decimal 22). Because this is a circular queue buffer, two pointers indicate the head and tail. It is not wise to manipulate this data.

0040:003EH (1 byte). This byte indicates whether a floppy disk drive needs to be recalibrated before seeking a track. Bits 0 through 3 correspond to drives 0 through 3. If a bit is clear, recalibration is needed. Generally, you will find that a bit is clear if there was any problem with the most recent use of a drive. For example, the recalibration bit will be clear if you try to request a directory (DIR) on a drive with no floppy disk inserted and then type *A* in response to the following message:

```
Not ready reading drive A
Abort, Retry, Fail?
```

0040:003FH (1 byte). This byte returns the floppy disk–drive motor status. Bits 0 through 3 correspond to drives 0 through 3. If the bit is set, the floppy disk–drive motor is running.

0040:0040H (1 byte). This byte is used by the ROM BIOS to ensure that the floppy disk–drive motor is turned off. The value in this byte is decremented with every tick of the system clock (that is, about 18.2 times per second). When the value reaches 0, the BIOS turns off the drive motor.

0040:0041H (1 byte). This byte contains the status code reported by the ROM BIOS after the most recent floppy disk operation. (See Figure 3-3.)

0040:0042H (7 bytes). These 7 bytes hold floppy disk controller status information.

A 30-byte area beginning at 0040:0049H is used for video control. This is the first of two areas in segment 40H that the ROM BIOS uses to track critical video information.

Although programs can safely inspect any of this data, you should modify the data only when you bypass the ROM BIOS video services and program the video hardware directly. In such cases, you should update the video control data to reflect the true status of the video hardware.

0040:0049H (1 byte). The value in this byte specifies the current video mode. (See Figure 3-4.) This is the same video-mode number used in the ROM BIOS video services. (See Chapter 11 for more on these services and page 83 for general information concerning video modes.)

Value	Meaning
00H	No error
01H	Invalid disk command requested
02H	Address mark on disk not found
03H	Write-protect error
04H	Sector not found; disk damaged or not formatted
06H	Disk change line active
08H	DMA disk error
09H	Attempt to cross 64-KB boundary with DMA
0CH	Media type not found
10H	Cyclical redundancy check (CRC) error in data
20H	Disk controller failed
40H	Seek operation failed
80H	Disk timed out (drive not ready)

Figure 3-3. *Floppy disk status codes in the ROM BIOS data area at 0040:0041H.*

We've already shown how to use DEBUG to determine the current video mode by inspecting the byte at 0040:0049H. Basic programs can use the following instructions to read this byte and determine the video mode:

```
DEF SEG = &H40             ' set Basic data segment to 40H
VIDEO.MODE = PEEK(&H49)    ' look at location 0040:0049H
```

0040:004AH (a 2-byte word). This word indicates the number of characters that can be displayed in each row of text on the screen.

0040:004CH (a 2-byte word). This word indicates the number of bytes required to represent one screenful of video data.

0040:004EH (a 2-byte word). This word contains the starting byte offset into video display memory of the current display page. In effect, this address indicates which page is in use by giving the offset to that page.

0040:0050H (eight 2-byte words). These words give the cursor locations for eight separate display pages, beginning with page 0. The first byte of each word gives the character column, and the second byte gives the row.

0040:0060H (a 2-byte word). These 2 bytes indicate the size of the cursor, based on the range of cursor scan lines. The first byte gives the ending scan line, and the second byte gives the starting scan line.

0040:0062H (1 byte). This byte contains the number of the current display page.

Number	Description
00H	40 × 25 16-color text (CGA composite color burst disabled)
01H	40 × 25 16-color text
02H	80 × 25 16-color text (CGA composite color burst disabled)
03H	80 × 25 16-color text
04H	320 × 200 4-color graphics
05H	320 × 200 4-color graphics (CGA composite color burst disabled)
06H	640 × 200 2-color graphics
07H	80 × 25 monochrome text
0DH	320 × 200 16-color graphics
0EH	640 × 200 16-color graphics
0FH	640 × 350 monochrome graphics
10H	640 × 350 16-color graphics
11H	640 × 480 2-color graphics
12H	640 × 480 16-color graphics
13H	320 × 200 256-color graphics

Figure 3-4. *BIOS video-mode numbers stored at address 0040:0049H.*

0040:0063H (a 2-byte word). This word stores the port address of the hardware display controller chip.

0040:0065H (1 byte). This byte contains the current setting of the display-mode register on the Monochrome Display Adapter and the Color Graphics Adapter.

0040:0066H (1 byte). This byte contains the current setting of the Color Graphics Adapter's CRT color register. This byte ends the first block of ROM BIOS video control data.

0040:0067H (5 bytes). The original IBM PC BIOS uses the 5 bytes starting at 0040:0067H for cassette tape control. In the PS/2 (except early models 25 and 30), the 4 bytes at 0040:0067H can contain the address of a system reset routine that overrides the usual BIOS start-up code. (See the BIOS technical reference manual for details.)

0040:006CH (4 bytes stored as one 4-byte number). This area is used as a *master clock count*, which is incremented once for each timer tick. It is treated as if it began counting from 0 at midnight. When the count reaches the equivalent of 24 hours, the ROM BIOS resets the count to 0 and sets the byte at 0040:0070H to 1. MS-DOS or Basic calculates the current time from this value and sets the time by putting the appropriate count in this field.

0040:0070H (1 byte). A nonzero value in this byte indicates that a clock rollover has occurred. When the clock count passes midnight (and is reset to 0), the ROM BIOS then sets this byte to 1, which means that the date should be incremented.

NOTE: *This byte is set to 1 at midnight and is not incremented further. Thus, there is no indication if two midnights pass before the clock is read.*

0040:0071H (1 byte). The ROM BIOS sets bit 7 of this byte to indicate that the Ctrl-Break key combination was pressed.

0040:0072H (a 2-byte word). This word is set to 1234H after the initial power-up memory check. When a warm boot is instigated from the keyboard (via Ctrl-Alt-Del), the memory check will be skipped if this location is already set to 1234H.

0040:0074H (4 bytes). These 4 bytes are used by various members of the PC family for floppy disk– and hard disk–drive control. See the *IBM BIOS Interface Technical Reference Manual* for details.

0040:0078H (4 bytes). Each of these bytes contains a time-out value for the respective parallel printers. (In the PS/2, only the first 3 bytes are used for this purpose.)

0040:007CH (4 bytes). Each of these bytes contains a time-out value for the respective RS-232 serial ports.

0040:0080H (a 2-byte word). This word is an offset into segment 40H that points to the start of the keyboard buffer area.

0040:0082H (a 2-byte word). This word is an offset into segment 40H that points to the end of the keyboard buffer area.

The next 7 bytes are used by the ROM BIOS in the EGA and VGA video adapters for video control:

0040:0084H (1 byte). The value of this byte is one less than the number of character rows displayed on the screen. The BIOS can refer to this value to determine how many character rows of data to erase when the screen is cleared or how many rows to print when Shift-PrtSc is pressed.

0040:0085H (a 2-byte word). This word indicates the height, in scan lines, of characters on the screen.

0040:0087H (4 bytes). These 4 bytes are used by the BIOS video support routines to indicate the amount of video RAM available and the initial settings of the EGA configuration switches, as well as other miscellaneous video status information.

0040:008BH (11 bytes). The ROM BIOS uses this data area for control and status information regarding the floppy disk and hard disk drives.

0040:0096H (2 bytes). Keyboard data area number 3. This data area is used to support the 101-key keyboards.

0040:0098H (9 bytes). This data area is used by the PC/AT and PS/2 BIOS to control certain functions of the real-time clock.

0040:00A8H (4 bytes). In the EGA and VGA BIOS, these bytes contain the segmented address of a table of video parameters and overrides for default ROM BIOS video configuration values. The actual contents of the table vary, depending on which video hardware you are using. The *IBM BIOS Interface Technical Reference Manual* describes this table in detail.

0050:0000H (1 byte). This byte is used by the ROM BIOS to indicate the status of a print-screen operation. Three possible hex values are stored in this location:

00H	Indicates OK status
01H	Indicates a print-screen operation is currently in progress
FFH	Indicates an error occurred during a print-screen operation

0050:0004H (1 byte). This byte is used by MS-DOS when a single–floppy disk system mimics a two–floppy disk system. The value indicates whether the single physical drive is acting as drive A or drive B. These values are used:

00H	Acting as drive A
01H	Acting as drive B

0050:0010H (a 2-byte word). This area is used by ROM Basic to hold its default data segment (DS) value.

Basic lets you set your own data segment value with the DEF SEG = *value* statement. (The offset into the segment is specified by the PEEK or POKE function.) You can also reset the data segment to its default setting by using the DEF SEG statement without a value. Although Basic does not give you a simple way to find the default value stored in this location, you can get it by using this little routine:

```
DEF SEG = &H50
DATA.SEGMENT = PEEK(&H11) * 256 + PEEK(&H10)
```

> NOTE: *ROM Basic administers its own internal data based on the default data segment value. Attempting to change this value is likely to sabotage Basic's operation.*

71

0050:0012H (4 bytes). In some versions of ROM Basic, these 4 bytes contain the segment and offset address of Basic's clock-tick interrupt handler.

NOTE: *In order to perform better, ROM Basic runs the system clock at four times the standard rate, so Basic must replace the ROM BIOS clock interrupt routine with its own. The standard BIOS interrupt routine is invoked by Basic at the normal rate; that is, once for every four fast ticks. There's more about this on page 178.*

0050:0016H (4 bytes). This area contains the address of ROM Basic's Break-key–handling routine.

0050:001AH (4 bytes). This area contains the address of ROM Basic's floppy disk error-handling routine.

The intra-application communications area

In the PC/XT/AT family, the 16 bytes starting at 0040:00F0H are reserved as an *intra-application communications area* (ICA). This data area provides an area of RAM at a known address that an application can use for sharing data among separate program modules. In the PS/2 BIOS, however, the ICA is no longer documented.

Few applications actually use the ICA because the amount of RAM is so small and because the data within the ICA can be unexpectedly modified when more than one program uses it. If you do write a program that uses the ICA, we recommend that you include a checksum and also a signature so that you can ensure that the data in the ICA is yours and that it has not been changed by another program.

WARNING: *The ICA is definitely located in the 16 bytes from 0040:00F0H through 0040:00FFH. A typographical error in some editions of the* IBM PC Technical Reference Manual *places the ICA at 0050:0000H through 0050:00FFH. This is incorrect.*

The BIOS extended data area

The IBM PS/2 ROM BIOS start-up routines allocate an additional area of RAM for their own use. This is also true of PS/2 clones. The BIOS routines use this *extended data area* for transient data storage. For example, the BIOS routines that support the pointing-device (mouse) controller hardware use part of the extended data area for temporary storage.

You can determine the starting address of the extended data area by using a system service that is available through ROM BIOS interrupt 15H. (See Chapter 13.) The first byte in the extended data area contains the size of the data area in kilobytes.

The ROM Version and Machine-ID Markers

Because the BIOS programs are fixed in read only memory, they can't easily be changed when additions or corrections are needed. This means that ROM programs must be tested very carefully before they are frozen onto ROM chips. Although there would seem to be a good chance for serious errors to exist in a system's ROM programs, IBM and other manufacturers have a fine track record; so far, only small and relatively unimportant errors have been found in the PC family's ROM programs. The few errors that have occurred have quickly been corrected by revising the BIOS.

The different versions of ROM software could present a small challenge to programmers who discover that the differences affect the operating characteristics of their programs. But an even greater challenge for programmers is that the different members of the PC family (PC, PC/XT, PC/AT, PS/2s, and clones) each have a slightly different set of ROM BIOS routines.

To ensure that programs can work with the appropriate ROM software, IBM has supplied two identifying markers that are permanently available at the end of memory in the system ROM. One marker identifies the ROM release date, which can be used to identify the BIOS version, and the other gives the machine model. These markers are always present in IBM's own machines, and you'll also find them supplied by the manufacturers of some PC compatibles. The following paragraphs describe these markers in detail.

The *ROM release date* can be found in an 8-byte storage area from F000:FFF5H to F000:FFFCH (2 bytes before the machine-ID byte). It consists of ASCII characters in the common American date format; for example, 06/01/93 stands for June 1, 1993. This release marker is a common feature of the IBM personal computers. It is almost universally present in modern clones but was present in only some of the early IBM compatibles.

You can look at the release date with DEBUG by using the following command:

```
DEBUG
D F000:FFF5 L 8
```

Alternatively, you can let your Basic program look at the bytes by using this technique:

```
10 DEF SEG = &HF000
20 FOR I = 0 TO 7
30 PRINT CHR$(PEEK(&HFFF5 + I));
40 NEXT
50 END
```

The *model ID* is a byte located at F000:FFFEH. This byte identifies the model of PC or PS/2 you are using. (See Figure 3-5.) In addition, a ROM BIOS service in the PC/AT and PS/2s returns more detailed identification information, including the submodel byte listed in the figure. (See Chapter 13.)

Machine	*Date*	*Model*	*Submodel*	*BIOS*	*Revision Notes*
PC	04/24/81	FFH	**	00	
	10/19/81	FFH	**	01	Some BIOS bugs fixed
	10/27/82	FFH	**	02	Upgrade of PC BIOS to XT level
PC/XT	11/08/82	FEH	**	00	
	01/10/86	FBH	00	01	256/640-KB system board
	05/09/86	FBH	00	02	
PC/AT	01/10/84	FCH	**	00	6-MHz 80286
	06/10/85	FCH	00	01	
	11/15/85	FCH	01	00	8-MHz 80286
PS/2 Model 25	06/26/87	FAH	01	00	
PS/2 Model 30	09/02/86	FAH	00	00	
	12/12/86	FAH	00	01	
PS/2 Model 50	02/13/87	FCH	04	00	
PS/2 Model 60	02/13/87	FCH	05	00	
PS/2 Model 80	03/30/87	F8H	00	00	16-MHz 80386
PS/2 Model 80	10/07/87	F8H	01	00	20-MHz 80386
PC*jr*	06/01/83	FDH	**	00	
PC Convertible	09/13/85	F9H	00	00	
PC/XT Model 286	04/21/86	FCH	02	00	

** not applicable

Figure 3-5. *Machine and ROM BIOS version identification for some IBM PCs and PS/2s.*

Many IBM-compatible computers can be identified in the same way, but we do not know of any reliable published information. You might need to rely on improvised methods to identify IBM compatibles.

You can examine the machine-ID byte with DEBUG by using the following command:

```
DEBUG
D F000:FFFE L 1
```

A Basic program can inspect this byte using a technique such as this:

```
10 DEF SEG = &HF000
20 MODEL = PEEK(&HFFFE)
30 IF MODEL < &HF8 THEN PRINT "I'm not an IBM computer" : STOP
40 ON (MODEL - &HF7) GOTO 100,110,120,130,140,150,160,170
100 PRINT "I'm a PS/2 Model 80" : STOP
110 PRINT "I'm a PC Convertible" : STOP
120 PRINT "I'm a PS/2 model 25 or 30" : STOP
130 PRINT "I'm a PC/XT" : STOP
140 PRINT "I'm an 80286-based machine (PC/AT, PS/2 model 50 or 60)" : STOP
150 PRINT "I'm a PCjr" : STOP
160 PRINT "I'm a PC/XT" : STOP
170 PRINT "I'm a PC" : STOP
```

The ROM Extensions

The third element of ROM has more to do with the PC's design than with the actual contents of its memory. The PC was designed to allow for installable extensions to the built-in software in ROM. The additional ROM is usually located on a plug-in adapter such as the Video Graphics Array or a hard disk controller card. Computers in the PC/XT/AT family also have empty sockets on their system boards to accommodate additional ROM chips. Because the original ROM BIOS could not include support programs for future hardware, the ability to add ROM extensions is obviously an important feature.

Several memory areas are reserved for ROM extensions. Addresses C000:0000H through C000:7FFFH are reserved for video adapter ROM. The area from C800:0000H through D000:FFFFH can be used by nonvideo adapters. (For example, the IBM PC/XT hard disk adapter occupies addresses starting at C800:0000H.) Finally, ROM extensions on chips placed onto the system board of a PC, PC/XT, or PC/AT occupy the address range E000:0000H through E000:FFFFH. In the PS/2 models using Micro Channel Architecture, you cannot add ROM chips to the system board. The system ROM in these computers occupies the entire address range from E000:0000H through F000:FFFFH.

ROM Basic

Now we move on to the fourth element of ROM: ROM Basic. Remember that ROM Basic is present only in IBM systems. ROM Basic acts in two ways. First, it provides the core of the Basic language, which includes most of the commands and the underlying foundation (such as memory management) that Basic uses. The disk versions of interpreted Basic, which are found in the program files BASIC.COM (available in PC-DOS versions 1 through 4) and BASICA.COM (available in PC-DOS versions 2 through 4), are essentially supplements to ROM Basic, and they rely on ROM Basic to get much of their work done. The second role of ROM Basic is to provide what IBM calls cassette Basic—the Basic that is activated when you start up your computer without a disk.

Whenever you use early versions of the interpreted, disk-based Basic, ROM Basic programs are also used—although there's nothing to make you aware of it. On the other hand, compiled Basic programs (such as those produced by Quick Basic) don't make use of ROM Basic.

Comments

As the PC family has evolved, the amount and complexity of the ROM software has increased to accommodate the greater sophistication of the computer hardware. The source code listings in the PC, PC/XT, and PC/AT technical reference manuals consist of tens of thousands of assembly language instructions. Despite the size of the ROM BIOS, a browse through the source code can be fun and enlightening. Note that these listings are not provided for the PS/2 family.

We have made every effort to point out when and how to use the ROM BIOS routines. We recommend that you read Chapters 10 through 13 before you begin your own exploration of the ROM BIOS.

Chapter 4

Video Basics

To many people, the video display *is* the computer. A program is often judged primarily by the quality and design of its display. In this chapter, you'll see what kinds of video display output the PC family can produce. More important, we'll explain how to manipulate the display to get the effects you want.

The Video Subsystems

Every PC has a *video subsystem* that is responsible for producing the image that appears on the display screen. At the heart of the video subsystem is the special-purpose circuitry that must be programmed to generate the electrical signals that control the video display. In most members of the PC family, this circuitry is located on a *display adapter,* a circuit board that plugs into one of the computer's expansion slots. In some other systems, including most IBM PS/2 models, the special video circuitry is built into the system board, and a plug-in display adapter is not required. In either case, plug-in or built-in, the circuits are functionally equivalent and are programmed the same way.

With the exception of a few highly specialized units, all PC video subsystems are *memory mapped.* This means that the video subsystem includes a block of dedicated memory, called the *video buffer,* that holds the text or graphics information displayed on the screen. Other components of the video subsystem translate the raw data in the video buffer into the signals that drive the video display. Thus, to display text or graphics on the screen, a program need only write the appropriate data to the video buffer. The video buffer can be written to directly, like any other area of RAM, or it can be written to by using special routines in the BIOS and MS-DOS.

The various video subsystems used in PCs and PS/2s evolved from the two video adapters designed for the original IBM PC: the Monochrome Display Adapter (MDA) and the Color Graphics Adapter (CGA). The CGA offers color capabilities and the ability to display graphics, but text quality is mediocre. The MDA provides excellent text display but does not have graphics or color capabilities. Following the introduction of the MDA and the CGA, the Hercules Corporation soon introduced the Hercules Graphics Card, which offers the same crisp text as the MDA and also, with special driver software, can be used to display graphics with many programs.

IBM later released the Enhanced Graphics Adapter (EGA), which offers more colors and a sharper screen display than the CGA. Other manufacturers soon followed with clones of the EGA.

When the IBM PS/2 line was introduced, two more video subsystems were made available: the Multi-Color Graphics Array (MCGA) and the Video

Graphics Array (VGA), both of which offer performance superior to that of the EGA. In most PS/2 models, the video subsystem is built into the system board. At the same time that IBM introduced these video subsystems, it introduced a VGA adapter that can be installed in an expansion slot in other members of the PC family. Consequently, the VGA quickly became the video system of choice.

Other manufacturers copied the VGA, and fierce competition had prices falling and manufacturers looking for ways to give their VGA adapters a competitive edge. They did so by adding capabilities, such as more colors or greater resolution, to the basic VGA standard. These adapters were called Super VGA (SVGA), but because there was no defined SVGA standard, adapters from various manufacturers differed. This was a headache for programmers, because a program written for one SVGA adapter might not work properly with another SVGA adapter.

To solve this problem, in 1989 a group of SVGA manufacturers formed the VESA (Video Electronic Standards Association) committee. This committee developed a set of standards, called the VESA standard, that would be followed by all SVGA manufacturers. This standard ensures that the SVGA BIOS expansion presents a consistent interface and permits programmers to write for SVGA adapters without concern about hardware differences among different manufacturers' products.

We'll discuss all six video subsystems—MDA, CGA, EGA, MCGA, VGA, and SVGA—in this chapter. Although clear differences in hardware design exist among the various video subsystems, their strong family resemblance should encourage you to consider what they have in common before worrying about the differences among them.

You might have heard about two other video subsystems: the Extended Graphics Array (XGA) and the 8514/A. Although these are capable designs, they have not achieved anywhere near the acceptance of the previously mentioned standards, and this book will not cover them.

All PC display screens are composed of a matrix of small, closely spaced dots, called *pixels* (an abbreviation for "picture element"). Any image you see on the screen, whether a page of text or a complex graphical image, is composed of pixels. The video control circuitry specifies whether each pixel is on or off and, in some systems, also specifies each pixel's brightness and color. This is fundamentally the same way that a television operates.

Five of the six PC video subsystems can operate in two fundamentally different modes, called *text mode* and *graphics mode*. (The exception is the MDA, which operates only in text mode.)

- In text mode you can display only characters from a predefined set (which includes letters, numbers, punctuation marks, and a variety of symbols). You cannot control individual screen pixels.

- In graphics mode you have complete control over every pixel on the screen. Graphics mode permits display of the predefined character set, but it is mainly used to display complex drawings and text characters in shapes and sizes not supplied by the predefined set.

When the PC was first introduced, buyers had to choose between the MDA and the CGA. The CGA can operate in both text and graphics modes to produce drawings and characters in several formats and colors. By contrast, the MDA can operate only in text mode, using the predefined set of alphanumeric and graphics characters and displaying them in only one color. The MDA works only with the IBM Monochrome Display (or its equivalent), and the CGA must be connected to either a direct-drive or a composite color monitor. (See page 86 for more on monitors.) For text work, many business and professional users prefer a monochrome display to a color display because a monochrome screen is easier on the eyes and less expensive than a color display. But by choosing monochrome, they sacrifice color, a valuable asset for any computer display.

The EGA was the first PC video subsystem to combine graphics, color, and high-quality text. The EGA can be used with either a monochrome or a color monitor. The EGA was also the first video subsystem with its own ROM BIOS extensions—BIOS video routines located in ROM chips on the adapter card.

The MDA, CGA, and EGA are all outdated today and are rarely seen on new systems. Many older systems with these video subsystems are still in use, however, so a programmer needs to be familiar with them.

The MCGA video subsystem is something of an orphan. It was designed by IBM for the early low-end models in the PS/2 line, and it has almost all of the capabilities of the VGA card. Other manufacturers never bothered to clone the MCGA, however, because they preferred to direct their resources toward the more powerful VGA standard. Today you'll find MCGA video subsystems on only a small minority of older IBM PS/2 systems.

The *de facto* video standard on almost all of today's new PC systems is VGA or SVGA. The cost of adapter cards and monitors has become reasonable, and the superior performance of VGA is highly desirable for modern graphically oriented applications programs. However, when you are writing a program, you cannot make any assumptions about the video subsystem that your program will be running on.

The best way to understand the video capabilities of the PC family is to learn about the features that their various video subsystems have in common. As we go along, we'll point out the differences and improvements that distinguish the newer and more complicated subsystems (EGA, MCGA, VGA, and SVGA) from their predecessors (MDA and CGA).

Memory and the Video Subsystems

The video buffer memory is connected directly to the display circuitry. This circuitry continuously scans the video buffer and updates the display. Remember, however, that the video buffer is also a part of the computer's main memory address space. A full 128 KB of the memory address space is reserved for use as a video buffer, at addresses A000:0000H through B000:FFFFH (decimal 655,360 through 786,431), but the two original display adapters use only two small parts of this memory area. The MDA provides a 4-KB video buffer located at segment B000H, and the CGA provides a 16-KB video buffer located at segment B800H.

With the other video subsystems, the address of the video buffer isn't fixed; instead, it depends on how the subsystem is configured. For example, when an EGA is used with a monochrome display, its text-mode video buffer is placed at B000H, exactly as with an MDA. When an EGA is attached to a color display, its video buffer is located at B800H. And when you use an EGA in non-CGA graphics modes, the starting buffer address is A000H. The MCGA and the VGA also support this chameleonlike method of buffer addressing.

Creating the Screen Image

You can describe the screen displays created by PC video subsystems as *memory-mapped displays* because each address in the display memory (the video buffer) corresponds to a specific location on the screen. (See Figure 4-1.) The display can be changed as quickly as the computer can write new data to video memory.

The display circuitry continually reads information from video memory and converts it to the control signals required to create the screen display. You learned earlier that the display is made up of pixels. Pixels are produced by an electron beam striking the phosphorescent coating on the inside surface of the display screen. The electron beam is produced by an electron gun that scans the screen line by line. As the gun moves across and down the screen in a fixed path called a *raster scan,* the video subsystem generates video control signals that turn the beam on and off, matching the pattern of the bits in memory.

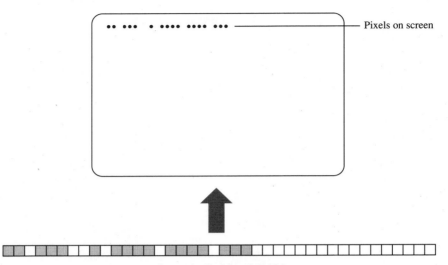

Figure 4-1. *The memory-mapped display.*

The video circuitry refreshes the screen from 50 to 72 times a second (depending on the video mode), making the changing images appear clear and steady. At the end of each screen-refresh cycle, the electron beam must move from the bottom right corner to the top left corner of the screen to begin a new cycle. This movement is called the *vertical retrace*. During the retrace, the beam is blanked and no pixels are written to the screen.

The vertical retrace period (about 1.25 milliseconds) is important to programmers for one main reason, which requires some explanation. The dual-ported design of the video memory gives the CPU and the display-refresh circuitry equal access to the display memory, which allows the CPU and the display circuitry to access video memory at the same time.

This causes a problem on the Color Graphics Adapter (CGA). If the CPU happens to read or write to the video buffer at the same time the display circuitry is copying data out of the buffer to display on screen, a "snow" effect might briefly appear on the screen. However, if you instruct the CPU to access memory only during vertical retrace, when the display circuitry is not accessing the video buffer, snow can be eliminated. To do this, a program running on a CGA can test the value of bit 3 in the adapter's I/O port at 3DAH. This bit is set to on at the beginning of vertical retrace and then set to off at the end. During this 1.25-millisecond pause, you can have your program write as much data as possible to the video display memory. At the end of the retrace, the display circuitry can write this data to the screen without causing snow.

This technique is useful for any application that directly accesses data in the video buffer in text mode on a CGA. Fortunately, the hardware design of all other PC video subsystems avoids such access conflict and makes this specialized programming technique unnecessary.

The Video Display Modes

With the exception of the MDA, all PC video subsystems can operate in multiple display modes. The display mode controls certain aspects of the video system's operation, such as the number of colors available and whether text or graphics can be displayed. Originally, 8 video modes were defined for PCs: 7 on the CGA and 1 on the MDA. The more sophisticated EGA, MCGA, and VGA introduced several new modes plus variations on the original 8. As a result, among these 5 PC video subsystems are 12 different text and graphics display modes and, depending how you count them, 7 or 8 variations. The VESA standard for SVGA added another 9 modes. You can see that there's plenty of variety when you're working with PC video subsystems!

The large number of display modes might seem confusing, but it's really quite logical. The display mode controls only three aspects of the video display:

- Whether text only, or both text and graphics, can be displayed

- The number of colors available

- The screen resolution—that is, the number of pixels vertically and horizontally on the screen

For example, on VGA systems, video mode 18 (12H) offers 640 × 480 resolution with 16 colors, and mode 19 (13H) offers 320 × 200 resolution with 256 colors.

Another thing you should know about video modes is that the "higher" video subsystems can imitate, or emulate, all the modes of the "lower" ones. For example, an EGA system can emulate all the modes of CGA and MDA systems, and a VGA system can emulate all MDA, CGA, and EGA modes. Don't let the seemingly redundant mode numbers in Figure 4-2 confuse you: The difference between mode 0 and mode 1, for example, is that the composite color signal on the CGA is modified for composite monochrome monitors in mode 0. (See page 86 for more on monitors.) With all other monitors and in all other video subsystems, modes 0 and 1 are the same, as are modes 2 and 3 and modes 4 and 5.

The evolutionary pattern is the same for graphics modes. The CGA supports two graphics modes: a 320 × 200–pixel, 4-color mode and a 640 × 200–pixel, 2-color mode. These same two modes are supported on the EGA,

MCGA, VGA, and SVGA. The EGA introduced three new graphics modes with more colors and better resolution than the original CGA graphics modes: the 320 × 200, 16-color; 640 × 200, 16-color; and 640 × 350, 16-color modes. The EGA also introduced a 640 × 350 monochrome graphics mode that could be used only with an MDA-compatible monochrome display.

When the VGA appeared, it supported the same modes as did the MDA, CGA, and EGA, but again, a few new graphics modes were introduced. The pattern continued with the SVGA, which supported all VGA (and lower) modes as well as its own.

Figure 4-2 provides details on the various video display modes.

BIOS Mode Number					
Hex	Dec	Type	Resolution	Colors	Video Subsystem
00H, 01H	0, 1	Text	40 × 25	16	CGA, EGA, MCGA, VGA, SVGA
02H, 03H	2, 3	Text	80 × 25	16	CGA, EGA, MCGA, VGA, SVGA
04H, 05H	4, 5	Graphics	320 × 200	4	CGA, EGA, MCGA, VGA, SVGA
06H	6	Graphics	640 × 200	2	CGA, EGA, MCGA, VGA, SVGA
07H	7	Text	80 × 25	Mono	MDA, EGA, VGA, SVGA
08H, 09H, 0AH	8, 9, 10	Graphics			(PC*jr* only)
0BH, 0CH	11, 12				(Used internally by EGA BIOS)
0DH	13	Graphics	320 × 200	16	EGA, VGA, SVGA
0EH	14	Graphics	640 × 200	16	EGA, VGA, SVGA
0FH	15	Graphics	640 × 350	Mono	EGA, VGA, SVGA
10H	16	Graphics	640 × 350	16	EGA, VGA, SVGA
11H	17	Graphics	640 × 480	2	MCGA, VGA, SVGA
12H	18	Graphics	640 × 480	16	VGA, SVGA
13H	19	Graphics	320 × 200	256	MCGA, VGA, SVGA
6AH	106	Graphics	800 × 600	16	SVGA
100H	256	Graphics	640 × 400	256	SVGA
101H	257	Graphics	640 × 480	256	SVGA
102H	258	Graphics	800 × 600	16	SVGA
103H	259	Graphics	800 × 600	256	SVGA
104H	260	Graphics	1024 × 768	16	SVGA
105H	261	Graphics	1024 × 768	256	SVGA
106H	262	Graphics	1280 × 1024	16	SVGA
107H	263	Graphics	1280 × 1024	256	SVGA

Figure 4-2. *Video modes available on PC video subsystems.*

How do you know which mode to use in a program? Clearly, if broad compatibility is a concern, the MDA and CGA modes are the least common denominators. If you need more colors or better graphics resolution than the CGA modes provide, you can turn to one of the EGA, VGA, or SVGA graphics modes. Of course, if your program requires an EGA or a VGA to run, users who have only a CGA will be out of luck.

Many commercial software vendors solve this problem by distributing installable video drivers along with their products. Before you can use a package like Microsoft Windows or a non-Windows version of Lotus 1-2-3, for example, you must run a special installation program that binds output routines for your particular video hardware to the software application. This approach is more work for both the people who write software and the people who use it, but it is a good way to make applications deliver the best possible video performance without stumbling over the diversity of video hardware and video modes.

Video-Mode Control

Before we get into the details about resolution and color in video modes, let's consider how you tell the hardware which video mode to use. The most efficient way to set up a video mode is to use assembly language to call the BIOS. BIOS interrupt 10H (decimal 16), service 00H, provides a way to select a video mode using the mode numbers listed in Figure 4-2. (See Chapter 11 for more details.)

Many programming languages also offer high-level commands that select video modes for you. For example, Basic gives you control over the video modes through the SCREEN statement but refers to them in its own way, using different mode numbers than do the BIOS routines. You can also control some of the video modes through the MS-DOS MODE command. (See Figure 4-3.)

Display Resolution

As you have already learned, a video image consists of a large number of closely spaced pixels. The display resolution is defined by the number of pixel rows, or *scan lines,* from top to bottom and the number of pixels from left to right in each scan line. The horizontal and vertical resolution are limited by the capabilities of the video monitor as well as by the display circuitry inside the computer. The video modes available on the different subsystems were carefully designed so that the horizontal and vertical resolution in each mode are within the limits imposed by the hardware.

Monitors

The type of video display, or monitor, that might be used with a program is an important consideration in program design. Monochrome monitors cannot produce color and most cannot produce graphics, and a few produce such a poor-quality image that you can use only the 40-column text display format. The many kinds of monitors that can be used with the PC family of computers can be broken down into five basic types.

Direct-drive monochrome monitors. These monitors are designed to work with the Monochrome Display Adapter (MDA), although you can also use them with an Enhanced Graphics Adapter (EGA). The green IBM Monochrome Display is reminiscent of IBM's 3270 series of mainframe computer terminals; it's no surprise that many business users are comfortable with the combination of an MDA and a green monochrome display.

Composite monochrome monitors. These monitors are still used and are the least expensive monitors available. They connect to the composite video output on the Color Graphics Adapter (CGA) and provide a fairly clear one-color image (usually green or amber). Don't confuse the composite monochrome monitor with the direct-drive monochrome monitor. The composite monochrome monitor can be attached only to the CGA, whereas the direct-drive monochrome monitor must be used with an MDA or an EGA.

Composite color monitors and TV sets. Composite color monitors use a single combined signal such as the composite video output of the CGA. The composite color monitor produces color and graphics but has limitations: An 80-column display is often unreadable; only certain color combinations work well; and graphics resolution is low quality, so graphics must be kept simple by the use of low-resolution graphics modes.

Although the standard television set (color or black-and-white) is technically a composite monitor, it usually produces an even lower-quality image than the dedicated composite monitor. Text displays must be in 40-column mode to ensure that the display is readable. TVs are connected to the composite video output of the CGA, but the composite signal must be converted by an RF adapter before going into the TV.

RGB color monitors. The RGB monitors are considered the best of both worlds. They combine the high-quality text display of the monochrome monitors with high-resolution graphics and color. RGB stands for "red-green-blue," and RGB monitors are so named because they use separate red, green, and blue color signals, unlike the composite monitors, which use only one composite signal. The image and color quality of an RGB monitor are much better than those produced on any screen that connects to the composite video output.

Variable-frequency monitors. One of the problems created by the proliferation of different video subsystems is that some subsystems produce color and timing signals with different frequencies or different encodings than those produced by other subsystems. For example, you cannot use a VGA-compatible monitor with a CGA because the color information in the monitor drive signals is encoded differently by a CGA than it is by a VGA video subsystem.

Monitor manufacturers have addressed this problem by designing variable-frequency RGB monitors that can be used with a wide range of signal frequencies and with more than one type of color signal encoding. For example, NEC's MultiSync monitors can adjust to the different signal frequencies generated by the CGA, the EGA, the VGA, and the SVGA video subsystems. These monitors also have a switch that lets you adapt them either to the digital color signal encoding used by the CGA and EGA subsystems or to the analog color signals used by the VGA and SVGA subsystems.

Many people use variable-frequency monitors because they anticipate the need to upgrade their video subsystems at some time in the future and they don't want to be stuck with an incompatible monitor.

Any specific monitor model has an upper limit to the screen resolution it can display, which determines which of the SVGA modes it can work with. Monitors also have a maximum refresh rate, which is the maximum number of times the screen image can be redrawn each second. Higher refresh rates provide clearer images with less apparent flicker; a refresh rate of at least 70 is considered desirable for today's graphics-intensive applications.

BIOS Mode Number		Basic Statement to	DOS Statement to
Hex	Dec	Change Mode	Change Mode
00H	0	SCREEN 0,0:WIDTH 40	MODE BW40
01H	1	SCREEN 0,1:WIDTH 40	MODE CO40
02H	2	SCREEN 0,0:WIDTH 80	MODE BW80
03H	3	SCREEN 0,1:WIDTH 80	MODE CO80
04H	4	SCREEN 1,0	n/a
05H	5	SCREEN 1,1	n/a
06H	6	SCREEN 2	n/a
07H	7	n/a	MODE MONO
0DH	13	SCREEN 7	n/a
0EH	14	SCREEN 8	n/a
0FH	15	SCREEN 10	n/a
10H	16	SCREEN 9	n/a
11H	17	SCREEN 11	n/a
12H	18	SCREEN 12	n/a
13H	19	SCREEN 13	n/a

Figure 4-3. *The Basic and DOS commands used to change video modes.*

The MDA's single text mode has 720 × 350–pixel resolution; that is, the screen has 350 scan lines, each of which contains 720 pixels. Because 25 rows of 80 characters of text are displayed in this mode, each character is 9 pixels wide (720 ÷ 80) and 14 pixels high (350 ÷ 25). The CGA's text modes are a bit lower resolution because the CGA's pixel resolution is only 640 × 200. Thus the 25 rows of 80-character text on a CGA consist of characters that are only 8 pixels wide (640 ÷ 80) and 8 pixels high (200 ÷ 25). That's why text looks sharper on an MDA screen than on a CGA.

The trend in the newer video subsystems has been to provide increased vertical resolution. For example, the EGA's 80 × 25 text mode has 640 × 350–pixel resolution, so text characters are 8 × 14 pixels. On the MCGA the default 80 × 25 text mode has 640 × 400 resolution (8 × 16 characters), and on the VGA the same text mode has 720 × 400 resolution, so each character is 9 pixels wide and 16 pixels high. From a program's point of view, the 80 × 25 text mode is the same on the CGA, the MCGA, and the VGA—it's display mode 3 in all cases—but a user sees much higher resolution when using a VGA or MCGA than when using one of the older graphics subsystems.

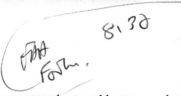

You see the same trend toward better resolution when you examine the graphics modes available with the newer video subsystems. The VGA's 640 × 480, 16-color mode has more than twice as many pixels on the screen as the original CGA's 640 × 200 graphics mode. (It's ironic that this CGA mode was known as a high-resolution mode when the CGA was new!) The SVGA standard provides resolution as high as 1280 horizontally by 1024 vertically, offering extremely sharp text and images.

The Use of Color

A variety of colors is available in every video mode except, of course, on a monochrome display. You might have noticed that among the various modes there are substantial differences in the number of colors available. In this section, we describe the color options for the video modes.

A color on the video display screen is produced by a combination of four elements: three color components—red, green, and blue—plus an intensity, or brightness, component. Text and graphics modes use the same colors and intensity options, but they combine them in different ways to produce their color displays. In text modes, where the basic display unit is an entire character, 1 byte is used to set the color, the intensity, and the blinking characteristics of the character and its background. In graphics modes, each screen pixel is represented by a group of 1 to 8 bits whose value determines the color and brightness of the displayed pixel.

In 16-color text and graphics modes, the four basic color and brightness components can be combined in 16 ways. Colors are specified by a group of 4 bits. Each bit designates whether a particular color component is on or off. The result is sixteen color combinations that correspond to the sixteen 4-bit binary numbers. (See Figure 4-4.)

In some video modes, the data in the video buffer consists of 4-bit attribute values that correspond exactly to the 16 possible color combinations on the screen. In other video modes, the attribute values do not directly specify colors. For example, on the EGA, each attribute value designates one of 16 palette registers, each of which contains a color value. (See Figure 4-5.) It is the palette color values that determine the color combinations displayed on the screen.

The use of palettes makes it possible to specify one of a broad range of colors using relatively few bits of data in the video buffer. Each of the EGA's 16 palette registers, for example, can contain one of 64 different 6-bit color values. In this way, any 2 of 64 different colors can be used in a 2-color EGA

Intensity	Red	Green	Blue	Binary	Hex	Description
0	0	0	0	0000B	00H	Black
0	0	0	1	0001B	01H	Blue
0	0	1	0	0010B	02H	Green
0	0	1	1	0011B	03H	Cyan (blue-green)
0	1	0	0	0100B	04H	Red
0	1	0	1	0101B	05H	Magenta
0	1	1	0	0110B	06H	Brown (or dark yellow)
0	1	1	1	0111B	07H	Light gray (or ordinary white)
1	0	0	0	1000B	08H	Dark gray (black on many screens)
1	0	0	1	1001B	09H	Light blue
1	0	1	0	1010B	0AH	Light green
1	0	1	1	1011B	0BH	Light cyan
1	1	0	0	1100B	0CH	Light red
1	1	0	1	1101B	0DH	Light magenta
1	1	1	0	1110B	0EH	Yellow (or light yellow)
1	1	1	1	1111B	0FH	Bright white

Figure 4-4. *Default colors available in 16-color text and graphics modes.*

video mode, any 4 of 64 can be used in a 4-color mode, and any 16 of 64 can be used in a 16-color mode.

All PC video subsystems except the MDA can use palettes to display colors. The CGA has three built-in, 4-color palettes for use in 320 × 200, 4-color mode. The EGA, as we have seen, has a 16-color palette in which each color can be selected from a set of 64 colors. The MCGA, the VGA, and the SVGA—which can display an even wider range of colors—use a separate palettelike component, the *video digital-to-analog converter* (video DAC), to send color signals to the screen.

The video DAC contains 256 color registers, each of which contains a 6-bit color value for each of the three primary colors: red, green, and blue. Because there are 64 possible values for each of the RGB components, each video DAC color register can contain one of 64 × 64 × 64, or 262,144, different color values. That wide range of colors can help you display subtle color shades and contours.

With the MCGA, the video DAC color registers serve much the same purpose as the palette registers do with the EGA. Attribute values in the

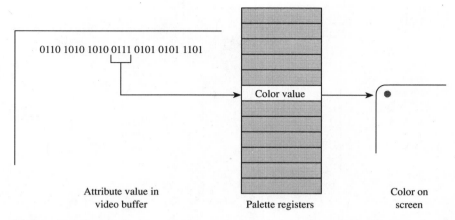

0110 1010 1010 0111 0101 0101 1101

Color value

Attribute value in
video buffer

Palette registers

Color on
screen

Figure 4-5. *How EGA colors are specified using palette registers. Each attribute value in the video buffer designates a palette register whose contents specify a color.*

video buffer designate video DAC color registers whose contents specify the colors that appear on the screen. Unfortunately, only one MCGA video mode can take full advantage of the video DAC's capabilities: 320 × 200, 256-color mode. Only this video mode uses 8-bit attribute values that can specify all 256 of the video DAC's color registers. All remaining video modes use attribute values that have no more than 4 bits, so only the first 16 video DAC color registers are used.

The VGA gets around this limitation (and complicates matters somewhat) by using a set of 16 palette registers as the EGA does, as well as a set of 256 video DAC color registers as the MCGA does. An attribute value in the video buffer selects one of the 16 palette registers, whose contents select one of the 256 video DAC color registers, whose contents determine the color displayed on the screen. (See Figure 4-6.) The same basic method is used for controlling color on SVGA subsystems.

Specifying colors on an EGA, an MCGA, a VGA, or an SVGA is clearly more complicated than it is on the CGA. To simplify this process, the ROM BIOS loads the palette registers (on the EGA, VGA, and SVGA) and the video DAC color registers (on the MCGA, VGA, and SVGA) with color values that exactly match those available on the CGA. If you use CGA-compatible text and graphics modes on the newer subsystems and ignore the palette and video DAC registers, you'll see the same colors you would on a CGA.

For this reason it's usually best to ignore the palette and video DAC registers when you start developing an application. Once your application

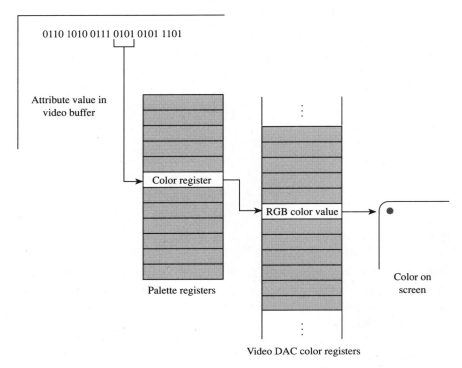

Figure 4-6. *How VGA colors are specified using palette registers and the video DAC.*

works properly with the CGA-compatible colors, you can add program code that changes the palette or the video DAC colors, or both. The BIOS provides a complete set of services that let you access the palette and video DAC registers. Chapter 11 covers these services in detail.

The next four sections discuss important color-related considerations.

Color-Suppressed Modes

In an effort to make the graphics modes compatible with a wide range of monitors, both color and monochrome, the CGA included a few display modes that do not produce color; these are called *color-suppressed modes*. There are three color-suppressed modes: modes 0, 2, and 5. In these modes, colors are converted into shades of gray or whatever color the screen phosphor produces. There are four gray shades in mode 5, and a variety of shades in modes 0 and 2. The CGA's color is suppressed in the composite output but *not* in its RGB output. This inconsistency is the result of an unavoidable technical limitation.

NOTE: *For each color-suppressed mode, there is a corresponding color mode, so modes 0 and 1 correspond to 40-column text, modes 2 and 3 to 80-column text, and modes 4 and 5 to medium-resolution graphics. Modes 4 and 5 reverse the pattern of modes 0 and 1 and modes 2 and 3, in which the color-suppressed mode comes first, and this fact has led to a complication in Basic. The burst parameter of the Basic SCREEN statement controls color. The meaning of this parameter is reversed for modes 4 and 5 so that the statement SCREEN,1 activates color in the text modes (0, 1, 2, and 3) but suppresses color in the graphics modes (4 and 5). This inconsistency might have been a programming error at first, but it is now part of the official definition of the SCREEN statement.*

Color in Text and Graphics Modes

Text and graphics modes use the same color-decoding circuitry but differ in the way they store the color attribute data in the video buffer. In text modes, no matter what video subsystem you use, the foreground and background colors of each character are specified by two 4-bit fields in a single attribute byte. (See Figure 4-7.) Together, the foreground and background attributes describe all of a character's pixels: All foreground pixels are displayed with the character's foreground attribute, and all background pixels assume the background attribute.

Bit 7 6 5 4 3 2 1 0	*Use*
1	Blinking of foreground character or intensity component of background color
. 1	Red component of background color
. . 1	Green component of background color
. . . 1	Blue component of background color
. . . . 1 . . .	Intensity component of foreground color
. . . . . 1 . .	Red component of foreground color
. . . . . . 1 .	Green component of foreground color
. . . . 1	Blue component of foreground color

Figure 4-7. *The coding of the color attribute byte.*

In graphics modes, each pixel's attribute is determined by the contents of a bit field in the video buffer. The size and format of a pixel's bit field depend on the video mode: The smallest bit fields are only 1 bit wide (as in 640 × 200, 2-color mode), and the largest bit fields are 8 bits wide (as in 320 × 200, 256-color mode).

The reason for having both text and graphics modes becomes clear if you think about how much data it takes to describe the pixels on the screen. In graphics modes, you need from 1 to 8 bits of data in the video buffer for every pixel you display. In 640 × 350, 16-color mode, for instance, with 4 bits per pixel, you need 640 × 350 × 4 ÷ 8 (112,000) bytes to represent one screenful of video data. But if you display 25 rows of 80 characters in a text mode with the same resolution, you need only 80 × 25 × 2 (4000) bytes.

The trade-off is clear: Text modes consume less memory and require less data manipulation than do graphics modes; however, you can manipulate each pixel independently in graphics modes, whereas in text modes, you can manipulate only entire characters.

Setting color in text modes

Let's take a closer look at how you control colors in text modes. (We'll get back to graphics modes later in this chapter.) In text modes, each character position on the display screen is controlled by a pair of adjacent bytes in the video buffer. The first byte contains the ASCII code for the character that will be displayed. (See Appendix D for a chart of characters.) The second byte is the character's *attribute byte*. It controls how the character will appear—that is, its colors, brightness (intensity), and blinking characteristics.

We've already mentioned two attributes that affect a character's appearance: color and intensity (brightness). You can assign several other attributes to text characters, depending on which video subsystem you're using. On all video subsystems, text characters can blink. On monochrome-capable subsystems (the MDA, EGA, VGA, and SVGA), characters can also be underlined. Also, on some non-IBM subsystems, such as the Hercules Graphics Card Plus, characters can have attributes such as overstrike and boldface.

In all cases, you assign these alternative attributes by using the same 4-bit attributes that specify color. A case in point is the blinking attribute. Character blinking is controlled by setting a bit in a special register in the video subsystem. (On the CGA, for example, this enable-blink bit is bit 5 of the 8-bit register mapped at input/output port 3D8H.) When this bit is set to 1, the high-order bit of each character's attribute byte is not interpreted as part of the character's background color specification. Instead, this bit indicates whether the character should blink.

If you have a CGA, run the following Basic program and watch what happens:

```
10 DEF SEG = &HB800          ' point to start of video buffer
20 POKE 0,ASC("A")           ' store the ASCII code for A in the buffer
30 POKE 1,&H97               ' foreground attribute = 7 (white)
                             ' background attribute = 9 (intense blue)
```

You'll see a blinking white letter *A* on a blue background. If you add the following statement to the program, you'll clear the enable-blink bit and cause the CGA to interpret the background attribute as intense blue:

```
40 OUT &H3D8,&H09            clear the enable-blink bit
```

The default attribute used by MS-DOS and Basic is 07H, normal white (7) on black (0), without blinking, but you can use any combination of 4-bit foreground and background attributes for each character displayed in a text mode. If you exchange a character's foreground and background attributes, the character is displayed in *reverse video*. If the foreground and background attributes are the same, the character is invisible.

Setting attributes in monochrome mode

The monochrome mode (mode 7) used by the Monochrome Display Adapter has a limited selection of attributes that take the place of color. Like the CGA, the MDA uses 4-bit foreground and background attributes, but their values are interpreted differently by the MDA attribute decoding circuitry.

Only certain combinations of foreground and background attributes are recognized by the MDA. (See Figure 4-8.) Other useful combinations, such as invisible (white-on-white) or a reverse-video and underlined combination, aren't supported by the hardware.

Again like the CGA, the MDA has an enable-blink bit that determines whether the high-order bit of each character's attribute byte controls blinking or the intensity of the background attribute. On the MDA, the enable-blink bit is bit 5 of the register at port 3B8H. As on the CGA, the enable-blink bit is set by the BIOS when it establishes monochrome text mode 7, so you must explicitly clear this bit if you want to disable blinking and display characters with an intensified background.

With the EGA, MCGA, VGA, and SVGA, text-mode attributes work the same as with the MDA and the CGA. Although the enable-blink bit is not in the same hardware register in the newer subsystems, interrupt 10H,

Attribute	Description
00H	Nondisplayed
01H	Underlined
07H	Normal (white on black)
09H	High-intensity underlined
0FH	High-intensity
70H	White background, black foreground (reverse video)
87H*	Blinking white on black (if blinking enabled) Dim background, normal foreground (if blinking disabled)
8FH*	Blinking high-intensity (if blinking enabled) Dim background, high-intensity foreground (if blinking disabled)
F0H	Blinking reverse video (if blinking enabled) High-intensity background, black foreground (if blinking disabled)

* Not displayed by all monochrome monitors

Figure 4-8. *Monochrome text-mode attributes. The appearance of some attributes depends on the setting of the enable-blink bit at I/O port 3B8H.*

service 09H, toggles the bit for the appropriate attribute on an EGA, MCGA, VGA, or SVGA. (See Chapter 11, page 335, for more information.)

Setting color in graphics modes

So far, we've seen how to set color (and the monochrome equivalent of color) in text modes. Setting color in graphics modes is quite different. In graphics modes, each pixel can have a different color. The color is set the same way attributes are set in text modes, but there are important differences. First, because each pixel is a discrete dot of color, there is no foreground or background; each pixel is simply one color or another. Second, pixel attributes are not always 4 bits in size; we've already mentioned that pixel attributes can range from 1 to 8 bits, depending on the video mode being used. These differences give graphics-mode programs a subtly different "feel" than they have in text modes, both to programmers and to users.

The most important difference between text-mode and graphics-mode attributes, however, is this: In graphics modes you can control the color of each pixel. This lets you use colors much more effectively than you can in text modes. This isn't so obvious with the CGA and its limited color capabilities, but with an EGA, MCGA, VGA, or SVGA it's quite apparent.

Let's start with the CGA. The CGA's two graphics modes are relatively limited in terms of color: In 320 × 200, 4-color mode, pixel attributes are only 2 bits wide, and you can display a maximum of four different colors at a time. In 640 × 200, 2-color mode, you have only 1 bit per pixel, so you can display a maximum of only two different colors (that is, "on" and "off," or monochrome) at one time. Also, the range of colors you can display in CGA graphics modes is severely limited.

In 320 × 200, 4-color mode, pixels can have value 0, 1, 2, or 3, corresponding to the 2-bit binary values 00B, 01B, 10B, and 11B. You can assign any one of the CGA's 16 color combinations to zero-value pixels, but colors for nonzero pixels are derived from one of three built-in palettes. (See Figure 4-9.) In 640 × 200, 2-color mode, nonzero pixels can be assigned any one of the 16 color combinations, but zero-value pixels are always black. In both modes, you can assign palette colors using the BIOS interrupt 10H services described in Chapter 11.

Pixel Bits	Pixel Value	Pixel Color
Mode 4, palette 0:		
0 1	1	Green
1 0	2	Red
1 1	3	Yellow or brown
Mode 4, palette 1:		
0 1	1	Cyan
1 0	2	Magenta
1 1	3	White
Mode 5:		
0 1	1	Cyan
1 0	2	Red
1 1	3	White

Figure 4-9. *Palettes in CGA 320 × 200, 4-color graphics mode.*

The EGA, MCGA, VGA, and SVGA are considerably more flexible in terms of color management because you can assign any color combination to any palette or video DAC color register. Equally important, you have larger pixel values and therefore more colors to work with on the screen. Frequently used graphics modes on the EGA and VGA are the 16-color modes with pixels that require 4 bits to define the colors. In most applications, 16 colors are adequate because you can select those 16 colors from the entire range of color combinations the hardware can display (64 colors on the EGA and 262,144 colors on the MCGA, VGA, and SVGA). Again, the BIOS provides services that let you assign arbitrary color combinations to the palette and video DAC color registers on the EGA, MCGA, VGA, and SVGA. See Chapter 11 for details.

Inside the Display Memory

Now we come to the inner workings of the video buffer map. In this section, you'll see how the information in the video memory is related to the display screen.

Although the video buffer memory map varies according to the video mode you use, a clear family resemblance exists among the video modes. In text modes, the video buffer map in all PC video subsystems is the same. In graphics modes, there are two general layouts, a *linear map* based on the map used with the original CGA graphics modes and a *parallel map* that was first used in EGA graphics modes.

Before we examine the map of the video buffer, let's look at the addresses where the video buffer is located. (See Figure 4-10.) The breakdown is straightforward: Color text modes start at paragraph address B800H, and monochrome text mode starts at B000H. CGA-compatible graphics modes start at B800H. All other graphics modes start at A000H. The amount of RAM required to hold a screenful of data varies according to the number of characters or pixels displayed and, in the case of graphics modes, according to the number of bits that represent a pixel.

Display Pages in Text Modes

The amount of RAM physically installed in the various video subsystems is frequently more than enough to contain one screen's worth of video data in text mode. In video modes where this is true, all PC video subsystems support multiple display pages. When you use display pages, the video buffer is mapped into two or more areas, or pages, each of which can hold a full screen of data. The video hardware displays only one of these pages on the screen at a time and can be switched among pages under program control.

You can write information to nondisplayed pages as well as directly to the displayed page. Using this technique, you can build a screen on a nonvisible page while another page is being displayed and then switch to the new page when the appropriate time comes. Switching screen images this way makes screen updates seem instantaneous.

Video Mode	Starting Paragraph Address (Hex)	Memory Used (Bytes)	Subsystem
00H, 01H	B800H	2000	CGA, EGA, MCGA, VGA, SVGA
02H, 03H	B800H	4000	CGA, EGA, MCGA, VGA, SVGA
04H, 05H	B800H	16,000	CGA, EGA, MCGA, VGA, SVGA
06H	B800H	16,000	CGA, EGA, MCGA, VGA, SVGA
07H	B000H	4000	MDA, EGA, VGA, SVGA
0DH	A000H	32,000	EGA, VGA, SVGA
0EH	A000H	64,000	EGA, VGA, SVGA
0FH	A000H	56,000	EGA, VGA, SVGA
10H	A000H	112,000	EGA, VGA, SVGA
11H	A000H	38,400	MCGA, VGA, SVGA
12H	A000H	153,600	VGA, SVGA
13H	A000H	64,000	MCGA, VGA, SVGA

Figure 4-10. *Video buffer addresses in PC video modes.*

The display pages are numbered 0 through 7, with page 0 starting at the beginning of the video buffer. Of course, the amount of available RAM may be insufficient to support eight full display pages; the actual number of pages you can use (see Figure 4-11) depends on how much video RAM is available and on how much memory is required for one screenful of data. Each page begins on an even-kilobyte memory boundary. The display page offset addresses are shown in Figure 4-12.

To select a display page, use BIOS interrupt 10H, service 05H. To determine which page is actively displayed, use interrupt 10H, service 0FH. (See Chapter 11 for information about these BIOS services.)

In any of these text modes, if the pages are not actively used (displayed on the screen) the unused part of the display memory can conceivably be used for data besides text or pixels, although this usage is neither normal nor advisable. Making any other use of this potentially free memory is asking for trouble in the future.

Video Mode	Subsystem	Number of Pages	Notes
00H, 01H	CGA, EGA, MCGA, VGA, SVGA	8	
02H, 03H	CGA	4	
	EGA, MCGA, VGA, SVGA	8	
04H, 05H	CGA, MCGA	1	
	EGA, VGA, SVGA	2	Not fully supported by ROM BIOS
06H	CGA, EGA, MCGA, VGA, SVGA	1	
07H	MDA	1	
	EGA, VGA, SVGA	8	
0DH	EGA, VGA, SVGA	8	
0EH	EGA, VGA, SVGA	4	
0FH	EGA, VGA, SVGA	2	
10H	EGA, VGA, SVGA	2	
11H	MCGA, VGA, SVGA	1	
12H	VGA, SVGA	1	
13H	MCGA, VGA, SVGA	1	

Figure 4-11. *Display pages available in PC video subsystems.*

Page	40 × 25, 16-color	80 × 25, 16-color	80 × 25 Mono
0	B800:0000H	B800:0000H	B000:0000H
1	B800:0800H	B800:1000H	B000:1000H*
2	B800:1000H	B800:2000H	B000:2000H*
3	B800:1800H	B800:3000H	B000:3000H*
4	B800:2000H	B800:4000H*	B000:4000H*
5	B800:2800H	B800:5000H*	B000:5000H*
6	B800:3000H	B800:6000H*	B000:6000H*
7	B800:3800H	B800:7000H*	B000:7000H*

* EGA, VGA, and SVGA only

Figure 4-12. *Start addresses for text-mode display pages in PC video subsystems.*

Display Pages in Graphics Modes

For the EGA, MCGA, VGA, and SVGA, the page concept is as readily available in graphics modes as in text modes. Obviously, there is no reason not to have multiple graphics pages if the memory is there to support them.

The main benefit of using multiple pages for either graphics or text is to be able to switch instantly from one display screen to another without taking time to build the display information from scratch. In theory, multiple pages could be used in graphics mode to produce smooth and fine-grained animation effects, but there aren't enough display pages to allow taking the animation very far.

Displaying Characters in Text and Graphics Modes

As you have learned, in text modes the pixel pattern of each character is not stored in the video buffer. Instead, each character is represented in the video buffer by a pair of bytes containing the character's ASCII value and display attributes. The pixel pattern that makes up each character is created by a character generator that is part of the display circuitry. The Color Graphics Adapter has a character generator that produces characters in an 8 × 8–pixel block format; the Monochrome Display Adapter's character generator uses a 9 × 14–pixel block format. The larger format is one of the factors that makes the MDA's display output easier to read.

The standard ASCII characters (01H through 7FH [decimal 1 through 127]) represent only half of the ASCII characters available in the text modes. An additional 128 characters and symbols (80H through FFH [decimal 128 through 255]) are available through the same character generator. The entire set of 255 characters and symbols is sometimes referred to as the IBM character set. Some of the symbols in this set can be used to make simple line drawings. A complete list of the IBM character set appears in Appendix D.

The graphics modes can also display characters, but they are produced quite differently than in text modes. Graphics-mode characters are drawn, pixel by pixel, by a BIOS software character generator instead of by a hardware character generator. (BIOS interrupt 10H provides this service; see Chapter 11.) The software character generator refers to a table of bit patterns to determine which pixels to use in drawing each character. The ROM of every PC contains a default table of character bit patterns, but you can also place a custom bit pattern table in RAM and instruct the BIOS to use it to display your own character set.

In CGA-compatible graphics modes (640 × 200, 2-color and 320 × 200, 4-color), the bit patterns for the second 128 ASCII characters are always found at the address stored in the interrupt 1FH vector at 0000:007CH. If you store a table of bit patterns in a buffer and then store the buffer's segment and offset at 0000:007CH, the BIOS will use the bit patterns in the buffer for ASCII characters 80H through FFH (decimal 128 through 255). In other graphics modes on the EGA, MCGA, VGA, and SVGA, the BIOS provides a service through interrupt 10H that lets you pass the address of a RAM-based table of character bit patterns for all 256 characters.

Mapping characters in text modes

In text modes, the memory map begins with the top left corner of the screen, with 2 bytes devoted to each character position. The memory bytes for successive characters immediately follow in the order in which you would read them—from left to right and from top to bottom.

Modes 0 and 1 are text modes with a screen format of 40 columns by 25 rows. Each row occupies 40 × 2 (80) bytes. A screen occupies only 2 KB in modes 0 and 1, which means the CGA's 16-KB memory can accommodate eight display pages. If the rows are numbered 0 through 24 and the columns are numbered 0 through 39, the offset to any screen character in the first display page is given by the following Basic formula:

```
CHARACTER.OFFSET = (ROW.NUMBER * 80) + (COLUMN.NUMBER * 2)
```

Because the attribute byte for any character is in the memory location next to the ASCII character value, you can locate it simply by adding 1 to the character offset.

Modes 2, 3, and 7 are also text modes, but with 80 columns in each row instead of 40. The byte layout is the same, but each row requires twice as many bytes, or 80 × 2 (160) bytes. Consequently, the 80 × 25 screen format uses 4 KB, and the CGA's 16-KB memory can accommodate four display pages. The offset to any screen location in the first display page is given by the following Basic formula:

```
CHARACTER.OFFSET = (ROW.NUMBER * 160) + (COLUMN.NUMBER * 2)
```

The beginning of each text display page traditionally starts at an even kilobyte boundary. Because each screen page in the text modes actually uses only 2000 or 4000 bytes, some unused bytes follow each page—either 48 or 96 bytes, depending on the size of the page. So, to locate any screen position on any page in text mode, use the general formula shown next:

```
LOCATION = (SEGMENT.PARAGRAPH * 16)
         + (PAGE.NUMBER * (PAGE.SIZE + PAD))
         + (ROW.NUMBER * ROW.WIDTH * 2)
         + (COLUMN.NUMBER * 2) + WHICH
```

■ *LOCATION* is the 20-bit address of the screen information.

■ *SEGMENT.PARAGRAPH* is the location of the video display memory (for example, B000H or B800H).

■ *PAGE.NUMBER* is a number in the range 0 through 3 or 0 through 7.

■ *PAGE.SIZE* is 2000 or 4000.

■ *PAD* is 24 if PAGE.SIZE = 2000, or 48 if PAGE.SIZE = 4000.

■ *ROW.NUMBER* is a number in the range 0 through 24.

■ *ROW.WIDTH* is 40 or 80.

■ *COLUMN.NUMBER* is a number in the range 0 through 39 or 0 through 79.

■ *WHICH* is 0 for the display character or 1 for the display attribute.

Mapping pixels in graphics modes

When you use a graphics mode, pixels are stored as a series of bit fields, with a one-to-one correlation between the bit fields in memory and the pixels on the screen. The actual mapping of bit fields in the video buffer depends on the video mode.

In CGA-compatible graphics modes, the display is organized into 200 lines, numbered 0 through 199. Each line of pixels is represented in the video buffer by 80 bytes of data. In 640 × 200, 2-color mode, each bit represents one pixel on the screen; in 320 × 200, 4-color mode, each pixel is represented by a pair of bits in the buffer. (See Figure 4-13.) Thus, there are eight pixels to each byte in 640 × 200, 2-color mode and 80 × 8, or 640, pixels per row. Similarly, there are four pixels to each byte in 320 × 200, 4-color mode and 80 × 4, or 320, pixels per row. The storage for the pixel rows is interleaved:

■ Pixels in even-numbered rows are stored in the first half of the video buffer, starting at B800:0000H.

■ Pixels in odd-numbered rows are stored starting at B800:2000H.

For example, in 640 × 200, 2-color mode, the first pixel in the first row (in the upper left corner of the screen) is represented by the leftmost bit (bit 7) in the byte at B800:0000H. The second pixel in the row is represented by

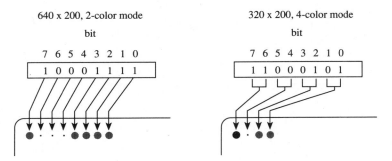

Figure 4-13. *Pixel mapping in CGA-compatible graphics modes.*

bit 6 of the same byte. Because of the interleaved buffer map, however, the pixel immediately below the first pixel is represented in bit 7 of the byte at B800:2000H.

In all other graphics modes, the buffer map is linear, as it is in text modes. Pixels are stored from left to right in each byte, and one row of pixels immediately follows another in the video buffer. On the MCGA, VGA, and SVGA, for example, the 1-bit pixels in 640 × 480, 2-color mode and the 8-bit pixels in 320 × 200, 256-color mode are stored starting at A000:0000H and proceed linearly through the buffer.

The catch is that pixel bit fields are not always mapped linearly in all video modes. On the EGA, VGA, and SVGA, the video buffer in 16-color graphics modes is arranged as a set of four parallel memory maps, called *bit planes*. In effect, the video memory is configured to have four 64-KB memory maps spanning the same range of addresses starting at A000:0000H. When data is written to the video buffer, the CPU must first send a signal to the video hardware specifying which of the four bit planes the data should go to. The EGA, VGA, and SVGA have special circuitry that accesses all four memory maps in parallel. Thus in 16-color EGA, VGA, and SVGA graphics modes, each 4-bit pixel is stored as 1 bit in each bit plane. (See Figure 4-14.) Another way to visualize this is that a 4-bit pixel value is formed by concatenating corresponding bits from the same address in each bit plane.

There is a good reason why the EGA, VGA, and SVGA were designed to use parallel memory maps in graphics modes. Consider the situation in 640 × 350, 16-color mode: With 4 bits per pixel, you need 640 × 350 × 4 (896,000) bits to store one screenful of pixels. That comes out to 112,000 bytes, which is bigger than the 64-KB maximum size of one 8086 segment. If you organize the pixel data in parallel, however, you need only 112,000 ÷ 4 (28,000) bytes in each memory map.

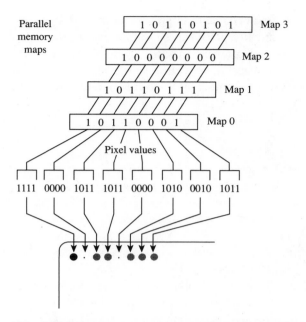

Figure 4-14. *Pixel mapping in 16-color EGA, VGA, and SVGA graphics modes.*

With this variety of memory maps and pixel sizes, it's fortunate that the BIOS provides services that let you read and write individual pixels regardless of the video mode. (Chapter 11 describes these services.) Unfortunately, BIOS pixel-manipulation services are pretty slow. If you're working in graphics modes, you'll probably find that the graphics drawing functions in your programming language (such as the PSET, LINE, and CIRCLE functions in Basic) are the best tools for creating graphics-mode screens.

Controlling the Video Display

In general, control of the display screen, like most other computer operations, can be obtained in four ways:

- By using the programming-language services (for example, Basic's SCREEN statement)

- By using the MS-DOS services (see Chapter 11)

- By using the BIOS video services (see Chapter 11)

- By directly manipulating the hardware via memory or I/O ports

The video services that are available through programming languages, MS-DOS, and the BIOS automatically place screen output data in the video buffer, with each type of service offering varying levels of control. The BIOS services are particularly powerful, providing nearly all the functions needed to generate display-screen output, control the cursor, and manipulate

About the Cursor

A blinking cursor is a feature of the text modes that is used to indicate the active location on the display screen. The cursor is actually a group of scan lines that fill the entire width of the character box. The size of the character box varies with the video hardware and video mode: The Monochrome Display Adapter uses a 9-pixels-wide-by-14-scan-lines-high format; the Color Graphics Adapter uses an 8-pixels-by-8-scan-lines format; the EGA's default text-mode character box is 8 pixels wide by 14 scan lines high; and the VGA's and SVGA's character boxes are 9 by 16. Because the higher-resolution video subsystems use character boxes with more scan lines, their text-mode characters appear sharper and more detailed, as you'll see in Appendix D.

The default cursor format uses two scan lines near the bottom of the character box, but it can be changed to display any number of scan lines within the character box. Because the blinking cursor used in text modes is a hardware-created feature, software has only limited control over it.

You can change the size of the cursor as well as its location on the screen by using the services provided by the BIOS. Interrupt 10H, service 01H lets you set the size of the cursor, and service 02H lets you move the cursor to any character position on the screen. The BIOS also provides a service (interrupt 10H, service 03H) that reports the current size and location of the cursor.

So far, we've been talking about the text-mode cursor. In graphics modes there is no hardware-generated cursor, but the BIOS routines keep track of a logical cursor location that tells you the active screen location. As in text modes, you can use BIOS services 02H and 03H to manage and monitor the graphics-mode cursor location.

To create a cursor in graphics modes, many programs, including Basic, simulate the block cursor by using a distinctive background color at the cursor location or by using an ASCII block character.

screen information. For maximum control over the video display, you also have the option of bypassing the software services and placing data directly in the video buffer—when you feel you have good reason to do so.

Direct video output certainly has speed advantages, and in the early days of relatively slow PCs it was a widely used technique. With today's faster hardware, the speed advantage is less significant. More important, direct video output is not compatible with windowing systems and more advanced multitasking operating environments. You can't mix programs that write directly to the display memory and windowing systems because two programs would be fighting over the control of the same memory and messing up each other's data. But because so many programs now generate direct video output, multitasking operating systems such as OS/2 go to great lengths to accommodate programs that write directly to the display memory. A system such as OS/2 can make this accommodation simply by keeping a copy of the program's display memory. When the program is running, the copy is moved into the display buffer; when the program is stopped, a fresh copy of the display buffer is made. This technique allows OS/2 to run programs that work directly with the display memory, but at a cost: First, computing and memory overhead go up; second, the program can't run in the background simultaneously with other programs; and third, the display information can't be windowed—it can't be moved or adjusted in size.

Programmers are faced with a conflict here: Direct output to the screen has the benefit of speed and power, but using BIOS or higher-level services for screen output has the benefit of more flexibility for adapting to windowing systems, new video hardware, and so on. For a program to be fully compatible with, say, OS/2 and Microsoft Windows, you must avoid direct video output.

Direct Hardware Control

Much of the information we've provided in this chapter, particularly the information on internal mapping of display memory, is meant to help you write video information directly to the display memory. But remember that direct programming has inherent risks, and you'll find it both safer and easier to use the highest available means to control the video display. Lower-level means, particularly direct manipulation, can be disruptive.

More important, it's not always easy to write well-behaved programs that access video hardware directly. There are several reasons for this. One is simply that there is a lot of different video hardware to worry about. Apart from the six IBM-standard video subsystems we've discussed here, many non-IBM video adapters and built-in video subsystems exist. If you write a program that accesses a particular IBM video subsystem directly, the program probably won't be portable to a different IBM subsystem or to non-IBM hardware.

We've already mentioned another reason to avoid direct video hardware programming: Multitasking or windowing operating systems must work overtime to accommodate programs that directly access video hardware. Of course, the designers of new PC operating environments are well aware of the need for good video performance, so modern operating systems generally offer faster and more flexible video output services than do older systems, such as MS-DOS. Direct hardware programming offers little advantage if the operating system's video I/O services are fast enough.

Also, direct video hardware control can get you into trouble with the BIOS if you aren't careful. The BIOS keeps track of the video hardware status in a set of variables in the data area in segment 40H. (See Chapter 3 for a list of BIOS video status variables.) If you program the video hardware directly, be careful to update the BIOS status variables accordingly.

For example, the simple routine presented earlier for resetting the CGA enable-blink bit bypasses a BIOS status variable. To update the enable-blink bit without causing the BIOS to lose track of the video hardware state, you would update the BIOS status variable at 0040:0065H:

```
10 DEF SEG = &HB800              ' (same as before)
20 POKE 0,ASC("A")
30 POKE 1,&H97
40 DEF SEG = &H0040             ' address the BIOS data area
50 POKE &H0065,(PEEK(&H0065) AND NOT &H20) ' update BIOS status variable
60 OUT &H3D8,PEEK(&H0065)       ' update hardware register
```

If you program carefully, controlling the video hardware directly can be very rewarding. You can maximize the speed of your video output as well as take full advantage of hardware capabilities such as smooth, pixel-by-pixel panning or hardware-generated interrupts. But when you write such a program, keep the pitfalls in mind.

Compatibility Considerations

If you want your program to run on a wide variety of PCs, you must design compatibility into the program. As the various PC video subsystems have evolved, programmers have developed several approaches to compatibility. These include

- Installable programs

- Self-installing programs

- Hardware-independent programming environments

We've already mentioned that many software vendors provide video compatibility by distributing software that has its video output routines in separate, installable modules: Before the software can be used, the video routines must be linked to the rest of the application. This lets you write programs that take full advantage of each video subsystem's capabilities without sacrificing compatibility.

However, the installation process can be cumbersome, both for a programmer who must write the installation program and for an end user who must install video routines properly. You can eliminate the installation process if you make your application self-installing. The key to doing this is to incorporate a routine in your program that automatically identifies which video subsystem the program is running on. The program can then tailor its video output to the capabilities and limitations of the video hardware.

You can use several different programming techniques to identify the video subsystem. The BIOS in EGA, VGA, and SVGA systems offers a service that reports the video hardware configuration (see Chapter 11), but for earlier video subsystems you must rely on improvised hardware identification techniques documented in the hardware technical manuals.

After a program has determined the video hardware configuration, it can produce appropriate output. For example, a program running on a Monochrome Display Adapter can use only one video mode with monochrome attributes. If the same program were running on a color subsystem, it could run with color attributes in text modes. If the program needed to produce graphics output, it could select a graphics mode with the highest possible resolution based on its identification of the video subsystem.

In the simplest case, your program can use whatever video mode is in use when the program starts up. BIOS interrupt 10H, service 0FH, reports the current video-mode number. If you're not using an assembly language interface to the BIOS, however, you might find it easier simply to use the following program to inspect the BIOS status variable at 0040:0049H that contains the video-mode number:

```
10 DEF SEG = &H0040
20 VIDEO.MODE = PEEK(&H0049)
```

You can avoid video hardware dependence in your programs if you use an operating environment such as Microsoft Windows or OS/2. These environments shield your program from the idiosyncrasies of video hardware by providing a set of consistent, hardware-independent subroutines to perform video I/O. The problem, of course, is that the end user must also have a copy of the operating environment to be able to run your program.

Whatever approach you take to video compatibility, be sure to consider several compatibility criteria. These criteria are not completely consistent with each other, reflecting the internal inconsistency in the design of the PC and the variety of display formats that can be used. Even so, there are overall guidelines for compatibility, and we'll outline them here.

First, text-only display output increases compatibility. Many PCs equipped with Monochrome Display Adapters are still in use, and such systems cannot show graphics output. If you are weighing a decision about text vs. graphics in the design of a program, there are two factors to consider. On one hand, as many programs have dramatically demonstrated, you can create very effective drawings using only symbols from the IBM character set. On the other hand, it is more and more common for today's PCs to have graphics capability. So, in the future, text-only output will probably lose its importance and you'll be able to use graphics in your programs without worrying about compatibility.

Second, the less your programs depend on color, the wider the range of computers with which they will be compatible. This does not mean that you need to avoid color for compatibility; it simply means that for maximum compatibility, programs should use color as an enhancement rather than as an essential ingredient. If programs can get along without color, they will be compatible with computers that use monochrome displays.

In general, you must weigh the advantage of broad compatibility against the convenience and simplicity of writing programs for a narrower range of displays. Our own experience and judgment tell us that far too often programmers err by opting for a narrower range of displays, thereby greatly reducing the variety of computers their programs can be used on. Be forewarned.

Chapter 5

Disk Basics

Most computer systems have some way to store information permanently, whether it is on punched paper tape, bar-coded print media, magnetic disks or tape, or laser disks. By far the most widely used media in the PC family are *floppy disks* and *hard disks* (called *fixed disks* by IBM). Floppy disks and hard disks come in various sizes and capacities, but they all work in basically the same way: Information is magnetically encoded on their surfaces in patterns determined by the disk drive and by the software that controls the drive.

When the PC family was introduced in 1981, it used one main type of storage device: the 5.25-inch floppy disk, which was double density, single sided, and soft sectored and which stored only 160 kilobytes (KB) of data. Since then, higher-capacity 5.25-inch and 3.5-inch floppy disks have come to be standard equipment on PCs, as have hard disks with capacities from 10 megabytes (MB) on the original IBM PC/XT to hundreds or even thousands of megabytes on today's advanced systems.

Although the type of storage device a program will be used with is important, it is the way stored information is laid out and managed that concerns programmers most. In this chapter, we'll provide some information about the hardware, but the focus will be on how information is organized and stored on both floppy disks and hard disks. Much of the information provided in this chapter applies as much to RAM disks—that is, the simulation of disk storage in memory—as it does to conventional floppy disks, hard disks, and disk cartridges.

Disk Data Mapping

To understand how data is organized on a disk, consider the physical structure of the disk itself and the drive mechanism that reads from and writes to it. We'll start with floppy disks, but both floppy disks and hard disks have the same basic geometry.

Inside a floppy disk's square, plastic case is a circular platter made of tough plastic coated with a magnetic medium. A floppy disk drive stores data on the disk by writing and reading magnetically encoded patterns that represent digital data. Because both sides of the disk are coated, both sides can be used to store data.

A floppy disk drive contains a motor that rotates the floppy disk at a constant speed. Except for the very early single-sided drives, the drive has two read/write heads, one for each side of the disk. The heads are mounted on an arm that moves them in unison to any position toward or away from the center of the disk. (The original IBM PC came with a floppy disk drive that had only one read/write head and could access only one side of a disk. Most PC users perceived this as wasteful, so single-sided disk drives gradually went the way of the dinosaur.)

Like the tape heads in an audio tape recorder, a floppy disk drive's read/write heads can store data on the disk by magnetizing the disk medium; they can also retrieve data from the disk by decoding the magnetically encoded patterns in the disk medium.

The geometry of a hard disk is similar to that of a floppy disk. The platters of a hard disk are made of magnetically coated metal or glass, which allows them to rotate much faster than floppy disks and also permits data to be stored at a higher density. In addition, a hard disk usually consists of a stack of several platters that rotate together, so hard disk drives have multiple read/write heads—one for each disk surface. As a result, a hard disk can store much more information than a floppy disk and can also access that information much more quickly.

Data Storage

The way data is mapped on floppy disks and on hard disks is a natural result of the geometry of the hardware. When a particular read/write head is held motionless over the rotating disk, a logical, or virtual, ring of magnetic medium moves past it as the disk rotates. For each position of the read/write head relative to the center of the disk, there is a corresponding ring of disk medium on which data can be stored. These concentric rings are called *tracks*. (See Figure 5-1.)

Each track is divided into a number of smaller units called *sectors*. All sectors on a given disk hold the same amount of data: 512 bytes for floppy disks and for most hard disks. The tracks are numbered sequentially, starting with the outermost track, which is always track 0. Within each track, sectors are also numbered sequentially, starting with 1. You can locate a piece of data on a disk surface by specifying the data's track number and sector number.

Because two-sided floppy disks and all hard disks have more than one disk surface, you need to think three-dimensionally to locate data. On multisurface disks, the position of the read/write heads is described by a *cylinder* number. A cylinder consists of one track per disk surface. Like tracks, cylinders are numbered sequentially. If you think of a cylinder as a stack of tracks at a given position of the read/write heads, you can see that the location of a particular track can be specified by a cylinder number plus a read/write head number.

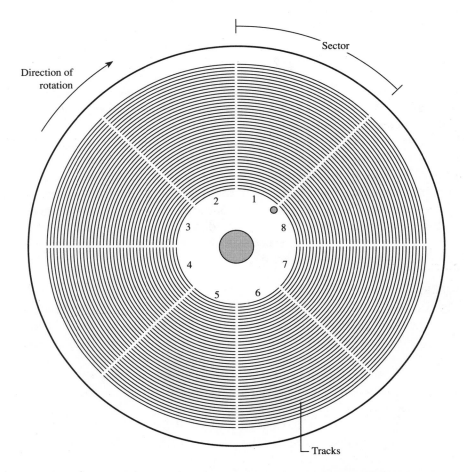

Figure 5-1. *One side of a floppy disk formatted with 40 concentric tracks and eight sectors per track.*

With this in mind, it's easy to make sense of the various floppy disk formats used in PC disk drives. (See Figure 5-2.) With the original single-sided IBM PC floppy disk drives, you could use disks formatted with 40 tracks. Each track contained eight 512-byte sectors of data, so the capacity of the disk was 40 × 8 × 512, or 160 KB. As technology has advanced, more accurate disk drives and better disk media have become available, permitting more tracks per surface and the storage of more data per track. Current standards are 1.2-MB capacity for 5.25-inch disks and 1.44-MB capacity for 3.5-inch disks. Hard disk drives are mechanically more accurate than floppy disk drives, and their magnetic media are of comparatively higher density,

Disk	Capacity	Cylinders	Sectors per Track	Heads
5.25-inch disk	160 KB	40	8	1
	180 KB	40	9	1
	320 KB	40	8	2
	360 KB	40	9	2
	1.2 MB	80	15	2
3.5-inch disk	720 KB	80	9	2
	1.44 MB	80	18	2
	2.88 MB	80	36	2

Figure 5-2. *PC floppy disk formats.*

so the number of tracks and the number of sectors per track are higher than for floppy disks.

Manufacturers' terminology regarding these variations of disk format and disk storage capacity is somewhat fuzzy. *Quad-density* refers to a floppy disk or drive that can use an 80-track disk format. *High-density* and *high-capacity* generally refer to the 1.2-MB 5.25-inch or 1.44-MB 3.5-inch disk format. *Double-density* disks can be formatted with eight or nine sectors per track, but they can't be used reliably with higher-capacity formats.

Bootable Disks

Regardless of the data they contain, all floppy disks and hard disks are potentially bootable; that is, they can contain the information necessary to get an operating system running at the time you start your computer. There is nothing special about the format of a bootable disk; it's merely a disk that contains information that lets the ROM BIOS boot the operating system. Here's how it works.

On all PC disks, the first sector on the disk—cylinder 0, head 0, sector 1—is reserved for a short bootstrap program. (The bootstrap program has to be short because the size of a sector is only 512 bytes.) The function of the bootstrap program is simply to read the bulk of the operating system into memory from elsewhere on the disk and then to transfer control to the operating system.

When you start or restart your computer, the last tasks performed by the start-up ROM BIOS routines are to read the contents of the disk boot sector into memory and to check for a bootstrap program. The BIOS does this checking by examining the last 2 bytes of the boot sector for a signature (55AAH) that indicates that the data in the boot sector represents a bootstrap

115

program. If the signature value isn't correct, the BIOS assumes that there's no bootstrap program in the boot sector and that the disk isn't bootable.

By default, on start-up all PCs check floppy disk drive A for a bootable disk. If no disk is found, the first hard disk (if present) is checked. If neither a bootable floppy disk nor a bootable hard disk is found, an error message is displayed, or on IBM systems, ROM Basic starts. Systems are designed to check floppy disk drive A first, rather than automatically booting from the hard disk, to enable you to boot from a floppy disk should the boot files on the hard disk become damaged.

If the bootstrap program is found, it is loaded into memory and executed. Its only job is to copy the start-up program for an operating system from the disk into memory. There's no restriction on the size and location of the operating system's start-up program; consequently, this stepwise transfer of control—from BIOS to boot sector to operating system—can be used to start any operating system: MS-DOS, XENIX, OS/2, or even a stand-alone application. *without an operating System!!*

MS-DOS Disk Formats

The disk formats listed in Figure 5-2 aren't the only ones you can use for floppy disks. Floppy disks are intended to be portable among PCs, but each operating system must provide support for the individual formats. MS-DOS recognizes only the listed disk formats. With the earliest releases of MS-DOS, only the 160-KB and 320-KB formats could be used. Later MS-DOS versions recognize higher-capacity disk formats and hard disks in addition to the original floppy disk formats. (See Figure 5-3.)

Disk	Capacity	MS-DOS Version	Media Descriptor
5.25-inch floppy disk	160 KB	1.0	FEH
	320 KB	1.1	FFH
	180 KB	2.0	FCH
	360 KB	2.0	FDH
	1.2 MB	3.0	F9H
3.5-inch floppy disk	720 KB	3.2	F9H
	1.44 MB	3.3	F0H
	2.88 MB	5.0	F0H
Hard disk		2.0	F8H

Figure 5-3. *Standard MS-DOS disk formats. The media descriptor value is used by MS-DOS to identify different disk formats.*

Floppy Disk Formats

Beginning with version 2.0, MS-DOS had the potential to recognize virtually any physical disk format. This became possible because MS-DOS versions 2.0 and later provided the necessary tools to write an installable device driver (a machine-language routine that can configure a disk drive to read or write different formats or that allows you to hook up a nonstandard disk drive to your system). See Chapter 8 for more on installable device drivers.

Fortunately, installable floppy disk device drivers have not led to a proliferation of nonstandard, incompatible disk formats. Instead, software vendors and programmers have relied on the standard MS-DOS formats listed in Figure 5-3. With 5.25-inch disks, the 360-KB, nine-sector format is used most frequently on machines with the 8088 CPU, and the 1.2-MB format is used on systems with an 80286 or higher processor. With 3.5-inch disks, the 720-KB format is rapidly being replaced by the 1.44-MB format. Note that lower-capacity disks of the same physical size can be read and written to by higher-capacity disk drives. For example, a high-density 3.5-inch drive can read and write to both 720-KB and 1.44-MB disks, whereas a low-density 3.5-inch drive can read and write to only 720-KB disks.

If you're interested in creating your own disk formats or in understanding MS-DOS disk formats in more detail, be sure to read about BIOS disk services in Chapter 10.

Hard Disk Formats

High-capacity hard disk systems present some special problems and opportunities. Hard disk formats vary much more than floppy disk formats. (See Figure 5-4.) Still, data is organized on hard disks by cylinder, head, and sector numbers, exactly as it is on floppy disks.

Because of a hard disk's large storage capacity, it is feasible to use only part of the disk space for MS-DOS and to use other portions of the disk

Disk	Capacity	Cylinders	Sectors per Track	Heads
Typical PC/XT hard disk	10 MB	306	17	4
PC/AT hard disk type 20	30 MB	733	17	5
PS/2 Model 30 hard disk, type 26	20 MB	612	17	4
PS/2 Model 60 hard disk, type 31	44 MB	732	17	7

Figure 5-4. *Some typical hard disk formats. All use 512 bytes per sector.*

Master Boot Sector. (handwritten)

for other operating systems. To facilitate this, the available space on a hard disk can be split into as many as four logical partitions, each of which is accessed separately. Each partition's data and programs can be kept completely separate from those of the other partitions. Each partition can contain its own boot sector and operating system.

The first sector on a hard disk contains a 64-byte partition table (Figure 5-5) and a disk bootstrap program. The partition table indicates where each partition is located on the disk. The table also designates one bootable partition. The first sector in the bootable partition is a partition boot sector that the BIOS can use to load an operating system.

NOT MBR (handwritten)

The disk bootstrap program examines the partition table to determine which one of the partitions is bootable. It then reads the partition's boot sector from the disk into memory. The partition boot sector contains a bootstrap program that reads the operating system from the disk into memory and then transfers control to the operating system.

Because bootable partitions are indicated in a table, you can select among bootable hard disk partitions simply by updating the table and restarting the computer. All operating systems capable of supporting hard disks provide a utility program that lets you update the partition table. (The MS-DOS utility FDISK is such a program.)

(handwritten left margin): Does this mean BIOS is in control of O/S loading OR BIOS Disc sector loading routine is called by disk bootstrap program and eventually returns control to bootstrap program.

Offset from Start of Entry	Size (Bytes)	Meaning
00H	1	Boot indicator (80H = bootable, 0 = not bootable)
01H	1	Starting head number
02H	2	Starting cylinder number (10 bits) and sector number (6 bits)
04H	1	System indicator: 1 = primary MS-DOS, 12-bit FAT 2 = XENIX 4 = primary MS-DOS, 16-bit FAT 5 = extended MS-DOS 6 = MS-DOS, larger than 32 MB 8 = other non-MS-DOS
05H	1	Ending head number
06H	2	Ending cylinder and sector numbers
08H	4	Starting sector (relative to beginning of disk)
0CH	4	Number of sectors in partition

(handwritten annotations around table): (8 bits) 256 hds. 1024 cyl. 64 sectors. Cylinder Head Sector. Correct. I think the latter is probably the case. i.e. Does the BIOS know of HD PARTITIONS!! Linux does not use CHS geometry only last two items starting sector & no. of sectors.

Figure 5-5. *The format of an entry in a hard disk partition table. The table consists of four such 16-byte entries, starting at offset 1BEH (decimal 446) in the disk boot sector.*

(handwritten): MBR

(handwritten bottom): Neither. disk boot sector bootstrap pgm calls BIOS disc reading pgm to read OS into memory & then passes control to OS.

1st sector
(Master Boot Record)
MBR

NOTE: *Be extremely careful if you access a hard disk boot sector. The information contained there is intended only for use by the ROM BIOS bootstrap loader. Should the data in a hard disk boot sector be erased or corrupted, the entire contents of the disk might become inaccessible.*

The Disk's Logical Structure

Although different disks have differing physical structures, all MS-DOS disks are logically formatted in the same way: The disk's sides, tracks, and sectors are identified numerically with the same notation, and certain sectors are always reserved for special programs and indexes that MS-DOS uses to manage disk operations. Before we describe how MS-DOS organizes space on a disk, we need to briefly cover the conventional notation used by MS-DOS and the ROM BIOS to locate information.

Physically, disk cylinder numbers start from 0 at the outside edge of the disk surface and increase toward the center of the disk. Read/write heads are also numbered starting with 0, but sector numbers start with 1. The location of any sector on the disk can thus be described by a unique combination of cylinder, head, and sector numbers. This is, in fact, how the BIOS services access disk data. But remember that different disks have different numbers of cylinders, heads, and sectors.

MS-DOS, however, does not recognize cylinders, heads, and sectors. Instead, MS-DOS sees a disk as a linear sequence of *logical sectors*. The sequence of logical sectors begins with the first sector on a disk: Sector 1, cylinder 0, head 0 (the boot sector) is MS-DOS logical sector 0.

Logical sectors are numbered from track to track in the same cylinder and then are numbered from cylinder to cylinder. Thus the last sector in cylinder 0, head 0 is followed by the first sector in cylinder 0, head 1; the last sector in a cylinder is followed by the first sector in the next cylinder. See page 247 for information on converting MS-DOS notation to ROM BIOS notation and vice versa.

The use of logical sector numbers lets MS-DOS avoid dealing with cylinder, head, and sector numbers that vary among different types of disk-drive hardware. However, this same feature meant that early versions of MS-DOS were limited in the amount of disk space that could be accessed on a disk drive. Before version 3.3, MS-DOS used 16-bit integers to maintain logical sector numbers. Because a 16-bit integer can have values only up to 65,536, that was the maximum number of logical sectors possible on a disk. Because the default size of a disk sector is 512 bytes, the largest disk MS-DOS could manage was 65,536 × 512, or 32 MB. This certainly was no problem on

119

floppy disks, but it became a serious problem when hard disks larger than 32 MB became popular.

To get around this restriction, MS-DOS version 3.3 introduced the *extended* MS-DOS partition. With MS-DOS 3.3, you could use the MS-DOS utility program FDISK to allocate a hard disk partition as an extended MS-DOS partition. You could format the extended partition as one or more separate logical drives. Thus, for example, you could use both a primary and an extended MS-DOS partition on a hard disk, with the primary partition as drive C and the extended partition as drives D and E. Each partition, however, was still limited to 32 MB.

MS-DOS 4 introduced support for hard disk partitions up to 2 gigabytes (2000 MB) in size. This is sufficient for all but the largest of today's hard disks. Even so, some users prefer to partition their hard disks into several moderate-size logical partitions because a single partition containing thousands of files can be difficult to manage.

Hard Disk Controllers

A hard disk must be interfaced to the system bus so that data can be transferred to and from the disk. This interface is provided by hardware circuitry called the *hard disk controller*. As computers have increased in speed, new controller designs have been introduced. Currently four types of hard disk controllers are in common use; they differ from each other in capacity, speed, and flexibility. From a programmer's perspective, the type of controller a program will be used with is of little consequence because the routines in the controller ROM BIOS or in an installable device driver will present a consistent software interface for applications programs. However, it is still worthwhile to know some details about the different kinds of controllers.

The ST-506 Controller

The first PC hard disks used the ST-506 controller developed by Seagate Corporation. The ST-506 controller is separate from the hard drive itself and is located on an adapter card that plugs into an expansion slot. It can control one or two hard disks and is connected to them by two cables. In some designs, a floppy disk controller and an ST-506 hard disk controller are combined on a single adapter card.

Initially, all ST-506 controllers used a recording method called MFM (Modified Frequency Modulation) to record data on the hard disk. This method allowed a maximum raw data transfer rate from the disk to the controller of approximately 5 Mb/sec (megabits per second). The raw data consisted of useful data intermixed with control information, and circuitry on the controller had to separate the two. The result was a useful data transfer rate of approximately 500 KB/sec (roughly equivalent to 4 Mb/sec). A more efficient recording method called RLL (Run Length Limited) was later introduced. By packing data more efficiently on the disk, RLL increased disk storage capacity and provided a raw data transfer rate of 7.5 Mb/sec and a useful data transfer rate of about 750 KB/sec. These transfer rates were more than adequate for early PCs.

The BIOS routines for hard disk access were originally written for the ST-506 controller. Because of the design of this controller, the BIOS routines still place certain constraints on hard disk systems. There can be a maximum of two drives, with no more than 1024 cylinders and 16 heads per drive and 63 sectors per track. Sector size is fixed at 512 bytes, so the maximum disk size with an ST-506 controller is 504 MB. Even today this size would usually be adequate, but the ST-506's relatively slow data transfer rate would be severely limiting on fast systems.

The ESDI Controller

ESDI stands for Enhanced Small Devices Interface. Essentially a "souped-up" ST-506 controller, ESDI was designed to retain ST-506 compatibility but provide faster data transfer rates. These higher rates are made possible by two innovations. First, a data separator located on the drive itself operates on the raw data stream and separates useful data from control data, sending only the former to the controller. Second, a temporary data-holding location called a sector buffer permits raw data to be read off the disk at the maximum possible rate. As a result, ESDI controllers permit effective transfer rates at least several times faster than those of ST-506 controllers.

ESDI controllers are used on a variety of PC systems, including a number of models in IBM's PS/2 line.

The SCSI Controller

SCSI (pronounced "scuzzy") is an acronym for Small Computer System Interface. A SCSI controller is not, strictly speaking, a hard disk interface. Rather, it is a high-performance generic interface that can be used as a liaison between a variety of peripheral devices and a PC. A SCSI controller can provide an interface between as many as eight devices and a PC. For example, you can have five hard disk drives, a CD-ROM drive, a tape backup unit, and a page scanner all daisy-chained to one SCSI controller. Because the SCSI interface is programmable, two peripherals on the same SCSI chain can interact without the intervention of the host computer. For example, a

SCSI hard disk can be backed up to a SCSI tape drive while the computer performs other tasks.

SCSI components are, in theory, interchangeable. You should be able to use a SCSI controller from one manufacturer with SCSI peripherals from other manufacturers. In practice, however, this is not always the case. The SCSI "standard" is loose enough to allow different manufacturers to implement it in slightly different ways, resulting in hardware incompatibilities. It's best to obtain a controller and peripherals from the same firm, or, if you must mix and match, to conduct compatibility tests before committing to a purchase.

With a SCSI hard disk drive, the disk-controller circuitry is located on the disk drive itself; the SCSI interface serves to connect the controller to the computer's bus. Having the controller circuitry and the hard disk drive as a single integrated unit provides several advantages, including a short analog data path and the ability to fully optimize the controller circuitry for each model of disk drive. SCSI drives use track caching, which permits a 1:1 disk interleave factor and correspondingly faster data access.

The original SCSI specification, which is still the most widely used, provides an 8-bit data path between a peripheral and the SCSI controller. The controller can handle data transfer rates of 4 to 5 MB/sec, but the limitations of most hard drives reduce the effective transfer rate to 1.5 to 2.0 MB/sec. The new SCSI II specification provides a 16-bit data path and correspondingly faster data transfer rates.

SCSI controllers have their own ROM BIOS, which does not directly support the ST-506 standard commands in a PC's ROM BIOS. The software interface among PC operating systems, PC programs, and a SCSI controller is handled by an installable device driver that is supplied with, and specific to, the SCSI controller.

The IDE Interface

On today's new PCs, the most common high-performance hard disk interface is the IDE interface. (IDE stands for Integrated Drive Electronics or Intelligent Drive Electronics, depending on whom you ask.) An IDE hard disk drive combines the drive and the controller in a single unit. A single cable connects the unit directly to the PC system bus. Some PCs provide an IDE connector on the system board. Others require a small expansion board, which contains no active circuitry and which serves simply as an electrical connection to the computer's bus.

By integrating the disk drive and the controller, IDE provides some of the same advantages as SCSI disk systems, such as track caching and the ability to emulate various drive formats. IDE disk systems are quite fast, equaling the performance of most ESDI and SCSI systems.

From the software standpoint, IDE controllers are fully compatible with the ST-506 standard, so they can be used in most PCs without the need for a special device driver. IDE goes beyond ST-506, however, providing features that are not supported by the standard ROM BIOS. As the IDE standard becomes more defined, access to these additional features will be included in the ROM BIOS of new systems.

How MS-DOS Organizes the Disk

When MS-DOS formats a floppy disk, it creates (or erases if the floppy disk has been previously formatted) and verifies the integrity of every sector. When MS-DOS formats a hard disk partition, it verifies the integrity of each sector without erasing preexisting data. (That is why a program such as the Norton Utilities' Format Recover can retrieve data from a hard disk after you have accidentally reformatted it.) On both floppy disks and hard disks, the format program reserves a certain amount of disk space in which to store control information and indexes that MS-DOS uses to organize and locate the data you store on the disk.

Every MS-DOS floppy disk or hard disk MS-DOS partition is mapped into four separate areas. These areas, in the order they are stored, are the *reserved area,* the *file allocation table* (FAT), the *root directory,* and the *files area.* (See Figure 5-6.) The size of each area varies among formats, but the structure of the areas and their order on the disk remain constant.

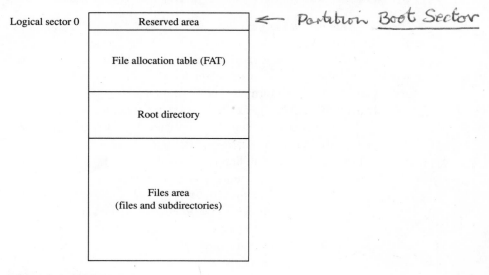

Figure 5-6. *MS-DOS disk map.*

The reserved area can be one or more sectors long; the first sector is always the *disk boot sector* (logical sector 0). A table within the boot sector specifies the size of the reserved area, the size (and number of copies) of the file allocation table, and the number of entries in the root directory. All floppy disks have a reserved area of at least one sector, even if they aren't bootable.

The file allocation table, or FAT, immediately follows the reserved area. The FAT maps the usage of all the disk space in the files area of the disk, including space used for files, space that hasn't been used, and space that is unusable because of defects in the disk medium. Because the FAT maps the entire usable data storage area of a disk, two identical copies of it are stored in case one is damaged. The size of a FAT depends on the size of the disk (or the size of the partition of a hard disk): Larger disks usually require larger FATs. Figure 5-7 shows FAT sizes for several floppy disk sizes.

Disk	*Capacity*	*Reserved Area*	*FAT**	*Root Directory*
5.25-inch disk	360 KB	1 sector	4 sectors	7 sectors
	1.2 MB	1 sector	14 sectors	14 sectors
3.5-inch disk	720 KB	1 sector	6 sectors	7 sectors
	1.44 MB	1 sector	18 sectors	14 sectors
	2.88 MB	1 sector	18 sectors	15 sectors

*Includes both copies.

Figure 5-7. *Reserved area, FAT, and root directory overhead for some common MS-DOS floppy disk formats.*

The root directory is the next item on any MS-DOS disk. It functions somewhat like a table of contents, identifying each file on the disk with a directory entry that contains several pieces of information, including the file's name, size, and starting location on the disk. The size of the root directory varies with the disk format. (See Figure 5-7.)

The files area, which occupies the bulk of the available disk space, is used to store files. In MS-DOS versions 2.0 and later, the files area can contain subdirectories as well as files. (MS-DOS considers a subdirectory to be a type of file.) For both files and subdirectories, space in the files area is allocated as needed in chunks of contiguous sectors called *clusters*. As with the sizes of the FAT and the root directory, an MS-DOS disk's cluster size varies with the disk format. (See Figure 5-8.) The number of sectors in a cluster is always equal to 2 raised to an integer power of 0 or greater; generally, the cluster size is one sector for single-sided floppy disks, two sectors for double-sided floppy disks, and four or more sectors for hard disks.

Disk	Capacity	Cluster Size
5.25-inch disk	360 KB	2 sectors
	1.2 MB	1 sector
3.5-inch disk	720 KB	2 sectors
	1.44 MB	1 sector
	2.88 MB	2 sectors
Typical PC/XT hard disk	10 MB	8 sectors
PC/AT hard disk, type 20	30 MB	4 sectors
PS/2 Model 30 hard disk, type 26	20 MB	4 sectors
PS/2 Model 60 hard disk, type 31	44 MB	4 sectors
PS/2 Model 80 hard disk, type 111	115 MB	8 sectors
PS/2 Model 80 hard disk, type 311	314 MB	16 sectors

Figure 5-8. *Cluster size for some common MS-DOS disk formats.*

The Logical Disk Structure in Detail

Now it's time to delve a little more deeply into each of the four sections of a disk: the boot sector, the root directory, the files area, and the FAT.

The Boot Sector

The boot sector on an MS-DOS floppy disk or in an MS-DOS partition on a hard disk consists primarily of a short machine-language program that starts the process of loading MS-DOS into memory. As we mentioned, to perform this task the BIOS checks to see whether the disk is bootable and then proceeds accordingly.

> NOTE: *A bootable disk contains the start-up programs for an operating system or for a stand-alone application that runs without operating system support. In the case of MS-DOS, a bootable disk contains two hidden files that provide the MS-DOS start-up routines and essential low-level MS-DOS functions. See Chapter 3, page 55, for details about these files.*

You can inspect the boot program by using the MS-DOS DEBUG utility, which combines the ability to read data from any sector on a disk with the ability to disassemble—or unassemble—machine-language code into assembly language statements. If you want to learn more about the boot program and you aren't intimidated by DEBUG's terse command format, place a bootable disk in drive A, and enter the following commands to display the disk's boot program:

```
DEBUG
L 0 0 0 1          ; load first logical sector
U 0 L 2            ; unassemble and list first and second bytes
```

At this point, DEBUG will display the first instruction in the boot program, a JMP to the address that contains the remainder of the program. Use DEBUG's U command with the address specified in the JMP to inspect the rest of the boot program. For example, if the first instruction is JMP 0036, enter

```
U 0036             ; unassemble and list next portion of boot program
```

For all disk formats except floppy disks formatted with eight sectors per track, you will find some key parameters in the boot sector, beginning with the eleventh byte. (See Figure 5-9.) These parameters are part of the BIOS parameter block (BPB) used by MS-DOS to control any disk-type device. If you're using DEBUG to inspect the boot sector of a floppy disk in

Offset in Boot Sector	Length	Description
0BH	1 word	Number of bytes per sector
0DH	1 byte	Number of sectors per cluster
0EH	1 word	Number of sectors in reserved area
10H	1 byte	Number of copies in FAT
11H	1 word	Number of root directory entries
13H	1 word	Total number of sectors
15H	1 byte	MS-DOS media descriptor
16H	1 word	Number of sectors per FAT
18H	1 word	Number of sectors per track
1AH	1 word	Number of heads (sides)
1CH	1 word	Number of hidden sectors

The system ID is an 8-byte system name at offset 03H in the boot sector. For disks formatted by MS-DOS 3.0, for example, this will be *MSDOS3.0.*

Figure 5-9. *The BIOS parameter block in the boot sector.*

(∂8, 0C)(0D)(0E,0F)
0002   08   2000

drive A, you can see a hexadecimal dump of the BPB by entering the following command:

```
D 0B L 1B
```

The extended BIOS parameter block

Starting with MS-DOS version 4.0, the BIOS parameter block contains an extra 4-byte entry that can contain the number of logical sectors on the disk. As with earlier versions, MS-DOS versions 4.0 and later store the number of logical sectors in the BPB field at offset 13H (decimal 19), and they store the number of hidden sectors in the field at offset 1CH (decimal 28). If, however, the sum of these two fields exceeds 65,535, MS-DOS stores a 0 at offset 13H and uses the additional field at offset 20H (decimal 32) to store the total number of logical sectors on the disk. The structure of the extended BPB is shown in Figure 5-10.

The volume serial number

Also starting with version 4.0, MS-DOS records a disk's volume label and serial number in a data structure that immediately follows the BPB in the

Offset in Boot Sector	Length (Bytes)	Description
0BH	2	Number of bytes per sector
0DH	1	Number of sectors per cluster
0EH	2	Number of sectors in reserved area
10H	1	Number of copies in FAT
11H	2	Number of root directory entries
13H	2	Total number of sectors
15H	1	MS-DOS media descriptor
16H	2	Number of sectors per FAT
18H	2	Number of sectors per track
1AH	2	Number of heads (sides)
1CH	4	Number of hidden sectors
20H	4	Total number of sectors (if field at offset 13H contains 0)

195, 428

The system ID is an 8-byte system name at offset 03H in the boot sector. For disks formatted by MS-DOS 5.0, for example, this will be *MSDOS5.0*.

Figure 5-10. *The extended BIOS parameter block in the boot sector; used by MS-DOS versions 4.0 and later.*

127

boot sector. The contents of this structure are shown in Figure 5-11. The volume label is the same 11-byte name that appears in a disk's volume label entry in the root directory. You specify the volume label with the MS-DOS FORMAT or LABEL command or with a call to interrupt 21H, function 16H.

MS-DOS itself calculates and stores the volume serial number when the disk is formatted. The serial number is derived from the current date and time, which means that serial numbers are always different for different disks. This permits MS-DOS to distinguish among different disks that have the same physical format. You can demonstrate this in MS-DOS version 4.0 or later by installing SHARE, opening a floppy disk file for input, and then replacing the current floppy disk with another floppy disk and trying to read from the open file. MS-DOS generates an ''invalid disk change'' critical error. In a program, you can write your own critical-error handler to deal with such situations, but it is much easier to rely on MS-DOS's built-in critical-error handler, which will display the volume label and serial number of the correct disk.

Offset in Boot Sector	Length (Bytes)	Description
24H	1	Physical drive number
25H	1	(Reserved)
26H	1	Signature byte (29H)
27H	4	Volume serial number
2BH	11	Volume label
36H	8	File system type (FAT12 or FAT16)

Figure 5-11. *Boot sector extensions in MS-DOS versions 4.0 and later.*

The Root Directory

The root directory on a floppy disk or in a hard disk partition is created by the MS-DOS FORMAT program when the disk is formatted. The root directory's size is determined by FORMAT, so the number of root directory entries is limited. (See Figure 5-12.)

In MS-DOS versions 1.x, which did not support subdirectories, the size of the root directory limited the total number of files that could be stored on a floppy disk. This restriction disappeared in MS-DOS versions 2.0 and later, where filenames could be placed in subdirectories as well as in the root directory. There is no limitation to the number of file entries contained in a subdirectory.

Disk	Capacity	Size	Number of Entries
5.25-inch floppy disk	180 KB	4 sectors	64
	360 KB	7 sectors	112
	1.2 MB	14 sectors	224
3.5-inch floppy disk	720 KB	7 sectors	112
	1.44 MB	14 sectors	224
Typical PC/XT hard disk	10 MB	32 sectors	512
PC/AT hard disk, type 20	30 MB	32 sectors	512
PS/2 Model 30 hard disk, type 26	20 MB	32 sectors	512
PS/2 Model 60 hard disk, type 31	44 MB	32 sectors	512
PS/2 Model 80 hard disk, type 111	115 MB	32 sectors	512
PS/2 Model 80 hard disk, type 311	314 MB	32 sectors	512

Figure 5-12. *Root directory sizes for some common MS-DOS disk formats.*

The root directory contains a series of 32-byte directory entries. Each directory entry contains the name of a file, the name of a subdirectory, or the disk volume label. The directory entry for a file contains such basic information as the file's size, its starting location on the disk, and the time and date it was most recently modified. This information is contained in the eight fields listed in Figure 5-13.

Offset	Description	Size (Bytes)	Format
00H	Filename	8	ASCII characters
08H	Filename extension	3	ASCII characters
0BH	Attribute	1	Bit coded
0CH	Reserved	10	Unused; zeros
16H	Time	2	Word, coded
18H	Date	2	Word, coded
1AH	Starting cluster number	2	Word
1CH	File size	4	Integer

Figure 5-13. *The eight parts of a directory entry.*

Offset 00H (decimal 0): the filename

The first 8 bytes in a directory entry contain the filename, stored in ASCII format. If the filename is fewer than eight characters, it is filled out to the right with blanks (*CHR$(32)*). Letters should be uppercase because lowercase letters will not be properly recognized. Normally, blanks should not be embedded in the filename, as in *AA BB*. Most MS-DOS command programs, such as DEL and COPY, will not recognize filenames with embedded blanks. Basic works successfully with these filenames, however, and MS-DOS services usually can too. (See Chapter 10.) This capability suggests some useful tricks, such as creating files that cannot easily be erased.

Two codes, used to indicate special situations, can appear in the first byte of the filename field. When a file is deleted, MS-DOS sets the first byte of the filename field in its directory entry to E5H to indicate that the directory entry can be reused for another filename. In MS-DOS versions 2.0 and later, the first byte of a directory entry can also be set to 00H to indicate the end of the list of directory entries.

When a file is erased, only two things on the disk are affected: The first byte of the directory entry is set to E5H, and the file's space allocation chain in the FAT is wiped out. (We'll cover this in the section on the FAT.) All other directory information about the file is retained, including the rest of its name, its size, and even its starting cluster number. The lost information can be recovered, in effect "unerasing" the file; in fact, this method is used by various file recovery utility programs. Such recovery is possible, however, only if the directory entry has not been used for another file. Because MS-DOS uses the first available directory entry whenever a new file is added, an erased file's entry is likely to be quickly overwritten, making file recovery problematic.

Offset 08H (decimal 8): the filename extension

Directly following the filename is the filename extension, stored in ASCII format. It is 3 bytes long and, like the filename, is padded with blanks if it is less than the full three-character length. Whereas a filename must contain at least one ordinary character (from the subset of characters acceptable to MS-DOS in the naming of files), an extension can be all blanks. Generally, the rules that apply to the filename also apply to the filename extension.

> NOTE: *When the directory contains a volume ID label entry, the filename and extension fields are treated as one combined field of 11 bytes. In this case, embedded blanks are permitted.*

Offset 0BH (decimal 11): the file attribute

The third field of the directory entry is 1 byte long. The bits of the attribute byte are individually coded as bits 0 through 7, as shown in Figure 5-14, and each bit is used to categorize the directory entry.

Bit *7 6 5 4 3 2 1 0*	*Meaning*
. . . . 1	Read-only
. . . . . . 1 .	Hidden
. . . . . 1 . .	System
. . . . 1 . . .	Volume label
. . . 1	Subdirectory
. . 1	Archive
. 0	Unused
0	Unused

Figure 5-14. *The 8 file-attribute bits.*

Bit 0, the low-order bit, is set to mark a file as read-only. In this state, the file is protected from being changed or deleted by any MS-DOS operation. But many MS-DOS services ignore this attribute, so even though bit 0 can provide worthwhile protection for data, it is not foolproof.

Bit 1 marks a file as hidden, and bit 2 marks a file as a system file. Files marked as hidden, system, or both cannot be seen by ordinary MS-DOS operations, such as the DIR command. Programs can gain access to such files only by using MS-DOS services to search explicitly for hidden or system files. There is no particular significance to the system attribute; it exists to perpetuate a feature of CP/M operating systems, and it has absolutely nothing to do with MS-DOS.

Bit 3 marks a directory entry as a volume label. A volume label entry is properly recognized only in the root directory and uses only a few of the eight fields available in the directory entry. The label itself is stored in the filename and extension fields, which are treated as one unified field for this purpose; the size and starting cluster fields are not used, but the date, time, and attribute fields are.

Bit 4, the subdirectory attribute, identifies a directory entry as a subdirectory. Because subdirectories are stored like ordinary data files, they need a supporting directory entry. All the directory fields are used for these entries, except the file-size field, which is 0. The actual size of a subdirectory can be found simply by following its space allocation chain in the FAT.

Bit 5, the archive attribute, was created to assist in making backup copies of the many files that can be stored on a hard disk. This bit is 0 on all files that haven't changed since they were last backed up; MS-DOS sets this bit to 1 whenever a file is created or modified.

Offset 0CH (decimal 12): reserved

This 10-byte area is set aside for possible future uses. All 10 bytes are normally set to 0.

Offset 16H (decimal 22): the time

This field contains a 2-byte value that indicates the time the file was created or last modified. It is used in conjunction with the date field, and the two together can be treated as a single 4-byte unsigned integer. This 4-byte integer can be compared to those in other directory entries for greater-than, less-than, or equal values. The time, by itself, is treated as an unsigned word integer. It is based on a 24-hour clock and is built out of the hour, minutes, and seconds with this formula:

$$Time=(Hour\times2048)+(Minutes\times32)+(Seconds\div2)$$

Subdirectories

There are two types of directories: *root directories* and *subdirectories.* The contents and use of each type are essentially the same (both store the names and locations of files on the disk), but their characteristics are different. The root directory has a fixed size and is stored in a fixed location on the disk. A subdirectory has no fixed size and can be stored anywhere on the disk. Any version of MS-DOS numbered 2.0 or later can use subdirectories.

A subdirectory is stored in a disk's files area, exactly like any other file. The format of directory entries in a subdirectory is identical to the format of entries in a root directory, but a subdirectory is not limited in size. Like an ordinary file, a subdirectory can grow without bounds as long as disk space is available to hold it.

A subdirectory is always attached to a parent directory, which can be either the root directory or another subdirectory. When you nest subdirectories, one within another, they are related in the form of a tree structure, as shown on the opposite page.

A parent directory contains one entry for each of its subdirectories. A subdirectory entry is exactly like a filename entry, except that the attribute byte marks the entry as a subdirectory and the file-size field is set to 0. The actual size of the subdirectory can be found by tracing its allocation chain through the FAT.

The 2-byte word used to store the time is 1 bit too short to store all the seconds, so seconds are stored in units of 2 seconds from 0 through 29. A value of 5, for example, would represent 10 seconds. The time 11:32:10 would be stored as the value 5C05H (decimal 23,557).

Offset 18H (decimal 24): the date

This field contains a 2-byte value that marks the date the file was created or last modified. It is used in conjunction with the time field, and the two together can be treated as a single 4-byte unsigned integer that can be compared to those in other directory entries for greater-than, less-than, or equal values. The date, by itself, is treated as an unsigned word integer that is built out of the year, month, and day with this formula:

$Date=((Year-1980)\times512)+(Month\times32)+Day$

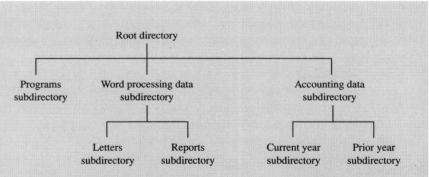

When MS-DOS creates a subdirectory, it places two special entries in it, with . and .. as filenames. These act like entries for further subdirectories, but . actually refers to the present subdirectory, and .. refers to its parent directory. The starting cluster number in each of these directory entries gives the location of the subdirectory itself or the location of its parent. When the starting cluster number is 0, the parent of the subdirectory is the root directory.

If the size of an ordinary file is reduced, you can generally count on MS-DOS to release any unused space. In the case of subdirectories, however, clusters of space that are no longer used (because the directory entries that occupied that space are erased) are not released until the entire subdirectory is deleted.

This formula compresses the year by subtracting 1980 from it. Thus, the year 1988 is represented by a value of 8. Using this formula, a date such as December 12, 1988, is stored by the formula as 118CH (decimal 4492):

```
(1988-1980)×512+12×32+12=4492
```

Although this scheme allows for years up through 2107, the highest year supported by MS-DOS is 2099.

Offset 1AH (decimal 26): the starting cluster number

The seventh field of a directory entry is a 2-byte value that gives the starting cluster number for the file's data space. This cluster number acts as the entry point into the file's space allocation chain in the FAT. For files with no space allocated and for volume label entries, the starting cluster number is 0.

Offset 1CH (decimal 28): the file size

The last field of a directory entry gives the size of the file in bytes. It is coded as a 4-byte unsigned integer, which allows file sizes to grow very large—4,294,967,295 bytes, to be exact, which is large enough for all practical purposes.

MS-DOS uses the file size in a file's directory entry to determine the *exact* size of the file. Because a file's disk space is allocated in clusters of 512 bytes or more, the actual disk space occupied by a file is usually greater than the value in the directory entry. On disk, the space between the end of the file and the end of the last cluster in the file is wasted.

The Files Area

All data files and subdirectories are stored in the files area, which occupies the last and largest part of each disk.

MS-DOS allocates space to files, one cluster at a time, as needed. (Remember that a cluster is one or more consecutive sectors; the number of sectors per cluster is a fixed characteristic of each disk format.) As a file is being created or as an existing file is extended, the file's allocated space grows. When more space is needed, MS-DOS allocates another cluster to the file. In MS-DOS versions 1 and 2, the first available cluster is always allocated to the file. Later versions of MS-DOS select clusters by more complicated rules that we won't go into here.

Under ideal conditions, a file is stored in one contiguous block of space. However, a file might be broken into several noncontiguous blocks, especially if information is added to an existing file or if a new file is stored in the space left by an erased file. So it's not unusual for one file's data to be scattered throughout the disk.

This file fragmentation slows access to the file's data to some degree. Also, it is much harder to "undelete" a file you have unintentionally deleted if it is fragmented, simply because you have to do a lot more searching for the individual clusters that make up the file's data space. But fragmentation has no other effect, and programs generally do not need to be concerned about where on a disk their data is stored. To determine whether a file is fragmented, use a program such as the Norton Utilities.

If you are concerned about floppy disk file fragmentation, the MS-DOS COPY command lets you transfer fragmented files to a newly formatted disk. MS-DOS allocates contiguous space for the copied files. This simple technique also works for hard disk files, but it is much less convenient unless you have an extra, newly formatted hard disk to use. If you think that hard disk file fragmentation is slowing down a particular application, you can purchase any of several hard disk defragmentation utility programs to rearrange fragmented hard disk files and make them contiguous. Most of the time, however, file fragmentation has little impact on the speed of your programs.

Whether or not you ever look at your fragmented files, you should know how MS-DOS uses the file allocation table (FAT) to allocate disk space and how the FAT forms a space allocation chain to connect all clusters that make up a file.

The File Allocation Table

The file allocation table (FAT) is MS-DOS's map of how space is utilized in the files area of a disk. We've already discussed how space for the FAT itself is reserved on a floppy disk or in a hard disk partition. Now we'll describe how the FAT is formatted and used.

For most disk formats, MS-DOS maintains two copies of the FAT, just in case one of them is damaged or becomes unreadable. Curiously, the CHKDSK program, which tests for most errors that can occur in the FAT and in directories, does not even notice if the two FATs are different.

The organization of the FAT is simple: There is one entry in the FAT for each cluster in the files area. A FAT entry can contain any of the values listed in Figure 5-15. If the value in a FAT entry doesn't mark an unused, reserved, or defective cluster, the cluster that corresponds to the FAT entry is part of a file, and the value in the FAT entry itself indicates the next cluster in the file.

This means that the space that belongs to a given file is mapped by a chain of FAT entries, each of which points to the next entry in the chain until a FAT entry containing a "last cluster" code is found. (See Figure 5-16.) Remember that the first cluster number in the chain is the starting cluster number in the file's directory entry. When a file is created or extended, MS-DOS allocates clusters to the file by searching the FAT for unused clusters (that is, clusters whose FAT entries are 0) and adding them to the chain. Conversely, when a file is truncated or deleted, MS-DOS frees the clusters that had been allocated to the file by clearing the corresponding FAT entries.

12-Bit Value	16-Bit Value	Meaning
000H	0000H	Unused cluster
FF0–FF6H	FFF0–FFF6H	Reserved cluster
FF7H	FFF7H	Bad cluster
FF8–FFFH	FFF8–FFFFH	Last cluster in a file
(Other values)		Next cluster in a file

Figure 5-15. *FAT values.*

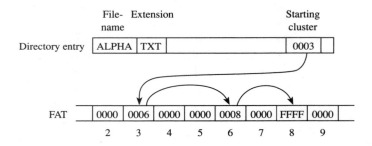

Figure 5-16. *Disk space allocation using the FAT.*

The FAT can be formatted with either 12-bit or 16-bit entries. The 12-bit format is used for floppy disks and for hard disk partitions that contain fewer than 4078 clusters. (A hard disk's partition table indicates whether an MS-DOS partition's FAT uses 12-bit or 16-bit entries.) The entries in a 12-bit FAT are harder to access because they don't fit neatly into the 16-bit word size of the 8086 family of microprocessors, but a 12-bit FAT takes up less room on a floppy disk, where disk space is scarcer.

The first two entries in the FAT are reserved for use by MS-DOS. The first byte of the FAT contains the same media descriptor value that appears in the BIOS parameter block in the disk boot sector. The remaining bytes of the first two entries are filled with the value FFH. Because the first two cluster numbers (0 and 1) are reserved, cluster number 2 corresponds to the first cluster of available disk space in the files area.

Reading the values in a 16-bit FAT is simple enough: Multiply a given cluster number by 2 to find the byte offset of the corresponding FAT entry.

In the 16-bit FAT in Figure 5-17a, for example, the byte offset of the FAT entry for cluster 2 is 04H, and the value in that entry is 0003; the byte offset of the FAT entry for cluster 3 is 06H, and the value in that entry is 0004; and so on.

For a 12-bit FAT, the computation is a bit trickier because each pair of FAT entries occupies 3 bytes (0 and 1 occupy the first 3 bytes, 2 and 3 occupy the next 3 bytes, and so forth). Given any cluster number, you can find the FAT entry by multiplying the cluster number by 3, dividing by 2, and then using the whole number part of the result as a displacement into the FAT. By grabbing a word at that address, you have the three hex digits of the FAT entry, plus one extraneous hex digit, which can be removed by any one of several quick machine-language instructions. If the cluster number is even, you discard the high-order digit; if it is odd, you discard the low-order digit. Try this on the 12-bit FAT in Figure 5-17b. You'll find that the entries are the same as in the 16-bit FAT in Figure 5-17a.

As we have said, the first two FAT entries, in both 12-bit and 16-bit formats, are not used to indicate the status of clusters. The very first byte of the FAT is used as a media descriptor byte, which indicates the format of the disk. (See Figure 5-18.) However, you should not assume that these IDs uniquely identify formats; they don't necessarily. If you considered every disk format in use, you'd find quite a few duplications. Beware.

Your programs can determine the format of a disk by reading and inspecting the FAT media descriptor byte. The easy way to do this is to use MS-DOS function 1BH (decimal 27). For more information about this function, see page 319.

(a) 16-bit FAT

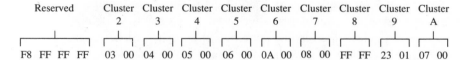

(b) 12-bit FAT

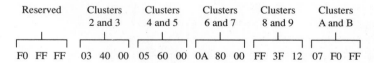

Figure 5-17. *The first few entries in a 16-bit FAT (a) and in a 12-bit FAT (b).*

Disk	Capacity	Heads	Sectors per Track	Media Descriptor
5.25-inch floppy disk	160 KB	1	8	FEH
	320 KB	2	8	FFH
	180 KB	1	9	FCH
	360 KB	2	9	FDH
	1.2 MB	2	15	F9H
3.5-inch floppy disk	720 KB	2	9	F9H
	1.44 MB	2	18	F0H
	2.88 MB	2	36	F0H
Hard disk				F8H

Figure 5-18. *MS-DOS media descriptor values.*

Special notes on the FAT

Normally programs do not look at or change a disk's FAT; they leave the FAT completely under the supervision of MS-DOS. The only exceptions are programs that perform space-allocation functions not supported by MS-DOS— for example, programs that recover deleted files, such as the UnErase program in the Norton Utilities program set.

Be aware that a FAT can be logically damaged. For example, an allocation chain can be circular, referring back to a previous link in the chain; or two chains can converge on one cluster; or a cluster can be orphaned, which means that it is marked as in use even though it is not part of any valid allocation chain. Also, an end-of-file marker (FFFH or FFFFH) may be missing. The MS-DOS programs CHKDSK and RECOVER are designed to detect and repair most of these problems as well as can reasonably be done.

For special notes on the interaction of the space allocation chain in the FAT and in MS-DOS's record of a file's size, see pages 135–37.

CD-ROM Discs

CD-ROM stands for Compact Disc—Read Only Memory, an optical disc storage device that provides access to huge amounts of data at a reasonable cost. CD-ROM discs have the term *compact disc* in their name because they use the same discs and data storage methods as music CDs. *Read only memory* refers to the fact that CD-ROM discs are read-only: You cannot erase data from or write new data to a CD-ROM disc. The most prevalent use for CD-ROM discs is to distribute large amounts of information, such as that contained in encyclopedias and telephone directories. CD-ROM discs are also commonly used to store the graphics, animation, and sound for multimedia. A single CD-ROM disc can hold approximately 600 MB of data.

CD-ROM discs are an optical medium. During manufacture, data is recorded on the surface of the disc as a pattern of microscopic pits, with the presence or absence of a pit signaling either a 0 or a 1 bit. During playback, a low-power laser beam tracks the disc as it rotates. The pits modulate the reflection of the laser beam, and the reflected light is decoded to reconstruct the original data.

In addition to using optical rather than magnetic encoding, CD-ROM discs differ from magnetic hard disks in two other ways. The data on a CD-ROM disc is recorded in a single, continuous spiral track that extends from the outer edge of the disc to the inner border, rather than in multiple concentric tracks as on a hard disk. Also, whereas a hard disk always spins at the same rate (usually 3600 rpm), a CD-ROM disc's rotation rate varies depending on where the read head is positioned. The rotation speed is adjusted to maintain a constant linear velocity under the read/write head— faster when data is being read from near the center of the disc and slower when data is being read from near the edge. These differences are largely responsible for the fact that CD-ROM discs have significantly slower data access rates than hard disks.

MS-DOS and the PC ROM BIOS were never intended to deal with devices such as CD-ROMs. For a system to access a CD-ROM drive, two software components are needed. The first is the Microsoft CD-ROM Extension (MSCDEX), a terminate-and-stay-resident program that allows MS-DOS to treat the CD-ROM drive as a remote network device. The second is the CD-ROM driver software, an installable device driver that is provided by the manufacturer of the CD-ROM drive. The device driver provides the necessary interface between MSCDEX and the CD-ROM hardware.

Comments

Although this chapter includes detailed information on direct manipulation of the logical structure of a disk, including the boot sector, FAT, and directories, it is not a good idea to manipulate these elements directly unless you have a compelling reason—and are sure that you know what you're doing! In fact, except where such manipulation is unavoidable (as, for example, in a copy-protection program), it's unwise to write programs that depend on any specific aspect of the disk format. On the whole, your best approach is to consider the standard hierarchy of operations and use the highest level of services that can satisfy your needs.

- First choice: Language services (the facilities provided by your programming language; for example, Basic's OPEN and CLOSE statements)

- Second choice: MS-DOS services (described in Chapter 10)

- Third choice: BIOS disk services (described in Chapter 10)

- Last choice: Direct control (for example, direct programming of the disk-drive controller through commands issued via I/O ports)

Most disk operations for the PC family can be handled quite easily with the services that your programming language provides. There are, however, two obvious circumstances that can call for more exotic methods. One, which we've already mentioned, occurs when your programming involves control of a disk on the same level exercised by MS-DOS. This level of control would be called for if you were writing a program similar to MS-DOS's CHKDSK or the Norton Utilities. The other circumstance involves copy protection. In one way or another, all floppy disk–copy-protection schemes involve some type of unconventional disk I/O. This type of control usually leads to the use of the ROM BIOS services but can also lead to the extreme measure of directly programming the disk-drive controller itself.

Copy Protection

The term *copy protection* generally refers to any method that makes it difficult or impossible for a user to install and run a program on more than one computer system. Copy protection is clearly of interest to software developers who want to prevent distribution of unauthorized, or pirated, copies of their programs. A variety of copy-protection schemes are commercially available. Most are based on some form of manipulation of disk format, file contents, or both. Some are simple; others are more complex. If you're interested in devising your own scheme, however, here are some things to consider.

For floppy disks, there are dozens of ways to approach copy protection. Perhaps the most common methods involve reformatting the sectors in certain tracks on the disk by using the BIOS format routines. Because MS-DOS cannot read sectors that don't conform to its specific formats, the MS-DOS COPY program can't copy a disk that has an occasional odd sector size interspersed with normal sectors. This limitation inspired a number of companies to produce copy programs that can read and copy sectors of any size, so it is not a particularly effective means of copy protection.

On a more advanced level, there are two special aspects of floppy disk copy protection that are worth noting. First, some of the most exotic and unbreakable protection schemes have been based on the discovery of undocumented abilities hidden in the floppy disk–drive controller. Second, some protection schemes are intentionally or unintentionally dependent on the particular characteristics of different floppy disk drives. This means that a copy-protected program might function on one model of computer but fail to function on another model, even though the copy protection has not been tampered with. If you use a copy-protection scheme, keep this in mind.

Many of the copy-protection techniques used on floppy disks are not appropriate for hard disks, mainly because most hard disk users need to be able to make backup copies of programs on their hard disks. This means that you should avoid copy-protection schemes that prevent hard disk backups by making it impossible for MS-DOS or the ROM BIOS to read part of the disk. Most of the hard disk copy-protection schemes in use today rely on data-encryption techniques, which discourage software piracy without preventing legitimate copying.

In an encrypted program, the program's executable code and data are stored on the disk in an enciphered, hard-to-unravel format. When you execute the program, a special start-up program decrypts the encrypted code and data so that it can be used. The start-up program might also rely on data saved in hidden files or in subdirectories to decrypt the main program.

There is no particular additional guidance that we can give you here, except to remind you that variety and ingenuity are the keys to successful copy protection. We also should mention that paying customers have proven to be very resistant to the added inconvenience that copy protection entails, and many major software publishers have abandoned copy protection in the belief that it costs them more customers than it's worth.

Chapter 6

Keyboard Basics

This chapter is about the PC keyboard. The first part of the chapter explains how the keyboard interacts with the computer on a hardware and software level. In the second part, we describe how the BIOS treats keyboard information and makes it available to programs.

> NOTE: *If you plan to play around with keyboard control, we urge you to read the comments on page 158 first and then apply the information in this chapter to your programs only if you have a strong reason for doing so. (For example, you might want to create a keyboard-enhancer program to modify the operation of the keyboard; see the sidebar on page 151 for more information on such programs.) If you have any such application in mind, take a look at the BIOS keyboard services in Chapter 12.*

The keyboard has undergone several modifications since the original IBM PC was released. The original PC keyboard had 83 keys. When the PC/AT was introduced, it had an 84-key keyboard that changed the locations of several keys on the 83-key keyboard and added one new key, Sys Req.

IBM later introduced a 101/102-key keyboard that provided extra function keys and a new keyboard layout. The 101/102-key keyboard is standard equipment in the IBM PS/2 series and is supplied with most other systems that have an 80286 or higher CPU. The 101/102-key layout includes two additional function keys (F11 and F12), duplicate shift and control keys, and modifications to several keys and keyboard combinations found in the 83-key and 84-key layouts (Pause, Alt-Sys Req, and Print Screen).

A trend in IBM's keyboard design has been to increase the similarity between the PC keyboard and the keyboards on IBM mainframe display terminals. For example, the 101/102-key keyboard's 12 function keys (F1 through F12) are reminiscent of the Program Function (PF) keys on IBM mainframe display terminals. Similarly, the Sys Req key is like the Sys Req key on IBM mainframe terminals: A mainframe terminal-emulator program running on a PC could use the Sys Req key for the same purpose a mainframe terminal would—to switch among terminal sessions or to initiate a keyboard reset function.

Another trend in IBM's keyboard design has been to accommodate non-English alphabets in the keyboard layout. The English-language version of the 101/102-key keyboard, released in the United States and the United Kingdom, has 101 keys, but for other languages the keyboard has an extra key next to the left Shift key, a different arrangement of keys around the Enter key, and a different map of ASCII characters to key locations. From a programmer's point of view, however, these two keyboards are so

similar that IBM describes them together in its technical documentation—
and we do the same in this chapter.

Keyboard Operation

The keyboard unit contains a dedicated microprocessor that performs a
variety of tasks, all of which help cut down on system overhead. The main
duty of the keyboard microprocessor is to monitor the keys and report to the
main computer whenever a key is pressed or released. If any key is pressed
continuously, the keyboard microprocessor sends out a repeat action at
specific intervals. The keyboard microprocessor controller also has limited
diagnostic and error-checking capabilities and has a buffer that can store key
actions in the rare instance that the main computer is temporarily unable to
accept them.

The 84-key and 101/102-key keyboards have more sophisticated keyboard control circuitry than the original 83-key keyboard and provide several additional features. These features include programmable typematic
control, programmable scan-code sets, and improved hardware for error
detection.

On the 83-key keyboard, the typematic delay and repeat rate are built
into the hardware: A key must be pressed for 0.5 second before auto-repeat
begins, and the repeat rate is about 10 characters per second. With the later
keyboards, you can modify the typematic delay and repeat rate by programming the keyboard controller. The most convenient way to do this is through
the BIOS keyboard services described in Chapter 12.

The keyboard controller in the 84-key and 101/102-key keyboards can
also assign any of three different sets of scan-code values to the keys. By
default, however, the BIOS establishes a scan-code set that is compatible with
the set used on the 83-key keyboard. You will probably find use for the alternative scan-code sets only if your program bypasses the BIOS and processes
scan codes directly. (See the PC/AT and PS/2 technical reference manuals for
details.)

The improved error-detection capability of the 84-key and 101/102-key
keyboard controllers is largely invisible to your programs, and the keyboard
hardware and BIOS service routines are very reliable. The most common errors you might encounter are a full BIOS keyboard buffer or a key combination that the BIOS cannot process. In both situations, the BIOS generates a
warning beep to inform you that something unusual has occurred. (For example, try holding down both pairs of Ctrl and Alt keys on a PS/2 keyboard.)

Keystrokes and Scan Codes

Each time you press or release one of the keys on the keyboard, the keyboard circuits transmit a sequence of one or more 8-bit numbers through the connector cable to the computer. This sequence, called a *scan code,* uniquely identifies the key you pressed. The keyboard produces different scan codes, depending on whether the key was pressed or released. Whenever you press a key, the scan-code byte contains a number ranging from 01H through E0H. When you release the key, the keyboard generates a scan code 80H higher than the "press" scan code by setting bit 7 of the scan-code byte to 1. For example, when you press the letter Z, the keyboard generates a scan code of 2CH; when you release it, the keyboard generates a scan code of ACH (2CH + 80H). On the PC/AT and later machines, the break code (the code generated when you release the key) is a 2-byte code: The first byte is F0H, and the second is the same as the scan code. On such machines, the break code for the letter Z would be F0H 2CH. The keyboard diagrams in Figures 6-1, 6-2, and 6-3 show the standard keyboard keys and their "press" scan codes.

Figure 6-1. *Scan codes for the 83-key keyboard (PC, PC/XT). Scan-code values are in hex.*

Figure 6-2. *Scan codes for the 84-key keyboard (PC/AT). Scan-code values are in hex.*

Figure 6-3. *Scan codes for the 101/102-key keyboard (PC/AT, PS/2, and most other 80286-or-later systems). Scan-code values are in hex.*

If you compare the scan codes for the 83-key, 84-key, and 101/102-key keyboards, you'll see that a given key generates the same scan code regardless of its location on the keyboard. For example, the Esc key has a scan code of 01H, whether it's next to the 1 key, next to the Num Lock key, or by itself in the upper left corner. (The 101/102-key keyboard can actually generate different scan codes, but the start-up ROM BIOS suppresses this by configuring the keyboard to be compatible with the 83-key keyboard.)

The 101/102-key layout contains duplicate shift and control keys that don't exist on the other keyboards. The 101/102-key keyboard distinguishes between duplicate keys by transmitting multiple-byte scan codes. For example, the two Alt shift keys have different scan codes: The left Alt key has a scan code of 38H, and the right Alt key has a 2-byte scan code, E0H 38H.

> NOTE: *The first byte of multiple-byte scan codes can vary depending on whether one of the shift keys (Ctrl, Alt, Shift), the Num Lock key, or the Caps Lock key is pressed at the same time. See IBM's PS/2 technical reference manuals for details.*

The 101/102-key keyboard also assigns special scan codes to certain keystroke combinations. The Alt-Sys Req ("Sys Req" appears on the front of the Print Screen key) combination is intended to be the same as the Sys Req key on the 84-key keyboard, so the 101/102-key keyboard transmits the same scan code, 54H. Because the Print Screen key has the same function as the Shift-PrtSc combination in the other keyboard layouts, the 101/102-key keyboard transmits a Shift-key scan code (E0H 2AH) followed by the PrtSc scan code (E0H 37H). The Pause key's scan code, E1H 1DH 45H, resembles the scan-code sequence for the Ctrl-Num Lock combination, but when you press Ctrl-Pause (that is, Ctrl-Break), the keyboard transmits E0H 46H E0H C6H, which is derived from the scan code for the Scroll Lock (Break) key on the 83-key and 84-key keyboards. Figure 6-4 lists these keystroke combinations and their associated codes.

101/102-Key Keyboard Keystroke Combination	84-Key Keyboard Equivalent	Scan Code Transmitted
Alt-Sys Req	Sys Req	54H
Print Screen	Shift-PrtSc	E0H 2AH
		E0H 37H
Ctrl-Break	Ctrl-Break	E0H 46H E0H C6H

Figure 6-4. *Scan codes for special keystroke combinations on the 101/102-key keyboard.*

NOTE: *The "compact" keyboard available for the PS/2 Model 25 is really a 101/102-key keyboard in disguise. The numeric keypad is mapped to a group of 14 keys on the main keyboard, and the Num Lock key is the shift state of the Scroll Lock key. However, keyboard scan codes and BIOS processing are the same for the compact keyboard as for the full-size 101/102-key keyboard.*

Any program that processes keyboard scan codes must be aware of which machine it's running on and which keyboard is in use. Fortunately, few programs need to respond directly to keyboard scan codes: The BIOS keyboard service routines translate scan codes into meaningful information that a program can use. The following sections describe this translation process more fully.

Communicating with the ROM BIOS

The keyboard-controller circuitry on the computer's system board monitors the keyboard for input. The keyboard controller generates interrupt 09H (decimal 9) each time it receives a byte of data from the keyboard. The BIOS contains a handler for interrupt 09H; the code in this handler reads the byte from the keyboard controller and processes it. (I/O port 60H contains the keyboard data byte.) The interrupt 09H handler translates scan codes into 2-byte values that are generally more useful to a program than the original scan codes.

When a standard ASCII character key is pressed, the low-order byte of the 2-byte value contains the ASCII code corresponding to the key pressed. The high-order byte usually contains the corresponding keyboard scan code.

When a special key, such as a function key or (with Num Lock turned off) a numeric-keypad key is pressed, the low-order byte is 0 and the high-order byte contains the keyboard scan code. (There will be more about this later, on page 153.)

The BIOS routines place the translated byte-pairs in a queue, called the keyboard buffer or the type-ahead buffer. This buffer is kept in low memory starting at location 0040:001EH. The byte-pairs are stored there until they are requested by a program that expects to read keyboard input.

Translating the Scan Codes

The scan-code translation job is moderately complicated because the IBM keyboard recognizes two types of keys that change the meaning of a keystroke: shift keys and toggle keys.

The shift keys

Three keys—Ctrl, Shift, and Alt—are known as *shift keys:* They change the shift state, and thereby the meaning, of whatever key they are used with. For example, when you press Shift-C, you get a capital *C;* when you press Ctrl-C, you generate the "break" character. The BIOS recognizes that all key actions are influenced by that shift state for as long as the shift key is held down.

The toggle keys

In addition to the shift keys, two *toggle keys* also affect the keyboard's shift state: the Caps Lock key and the Num Lock key. When activated, Caps Lock reverses the shift state of the alphabet keys; it doesn't affect the other keys. When activated, the Num Lock key disables cursor-control functions on the numeric keypad. Toggle keys are activated with a single keystroke and remain active until released by a second keystroke. The Ins (Insert) and Scroll Lock keys are also toggle keys, but they do not affect the state of other keys.

The 2-byte shift-key and toggle-key status information is kept by the BIOS in a low-memory location starting at 0040:0017H, where you can use it or change it. When you press a shift key or a toggle key, the BIOS sets a specific bit in one of these two bytes. When the BIOS receives the release scan code of a shift key, it switches the status bit back to its original shift state.

Whenever the BIOS receives a scan code for an ordinary keystroke, such as the letter Z or a Right direction key, it first checks the shift state and then translates the key into the appropriate 2-byte code. (We discuss the status bytes in more detail on page 155.)

The combination keys

While the ROM BIOS routine is translating scan codes, it checks for Sys Req keystrokes and for certain shift-key combinations; specifically, it checks for the Ctrl-Alt-Del, Shift-PrtSc, Ctrl-Num Lock, and Ctrl-Break combinations. These five command-like key actions cause the BIOS to perform a specific task immediately.

Sys Req (on the 84-key keyboard) and **Alt-Sys Req** (on the 101/102-key keyboard) cause the BIOS to issue interrupt 15H (decimal 21) with AH = 85H. Your program can provide its own interrupt 15H handler that intercepts and processes Sys Req keystrokes. (See Chapter 13 for details.)

Ctrl-Alt-Del causes the computer to reboot. Ctrl-Alt-Del is probably used more often than any other key combination. It works dependably as long as the keyboard interrupt service is working. If the interrupt service is not working, to reboot you must press the system reset button or turn off the power, wait a few seconds, and then turn it on again; the power-on program resets all interrupt vectors and services.

Shift-PrtSc (**Print Screen** only on the 101/102-key keyboard) causes the BIOS interrupt 09H handler to execute software interrupt 05H (decimal 5). The default interrupt 05H handler is also part of the BIOS; it sends a "snapshot" of the current contents of the screen to the printer.

Ctrl-Num Lock (**Pause** only on the 101/102-key keyboard) suspends operation of a program until another keystroke occurs.

Ctrl-Break causes the BIOS to generate software interrupt 1BH (decimal 27) and to set bit 7 of the byte at 0040:0071H to 1. The default MS-DOS handler for interrupt 1BH simply sets a flag internal to MS-DOS that causes MS-DOS to interpret Ctrl-Break as Ctrl-C. You can override the default MS-DOS action for Ctrl-Break by pointing the interrupt 1BH vector (located at 0000:006CH) to your own interrupt handler.

These are the only key combinations that are especially meaningful to the BIOS. When an invalid combination is reported from the keyboard, the BIOS simply ignores it and moves on to the next valid key action.

Two more features of the PC keyboard should be presented before we discuss the details of keyboard coding: *repeat key action* and *duplicate keys.*

Repeat key action

The PC keyboard features automatic repeat key action, a process called *typematic* by IBM. The circuitry inside the keyboard monitors how long each key is pressed; if a key is held down longer than a defined interval, the circuitry generates repeat key actions. These are reported as successive keystroke scan codes, without the intervening key-release codes. This makes it possible for an interrupt 09H handler to distinguish between regular keystrokes and typematic action. However, the BIOS does not always distinguish between the two. The BIOS keyboard-handling routine treats each automatic repeat key action as though the key were actually pressed and interprets the key accordingly.

For example, if you press and hold the A key long enough for the keyboard to begin generating successive keystroke signals, the BIOS will create a series of *A*'s to be passed on to whatever program is reading keyboard data. On the other hand, when you press and hold a shift key, the BIOS sets the

Keyboard-Enhancer Programs

Thanks to the flexible software design of the PC, it's possible to create programs that customize the keyboard. Such programs are known as *keyboard-enhancer programs.*

Keyboard-enhancer programs monitor the scan codes that come in from the keyboard and respond to them in ways that aren't supported by the BIOS or by MS-DOS. Typically, these programs are fed instructions, called *keyboard macros,* that tell them what keystrokes to look for and what changes to make. The changes might involve suppressing a keystroke (acting as if it never happened), replacing one keystroke with another, or replacing one keystroke with a long series of keystrokes. The most common use of keyboard macros is to abbreviate frequently used phrases. For example, you might instruct a keyboard enhancer to convert a key combination, such as Alt-S, into a salutation, such as *Sincerely yours,* that you use in correspondence. You can also use keyboard macros to condense multiple-keystroke program commands to a single keystroke.

Keyboard enhancers work by combining the powers of two special facilities—one that's part of MS-DOS and one that's part of the PC's BIOS. The MS-DOS facility allows the enhancer program to remain resident in the computer's memory, quietly monitoring the operation of the computer while the ordinary control of the computer is turned over to a conventional program, such as a word processor. The BIOS facility lets programs divert the stream of keyboard information so that it can be inspected and changed before it is passed on to a program. Keyboard enhancers use the MS-DOS terminate-and-stay-resident facility to stay active in memory while other programs are running; then they use the BIOS keyboard-monitoring facility to preview keyboard data and change it as needed.

appropriate bit in its status byte in segment 40H to 1. While you hold the shift key down, the BIOS continues to set the same bit to 1. When you release the key, the BIOS resets the status bit. All this boils down to the simple fact that the BIOS treats repeat key actions in a sensible way, acting on them or ignoring them as needed.

Duplicate keys

We've already described how the keyboard differentiates duplicate keys by assigning different scan codes to each. The BIOS translates duplicate keys into the same ASCII character codes. For example, if you press either of the two asterisk (*) keys, the BIOS returns ASCII 2AH (the ASCII code for an asterisk); if you press either of the two Ctrl keys on a 101/102-key keyboard, the BIOS sets the appropriate bit in its respective shift-state byte.

In some cases, the BIOS also lets programs differentiate between duplicate keys. Remember that the BIOS translates each keystroke into a scan code as well as an ASCII code. A program that requests a keystroke from the BIOS can inspect the scan code to determine which key was pressed. In the case of shift keys, a program can inspect the BIOS shift-state bytes at 0040:0017H and 0040:0018H to determine exactly which shift keys are pressed. (See the discussion of the shift-state bytes on page 157.)

Entering ASCII Codes Directly

We should mention that the PC keyboard, in conjunction with the ROM BIOS, provides an alternative way to enter nearly any ASCII character code. This is done by holding down the Alt key and then entering the decimal ASCII character code from the numeric keypad on the right side of the keyboard. This method lets you enter any ASCII code from 01H through FFH (decimal 1 through 255).

Keyboard Data Format

After a keyboard action has been translated by the BIOS keyboard service routine, it is stored as a pair of bytes in the keyboard buffer. We call the low-order byte of each pair the *main byte* and the high-order byte of each pair the *auxiliary byte*. The composition of these bytes will vary depending on whether an ASCII key or a special key was pressed.

The ASCII Keys

When the main byte is an ASCII character value from 01H through FFH, one of two events has occurred: One of the standard character keys was pressed, or an ASCII character was entered directly using the Alt-*number* method mentioned previously. (See Appendix D for the complete ASCII character set.) For these ASCII characters, the auxiliary byte contains the scan code of the pressed key. (The scan code is 0 for characters entered with Alt-*number*.) Usually you can ignore this scan code. MS-DOS does not report keyboard scan codes, nor do high-level programming language functions such as *getch()* in C or INKEY$ in Basic. However, a program can examine the auxiliary byte (scan code) to differentiate between duplicate keyboard characters.

The Special Keys

When the main byte is null (00H), it means that a special, non-ASCII key was pressed. The special keys include the function keys, shifted function keys, cursor-control keys such as Home and End, and some of the Ctrl-key and Alt-key combinations. When any of these keys are pressed by themselves or in combination with other keys, the auxiliary byte contains a single value that indicates which key was pressed. Figure 6-5 lists these values in a rough mixture of logical and numeric order. (For a complete breakdown of ROM BIOS key codes, see the *IBM BIOS Interface Technical Reference Manual*.)

NOTE: *With the 101/102-key keyboard, the main byte value for the gray cursor-control keys is E0H. This value distinguishes these keys from their counterparts on the numeric keypad, which have a main byte value of 00H.*

| Value | | | Value | | | Value | | |
Hex	Dec	Keys Pressed	Hex	Dec	Keys Pressed	Hex	Dec	Keys Pressed
3BH	59	F1	55H	85	Shift-F2	60H	96	Ctrl-F3
3CH	60	F2	56H	86	Shift-F3	61H	97	Ctrl-F4
3DH	61	F3	57H	87	Shift-F4	62H	98	Ctrl-F5
3EH	62	F4	58H	88	Shift-F5	63H	99	Ctrl-F6
3FH	63	F5	59H	89	Shift-F6	64H	100	Ctrl-F7
40H	64	F6	5AH	90	Shift-F7	65H	101	Ctrl-F8
41H	65	F7	5BH	91	Shift-F8	66H	102	Ctrl-F9
42H	66	F8	5CH	92	Shift-F9	67H	103	Ctrl-F10
43H	67	F9	5DH	93	Shift-F10	89H	137	Ctrl-F11
44H	68	F10	87H	135	Shift-F11	8AH	138	Ctrl-F12
85H	133	F11	88H	136	Shift-F12	68H	104	Alt-F1
86H	134	F12	5EH	94	Ctrl-F1	69H	105	Alt-F2
54H	84	Shift-F1	5FH	95	Ctrl-F2	6AH	106	Alt-F3

*The second key in this combination is located on the numeric keypad.

Figure 6-5. *ROM BIOS auxiliary byte values for the special keys.*   *(continued)*

Figure 6-5. *continued*

Value			Value			Value		
Hex	Dec	Keys Pressed	Hex	Dec	Keys Pressed	Hex	Dec	Keys Pressed
6BH	107	Alt-F4	19H	25	Alt-P	74H	116	Ctrl-Right direction key
6CH	108	Alt-F5	1EH	30	Alt-A	75H	117	Ctrl-End
6DH	109	Alt-F6	1FH	31	Alt-S	76H	118	Ctrl-PgDn
6EH	110	Alt-F7	20H	32	Alt-D	77H	119	Ctrl-Home
6FH	111	Alt-F8	21H	33	Alt-F	84H	132	Ctrl-PgUp
70H	112	Alt-F9	22H	34	Alt-G	8DH	141	Ctrl-Up direction key*
71H	113	Alt-F10	23H	35	Alt-H	8EH	142	Ctrl-minus sign*
8BH	139	Alt-F11	24H	36	Alt-J	8FH	143	Ctrl-5*
8CH	140	Alt-F12	25H	37	Alt-K	90H	144	Ctrl-plus sign*
78H	120	Alt-1	26H	38	Alt-L	91H	145	Ctrl-Down direction key*
79H	121	Alt-2	2CH	44	Alt-Z	92H	146	Ctrl-Ins*
7AH	122	Alt-3	2DH	45	Alt-X	93H	147	Ctrl-Del*
7BH	123	Alt-4	2EH	46	Alt-C	94H	148	Ctrl-Tab
7CH	124	Alt-5	2FH	47	Alt-V	95H	149	Ctrl-forward slash*
7DH	125	Alt-6	30H	48	Alt-B	96H	150	Ctrl-asterisk*
7EH	126	Alt-7	31H	49	Alt-N	97H	151	Alt-Home*
7FH	127	Alt-8	32H	50	Alt-M	98H	152	Alt-Up direction key*
80H	128	Alt-9	0FH	15	Shift-Tab	99H	153	Alt-PgUp*
81H	129	Alt-0	47H	71	Home	9BH	155	Alt-Left direction key*
82H	130	Alt-hyphen	48H	72	Up direction key	9DH	157	Alt-Right direction key*
83H	131	Alt-equal sign	49H	73	PgUp	9FH	159	Alt-End*
10H	16	Alt-Q	4BH	75	Left direction key	A0H	160	Alt-Down direction key*
11H	17	Alt-W	4DH	77	Right direction key	A1H	161	Alt-PgDn*
12H	18	Alt-E	4FH	79	End	A2H	162	Alt-Ins*
13H	19	Alt-R	50H	80	Down direction key	A3H	163	Alt-Del*
14H	20	Alt-T	51H	81	PgDn	A4H	164	Alt-forward slash*
15H	21	Alt-Y	52H	82	Ins	A5H	165	Alt-Tab
16H	22	Alt-U	53H	83	Del	A6H	166	Alt-Enter*
17H	23	Alt-I	72H	114	Ctrl-PrtSc	E0H	224	Ctrl-Enter*
18H	24	Alt-O	73H	115	Ctrl-Left direction key			

Codes generated by the BIOS for the complete set of characters and special keys are handled differently in different programming languages. The Basic language, for example, takes a mixed approach to the special keys. When you use ordinary input statements, Basic returns the ASCII characters and filters out any special keys. Some of these keys can be acted on with the ON KEY statement, but you can use the Basic INKEY$ function to get directly to the BIOS coding for keyboard characters and find out immediately which special key was pressed. If the INKEY$ function returns a 1-byte string, it is reporting an ordinary or extended ASCII keyboard character. If INKEY$ returns a 2-byte string, the first byte in the string is the BIOS's main byte and will always be 00H; the second byte is the auxiliary byte and will indicate which special key was pressed.

ROM BIOS Keyboard Control

The BIOS stores keyboard status information in several portions of the BIOS data area in segment 40H in low memory. Your programs can use some of the BIOS status variables to check the keyboard status or to modify BIOS keyboard processing.

The two keyboard status bytes at locations 0040:0017H (shown in Figure 6-6) and 0040:0018H (shown in Figure 6-7) are coded with individually meaningful bits that indicate which shift keys and toggle keys are active. All the standard models of the PC family include these two bytes, although the bits representing the Sys Req, left Alt, and left Ctrl keys are updated only for the keyboards that support these keys.

The status byte at 0040:0017H is particularly useful because it establishes the state of BIOS keystroke processing. Changes to this status byte affect the next keystroke that the BIOS processes.

Bit *7 6 5 4 3 2 1 0*	*Meaning*
X	Insert state: 1 = active; 0 = inactive
. X	Caps Lock: 1 = active; 0 = inactive
. . X	Num Lock: 1 = active; 0 = inactive
. . . X	Scroll Lock: 1 = active; 0 = inactive
. . . . X . . .	1 = Alt pressed
. . . . . X . .	1 = Ctrl pressed
. . . . . . X .	1 = left Shift pressed
. . . . X	1 = right Shift pressed

Figure 6-6. *The coding of the keyboard status byte at location 0040:0017H. Bits 4 through 7 are toggles; their values change each time the key is pressed. Bits 0 through 3 are set only while the corresponding key is pressed.*

Bit 7 6 5 4 3 2 1 0	Meaning
X	1 = Ins pressed
. X	1 = Caps Lock pressed
. . X	1 = Num Lock pressed
. . . X	1 = Scroll Lock pressed
. . . . X . . .	1 = hold state active (Ctrl-Num Lock or Pause pressed)
. . . . . X . .	1 = Sys Req pressed
. . . . . . X .	1 = left Alt pressed
. . . . X	1 = left Ctrl pressed

Figure 6-7. *The coding of the keyboard status byte at location 0040:0018H. These bits are set only while the corresponding key is pressed.*

The Insert State

The insert state is toggled by pressing the Ins key. The BIOS keeps track of the insert state in bit 7 of byte 0040:0017H. However, every program we know of ignores this bit and keeps its own record of the insert state. This means that you should not rely on this status bit to tell you anything about the current state of Ins key processing.

The Caps Lock State

Some programmers force the Caps Lock state to be active by setting bit 6 of byte 0040:0017H. This can confuse or irritate some program users, so we don't recommend it. However, this trick works reliably, and precedent exists for using it. If you do, you'll see that the BIOS updates the LED indicator on the 84-key and 101/102-key keyboards accordingly. This also occurs when you update the Num Lock or Scroll Lock states.

The Num Lock State

Because the Num Lock key's location on the keyboard makes it susceptible to inadvertent keystrokes, some programmers force the Num Lock toggle (bit 5 of byte 0040:0017H) to a predetermined state at the beginning of a program. For example, clearing the Num Lock status bit before requesting user input from the keypad forces keypad keystrokes to be processed as direction keys instead of numbers, even if the Num Lock key was pressed accidentally. This can be particularly helpful with the old 83-key keyboards that have no status LEDs and provide no visual indication of the Num Lock state.

The Keyboard-Hold State

The BIOS establishes the keyboard-hold (pause) state when it detects a Ctrl–Num Lock or Pause keystroke. During keyboard hold, the BIOS executes a do-nothing loop until a printable key is pressed; it doesn't return control of the computer to whatever program is running until this happens. This feature is used to suspend the operation of the computer—for example, to stop text scrolling on the screen so that you can read it.

During keyboard hold, all hardware interrupts are handled normally. For example, if a disk drive generates an interrupt (signaling the completion of a disk operation), the disk interrupt handler receives the interrupt and processes it normally. But when the interrupt handler finishes working, it passes control back to whatever was happening when the interrupt took place—which is that do-nothing loop inside the ROM BIOS. So, during the keyboard hold the computer can respond to external interrupts, but programs are normally completely suspended. The keyboard BIOS continues to handle interrupts that signal key actions, and when it detects a normal keystroke (for example, the Spacebar or a function key, but not a shift key by itself), it ends the keyboard hold, finally returning control to whatever program was running.

The keyboard-hold state is of no practical use in programming, except that it provides a standard way for users of our programs to suspend a program's operation.

Be aware that the keyboard-hold state is not "bulletproof." A program can continue working through the keyboard hold by acting on an external interrupt, such as the clock-tick interrupt. If you really want a program to avoid being put on hold, the program could set up an interrupt handler that would work through the hold state, or it could simply turn off the hold state whenever the hold state was turned on.

The Toggle-Key States

Notice that bits 4 through 7 in the bytes at 0040:0017H and 0040:0018H refer to the same keys. In the first byte, the bits show the current state of the toggle keys; in the second byte, they show whether the corresponding toggle key is pressed.

You can read the status of any of these bits to your heart's content, but few, if any, are likely to be useful in your programs. With the possible exception of controlling the Caps Lock state, we don't think it's wise to change any of the shift-state bits (bits 4 through 6 of byte 0040:0017H). And it is potentially disruptive to change any of the "key is pressed" bits (bits 0 through 3 of byte 0040:0017H or any bits in byte 0040:0018H).

Comments

If you want to gain a deeper understanding of the PC's keyboard operation, study the ROM BIOS program listing in the IBM technical reference manual for the PC, PC/XT, or PC/AT. If you do this, be careful to avoid making a simple mistake that is common when anyone first studies the ROM BIOS, particularly the interrupts used by the BIOS. The BIOS provides two different interrupts for the keyboard: one that responds to keyboard hardware interrupts (interrupt 09H, decimal 9) and collects keyboard data into the low-memory buffer; and one that responds to a software interrupt requesting keyboard services (interrupt 16H, decimal 22) and passes data from the low-memory buffer to MS-DOS and your programs. It is easy to confuse the operation of these two interrupts, and it is just as easy to further confuse them with the break-key interrupts—1BH and 23H (decimals 27 and 35). The table in Figure 6-8 lists the keyboard interrupts.

| Interrupt | | Origin of Interrupt | Use |
Hex	Dec		
09H	9	Keyboard	Signals keyboard action.
16H	22	User program	Invokes standard BIOS keyboard services. (See Chapter 12.)
1BH	27	ROM BIOS	Occurs when Ctrl-Break is pressed while under BIOS control; a routine is invoked if you create it.
23H	35	MS-DOS	If you create it, an interrupt routine is invoked when a break-key combination is pressed while under MS-DOS control.

Figure 6-8. *The interrupts related to keyboard action.*

A general theme running throughout this book advises you not to play fast and loose but to play by the rules. This means, again, to write programs that are general to the PC family rather than tied to the quirks of any one model and to write programs that use portable means (such as MS-DOS or ROM BIOS services) to manipulate data instead of direct hardware programming. These rules apply to keyboard programming as much as they do to any other aspect of programming.

Chapter 7

Ports, Clocks, Sound Generation, and CMOS Memory

In this chapter we cover some important components of PC hardware that you need to know about: parallel and serial ports, clocks and timers, sound generation, and CMOS memory.

Ports

A port is a channel by which a computer can communicate with the outside world. PCs can be equipped with two types of ports: parallel and serial. Note that although the same term is used, these ports are different from the I/O ports you learned about in Chapter 2. A parallel or serial port is a physical connection that lets you hook your system to a peripheral device such as a printer or a modem.

Parallel Ports

A parallel port is so called because it transmits data in parallel fashion, 8 bits (1 byte) at a time. A parallel port connection consists of a 25-pin D-shell connector (so called because of its shape), comprising eight data lines, nine control lines, and eight ground lines. A parallel port can be used for both sending and receiving data. Some manufacturers have used this capability to design external components, such as portable hard disks, that interface with the computer via a parallel port. In the overwhelming majority of systems, however, a parallel port is used exclusively to connect a PC to a printer. For this reason, a parallel port is sometimes called a printer port. We will limit the discussion in this book to using a parallel port to send data to a printer.

A PC can have as many as three parallel ports installed, although most systems have only one or two. In early systems, one parallel port was often located on the video adapter card (Monochrome Display Adapter or Hercules Graphics Card). Today it is more common to have a parallel port on its own adapter card (sometimes along with a serial port) or built into the system board.

Parallel port assignments

Three blocks of I/O ports are reserved for parallel ports. The I/O addresses of these blocks are shown in Figure 7-1.

I/O Addresses (Hex)	Parallel Port
3BCH–3BFH	Port on MDA
378H–37FH	Second parallel port (378H–37BH on IBM PS/2)
278H–27FH	Third parallel port (278H–27BH on IBM PS/2)

Figure 7-1. *The I/O addresses reserved for parallel ports.*

Attentive readers might notice that the parallel port on the MDA is allocated only four I/O ports, whereas for machines other than the IBM PS/2, parallel ports are each allocated eight I/O ports. In fact, only the first three of the assigned I/O ports are actually used for any parallel port; the others are unused. For example, the parallel port on the MDA uses only I/O addresses 3BCH, 3BDH, and 3BEH.

During the system start-up procedure, the ROM BIOS checks these three I/O port blocks to see whether parallel port hardware is installed. The block starting at 3BCH is checked first, followed by the block at 378H and the block at 278H. The first parallel port that is found is addressed as interface 0 by the BIOS and as LPT1 by MS-DOS. The second and third ports, if present, are addressed as interface 1 and interface 2 by the BIOS and as LPT2 and LPT3 by MS-DOS. The BIOS assigns these logical names by storing each port's base I/O address in the BIOS data area, a reserved area of low memory. An 8-byte array holds these addresses, as shown in Figure 7-2.

Address (Hex)	Interface (BIOS)	Device (MS-DOS)
0040:0008H	0	LPT1
0040:000AH	1	LPT2
0040:000CH	2	LPT3
0040:000EH	3	n/a

Figure 7-2. *The base I/O addresses in the BIOS data area for parallel ports.*

Although the ROM BIOS start-up routine looks for only three parallel ports, the BIOS data area can hold the I/O assignments of four parallel ports. If you install hardware for a fourth parallel port, you can access it as interface 3, by using BIOS functions, if you place its base I/O address at address 0040:000EH in the BIOS data area. MS-DOS, however, cannot access a fourth parallel port.

The parallel port registers

Each parallel port has three registers that are accessed via the three I/O ports assigned to the parallel port. These registers are used to send data to the printer to determine the printer's status and to control the printer's operation. The data register is accessed at the base port address. (For example, the base port address for a parallel port on an MDA is 3BCH.) On early machines, this is a write-only register; data in this register is communicated directly to the printer. On most systems in use today, this register can be used both to read and write data, allowing the parallel port to be used for many applications beyond the simple sending of data to the printer.

The printer status register is accessed at the base port address plus 1. (This is 3BDH for a parallel port on an MDA, for example.) The printer status register is a read-only register; its bits signal the printer's current status, as shown in Figure 7-3. You can read the status byte directly, or you can use the BIOS service interrupt 17H, function 02H, as explained in Chapter 13.

Bit 7 6 5 4 3 2 1 0	Meaning
X	1 = printer is not busy
. X	0 = printer is ready for the next character
. . X	1 = printer is out of paper
. . . X	1 = printer is on line
. . . . X . . .	0 = error has occurred
. . . . . X . .	Not used
. . . . . . X .	Not used
. . . . X	Not used

Figure 7-3. *The coding of the printer status register.*

The printer control register is accessed at the base port address plus 2. (This is 3BEH for a parallel port on an MDA, for example.) This register can be both read and written. Its bits are as shown in Figure 7-4.

Bit 4 might require some explanation. If this bit is on, the parallel port hardware executes hardware interrupt IRQ 7 or IRQ 5 when the ACK line

Bit 7 6 5 4 3 2 1 0	Meaning
X	Not used
. X	Not used
. . X	Not used*
. . . X	1 = execute interrupt when ACK = 0 , *0 = IRQ disabled.*
. . . . X . . .	1 = select printer (on line)
. . . . . X . .	0 = initiate printer reset
. . . . . . X .	1 = auto linefeed
. . . . X	1 = data transfer on , *0 = no data transfer*

* In the IBM PS/2, bit 5 is the "direction" bit, which is used to determine how to process the data in the data register when the port is operating in extended mode. If the bit is off, the data register is processed as for earlier machines. If the direction bit is on, the data register is considered to contain new data received from the I/O device.

Figure 7-4. *The coding of the printer control register.*

not a printer itself, but on the motherboard.

from the printer signals that the printer has received the last character. (You can set which interrupt will be executed by using switches on the printer adapter card.) This feature is rarely used because PC printer control is almost always performed by using polling (discussed on page 168) rather than interrupts. Neither the BIOS nor MS-DOS uses this interrupt vector.

Printer time-out errors

A *time-out error* occurs when the BIOS tries to send data to the printer for a period of time and the printer is not accepting characters because it is busy (as signaled by bit 7 of the status register) or for some other reason. A time-out error is signaled by bit 0 of the printer status byte, which you can obtain by calling interrupt 17H, function 02H. (See Chapter 13.) High-level languages and MS-DOS check the printer status byte and signal time-out errors. If you're programming a parallel port directly, your program will have to perform its own checking.

Because a parallel port can send characters much faster than a printer can print, it will often find that the printer reports "busy" during a print job. The BIOS will repeatedly try to send the data, and if things are functioning normally, the printer will eventually be able to accept it. A time-out error occurs only when the printer does not accept data for an extended time period. The BIOS specifies this time period by values kept at 0040:0078H in the BIOS data area. These values do not specify a fixed time interval but rather specify the number of unsuccessful attempts to send data that is allowed before a time-out error occurs.

There is a separate retry value for each of the three parallel ports, as listed in Figure 7-5. The default retry value, 20, is entered in the three memory locations during system start-up. The BIOS multiplies the retry value by a constant (262,140 in many PCs) to obtain the actual retry count. Thus, the default is for a time-out error to occur only after a parallel port has tried unsuccessfully to send data more than 5,000,000 times. This sounds like a lot, but because the BIOS retry loop executes very quickly, it corresponds to only a few seconds.

Port	*Address of Retry Value*
First parallel port	0040:0078H
Second parallel port	0040:0079H
Third parallel port	0040:007AH

Figure 7-5. *The addresses of the retry values for the parallel ports. If you are supporting a fourth printer by using BIOS interface 3, the byte at 0040:007BH is used for the retry value.*

Because the time-out error is dependent on the number of retries rather than on a fixed time interval, the actual interval depends on CPU speed (that is, the rate at which BIOS retry loops execute). To prevent unnecessary time-out errors, the ROM BIOS on fast systems usually multiplies the retry value by a larger constant to obtain a higher retry count and thus a more realistic time-out interval. These systems change the constant instead of changing the default retry value because the retry value is a single byte and can take a maximum value of only 255, which does not offer sufficient flexibility for setting long time-out intervals on fast systems. A program, however, can modify the retry value for a parallel port. The multiplication constant cannot be changed because it is hard-coded into the ROM BIOS.

Programming parallel ports

Programming of printer output can be approached at four levels. The highest level, which is usually the best approach, is to use the printer statements that are part of your high-level language. It's unusual for a program to require functionality beyond that provided by these statements, and they provide the additional advantages of portability and compatibility with any future hardware or software changes.

The next level is to use MS-DOS services. You can send a multiple-character string to LPT1 by making a single call to interrupt 21H, function 40H, using handle value 4, which is MS-DOS's predefined handle for LPT1. To use this function to send data to another printer port, you must use interrupt 21H, function 3DH, to open the desired port (LPT2 or LPT3) as a device and then pass the port's device handle when you call interrupt 21H, function 40H. You can send a single character to LPT1 by using interrupt 21H, function 05H. Please see Chapter 13 for more information on these services.

Note that the interrupt 21H MS-DOS printer services are relatively slow, although they are usually fast enough to keep up with a printer. A more serious disadvantage is that they do not permit a program to determine the printer's status. Thus, the interrupt 17H BIOS printer services—the third level—are preferred over the MS-DOS services. The three interrupt 17H BIOS printer services are listed in Figure 7-6.

Interrupt 17H Service	*Action*
Function 00H	Writes one character to a parallel port and returns the port status
Function 01H	Initializes a parallel port and returns the port status
Function 02H	Returns the port status

Figure 7-6. *The interrupt 17H BIOS printer services.*

These BIOS printer functions can work with any parallel port. When you call the function, you pass the port's device number, which is assigned by the BIOS. (Device 0 is LPT1, device 1 is LPT2, and so on.) The port status is returned as the printer status byte. The meaning of each bit in this byte is listed in Figure 7-7. See Chapter 13 for further information on the BIOS printer functions.

Bit 7 6 5 4 3 2 1 0	Meaning
X	1 = printer not busy
. X	1 = receive mode selected
. . X	1 = printer out of paper
. . . X	1 = printer on line
. . . . X . . .	1 = transfer error
. . . . . X . .	Not used
. . . . . . X .	Not used
. . . . X	1 = time-out error

Figure 7-7. *The coding of the printer status byte.*

The lowest level of parallel port programming is direct hardware programming. By writing and reading the I/O ports associated with a particular printer port, you can send data, check the port's status, and so on. Direct hardware programming should never be necessary for sending data to a printer; the BIOS services provide all the functionality you will ever need. However, direct hardware programming is needed for highly specialized tasks, such as using a parallel port for bidirectional data transfer between two computers.

Serial Ports

As you may have guessed, the name "serial port" arises from the fact that this type of port transmits data in serial fashion, 1 bit at a time. Serial ports are also referred to as asynchronous communications ports and RS-232 ports. Serial ports are bidirectional; they are commonly used to enable a PC to communicate with networks, other PCs, and a variety of peripheral devices, including modems, some printers, mice, and pen plotters. Compared to parallel ports, serial ports are relatively slow, but they can communicate over much longer distances and are more flexible with regard to bidirectional data transfer.

As a theoretical minimum, a serial port connection requires three wires: one to transmit data, one to receive data, and a ground. In practice, serial links have a number of additional wires, which are used to transmit *handshaking* signals between the computer and the device. Because a serial link is bidirectional, the devices on the two ends of the connection use handshaking signals to coordinate with each other.

A serial port connector is a 9-pin or 25-pin connector on the back of the system. Inside, the serial port circuitry can be located on a plug-in adapter card, or it can be built into the system board. With the exception of IBM's PS/2 line, all PCs can "officially" support a maximum of two serial ports, called COM1 and COM2. Because many PC users needed more than two ports, some manufacturers of peripherals created an unofficial standard for two additional serial ports, COM3 and COM4. PS/2 systems can support as many as seven ports.

Serial port communications protocols

A serial port offers flexibility as to how fast data is transmitted and received and how data is encoded in the serial stream of bits. For two serial ports to communicate with each other, the speed and data encoding settings, collectively called *communications parameters,* must be identical for both ports.

A serial port's transmission speed is specified as a *baud rate;* the baud rate is roughly equivalent to the number of bits transmitted per second. Serial ports on all PCs can be set to 110, 300, 1200, 2400, 4800, or 9600 baud. A setting of 19,200 baud is possible on some systems.

The other communications parameters are *word length, parity checking,* and number of *stop bits:*

- Word length specifies the number of bits that make up each unit of data transmitted; serial port hardware can work with word lengths from 5 through 8 bits, but the PC BIOS supports only lengths of 7 or 8 bits. A word length of 7 is fine for transmitting text made up of characters with ASCII values in the range 0 through 127. A word length of 8 must be used for transmitting the extended ASCII set (ASCII values 0 through 255) or for transmitting binary data.

- Parity checking, when used, adds 1 bit to each data word. Serial port hardware can use the parity bit to verify that the data was received correctly.

- A stop bit is used, in conjunction with a start bit, to delineate the beginning and end of each data word. Serial ports always use 1 start bit, and they can be set to use 1 or 2 stop bits. Most communications software uses 1 stop bit.

Most high-level languages offer convenient methods for configuring serial port communications parameters. You can also configure a serial port by using BIOS functions or by accessing the port registers directly.

I/O port and IRQ assignments

Each serial port interacts with the CPU by means of I/O ports and hardware interrupts. Each serial port is allocated eight I/O ports (only seven of which are actually used) and one IRQ line. Figure 7-8 shows the I/O port and IRQ assignments of COM1 through COM4.

Serial Port	Interrupt	I/O Addresses (Hex)
COM1	IRQ 4	3F8H–3FFH
COM2	IRQ 3	2F8H–2FFH
COM3	IRQ 4	3E8H–3EFH
COM4	IRQ 3	2E8H–2EFH

Figure 7-8. *The I/O port and IRQ assignments for COM1 through COM4.*

During system start-up, the BIOS looks for installed serial ports and places their I/O base addresses in an 8-byte table in low RAM, in the BIOS data area. (See Figure 7-9.) If a port is not available (not installed), its entry in the table is set to 0. A program can inspect the entries to see which serial ports are available. Some programs that use a serial port, such as a serial mouse driver, zero the table entry of the port they are using in order to lessen the chance that another program will try to use the same port.

Serial Port	Location of I/O Base Address
COM1	0040:0000H
COM2	0040:0002H
COM3	0040:0004H
COM4	0040:0006H

Figure 7-9. *The locations of the I/O base addresses for installed serial ports.*

Note that the BIOS reserves space for the addresses of four serial ports, even though the PC "officially" supports only two. This suggests that the designers of the PC originally planned to support four ports but found themselves limited to two because there were only two unused IRQ lines on the original PC bus. You can see from Figure 7-8 that the "unofficial" COM3 and COM4 ports use the same IRQ lines as COM1 and COM2, which can cause problems. We'll explain these problems in the next section.

Serial port interrupts

One programming technique for reading data from a serial port is to use *polling*. With this method, the program executes a loop that repeatedly checks the port to see whether a character has been received; if so, the character is read into memory. Polling is simple to program, and it works fine at slow communication speeds. At speeds above 1200 baud, however, data might be lost because the serial port receives characters faster than the program can fetch them.

To maximize efficiency and prevent data loss, the preferred technique is to use interrupt-driven programming. Each serial port is attached to one of the PC's hardware interrupt lines. An interrupt is signaled whenever a character is received by the port. With interrupt-driven programming, the program includes an interrupt service routine whose address is placed in the interrupt vector for the desired serial port. The code in the service routine has only one job: to fetch the waiting character from the serial port and place it in a memory buffer where the program's main code can access it. All commercial communications programs are interrupt driven.

As you saw in Figure 7-8, only two hardware interrupt lines, IRQ 3 and IRQ 4, are available for serial ports. Thus, if COM3 and COM 4 are installed, they must share these IRQ lines with COM1 and COM2.

When more than two serial ports are installed in a PC (other than a PS/2 model), a problem arises because the interrupt lines on the PC bus were not designed to be shared. If two serial cards attempt to use the same IRQ line, it's possible for them to miss interrupts or even, in some cases, to cause damage to the hardware.

The reason that COM3 and COM4 can be supported at all is that many uses of serial ports do not employ interrupts. For example, using COM1 to send data to a printer does not involve interrupts. It would then be OK for an interrupt-driven communications program to use COM3. Generally speaking, however, it's best to avoid using COM3 and COM4. If you must use them, ensure that there will be no IRQ conflicts.

The UART

At the heart of every serial port is a chip called a *universal asynchronous receiver transmitter,* or UART for short. The original IBM PC uses the 8250 UART. Systems with 80286 and higher CPUs (except for PS/2 systems) use the downward-compatible 16450 UART, which has added features and increased speed. IBM PS/2 systems use the 16550 UART, which is also compatible with the 8250. The primary function of the UART is to convert data from parallel format to serial format and vice versa. Outgoing data must be converted from the parallel format used by the computer to the serial format used by the serial port; and start bits, stop bits, and parity bits must be added. Incoming data must be converted in the opposite direction.

UART functions are controlled by 10 data and control registers that are mapped to the I/O ports. These registers are summarized in Figure 7-10. Note that in some cases more than one register is mapped to the same I/O port. Which register is accessed at the port is controlled by the setting of a bit in another register.

I/O Address	Register	Comments
Base + 0	Transmit buffer	If bit 7 of line control register = 0
Base + 0	Receive buffer	If bit 7 of line control register = 0
Base + 0	Divisor latch low byte	If bit 7 of line control register = 1
Base + 1	Divisor latch high byte	If bit 7 of line control register = 1
Base + 1	Interrupt enable	If bit 7 of line control register = 0
Base + 2	Interrupt identification	
Base + 3	Line control	
Base + 4	Modem control	
Base + 5	Line status	
Base + 6	Modem status	

Figure 7-10. *The I/O addresses of the data and control registers that control UART functions.*

This section describes the functions of the various UART registers. We do not attempt to provide a complete treatment of UART programming, a complex topic that can take up an entire book. But the information here should allow you to get started. Note that in many registers, some of the bits are not currently used. You cannot assume they will not be used in the future, however, so your programs should not change their values.

The functions of the transmit buffer and the receive buffer are self-evident. Data written to the transmit buffer is transmitted by the UART, and data received by the UART is made available in the receive buffer.

The bits in the interrupt enable register determine which UART events trigger an interrupt. You can see from Figure 7-11 that there are four possible events, all of which trigger the same interrupt. The interrupt service routine must examine the interrupt identification register to determine which of the events has occurred. All bits in the interrupt enable register are set to 0 upon UART reset.

Bit 7 6 5 4 3 2 1 0	Meaning
X	Not used (always 0)
. X	Not used (always 0)
. . X	Not used (always 0)
. . . X	Not used (always 0)
. . . . X . . .	1 = interrupt when modem status register changes
. . . . . X . .	1 = interrupt when line status register changes
. . . . . . X .	1 = interrupt when transmit register empty
. . . . X	1 = interrupt when data received

Figure 7-11. *The coding of the interrupt enable register.*

The two divisor latch registers are used to set the UART baud rate. Note that these two registers are mapped to the same I/O ports as the transmit buffer, receive buffer, and interrupt enable registers. To write data to the divisor latch registers, you must set bit 7 of the line control register to 1. Figure 7-12 shows the hex values you must write to these registers to set the most commonly used baud rates. Be sure to write the high byte to the high byte register (at I/O base plus 1) and the low byte to the low byte register (at I/O base plus 0).

Baud Rate	Hex Value
300	0180H
1200	0060H
2400	0030H
4800	0018H
9600	000CH

Figure 7-12. *The hex values you must write to the divisor latch registers to set the most commonly used baud rates.*

After the UART has triggered an interrupt, the interrupt identification register contains information about which event was responsible. It also contains the interrupt-pending bit, which indicates whether other data in the register should be used. The bits in this register are listed in Figure 7-13.

The line control register is used to control various aspects of data transmission, including setting communications parameters. Bit 7 in this register is used to specify which registers will be accessed via I/O addresses base plus 0 and base plus 1. All bits in this register are set to 0 upon UART reset. The bits in the line control register are listed in Figure 7-14.

Bit 7 6 5 4 3 2 1 0	Function	Meaning
X	Not used	Always 0
. X	Not used	Always 0
. . X	Not used	Always 0
. . . X	Not used	Always 0
. . . . X . . .	Not used	Always 0
. . . . . X X .	Interrupt ID	00 = modem status interrupt 01 = transmit holding buffer empty interrupt 10 = received data available interrupt 11 = line status interrupt
. . . . X	Interrupt pending	0 = interrupt pending, use bits 1 and 2 1 = interrupt not pending, ignore bits 1 and 2

Figure 7-13. *The coding of the interrupt identification register.*

Bit 7 6 5 4 3 2 1 0	Function	Meaning
X	Divisor latch access	1 = access divisor latch bytes
. X	Break control	0 = disabled 1 = enabled
. . X	Override parity	0 = force parity bit to 0 1 = force parity bit to 1
. . . X	Parity select	0 = odd parity 1 = even parity
. . . . X . . .	Parity enable	0 = parity disabled 1 = parity enabled
. . . . . X . .	Stop bits	0 = 1 stop bit 1 = 1.5 stop bits (only if word length = 5 bits) 1 = 2 stop bits
. . . . . . X X	Word length	00 = 5 bits 01 = 6 bits 10 = 7 bits 11 = 8 bits

Figure 7-14. *The coding of the line control register.*

The line status register contains information about the status of the data transmission line; it indicates the operation currently in progress and the occurrences of any errors. Its bits are listed in Figure 7-15.

Bit 7 6 5 4 3 2 1 0	Function	Meaning
X	Not used	Always 0
. X	Transmitter shift register	0 = data transfer 1 = transmitter idle
. . X	Transmitter hold register	0 = ready 1 = transmitting character
. . . X	Break indicator	0 = normal receive 1 = break received
. . . . X . . .	Framing error	0 = normal receive 1 = framing error
. . . . . X . .	Parity error	0 = normal receive 1 = parity error
. . . . . . X .	Overrun error	0 = normal receive 1 = overrun error
. . . . X	Receiver data	0 = no data received 1 = data received

Figure 7-15. *The coding of the line status register.*

The modem status register provides a variety of status bits that are used to control handshaking with another serial port. (See Figure 7-16.) The name ''modem status register'' reflects the fact that these signals are involved when the serial port is being used to drive a modem, which is used to

Bit 7 6 5 4 3 2 1 0	Function
X	Receiver line signal detect (RLSD)
. X	Ring indicator (RI)
. . X	Data set ready (DSR)
. . . X	Clear to send (CTS)
. . . . X . . .	Delta RLSD
. . . . . X . .	Delta RI
. . . . . . X .	Delta DSR
. . . . X	Delta CTS

Figure 7-16. *The coding of the modem status register.*

transmit serial data over phone lines. The modem status register contains 4 bits that signal various aspects of the current modem status. The other 4 bits in this register, the *delta* bits, indicate whether any aspect of the modem status has changed since the last time the register was read. These bits are set to 1 if the status has changed and 0 if it has not.

The bits in the modem control register are used to control the state of the serial port handshaking lines. These bits are listed in Figure 7-17.

Bit 7 6 5 4 3 2 1 0	Function	Meaning
X	Not used	Always 0
. X	Not used	Always 0
. . X	Not used	Always 0
. . . X	Loopback test mode	0 = disabled 1 = enabled
. . . . X . . .	OUT2 signal (often used to enable PC interrupts)	0 = OUT2 forced inactive 1 = OUT2 forced active
. . . . . X . .	OUT1 signal (used to reset some internal modems)	0 = OUT1 forced inactive 1 = OUT1 forced active
. . . . . . X .	RTS signal (request to send)	0 = RTS forced inactive 1 = RTS forced active
. . . . X	DTR signal (data terminal ready)	0 = DTR forced inactive 1 = DTR forced active

Figure 7-17. *The coding of the modem control register.*

Programming the serial ports

Directly programming serial port hardware can be a tricky business. As we mentioned earlier, you must use interrupt-driven programming for any serious serial communications task. You've also seen that there is quite a range of control and status information you must keep track of. Finally, your communications programs must be able to coordinate their activities with the hardware and software at the other end of the line. All of these factors make direct serial port programming a task that even the most seasoned programmers hesitate to take on.

Fortunately, there's rarely a need to do so. Most high-level languages provide serial port input and output statements that are more than adequate for most programmers. For more demanding applications, numerous add-on libraries of serial port functions are available. The time and frustration that one of these add-on libraries can save make it well worth the purchase cost.

MS-DOS and BIOS serial port services can sometimes be useful for relatively simple tasks. But because these services are not interrupt driven, the maximum communication speed they can support is limited.

MS-DOS has services available via interrupt 21H for reading data from and writing data to a serial port. There are no MS-DOS services for configuring a serial port, however, so you must use your high-level language or the BIOS services (described in Chapter 13) to set baud rate and other communications parameters.

To read or write blocks of data, you can use the handle-based services interrupt 21H, functions 3FH and 40H. MS-DOS automatically associates handle 3 with serial port COM1. (COM1 is also known as AUX.) To use these services with another serial port, such as COM2, you must use interrupt 21H, function 3DH to open the port and obtain a handle for it. Please refer to Chapter 10 for more information on these MS-DOS services.

The BIOS serial port services offer much more flexibility than the MS-DOS services. Using these services on a relatively fast system, you can usually achieve reliable serial port communications at speeds as high as 2400 baud. The BIOS serial port services are summarized in Figure 7-18. Please see Chapter 13 for details.

BIOS Service	*Description*
Interrupt 14H, function 00H	Initializes and configures a serial port
Interrupt 14H, function 01H	Writes one character to a serial port
Interrupt 14H, function 02H	Reads one character from a serial port
Interrupt 14H, function 03H	Gets serial port status
Interrupt 14H, function 04H	Performs an extended initialization of a serial port (PS/2 only)
Interrupt 14H, function 05H	Performs an extended control of a serial port (PS/2 only)

Figure 7-18. *The BIOS serial port services.*

Clocks and Timers

Clocks and timers create the computer's heartbeat. The computer's essential functions of computation and data transfer take place in step with the pulses generated by electronic clocks. PCs play host to several clocks and timers you should know about:

- The **system timer** generates clock ticks and other timing pulses at precisely controlled intervals.

- The **sound generator** can produce a variety of sounds through the computer's built-in speaker.

- The **real-time clock** keeps track of the date and time and can also serve as an "alarm clock." (This is supported only in systems with an 80286 or higher CPU.)

To understand how to use the system timer, the sound generator, and the real-time clock, you need to know about the basic clock and timing mechanisms in PCs. That is what we'll outline in this section.

PCs have several clocks and timers that run at different rates and perform different functions. Some of them are intrinsic to the circuit design of the computer; their operation is independent of software control. Others are designed to support timing functions in software; the operation of these timers can be controlled by software through BIOS services or by direct hardware programming.

The CPU Clock

Probably the most basic of the timed events in a PC is the step-by-step operation of the computer's CPU, whose speed is determined by the frequency of a special oscillator circuit that generates high-frequency pulses at regular intervals. This frequency is the CPU's *clock speed,* and it determines how quickly the CPU can carry out its functions.

The CPU oscillator keeps time for the CPU in much the same way a metronome keeps time for a musician. At each tick of the CPU clock (that is, at each pulse in the CPU oscillator's signal), the CPU carries out part of one machine instruction. All CPU instructions require one or more clock cycles to execute. For example, the register INC instruction requires two clock cycles to execute, except on the 80486, where it requires only one; more complicated instructions such as CALL and MUL take a longer amount of time.

In the original IBM PC and PC/XT, the CPU's clock speed is 4,772,727 cycles per second, or about 4.77 megahertz. (A *megahertz,* or MHz, is one million cycles per second.) One CPU clock cycle thus lasts about 1/4,772,727 of a second, or about 210 *nanoseconds* (billionths of a second). With this clock frequency, a two-cycle INC instruction executes in roughly 420 nanoseconds (0.42 *microseconds,* or millionths of a second).

The odd clock speed of 4.77 MHz was actually a convenient frequency for the designers of the original PC to use. In fact, the CPU clock speed is derived from a basic oscillator frequency of 14.31818 MHz, which is commonly used in television circuitry. Dividing the basic frequency by 3 gives the 4.77 MHz CPU clock speed. Dividing by 4 gives a clock speed of 3.57955 MHz, which is the frequency of the color burst signal used in color televisions and in the PC's Color Graphics Adapter. Dividing the basic frequency by 12 gives 1.19318 MHz, which is the clock frequency used by the PC's system timers.

In later, faster members of the PC family, the CPU clock speed is higher, so the overall computational speed of these computers is greater. The 80286, 80386, and 80486 processors also execute many machine instructions in fewer clock cycles than the 8088 uses in the PC and PC/XT. For example, the register PUSH instruction in the 8088 executes in 15 clock cycles; in the 80286 the same instruction takes 3 cycles; in the 80386 it takes only 2 cycles; and in the 80486 it takes only 1 cycle. The combination of a higher CPU clock speed and faster machine instructions means that the 80286-based, 80386-based, and 80486-based members of the PC family execute programs significantly faster than do the 8088-based and 8086-based machines. For example, a 20-MHz 80386 system is approximately 15 times faster than the original PC, and today's systems based on 50-MHz 80486 CPUs are roughly 50 times faster.

System Timers

Not only the CPU but many other basic hardware and software functions occur at regular intervals based on a preset clock frequency. For example, the dynamic RAM chips that constitute the computer's main memory must be accessed at regular intervals in order to refresh the information represented in them. Also, ROM BIOS and operating system functions such as keeping track of the time of day require the computer to generate a clock-tick signal at a predetermined rate. All PCs have circuitry that generates the necessary timing signals.

In the PC and PC/XT, an Intel 8253-5 programmable timer/counter chip produces the RAM refresh and clock-tick signals. In the PC/AT, an Intel 8254-2 chip is used in the same way. The PS/2 models 25 and 30 use an 8253-5 chip for the clock tick, but RAM refresh timing is a function of a custom integrated circuit. In PS/2 models that use Micro Channel Architecture (MCA), all timing functions are implemented in custom chips. Clones from other manufacturers use a variety of methods to generate timing signals.

Despite these hardware variations, the timer programming interface is the same in all PCs.

In all members of the PC family, the timer chip has three output channels, each with a dedicated function:

- **Channel 0** is the system clock-tick timer. When the computer is coldbooted, the ROM BIOS programs the timer to oscillate with a frequency of about 18.2 ticks per second. This signal is tied to the computer's interrupt controller in such a way that interrupt 08H (decimal 8) is generated each time the clock ticks.

- **Channel 1** is always dedicated to producing the RAM refresh timing signal; it's not intended for use in software applications.

- **Channel 2** is used to control the computer's speaker. The frequency of the timer's channel 2 signal determines the frequency of the sound that is emitted by the loudspeaker. (We'll come back to this later.)

PS/2 models that use Micro Channel Architecture also have a timer channel 3. The signal produced on channel 3 is tied to the computer's non-maskable interrupt (interrupt 02H, decimal 2) and can be used by an operating system as a "watchdog" to ensure that some other critical function, such as servicing a clock-tick interrupt, does not crash the computer by taking too long to execute.

Using the System Timer Tick

In all PCs, the input oscillator to the system timer circuit has a frequency of 1.19318 MHz. On each cycle, the timer chip decrements the values in a set of internal 16-bit counters, one for each of the timer's output channels. When the value in a counter reaches 0, the chip generates a single output pulse on the corresponding channel, resets the count, and starts counting down again.

When the ROM BIOS initializes the system timer, it stores a countdown value of 0 in the count register for channel 0. This means that the timer chip decrements the counter 2^{16} times between output pulses on channel 0, so output pulses occur at a rate equal to 1,193,180/65,536, or roughly 18.2 times per second. The output from timer channel 0 is used as the signal on interrupt request level 0 (IRQ 0), so interrupt 08H occurs whenever channel 0 of the system timer counts down to 0—that is, 18.2 times per second.

The BIOS contains an interrupt handler for interrupt 08H that increments a running count of clock ticks at 0040:006CH in the BIOS data area. This interrupt handler also decrements the byte at 0040:0040H; if the value in the byte reaches 0, the interrupt handler issues a command to the floppy disk–drive controller to turn off the disk-drive motor if it's on.

The BIOS interrupt 08H handler also issues software interrupt 1CH (decimal 28), which is intended for use in programs that must be notified when a system timer tick occurs. A program can detect when each timer tick occurs simply by pointing the interrupt 1CH vector at 0000:0070H to its own interrupt handler. If you use an interrupt 1CH handler in a program, however, be aware that the BIOS interrupt 08H handler does not allow subsequent clock-tick interrupts on IRQ 0 to occur until your interrupt 1CH handler returns. If you install an interrupt 1CH handler, ensure that it doesn't keep IRQ 0 disabled for too long or the system might crash.

The system timer tick and its interrupt are useful in programs that must perform a simple task at a regular interval regardless of what else is going on in the computer. The timer-tick interrupt has the highest priority of any of the hardware interrupts (except the nonmaskable interrupt), so the code in the corresponding interrupt 08H and 1CH handlers takes precedence over all other system software.

For this reason, the timer tick is used primarily in operating system software and in memory-resident "pop-up" programs such as Sidekick and the Norton Guides. Such programs have their own timer-tick interrupt handlers that check whether it is time to pop up on the screen. These programs generally rely on the system timer tick to occur at the default frequency of 18.2 ticks per second.

Because timer-tick function is so essential to the proper operation of the computer, you should change the output frequency of system timer channel 0 only if you are careful to preserve the functionality of the BIOS interrupt 08H handler. For example, Basic uses the timer tick to measure the duration of tones created with the PLAY or SOUND command. However, because the standard rate of 18.2 ticks per second is not fast enough to provide the precision that some kinds of music demand, Basic reprograms the timer to tick four times faster, which causes interrupt 08H to occur 72.8 times per second instead of 18.2 times per second. When Basic counts against the quadruple rate, it is able to more accurately reproduce the proper tempo of a piece of music.

Basic can do this because it has a special interrupt 08H handler that calls the default interrupt 08H handler on every fourth timer tick. This ensures that the usual interrupt 08H functions still occur 18.2 times per second.

If you reprogram system timer channel 0 to a nonstandard rate, your program should use the same technique in order to preserve interrupt 08H functionality.

Programming system timer channel 2, the sound frequency generator, is not as demanding, because no BIOS or operating system functions rely on it. Before we cover the programming details, however, we'll describe some of the basic mechanics of creating sounds with a computer.

The Physics of Sound

Sounds are simply regular pulses or vibrations in air pressure. Sound is produced when air particles are set into motion by a vibrating source. When the vibrating source pushes out, it compresses the air particles around it, increasing air pressure. As it pulls in, the particles pull apart, decreasing air pressure. These alternating waves of increased and decreased pressure, called *sound waves,* travel through the air away from the source.

The speaker in a PC can be made to vibrate by electrical impulses generated by the computer. Because computers normally deal with binary numbers, the voltages they produce are either high or low. Every transition from one voltage state to another either pushes the speaker cone out or relaxes it. A sound is produced when the voltage to the speaker goes from low to high to low again, causing the speaker to move out and then in. This single vibration, consisting of a pulse out and a pulse in, is called a *cycle.* Through the speaker, a single cycle of sound is heard as a click. A continuous sound is produced when a continuous stream of pulses is sent to the speaker. As the pulse rate increases, so does the pitch of the tone. For example, if you pulse the speaker in and out 261.63 times per second (that is, at a rate of 261.63 *hertz,* or cycles per second), you hear the musical note known as middle C. Figure 7-19 lists the frequencies required to generate other musical notes.

The average adult can hear sounds ranging from roughly 20 through 15,000 hertz. Human speech falls almost entirely within the range of 125 through 2500 hertz. A PC can send electrical signals to its speaker that can range from about 18 to more than a million hertz, although mechanical limitations of a PC's speaker preclude it reproducing anything higher than perhaps 10,000 hertz. The speaker has no volume control and is not really intended for accurate sound reproduction. As a result, different frequencies produce different effects; some may sound louder than others, and some may have a more accurate pitch. This variation is a by-product of the speaker design and is not something you can control.

Note	Frequency	Note	Frequency	Note	Frequency	Note	Frequency
C_0	16.35	C_2	65.41	C_4	261.63	C_6	1046.50
$C_{\#0}$	17.32	$C_{\#2}$	69.30	$C_{\#4}$	277.18	$C_{\#6}$	1108.73
D_0	18.35	D_2	73.42	D_4	293.66	D_6	1174.66
$D_{\#0}$	19.45	$D_{\#2}$	77.78	$D_{\#4}$	311.13	$D_{\#6}$	1244.51
E_0	20.60	E_2	82.41	E_4	329.63	E_6	1318.51
F_0	21.83	F_2	87.31	F_4	349.23	F_6	1396.91
$F_{\#0}$	23.12	$F_{\#2}$	92.50	$F_{\#4}$	369.99	$F_{\#6}$	1479.98
G_0	24.50	G_2	98.00	G_4	392.00	G_6	1567.98
$G_{\#0}$	25.96	$G_{\#2}$	103.83	$G_{\#4}$	415.30	$G_{\#6}$	1661.22
A_0	27.50	A_2	110.00	A_4	440.00	A_6	1760.00
$A_{\#0}$	29.14	$A_{\#2}$	116.54	$A_{\#4}$	466.16	$A_{\#6}$	1864.66
B_0	30.87	B_2	123.47	B_4	493.88	B_6	1975.53
C_1	32.70	C_3	130.81	C_5	523.25	C_7	2093.00
$C_{\#1}$	34.65	$C_{\#3}$	138.59	$C_{\#5}$	554.37	$C_{\#7}$	2217.46
D_1	36.71	D_3	146.83	D_5	587.33	D_7	2349.32
$D_{\#1}$	38.89	$D_{\#3}$	155.56	$D_{\#5}$	622.25	$D_{\#7}$	2489.02
E_1	41.20	E_3	164.81	E_5	659.26	E_7	2637.02
F_1	43.65	F_3	174.61	F_5	698.46	F_7	2793.83
$F_{\#1}$	46.25	$F_{\#3}$	185.00	$F_{\#5}$	739.99	$F_{\#7}$	2959.96
G_1	49.00	G_3	196.00	G_5	783.99	G_7	3135.96
$G_{\#1}$	51.91	$G_{\#3}$	207.65	$G_{\#5}$	830.61	$G_{\#7}$	3322.44
A_1	55.00	A_3	220.00	A_5	880.00	A_7	3520.00
$A_{\#1}$	58.27	$A_{\#3}$	233.08	$A_{\#5}$	932.33	$A_{\#7}$	3729.31
B_1	61.74	B_3	246.94	B_5	987.77	B_7	3951.07
						C_8	4186.01

Note: Equal Tempered Chromatic Scale; $A_4 = 440$
Note: American Standard pitch — adopted by the American Standards Association in 1936

Figure 7-19. *Eight octaves of musical note frequencies.*

How the Computer Produces Sound

You can generate sounds through the speaker in two ways, using one or both of two different sound sources. One method is to write a program that turns the speaker on and off by manipulating two speaker bits in the I/O port that provides access to the speaker-control circuitry. When you use this method, your program controls the timing of the pulse and the resulting sound frequency. The other method is to use channel 2 of the system timer chip to pulse the speaker at a precise frequency. Using the timer chip is a more popular method for two reasons: Because speaker pulses are controlled by the timer chip instead of by a program, the CPU can devote its time to the other demands of the computer system; and the timer chip is not dependent on the working speed of the CPU, which varies according to which PC model you use. The program method and the timer method can be used together or separately to create many simple and complex sounds.

Timer-Chip Sound Control

The programmable timer chip is the heart of the standard PC models' sound-making abilities. As we have seen, channel 2 of the timer chip is dedicated to sound generation. To create sounds, you must program channel 2 properly and then use the pulses from channel 2 to drive the speaker.

The timer can be programmed to produce pulses at whatever frequency you want, but because it does not keep track of how long the sound continues, the sound will continue forever unless it is turned off. Therefore, your programs must end a sound by using some sort of timing instruction.

Programming the timer chip

To program timer channel 2, load the timer chip with an appropriate countdown value for the channel 2 counter. (The timer chip holds this value in an internal register so that it can reset the counter each time it reaches 0.) The countdown value takes effect immediately after you load it into the timer chip. The timer chip decrements the counter with each cycle of its 1.19318 MHz clock until the counter reaches 0; then it sends an output pulse on channel 2 to the sound generator circuitry and starts counting down once again.

In effect, the timer "divides" the countdown value into the clock frequency to produce an output frequency. The result is that the timer sends out a series of pulses that produce a sound of a certain frequency when you turn on the speaker.

The controlling count and the resulting frequency have a reciprocal relationship, as shown by these formulas:

Count = 1,193,180 ÷ Frequency
Frequency = 1,193,180 ÷ Count

You can see that a low-frequency (low-pitched) sound is produced by a high count and that a high-frequency (high-pitched) sound is produced by a low count. A count of 100 produces a high pitch of roughly 11,931 cycles per second, whereas a count of 10,000 produces a low pitch of about 119 cycles per second.

You can produce just about any frequency within the limitations of 16-bit arithmetic. The lowest frequency is 18.2 hertz, with a divisor of 65,535 (FFFFH); the highest is 1.193 megahertz, with a divisor of 1. The Basic language holds this to a practical range of 37 through 32,767 hertz. The following program demonstrates that the actual frequency range of the internal speaker is even less than Basic provides.

After you calculate the count that you need for the frequency you want, you send it to the timer channel 2 registers. This is done by using three port outputs. The first port output notifies the timer that the count is coming by sending the value B6H (decimal 182) to port 43H (decimal 67). The next two outputs send the low-order and high-order bytes of the count, a 16-bit unsigned word, to port 42H (decimal 66)—the low-order byte followed by the high-order byte. The following Basic program illustrates the process:

```
10 COUNT = 1193180! / 3000      ' 3000 is the desired frequency
20 LO.COUNT = COUNT MOD 256     ' calculate low-order byte value
30 HI.COUNT = COUNT / 256       ' calculate high-order byte value
40 OUT &H43, &HB6               ' get timer ready
50 OUT &H42, LO.COUNT           ' load low-order byte
60 OUT &H42, HI.COUNT           ' load high-order byte
```

Activating the speaker

After you have programmed the timer, you still need to activate the speaker circuitry in order to use the signal that the timer is generating. As with most other parts of the PC, the speaker is manipulated by sending data to a specific port, a process illustrated in Figure 7-20. The speaker is controlled

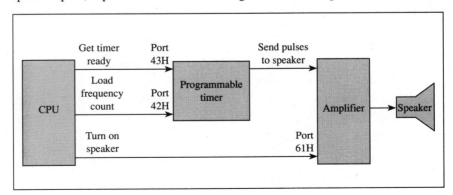

Figure 7-20. *How sound frequencies are generated by the system timer and speaker.*

by changing the values of bits 0 and 1 at I/O port 61H (decimal 97). Only 2 of the port's 8 bits are used by the speaker: the low-order bits numbered 0 and 1. The other 6 bits are used for other purposes, so it is important that you don't disturb them while working with the speaker.

The lowest bit, bit 0, controls transmission of the timer chip's output signal to the speaker. The second bit, bit 1, controls the pulsing of the speaker. Both bits must be set to make the speaker respond to the timer chip's signal. You can turn them on without disturbing the nonspeaker bits by reading the present value from the port, setting the first 2 bits, and then writing the modified value back to the port. This is accomplished in Basic as shown here:

```
70 OLD.PORT = INP (&H61)            ' read the value at port 61H
80 NEW.PORT = (OLD.PORT OR &H03)    ' set bits 0 and 1
90 OUT &H61, NEW.PORT               ' turn speaker on
```

Direct Speaker Control

The timer controls the speaker by sending periodic signals that pulse the speaker. You can do the same thing with a program that sends in and out signals directly to the speaker. You do this by setting bit 0 of port 61H (decimal 97) to 0 to turn the speaker off and then alternately setting bit 1 on and off to pulse the speaker. When you use this method, the speed of the program determines the frequency of the sound; the faster the program executes, the higher the pitch. The following Basic program is an example of this method:

```
10 X = INP (&H61) AND &HFC         ' read port value,
                                     turn off bits 1 and 0
20 OUT &H61, X                     ' pull speaker in
30 OUT &H61, X OR 2                ' push speaker out
40 GOTO 20
```

The actions in lines 20 and 30 pulse the speaker in and out. Each is a half-cycle, and the two together produce one complete sound cycle.

This example runs as fast as Basic can process it, producing as high a note as possible. If you needed more range in your application, you could use a faster language and insert deliberate delays, equal to half the frequency cycle time, between each complete cycle. (These delays would be half the cycle time because each ON or OFF operation is a half-cycle.) No matter which language you use, you must include a duration count to end the sound. To produce different sounds at particular frequencies, such as clicking or buzzing sounds, simply vary the delays between pulses.

Despite all these wonderful possibilities, generating sounds through the speaker by direct program action is not a good way to make sounds. It has three big disadvantages compared to the use of the timer:

- A program requires the constant attention of the CPU, so the computer has a hard time getting any other work done.

- The frequency of the sound is at the mercy of the speed of the computer; that is, the same program makes a lower or higher sound on a slower or faster computer.

- The clock-tick interrupts interfere with the smoothness of the sound, making a warble. The only way to avoid this is to suspend the clock tick by disabling the interrupts—and that disrupts the computer's sense of time.

As far as we know, there is only one advantage to making sounds using the direct method: With the proper control over the program delays, the direct method lets you make a low-fidelity polyphonic sound. Be forewarned, though, that this requires some clever and tedious programming and, all in all, may not be worth the trouble.

Speaker Volume and Sound Quality

The computer's internal speaker has no volume control of any kind and, like all speakers, varies in how well it responds to different frequencies; the speaker reproduces some frequencies louder than others. In the case of a crude speaker like that found in most PCs, the loudness of the sound varies widely with the frequency. You can use the following program to test this— it might help you choose the best sound pitch for your purpose:

```
10 PLAY "MF"                          ' plays each sound separately
20 FREQUENCY = 37
30 WHILE FREQUENCY < 32000            ' use all frequencies to
                                        32000 Hz
40    PRINT USING "##,###"; FREQUENCY ' display frequency
50    SOUND FREQUENCY, 5              ' produce sound with
                                        duration of 5
60    FREQUENCY = FREQUENCY * 1.1     ' increment frequency by 1/10
70 WEND
```

Be aware that the speakers in the various PC models might not sound alike, partly because the materials of each system housing resonate differently as speaker enclosures. Try the following samples on two different computer models and be prepared for these variations in sound:

```
100 'sound samples
110 '
120 'warble (two rapidly alternating tones)
130 FOR N% = 0 TO 5
140   SOUND 440, .7
150   SOUND 466.16, .5
160 NEXT
170 WHILE(INKEY$="") : WEND       ' wait for a keystroke
180 '
190 'two tones played quickly
200 SOUND 900, .1
210 SOUND 760, 1
220 WHILE(INKEY$="") : WEND
230 '
240 'random noise
250 X = INP(&H61) AND &HFC
260 I=20                          ' changing I changes the noise
270 FOR N% = 0 TO 500
280   IF (RND * 100 < I) THEN OUT &H61,X OR 2 : OUT &H61,X
290 NEXT
```

CMOS Memory

All PCs with 80286 or higher processors have 64 bytes of special memory that is maintained by a battery so that it keeps its information even when the computer is turned off. This is often referred to as CMOS memory. (CMOS stands for complementary metal oxide semiconductor.) This permanent storage is used to maintain a real-time clock and certain configuration data about the system and its peripherals. In the PC/AT, the CMOS memory is part of a Motorola MC146818 chip. In the PS/2s, the real-time clock is in custom silicon. Many 8088 PCs have a battery-operated real-time clock. This clock is part of a plug-in adapter card, not part of the original PC design.

The 64 bytes of CMOS memory are not mapped into the CPU's address space. Rather, they are accessed via two I/O ports, at addresses 70H and 71H (decimal 112 and 113). A program writes the configuration address (00H through 3FH) to I/O port 70H and then writes a new byte value or reads the current byte value at I/O port 71H. (See Figure 7-21.)

Configuration Information

Part of CMOS memory is used to maintain certain information about the system configuration, such as the type of hard disk and the amount of memory. At boot time the ROM BIOS reads the configuration information from CMOS memory and uses it in various ways during operations. To ensure that the data is accurate, some bytes of CMOS memory are devoted to *checksum*

185

bytes, which the ROM can use to verify that other data in CMOS memory has not been corrupted. If the checksum bytes compare OK, the boot process proceeds normally. If not, the computer displays an error message. In either case, you can access the ROM BIOS setup program that is used to examine and change data in CMOS memory. On non-IBM PCs, the setup program is usually called up by pressing a special key combination during booting.

Figure 7-21 presents a map of the configuration portion of CMOS memory in the IBM PC/AT.

CMOS Address	Contents
0EH	Diagnostic byte
0FH	Power-down system status
10H	Bits 4–7: first floppy disk–drive type Bits 0–3: second floppy disk–drive type
11H	Reserved
12H	Bits 4–7: hard drive 1 type Bits 0–3: hard drive 2 type
13H	Reserved
14H	Configuration byte
15H	Low byte of base memory size

16H	High byte of base memory size:
	    100H = 256 KB
	    200H = 512 KB
	    280H = 640 KB

17H	Low expansion memory byte

18H	High expansion memory byte:
	    200H = 512 KB
	    400H = 1024 KB
	    600H–3C00H = 1536–15,360 KB

19H	Extended type byte: hard disk 1
1AH	Extended type byte: hard disk 2
1BH–2DH	Reserved
2EH–2FH	Checksum for addresses 10H–2DH
30H	Low expansion memory byte

31H	High expansion memory byte:
	    200H = 512 KB
	    400H = 1024 KB
	    600H–3C00H = 1536–15,360 KB

33H	Information flag

Figure 7-21. *A map of the configuration portion of CMOS memory in the IBM PC/AT.*

The bits in the diagnostic byte are set depending on certain errors that may occur during the Power On Self Text (POST). (See Figure 7-22.)

Bit 7 6 5 4 3 2 1 0	Meaning
X	1 = CMOS battery dead
. X	1 = checksum incorrect
. . X	1 = configuration byte incorrect
. . . X	1 = memory size incorrect
. . . . X . . .	1 = hard drive or controller error
. . . . . X . .	1 = date or time incorrect
. . . . . . X .	Not used
. . . . X	Not used

Figure 7-22. *The coding of the diagnostic byte.*

The bits in the configuration byte specify certain information about the system hardware. (See Figure 7-23.)

Bit 7 6 5 4 3 2 1 0	Function	Meaning
X X	Number of disk drives	00 = 1 drive 01 = 2 drives
. . X X	Primary display type	00 = display has its own BIOS 01 = 40-column CGA 10 = 80-column CGA 11 = MDA
. . . . X . . .	Not used	
. . . . . X . .	Not used	
. . . . . . X .		1 = math coprocessor installed
. . . . X		0 = no floppy disk drive available 1 = floppy disk drive(s) available

Figure 7-23. *The coding of the configuration byte.*

The byte at CMOS address 10H (decimal 16) encodes the types of two floppy disk drives, devoting 4 bits to each drive. Bits 4 through 7 are for drive 0, and bits 0 through 3 are for drive 1. The possible 4-bit codes are

0000 = no disk drive

0001 = 5.25-inch 320-KB or 360-KB

0010 = 5.25-inch 1.2-MB

0011 = 3.5-inch 720-KB

0100 = 3.5-inch 1.44-MB

0110 = 3.5-inch 2.88-MB

The reserved portions of the CMOS memory area might be used in different ways by the BIOS manufacturer. You cannot assume that this is a safe place to store data.

The Real-Time Clock

Portions of CMOS memory are used to store the real-time clock's time and date information and also to store the alarm settings. Figure 7-24 maps these CMOS addresses.

When you boot a PC, the ROM BIOS start-up routines read the time of day from the real-time clock and convert it into the corresponding number of timer ticks. This value is used to initialize the 4-byte count that is stored at

CMOS Address	Contents
00H	Current second
01H	Second alarm
02H	Current minute
03H	Minute alarm
04H	Current hour
05H	Hour alarm
06H	Day of the week
07H	Day of the month
08H	Month
09H	Year (00–99)
0AH	Clock status register A
0BH	Clock status register B
0CH	Clock status register C
0DH	Clock status register D
32H	Century in BCD (19 or 20)*

*In the IBM PS/2, the century byte is at 37H. 32H and 33H are used for a CRC value for bytes 10H through 31H.

Figure 7-24. *A map of the CMOS addresses used to store the real-time clock's time and date information and the alarm settings.*

0040:006CH in the ROM BIOS data area. All versions of MS-DOS use this count value to determine the current time of day. Starting with version 3.0, MS-DOS also obtains the current date from the real-time clock and initializes its own internal record of the date at boot time.

To work with the current date and time in a program, we recommend that you use the MS-DOS date and time services (Chapter 13) to get and set the current values. You can also use BIOS services to access the real-time clock (Chapter 13). However, if you call the BIOS to change the date or time, MS-DOS might not be aware of the change and might assume an incorrect time or date.

Setting the Alarm

The real-time clock has an alarm feature that can be used to generate an interrupt at a specific time of day. To take advantage of this feature, you must create an interrupt handler that performs an action when the alarm interrupt occurs. You can even make this action independent of other programs by leaving the interrupt handler resident in memory with an MS-DOS terminate-and-stay-resident service. (See Chapter 13.)

The BIOS provides a set of services through interrupt 1AH (decimal 26) that gives you access to the real-time clock's alarm feature. See Chapter 13 for details.

Chapter 8

Device Drivers and Peripherals

A major feature of the PC is that it lets the user expand its functionality by adding specialized devices that perform tasks the user requires. The devices, also called *peripherals,* are the subject of this chapter. First we cover installable device drivers, the software often used to communicate with devices. Then we present basic information about the most popular devices.

Installable Device Drivers

MS-DOS has the ability to use hardware device drivers that are not part of the BIOS. These are called *installable device drivers,* and they are loaded from disk at boot time. When you add a peripheral device to your computer, the device manufacturer usually supplies an installable device driver that provides an interface with the new hardware (if a device driver is necessary). An installable device driver might take the place of an existing BIOS driver, or it might provide a function not in the BIOS. There are also installable device drivers that are not supplied with devices; some, such as ANSI.SYS and HIMEM.SYS, are supplied as part of the MS-DOS package.

The ANSI device driver (ANSI.SYS), which provides flexible screen display control, is an installable driver. Although the ANSI device driver is similar to other installable drivers in some regards, it is radically different from a programming perspective and will therefore be treated separately. We begin by looking at installable device drivers in general and giving you some details about how MS-DOS device drivers are implemented. Next we show you how a typical MS-DOS device driver, ANSI.SYS, can be used in MS-DOS applications.

Overview

The PC BIOS and MS-DOS provide the necessary routines to work with most common computer devices, such as standard disk drives, serial communications ports, printers, and, of course, the keyboard and the display screen. However, many other specialized devices can be attached to PCs. As previously mentioned, most of these devices require additional software support—device drivers—to enable them to work with MS-DOS and MS-DOS programs.

Since the release of version 2.0, MS-DOS has been able to incorporate into its own operations any device driver that follows a standard set of integration rules. During start-up, a DEVICE command in CONFIG.SYS tells MS-DOS when there is a device driver to be loaded. The syntax of the DEVICE command is DEVICE = *filespec* or DEVICEHIGH = *filespec.* (DEVICEHIGH is a DEVICE command that loads a device driver into upper memory rather than conventional memory.) For each DEVICE = command in

CONFIG.SYS, MS-DOS locates the device driver, loads it into memory, and goes through the series of steps necessary to integrate the functions provided by the device driver into MS-DOS itself.

Typically, a device driver supports a new kind of device in an old way. For example, a device driver that supports a disk drive whose detailed control commands are new to MS-DOS but whose overall features are similar to other kinds of disk drives will most likely follow the program format laid down by the device driver's predecessors. Likewise, a device driver that supports the addition of a mouse or a joystick might treat the peripheral as a keyboardlike device.

On the other hand, device drivers can perform functions that have little or nothing to do with the addition of hardware devices to the computer; witness the expanded memory manager and extended memory manager device drivers as well as the ANSI device driver, which we discuss in a following section. The ANSI device driver doesn't work with new hardware in the computer; instead, it modifies the operation of the keyboard and the display screen, part of the computer's standard hardware.

The technical details of writing a device driver really belong in a book specializing in MS-DOS systems programming, but we can give you an understanding of how device drivers work.

How Device Drivers Work

There are two kinds of device drivers: those for *character devices,* such as the keyboard, printer, and communications port, which work with a serial stream of characters; and those for *block devices,* such as the disk drive, which read and write blocks of data that are identified by some form of block address. Character devices are identified by their own names. (These names are similar to the names LPT1 and COM1.) Block devices are identified by a drive letter that MS-DOS assigns (A, B, C, and so on).

When writing a program, you generally treat a character device as a device that inputs or outputs data one character at a time, similar to a terminal or printer. A character device can be opened by using its name and then can be read from or written to. On the other hand, your program sees a block device as if it were a random access device, similar to a disk drive. This is the point of using installable device drivers—the usual MS-DOS interrupt 21H (decimal 33) function for printers and disk drives lets you access any device as long as the device driver conforms to MS-DOS's rules.

MS-DOS maintains a chained list of device drivers in which each device driver points to the address of the next device driver in the list. The chain starts in the heart of the MS-DOS kernel, beginning with the NUL device. When you use an interrupt 21H function to identify a character device, MS-DOS searches the list of device drivers before it searches disk directories.

Every installable device driver consists of three main structural elements: a *device header,* a *strategy routine,* and an *interrupt routine.* The device header is a data structure that contains a device attribute word as well as the addresses of the strategy and interrupt routines. MS-DOS communicates with a device driver by using a data structure called a *request header.* MS-DOS uses the request header to pass I/O function numbers to the device driver. (Buffer addresses are in the request packet, appended to the header.) The device driver uses the same data structure to return status and error codes to MS-DOS.

To initiate an I/O request, MS-DOS builds a request packet (consisting of a request header plus a function-specific structure), calls the device driver's strategy routine to pass it the request header's address, and then calls the driver's interrupt routine. The interrupt routine examines the request packet, initiates the data transfer to or from the hardware device, waits for the completion of the data transfer, and updates the request header with a status code before it returns to MS-DOS.

> NOTE: *It might seem curious that MS-DOS makes two separate calls to a device driver for each input or output request. This somewhat redundant design is actually similar to that used in device drivers in multitasking operating systems such as UNIX (after which the MS-DOS design is modeled) and OS/2.*
>
> *In a multitasking system, the two-part design makes good sense because it allows I/O operations to take place in parallel with other system functions. The strategy routine starts the I/O operation and then returns control to the operating system, which can perform other tasks without waiting for the hardware device to transfer data. When the data transfer is complete, the interrupt routine gains control and cleanly terminates the operation.*

Writing a device driver is similar to writing the I/O service programs that are at the heart of MS-DOS and at the heart of the computer's built-in ROM BIOS. Writing a device driver is among the most sophisticated and intricate programming tasks you can perform. For more information, see Chapter 9, ''Device Drivers,'' in *Microsoft MS-DOS Programmer's Reference.*

The ANSI Device Driver

The ANSI device driver that comes with MS-DOS enhances the handling of keyboard input and screen output. As with any installable device driver, the ANSI device driver is active only when you load it into MS-DOS with a command in the CONFIG.SYS file. The following CONFIG.SYS command loads the ANSI device driver into MS-DOS:

```
device = ANSI.SYS
```

The ANSI device driver monitors both the screen output and the keyboard input that pass through the standard MS-DOS screen and keyboard services. Keyboard data and screen data that bypass MS-DOS—a program that uses the BIOS services, for example—are never seen or processed by the ANSI device driver.

When monitoring the screen output, the ANSI device driver is looking for special codes that identify ANSI commands. The device driver intercepts and executes these commands, and the commands never appear on the display screen.

ANSI commands are identified by a special 2-byte code: The first byte is the "escape" character, ASCII 1BH (decimal 27); and the second byte is the left-bracket character ([), ASCII 5BH (decimal 91). Following these identifying bytes are the command parameters and finally the command code itself. The command parameters are either numbers (in the form of ASCII numeric characters interpreted as decimal digits) or strings of ASCII characters enclosed in quotes, like this: "a string parameter". Multiple command parameters are separated by semicolons. The command code itself, which completes the ANSI command, is always a single alphabetic character. Command codes are case sensitive; for example, lowercase *h* is one command code, and uppercase *H* is a different one.

Two examples, one simple and one complex, show what these command codes look like. (The caret stands for the escape character, 1BH.)

```
^[1C
^[65;32;66;"Remapped B"p
```

The first ANSI command moves the cursor one character forward (on the same line). The second ANSI command redefines the A key so that the string "Remapped B" appears on the computer's screen whenever the A key is pressed.

The ANSI device driver recognizes a large number of ANSI commands, but they all fall into two broad categories: *screen control commands* and *keyboard translation commands*. Let's look at screen control commands first.

ANSI screen control commands

Although the BIOS services for the PC let you move the cursor anywhere on the screen and basically give you full-screen control, the standard MS-DOS services do not. In fact, the MS-DOS screen output services are completely oriented to "glass teletype" output—output similar to that of a typewriter. This, of course, ignores the richer potential of a display screen. This lack of full-screen output in MS-DOS forces most programs to bypass the MS-DOS services and use lower-level services, such as the BIOS services.

The ANSI device driver remedies this situation by providing a set of full-screen commands that can be used to do nearly anything that the display screen is capable of doing. This includes moving the cursor, clearing the screen, setting the display attributes (color, underscore, blinking, and so on), and changing the display mode from text to graphics and vice versa. Some commands are more sophisticated and can remember the current cursor location so that you can move the cursor to display information at a different location on the screen and then return it to its original location.

ANSI keyboard translation commands

The other type of command accepted by the ANSI device driver is a keyboard translation command. When a keyboard translation command is intercepted by the ANSI device driver, the device driver monitors keyboard input and replaces one character with another character or with a string of characters. This allows the ANSI device driver to function as a crude but effective keyboard-enhancer program.

The two types of ANSI commands are different in their purpose and use, but they are both passed to the device driver in the same way—by a stream of screen output characters.

The pros and cons of the ANSI device driver

You can look at the ANSI device driver in two ways: from the perspective of the user, who can use it to perform a few beneficial tricks, and from the perspective of the programmer, who can use it as an aid to program development.

Prior to the introduction of the DOSKEY command in MS-DOS 5, users often employed the ANSI device driver as a poor man's keyboard enhancer. The keyboard translation commands, as we mentioned, let you roughly simulate the keyboard "macro" features of commercial keyboard-enhancer programs.

You can also use the ANSI device driver as an MS-DOS command-prompt enhancer. Usually the keyboard-oriented ANSI commands are activated by placing them in a text file and sending them to the screen (and therefore to the ANSI driver) with the MS-DOS TYPE command. By embedding ANSI commands in the prompt string, however, you can tell the ANSI device driver to remember the cursor's location, move the cursor to the top of the screen, display the date and time in reverse video, and then return the cursor to its previous location; or you can even clear the screen and then display a menu of commands. The possibilities are endless.

From a programmer's point of view, the ANSI device driver has two main benefits to offer:

- It makes the most crucial BIOS-type services available to any programming language.

- It lets you write programs for any MS-DOS–based computer (not just the PC family) that uses the ANSI device driver.

Despite these apparent advantages, we generally believe that relying on ANSI commands in your programs is not a good idea. For one thing, this programming method requires that the ANSI device driver be installed in any computer on which your programs are used, which complicates the instructions you must prepare to accompany the programs. It is difficult enough to explain the setup and use of your programs to both novices and experts without adding extra layers of complexity, such as the explanation of how to install the ANSI device driver.

More important, however, is that, compared to other available methods, the ANSI device driver is pathetically slow in generating full-screen output. For a direct comparison of the speed of the ANSI device driver, the BIOS services, and direct-to-memory screen output, run the NU program in version 4.0 of the Norton Utilities set. The NU program contains three screen drivers that use these three output methods. If you try them all, you'll quickly see how much slower the ANSI device driver method is. Unless little screen output will be displayed, the ANSI device driver is too slow to be satisfactory.

Multimedia

Multimedia is one of the hottest buzzwords in the computer industry today. If you're wondering exactly what multimedia is, you're not alone! In a broad sense, multimedia is an exciting attempt to revolutionize the means by which a computer can present information, using animated graphics, analog and digital video, and high-quality sound.

Because a standard PC is limited to text, static graphics, and poor-quality beeps and chirps from the built-in speaker, a multimedia computer system requires specialized hardware and software. But until recently, there were no standards that defined a multimedia computer system. This caused problems for users and developers alike because multimedia programs wouldn't work on every type of system. Then a group of hardware and software vendors joined together to form the Multimedia PC Marketing Council (MPC), whose first job was to define a minimum set of hardware and software standards for multimedia. Computer systems that meet the standards set by this organization are permitted to have the MPC logo attached to the face of the system. The minimum system that qualifies as an MPC multimedia computer system includes an 80386SX or better CPU, a fast CD-ROM drive, MIDI (Musical Instrument Digital Interface) and waveform audio capability, and Microsoft Windows 3.0 with Multimedia Extensions 1.0 (sometimes called Windows with Multimedia) or Microsoft Windows 3.1.

Multimedia Hardware

In this section we briefly discuss the major hardware components of a multimedia computer system. Figure 8-1 shows the sound, video, and storage peripherals that can be used in a multimedia computer system.

CD-ROM

Of primary importance in any multimedia computer system is the ability to access large quantities of information. The high-quality graphics, animated images, and high-fidelity sound of multimedia all require large amounts of data storage. For this reason, the CD-ROM disc has been adopted as the standard multimedia storage device. CD-ROM encodes information optically, using basically the same method as the audio CDs that are used for music. A CD-ROM disc can hold roughly 600 MB of data. In a multimedia system, the data on a CD-ROM disc can include sound, graphics images, digitized full-motion video, and text. Thus, for example, a multimedia encyclopedia on a CD-ROM disc can include an entry on gorillas that contains a text description of gorillas, a map graphic of their geographical distribution, a full-motion video of gorilla behavior, and a recording of gorilla calls.

> NOTE: *A CD-ROM drive is not a replacement for a hard disk drive. CD-ROM discs are read only, so you can't record information on them by using your computer system. However, because of their capacity and low cost to manufacture, CD-ROM discs are an ideal medium for distributing large quantities of information. Please refer to Chapter 5 for more details on CD-ROM drives.*

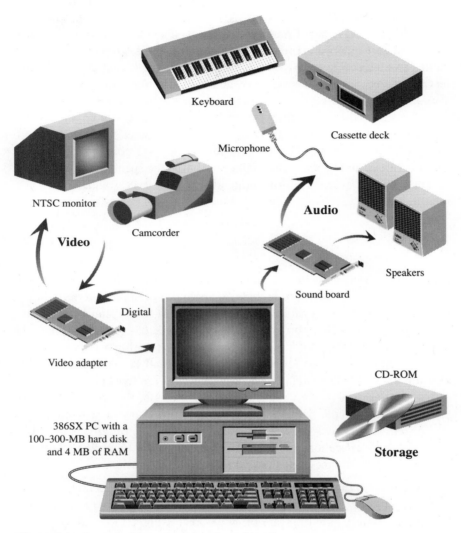

Figure 8-1. *Some possible components of a multimedia computer system.*

Sound boards

The sound board, or audio board, in a multimedia system is responsible for routing and processing stereophonic sound signals. To generate sound, the sound board is connected to an amplifier and one or two speakers that are external to the PC. (Many multimedia systems use *powered speakers* that contain a built-in amplifier.) In multimedia, there are three possible sources for sounds: waveform audio, CD audio, and MIDI audio.

Waveform audio Waveform audio is Microsoft's name for one form of digital audio that is part of multimedia; sampled sound is another name for it. To create waveform audio, an analog sound signal is sent through an analog-to-digital converter (ADC), which samples the signal at discrete intervals and converts it to a series of numbers. The resulting digital representation can be stored on disk (hard disk or CD-ROM disc); it is usually stored in a file with the .WAV extension. To play waveform audio, the digital data is read from the .WAV file and sent over the computer's bus to the sound card. A digital-to-analog converter in the sound card converts the digital data back to an analog waveform, which is sent to the speakers. Some sound boards support stereo waveform audio, although the MPC standard does not require this.

> NOTE: *.WAV files are often supplied with multimedia software that you purchase; for example, Microsoft Windows 3.1 comes with a few .WAV files.*

Although all multimedia sound boards have the ability to play .WAV files, some sound boards also include an analog-to-digital converter, allowing you to create your own .WAV files. The sound source can be a microphone, a cassette deck, or any device that is capable of converting sound to an analog signal. The standard sampling rates for creating waveform audio are 11.025 kHz (kilohertz) for monophonic sound and 11.025 kHz and 22.050 kHz for stereophonic sound. These sampling rates are low compared to the 44.100 kHz used for audio compact discs. In addition, the waveform audio standard uses a sample size of 8 bits (1 byte), which allows a dynamic range (the difference between the loudest and softest sounds) of only 48 decibels (dB). These specifications provide adequate fidelity for recording and playing back speech, but they fall short when it comes to music.

CD audio CD audio (sometimes called Redbook audio) is identical to that on standard audio compact discs. CD audio is digital stereophonic audio that was digitized at a sampling rate of 44.100 kHz using a 16-bit sample size, providing excellent fidelity for reproduction of all types of sounds, including music. CD-ROM discs typically provide CD audio along with other data. In addition, most CD-ROM drives can play standard audio CDs. When you are playing CD audio, the digital-to-analog conversion is performed by circuits in the CD-ROM player. In nonmultimedia systems, the analog audio signal is sent directly from the CD-ROM player to the speakers; in multimedia systems, the output is routed through the sound board (without any further processing) to the speakers.

MIDI audio MIDI stands for Musical Instrument Digital Interface. MIDI is a protocol for connecting electronic musical instruments (synthesizers) and keyboards to each other and to computers. A standard MIDI file format is used to store MIDI information on disk; such files usually have a .MID extension, although MIDI files for Windows with Multimedia can have a .RMI extension. The MIDI standard is maintained by the International MIDI Association (IMA).

A MIDI audio file is different from both waveform audio and CD audio files. The waveform audio and CD audio formats store a direct digital representation of sounds. In contrast, a MIDI file contains a sequence of commands, or messages, that instruct a MIDI synthesizer to produce certain sounds. For a given duration of sound, a MIDI file is much smaller than the corresponding waveform or CD file. MIDI, however, is limited to those sounds that a MIDI synthesizer can create.

A MIDI synthesizer can support as many as 128 different instrumental voices (percussion, trumpet, piano, violin, and so on). The MIDI message format has the ability to control, or play, a maximum of 16 channels at a time. Each channel is associated with one of the 128 voices, and one channel is often reserved for percussion. The MIDI messages specify the notes to play, their duration and loudness, which instrumental voice is used by each of the 16 channels, and other information about the sounds.

Not all MIDI synthesizers are created equal. They differ in the number of voices and channels they support as well as in the quality of the reproduced sound. To meet the MPC standard, a sound board must contain a MIDI synthesizer capable of three simultaneous melodic voices, an overall six-note polyphony, and a two-note percussion voice. External synthesizers offer much more flexibility, and they usually sound better. They are also more expensive. External MIDI synthesizers are usually packaged with a keyboard.

Sound boards have a MIDI In port to which you can connect an external MIDI controller (typically a keyboard). You can use the keyboard to play the internal synthesizer, and with the proper software, you can capture the MIDI messages from the keyboard for later manipulation or playing or both. Sound boards also have a MIDI Out port for connection to an external synthesizer. Figure 8-2 shows the required and optional MIDI components in a multimedia computer system.

You can record and play MIDI files with the basic multimedia computer system. If you want to edit MIDI files or create them without the use of a MIDI controller, you will need specialized software called a MIDI sequencing package. A variety of commercial sequencing packages is available.

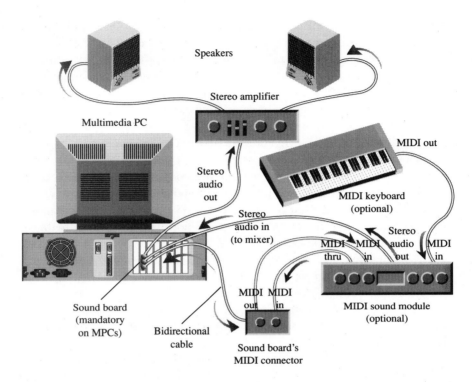

Speakers

Stereo amplifier

Multimedia PC

MIDI out

Stereo
audio
out

MIDI keyboard
(optional)

Stereo
audio in
(to mixer)

Stereo
audio
out

MIDI
thru

MIDI
in

MIDI
in

MIDI MIDI
out   in

Sound board
(mandatory
on MPCs)

Bidirectional
cable

MIDI sound module
(optional)

Sound board's
MIDI connector

Figure 8-2. *Components of a multimedia MIDI setup.*

Video

Good graphics or presentation software running on a multimedia computer
system provides a great deal of flexibility in working with digital images.
These images can be graphics that you create on your PC, such as charts or
computer-generated drawings. They can also be digitized images of real-
world objects that you create with either a scanner or a video camera. For example, you could overlay a graph of your company's profits on a digitized
video image of the company headquarters building. With the ability to manipulate, edit, and combine images, you can create effective presentations.

So far we have talked only about still images. In discussions of multimedia you also hear about full-motion video—that is, video similar to what
you see on television. (This is called NTSC video, which stands for National
Television System Committee video.) PC hardware cannot yet deliver on all
the promises of multimedia video, however, and the present MPC multimedia standard requires only a 16-color VGA card and has no provisions for
full-motion video. In theory, a 256-color Super VGA video system can display NTSC video. However, the data requirements for NTSC video are stag-
gering. Storing a single frame of color NTSC video in digital format can

require as much as 1.5 MB of disk space. When you consider that full-motion video uses 30 frames per second, it's clear that even a short full-motion video presentation would fill up the largest of hard disks. Add to this the necessity of converting the analog NTSC signal to digital form and transmitting the digital information at rates well beyond the capability of even the fastest PC bus, and you can see why multimedia video has yet to live up to its promise. The field is advancing rapidly, however, and by the time you read this, full-motion video on PCs might be a reality.

Despite these problems, there are some interesting video options available. Some manufacturers offer NTSC video cards that allow you to view a television picture in a small window on the screen. More useful are NTSC/VGA boards that convert a VGA graphics image to an NTSC signal that can be viewed on a television or recorded on a video cassette recorder. Some of these boards also have an NTSC input that permits computer-generated graphics to be combined with full-motion television images; the result can be viewed or recorded for later presentation.

Programming Multimedia

A multimedia computer system that meets the MPC standard must be equipped with Windows with Multimedia—Microsoft Windows 3.0 with special extensions and enhancements for multimedia. Starting with version 3.1 of Windows, the multimedia extensions are built-in, so you don't need to purchase any software add-ons. Programming multimedia, therefore, means programming for Windows with Multimedia.

> NOTE: *IBM has decided to go its own way with multimedia. Instead of following the MPC standards, IBM designed its own standard, called Ultimedia. In technical terms, Ultimedia is superior to the current MPC standard because it calls for more capable hardware. (The next level of the MPC standard will likely catch up, however.) In practice, the two standards are not compatible; an MPC system cannot play an Ultimedia title, and vice versa. However, an Ultimedia system uses the OS/2 operating system, and because OS/2 2.0 can run most applications for Windows, it should, at least in theory, be able to play an MPC multimedia title. IBM has announced plans to add multimedia extensions to OS/2 in the near future, allowing multimedia to run directly on OS/2, rather than on the integrated Windows-like environment.*

Windows with Multimedia

The purpose of Windows with Multimedia is to provide the underlying software support for multimedia applications. Just as MS-DOS provides support routines that allow applications to interface with standard PC hardware (for example, disk access and screen control), Windows with Multimedia provides support routines that allow multimedia applications to interface with specialized multimedia hardware. Among the more important parts of Windows with Multimedia are

- Support for MIDI devices and digital audio (both waveform and CD). Both MIDI and digital audio files can be played in the background while an application is running.

- The Media Control Interface (MCI), which allows you to control media-related devices, such as sound cards, video overlay cards, and videotape players.

- Improved VGA video drivers.

- An extensible control panel that permits programmers to create customized control panel applications called *applets.*

Creating a multimedia application is basically similar to regular programming, but it is significantly more involved because of the many different components of a multimedia system. The main items you'll need for multimedia programming are the Microsoft Multimedia Development Kit, which contains the required application development tools, and the Microsoft Windows 3.1 Software Development Kit. For more information on multimedia programming, refer to Microsoft Press's three-volume set on the topic (*Microsoft Windows Multimedia Programmer's Reference, Microsoft Windows Multimedia Programmer's Workbook,* and *Microsoft Windows Multimedia Authoring and Tools Guide*).

Mice and Other Pointing Devices

More and more PCs are equipped with a pointing device of some kind, such as a mouse or a trackball. Although people's opinions of these devices vary, there's little doubt that they speed and simplify the performance of many computer tasks. As a programmer, you should be aware of what's involved in including mouse support in your programs. (Mice are the most popular pointing device, and other variations, such as trackballs, are almost always configured to appear as a mouse to the program.) In this section we can provide only a general outline of mouse programming. For complete details, refer to *Microsoft Mouse Programmer's Reference,* second edition, published by Microsoft Press. (An easy solution is to develop your programs with either Visual Basic for MS-DOS or Visual Basic for Windows. These products provide mouse support with no extra programming required.)

Mouse Hardware

A mouse can be connected to the computer in several different ways. The *bus mouse* is connected to its own adapter card, which is plugged into the computer's expansion bus. The *serial mouse* connects directly to one of the PC's serial ports, so you don't need to devote an expansion slot to a mouse adapter card. The *InPort mouse* connects to a special InPort connector, which can be located on its own adapter card or can be part of an adapter card that has multiple functions. On IBM PS/2s and some clones, the mouse is attached to a "pointing device" connector, which is attached directly to supporting circuitry on the system board. Fortunately, unless a programmer is writing device-driver code for a mouse, he or she doesn't need to be concerned with the hardware differences among these three types of mice. In keeping with the principle of hardware independence, mouse driver software handles hardware differences automatically and presents a consistent mouse software interface regardless of the type of mouse installed.

Microsoft Corporation introduced the first mouse for the PC. It had a two-button design that, with some modifications, remains the most popular mouse for the PC to this day. Figure 8-3 shows the Microsoft mouse and the Microsoft BallPoint mouse. Other manufacturers have entered the mouse business and offer their own mouse designs, which sometimes provide features not found on the Microsoft mouse, such as a third mouse button or increased resolution for movement of the on-screen mouse pointer. However, the two-button Microsoft mouse has become the standard, so all mice, regardless of manufacturer, have the ability to emulate the Microsoft mouse. If these mice have additional features, a special device driver is provided to allow programs to take advantage of them.

Figure 8-3. *The Microsoft mouse and the Microsoft BallPoint mouse.*

Programming Mouse Support

With rare exceptions, writing a program to support a mouse means dealing, directly or indirectly, with the mouse driver. The driver provides *mouse services* that a program uses to interact with the mouse. The mouse services can be divided into two categories. *Control services* are used to modify the operation of the mouse—for example, to change the appearance of the mouse pointer or to set how fast the mouse pointer moves relative to mouse movement. *Inquiry services* are used to obtain information about the mouse status, such as the position of the mouse pointer and whether the user has pressed one of the mouse buttons.

As you might expect, the mouse services are accessed via a software interrupt: interrupt 33H (decimal 51). You place the number of the desired service in register AX, place any other necessary control information in one or more other registers, and then call the interrupt. The inquiry services return information, usually in registers BX, CX, and DX.

Programming for a mouse can be accomplished at one of three levels. At the most basic level, the program accesses the mouse driver directly via interrupt 33H calls. This access can be performed with an assembly language interface, but it can also be done from many high-level languages. This direct approach provides the greatest flexibility, but it can be somewhat difficult because the programmer must write the code that enables the program to respond appropriately to mouse input.

The second level of mouse programming is via a mouse function library that works with a high-level language. Such a library might be part of a compiler package, or it can be an add-on product that you purchase separately. The library functions often provide services that go beyond those available via the mouse driver interrupts, which makes it easier to incorporate mouse support into your programs.

For the highest level of mouse programming, you must use a programming language that provides integrated mouse support, such as Microsoft Visual Basic. When you write a program with one of these languages, full mouse support is automatically included in the program without any special action on your part. This is certainly the easiest way to create a program with mouse support.

Printers

We all know what a printer is, and almost every PC has a printer connected to it. However, not everyone is aware of the basics of how printers work or how they are controlled by the computer. Those are the subjects of this section. First we'll explain the inner workings of the three main types of printers. We will limit the discussion to black-on-white printers. There are some color printers available, but they are fairly uncommon and very expensive.

Printer Hardware

Perhaps the most often used type of printer is the *dot-matrix printer*. The print head of a dot-matrix printer moves back and forth across the paper as the paper is pulled through the printer. The print head contains a vertical array of fine pins, or wires, as shown in Figure 8-4. There are most commonly 9 or 24 pins. Each pin is held away from the paper by a spring; the pin can be pressed against the paper (through an inked ribbon) by a miniature electromagnet. The control circuitry in the printer causes the pins to "fire" in the proper sequence and pattern to create the desired letters or graphics on the page. The image is made up of a matrix of tiny dots—hence the name dot-matrix printer. Output quality can be quite good, particularly on models with 24 pins. The advantages of dot-matrix printers include affordability and the ability to print multipart forms (computer printer paper in sets with carbon paper between the sheets). On the other hand, they are relatively noisy and print graphics and high-quality text slowly.

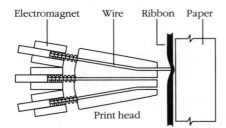

Figure 8-4. *In a dot-matrix printer, electromagnets drive wires against ribbon and paper.*

An *ink-jet printer* operates in essentially the same manner as a dot-matrix printer. However, instead of an array of wires, the print head contains an array of small nozzles that spurt ink onto the paper as the print head moves. Ink-jet printers are much quieter than dot-matrix printers, but they cannot print multipart forms.

For many applications, the *laser printer* is the printer of choice. This type of printer gets its name from the way it forms images. (See Figure 8-5.) Inside the printer is a photosensitive drum whose surface is given a uniform electrostatic charge before each page is printed. As the drum rotates, its surface is scanned by a low-power laser that is rapidly pulsed on and off by the printer controller circuitry to form the desired image on the drum. (Some "laser" printers actually use an array of light-emitting diodes to form the image.) The laser light affects the electrostatic charge so that the drum is charged only where the image is to be black. The drum rotates further, and the areas that are charged attract powdered ink, or toner, to the drum surface. Finally the drum is pressed against the paper to transfer the image. Laser printers are fast and offer excellent print quality, but they are expensive and periodically require expensive replacement toner and image drums. Like ink-jet printers, laser printers are nonimpact printers and cannot produce multipart forms.

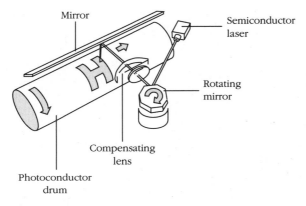

Figure 8-5. *In a laser printer, an electrostatic charge attracts toner to form an image that is then transferred to paper.*

Printer Control

Whatever type of printer you have, your computer must send it the proper data to create a printout. You can send ASCII text to most types of printers, and they will print it using the printer's default font and line spacing. This is rarely satisfactory, however. In most of your print jobs, you'll want to use special printer features such as the ability to print different fonts, special symbols, boldface, italics, underlining, or graphics.

The special printer features differ from model to model, but all printers have at least some of these capabilities. To access the special features, a program must send *printer control commands* to the printer. For example, to print part of a page in boldface, a program would have to send the "turn boldface on" command, followed by the text to be printed and then by the "turn boldface off" command. Because of the many printer features that must be controllable, there are a huge number of printer control commands.

To make matters worse, printer control commands are not standardized. Almost every printer manufacturer has its own language, so to speak; to have complete access to all of a printer's features, you must speak to it in its own language. This is the reason for the long list of printers that you must select from when installing many programs.

Fortunately, the situation is not as bad as it might be. To some degree, the printer industry has recognized the value of *printer emulations*. This means that a given printer might have its own obscure set of printer control commands, but it can also be made to recognize another, more popular, set of printer control commands; in other words, it can emulate another printer. The printer control commands that other manufacturers most often emulate are the Epson and the IBM ProPrinter commands for dot-matrix printers and the Hewlett-Packard LaserJet commands for laser printers. Because essentially all software packages support these popular printer control command sets, you can use almost any printer with almost any program, although you might not be able to use all the features available in the printer.

The final printer control method we'll mention is the PostScript page-description language, which was developed by Adobe Systems. PostScript is fundamentally different from printer control commands. Instead of using a sequence of discrete commands that instruct the printer to perform specific actions, PostScript uses its own special language to describe an entire page of output at a time. The computer sends the printer a set of commands that are not too different from those in a regular programming language. A specialized computer in the printer, called the PostScript interpreter, interprets those commands to create the image. PostScript offers great flexibility in both text and graphics output; laser printers from various manufacturers are capable of PostScript printing.

Programming Printer Support

After reading the information in the previous section, you might be thinking that writing a program to support a reasonable assortment of printers is a difficult task. If you're programming for Windows, it's actually easy because printer support is provided by the Windows environment rather than by the application program. Programming for MS-DOS, however, does present some problems. One approach is to include support for only a few popular printer control command sets, taking advantage of the emulations that are built into most printers. Programming PostScript printers requires no effort if your program will run under Windows. But if the program will run under MS-DOS, you should refer to the PostScript language-design and reference books by Adobe Systems, Inc., the owners of PostScript.

Modems

A modem is a device that allows computers to send digital data over telephone lines. The word *modem* is an abbreviation of *modulator/demodulator*. The original term reflected the fact that early modems actually converted digital data to sound, which was fed into a telephone handset for transmission. Modern modems feed the data signal directly into the phone line, but the principle is the same. For modem transmission, you need a modem connected to both the sending and receiving computers.

PC modems come in two styles. An *internal modem* consists of an adapter card that plugs into one of the PC's expansion slots, with connectors, accessible from the rear of the computer, for both the telephone line and a telephone. An *external modem* has the same phone connectors, but it is housed in a separate box with its own power supply. Figure 8-6 shows an external modem. An external modem connects to one of the computer's serial ports via a cable, whereas an internal modem has its own built-in serial port circuitry.

The most important characteristic of a modem is its transmission speed. Speed used to be measured as *baud rate;* this is an obsolete term, but it is sometimes still seen. Technically, a modem's baud rate is the number of signal transitions it can transmit per second. Baud rate is not, as is often

Figure 8-6. *An external modem.*

assumed, the number of bits per second that a modem can transmit. Manufacturers now more frequently rate their modems in bits per second (bps), which is a more accurate measure of how quickly data can be transferred.

Comparing and selecting modems used to be straightforward: You decided whether you wanted an internal or external modem, chose the desired speed, and that was about it. Today, however, a variety of data-compression and error-correction protocols is available on modems. Data compression is a technique by which the sending modem compresses data to a compact form before sending it, and the receiving modem decompresses the data to its original state. Error correction is a method by which the receiving modem can determine whether data has been received free of errors; if an error is detected, the data can be either reconstructed or retransmitted.

Modem Standards and Protocols

The standards for data compression, error correction, and modem signaling speed can be confusing, so here's a brief glossary of the most commonly encountered terms to help you make sense of the alphabet soup that you often see in modem ads.

Signaling speed standards

V.22. A standard that governs signaling at 1200 bps.

V.22bis. A standard that governs signaling at 2400 bps.

V.32. A standard that governs signaling at 4800 bps.

V.32bis. A standard that encompasses signaling at 14,400 bps.

Data-compression protocols and standards

MNP 5. A proprietary data-compression protocol that compresses data to approximately two-thirds its original size. MNP stands for Microcom Network Protocol.

V.42bis. An international data-compression standard that compresses data to approximately one-third its original size.

Error-correction protocols

MNP 2, MNP 3, and MNP 4. Three levels of an error-correction protocol that was developed by Microcom, Inc., and placed in the public domain.

V.42. An international standard that includes its own error-correction protocol plus a fallback to MNP 2, MNP 3, or MNP 4 if the primary protocol is not available on the other end of the line.

Modern modems are quite clever, and when a connection is made the modems at the two ends "negotiate" and decide on the most efficient transmission speed, data-compression method, and error-correction protocol that both modems support. If problems arise during data transfer (because of noise on the phone lines, for example), the modems can renegotiate and fall back to a slower speed.

Programming Modems

All modems have a command set—a set of instructions that tells the modem to carry out various actions, such as dialing a phone number, setting a particular transmission speed, or hanging up the phone line. Most modems recognize the Hayes Standard AT Command Set. This command set was developed by Hayes Microcomputer Products for its own modems and has become a de facto industry standard. When you're using a modem, communications programs take care of the modem commands for you. If you want to write your own program to control a modem directly, you'll need to refer to the modem manual for details on the command set. In almost all cases, this will be the AT command set.

Networks

A network is any arrangement in which two or more computers are connected so that they can share data or peripheral devices, or both. A network can contain only a few computers, or it can encompass hundreds. Reasons to network computers include the following:

- Peripheral sharing. Multiple users can access the same printer, modem, or plotter.

- File sharing. Data files needed by many workers, such as customer databases, can be maintained on one system and accessed over the network. Updates to the data are available to everyone. Files can be shared among different types of computers: PCs, mainframes, Macintoshes, and so on.

- Security. Sensitive data can be kept centrally and accessed only by users with the proper authority.

The field of PC networks is complex and constantly changing. Any sort of comprehensive coverage is well beyond the scope of this book. We can, however, provide you with a brief primer on network hardware and software so that you'll have some foundation on which to build if you decide to investigate networks further.

Network Hardware and Software

The term *LAN* is often used to refer to a network. LAN is an acronym for local area network. There are also WANs, or wide area networks, which cover a larger geographic area than LANs. There is no strict rule as to what constitutes a LAN and what constitutes a WAN. For example, a network that connects the 50 PCs at your downtown headquarters would be considered a LAN. If the network also included the 20 PCs at your suburban warehouse, it would be a WAN. Figure 8-7 shows a typical network configuration.

Some networks are nothing more than a way for two or more PCs to use the same printer. These systems link the computers via their parallel or serial ports. They are sometimes referred to as *zero-slot LANs* because they do not require that one of the expansion slots in each PC be taken up with a special network adapter card.

Other LANs are much more powerful, providing not only peripheral sharing but also data and program file sharing, electronic mail, workgroup applications, and more. These LANS require that each PC, or workstation,

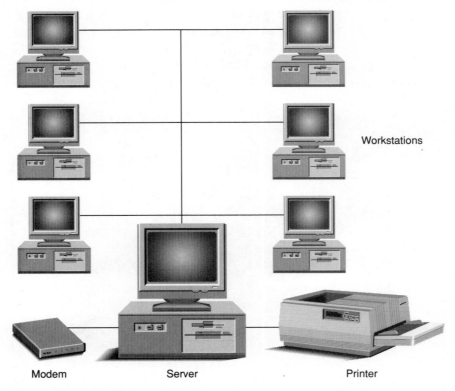

Workstations

Modem   Server   Printer

Figure 8-7. *A typical LAN configuration.*

include a network adapter card that connects the PC to the network. A network adapter card is shown in Figure 8-8. Somewhere in the network will be one or more *file server* computers. A file server is typically a powerful PC with a large hard disk and a lot of memory. Its job is to store the network's programs and data files, to handle requests for peripheral sharing, to respond to requests from users, and to generally mediate network traffic and operations. Requests, messages, and files are transferred in both directions between the workstations and the file server.

A type of LAN called a *peer-to-peer network* does away with the need for a dedicated file server by having one of the users' PCs serve double duty, acting as a workstation and as the network file server. This type of arrangement is suitable only for relatively small networks where security considerations are not of paramount importance.

In addition to the workstations and file servers, LANs require three components: cabling to connect the workstations and file servers together, network adapter cards to connect the PCs to the cabling, and network software to make everything work.

Cabling is an important part of any LAN. The type used (which need not be the same in all parts of a LAN) determines the speed at which data can be transferred, the maximum distance between PCs, and the immunity of the system to electrical interference. Cabling type also has a large impact on system cost. The available types are listed on the next page.

Figure 8-8. *A network, or LAN, adapter card.*

- **Unshielded twisted-pair** (UTP) is simply a pair of wires twisted around each other. UTP comes in two types. Voice-grade UTP, used for telephone systems, has a low bandwidth (maximum data transmission speed) that can place serious restrictions on LAN performance. Data-grade UTP has a significantly higher bandwidth.

- **Shielded twisted-pair** (STP) is data-grade twisted-pair encased in an electrical shield for protection from electromagnetic interference. Because it is more resistant to noise from outside sources, STP can carry higher data rates than data-grade UTP.

- **Coaxial cable** consists of a single central conductor surrounded by an insulating layer and a braided metal shield. Coaxial cable is sometimes referred to as Ethernet trunk cable. It comes in both thick and thin versions, both of which offer good data bandwidth. Thin coaxial cable, however, is less suitable for connections over long distances.

- **Fiber-optic cable** consists of transparent glass fibers and uses light rather than electricity to transmit data. It has the highest bandwidth, and it offers excellent reliability, flexibility, and freedom from interference. It is also the most expensive type of network cabling.

Wireless LANs use radio or infrared links between some or all network components. A wireless link makes cabling unnecessary, but it can be sensitive to outside interference.

Each PC on a network requires a network adapter card to connect it to the cabling. The network adapter card converts data from the low-power signals used in the computer to the high-power signals transmitted over the network, and vice versa. The network adapter card, in cooperation with the network software, also specifies the *media access control,* the protocol used to send data over the network. Three network adapter card types are in common use today:

- **Ethernet** uses a listen-before-transmitting method of sharing the network. If a PC wants to transmit over the network, it "listens" to determine whether the network is busy and then transmits only when the network is not busy. Ethernet can use various cabling types, and it offers a maximum data transmission rate of 10 Mb per second (Mbps). Effective transmission rates are, however, significantly lower because of various overhead factors (such as two computers simultaneously trying to transmit over the network).

- **Token Ring** uses a deterministic method of controlling network access. A special message, called the *token,* is continually passed around the network from computer to computer. Only when a PC has the token can it transmit data on the network. Data transfer rates can be either 4 or 16 Mbps. Token Ring can use either UTP or STP for cabling.

- **FDDI (Fiber Distributed Data Interface)** is by far the fastest network protocol, with a data transmission rate of 100 Mbps. At present FDDI requires fiber-optic cabling, although efforts are under way to extend the protocol to other cabling types. FDDI utilizes a double-ring cabling configuration, with the two rings simultaneously sending data in opposite directions. This provides excellent reliability.

All three of these network protocols use packet-based technology. A packet, or frame, is a discrete message that contains the network address of the sending PC, the network address of the intended recipient PC, and whatever data, files, or requests are being transmitted. Each protocol has its own specifications as to the exact format and size of the packet, how it travels over the network, and how permission to transmit is decided.

The final component of a LAN is the network software. Network software has two parts: the client software that runs on each workstation; and the server software that runs on the file servers. At the client end, requests from a user or an application program that require network attention are intercepted by a part of the network software called the redirector. The request is passed to that part of the server software called the network communications software, which packages it for transmission on the network. An installable device driver provides the software interface with the network adapter card. Data received from the network is unpackaged by the network communications software and made available to the client operating system or application program.

A file server has its own device driver, compatible with the server's network adapter card. The server also runs network communications software that takes care of packaging and unpackaging data. When a request is received from a client, the server software checks its security level to be sure that the client has the proper access rights. If everything checks out, the request is passed to the server's operating system for action.

A variety of vendors market LAN software. All LAN software can be divided into two categories. MS-DOS–based LAN software works in conjunction with the MS-DOS operating system, whereas non-MS-DOS LAN software uses another operating system, such as OS/2 or its own proprietary operating system. Generally speaking, MS-DOS–based LAN software is less powerful and is suitable for networks that have few users (typically 50 users or fewer) and undemanding data transfer needs. Non-MS-DOS LAN software provides greater capabilities at greater cost.

PART II:

PC OPERATING SYSTEMS

Chapter 9

Operating System Fundamentals

An operating system is what runs a computer. Specifically, it is the system of software that operates the computer hardware, enabling it to perform the tasks that the user requires. All computers have some sort of operating system, and as you'll see, various operating systems can be used on members of the PC family. Although PC operating systems differ in significant ways, they also have much in common.

An operating system is software—a collection of instructions that tell the computer hardware what to do. One of the operating system software's primary functions is to act as an interface between the user and the hardware. For example, if you enter the command to copy a file from one disk to another, it's the operating system that interprets the command, locates the file on one disk, copies it to the second disk, and displays ''copy completed'' or some similar message on the screen.

Another main function of the operating system is to serve as an interface between application programs and the computer hardware. The term *application program* refers to a program designed to perform a specific task, such as word processing or database management. When an application program needs to interact with the hardware, it usually does so by means of services provided by the operating system.

These relationships are illustrated schematically in Figure 9-1. There is a dotted line between *Application programs* and *Computer hardware* because, as you have learned in the first eight chapters of this book, a program can interact with the hardware directly.

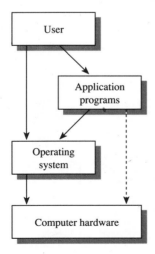

Figure 9-1. *The main task of any operating system is to serve as an interface between the computer hardware and the user and application programs.*

PC Operating Systems

We, of course, are interested in operating systems for the PC family of computers. This section provides a brief description of the major operating systems used on PCs.

MS-DOS

Microsoft's MS-DOS operating system is by far the preeminent PC operating system. MS-DOS was introduced with the original IBM PC back in 1981, and it is in use on the vast majority of PCs worldwide. MS-DOS has undergone numerous revisions and improvements, and it can be used on all members of the PC family. MS-DOS is starting to show its age, however. Because it is a real-mode operating system, it cannot take advantage of some of the more advanced features found on modern CPUs. Nor is MS-DOS well suited for multitasking. Nevertheless, MS-DOS remains the largest player in the PC–operating system world, with more users, applications, and programming tools than any other operating system.

Microsoft Windows

Strictly speaking, Microsoft Windows is not an operating system. Rather, it works in conjunction with MS-DOS to provide a variety of additional capabilities to users and application programs. Windows presents a consistent graphical interface to the user; each application program runs in its own window, which can occupy the whole screen or part of the screen or can be hidden. Because all Windows programs share certain features, after you learn to use one, you know the basics for all the others.

In many respects, however, Windows should be thought of as an operating system. It brings new features to MS-DOS and, in fact, sometimes bypasses MS-DOS and controls the hardware directly. On some hardware platforms, Windows can overcome the real-mode limitations of MS-DOS to tap the enhanced capabilities of the 80386 and higher CPUs. Windows has become very popular, and more and more applications and programming tools are becoming available for it. Microsoft Windows is currently available in version 3.1.

The newest version of Windows, which is in testing as this is being written, is Windows NT. Rather than building on MS-DOS, Windows NT is a new-from-the-ground-up operating system designed to take advantage of the latest hardware advances. You'll learn more about Windows and Windows NT in Chapter 14.

OS/2

OS/2 was introduced in 1987 and was originally intended to be the successor to MS-DOS. At first OS/2 was a joint project of Microsoft and IBM, but it has now been taken over by IBM. OS/2 is a protected-mode, multitasking operating system that requires at least an 80386 CPU. Initially a 16-bit operating system, it is a 32-bit system in its current incarnation (version 2.0). With some limitations, OS/2 can run applications written for MS-DOS or Microsoft Windows. To obtain the full benefits of OS/2, however, an application must be specifically written for OS/2.

OS/2 is a large, complex, and powerful operating system that has, in broad outline, many of the same features and capabilities that are planned for Windows NT. And like Windows NT, OS/2 is not really aimed at every user's machine. Rather, it is appropriate for high-end users and for network servers, where its power and security features justify the required hardware expense. OS/2 is covered in more detail in Chapter 15.

Other Operating Systems

A few other operating systems and environments are available for PCs. They are described here briefly, although we do not cover programming for them.

- UNIX is a multiuser, multitasking operating system originally developed at AT&T Bell Labs for use on minicomputers. As soon as PC hardware became powerful enough, UNIX was ported to PCs. UNIX has long been a favorite of users in the scientific and engineering communities, and as a result, a wide array of specialized technical application programs is available for it. However, UNIX has yet to make any significant headway in the mainstream business PC market.

- DR DOS is an MS-DOS clone developed by Digital Research Corporation. Its intention is to provide complete compatibility with MS-DOS and to provide some additional utilities to attract customers. Any program written for MS-DOS should run under DR DOS.

- DESQview is a product of Quarterdeck Office Systems. It is not an operating system per se but rather an operating system enhancer that runs on top of MS-DOS to provide limited multitasking and windowing capabilities.

Despite the existence of a variety of powerful operating systems and operating system enhancers, the PC world is still overwhelmingly an MS-DOS world, with the MS-DOS and Windows combination placing second.

The remainder of this book is devoted primarily to aspects of MS-DOS and Windows that you need to know about.

The History of MS-DOS

The origins of MS-DOS date back to 1980, when an operating system called 86-DOS was written for a line of 8086 computers manufactured by Seattle Computer Products. At that time IBM was developing its original PC, and it had asked Microsoft Corporation to provide an operating system. Microsoft purchased 86-DOS and made some modifications to suit the IBM hardware. This product was released as MS-DOS 1.0. (It was called PC-DOS 1.0 when it was sold by IBM.)

Most versions of MS-DOS were released in two variations: PC-DOS when sold by IBM and MS-DOS when sold by Microsoft or by third-party manufacturers. Except for the name, PC-DOS and MS-DOS were essentially identical. (In releases prior to release 5.0, they differed only in a few minor details, such as the names of some operating system files.) We refer to MS-DOS throughout this book, but everything we say applies equally to PC-DOS.

Since its first release, MS-DOS has undergone extensive improvements and revisions. MS-DOS version 6.0 is now available. Even though each new release has contained both improvements and bug-fixes, the driving force behind most releases has been a hardware change, often involving a disk-drive change. (See Figure 9-2.)

Not all MS-DOS versions are listed in Figure 9-2. Some minor versions, such as 2.11 and 4.01, involved only bug-fixes from the previous version.

Version	Release Date	Hardware Change
1.0	August 1981	Original IBM PC (single-sided floppy disk drive)
1.1	May 1982	Double-sided floppy disk drive
2.0	March 1983	PC/XT
2.1	October 1983	PC*jr* and Portable PC
3.0	August 1984	PC/AT
3.1	March 1985	PC Network
3.2	January 1986	Support for 3.5-inch floppy disk drives
3.3	April 1987	PS/2s
4.0	June 1988	Hard disks larger than 32 MB
5.0	June 1991	Larger hard disk partitions

Figure 9-2. *MS-DOS releases and associated changes to hardware.*

Also note that this figure lists only the major hardware change behind each MS-DOS version. Each new version also included a variety of other improvements and enhancements, which are summarized here:

Version 1.0 supported the single-sided, eight-sector floppy disk format. All basic MS-DOS services were included in this release.

Version 1.1 added support for double-sided floppy disks. The MS-DOS services remained the same.

Version 2.0 added support for nine-sector floppy disks (both single-sided and double-sided), for the PC/XT hard disk, and for the hierarchical directory structure. The MS-DOS services were enhanced extensively in this version. (See Chapter 10.)

Version 2.1 added neither new disk formats nor new MS-DOS services; it did, however, adjust its disk operation timing to benefit the PC*jr* and the Portable PC.

Version 3.0 added support for the PC/AT's 1.2-MB floppy disk drive and additional hard disk formats. It also laid the groundwork for network disks.

Version 3.1 added network disks, which included a file-sharing capability.

Version 3.2 introduced support for 3.5-inch floppy disk drives.

Version 3.3 was announced concurrently with IBM's introduction of the PS/2s. Several new commands and functions were included specifically to support the PS/2 hardware.

Version 4.0 provided integration of enhanced memory capabilities and added a visual shell user interface.

Version 5.0 included significantly improved memory management capabilities and an improved visual shell.

Version 6.0 added major new utilities, including file compression, anti-virus tools, memory optimization, and disk-defragmenting software.

NOTE: *Each version of MS-DOS is compatible with prior versions, except in some very detailed respects that are rarely of concern to applications programmers.*

With each release of MS-DOS, software developers had to decide which version of MS-DOS to target. From the programmer's perspective, the major change to MS-DOS came with version 2.0, which added a wide variety of support services for hard disks. Since version 2.0, changes in programming services have been relatively minor and usually can be accommodated by including code that verifies which version of MS-DOS is running. A program can do this by calling MS-DOS interrupt 21H, function 30H or (for MS-DOS versions 5.0 and later) function 3306H. (See Chapter 13.) You can determine your MS-DOS version number by typing *VER* at the MS-DOS prompt.

The Structure of MS-DOS

As a programmer, you must understand the internal structure of MS-DOS. MS-DOS has a hierarchical structure, comprising three layers that isolate the user and the application programs from the computer hardware. These layers are the BIOS (basic input/output system), the MS-DOS kernel, and the command processor.

The BIOS

The BIOS can be thought of as the lowest layer of MS-DOS because it interacts directly with the hardware. It is concerned primarily with input and output. The BIOS contains the drivers, or software interfaces, for the following five hardware devices: the console (keyboard and display), a generic printer, the auxiliary device (serial port), the computer's clock, and the boot disk device.

Part of the BIOS is built into each computer by the computer manufacturer. This part of the BIOS is called the *resident* portion. It is also called the ROM BIOS because it is contained in read only memory (ROM) chips located on the computer system board. As you learned in Chapter 3, the ROM BIOS serves as an interface with the computer hardware; it controls the hardware devices installed in a computer. It also presents a standardized interface with software.

The second part of the BIOS is nonresident; it is read into random access memory (RAM) from disk when a computer boots. In MS-DOS this file is called IO.SYS; in PC-DOS it is called IBMBIO.COM. Despite the different names, IO.SYS and IBMBIO.COM serve the same function; we will refer to both by the name IO.SYS. Note that this file has the file attributes *hidden* and *system,* which means that you won't see the file in your directory listing unless you have MS-DOS 5.0 or later and use the /ah switch with the DIR command or unless you use a utility program that displays hidden filenames.

The MS-DOS Kernel

The next component of MS-DOS is the *MS-DOS kernel,* which is loaded from disk during the boot procedure. The kernel is located in a disk file named MSDOS.SYS (IBMDOS.COM in PC-DOS), which, like IO.SYS, has the attributes *hidden* and *system.* Application programs interact with the MS-DOS kernel; it can be thought of as the heart of the operating system. The kernel provides hardware-independent functions, called *system functions,* that are accessed by means of a software interrupt. The functions provided by the kernel include file and directory management, memory management, character device input/output, and time and date support.

The fact that the system functions are hardware independent is important. This independence permits any program running under MS-DOS to use the system functions without regard for the specific hardware that is being used. The MS-DOS kernel can provide hardware-independent functions because it relies on the drivers in the BIOS to deal, on a physical level, with the hardware.

The Command Processor

The final component of MS-DOS is the *command processor*. It is the command processor that you are interacting with at the familiar A> or C> prompt. The function of the command processor is to carry out user commands. For example, if you enter *DIR* to get a directory listing or *VER* to display the MS-DOS version number, the command processor carries out your command. Similarly, if you enter *WP* to run the WordPerfect word processing program, the command processor loads WordPerfect from disk, turns control over to the program, and then regains control when you exit.

The command processor is loaded into memory at boot time from the disk file COMMAND.COM. There are three modules in COMMAND.COM:

- The *resident* module is loaded into low memory, directly above the MS-DOS kernel, and remains there as long as the computer is on. The resident module processes Ctrl-Break and Ctrl-C, issues error messages (for example, the infamous ''Abort, Retry, Fail'' message), and deals with the termination of application programs.

- The *initialization* module of COMMAND.COM is loaded at boot time. Its only function is to load and process the commands in the AUTOEXEC.BAT file. After this is done, the memory allocated to the initialization module is freed for other purposes.

- The *transient* module of COMMAND.COM is loaded into the high end of conventional memory at boot time. Its tasks include issuing the familiar A> or C> prompt, reading commands from the keyboard, and executing these commands. An application program can use the memory occupied by this module if necessary. When the program terminates, the resident COMMAND.COM module determines whether the transient module is still loaded. If not (that is, if the application program used that memory), the transient module is reloaded from disk.

You may have noticed that the components of MS-DOS and the computer hardware form a layered structure. At the top is the user interacting with an application program or with the command processor. Below that is the MS-DOS kernel, which, in turn, uses the BIOS to interact with the hardware. This relationship is illustrated in Figure 9-3.

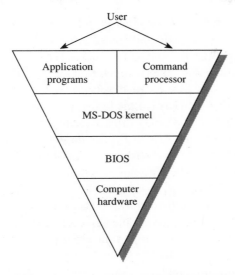

Figure 9-3. *The components of MS-DOS form several layers between the user and the computer hardware.*

BIOS Services

One secret of successful programming for the PC family lies in the effective use of the software that is built into the BIOS services. As you learned earlier, the BIOS services are sandwiched between the hardware and the higher-level software, including programming languages, application programs, and the MS-DOS kernel.

> NOTE: *Remember that part of the BIOS is built into the hardware and called the ROM BIOS, whereas other parts of the BIOS are loaded into RAM from disk at boot time. For the programmer, it makes no difference whether a particular routine is in the ROM BIOS or is loaded from IO.SYS. We will use the term BIOS generically to refer to all BIOS routines, whatever their origin.*

The BIOS services work directly with the computer's hardware and peripheral devices; they perform some of the computer system's most fundamental tasks, such as reading and writing individual bytes of data from and to the display screen or disk. MS-DOS services and programming-language services are often built from these basic functions and enhanced to make a particular process more efficient. You can enhance your programs in the same way by directly accessing the BIOS, thereby gaining access to an extremely powerful set of tools and using your computer in the way that IBM intended it to be used.

That last point is worth emphasizing. IBM and other PC manufacturers have gone to considerable lengths to create a clean and well-defined method for directing the operation of the computer by using the BIOS services. As each new PC model is designed, IBM (and any other computer maker who is faithfully extending the PC family) makes sure its BIOS services are thoroughly compatible with those of the other members of the family. As long as you control your computer by using the BIOS, whether directly or indirectly, you are safe from any compatibility problems. If you bypass the BIOS and program directly to the hardware, you are not only asking for trouble, you are also severely limiting the range and viability of your programs.

That's not to say that you should always use BIOS services when they're available. The input/output functions provided by the MS-DOS kernel and high-level programming languages often provide the same services as the BIOS and do so in a form that is easier to use within your programs. But when a program needs more direct access to the computer's input/output devices than MS-DOS or your programming language can provide, the BIOS services are usually the answer.

The following four chapters discuss the BIOS service routines and the MS-DOS service routines. The routines fall naturally into groups derived from the hardware devices they support, so we will review the video services, disk services, and keyboard services separately. But before you take a closer look at the individual services, you need to know how to incorporate them into your programs. This chapter sets the stage by explaining what goes into writing an *interface routine,* the bridge between programming languages and the BIOS services. Let's begin with a word on how the BIOS operates.

The BIOS Philosophy

All BIOS services are invoked by interrupts. Each interrupt instruction selects a particular entry in the interrupt vector table in low memory. The addresses of all BIOS service routines are stored in this table. This design makes it possible for a program to request a service without knowing the specific memory location of the BIOS service routine. It also allows the services to be moved around, expanded, or adapted without affecting the programs that use the services. Although IBM has tried to maintain the absolute memory locations of some parts of the BIOS, it would be foolish to use these addresses because they may change in the future. The standard, preferred, and most reliable way to invoke a BIOS service is to use its interrupt rather than its absolute address.

The BIOS services could be supervised by one master interrupt handler, but instead they are divided into subject categories, and each category has its own interrupt handler. This design lets each interrupt handler be easily replaced. For example, if a hardware manufacturer created a radically different video display that operated under a completely new BIOS program, the manufacturer could provide the new BIOS program along with the hardware. The new BIOS program could be stored in RAM (as an installable device driver) or in ROM (as ROM chips on an adapter card). When the new service routine's address was inserted in the proper location in the interrupt vector table, the new routine would effectively replace the part of the original BIOS that was used with the old hardware. By making the BIOS modular, IBM has made it easier to improve and extend the capabilities of its computers.

The BIOS Service Interrupts

The 12 BIOS interrupts fall into 5 groups, as shown in Figure 9-4:

- Six interrupts serve specific peripheral devices.
- Two interrupts report on the computer's equipment.
- One interrupt works with the real-time clock.
- One interrupt performs the print-screen operation.
- Two interrupts place the computer into another state altogether by activating ROM Basic or the system start-up routine.

As you'll see, most of the interrupts are tied to a group of subservices that actually do the work. For example, the video service interrupt 10H (decimal 16) has 25 subservices that do everything from setting the video mode to changing the size of the cursor. You call a subservice by invoking its governing interrupt and specifying the subservice number in register AH. This process is explained in the example at the end of this chapter.

BIOS Service Operating Characteristics

The BIOS services use some common calling conventions that provide consistency in the use of registers, flags, the stack, and memory. We outline the characteristics of these operating conventions next, beginning with the segment registers.

Interrupt		Use
Hex	Dec	

Peripheral Devices Services

10H	16	Video display services. (See Chapter 11.)
13H	19	Disk services. (See Chapter 10.)
14H	20	Communications services. (See Chapter 13.)
15H	21	System services. (See Chapter 13.)
16H	22	Standard keyboard services. (See Chapter 12.)
17H	23	Printer services. (See Chapter 13.)

Equipment Status Services

11H	17	Equipment-list service. (See Chapter 13.)
12H	18	Memory-size service. (See Chapter 13.)

Time/Date Service

1AH	26	Time and date service. (See Chapter 13.)

Print-Screen Service

05H	5	Print-screen service. (See Chapter 13.)

Special Services

18H	24	Activate ROM Basic. (See Chapter 13.)
19H	25	Activate bootstrap start-up routine. (See Chapter 13.)

Figure 9-4. *The 12 BIOS service interrupts.*

The *code segment register* (CS) is automatically reserved, loaded, and restored as part of the interrupt process. Consequently, you don't have to worry about your program's CS. The DS and ES registers are preserved by the BIOS service routines, except in the few cases in which they are explicitly used. The *stack segment register* (SS) is left unchanged, and the BIOS services depend on the calling program to provide a working stack. (Everything depends on a working stack!)

The stack requirements of the BIOS services are not spelled out and can vary considerably, particularly because some services invoke other services. Generally, however, most programs ought to be working with a much larger stack than the BIOS services need.

The BIOS varies in its usage of the other CPU registers. The *instruction pointer* (IP) is preserved by the same mechanism that preserves the code segment. In effect, the *stack pointer* (SP) is preserved because all the BIOS services leave the stack clean, popping off anything that was pushed on during the service-routine execution.

As usual, the general-purpose registers, AX through DX, are considered fair game. The standard rule is not to expect any contents of these registers to be maintained when you pass control to another routine, and that applies to the BIOS services as well. If you closely inspect the coding of the services in the IBM technical reference manuals, you will find that one or more registers are left undisturbed in one service or another, but you would be foolish to try to take advantage of this. As a general rule, when a simple result is returned from a subroutine, it is left in the AX register; this applies to both the BIOS and to all programming languages. We'll see how often this really happens when we cover the BIOS services in detail.

The *index registers* (SI and DI) can be changed, exactly like the AX through DX registers. The *stack frame register* (BP) can also be changed by a few BIOS service routines.

The flags in the flag register are routinely changed as a by-product of the instruction steps in the BIOS routines. You should not expect any of them to be preserved. In a few instances, the *carry flag* (CF) or the *zero flag* (ZF) is used to signal the overall success or failure of a requested operation.

These details are important but rather tedious, and there is little reason for you to pay much attention to them. If your programs follow the general interface rules given in the next section and if they follow the specific requirements of your programming language, you may not need to be concerned with them at all.

NOTE: *If you set out to use the BIOS services in your programs, you'll naturally be concerned about the possible conflicts between the services and the operating conventions that your language follows. Put your mind at ease. You will find that you do not have to take any extraordinary precautions to protect your programming language from the BIOS or vice versa.*

Creating an Assembly Language Interface

For your programs to use the BIOS services directly, you sometimes need to create an assembly language interface routine to link the programming language to the BIOS. When we say "interface routine," we are referring to the conventional program-development subroutines—subroutines that are assembled into object modules (.OBJ files) and then linked to form working programs (.EXE or .COM files in MS-DOS). For more on this subject, see Chapter 16.

Working with assembly language can seem a fearsome task if you are not already comfortable with it. Although there are plenty of good reasons to be intimidated by assembly language—after all, it is the most difficult and demanding kind of programming—it's really not that difficult to create an assembly language interface routine.

To create your own interfaces, you need to have an assembler that is compatible with the MS-DOS standards for object files. All the examples we

NOTE: *Interpreted Basic can work with machine-language subroutines that are put directly into memory. It is as easy to prepare the sort of assembler subroutine that will work with Basic by using DEBUG's A (assemble) command as it is to prepare the subroutine by using an ordinary assembler.*

BIOS Interrupt Conflicts

In the hardware specification for the 8086 family of microprocessors, Intel reserved interrupt numbers 00H through 1FH (decimal 0 through 31) for use by the microprocessor itself. (See Figure 9-5.) Unfortunately, IBM had appropriated several of these reserved interrupt numbers for its own use in the design of the IBM PC. This wasn't a problem with the PC and the PC/XT, which used the Intel 8088 microprocessor, because the 8088 predefined only interrupts 00H through 04H.

When the PC/AT appeared, however, IBM's use of Intel's reserved interrupt numbers led to a conflict. The reason is that the AT's 80286 chip predefines some of the same interrupt numbers that IBM's BIOS uses. The conflict appears when you use the 80286 BOUND instruction to validate an array index. The 80286 signals an out-of-bounds array index by executing interrupt 05H; IBM had previously assigned interrupt 05H to the BIOS print-screen function. If you aren't careful, a program that executes the BOUND instruction can unexpectedly print the screen.

To resolve the conflict, you must install an interrupt 05H handler that inspects the code that caused the interrupt. This handler can determine whether the interrupt was executed in software or by the CPU. You can also avoid this problem by using a protected-mode operating system such as OS/2, which bypasses the BIOS. If you use MS-DOS, however, be aware that a programming error can occasionally lead to unexpected execution of a BIOS routine.

give here are for the Microsoft Macro Assembler, and they should also work fine with Borland's Turbo Assembler.

The basic form of an interface routine

An interface routine's form varies with its intended use. An assembly language interface is a handshaker between your programming language and a BIOS service, so it has to be tailored to meet the needs of both ends. *It matters* which programming language is being used; *it matters* which ROM BIOS service is being invoked; and *it matters* whether any data is being passed in one direction or the other. However, the general outline of an assembly language interface is basically the same no matter what you are doing.

One of the best ways to understand how an assembly language interface is coded is to view it as five nested parts, which are outlined on the following page.

Interrupt	CPU	Function
00H	8088, 8086, 80286, 80386, 80486	Divide error
01H	8088, 8086, 80286, 80386, 80486	Single-step
02H	8088, 8086, 80286, 80386, 80486	NMI (nonmaskable interrupt)
03H	8088, 8086, 80286, 80386, 80486	Breakpoint (INT 3)
04H	8088, 8086, 80286, 80386, 80486	Overflow (INTO)
05H	80286, 80386, 80486	BOUND out of range
06H	80286, 80386, 80486	Invalid opcode
07H	80286, 80386	Coprocessor not available
07H	80486	Device not available
08H	80286, 80386, 80486	Double exception (double fault)
09H	80286, 80386	Coprocessor segment overrun
09H	80486	Reserved
0AH	80386, 80486	Invalid task-state segment
0BH	80386, 80486	Segment not present
0CH	80386, 80486	Stack fault
0DH	80286, 80386, 80486	General protection exception
0EH	80386, 80486	Page fault
10H	80286, 80386, 80486	Coprocessor error
11H	80486	Alignment check interrupt

Figure 9-5. *Predefined hardware interrupts in Intel microprocessors.*

Level 1: General assembler overhead
  Level 2: Subroutine assembler overhead
    Level 3: Entry code
      Level 4: Get parameter data from caller
        Level 5: Invoke BIOS service
      Level 4: Pass back results to caller
    Level 3: Exit code
  Level 2: Finish subroutine assembler overhead
Level 1: Finish general assembler overhead

In the outline, Levels 1 and 2 tell the assembler what's going on, but they don't produce any working instructions. Levels 3 through 5 produce the actual machine-language instructions. We'll examine each level to show you the rules and explain what's going on. Don't forget that the specific requirements of an interface routine change for different circumstances. We'll point out the few design elements that are universal to all routines.

Here is a simple BIOS interface routine. It's designed to be called from a C program, but the elements of the interface design are the same whether you use this routine as is or adapt it to another programming language.

```
_TEXT           SEGMENT     byte public 'CODE'
                ASSUME      cs:_TEXT

                PUBLIC      _GetMemSize
_GetMemSize     PROC        near

                push        bp
                mov         bp,sp

                int         12H
                pop         bp
                ret

_GetMemSize     ENDP

_TEXT           ENDS

                END
```

In the next few pages we examine the construction of this routine.

Level 1: General assembler overhead

Here is an outline of a typical Level-1 section of an interface routine, with the lines numbered for reference:

```
1-1   _TEXT        SEGMENT    byte public 'CODE'
1-2                ASSUME     cs:_TEXT
```

(Levels 2 through 5 appear here)

```
1-3   _TEXT        ENDS
1-4                END
```

Line 1-1 is a SEGMENT directive that declares the name of a logical grouping of executable machine instructions and informs the assembler (and any person who reads the source code) that what follows consists of executable code. Line 1-2, the ASSUME directive, tells the assembler to associate the CS register with any address labels in the _TEXT segment. This makes sense because the CS register is used by the microprocessor to address executable code.

Line 1-3 ends the segment started in line 1-1, and line 1-4 marks the end of the source code for this routine.

The names _TEXT and CODE conform to the conventions used by virtually all C language compilers for PCs, as do the byte and public attributes of the SEGMENT directive. Alternative names and attributes are available to advanced programmers, but for now we'll stick with the simplest.

Level 2: Subroutine assembler overhead

Next let's look at an outline of a typical Level 2, the assembler overhead for a subroutine, which is called a *procedure* in assembler parlance. The following sample shows some typical Level-2 coding:

```
2-1                PUBLIC    _GetMemSize
2-2   _GetMemSize  PROC      near
```

(Levels 3 through 5 appear here)

```
2-3   _GetMemSize  ENDP
```

Line 2-1 instructs the assembler to make the name of the procedure, _GetMemSize, public information, which means that the link program can then connect it to other routines that refer to it by name.

Lines 2-2 and 2-3 bracket the procedure named _GetMemSize. PROC and ENDP must surround each procedure, with PROC defining the beginning of the procedure and ENDP signaling the end of it. Again, the near attribute in the PROC statement adheres to the conventions established for linking assembly language routines to C programs. In more advanced C programs and in routines linked with programs written in languages such as FORTRAN and Basic, you must sometimes use a different attribute, far. (You will find more about this in Chapter 17.)

Level 3: Entry and exit code

Levels 3, 4, and 5 contain executable instructions. In Level 3, the assembly language routine handles the housekeeping overhead that is required if a subroutine is to work cooperatively with the calling program. The key to this cooperation is the stack.

When the calling program transfers control to the subroutine, it does so by means of a CALL instruction. (In this example, the instruction would be CALL _GetMemSize.) When this instruction executes, the microprocessor pushes a return address—the address of the instruction following the CALL instruction—onto the stack. Later the assembly language routine can return control to the calling program by executing a RET instruction, which pops the return address off the stack and transfers control to the instruction at that address.

If any parameters are to be passed to the assembly language routine, the calling program pushes them on the stack before it executes the CALL instruction. Thus, when the routine gets control, the value on top of the stack is the return address, and any parameters are found on the stack below the return address. The stack grows from higher to lower addresses, and each value on the stack is 2 bytes in size, so you end up with the situation depicted in Figure 9-6.

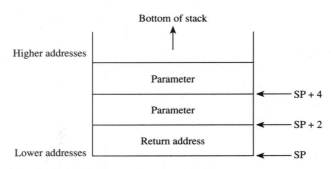

Figure 9-6. *The stack at the time a subroutine is called.*

To access the parameters on the stack, most compilers and assembly language programmers copy the value in SP into register BP. In this way the values on the stack can be accessed even within a routine that changes SP by pushing parameters or calling a subroutine. The conventional way of doing this is shown by the following code:

```
3-1        push      bp          ; preserve the current contents of BP
3-2        mov       bp,sp       ; copy SP to BP
```

(Levels 4 and 5 appear here)

```
3-3        pop        bp
3-4        ret
```

After lines 3-1 and 3-2 have executed, the stack is addressable, as shown in Figure 9-7. (In a moment we'll show how useful this is.) When it's time to return control to the calling program, the routine restores the caller's BP register value (line 3-3) and executes a RET instruction (line 3-4).

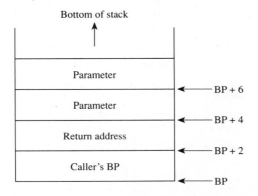

Figure 9-7. *The stack after register BP is initialized.*

If you think about it, you'll realize that things could be more complicated. For example, a calling program might use either a near or a far CALL instruction to transfer control to a subroutine. If your program uses far subroutine calls by convention (instead of the near calls used by default in C), the PROC directive (line 2-2) would require the far attribute instead of near. This would instruct the assembler to generate a far RET instruction instead of a near RET.

Furthermore, with a far calling convention, the return address on the stack would be 4 bytes in size instead of 2 bytes, so the first parameter would be at address [BP + 6] instead of [BP + 4], as shown in Figure 9-7. In this book, however, we'll stick to the most straightforward case: near PROCs and 2-byte return addresses.

Level 4: Get parameter data from caller

Level 4 passes the parameters from the caller to the BIOS, and it passes the results from the BIOS to the caller. (Note, however, that the sample program contains no parameters from the caller.) The caller's parameters are on the stack, either in the form of data or addresses. (See Chapter 17 for help with this.) The registers, mostly AX through DX, are used for BIOS input and output. The trick here—and it can be tricky—is to use the correct stack off-sets to find the parameters. We'll sneak up on this problem in stages.

You get to the parameters on the stack by addressing relative to the address stored in BP in lines 3-1 and 3-2. (Refer to Figure 9-7 to determine how items on the stack relate to the value in BP.) When more than one parameter is present on the stack, you must decide which parameter is which. Most languages push their parameters on the stack in the order they are written. This means that the *last* parameter is the one closest to the top of the stack, at [BP + 4]. However, C uses the reverse order so that the parameter at [BP + 4] is the *first* one written in the calling program.

Parameters normally take up 2 or 4 bytes on the stack, although 2 bytes is more common. If any of these parameters were 4 bytes in size, you would need to adjust the subsequent references accordingly.

If *data* were placed on the stack, you could get it immediately by addressing it like this: [BP + 4]. If an *address* were placed on the stack, two steps would be needed to access the desired data: You would get the address, and then you would use the address to get the data. Following is a Level-4 example showing both data ([BP + 4]) and address ([BP + 6]) retrieval:

```
4-1        mov      ax,[bp+4]      ; value of parameter1
4-2        mov      bx,[bp+6]      ; address of parameter2
4-3        mov      dx,[bx]        ; value of parameter2
```

(Level 5 appears here)

```
4-4        mov      bx,[bp+6]      ; address of parameter2 (again)
4-5        mov      [bx],dx        ; store new value at
                                   ; parameter2 address
```

All these MOV instructions move data from the second operand to the first operand. Line 4-1 grabs data right off the stack and slaps it into the AX register. Lines 4-2 and 4-3 get data by means of an address on the stack: Line 4-2 gets the address and parks it in BX, and then line 4-3 uses that address to get to the actual data, which is moved into DX. Lines 4-4 and 4-5 reverse this process: Line 4-4 gets the address again, and then line 4-5 moves the contents of DX into that memory location.

NOTE: *A crucial bit of assembler notation is demonstrated here: BX refers to what's in BX, and [BX] refers to a memory location whose address is in BX. A reference such as [BP + 6] indicates a memory location 6 bytes past the address stored in register BP.*

Although sorting out these references may not be a snap, if you think them through carefully, they work out right.

Level 5: Invoke BIOS service

Level 5 is our final step: It simply invokes the BIOS service.

When all registers contain appropriate values (usually passed from the calling program and copied into registers by means of the stack), the routine can transfer control to the BIOS by using an interrupt:

```
5-1        int     12h
```

In this example, this single INT instruction does all the work for you. The BIOS returns the computer's memory size in register AX, where C expects the routine to leave it when the routine returns control to the calling program. In other cases, you might need to leave a result elsewhere, as in lines 4-4 and 4-5 in the previous examples.

Most BIOS interrupts, however, provide access to several different services. In such cases, you must specify a service number in register AH before you execute the interrupt. For example, to access the first video service, you would execute these commands:

```
mov     ah,0         ; AH = service number 0
int     10h          ; BIOS video services interrupt
```

This five-step process outlines the basic principles of almost all aspects of an assembly language interface. In the following chapters, you'll see how this design is used in specific examples.

An Advanced BIOS Interface

To conclude this discussion of BIOS services, we'd like to mention the alternative BIOS interface that IBM introduced in the PS/2 models that use Micro Channel Architecture. This *Advanced BIOS* (ABIOS) *interface* addresses some of the major design shortcomings of the interrupt-based interface described previously.

The traditional, interrupt-based ROM BIOS interface is limited in two important ways:

■ It cannot be used in protected mode in a PS/2 with Micro Channel Architecture.

■ It provides poor support for multitasking; consequently, an operating system that offers multitasking cannot rely on the traditional BIOS interface.

IBM's solution to these problems is the Advanced BIOS interface in the PS/2 models with Micro Channel Architecture. Through the Advanced BIOS interface, BIOS services are accessed by using a set of address tables and common data areas designed for use in protected mode as well as with a multitasking operating system. However, the complexity of the ABIOS interface makes it better suited to supporting an operating system than to supporting application programs. Unless you are writing a protected-mode, multitasking operating system, we recommend that you keep using the traditional BIOS interface that is common to all computers in the PC family.

MS-DOS Services

Chapters 10 through 13 cover the program support services provided by MS-DOS. These *MS-DOS services* constitute the entire set of operations that MS-DOS provides to programs. Appendix B summarizes their technical details. In this section, we introduce some of the main concerns a programmer often faces when working with the MS-DOS services.

Programs access MS-DOS services by using a set of interrupts. Interrupt numbers 20H through 3FH (decimal 32 through 63) are reserved for use by MS-DOS. Although 10 of these interrupts can be used in programs, most MS-DOS services are invoked in much the same way as the BIOS services: through one umbrella interrupt, interrupt 21H (decimal 33). You can access a variety of MS-DOS functions by specifying a function number in register AH at the time you call interrupt 21H.

The Pros and Cons of Using the MS-DOS Services

The question of whether to use the MS-DOS services arises naturally during the design and development of sophisticated programs. Our general advice, echoed throughout this book, is for you to use the highest available service that will accomplish what you need. This means that, whenever possible, you should use the built-in services of your programming language first, resorting only when necessary to direct use of the MS-DOS services or the BIOS services and resorting only in extreme circumstances to direct programming of the computer's hardware.

In practical terms, either a program can be written entirely within the confines of the programming language's facilities or nearly all of its I/O work must be done outside the programming language, at a lower level. When a lower level of programming is needed, with very few exceptions the MS-DOS services are best suited for disk operations. When you are working with the keyboard or other I/O devices, either the MS-DOS routines or the

BIOS routines will be adequate, depending on the application. But for low-level video-display programming, the situation is more complex. Satisfactory screen output almost always seems to call for the BIOS services and direct hardware programming, even though in some cases screen output is best left in the hands of MS-DOS. We'll see why in a moment.

MS-DOS: A Disk-Service Cornucopia

When you inspect the full range of tools and services placed in your hands by programming languages, by MS-DOS, by the BIOS, and by the computer's hardware, it becomes quite clear that the richest concentration of disk-oriented services exists at the MS-DOS level. This almost goes without saying because MS-DOS is a disk operating system and is inherently strongest in its support of disk operations.

The majority of services that MS-DOS performs are directly connected to the manipulation of disk files. (These services are discussed in Chapter 10.) Even some services that are nominally controlled by a program, such as loading and executing another program (interrupt 21H, function 4BH), involve disk-file operations. From this perspective, MS-DOS is not so much a disk operating system as it is a system of disk services designed for use by your programs. When you are developing programs for PCs, you should approach MS-DOS from this standpoint: Think of MS-DOS as a cornucopia of disk operations placed at your service.

MS-DOS and Video: A Difficult Match

Unfortunately, MS-DOS does not provide much in the way of video output services. In fact, the available MS-DOS services are limited to a character-only, "glass teletype" interface that is rapidly becoming an anachronism in these days of high-resolution color graphics.

To achieve attractive, high-performance video output, you must rely on the BIOS or on direct programming of the video hardware. Because IBM and the clone manufacturers have maintained a fairly consistent programming interface to their video hardware, many programmers feel comfortable about bypassing MS-DOS and using lower-level video programming techniques.

But when you bypass MS-DOS, you encounter a problem: Two different programs can't reliably share the video hardware. Consider what can happen, for example, if you write a program that configures the video hardware in a way that conflicts with the configuration used by a memory-resident "pop-up" program such as SideKick. If your program runs in a video mode that the pop-up program doesn't recognize, the pop-up program's output might appear incomprehensible on the screen. Worse, the pop-up program might reconfigure the video subsystem for its own purposes and leave your program's video output in limbo.

The problem is amplified in multitasking operating environments, such as Microsoft Windows and OS/2, where programs generally share access to the screen. In these environments, a program can bypass the operating system and gain complete control of the screen only if the operating system suspends video output from all other concurrently executing programs. Thus a program that ties up the video hardware can delay the multitasking execution of background programs.

The designers of OS/2 and Microsoft Windows attacked this problem by providing a sophisticated gamut of video output services. These video output services not only resolve conflicts among programs that want to access the video display, they also provide good performance. To get the best video performance in the world of MS-DOS, however, you must either resort to BIOS calls and direct hardware programming or else rely on the video output services provided by your programming language (which themselves bypass MS-DOS).

When trying to decide which method to use, you should consider the probable lifetime of your programs and the range of machines they might be used on. For a PC-specific game program with an expected life of a few months (common for games), you have little reason to worry about these issues. This is not the case for a generalized business or professional application, which should be usable for many years and in many environments.

Floppy Disk Format Considerations

If you're planning to share or sell your programs, you must decide which floppy disk format you'll use to distribute your software. Initially most software vendors used single-sided 5.25-inch floppy disks with eight sectors per track because this format was the lowest common denominator that could be read by all versions of MS-DOS. Later, as single-sided floppy disk drives became virtually extinct, software publishers adopted the double-sided 5.25-inch floppy disk format as an acceptable medium.

Today you must contend with 3.5-inch as well as 5.25-inch floppy disk formats. You should probably stick to the 720-KB format for 3.5-inch disks and to the 360-KB format for 5.25-inch disks. You should also offer a choice of disk sizes because both 5.25-inch and 3.5-inch formats are in widespread use and will be for some time to come.

Comments

Technical information about MS-DOS has become much easier to find since the early days, when the only reliable sources of information were the

MS-DOS technical reference manuals. Nowadays many PC programming magazines discuss MS-DOS programming techniques. Several good reference books on various, detailed aspects of MS-DOS programming, including memory-resident programs, installable device drivers, and exception handlers, are also available.

In this section we describe how to communicate with MS-DOS by using interrupts. (See Figure 9-8.) MS-DOS reserves all 32 interrupt numbers from 20H through 3FH (decimal 32 through 63) for its own use. MS-DOS provides system services through 5 of these interrupts (20H, 21H, 25H, 26H, and 27H). These interrupts can be called directly from a program by using the INT instruction. MS-DOS uses the interrupt vectors for 4 others (22H, 23H, 24H, and 28H) to contain the addresses of routines called by MS-DOS itself; you can substitute your own routines for the default MS-DOS routines by updating one of these interrupt vectors. Interrupt 2FH is reserved for communication between memory-resident programs. The other 22 interrupts reserved by MS-DOS are not intended for use in your programs.

Interrupt Number		
Hex	**Dec**	**Description**
20H	32	Program Terminate
21H	33	General MS-DOS Services
22H	34	Terminate Address
23H	35	Ctrl-C Handler Address
24H	36	Critical-Error Handler Address
25H	37	Absolute Disk Read
26H	38	Absolute Disk Write
27H	39	Terminate and Stay Resident
28H	40	MS-DOS Idle Interrupt
2FH	47	Multiplex Interrupt

Figure 9-8. *MS-DOS interrupts.*

NOTE: *You can use any of the 10 interrupts described in this chapter in your programs. Nevertheless, there is some overlap between the services provided through the separate interrupts described in this chapter and the functions available through interrupt 21H. When you have a choice, use the interrupt 21H functions described in Chapters 10 through 13. We point out why as we describe each MS-DOS interrupt.*

The Five Main MS-DOS Interrupts

Of the MS-DOS interrupts described in this chapter, five have built-in interrupt-handling programs, each of which performs a particular task.

Interrupt 20H (decimal 32): Program Terminate

Interrupt 20H (decimal 32) is used to exit from a program and pass control back to MS-DOS. It is similar to interrupt 21H, function 00H. (See page 396.) These services can be used interchangeably with any version of MS-DOS to end a program. Interrupt 20H does not automatically close files opened with interrupt 21H, function 0FH or 16H when it terminates a program, so you should always use interrupt 21H, function 10H to close such files before exiting via interrupt 20H. If a modified file is not formally closed, its new length will not be recorded in the file directory.

A program can set three operational addresses by using MS-DOS interrupts 22H, 23H, and 24H, as we will see shortly. As part of the cleanup operations performed by MS-DOS for interrupt 20H, these addresses are restored to the values they had before the program was executed. Resetting these addresses is essential if the program that invoked interrupt 20H was executed as the "child" of another program. It serves to protect the "parent" program from using routines intended for the "child." (See MS-DOS function 4BH in Chapter 13.)

> NOTE: *When MS-DOS executes a program, it constructs a* program segment prefix *(PSP), a 256-byte block of memory that contains control information that, among other things, is referenced by MS-DOS when a program is terminated. (We discuss the PSP in detail at the end of this chapter.) MS-DOS depends on the CS register to point to the PSP when the interrupt 20H terminate service is invoked. If the CS register points elsewhere, MS-DOS may crash.*
>
> *In practice, you should terminate your programs with interrupt 21H, function 4CH, which is more flexible and less restrictive than interrupt 20H. The only reason to use interrupt 20H is to maintain compatibility with MS-DOS version 1.0.*

Interrupt 21H (decimal 33): General MS-DOS Services

You can take advantage of a wide range of MS-DOS functions by using interrupt 21H (decimal 33). Each function is accessed by a unique number that you specify when you execute interrupt 21H. Chapters 10 through 13 cover the interrupt 21H services in detail.

Interrupts 25H and 26H (decimals 37 and 38): Absolute Disk Read and Write

Interrupt 25H (decimal 37) and its companion, interrupt 26H (decimal 38), are used to read and write specific disk sectors. They are the only MS-DOS services that ignore the logical structure of a disk and work only with individual sectors, paying no attention to the locations of files, file directories, or the file allocation table.

Interrupts 25H and 26H are similar to the corresponding BIOS disk services, except that the sectors are located by a different numbering method. With the BIOS services, the sectors are selected by their three-dimensional coordinate locations (cylinder, head, and sector), whereas with interrupts 25H and 26H, the sectors are selected by their sequential logical sector numbers. (MS-DOS's sector-numbering system is discussed on page 119.)

The following Basic formula converts three-dimensional coordinates used by the BIOS to logical sector numbers used by MS-DOS:

```
LOGICAL.SECTOR = (SECTOR - 1) + (HEAD * SECTORS.PER.TRACK) +
(CYLINDER * SECTORS.PER.TRACK * NUMBER.OF.HEADS)
```

And here are the formulas for converting logical sector numbers to three-dimensional coordinates:

```
SECTOR = 1 + LOGICAL.SECTOR MOD SECTORS.PER.TRACK

HEAD = (LOGICAL.SECTOR \ SECTORS.PER.TRACK) MOD NUMBER.OF.HEADS

CYLINDER = LOGICAL.SECTOR \ (SECTORS.PER.TRACK * NUMBER.OF.HEADS)
```

> NOTE: *Remember, the BIOS counts heads and cylinders from 0 but counts sectors from 1; MS-DOS logical sectors are numbered from 0.*

To use interrupt 25H or 26H to read or write a block of logical sectors, load the necessary parameters into the CPU registers and execute the interrupt. The number of sectors to be read or written is specified in the CX register; the starting sector number is specified in DX; and the memory address for data transfer is specified in DS:BX. The disk drive is selected by placing a number in the AL register: Drive A is 0, drive B is 1, and so on.

Although BIOS services work with true physical drives, MS-DOS services work with logical drive numbers. MS-DOS assumes every computer has at least two logical drives. If no physical drive B exists, MS-DOS simulates it by using the one physical drive as either drive A or drive B, whichever is needed. You can then remap these logical drives by using the MS-DOS ASSIGN command.

The results of interrupts 25H and 26H are reported in the carry flag (CF) register and in the AL and AH registers. If no error occurred, CF = 0. If an error did occur (CF = 1), AL and AH contain the error codes in two somewhat redundant groups. The AL codes in Figure 9-9 are based on those used by the MS-DOS critical-error handler through interrupt 24H (see page 255), and the AH codes in Figure 9-10 are based on the error codes reported by the BIOS (see page 273).

| Error Code | | |
Hex	Dec	Meaning
00H	0	Write-protect error: attempt to write to protected floppy disk
01H	1	Unknown unit: invalid drive number
02H	2	Drive not ready (for example, no disk, or door open)
04H	4	CRC (cyclical redundancy check) error: parity error
06H	6	Seek error: move to requested cylinder failed
07H	7	Unknown media: disk format not recognized
08H	8	Sector not found
0AH	10	Write error
0BH	11	Read error
0CH	12	General, nonspecific error
0FH	15	Invalid disk change (MS-DOS version 3.0 or later)

Figure 9-9. *The error-code values and meanings returned in the AL register following an error in a disk read or write through MS-DOS interrupt 25H or 26H.*

| Error Code | | |
Hex	Dec	Meaning
01H	1	Bad command
02H	2	Bad address mark: sector ID marking invalid or not found
03H	3	Write-protect error: attempt to write to protected disk
04H	4	Bad sector: requested sector not on disk
08H	8	DMA (direct memory access) failure
10H	16	Bad CRC: read found invalid parity check of data
20H	32	Controller failed: disk drive controller malfunction
40H	64	Bad seek: move to requested track failed
80H	128	Time-out: drive did not respond

Figure 9-10. *The error-code values and meanings returned in the AH register following an error in a disk read or write through MS-DOS interrupt 25H or 26H.*

Normally interrupt handlers and other service routines leave the stack clean when they exit, returning it to its original size and contents. MS-DOS interrupts 25H and 26H deliberately do not clean up the stack. Instead, they finish and return to the program with one word left on the stack. This word holds the contents of the flag register, which show how the flags were set when the program invoked the service. This is purportedly done to preserve the program's flag status before the service was used because interrupts 25H and 26H use the flags for their return codes. We think this is a silly precaution because any program that needs to preserve the flags can simply do what programs normally do when they need something saved: push them on the stack themselves. Any program that uses interrupts 25H and 26H should pop the two extra flag-status bytes off the stack after the interrupt returns. These bytes can either be placed in the flags register with a POPF command (which should be done after testing CF for an error) or be discarded by incrementing the stack pointer register by 2 (ADD SP,2).

Interrupt 27H (decimal 39): Terminate and Stay Resident

Interrupt 27H (decimal 39) invokes one of the most interesting of all the services provided by MS-DOS.

Like interrupt 20H, interrupt 27H ends a program, but it does not erase the program from memory. Instead, it leaves a specified portion of the program in memory. (The program *stays resident.*) The program and data that are made resident using interrupt 27H become, in effect, an extension of MS-DOS and will not be overwritten by other programs.

> NOTE: *As with interrupt 20H, MS-DOS versions 2.0 and later provide a more flexible alternative to interrupt 27H. This is interrupt 21H, function 31H, which we recommend instead of interrupt 27H unless you are concerned about compatibility with MS-DOS version 1.0. See Chapter 13 for more about interrupt 21H, function 31H.*

Interrupt 27H (or its function-call equivalent) is used by a number of sophisticated pop-up programs, such as SideKick. Terminate-and-stay-resident (TSR) programs typically use this service for establishing new interrupt-handling routines that are meant to stay in effect indefinitely. Most often, these interrupt-handling routines replace existing MS-DOS or BIOS interrupt handlers in order to change or extend their operation. But the resident item is not limited to interrupt handlers and program instructions; it could just as easily be data. For example, the same programming technique could be used to load status information into a common area that various programs would share, allowing them to communicate indirectly.

Normally a TSR program is designed in two parts, consisting of a *resident portion* that remains in memory and a *transient portion* that installs the resident portion by updating interrupt vectors, initializing data, and calling the terminate-and-stay-resident service. The transient portion does not remain in memory after interrupt 27H is executed.

To accommodate this process, TSR programs are designed with the resident portion first (that is, at lower addresses). The transient portion computes the size of the resident portion and places this value in register DX when it executes interrupt 27H. MS-DOS then leaves the resident portion in memory but reclaims the memory occupied by the transient portion for executing other programs.

Anything left resident by this service normally remains resident as long as MS-DOS is also resident. It is not unusual for several different programs to leave part of themselves resident. Programs that use this technique are usually sophisticated and complicated, so it is also not unusual for them to interfere with each other. To operate such a group of resident programs successfully, a user must sometimes load them in a particular order—an order he or she may have to discover through experimentation. (This is an unfair trick to play on an unsuspecting user.)

As it does with interrupt 20H, the ordinary terminate service, MS-DOS resets the address vectors for interrupts 22H through 24H when it performs this terminate-and-stay-resident service. Therefore, you can't use this service to create resident interrupt handlers for the address interrupts. This might seem to be a limitation, but it is actually fairly reasonable. The address interrupts are not meant to be used globally; they are meant to be used only by individual programs. (See the MS-DOS address interrupts section on page 253 for further discussion.)

The Multiplex Interrupt

The *multiplex interrupt,* interrupt 2FH (decimal 47), is used to communicate with memory-resident programs. This interrupt wasn't used in MS-DOS version 1, but in MS-DOS version 2 the RAM-resident print spooler PRINT used it. In MS-DOS versions 3.0 and later, the protocol for using interrupt 2FH was standardized to allow multiple memory-resident programs to share the interrupt. (That's why this interrupt is called the multiplex interrupt.)

NOTE: *Most of the material in this section applies to all versions of MS-DOS; however, interrupt 2FH is available only with MS-DOS versions 3.0 and later.*

To use the multiplex interrupt, you must write a TSR program that contains an interrupt handler for interrupt 2FH. (To accomplish this, use the MS-DOS terminate-and-stay-resident service.) The transient portion of the TSR program must copy the address of the previous interrupt 2FH handler from the interrupt 2FH vector (0000:00BCH) to a variable in the resident portion. The transient portion then updates the interrupt 2FH vector with the address of the resident portion's interrupt 2FH handler so that when interrupt 2FH is subsequently executed, the TSR's handler gets control.

When interrupt 2FH is executed, the resident interrupt 2FH handler does the following:

```
IF      AH=IDnumber
THEN    process the value in AL
        return from the interrupt (IRET)
ELSE    jump to the previous interrupt 2FH handler
```

This simple logic lets several memory-resident programs use the multiplex interrupt to communicate. The key is that every memory-resident program must have a unique ID number. Your program's interrupt 2FH handler should recognize one of the 64 values from C0H through FFH. (There are 256 possible ID numbers, of course, but Microsoft and IBM reserve numbers 00H through BFH for use by MS-DOS utilities.)

When your program's interrupt 2FH handler gains control, it must first check the value in register AH. If the value in AH matches the program's ID number, the handler looks in AL to decide what to do next. If the values don't match, the handler simply jumps to the address of the previous interrupt 2FH handler. The interrupt 2FH handler considers the value in AL to be a function number and processes it accordingly, as described in the following paragraphs.

For interrupt 2FH, **function 00H** has a special meaning. It instructs the interrupt handler to return one of two values in AL:

- A value of FFH indicates that an interrupt 2FH handler is resident in memory and available to process other function numbers.

- A value of 01H indicates that the ID number in AH is in use.

So, to detect whether a particular TSR program is installed in memory, a program executes interrupt 2FH with the TSR's ID number in AH and with AL = 00H. If the TSR is present in memory, it returns AL = FFH. If another TSR is using the ID number for its own purposes, that TSR returns AL = 01H. Otherwise, any interrupt 2FH handlers in memory simply ignore the interrupt, causing the interrupt to return AL = 00H.

The best-documented example of how to use the multiplex interrupt is the PRINT program supplied with MS-DOS versions 3.0 and later. By examining how PRINT uses the multiplex interrupt, you can make better use of this interrupt in your own memory-resident programs.

PRINT's multiplex ID number is 1. Any time interrupt 2FH is executed with this ID number in AH, PRINT's memory-resident interrupt handler processes the interrupt. Because seven different functions are defined by the PRINT program, a call to PRINT consists of executing interrupt 2FH with AH = 01H and a function number in AL. (See Figure 9-11.)

Each time you run PRINT, the program executes interrupt 2FH with AH = 01H and AL = 00H. The first time you run the program, the value returned in AL by the interrupt is 00H, so the program installs itself in memory. When you invoke PRINT a second time, the value returned in AL as a result of executing the multiplex interrupt with AX = 0100H is FFH. This value is placed there by the memory-resident copy of PRINT, so the second invocation of the program knows not to install itself in memory.

The second and subsequent invocations of PRINT can request any of six functions by passing a function number to the memory-resident copy of the program. You could also use these functions in your own programs by placing the value 01H (PRINT's multiplex ID) in register AH, placing the function number in register AL, and then issuing interrupt 2FH.

Function Number	Description
00H	Get installed status.
01H	Submit file to print.
02H	Remove file from print queue.
03H	Cancel all files in print queue.
04H	Hold print queue.
05H	Release print queue.
06H	Get printer's device header.

Figure 9-11. *PRINT functions defined through the multiplex interrupt.*

For PRINT, **function 01H** submits a file to the print spooler for printing. To tell PRINT what is to be printed, you set the register pair DS:DX to point to a 5-byte area called a *submit packet*. The first byte of the submit packet is a level code (which should be 0). The remaining 4 bytes of the submit packet are the segmented address of an ASCIIZ string that defines the pathname of the file to be printed. (See page 300.) The pathname must be a single file. The global filename characters * and ? are not allowed.

When a file is submitted by using this function, it is added to the end of the queue, or list, of files to be printed. The files are printed in turn and are dropped from the queue after they're printed.

For PRINT, **function 02H** cancels individual files that are queued for printing. The register pair DS:DX points to the ASCIIZ string that defines which file is to be removed from the queue. In this case, the global filename characters * and ? can be used. In function 02H, DS:DX points directly to the filename string rather than to a submit packet that points to the string.

For PRINT, **function 03H** cancels all files queued for printing. For both functions 02H and 03H, if the file currently being printed is canceled, PRINT stops printing the file and prints a short message to that effect.

For PRINT, **function 04H** gives programs access to the print queue so that they can inspect it. The queue is frozen when this function is requested, so you don't have to worry about the list changing while you inspect it. Issuing any other PRINT function call unfreezes the queue. Function 04H returns a pointer in the register pair DS:SI that points to a list of filenames that are queued for printing. Entries in the list are strings with a fixed length of 64 bytes. The end of the list is indicated by an entry that begins with a zero byte.

The queue freeze imposed by function 04H doesn't need to halt the printing operation. But function 04H suspends the removal from the queue of a file that has finished printing.

For PRINT, **function 05H** is essentially a null function; it doesn't do anything except unfreeze the queue of filenames frozen by function 04H. (The other four functions can do this, too.)

For PRINT, **function 06H** sets the carry flag (CF) if the print queue is not empty and loads registers DS:SI to point to the printer device header. If the queue is empty, function 06H clears the carry flag and sets AX to zero.

The Three MS-DOS Address Interrupts

MS-DOS uses three interrupts, 22H through 24H (decimal 34 through 36), to handle three exceptional circumstances: the end of a program, a "break" keyboard action (Ctrl-Break or Ctrl-C on the standard PC keyboard), and the occurrence of any "critical" error (usually a disk error of some kind). Your programs can affect the action taken in each of these three circumstances by changing the corresponding interrupt vector to point to any operation you choose. This is why we call these interrupts the *address interrupts*.

MS-DOS maintains a default address setting for each of these three interrupts. This default address setting is preserved at the beginning of a program's operation and is restored after the program has finished. This procedure allows your programs to freely change these vectors as needed without disturbing the operation of subsequent programs or the operation of MS-DOS itself.

Interrupt 22H (decimal 34): Termination Address

The address that is associated with interrupt 22H (decimal 34) specifies where control of the computer will be passed when a program's execution ends with a call to MS-DOS interrupt 20H or 27H or with interrupt 21H, function 00H, 31H, or 4CH. Interrupt 22H isn't designed to be executed directly by a program by using the INT instruction. Instead, MS-DOS uses the interrupt 22H vector to store the address of its own program termination routine.

It's not a good idea to manipulate the MS-DOS termination address. The inner workings of the default MS-DOS program-termination routine are not documented, so writing a substitute routine that terminates a program cleanly without confounding MS-DOS is difficult. If you are qualified to use this feature, you probably understand it better than we can explain it.

Interrupt 23H (decimal 35): Ctrl-C Handler Address

The address that is associated with interrupt 23H (decimal 35) points to the interrupt-handling routine that MS-DOS invokes in response to the Ctrl-C key combination. (For most computers, MS-DOS will convert Ctrl-Break to Ctrl-C.) Thus, interrupt 23H is intended to be executed only by MS-DOS, not by an application program. A few old-fashioned programs, such as the MS-DOS editor EDLIN, use Ctrl-C as a command keystroke, but in most applications the Ctrl-C combination signals that the user wants to interrupt an ongoing process.

MS-DOS is a bit quirky about when it will respond to a Ctrl-C keystroke. Normally MS-DOS acts on a break only when it is reading from or writing to a character I/O device (the screen, keyboard, printer, or communications port). However, the BREAK ON command allows MS-DOS versions 2.0 and later to act on Ctrl-C at the time of most other MS-DOS system calls.

MS-DOS's default Ctrl-C handler terminates the program or batch file you are executing. However, if your program provides its own interrupt 23H handler, it can have MS-DOS take any action you want.

In general, a Ctrl-C handler can take three different courses of action:

- It can perform some useful action, such as setting a flag, and then return to MS-DOS by using an interrupt return (IRET) instruction. In this case, MS-DOS picks up where it left off, without terminating your program's execution.

■ It can set or clear the carry flag and then return to MS-DOS with a far return instruction (RET 2) that discards the flags pushed on the stack when the interrupt 23H handler was called by MS-DOS. If the carry flag is set, MS-DOS terminates the interrupted program. If the carry flag is clear, MS-DOS continues execution.

■ It can keep control without returning to MS-DOS. This option is tricky, however, because you don't usually know what was on the stack at the moment MS-DOS detected the Ctrl-C keystroke. An interrupt 23H handler that doesn't return to MS-DOS should generally restore the stack pointer register (SP) to a predetermined value. It should also execute interrupt 21H, function 0DH, to flush the MS-DOS file buffers so that the MS-DOS disk I/O system will be in a known state.

The usual reason to write your own Ctrl-C handler is to let your program handle a keyboard break itself. Even if you want your program to terminate immediately after Ctrl-C is pressed, you might still need to clean up before your program terminates. For example, if you use interrupt 21H, function 0FH or 16H to open a file, you should write your own Ctrl-C handler to close it because the default MS-DOS Ctrl-C handler won't do so. Also, if you installed your own interrupt handlers for BIOS or hardware interrupts, the MS-DOS Ctrl-C handler won't restore them before it terminates your program. Again, your Ctrl-C handler should do this, if necessary.

If you do write your own Ctrl-C handler, don't forget the relationship between Ctrl-C and the keyboard Ctrl-Break combination. When you press Ctrl-Break, the BIOS keyboard interrupt handler generates interrupt 1BH. MS-DOS's interrupt 1BH handler inserts a Ctrl-C key code into the keyboard input buffer. The next time MS-DOS checks the keyboard buffer, it finds Ctrl-C and executes interrupt 23H. Thus, pressing Ctrl-Break has the same effect as pressing Ctrl-C, except that MS-DOS detects the break generated by Ctrl-Break without first processing the intervening characters in the keyboard buffer.

Interrupt 24H (decimal 36): Critical-Error Handler Address

The address that is associated with interrupt 24H (decimal 36) points to the interrupt-handling routine invoked whenever MS-DOS detects the occurrence of a *critical error*—an emergency situation that prevents MS-DOS from continuing with normal processing. Typically, the critical error is a disk error, but other errors are also reported, as we'll see.

Like interrupt 23H, interrupt 24H is intended to be invoked only by MS-DOS, not by an application program. However, an application can substitute its own interrupt 24H handler for the default MS-DOS handler. The MS-DOS default handler produces a familiar message:

```
Abort, Retry, Ignore?
```
(in MS-DOS versions prior to 3.3)

or

```
Abort, Retry, Fail?
```
(in MS-DOS versions 3.3 and later)

If you substitute a customized interrupt 24H handler for the one MS-DOS provides, you can tailor critical-error handling to the needs of your program.

When MS-DOS transfers control to a critical-error handler, it provides several sources of information about the error itself and about the state of the system at the time the error occurred. These sources include the register pair BP:SI, the stack, the AX register, and the DI register. We will cover them one by one because this process is quite complicated.

If you are operating under MS-DOS version 2.0 or later, the register pair BP:SI is set to point to a device-header control block. Your critical-error handler can inspect the device header to learn more about the device (disk drive, printer, and so forth) that experienced the error. (See the MS-DOS technical reference manuals or the *MS-DOS Programmer's Reference* for more about the device header.)

When the critical-error handler gains control, the stack contains the complete register set of the program that issued the MS-DOS function call that ended in the critical error. This information can be quite useful to an error handler that is intimately integrated with the active program. The usual method of accessing the information on the stack is to address the stack by using register BP. You can access the stack as shown in Figure 9-12 if the first two instructions in your critical-error handler are as follows:

```
PUSH    BP
MOV     BP,SP
```

MS-DOS indicates the nature of a critical error primarily through a combination of the high-order bit of the AH register and the low-order byte of the DI register (a curious choice, for sure). If the high-order bit of AH is 0, the error is related to a disk operation. If the same bit (bit 7 of AH) is 1, the error is something other than a disk error, as we discuss shortly.

When the error is a disk-device error (high-order bit of AH is 0), register AL identifies the drive number (0 is drive A, 1 is drive B, and so on). Bits 0 through 5 of AH contain further information about the error, as shown in Figure 9-13.

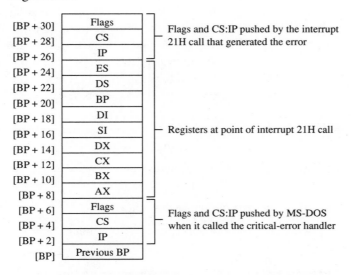

Figure 9-12. *Information passed on the stack to an interrupt 24H (critical-error) handler.*

Bit 5 4 3 2 1 0	Meaning
. 0	Read error.
. 1	Write error.
. . . 0 0 .	Error involved DOS system files.
. . . 0 1 .	Error involved file allocation table.
. . . 1 0 .	Error involved root directory.
. . . 1 1 .	Error involved files area of disk.
. . 1 . . .	Fail response allowed.
. 1	Retry response allowed.
1	Ignore response allowed.

Figure 9-13. *The bits and associated errors indicated in the AH register when MS-DOS invokes interrupt 24H.*

MS-DOS returns additional information about the error in the low-order byte of register DI. (See Figure 9-14.) The error codes in DI cover a variety of input/output devices, so you must rely on a combination of the information in AH and in DI to determine the exact nature of the critical error.

257

If bit 7 of AH is set, the error is probably not a disk error, although it may be disk related. One disk-related error normally reported when bit 7 of AH is set is an error in the disk's FAT. In MS-DOS version 1, this is always the case. For versions 2.0 and later, the error handler should inspect bit 15 of the word that is offset 4 bytes into the device header (BP: [SI + 4]). If this bit is clear, the device is a block device (disk) and the error is a FAT error. If this bit is set, the device is a character device, in which case the low-order byte of DI defines the exact problem. (Regardless of device type, the high-order byte should be ignored.) DI error-code values shown in Figure 9-14 are essentially the same as the values reported in AL for interrupts 25H and 26H (decimals 37 and 38).

You can use the following interrupt 21H functions in your critical-error handler to report what's going on to the program's user:

- Functions 01H through 0CH, which provide simple keyboard and display services

- Function 30H, which returns the MS-DOS version number

- Function 59H, which returns extended error information in MS-DOS versions 3.0 and later

Error Code		
Hex	*Dec*	*Description*
00H	0	Write-protect error: attempt to write to protected floppy disk
01H	1	Unknown unit: invalid drive number
02H	2	Drive not ready (no floppy disk or drive door open)
03H	3	Unknown command requested
04H	4	Data error (CRC)
05H	5	Bad request structure length
06H	6	Seek error: move to requested cylinder failed
07H	7	Unknown disk format
08H	8	Sector not found
09H	9	Printer out of paper
0AH	10	Write fault
0BH	11	Read fault
0CH	12	General, nonspecific error
0FH	15	Invalid disk change (MS-DOS version 3.0 or later)

Figure 9-14. *Errors indicated in the low-order byte of register DI when MS-DOS invokes interrupt 24H.*

Don't call other MS-DOS services within your critical-error handler, however, because other services may overwrite internal buffers or stacks that MS-DOS will need when the error handler returns.

Normally an error-handler routine returns to MS-DOS after doing whatever it chooses to do. MS-DOS can then take one of four courses of action: It can ignore the error, try the operation again, terminate the program, or fail the requested operation and return to the program (MS-DOS versions 3.1 and later). You tell MS-DOS which course you want it to take by loading one of the values shown in Figure 9-15 into the AL register before executing an IRET to return to MS-DOS.

If you use a custom critical-error handler, it will remain in effect only as long as the program that installs it is running. When the program terminates, MS-DOS replaces the contents of the interrupt 24H vector with the address of the default critical-error handler.

AL	Description
00H	Ignore the error and press onward.
01H	Retry the operation.
02H	Terminate the program.
03H	Fail the operation (MS-DOS versions 3.1 and later).

Figure 9-15. *Values that can be returned to MS-DOS in register AL by an interrupt 24H (critical-error) handler.*

The MS-DOS Idle Interrupt

MS-DOS executes interrupt 28H (decimal 40) within interrupt 21H services that loop while waiting for an expected event, such as a keystroke. For example, if you execute the MS-DOS keyboard input service (interrupt 21H, service 01H), MS-DOS executes interrupt 28H within an idle loop that waits for the next keystroke.

The default MS-DOS handler for interrupt 28H is merely an IRET instruction; that is, executing interrupt 28H normally does nothing at all. You can substitute your own interrupt 28H handler, however, that does something useful while MS-DOS is otherwise idle. In particular, a memory-resident program can contain an interrupt 28H handler that is executed repeatedly whenever MS-DOS is waiting for keyboard output.

The biggest problem with installing your own interrupt 28H handler is that the handler can execute interrupt 21H to access MS-DOS services only under very specific circumstances. Unfortunately, you must know many details about the way MS-DOS internally processes interrupt 21H requests in order to use these safely within an interrupt 28H handler.

The Program Segment Prefix (PSP)

When MS-DOS loads a program, it sets aside a 256-byte block of memory for the program called the *program segment prefix* (PSP). The PSP contains a hodgepodge of information that MS-DOS uses to help run the program. A PSP is associated with every MS-DOS program, no matter what language the program is written in. However, for programming purposes, the information stored in the PSP is more relevant to programs written in assembly language than to programs written in high-level languages. With a high-level language, the language is normally in charge of the program's working environment, memory usage, and file control—all the information that the PSP is concerned with. Therefore, you can normally make good use of the PSP only if your program is assembly language based.

Before we describe the elements of the PSP, we need to look at the relationship between the PSP and the program it supports.

MS-DOS always builds a program's PSP in memory just below the memory area allocated to the program itself. When the program receives control from MS-DOS, segment registers DS and ES point to the beginning of the PSP. Because it sometimes needs to locate PSP information, MS-DOS keeps a copy of the PSP segment value internally.

The best way to explain how the PSP and the program work together is to jump right into the PSP's internal structure. We will reveal the purpose and potential use of each element as we explain it.

The internal structure of the PSP

As you will soon discover, the PSP contains a rather confusing mixture of items. (See Figure 9-16.) The background and history of MS-DOS pull it in different directions—backward to the earlier CP/M system and forward to UNIX-type operating environments. As a result, the PSP contains elements that serve different purposes and are oriented to different programming methods. We discuss the elements in the order in which they appear.

The field at offset 00H (2 bytes) contains bytes CDH and 20H, the interrupt 20H instruction. As we saw in the discussion of interrupt 20H in this chapter, this interrupt is only one of several standard ways for a program to terminate. This instruction is placed at the beginning of the PSP (at offset 00H) so that a program can end itself simply by jumping to this location when the CS points to the PSP. As you might guess, this is not the most sensible thing for a program to do; it's always best to go through the appropriate interrupt or function call. This odd method of terminating a program is a relic of the days when CP/M compatibility was important.

Offset Hex	Offset Dec	Length (Bytes)	Description
00H	0	2	INT 20H instruction
02H	2	2	Address of paragraph following the program
04H	4	1	(Reserved; normally 0)
05H	5	5	Call to MS-DOS function dispatcher
0AH	10	4	Interrupt 22H (termination) address
0EH	14	4	Interrupt 23H (Ctrl-C) address
12H	18	4	Interrupt 24H (critical-error) address
16H	22	22	(Reserved)
2CH	44	2	Segment address of the environment block
2EH	46	34	(Reserved)
50H	80	3	INT 21H, RETF instructions
53H	83	9	(Reserved)
5CH	92	16	FCB #1
6CH	108	20	FCB #2
80H	128	128	Command-line parameters and default disk transfer area (DTA)

Figure 9-16. *The parts of the program segment prefix (PSP).*

The field at offset 02H (2 bytes) contains the segment address of the paragraph following the last paragraph of memory allocated to the program. MS-DOS normally loads a program in the first free area of memory large enough to contain the program. A program can use this field to determine the actual size of the memory area allocated to it.

In practice, there's a better way to determine the amount of memory allocated to a program. Interrupt 21H, function 4AH, can return the size of any block of memory, not just the block into which a program is loaded. (See Chapter 13 for more on this MS-DOS service.)

The field at offset 05H (5 bytes) contains a long call to the *MS-DOS function dispatcher*, the internal MS-DOS routine that examines the function number you pass to MS-DOS and executes the corresponding service routine. This field, too, is a remnant of the days when CP/M compatibility was important to MS-DOS programmers. A program can make a near call to offset 05H in the PSP with a function number in register CL and get the same result as if it had loaded AH with the function number and executed interrupt 21H.

Needless to say, this technique is not very useful in real-world MS-DOS programs.

The fields at offsets 0AH, 0EH, and 12H (4 bytes each) contain the segmented addresses of the default handlers for interrupts 22H (termination), 23H (Ctrl-C), and 24H (critical-error). These addresses are stored in the PSP for your convenience. If you substitute a customized interrupt handler for one of the MS-DOS handlers, you can restore the default handler by copying its address from the PSP into the corresponding interrupt vector.

In MS-DOS versions 2.0 and later, the field at offset 2CH (2 bytes) contains the paragraph address of the program's *environment block*. The environment block contains a list of ASCIIZ strings (strings of ASCII characters, each terminated with a zero byte) that define various kinds of information. The end of the environment block is marked by a zero-length string (that is, a single zero byte) where you would expect to find the first byte of the next string. Environment blocks that begin with a zero-length string do not contain any strings.

Each environment string is of the form *NAME=value*, where *NAME* is capitalized and of any reasonable length and *value* can be almost anything. The environment thus consists of a list of global variables, each of which contains information that your program might be able to use. For example, if the environment block contains the PATH environment variable (that is, a string that starts with PATH=), any program—including MS-DOS itself—can examine its environment block to determine which directories to search for executable files (and in what order). In this way, the environment block provides a simple means of passing information to any program that examines it. (You can change the contents of the environment block with the MS-DOS SET command.)

MS-DOS makes a copy of the environment block whenever it loads a program to be executed, and it places the copy's paragraph address (segment) in the program's PSP. To obtain information from the environment block, a program must first obtain its segment from the PSP and then examine each of the zero-terminated strings. Some high-level languages contain functions that do this for you. For example, in C, the *getenv()* library function does all the work.

Many sophisticated MS-DOS programs rely on information in the environment block. Also, the concept of the environment is found in other powerful operating systems, including UNIX and OS/2. We recommend the use of the environment block whenever you need to pass user-configurable information to a program.

The field at offset 50H contains two executable 8086 instructions: INT 21H and RETF (far return).

This is another kludge that lets you invoke MS-DOS functions some-what indirectly. To use this feature, you set up everything necessary to in-voke an MS-DOS interrupt 21H function (by selecting the function in AH, and so forth). Then, instead of bravely performing an interrupt 21H (a 2-byte instruction), do a far call to offset 50H in the PSP (a 5-byte instruction).

You might expect that this feature is another flash from the past, a bit of CP/M compatibility, but actually it was introduced with MS-DOS version 2.0 and will not work with previous versions of MS-DOS. You might find that making a far call to offset 50H in the PSP is handy if you intend to patch the address of a different function dispatcher into your code; but in most cases, a simple INT 21H instruction will suffice.

The fields at offsets 5CH and 6CH support old-fashioned file process-ing, using file control blocks, or FCBs. FCBs can be used for file I/O with any version of MS-DOS, but their use is discouraged with MS-DOS versions 2.0 and later, where more modern file I/O is available through the use of file handles. See page 288 for more on file control blocks, and see page 300 for more on file handles.

This area of the PSP was designed to make life easier for programs that receive one or two filenames as parameters. The basic idea, and a good one, we think, is to let MS-DOS construct the necessary FCBs out of the first two command-line parameters (the parameters given on the command line, following the program name). If a program needs either or both FCBs, it can open and use them without having to decode the command-line parameters and construct the FCBs itself.

If you use this feature of the PSP, you should be aware of three poten-tial complications. First, the two FCBs overlap where they are placed. If your program needs only the first, fine; but if it needs the second FCB as well, one or both of them should be moved elsewhere before they are used. Second, these FCBs can involve FCB extensions, a fact that is overlooked in most MS-DOS documentation for the PSP. Finally, if you use an MS-DOS function that requires an extended FCB, you should copy the default FCBs to another area of memory where the FCB extensions won't overlap other data in the PSP.

Keep in mind that the use of FCBs is considered obsolete, but if you want to use them, this information should help.

The field at offset 80H serves two purposes. When MS-DOS first builds the PSP, it fills this field with the command-line parameters typed by the user when the program was invoked. The length of the command line is in the byte at offset 80H. A string containing the command-line parameters follows at offset 81H.

This string has some peculiarities. It does not contain the name of the program that was invoked. Instead, it begins with the character that immediately follows the program name, which is usually a blank. Separators, such as blanks and commas, are not stripped out or compressed. If you use the command line, you have to be prepared to scan through it and recognize standard separators. Fortunately, high-level languages often provide functions that parse the command-parameter string for you. In C, for example, the values *argc* and *argv* are passed to the main start-up routine in every C program. These two values contain the number of command-line parameters and the address of a list of individual parameters. It's usually easier to rely on your high-level language to extract command-line parameters from the PSP than it is to do it yourself in assembly language.

Starting with MS-DOS version 2.0, the command line is modified in a particular way: MS-DOS strips any redirection parameters (such as < or >) and reconstructs the parameter line as if these items were not there. The result of these two operations on the command string is that a program can neither find out whether its standard I/O is being redirected nor find out its own name.

The other purpose served by the field at offset 80H in the PSP is that of the default disk transfer area. This default buffer area is established by MS-DOS just in case you use an MS-DOS service that calls for a DTA and you haven't yet set up your own DTA buffer. See Chapter 10 for descriptions of the services that use or manipulate the DTA.

An Example

The following interface example shows how you can use an interrupt handler to process Ctrl-C keystrokes. The example consists of two assembly language routines.

The first routine, *INT23Handler*, gains control when MS-DOS executes INT 23H in response to a Ctrl-C keystroke. This handler simply increments the value in a flag and then returns to MS-DOS with an IRET instruction.

Note how the flag *_INT23Flag* is addressed through the segment group DGROUP. In many languages, segments with different names are grouped together in one logical group so that they can all be addressed with the same segment register. In the case of Microsoft C, this group of segments is named DGROUP, and it includes the data segment (*_DATA*) used by the compiled C program.

The second assembly language routine, *_Install()*, is designed to be called by a C program. This short routine calls an MS-DOS interrupt 21H function that updates the interrupt 23H vector with the address of the interrupt handler. (Chapters 10 through 13 and Appendix B contain more about this MS-DOS function and about interrupt 21H services in general.)

```
DGROUP          GROUP   _DATA

_TEXT           SEGMENT byte public 'CODE'
                ASSUME  cs:_TEXT,ds:DGROUP

;
; the interrupt 23H handler:

INT23Handler    PROC    far
                push    ds                      ; preserve all registers used
                push    ax                      ; ... in this interrupt handler

                mov     ax,seg DGROUP           ; set DS to the segment where
                mov     ds,ax                   ; ... the flag is located
                inc     word ptr _INT23flag     ; increment the flag

                pop     ax                      ; restore regs and return
                pop     ds
                iret

INT23Handler    ENDP

;
; the C-callable installation routine:

                PUBLIC  _Install
_Install        PROC    near

                push    bp                      ; the usual C prologue
                mov     bp,sp
                push    ds                      ; preserve DS

                push    cs                      ; set DS:DX to point to ...
                pop     ds
                mov     dx,offset INT23Handler  ; ... the interrupt handler
                mov     ax,2523h                ; AH = MS-DOS function number
                                                ; AL = interrupt number
                int     21h                     ; call MS-DOS to update the
                                                ; interrupt vector

                pop     ds
                pop     bp                      ; restore regs and return
                ret

_Install        ENDP

_TEXT           ENDS
```

(continued)

```
                ;
                ; the flag set by the interrupt 23H handler when Ctrl-C is pressed:

_DATA             SEGMENT word public 'DATA'

                  PUBLIC  _INT23flag
_INT23flag        DW     0                          ; flag (initial value = 0)
_DATA             ENDS
```

The snippet of C code that follows shows how you could use this interrupt 23H handler in a program. This C program does nothing but wait for you to press Ctrl-C. When you do, the assembly language interrupt 23H handler increments the flag. When the loop in the C program sees that the flag is nonzero, it displays a message and decrements the flag.

```c
extern int INT23flag;                       /* flag set when Ctrl-C is pressed */

main()
{
        int     KeyCode;


        Install();                          /* install the interrupt 23H
                                               handler */

        do
        {
          while( INT23flag > 0 )
          {
            printf( "\nCtrl-C was pressed" );  /* show a message ... */
            --INT23flag;                       /* ... and decrement the flag */
          }

          if( kbhit() )                     /* look for a keypress */
            KeyCode = getch();
          else
            KeyCode = 0;
        }
        while( KeyCode != 0x0D );            /* loop until Enter
                                               is pressed */

}
```

Although the C code is short, it suggests two important points. One is that you must give MS-DOS the chance to detect a Ctrl-C keystroke each time you test your interrupt 23H flag. (Remember that MS-DOS is guaranteed to check for Ctrl-C only when it reads from or writes to a character input/output device.) In this program, C's *kbhit( )* function calls MS-DOS to check for keyboard activity and, at the same time, lets MS-DOS check for Ctrl-C as well.

Also, note how the interrupt handler increments the flag instead of merely setting it to "true" or "false." This lets the loop in the C program process rapid, successive interrupts without losing track of how many interrupts have occurred.

Chapter 10

BIOS and MS-DOS Disk Services

We're now going to cover the disk services provided by the BIOS and by MS-DOS. To understand this chapter, you should be familiar with the logical structure of the contents of a disk, which is covered in Chapter 5; pages 123 through 138 are especially important.

Generally speaking, the MS-DOS services are preferred over the BIOS services for disk operations. If you decide to use any of the BIOS disk services, we recommend that you read the section entitled "Comments and Examples" later in this chapter.

One of the major new features introduced with MS-DOS version 6.0 is DoubleSpace file compression. If you elect to use this feature, all files are automatically compressed as they are written to disk and decompressed as they are read from disk. The result is an effective doubling of disk capacity with relatively little performance penalty. (The time saved because fewer bytes need to be written to or read from the disk almost compensates for the time required to compress and decompress information.)

How does the DoubleSpace technology affect the programmer? The answer, in a nutshell, is that it doesn't. The compression and decompression is completely transparent to a program regardless of whether it uses high-level language statements, MS-DOS calls, or BIOS routines for disk access. This is the way it must be, of course, because a program cannot know in advance whether it is using a compressed disk. There are a few specialized DoubleSpace ISR routines in MS-DOS 6.0, but these are required only for writing disk utilities, such as defragmenters; they are not needed by the majority of programmers.

The BIOS Disk Services

The original IBM PC BIOS offered only six disk services. As the floppy disk and hard disk subsystems of the PC family became increasingly sophisticated, the number of BIOS services that support disk I/O increased from 6 in the original IBM PC to 22 in the PS/2s. (See Figure 10-1.) To keep the BIOS software modular and flexible, IBM separated the support routines for hard disks from the floppy disk support routines.

All BIOS disk services are invoked by using interrupt 13H (decimal 19) and are selected by loading the service number into the AH register. Disk drives are identified by a zero-based number passed in DL, with the high-order bit set to 1 to indicate a hard disk. Thus, the first floppy disk drive in the computer is identified by drive number 00H, and the first hard disk drive is designated by drive number 80H.

The BIOS uses a set of descriptive parameter tables called *disk-base tables* to gain information about the capabilities of the disk controller hardware and the disk media. The BIOS maintains the segmented addresses of the disk-base tables it uses in interrupt vectors. The address of the table for the current floppy disk drive is in the interrupt 1EH vector (0000:0078H); addresses of tables for the first and second hard drives are in interrupt vectors 41H (0000:0104H) and 46H (0000:0118H).

For most programmers, the disk-base tables are an invisible part of the disk services. However, some disk-base parameters might occasionally need to be changed for special purposes. For this reason we include a brief description of the disk-base tables in the middle of this chapter.

The following sections describe the BIOS services listed in Figure 10-1.

Service	Description	Floppy Disk	Hard Disk
00H	Reset Disk System	x	x
01H	Get Disk Status	x	x
02H	Read Disk Sectors	x	x
03H	Write Disk Sectors	x	x
04H	Verify Disk Sectors	x	x
05H	Format Disk Track	x	x
06H	Format PC/XT Bad Disk Track		x
07H	Format PC/XT Hard Disk, Starting at Cylinder ''n''		x
08H	Get Disk-Drive Parameters	x	x
09H	Initialize Hard Disk Parameter Tables		x
0AH	Read Long		x
0BH	Write Long		x
0CH	Seek to Cylinder		x
0DH	Alternate Hard Disk Reset		x
10H	Test for Drive Ready		x
11H	Recalibrate Drive		x
15H	Get Disk Type	x	x
16H	Get Floppy Disk Change Status	x	
17H	Set Floppy Disk Type	x	
18H	Set Media Type for Format	x	
19H	Park Heads		x
1AH	Format ESDI Unit		x

Figure 10-1. *The BIOS disk services.*

Service 00H (decimal 0): Reset Disk System

Service 00H (decimal 0) resets the disk controller and drive. This service does not affect the disk media itself. Instead, a reset through service 00H forces the BIOS disk-support routines to start from scratch for the next disk operation by recalibrating the disk drive's read/write head—an operation that positions the head on track zero. This reset service is normally used after an error in any other drive operation.

When you call service 00H for a hard disk drive, the BIOS also resets the floppy disk–drive controller. If you want to reset the hard disk controller only, use service 0DH. (See page 280.)

Be sure to look at the discussion of disk-base tables on page 282 for the effect of the disk-base table on the reset operation.

Service 01H (decimal 1): Get Disk Status

Service 01H (decimal 1) reports the disk status in register AH. The status is preserved after each disk operation, including the read, write, verify, and format operations. By preserving the disk status, an error-handling or error-reporting routine can be completely independent of the routines that operate the disk. This can be quite useful. Under the right circumstances, you can rely on MS-DOS or your programming language to drive the disk (a wise choice; see ''Comments and Examples'' on page 284), and at the same time have your program find out and report the details of what went wrong. See Figure 10-2 for details about the status byte.

Value (Hex)	Meaning	Value (Hex)	Meaning
00H	No error	08H	DMA overrun (F)
01H	Bad command	09H	DMA across 64-KB boundary
02H	Address mark not found	0AH	Bad sector flag (H)
03H	Write attempted on write-protected disk (F)	0BH	Bad track (H)
		0CH	Bad media type (F)
04H	Sector not found	0DH	Invalid number of sectors on format (H)
05H	Reset failed (H)	0EH	Control data address mark detected (H)
06H	Floppy disk removed (F)	0FH	DMA arbitration level out of range (H)
07H	Bad parameter table (H)	10H	Bad CRC or ECC

(H) = hard disk only
(F) = floppy disk only

Figure 10-2. *The value of the disk status byte returned in register AH by service 01H.* *(continued)*

Figure 10-2. *continued*

Value (Hex)	Meaning	Value (Hex)	Meaning
11H	ECC corrected data error (h)	BBH	Undefined error (H)
20H	Controller failed	CCH	Write fault (H)
40H	Seek failed	E0H	Status error (H)
80H	Time out	FFH	Sense operation failed (H)
AAH	Drive not ready (H)		

Service 02H (decimal 2): Read Disk Sectors

Service 02H (decimal 2) reads one or more disk sectors into memory. If you want to read more than one sector, every sector must be on the same track and read/write head. This is largely because the BIOS doesn't know how many sectors might be on a track, so it can't know when to switch from one head or track to another. Usually this service is used for reading either individual sectors or an entire trackful of sectors for bulk operations such as DISKCOPY in MS-DOS. Various registers are used for control information in a read operation. They are summarized in Figure 10-3.

Parameters	Status Results
DL = drive number	If CF = 0, then no error and AH = 0,
DH = head number	AL = number of sectors used
CH = cylinder number (F) low-order 8 bits of cylinder number (H)	If CF = 1, then error and AH contains service 01H status bits
CL = sector number (F) high-order 2 bits of cylinder number plus 6-bit sector number (H)	
AL = number of sectors to be read, written, verified, or formatted	
ES:BX = address of buffer	

(H) = hard disk only
(F) = floppy disk only

Figure 10-3. *The registers used for control information by the read, write, verify, and format services.*

DL contains the drive number, and **DH** contains the read/write head number.

CH and **CL** identify, for floppy disks, the cylinder and sector numbers to be read. CH contains the cylinder number, which should be less than the total number of cylinders on the formatted floppy disk. (See Chapter 5 for a table of standard IBM formats.) Of course, the cylinder number can be higher with non-IBM formats or with some copy-protection schemes. CL contains the sector number.

For hard disks, there might be more than 256 cylinders, so the BIOS requires you to specify a 10-bit cylinder number in CH and CL. You must place the 8 low-order bits of the cylinder number in CH. The 2 high-order bits of CL contain bits 8 and 9 (relative to zero) of the cylinder number. For Award AT BIOS and AMI BIOS, if there are more than 1024 cylinders on the hard disk, bits 10 and 11 of the cylinder number are stored in the high-order 2 bits of DH. The 6 low-order bits of CL designate the sector number to be read. Don't forget that sectors are numbered from 1, unlike drives, cylinders, or heads (sides).

AL contains the number of sectors to be read. For floppy disks, this is normally 1, 8, 9, 15, 18, or 36. We are warned by IBM not to request 0 sectors.

ES:BX contains the buffer location. The location of the memory area where the data will be placed is provided by a segmented address given in this register pair.

The data area should be big enough to accommodate as much as is read; keep in mind that although normal MS-DOS sectors are 512 bytes, sectors can be as large as 1024 bytes. (See service 05H on page 276.) When this service reads more than one sector, it lays out the sectors in memory one right after another.

CF (the carry flag) contains the error status of the operation. The result of the operation is actually reported through a combination of the carry flag and the AH register. If CF = 0, no error occurred, AH will also be 0, and, for a floppy disk, the number of sectors read will be returned in AL. If CF = 1, an error did occur, and AH will contain the status value detailed under service 01H, the status service.

When you use any other floppy disk service, remember that the disk-drive motor takes some time to reach a working speed and that none of these services waits for this to happen. Although our own experience with the BIOS floppy disk services suggests that this is rarely a problem, IBM recommends that any program using these services try three times before assuming an error is real and that the reset service be used between tries.

The logic (partly expressed in Basic) is as follows:

```
10 ERROR. COUNT = 0
20 WHILE ERROR.COUNT < 3
30 ' do read/write/verify/format operation
40 ' error checking here: if no error goto 90
50   ERROR.COUNT = ERROR.COUNT + 1
60 ' do reset operation
70 WEND
80 ' act on error
90 ' carry on after success
```

Service 03H (decimal 3): Write Disk Sectors

Service 03H (decimal 3) writes one or more sectors to a disk—the reverse of service 02H. All registers, details, and comments given for service 02H also apply to service 03H. (Also see Figure 10-3.) The disk sectors must be formatted before they can be written to.

Service 04H (decimal 4): Verify Disk Sectors

Service 04H (decimal 4) verifies the contents of one or more disk sectors. This operation is not what many people think it is: No comparison is made between the data on the disk and the data in memory. This service simply checks that the sectors can be found and read and that the cyclical redundancy check (CRC) is correct. The CRC acts as a sophisticated parity check for the data in each sector and reliably detects most errors, such as lost or scrambled bits.

Most programmers use the verify service to check the results of a write operation after using service 03H, but you can verify any part of a disk at any time. The MS-DOS FORMAT program, for example, verifies each track after it is formatted. However, many people regard verification as an unnecessary operation because disk drives are so reliable and because ordinary error reporting works so well. Even MS-DOS doesn't verify a write operation unless you ask it to with the VERIFY ON command.

> NOTE: *It's worth pausing to mention that there is nothing unusual or alarming about having "bad tracks" marked on a disk, particularly a hard disk. In fact, it is quite common for a hard disk to have a few bad patches on it. The MS-DOS FORMAT program notices bad tracks and marks them as such in the disk's file allocation table. Later the marking tells MS-DOS that these areas should be bypassed. Bad tracks are also common on floppy disks; with floppy disks, however, you have the option of throwing away the defective media.*

The verify service operates exactly as do the read and write services, and it uses the same registers. The only difference between them is that the verify operation does not use any memory area and therefore does not use the register pair ES:BX.

Service 05H (decimal 5): Format Disk Track

Service 05H (decimal 5) formats one track. The format service operates as do the read and write services except that you need not specify a sector number in CL. All other parameters are as shown in Figure 10-3.

Because formatting is done one full track at a time, you cannot format individual sectors. However, on a floppy disk you can specify individual characteristics for each sector on a track.

Every sector on a floppy disk track has 4 descriptive bytes associated with it. You specify how the 4 bytes for each sector are to be formatted by creating a table of 4-byte groups and passing the table's address in the register pair ES:BX. When you format a disk track, the 4-byte groups are written to the disk immediately in front of the individual sectors on the track. The 4 bytes of data associated with a sector on the disk are known as *address marks* and are used by the disk controller to identify individual sectors during the read, write, and verify operations. The 4 bytes are referred to as C for cylinder, H for head, R for record (or sector number), and N for number of bytes per sector (also called the *size code*).

When a sector is being read or written to, the floppy disk controller searches the disk track for the sector's ID, the essential part of which is R, the record or sector number. The cylinder and head parameters are not actually needed in this address mark because the read/write head is positioned mechanically at the proper track and the side is selected electronically, but they are recorded and tested as a safety check.

The size code (N) can take on any one of the four standard values shown in Figure 10-4. The normal setting is code 2 (512 bytes).

N	Sector Size (Bytes)	Sector Size (KB)
0	128	1/8
1	256	1/4
2	512	1/2
3	1024	1

Figure 10-4. *The four standard sizes of the N size code.*

Sectors are numbered on the disk in the order specified by R. On floppy disks the sectors are normally numbered in numeric sequence (unless rearranged for copy protection), but on hard disks the order of the sectors can be rearranged (interleaved) either for better performance or to create timing differences for copy-protection purposes. The interleave used on a hard disk depends on the capabilities of the disk-controller hardware. For example, the PC/XT's hard disk has its sectors interleaved so that logically consecutive sectors are physically located six sectors apart.

To format a floppy disk track by using service 05H, you perform the following steps:

1. Call service 17H to inform the BIOS what kind of floppy disk is to be formatted. (See page 281 for more about service 17H.) This service needs to be called only once for each disk being formatted.

2. Call service 18H to describe the disk media to the BIOS. (See page 281 for more about service 18H.)

3. Create a table of address marks for the track. There must be a 4-byte entry in the table for each sector. For example, for track 0, side 1 of a typical nine-sector MS-DOS disk, the table would contain nine entries:

    0 1 1 2   0 1 2 2   0 1 3 2   ...   0 1 9 2

4. Call service 05H to format the track.

The method for formatting a hard disk track is somewhat different. You should omit the calls to services 17H and 18H (steps 1 and 2 in the previous list) because there is no need to describe the disk media to the BIOS. Also, with a PC/AT or a PS/2, the table whose address you pass in step 3 has a format that consists only of a flag byte (00H = good sector, 80H = bad sector) and a sector number (R) byte, one pair for each sector. With a PC/XT, you don't need a table at all. Instead, you call service 05H with an interleave value in AL, and the BIOS does the rest.

You might want to verify the formatting process by following each call to service 05H with a call to service 04H.

When a floppy disk track is formatted, the disk drive pays attention to the disk's index hole and uses it as a starting marker to format the track. The index hole is ignored in all other operations (read, write, or verify), and tracks are simply searched for by their address marks.

Nothing in this format service specifies the initial data value written to each formatted sector of a disk. That is controlled by the disk-base table. (See page 282.)

NOTE: *Service 05H should not be used with ESDI drives. Use service 1AH instead.*

Using service 05H for copy protection

Floppy disk tracks can be formatted in all sorts of ways, but MS-DOS can read only certain formats. Consequently, some copy-protection schemes are based on an unconventional format that prevents the operating system from successfully reading and copying data. You can choose from several copy-protection methods:

- You can rearrange the order of the sectors, which alters the access time in a way that the copy-protection scheme can detect.

- You can squeeze more sectors onto a track. (Ten is about the outside limit for 512-byte sectors on a 360-KB disk.)

- You can simply leave out a sector number.

- You can add a sector with an oddball address mark. For example, you can make C = 95 or R = 42.

- You can specify one or more sectors to be an unconventional size.

Any of these techniques can be used either for copy protection or for changing the operating characteristics of the disk. Depending on what options are used, a conventionally formatted disk can have its copy-protection characteristics hidden from MS-DOS.

Service 06H (decimal 6): Format PC/XT Bad Disk Track

Service 06H (decimal 6) is provided only in the PC/XT hard disk BIOS. This service commands the XT's hard disk controller to format a track in which the disk media is defective. The disk controller records which sectors are defective in a table located in a reserved cylinder. The register parameters are the same as those shown in Figure 10-3, except that register AL contains a sector interleave value, and no address need be specified in ES:BX.

Service 07H (decimal 7): Format PC/XT Hard Disk

Service 07H (decimal 7), like service 06H, is supported only in the PC/XT hard disk BIOS. It formats the entire hard disk drive, starting at the cylinder number specified in CH and CL. Register parameters for service 07H are the same as for service 05H except that register AL contains a sector interleave value, and no head number need be specified in register DH. (Also see Figure 10-3.) Note that if the Award AT BIOS or the AMI BIOS is installed and the drive supports more than 1024 cylinders, bits 10 and 11 of the cylinder number will be stored in the high-order bits of DH.

Service 08H (decimal 8): Get Disk-Drive Parameters

Except for the PC/XT BIOS, service 08H (decimal 8) returns disk-drive parameters for the drive whose number you specify in DL. DL reports the number of disk drives attached to the disk controller, so floppy disk and hard disk drive counts are reported separately. DH reports the maximum head number, CH returns the maximum cylinder number, and CL returns the highest valid sector number plus the 2 high-order bits of the maximum cylinder number.

For floppy disk drives, the PC/AT BIOS (after January 10, 1984) and the PS/2 BIOS also report the drive type in BL: 01H = 360-KB, 5.25-inch; 02H = 1.2-MB, 5.25-inch; 03H = 720-KB, 3.5-inch; 04H = 1.44-MB, 3.5-inch; and 06H = 2.88-MB, 3.5-inch.

Service 09H (decimal 9): Initialize Hard Disk Parameter Tables

Service 09H (decimal 9) establishes the disk-base tables for two hard disk drives. You call this service with a valid hard disk–drive number in DL and with the interrupt 41H and 46H vectors containing the addresses of disk-base tables for two different hard disk drives. If DL = 80, interrupt 41H vector is used; if DL = 81, interrupt 46H vector is used. (The PC/XT BIOS applies the data in the table addressed by the interrupt 41H vector to both drives; no reference is made to the interrupt 46H vector.) Because hard disks are nonremovable, this service should be used only to install a ''foreign'' disk drive not recognized by the BIOS or by the operating system. For more details, see the *IBM BIOS Interface Technical Reference Manual*.

NOTE: *Do not use service 09H for ESDI drives.*

Services 0AH and 0BH (decimals 10 and 11): Read and Write Long

Service 0AH (decimal 10) reads, and service 0BH (decimal 11) writes, *long sectors* on PC/AT or PS/2 hard disks. A long sector consists of a sector of data plus a 4-byte or 6-byte error-correction code (ECC) that the hard disk controller uses for error checking and error correction of the sector's data. These services use the same register parameters as do parallel services 02H and 03H.

NOTE: *The* IBM BIOS Interface Technical Reference Manual *states that services 0AH and 0BH are ''reserved for diagnostics,'' so avoid these services unless you have a good reason for using them.*

Service 0CH (decimal 12): Seek to Cylinder

Service 0CH (decimal 12) performs a seek operation that positions the disk read/write heads at a particular cylinder on a hard disk. Register DL provides the drive ID, register DH provides the head number, and registers CH and CL provide the 10-bit cylinder number.

Service 0DH (decimal 13): Alternate Hard Disk Reset

For hard disk drives, service 0DH (decimal 13) is the same as service 00H (Reset Disk System) except that the BIOS does not automatically reset the floppy disk–drive controller. This service is not available in the PC/XT BIOS; it should not be used with ESDI drives.

Service 10H (decimal 16): Test for Drive Ready

Service 10H (decimal 16) tests to see if a hard disk drive is ready. The drive is specified in register DL, and the status is returned in register AH.

Service 11H (decimal 17): Recalibrate Drive

Service 11H (decimal 17) recalibrates a hard disk drive. The drive is specified in register DL, and the status is returned in register AH.

Service 15H (decimal 21): Get Disk Type

Except for the PC and early PC/XT BIOS, service 15H (decimal 21) returns information about the type of disk drive installed. Given the drive ID in register DL, it returns in register AH one of four disk-type indicators. If AH = 00H, no drive is present for the specified drive ID; if AH = 01H, a floppy disk drive that cannot sense when the disk has been changed is installed; if AH = 02H, a floppy disk drive that can sense a change of disks (drives such as the AT's high-capacity disk drives) is installed; finally, if AH = 03H, a hard disk drive is installed. When the drive type is 3, the register pair CX:DX contains a 4-byte integer that indicates the total number of disk sectors on the drive.

Service 16H (decimal 22): Get Floppy Disk Change Status

In the BIOS, on most machines that use an 80286, 80386, or 80486 processor, service 16H (decimal 22) reports whether the floppy disk in the drive specified in DL was changed. The status is reported in AH. (See Figure 10-5.)

There are several important points to keep in mind about service 16H. Before you use this BIOS service, call service 15H to ensure that the floppy disk–drive hardware can sense when a disk is changed. You should follow a call to service 16H with a call to service 17H (Set Floppy Disk Type) whenever you detect a disk change.

Keep in mind that the hardware can detect only whether the disk-drive door was opened; it cannot tell whether a different disk was placed in the drive. You must still read data from the disk to determine whether a different floppy disk is in the drive. Data such as a volume label, the volume serial number, the root directory, or a file allocation table can help to uniquely identify a disk.

Value	Meaning
AH = 00H	No floppy disk change.
AH = 01H	Service called with invalid parameter.
AH = 06H	Floppy disk has been changed.
AH = 80H	Floppy disk drive not ready.

Figure 10-5. *Status values returned in AH by floppy disk service 16H.*

Service 17H (decimal 23): Set Floppy Disk Type

In the PC/AT and PS/2 BIOS, service 17H (decimal 23) describes the type of floppy disk in use in a specified drive. You call this service with a drive ID in register DL and a floppy disk–type ID in register AL. (See Figure 10-6.) The BIOS resets the disk change status if it was previously set. It then records the disk type in an internal status variable that can be referenced by other BIOS services.

Notice that for AL = 04H, there is no means of distinguishing the disk type or even the disk capacity. Further, this service does not support 2.88-MB drives. Therefore, it is recommended that service 18H be used for all 3.5-inch disks and drives.

Value	Meaning
AL = 01H	320/360-KB disk in 360-KB drive
AL = 02H	360-KB disk in 1.2-MB drive
AL = 03H	1.2-MB disk in 1.2-MB drive
AL = 04H	720-KB disk in 720-KB drive (PC/AT or PS/2), or 720-KB or 1.44-MB disk in 1.44-MB drive (PS/2)

Figure 10-6. *Disk-type ID values for floppy disk service 17H.*

Service 18H (decimal 24): Set Media Type for Format

Service 18H (decimal 24) describes the number of tracks and sectors per track to the BIOS before it formats a floppy disk in a specified drive. These values are placed in registers CH, CL, and DL when you call this service. (See Figure 10-3.) This service is available only in the PC/AT and PS/2 BIOS.

Service 19H (decimal 25): Park Heads

Service 19H (decimal 25) parks the drive heads for the PS/2 hard disk whose drive ID you specify in register DL. Calling this function causes the disk controller to move the drive heads away from the portion of the disk media where data is stored. This is a good idea if you plan to move the computer because it can prevent mechanical damage to the heads or to the surfaces of the disk media. On the Reference Diskette that accompanies every PS/2, IBM supplies a utility program that uses this BIOS service to park the heads.

Service 1AH (decimal 26): Format ESDI Unit

This service is provided only in the BIOS of the ESDI (Enhanced Small Device Interface) adapter for high-capacity PS/2 hard disks. It formats a hard disk attached to this adapter. See the *IBM BIOS Interface Technical Reference Manual* for details.

Disk-Base Tables

As we mentioned near the beginning of this chapter, the BIOS maintains a set of disk-base tables that describe the capabilities of each floppy disk drive and hard disk drive in the computer. During system start-up, the BIOS associates an appropriate disk-base table with each hard disk drive. (In the PC/AT and PS/2s, a data byte in the nonvolatile CMOS RAM designates which of several ROM tables to use.) There is no reason to change the parameters in the hard disk tables after they have been set up by the BIOS. Doing so might lead to garbled data on the disk.

The situation is different in the case of floppy disk drives. The parameters in the disk-base table associated with a floppy disk drive might need to be updated to accommodate different disk formats. We spend the next few pages describing the structure of a disk-base table for a floppy disk drive and showing how a modified table can be useful.

The disk-base table comprises the 11 bytes shown in Figure 10-7.

Bytes 0 and 1 are referred to as the *specify bytes*. They are part of the command strings sent to the floppy disk–drive controller, which in IBM's technical reference manuals is also called the *NEC* (Nippon Electric Company) *controller*. The 4 high-order bits of byte 0 specify the *step-rate time* (SRT), which is the time the drive controller allows for the drive heads to move from track to track. The default BIOS SRT value for floppy disk drives is conservative; for some drives, MS-DOS reduces this value to speed up drive performance.

Offset	Use
00H	Specify byte 1: step-rate time, head-unload time
01H	Specify byte 2: head-load time, DMA mode
02H	Wait time until floppy disk motor turned off
03H	Bytes per sector: 0 = 128; 1 = 256; 2 = 512; 3 = 1024
04H	Last sector number
05H	Gap length between sectors for read/write operations
06H	Data length when sector length not specified
07H	Gap length between sectors for formatting operations
08H	Data value stored in formatted sectors
09H	Head-settle time
0AH	Motor start-up time

Figure 10-7. *The use of the 11 bytes in the disk-base table for a floppy disk drive.*

Byte 2 specifies how long the disk motor is to be left running after each operation. The motor is left on in case the disk is needed again. The value is in units of clock ticks. (There are roughly 18.2 clock ticks per second.) All versions of the table have this set to 37 (25H)—meaning that the motor stays on for about 2 seconds.

Byte 3 gives the sector length code—the same N code that is used in the format operation. (See service 05H, page 276.) This is normally set to 2, which represents the customary sector length of 512 bytes. In any read, write, or verify operation, the length code in the disk base must be set to the proper value, especially when working with sectors of unconventional length.

Byte 4 gives the sector number of the last sector on the track.

Byte 5 specifies the gap length between sectors, which is used when reading or writing data. In effect, it tells the floppy disk–drive controller how long to wait before looking for the next sector's address marking so that it can avoid looking at nonsense on the disk. This length of time is known as the *search gap*.

Byte 6 is called the *data transfer length* (DTL) and is set to FFH (decimal 255). This byte sets the maximum data length when the sector length is not specified.

Byte 7 sets the gap length between sectors when a track is formatted. Naturally the format gap is bigger than the search gap at offset 05H. The normal format gap-length value varies with the floppy disk drive. For example, the value is 54H for the PC/AT's 1.2-MB drive and 6CH for 3.5-inch PS/2 floppy disk drives.

Byte 8 provides the data value stored in each byte of the sectors when a floppy disk track is formatted. The default value is F6H, the division symbol. You can change the value to anything you want if you can think of a good reason to do so.

Byte 9 sets the *head-settle* time, which is how long the system waits for vibration to end after seeking to a new track. This value also depends on the drive hardware. On the original PC, the value was 19H (25 milliseconds), but the BIOS default for the PC/AT 1.2-MB drive and the PS/2 floppy disk drives is only 0FH (15 milliseconds).

Byte 0AH (decimal 10), the final byte of the disk-base table, sets the amount of time allowed for the floppy disk–drive motor to get up to speed; it is measured in eighths of a second.

It's fun to tinker with the disk-base values; there are enough of them to give you an opportunity for all sorts of excitement and mischief. To do this, you need to write a program that builds your customized disk-base table in a buffer in memory. Then tell the BIOS to use your table by carrying out the following steps:

1. Save the segmented address of the current disk-base table. (This is the value in the interrupt 1EH vector, 0000:0078H.)

2. Store the segmented address of your modified table in the interrupt 1EH vector.

3. Call BIOS disk service 00H to reset the disk system. The BIOS will reinitialize the floppy disk–drive controller by using parameters from your table.

When you've finished, be sure to restore the address of the previous disk-base table and reset the disk system.

Comments and Examples

In Chapter 11, where we cover the BIOS video services, we recommend that you make direct use of the BIOS services when MS-DOS or your programming language does not provide the support you need. But in the case of the BIOS disk services, our advice is different.

For the disk operations that a program would normally want performed, the manipulation and supervision of disk input/output should be left to MS-DOS and performed either by using the conventional file services of a programming language or by using the MS-DOS services. There are several reasons for this. The main reason is that it is far easier to let MS-DOS do the work. The MS-DOS facilities take care of all fundamental disk operations, including formatting and labeling disks, cataloging files, and performing basic read and write operations. Most of the time it isn't necessary to go any deeper into the system software. However, there are times when you might want to work with disk data in an absolute and precise way, usually for copy protection. This is when you should use the BIOS services.

For our example, we use C to call a couple of subroutines that use BIOS functions 02H and 03H to read and write absolute disk sectors. We start by defining how we want the interface to look from the C side, which the following program illustrates. If you are not familiar with C and don't want to decipher this routine, you can pass it by and study the assembly language interface example that follows it without missing any information.

```
main()
{
        unsigned char Buffer[512];      /* a 512-byte buffer for reading */
                                        /*  or writing one sector */

        int     Drive;
        int     C,H,R;                  /* address mark parameters */
        int     StatusCode;             /* status value returned by BIOS */

        StatusCode = ReadSector( Drive, C, H, R, (char far *)Buffer );
        StatusCode = WriteSector( Drive, C, H, R, (char far *)Buffer );

}
```

This C fragment shows how you would call the BIOS read and write services from a high-level language. The functions *ReadSector()* and *WriteSector()* are two assembly language routines that use interrupt 13H to interface with the BIOS disk services. The parameters are familiar: C, H, and R are the cylinder, head, and sector numbers we described earlier. The C compiler passes the buffer address as a segment and offset because of the explicit type cast (char far *).

The form of the assembly language interface should be familiar if you read the general remarks in Chapter 9 on page 235 or looked ahead to the example in Chapter 11 on page 355. The assembly language routines themselves copy the parameters from the stack into the registers. The trick is in how the cylinder number is processed: The 2 high-order bits of the 10-bit cylinder number are combined with the 6-bit sector number in CL.

```
_TEXT           SEGMENT byte public 'CODE'
                ASSUME  cs:_TEXT
```

(continued)

```
                PUBLIC  _ReadSector
ReadSector      PROC    near            ; routine to read one sector

                push    bp
                mov     bp,sp           ; address the stack through BP

                mov     ah,2            ; AH = BIOS service number 02h
                call    DiskService

                pop     bp              ; restore previous BP
                ret

_ReadSector     ENDP


                PUBLIC  _WriteSector
_WriteSector    PROC    near            ; routine to write one sector

                push    bp
                mov     bp,sp

                mov     ah,3            ; AH = BIOS service number 03h
                call    DiskService

                pop     bp
                ret

_WriteSector    ENDP

DiskService     PROC    near            ; call with AH = BIOS service number

                push    ax              ; save service number on stack
                mov     dl,[bp+4]       ; DL = drive ID
                mov     ax,[bp+6]       ; AX = cylinder number
                mov     dh,[bp+8]       ; DH = head number
                mov     cl,[bp+10]      ; CL = sector number
                and     cl,00111111b    ; limit sector number to 6 bits
                les     bx,[bp+12]      ; ES:BX -> buffer

                ror     ah,1            ; move bits 8 and 9
                ror     ah,1            ;  of cylinder number
                                        ;  to bits 6 and 7 of AH
                and     ah,11000000b
                mov     ch,al           ; CH = bits 0-7 of cylinder number
                or      cl,ah           ; copy bits 8 and 9
                                        ;  of cylinder number
                                        ;  to bits 6 and 7 of CL
```

```
            pop     ax              ; AH = BIOS service number
            mov     al,1            ; AL = 1 (# of sectors to read/write)
            int     13h             ; call BIOS service

            mov     al,ah           ; leave return status
            xor     ah,ah           ; # in AX

            ret

DiskService ENDP

_TEXT       ENDS
```

Note how the code that copies the parameters from the stack to the registers is consolidated in a subroutine, *DiskService*. When you work with the BIOS disk services, you'll find that you can often use subroutines similar to *DiskService* because most of the BIOS disk services use similar parameter register assignments.

The MS-DOS Disk Services

When MS-DOS 1.0 was introduced, PCs had no hard disk drives and, at most, two floppy disk drives. There was no need to deal with large numbers of files or to navigate among subdirectories. The disk services that were part of MS-DOS version 1.0 were perfectly adequate for the available hardware. These services are called the *file control block* services because they utilize an area of memory, the file control block (FCB), that is used to pass file-related information back and forth between a program and MS-DOS.

With the introduction of the PC/XT and its hard disk, there was a need for more sophisticated file manipulation functions. MS-DOS 2.0 provided the required functionality with the *handle* functions. These disk functions are independent of the FCB functions, and they provide a number of significant advantages:

- They support the hierarchical directory structure.

- They make it unnecessary for programs to devote memory to file information.

- They support file locking, file sharing, and record locking in network environments.

- They support input and output redirection.

- They offer superior error handling and reporting.

287

In versions prior to MS-DOS version 4.0, the handle functions have a few minor disadvantages, however. With MS-DOS versions 2.0 through 3.2, a program can have a maximum of 20 files open at once by using the handle functions. In versions 2.0 through 3.3, some tasks, such as changing a disk's volume label or directly accessing directory information, require the use of the FCB functions. Starting with MS-DOS version 4.0, all the FCB functions have been superseded by handle functions.

MS-DOS versions 2.0 and later include support for both sets of disk functions. If you want to use MS-DOS functions for disk access, you should use the handle functions. It's a good idea to be familiar with the FCB functions, however, because you might occasionally need to use them in support of an older version of MS-DOS.

The FCB Functions

To use the FCB functions, a program must allocate memory space for one FCB for each file to be opened. A program uses the fields in the FCB to pass information to the FCB functions, and the FCB functions use these fields to pass information back to a program. There is also a memory region, the *disk transfer area* (DTA), that is used as a temporary holding area for the data being written to and read from a file. You need to understand the FCB and DTA in order to use the FCB functions.

The structure of the FCB

The normal FCB is a 37-byte data structure that contains a variety of information MS-DOS can use to control file input/output. (See Figure 10-8.) A 44-byte, extended FCB is used by some MS-DOS functions: 7 bytes are tacked onto the beginning of the normal FCB data structure. (See Figure 10-9.)

The use of the FCB extension is more than a little peculiar. The extension is used only when you work with the attribute field in a directory entry in which read-only files, hidden files, system files, volume labels, and subdirectories are identified. In general, you need to use extended FCBs only if you are performing directory searches or otherwise working with directory entries rather than with the contents of files. However, all FCB-based functions recognize the extended FCB format if you should choose to use it.

With two exceptions, all fields in an extended FCB are identical to those in a normal FCB. Only the offsets are different: In an extended FCB, the offset of a particular field is 7 bytes greater than the offset of the same field in a normal FCB.

Offset			
Hex	Dec	Field Width	Description
00H	0	1	Drive identifier
01H	1	8	Filename
09H	9	3	File extension
0CH	12	2	Current-block number
0EH	14	2	Record size in bytes
10H	16	4	File size in bytes
14H	20	2	Date
16H	22	2	Time
18H	24	8	(Reserved)
20H	32	1*	Current-record number
21H	33	4	Random-record number

*Only the low-order 7 bits are used.

Figure 10-8. *The structure of a normal file control block.*

Offset			
Hex	Dec	Field Width	Description
00H	0	1	Extended FCB flag (always FFH)
01H	1	5	(Reserved)
06H	6	1	Attribute
07H	7	1	Drive identifier
08H	8	8	Filename
10H	16	3	File extension
13H	19	2	Current-block number
15H	21	2	Record size in bytes
17H	23	4	File size in bytes
1BH	27	2	Date
1DH	29	2	Time
1FH	31	8	(Reserved)
27H	39	1*	Current-record number
28H	40	4	Random-record number

*Only the low-order 7 bits are used.

Figure 10-9. *The structure of an extended file control block. The first three fields distinguish this data structure from a normal FCB.*

The following sections describe the fields in normal FCBs.

Offset 00H (decimal 0). The first field in a normal (nonextended) FCB is the *disk-drive identifier*. Values for the drive identifier start at 1; a value of 1 indicates drive A, a value of 2 indicates drive B, and so on. If this field contains 0 at the time an FCB is opened, MS-DOS uses the current default drive and updates this field with the corresponding drive identifier.

Offsets 01H and **09H (decimals 1 and 9).** The two fields at offsets 01H and 09H contain an 8-byte name and a 3-byte extension. These fields are left justified and padded on the right with blanks. Following MS-DOS convention, either uppercase or lowercase letters may be used. If the filename is a device name that MS-DOS recognizes, such as CON, AUX, COM1, COM2, LPT1, LPT2, LPT3, PRN, or NUL, MS-DOS will use that device rather than a disk file.

> NOTE: *This is a reasonably good place to point out that the FCB mechanism has no provision for working with pathnames. When you use FCBs, they always apply to the current directory in any drive. For flexible use of paths and subdirectories, see the new, extended functions described later in this chapter.*

Offsets 0CH and **20H (decimals 12 and 32).** For sequential file operations, the current-block and current-record fields keep track of the location in the file. The use of these fields is rather odd. Instead of using one integrated record number, the record number is divided into a high portion and a low portion, which are referred to as the *block number* and the *record number*. The record number is a 7-bit value, so record numbers range from 0 through 127. Thus, the first record in a file is block 0, record 0; the 128th record is block 1, record 0.

Before you use the sequential read and write functions 14H and 15H, be sure to initialize the current-block and current-record fields to the desired starting location in the file.

Offset 0EH (decimal 14). The record-size field contains a 2-byte value that specifies the size, in bytes, of the logical records in the file. When MS-DOS reads or writes a record, the *logical size* of the record is the number of bytes transferred between MS-DOS's disk buffers and the DTA.

The same file data can be worked on by using a variety of record sizes. When a file is opened by using function 0FH or 16H, MS-DOS sets the record size to 128 bytes by default. If you want another size, such as 1 for single-byte operations, you must change the record-size field *after* the file is opened.

Offset 10H (decimal 16). The file-size field at offset 10H indicates the file size in bytes. The value is taken from a file's directory entry and is placed in the FCB when MS-DOS opens the file. For an output file, this field is changed by MS-DOS as the file grows. When the file is closed, the value is copied from the FCB to the file's directory entry.

By changing this field, you can gain some last-minute control over the size of an output file, but be careful when doing this. You can, for example, truncate a file you have updated by decreasing the file-size value in this field. Also, be careful not to use function 17H to rename an open file: This function requires that you specify the file's new name in the same part of the FCB used for the file size.

Offsets 14H and **16H (decimals 20 and 22).** The 2-byte fields at offset 14H (date) and offset 16H (time) record when a file was last updated. These fields use the same format as the corresponding fields in a directory entry. (See Chapter 5.) The initial values in these fields are copied from a file's directory entry when the file is opened. They are subsequently updated each time you write to the file. If the file is updated, MS-DOS copies the values from the FCB to the directory entry when the file is closed.

Offset 21H (decimal 33). The random-record field is used during random read and write operations, exactly as the current-record and current-block numbers are used during sequential operations. This 4-byte field is in the form of a 32-bit integer. Records are numbered from 0, which makes it easy to calculate the file offset to any record by multiplying the random-record number by the record size. You must set this field before any random file operation. MS-DOS leaves it undisturbed.

An extended file control block has three additional fields not found in a normal FCB:

- The first field of an extended FCB is a flag byte whose contents must be FFH. MS-DOS distinguishes between normal and extended FCBs by examining this byte. (In a normal FCB, the first field is the disk-drive identifier, which should never be FFH.)

- Offset 01H through 05H are reserved bytes.

- Offset 06H in an extended FCB is a 1-byte field that consists of an attribute byte whose bits signify file, volume label, and subdirectory attributes. This byte's format is identical to the attribute byte in a directory entry. (See Chapter 5.)

NOTE: *One rare situation in which you would use FCB-based functions instead of handle-based functions is when you work with a disk's volume label in versions of MS-DOS prior to version 4.0. MS-DOS versions 2.0 through 3.3 do not provide any special services for manipulating a volume label. You must use function 16H with an extended FCB to create a volume label, function 17H to rename it, and function 13H to delete it. In MS-DOS versions 4.0 and later, subfunctions at interrupt 21H, function 440DH are used.*

The DTA

The FCB disk functions use the disk transfer area, or DTA. This is a region of memory that serves as a buffer between an application program and a disk. To write data to a disk, you place the data in the DTA and then call one of the FCB disk write functions, which reads the data from the DTA and writes it to the disk. In a similar fashion, FCB disk-read functions read data from the disk and place it in the DTA, where the program can access it. (A couple of the handle-based disk functions also use the DTA; this is covered later in the chapter.)

MS-DOS provides a default DTA in the program segment prefix (PSP), a reserved area of memory that is set up whenever MS-DOS loads and executes a program. (Please refer to Chapter 9 for details on the PSP.) This default DTA is 128 bytes in size, which is sufficient for most disk operations. Your program need take no special action to use the default DTA; the FCB functions automatically use it. If your program requires a DTA larger than 128 bytes, it must explicitly allocate the buffer space and then take these steps:

1. Obtain the current DTA address by calling interrupt 21H, function 2FH.

2. Inform MS-DOS of the new DTA address by calling interrupt 21H, function 1AH.

3. Before terminating, restore the original DTA address with another call to interrupt 21H, function 1AH.

Figure 10-10 summarizes the MS-DOS FCB functions, and the following section provides a full description of each function.

Function 0FH (decimal 15): Open File

Function 0FH (decimal 15) opens a file by using a file control block (FCB). An FCB is a data structure used by MS-DOS to track input and output for a particular file. Among other information, an FCB contains a file's name and disk-drive number. (See page 288 in this chapter for details on the contents of FCBs.)

| Function | | |
Hex	Dec	Description
0FH	15	Open File
10H	16	Close File
11H	17	Find First Matching Directory Entry
12H	18	Find Next Matching Directory Entry
13H	19	Delete File
14H	20	Sequential Read
15H	21	Sequential Write
16H	22	Create File
17H	23	Rename File
21H	33	Read Random Record
22H	34	Write Random Record
23H	35	Get File Size
24H	36	Set FCB Random-Record Field
27H	39	Read Random Records
28H	40	Write Random Records
29H	41	Parse Filename

Figure 10-10. *The FCB functions. All are called by placing the function number in register AH and then calling interrupt 21H.*

NOTE: *Function 0FH is one of several MS-DOS functions that use an FCB to track file input and output. However, you should avoid the MS-DOS functions that use FCBs because these functions were made obsolete by the more powerful handle-based file functions introduced in MS-DOS version 2.0. Furthermore, unlike handle-based functions, FCB-based functions are not supported in OS/2 protected mode. Use the FCB-based functions only if compatibility with MS-DOS version 1 is important.*

To use an FCB to open a file, you must reserve memory for the FCB and place the file's name and disk-drive number in the proper fields in the data structure. Then you call function 0FH with the segmented address of the FCB in the register pair DS:DX. MS-DOS attempts to open the file, using the drive and filename you specified in the FCB. If the file is opened, AL = 00H; if the file cannot be opened, AL = FFH.

If the file is opened successfully, MS-DOS initializes several fields in the FCB, including the date and time fields and the logical record-size field (which is set to 128). You can either use this record size or change it, depending on your application.

Function 10H (decimal 16): Close File

Function 10H (decimal 16) closes a file and updates the file's directory entry. You call this function with the segmented address of the file's FCB in DS:DX. MS-DOS returns AL = 00H if the function successfully closed the file or AL = FFH if an error occurred.

It is good practice to use function 10H to explicitly close all files you opened with function 0FH or 16H. This ensures that the file contents are updated from MS-DOS internal file buffers and that the corresponding directory entries are current.

Function 11H (decimal 17): Find First Matching Directory Entry

Function 11H (decimal 17) searches the current directory for a specified directory entry. The name you specify to function 11H can contain the wildcard characters ? and *. The ? character matches any single ASCII character (as a wildcard in a poker game matches any other card), and the * matches any string of characters, so MS-DOS can match a name that contains one or more wildcard characters with several different directory entries. If more than one directory entry matches, MS-DOS reports only the first match. You must then use function 12H to search for subsequent matching entries.

Before you call function 11H, store the address of an FCB in DS:DX. The filename field of this FCB must contain the name you want MS-DOS to search for. MS-DOS reports a successful match by returning AL = 00H; if no directory entries match the specified name, MS-DOS returns AL = FFH. When MS-DOS finds a matching directory entry, it stores the drive number in the current disk transfer area (DTA) and copies the directory entry to the DTA, starting at the second byte.

If the FCB has an FCB extension (see page 288), you can specify the attributes of the file that you want to search for. If you specify any combination of the hidden, system, or directory attribute bits, the search matches normal files and also any files with those attributes. If you specify the volume label attribute, function 11H searches only for a directory entry with that attribute. With MS-DOS versions prior to 2.0, neither the directory nor the volume label attributes can be used in the file search operation. The archive and read-only attributes cannot be used as search criteria in any MS-DOS release.

Function 12H (decimal 18): Find Next Matching Directory Entry

Function 12H (decimal 18) finds the next of a series of files, following the set-up preparation performed by function 11H. As with function 11H, you must call function 12H with the address of an FCB in DS:DX. For function 12H, the FCB should be the same as the one you used for a successful call to function 11H.

MS-DOS reports a successful match by returning AL = 00H; if no match exists, MS-DOS returns AL = FFH. This lets you combine functions 11H and 12H to perform a complete directory search by using the following logic:

```
initialize FCB
call function 11H
WHILE AL = 0
        process data returned in DTA
        use current contents of FCB
        call function 12H
```

Function 13H (decimal 19): Delete File

Function 13H (decimal 19) deletes all files that match the name specified in the FCB that is pointed to by the register pair DS:DX. The filename in the FCB can contain wildcard characters so that multiple files can be deleted with a single call to function 13H. The function returns AL = 00H if the operation is a success, and all matching file directory entries are deleted. The function returns AL = FFH if the operation is a failure, meaning that no directory entries matched.

Function 14H (decimal 20): Sequential Read

Function 14H (decimal 20) reads records sequentially from a file. To use this function, open a file by using function 0FH. Then initialize the current-block, current-record, and record-size fields of the FCB. For example, to read the first 256-byte record from a file, set the record-size field to 100H (decimal 256) and both the current-block field and the current-record field to 00H before you call function 14H.

After the FCB is initialized, you can call function 14H once for each record you want to read. Each time you call function 14H, pass the address of the file's FCB in DS:DX. MS-DOS reads the next record from the file and stores the data in the current disk transfer area (DTA). At the same time, MS-DOS tracks its current position in the file by updating the current-block and current-record fields in the FCB.

AL reports the results of the read. A successful read is signaled when AL = 00H. AL = 01H signals an end of file, indicating that no data was read. AL = 02H signals that data could have been read but wasn't because insufficient memory remained in the DTA segment. AL = 03H signals an end of file with a partial record read. (The record is padded with zero bytes.)

Function 15H (decimal 21): Sequential Write

Function 15H (decimal 21) writes a sequential record; it is the companion to function 14H. As with function 14H, MS-DOS tracks its current position in the file by updating the FCB whose address you pass in DS:DX. MS-DOS copies the data from the current DTA to the file and reports the status of the write operation in AL.

If AL = 00H, the write operation was a success. If AL = 01H, the disk was full and the record was not written. If AL = 02H, the amount of memory remaining in the DTA's segment was less than the record size, so MS-DOS aborted the write operation.

It's important to note that data is logically written by this function, but it is not necessarily physically written. MS-DOS buffers output data until it has a complete disk sector to write; only then does MS-DOS actually transfer the data to the disk.

Function 16H (decimal 22): Create File

Function 16H (decimal 22) opens an empty file with a specified name. If the file exists in the current directory, function 16H truncates it to zero length. If the file does not exist, function 16H creates a directory entry for the new file. As with most other FCB-based file functions, you call function 16H with DS:DX pointing to an FCB that contains the name of the file. The function returns AL = 00H to indicate successful operation. If AL = FFH, the function failed, possibly because you specified an invalid filename in the FCB.

If you want to avoid inadvertently losing the contents of an existing file, you should determine whether the file already exists by calling function 11H before you use function 16H.

Function 17H (decimal 23): Rename File

Function 17H (decimal 23) renames files or subdirectories in a modified FCB pointed to by DS:DX. For the rename operation, the FCB has a special format. The drive and original name are located in their usual positions, but the new name and extension are placed at offsets 11H through 1BH in the FCB.

AL = 00H signals complete success, and AL = FFH signals that the original name wasn't found or that the new name is already in use.

If the new name contains ? wildcard characters, they are interpreted as *ditto-from-old-name,* and the characters in the original name that correspond to the positions of the wildcard characters are not changed.

Function 21H (decimal 33): Read Random Record

Function 21H (decimal 33) reads one record from a random location in a file. To use this function, open a file with an FCB. Then store the record number of the record you want to read in the random-record field of the FCB. When you call function 21H with DS:DX pointing to the FCB, MS-DOS reads the specified record into the DTA. MS-DOS does not update the random-record field in the FCB.

AL is set with the same codes as it is for a sequential read: AL = 00H indicates a successful read; AL = 01H indicates an end of file, with no more data available; AL = 02H means that insufficient space exists in the DTA segment; and AL = 03H indicates an end of file, with a partial data record available.

Contrast this function with function 27H, which can read more than one random record at a time, or with function 14H, which reads sequential records. See function 24H for more on setting the random-record field.

Function 22H (decimal 34): Write Random Record

Function 22H (decimal 34) writes one record to a random location in a file. As with function 21H, you must initialize the random-record field in the file's FCB and then call this function with DS:DX pointing to the FCB. MS-DOS then writes data from the DTA to the file at the position specified in the FCB. MS-DOS does not update the random-record field in the FCB.

AL is set with the same codes used for a sequential write: AL = 00H indicates a successful write; AL = 01H means the disk is full; AL = 02H indicates insufficient space in the DTA segment.

Contrast this function with function 28H, which can write more than one random record, or with function 15H, which writes sequential records. See function 24H for more on setting the random-record field.

Function 23H (decimal 35): Get File Size

Function 23H (decimal 35) reports the size of a file in terms of the number of records in the file. DS:DX points to the FCB of the file you want to know about. Before calling the function, the FCB should be left unopened and the record-size field, the drive-number field, and the filename field in the FCB filled in. If you set the record size to 1, the file size is reported in bytes, which is most likely what you want.

If the operation is successful, AL = 00H and the file size is inserted into the FCB. If the file is not found, AL = FFH.

Function 24H (decimal 36): Set FCB Random-Record Field

Function 24H (decimal 36) sets the random-record field to correspond to the current sequential block and record fields in an FCB. This facilitates switching from sequential to random I/O. The DS:DX registers point to the FCB of an open file, and the random-record field must be set to zero.

Function 27H (decimal 39): Read Random Records

Function 27H (decimal 39) reads one or more records, starting at a random file location. DS:DX points to the FCB of the file to be read. A combination of the FCB's record-size field and relative-record number field specifies the file location from which the records are read. CX contains the number of records wanted, which should be more than 0.

The return codes are the same as they are for function 21H: AL = 00H means the read was successful; AL = 01H indicates an end of file, with no more data (if the records were read, the last record is complete); AL = 02H indicates that the DTA segment was too small; and AL = 03H indicates an end of file in which the last record read is incomplete and padded with zeros.

No matter what the result, CX is set to the number of records read, including any partial record, and the current-block and current-record fields in the FCB are set to the next sequential record; successive calls to function 27H will read sequential groups of records from the file until end of file is reached.

Contrast this function with function 21H, which reads only one record.

Function 28H (decimal 40): Write Random Records

Function 28H (decimal 40) writes one or more records, starting at a specified random file location. DS:DX points to the FCB of the file to be written, and MS-DOS converts the random-record number in this FCB to current-block number and current-record number, which are then stored in the FCB. CX contains the number of records wanted, and in this case, CX can be 00H. CX = 00H signals MS-DOS to adjust the file's length to the position of the specified random record. This adjustment makes it easier for a program to manage random files: If you have logically deleted records at the end of a file, this service allows you to truncate the file at that point by setting the file's length in CX, thereby freeing disk space.

The return codes are the same as they are for function 22H: AL = 00H indicates a successful write; AL = 01H means that no more disk space is available; and AL = 02H indicates that the DTA segment was too small. No matter what the result, CX is always set to the number of records written.

Contrast this function with function 22H, which writes only one random record.

Function 29H (decimal 41): Parse Filename

Function 29H (decimal 41) parses a string for a filename with the form DRIVE:FILENAME.EXT. You call this function with DS:SI pointing to a text string and ES:DI pointing to the drive-identifier byte in an unopened FCB. Function 29H attempts to extract the drive and filename information from the string and to use it to initialize the drive and name fields of the FCB. The string is an ASCIIZ string, which requires that the last byte of the string be set to 00H; this allows the string to be variable in length, containing more than one DRIVE:FILENAME.EXT set. If AL = 00H, the current-block number and current-record number fields are updated, allowing the successive writing of sequential groups of records. If the function executes successfully, it returns AL = 00H if the string contains no wildcard characters or AL = 01H if the string contains at least one * or ? wildcard character. If the drive letter specifies an invalid drive, the function returns AL = FFH.

Function 29H also updates DS:SI to point to the byte after the end of the filename in the string. This facilitates processing a string that contains multiple filenames. Also, if the parsing was unsuccessful, the FCB contains a blank filename.

Function 29H lets you control four aspects of the filename parsing. When you call the function, the 4 low-order bits of the value in AL specify how function 29H parses the string:

- If bit 0 is set, the function scans past separator characters (for example, leading blank spaces) to find the file specification. If bit 0 is 0, the scan operation is not performed, and the file specification is expected to start in the first byte of the string.

- If bit 1 is set, the drive byte in the FCB will be set only if the DRIVE parameter is provided in the file specification being scanned. This allows the FCB to specify a default drive.

- If bit 2 is set, the filename in the FCB is changed only if a valid filename is found in the string. This lets the FCB specify a default filename, which can be overridden by the filename in the string.

- If bit 3 is set, the filename extension in the FCB is changed only if a valid extension is found in the file specification. This allows the FCB to specify a default extension.

NOTE: *Although this service can be handy, it is intended for use only with FCB-based file functions. You don't need this function if you rely on the handle-based file functions.*

The Handle Functions

MS-DOS 2.0 introduced the handle-based file functions. As we discussed earlier in this chapter, these functions have several advantages over the FCB-based file functions. From a programmer's point of view, the handle-based functions have three important new features that directly affect the way you use MS-DOS disk services:

- To work with a file or directory, the program need only pass MS-DOS the pathname or filename as a string in the ASCIIZ format—a string of ASCII characters terminated by a single zero (00H) byte.

- When a file is opened or created, MS-DOS provides a 16-bit number called a handle, which the program uses to identify the file for subsequent operations.

- The handle functions return a set of consistent error codes in the AX register.

We discuss these enhancements in the next few pages.

ASCIIZ strings

Some of the handle-based file functions require you to pass file and directory names in the form of *ASCIIZ strings*. An ASCIIZ string is simply a string of ASCII characters terminated by a single zero byte that marks the end of the string. For example, the ASCIIZ representation of the pathname C:\COMMAND.COM would consist of the 15 hexadecimal bytes shown in Figure 10-11.

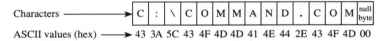

Characters → | C | : | \ | C | O | M | M | A | N | D | . | C | O | M | null byte |

ASCII values (hex) → 43 3A 5C 43 4F 4D 4D 41 4E 44 2E 43 4F 4D 00

Figure 10-11. *An ASCIIZ string is a sequence of ASCII characters terminated by a zero byte.*

The ASCIIZ string format is used by the C programming language. It's simple to create ASCIIZ strings in other languages. For example, in Basic, to create an ASCIIZ string containing a filename you would write

```
FileName$ = "myfile.dat" + CHR$(0)
```

In assembly language you would write

```
filename    db      'myfile.dat',0
```

File handles

The handle-based file functions get their name from the fact that they rely on *handles*, 16-bit numbers that MS-DOS (versions 2.0 and later) uses to identify open files. When you open an existing file or create a new file, MS-DOS returns a handle that it uses to identify the file for subsequent operations, such as reading and writing data. The use of handles allows MS-DOS to be more flexible in its file management services than it was with FCB-based file services. In particular, capabilities such as file redirection and support for hierarchical directories would have been very difficult to graft onto the fixed-format FCB data structure. Furthermore, the use of handles actually simplifies file management by making the mechanics of file input/output—parsing filenames, keeping track of the current file position, and so on—the responsibility of MS-DOS rather than of your programs.

The flexibility of the handle-based functions is further increased by the fact that handles can identify nondisk sources of input and output for a program, such as the keyboard and the video display. For example, interrupt 21H, function 40H can be used to write data to a disk file, to the screen, or to a printer, depending on the handle that is passed to it. Five standard, predefined handles, numbered 0 through 4, are available to every program. (See Figure 10-12.) Other handles, with higher handle numbers, are issued by MS-DOS as needed for files and other devices.

Handle	Use	Default Device
0	Standard input (normally keyboard input)	CON
1	Standard output (normally screen output)	CON
2	Standard error output (always to the screen)	CON
3	Standard auxiliary device (AUX device)	AUX
4	Standard printer (LPT1 or PRN device)	PRN

Figure 10-12. *The five standard MS-DOS handles.*

NOTE: *Of the five standard MS-DOS handles, only the first three are supported in OS/2 protected mode. If you are programming with upward compatibility in mind, you should avoid using handles 3 and 4 by default. Instead, open the serial port and printer devices explicitly, as you would any other file or input/output device.*

MS-DOS limits the use of handles with regard to how many files or devices your program can open at one time:

- MS-DOS maintains an internal data structure that controls I/O for each file or other input/output device associated with a handle. The default size of this data structure allows for only 8 handles. Fortunately, the FILES command in the CONFIG.SYS file lets you increase the number of possible handles to a maximum of 99 in MS-DOS versions prior to 3.0 and 255 in versions 3.0 and later.

■ MS-DOS uses a reserved area in each program's PSP to maintain a table of handles associated with the program. This table has room for a maximum of 20 handles. Thus, even if you specify FILES = 30 in your CONFIG.SYS file, your programs will still be able to use only 20 handles at a time. (Beginning with version 3.3, MS-DOS provides a way around this through interrupt 21H, function 67H. See page 312 for details.) Fortunately, few applications require more than 20 files to be open at once, so these limitations are not usually important.

Consistent error codes

In the event of an error, each of the handle-based functions returns an error status code in the AX register. These functions also set the carry flag to signal that an error has occurred. You should generally follow each call to a handle-based function with a test of the carry flag; if the flag is set, the value in AX describes what caused the error.

In MS-DOS versions 3.0 and later, you can also use interrupt 21H, function 59H to obtain extended error information from MS-DOS. You can call function 59H after any interrupt 21H function reports an error; you can also use it inside a critical-error (interrupt 24H) handler to determine the nature of an MS-DOS critical error. In both situations, function 59H returns an extended error code and also suggests possible actions to alleviate the problem.

For a complete list of extended error codes and how to use them, see the discussion of function 59H on page 417.

Now let's look at the handle-based file functions. Figure 10-13 summarizes the functions, and the following sections provide details.

All MS-DOS function calls described in the following sections are invoked through interrupt 21H (decimal 33). The individual functions are selected by placing the function number in the AH register. Any program that uses these functions should test the MS-DOS version number first to be sure the functions are supported. (Functions 30H and 3306H provide this service.)

Function 3CH (decimal 60): Create File

Function 3CH (decimal 60) opens an empty file by using a specified name. If the file exists, function 3CH truncates it to zero length. If the file does not exist, function 3CH creates a new file. This function supersedes function 16H (discussed on page 296).

To invoke this function, create an ASCIIZ string containing the pathname and filename. The register pair DS:DX contains the address of the ASCIIZ string. CX contains the file attribute. (See page 130 for more on file attributes and attribute bit settings.) When function 3CH executes

Function		
Hex	**Dec**	**Description**
3CH	60	Create File
3DH	61	Open File or Device
3EH	62	Close File or Device
3FH	63	Read from File or Device
40H	64	Write to File or Device
41H	65	Delete File
42H	66	Move File Pointer
43H	67	Get/Set File Attributes
45H	69	Duplicate File Handle
46H	70	Force Duplicate File Handle
56H	86	Rename File
57H	87	Get/Set File Date and Time
5AH	90	Create Temporary File
5BH	91	Create New File
5CH	92	Lock/Unlock File Region
67H	103	Set Handle Count
68H	104	Commit File
6CH	108	Extended File Open/Create

Figure 10-13. *The handle-based MS-DOS file functions.*

successfully, it clears the carry flag and returns a handle in AX. Otherwise, this function sets the carry flag and leaves an error code in AX. Possible error codes are 03H (path not found), 04H (no handle available), and 05H (access denied). Code 05H can indicate either that there is no room for a new directory entry or that the existing file is marked read-only and can't be opened for output.

Be aware that by using function 3CH you can accidentally truncate an existing file to zero length. The best way to avoid this mistake is simply to call function 4EH to search the directory for an existing file before you call function 3CH. Or, if you are using MS-DOS 3.0 or later, you have two alternatives: You can call function 5BH, which works like function 3CH but won't open an existing file; or you can use function 5AH to create a temporary file with a unique filename.

Function 3DH (decimal 61): Open File or Device

Function 3DH (decimal 61) opens an existing file or device. You provide the pathname and filename in the form of an ASCIIZ string. As with all other handle-related functions, DS:DX points to this string. You indicate how you want to use the file by placing a file-access code in register AL. The 8 bits of AL are divided into the four fields shown in Figure 10-14.

Bit								Use
7	6	5	4	3	2	1	0	
I	.	.	.	.	.	.	.	Inheritance flag (MS-DOS versions 3 and later)
.	S	S	S	.	.	.	.	Sharing mode (MS-DOS versions 3 and later)
.	.	.	.	R	.	.	.	(Reserved)
.	.	.	.	.	A	A	A	Access code

Figure 10-14. *File-access and sharing codes for function 3DH.*

The file-access code for MS-DOS version 2 is simple: Only the access bits (bits 0 through 2) are used; all other bits are set to 0. The three access-code settings, used by all versions of MS-DOS beginning with version 2.0, are defined in Figure 10-15.

Bit			Use
2	1	0	
0	0	0	Read-only access
0	0	1	Write-only access
0	1	0	Read and write access

Figure 10-15. *File-access modes for function 3DH.*

MS-DOS versions 3.0 and later use the *inheritance* and *sharing codes* as well as the access code. The inheritance and sharing codes give you control over how different programs access the same file at the same time.

Bit 7, the inheritance bit, indicates whether a child process can inherit the use of this file. (For more about parent and child processes, see the discussion of function 4BH in Chapter 13.) When a child process inherits a handle, it inherits the file's access and sharing codes: If bit 7 = 0, a child process can use the same handle as the parent process to access the file; if bit 7 = 1, the child process must itself open the file to obtain a different handle.

Bits 4 through **6,** the sharing-mode bits (SSS in Figure 10-14), define what happens when more than one program tries to open the same file. There are five sharing modes: compatibility mode (SSS = 000), deny read/ write mode (SSS = 001), deny write mode (SSS = 010), deny read mode (SSS = 011), and deny none mode (SSS = 100). When a second attempt is made to open the file, MS-DOS compares the file's sharing code to the access requested in the second open operation. MS-DOS allows the second open operation to succeed only if the sharing mode and the requested access mode are compatible.

> NOTE: *MS-DOS performs this file-sharing validation only if it is running on a network or if the SHARE utility is installed. See the MS-DOS technical reference manual for more details on networking and the SHARE utility.*

Bit 3, marked as "Reserved" in Figure 10-14, should be set to 0.

Like function 3CH, function 3DH clears the carry flag and returns a handle in AX when it successfully opens a file or device. Otherwise, this function sets the carry flag and leaves an error code in AX. The possible return codes from function 3DH are 02H (file not found), 03H (path not found), 04H (no handles available), 05H (access denied), and 0CH (invalid access code).

If SHARE or network file sharing is in force in MS-DOS versions 3.0 and later, MS-DOS signals a sharing violation by executing interrupt 24H.

Function 3EH (decimal 62): Close File or Device

Function 3EH (decimal 62) closes a file or device associated with the handle in BX. This function flushes all file buffers and updates the directory if necessary. The only error code this function can return is 06H (invalid handle).

Function 3FH (decimal 63): Read from File or Device

Function 3FH (decimal 63) reads the file or device associated with the handle in BX. The CX register specifies the number of bytes to read; DS:DX points to the buffer where data that is read will be placed. If the read operation is successful, function 3FH clears the carry flag and returns the number of bytes read in AX. If this value is 0, the function has tried to read from the end of a file. If AX is nonzero but less than CX, end of file was reached during the read operation. If the read operation fails, this function sets the carry flag and leaves an error code in AX. The possible error codes are 05H (access denied) and 06H (invalid handle).

Function 40H (decimal 64): Write to File or Device

Function 40H (decimal 64) writes to the file or device associated with the handle in BX. CX specifies the number of bytes to be written; DS:DX points to the address of the data buffer.

When the write operation is complete, function 40H updates the file pointer to point past the data just written.

You must examine both the carry flag and the value in AX returned by function 40H to determine the success of the write operation:

- If the carry flag is clear and AX = CX, the operation was completed successfully.

- If the carry flag is clear but AX < CX, the output was written to a disk file that had insufficient disk space to complete the write operation.

- If the carry flag is set, AX contains an error code of 05H (access denied) or 06H (invalid handle).

The fact that function 40H updates the file pointer has an interesting side effect: You can set the size of a file to any arbitrary value by executing function 40H with CX = 00H. The usual technique is to call function 42H to set the file pointer location and then to immediately call function 40H with CX = 00H to update the file size.

Function 41H (decimal 65): Delete File

Function 41H (decimal 65) deletes the directory entry of a file. The file is specified by an ASCIIZ string containing the pathname and filename. The register pair DS:DX points to the string. Unlike function 13H, function 41H does not support wildcard characters in the file specification: With function 41H you can delete only one file at a time.

You cannot delete read-only files with this function. To delete a read-only file, first remove the read-only attribute by using function 43H, and then use function 41H.

Function 41H can return three error codes in AX: 02H (file not found), 03H (path not found), and 05H (access denied).

Function 42H (decimal 66): Move File Pointer

Function 42H (decimal 66) changes the logical read/write position in a file. To invoke this service, you load BX with a handle and then specify the new pointer location by placing a reference location in AL and an offset relative to the reference location in register pair CX:DX. The byte offset in CX:DX is a 32-bit, signed long integer. CX is the high-order part of the offset (which is 0, unless the offset amount is more than 65,535), and DX is the low-order part.

You can specify the reference location in AL in three different ways. If AL = 00H, the offset is taken relative to the beginning of the file, and the file pointer is moved CX:DX bytes from that point. If AL = 01H, the offset is taken relative to the current file pointer location. And finally, if AL = 02H, the offset is taken from the current end of file.

If the function executes successfully, it clears the carry flag and returns in the register pair DX:AX the current file pointer location relative to the beginning of the file. The pointer is returned as a 32-bit, long integer, with the high-order part in DX and the low-order part in AX. If the function fails, it sets the carry flag and returns an error code in AX. Possible error codes are 01H (invalid function number, which means AL did not contain 00H, 01H, or 02H) and 06H (invalid handle).

You can use function 42H in several ways:

- To place the file pointer at an arbitrary location in the file, call function 42H with AL = 00H and CX:DX specifying the desired offset relative to the start of the file.

- To position the file pointer at the end of the file, call function 42H with AL = 02H and 00H in CX:DX.

- To determine the current location of the file pointer, use AL = 01H and place 00H in CX:DX; the value returned in DX:AX is the current file pointer location.

MS-DOS does not validate the resulting location of the file pointer. In particular, if AL = 01H or 02H, you can end with a *negative file pointer offset* (that is, a file pointer at a position before the logical start of the file). However, it's not a good idea to use negative file pointers, for two reasons: If you perform a subsequent read or write operation, you'll be in error; and your program will be harder to adapt for OS/2, where an attempt to move a file pointer to a negative offset generates an error.

NOTE: *The operation of moving a logical file pointer to a specified location in a file is sometimes called a* seek, *but the same word is also used to refer to moving the read/write heads of a disk drive to a specified cylinder on a disk. The two operations aren't the same.*

Function 43H (decimal 67): Get/Set File Attributes

Function 43H (decimal 67) gets or sets the attributes of a file. (See page 130 for details about file attributes.) DS:DX points to an ASCIIZ string that specifies the file in question. (Wildcard characters cannot be used.) Calling function 43H with AL = 00H returns the file's attributes in CX; AL = 01H sets the attribute values you specify in CX.

If function 43H fails, the carry flag is set and AX contains one of four error codes: 01H (invalid function), 02H (file not found), 03H (path not found), or 05H (access denied).

Function 45H (decimal 69): Duplicate File Handle

Function 45H (decimal 69) duplicates an open file handle and returns a new handle number that refers to the same file or device. All actions performed with one handle will be reflected in the other handle—the new handle does not act independently in any way.

You call function 45H with an open handle in BX. If the function executes successfully, it clears the carry flag and leaves a new handle number in AX. If an error occurs, the carry flag is set and AX contains an error code: 04H (no more handles) or 06H (invalid handle).

You can use function 45H along with function 46H to implement input/output redirection. You can also use it to commit an open file to disk by duplicating the open file's handle and then closing the duplicate handle. This operation flushes the file's disk buffers and updates the directory without the overhead of closing the file, reopening it (which involves a directory search), and repositioning the file pointer:

```
mov bx,Handle        ; BX = handle of open file
mov ah,45h
int 21h              ; get duplicate handle into AX
jc  Error
mov bx,ax            ; BX = duplicate handle
mov ah,3Eh
int 21h              ; close duplicate handle
                     ;   (original handle remains open)
```

Function 46H (decimal 70): Force Duplicate File Handle

Function 46H (decimal 70) has a somewhat misleading name because it really does not create a duplicate handle, as function 45H does. Instead, function 46H associates an existing open handle with a different device. This is the key to implementing input/output redirection in MS-DOS.

You call function 46H with an open handle in BX and a second handle in CX. When function 46H returns, the handle in CX is associated with the same device as the open handle in BX. If the handle in CX was previously associated with an open device, function 46H closes the device, which might otherwise be without a handle. If no errors occur, the function clears the carry flag. Otherwise, the carry flag is set, and AX contains an error code: 04H (no more handles) or 06H (invalid handle).

To see how function 46H works, consider how you would redirect output from the standard output device (the video screen) to a file:

```
mov bx,stdout            ; BX = handle of standard output device
mov ah,45h               ; AH = function number ("Duplicate File Handle")
int 21h                  ; get duplicate handle into AX
jc  Error                ; (trap errors)

mov stdoutDup,ax         ; save the duplicate handle in a memory variable
mov bx,FileHandle        ; BX = handle of open file
mov cx,stdout            ; CX = handle to be redirected
mov ah,46h               ; AH = function number ("Force Duplicate File Handle")
int 21h                  ; redirect stdout to the file
jc  Error

                         ; at this point, all output to stdout
                         ;   goes into the file
```

To undo this redirection, associate the standard output device with the saved duplicate:

```
mov bx,stdoutDup         ; BX = duplicate of previous stdout
mov cx,stdout            ; CX = handle to be redirected
mov ah,46h               ; AH = function number ("Force Duplicate File Handle")
int 21h                  ; restore stdout to what it was
jc  Error

mov bx,stdoutDup         ; BX = duplicate handle
mov ah,3Eh               ; AH = function number ("Close")
int 21h                  ; discard duplicate handle
```

Function 56H (decimal 86): Rename File

Like the standard MS-DOS RENAME command, function 56H (decimal 86) changes the name of a file; unlike the RENAME command, this function can also change the name of a directory. But it can also move a file's directory entry or subdirectory entry from one directory to another. The file itself is not moved, only the directory entry, which means that the new and old directory paths must be on the same drive. This is a truly fabulous and useful feature, and it is available in MS-DOS version 6.0 as the MOVE command; earlier versions of MS-DOS do not provide such a command.

This function needs two pieces of information: the old and new pathnames and filenames. These can be full-blown file specifications, with drive and path components. The specified or implied drives must be the same so that the new directory entry will be on the same drive as the file. The wildcard characters * and ? cannot be used because this function works on single directory entries only. As usual, both file specifications are supplied in the form of ASCIIZ strings. The register pair DS:DX points to the old name string, and ES:DI points to the new string.

Function 56H clears the carry flag when it successfully renames a file or directory. If an error occurs, the carry flag is set, and AX contains an error code: 02H (file not found), 03H (path not found), 05H (access denied), or 11H (not the same device). One error that might not be reported occurs if you use function 56H to rename an open file. Be sure to close an open file with function 10H or 3EH before you use function 56H to rename it.

Function 57H (decimal 87): Get/Set File Date and Time

Function 57H (decimal 87) gets or sets a file's date and time. Normally a file's directory entry contains the date and time the file was created or last changed. This function lets you inspect or explicitly update the recorded date and time. AL selects the operation: AL = 00H gets the date and time, and AL = 01H sets the date and time.

The file is selected by placing the file handle in BX, which makes this function applicable only to files that were opened using the handle-based MS-DOS functions. Setting a file's time stamp with this function will take effect only if the file is successfully closed.

The date and time are placed in registers CX and DX in the same format used in the disk directory entries, although in a slightly different order. In this function, the time is placed in CX and the date in DX.

Use the following formulas to build or break down the date and time:

$$CX = (HOUR * 2048) + (MINUTE * 32) + (SECOND / 2)$$
$$DX = ((YEAR - 1980) * 512) + (MONTH * 32) + DAY$$

If this function fails, it returns an error code in AX: 01H (invalid function number—based on the subfunction selected in AL, not the main function number) or 06H (invalid handle).

Function 5AH (decimal 90): Create Temporary File

Function 5AH (decimal 90) was introduced in MS-DOS version 3.0. It creates a file for temporary use. It generates a unique filename for the file by building the name from the current time of day. You provide two parameters: the file attribute, which is placed in the CX register, and the pathname of the directory where the file will be created. The pathname must be an ASCIIZ string and is pointed to by the register pair DS:DX.

The pathname string must be ready to have the filename of the created file appended to it: The string must end with a backslash character and be followed by 13 bytes to allow enough room for MS-DOS to add a filename to the string. If you don't want to specify a path, you can give MS-DOS a null string, which tells it to use the current directory of the current drive.

If function 5AH successfully creates a file, it clears the carry flag, places the handle for the file in AX, and returns the name of the file appended to the pathname you specified in DS:DX. If the function fails, it sets the carry flag and returns an error code in AX: 03H (path not found), 04H (no more handles), or 05H (access denied).

This function is called Create Temporary File only to suggest its intended purpose. Actually, there is nothing temporary about the file that is created because MS-DOS does not automatically delete it; your programs must look after that chore.

Function 5BH (decimal 91): Create New File

Function 5BH (decimal 91) was introduced in MS-DOS version 3.0. It is similar to function 3CH, which is (inaccurately) called the Create File function. Function 3CH is actually designed to find a file or to create one if the requested file does not exist. By contrast, function 5BH is a pure create file function and will fail if the file already exists.

As with function 3CH, the CX register is set to the file attribute, and DS:DX contains the address of the pathname and filename (which is stored as an ASCIIZ string). On return, if CF = 0, AX = file handle for the new file. If CF = 1, AX contains an error code: 03H (path not found), 04H (no more handles), 05H (access denied), or 50H (file already exists).

You should use function 3CH if you want to reuse an existing file with a particular filename or to create a file with that name if the file doesn't exist. If, however, you want to open a new file only if the specified filename does not already exist, use function 5BH.

Function 5CH (decimal 92): Lock/Unlock File Region

Function 5CH (decimal 92) locks certain parts of a file so that the file can be shared by several programs without one program interfering with the operations of another. If one program locks one part of a file, it can use or change that part of the file while it is locked, safe in the knowledge that no other program will be able to use that part while it remains locked. As you might guess, file locking is used only in conjunction with file-sharing operations, such as those that can occur in a network.

When you call function 5CH, AL indicates whether you are locking (AL = 00H) or unlocking (AL = 01H) a portion of a file. BX gives the file handle. CX and DX are treated as a 4-byte integer that specifies the byte offset of the start of the locked portion of the file. SI and DI form a 4-byte integer that specifies the length of the locked portion. The first register in each of these register pairs (CX and SI) gives the high-order part of the integer. When function 5CH successfully locks a portion of a file, it clears the carry flag. If an error occurs, the carry flag is set, and AX contains an error code: 01H (invalid function), 06H (invalid handle), 21H (file-locking violation), or 24H (sharing buffer overflow).

You are not allowed to unlock file portions piecemeal or in combination; an unlock request should exactly match a previous lock request. You must also explicitly remove all locks before closing a file or terminating a program that does file locking.

Use function 5CH to lock a file region before you read or write a file that may have been locked by another program; use function 5CH again to unlock the region after the read or write operation is complete. The first call to function 5CH tells you if the part of the file you intend to access is already locked; you should not rely on the read and write functions to return error codes if they access a previously locked region.

Function 5CH is supported only in MS-DOS versions 3.0 and later.

Function 67H (decimal 103): Set Handle Count

Function 67H (decimal 103) was introduced in MS-DOS version 3.3; it lets a program specify the maximum number of handles it can keep open at any one time. MS-DOS maintains a table of the handles used by a program in a reserved area in the program's PSP. Normally the limit is 20 handles, of which 5 are automatically opened by MS-DOS for the standard input, output, error, auxiliary, and printer devices.

To increase the maximum number of open handles, call function 67H with the maximum number of desired handles in BX. MS-DOS will allocate a new block of memory and use it to store an expanded table of handles. The function clears the carry flag to indicate success; if the carry flag is set, AX contains an error code.

Keep in mind two points about function 67H:

- If you are running a COM program that uses all available memory, it must call function 4AH to shrink its memory allocation before MS-DOS can allocate a memory block for the handle table.

- The size of MS-DOS's internal file table imposes an upper limit on the number of handles you can open. You can increase the size of that table with the FILES command in your CONFIG.SYS file.

Function 68H (decimal 104): Commit File

Function 68H (decimal 104) was first supported in MS-DOS version 3.3. When you call this function with an open file handle in BX, MS-DOS flushes the disk buffer associated with the handle and updates the disk directory accordingly. This procedure ensures that data written to the disk buffer but not yet physically written on a disk will not be lost should a power failure or other mishap occur.

By executing function 68H, you obtain the same result that you would by using function 45H to duplicate a file handle and then using function 3EH to close the duplicate handle.

Function 6CH (decimal 108): Extended File Open/Create

Function 6CH (decimal 108) was introduced with version 4.0 of MS-DOS. It combines the capabilities of several previous MS-DOS functions, permitting you to specify several actions when you open a file:

- You can open an existing file (as with function 3DH).

- You can create a new file or truncate an existing file (as with function 3CH).

- You can create a file that is guaranteed to be new (as with function 5BH).

- You can open a file for which every write operation is committed to disk (as if you called function 68H after each write).

- You can disable critical-error processing (interrupt 24H) for the file.

When you call function 6CH, you specify what combination of actions are to be taken by setting bits in registers BX and DX. The other registers specify other information required by MS-DOS: CX contains the file attributes if you are creating a file, and DS:SI points to an ASCIIZ filename. Note that AL must contain 0 when this function is called. The values for BX and DX are listed in Figures 10-16 and 10-17.

Bit 15 14 13 12 11 10 9 8	7 6 5 4 3 2 1 0	Field Value	Meaning
. . . .	. . . . . 0 0 0	0	Access code: read only
. . . .	. . . . . 0 0 1	1	Access code: write only
. . . .	. . . . . 0 1 0	2	Access code: read/write
. . . .	. . . . 0 . . .		(Reserved)
. . . .	. 0 0 0	0	Sharing mode: compatibility
. . . .	. 0 0 1	1	Sharing mode: deny read/write
. . . .	. 0 1 0	2	Sharing mode: deny write

Figure 10-16. *Bit-field values in register BX for interrupt 21H, function 6CH.*   *(continued)*

Figure 10-16. *continued*

15	14	13	12	11	10	9	8	7	6	5	4	3	2	1	0	Field Value	Meaning
.	.	.	.	.	.	.	.	.	0	1	1	.	.	.	.	3	Sharing mode: deny read
.	.	.	.	.	.	.	.	.	1	0	0	.	.	.	.	4	Sharing mode: deny none
.	.	.	.	.	.	.	.	0	.	.	.	.	.	.	.	0	Inherit: child inherits handles
.	.	.	.	.	.	.	.	1	.	.	.	.	.	.	.	1	Inherit: no inherited handles
.	.	.	0	0	0	0	0	.	.	.	.	.	.	.	.		(Reserved)
.	0	.	.	.	.	.	.	.	.	.	.	.	.	.	.	0	INT 24H: enabled
.	1	.	.	.	.	.	.	.	.	.	.	.	.	.	.	1	INT 24H: disabled
.	.	0	.	.	.	.	.	.	.	.	.	.	.	.	.	0	Auto-commit: disabled
.	.	1	.	.	.	.	.	.	.	.	.	.	.	.	.	1	Auto-commit: enabled
0	.	.	.	.	.	.	.	.	.	.	.	.	.	.	.		(Reserved)

15	14	13	12	11	10	9	8	7	6	5	4	3	2	1	0	Field Value	Meaning
.	.	.	.	.	.	.	.	.	.	.	.	0	0	0	0	0	If file exists: fail
.	.	.	.	.	.	.	.	.	.	.	.	0	0	0	1	1	If file exists: open
.	.	.	.	.	.	.	.	.	.	.	.	0	0	1	0	2	If file exists: truncate and open
.	.	.	.	.	.	.	.	0	0	0	0	.	.	.	.	0	If file not found: fail
.	.	.	.	.	.	.	.	0	0	0	1	.	.	.	.	1	If file not found: create
0	0	0	0	0	0	0	0	.	.	.	.	.	.	.	.		(Reserved)

Figure 10-17. *Bit-field values in register DX for interrupt 21H, function 6CH.*

If the call to function 6CH is successful, it returns with the carry flag clear, a file handle in AX, and a result code in CX. The possible result codes are 01H (existing file opened), 02H (new file created and opened), and 03H (existing file truncated and opened). If an error occurs, the function sets the carry flag and returns an error code in AX. Possible error codes depend on the type of operation that you requested. They include 01H (invalid function), 02H (file not found), 03H (path not found), 04H (no handles available), 05H (access denied), and 50H (file already exists).

The Directory Functions

MS-DOS provides a number of functions for the management of directories and their contents, as shown in Figure 10-18.

| Function | | Description |
Hex	Dec	
39H	57	Create Directory
3AH	58	Remove Directory
3BH	59	Change Current Directory
47H	71	Get Current Directory
4EH	78	Find First Matching Directory Entry
4FH	79	Find Next Matching Directory Entry

Figure 10-18. *The MS-DOS directory functions.*

Function 39H (decimal 57): Create Directory

Function 39H (decimal 57) creates a subdirectory exactly as the MS-DOS command MKDIR does. To invoke this service, you create an ASCIIZ string containing the pathname of the new directory. The register pair DS:DX contains the address of the ASCIIZ string. If an error occurs, function 39H sets the carry flag and returns an error code in AX. The possible error codes are 03H (path not found) and 05H (access denied).

Function 3AH (decimal 58): Remove Directory

Function 3AH (decimal 58) removes (deletes) a subdirectory exactly as the MS-DOS command RMDIR does. To invoke this function, create an ASCIIZ string containing the pathname of the directory you want to remove. The register pair DS:DX points to the ASCIIZ string. If an error occurs, function 3AH sets the carry flag and returns an error code in AX. The possible error codes are 03H (path not found), 05H (access denied), and 10H (attempt to remove current directory).

Function 3BH (decimal 59): Change Current Directory

Function 3BH (decimal 59) changes the current directory exactly as the MS-DOS command CHDIR does. To invoke this function, create an ASCIIZ string containing the pathname of the new directory. DS:DX contains the address of the ASCIIZ string. If an error occurs, function 3BH sets the carry flag and returns an error code in AX. The one possible error code returned is 03H (path not found).

Function 47H (decimal 71): Get Current Directory

Function 47H (decimal 71) reports the current directory in the form of an ASCIIZ string. You call function 47H with a drive number in DL (00H = default drive, 01H = drive A, and so on) and the address of a 64-byte buffer in

DS:SI. The function normally clears the carry flag and fills the buffer with an ASCIIZ string that indicates the path from the root to the current directory. If you specify an invalid drive number, the function sets the carry flag and returns an error code of 0FH in AX.

Because the path returned by this function starts at the root directory, the string at DS:SI includes neither the drive letter (as in A:) nor the start-from-the-root backslash (as in A:\). By these rules, if the current directory is the root directory, this function returns a null string. If you want an intelligible display of the current directory, you can prefix the information returned by this function with the drive and root indicators (as in A:\).

Function 4EH (decimal 78): Find First Matching Directory Entry

Function 4EH (decimal 78) searches a directory for a specified name and attribute. You call function 4EH with DS:DX pointing to an ASCIIZ string that contains the path and name to be matched. (You can use * and ? wildcard characters in the search name you specify.) In addition, you must place a directory attribute for the search in CX. You can search for hidden, system, subdirectory, and volume-label directory entries by setting the appropriate bits in CX. (See page 131 for a table of attribute bits.)

> NOTE: *Before you call function 4EH, ensure that the current disk transfer area (DTA) is at least 43 bytes in size.*
>
> *If this function successfully matches the name you specify to a directory entry, it clears the carry flag and fills the DTA with the data shown in Figure 10-19. If the function fails, it sets the carry flag and returns an error code in AX: 02H (file not found), 03H (path not found), or 12H (no more files; no match found).*
>
> *This function is similar to function 11H. The file attributes in this search function are the same as they are with an extended FCB in function 11H. (See page 294.)*
>
> *The attribute search follows a particular logic. If you specify any combination of the hidden, system, and directory attribute bits, the search matches normal files and also any files with the specified attributes. If you specify the volume label attribute, the search matches only a directory entry with that attribute. The archive and read-only bits do not apply to the search operations.*

Function 4FH (decimal 79): Find Next Matching Directory Entry

Function 4FH (decimal 79) continues a directory search when you're using a name that may match more than one directory entry because it contains wildcard characters. When you call this function, the DTA must contain the data returned by a previous call to function 4EH or 4FH.

Offset		Size	
Hex	**Dec**	**(Bytes)**	**Description**
00H	0	21	Area used by MS-DOS for find-next function 4FH
15H	21	1	Attribute of file found
16H	22	2	Time stamp of file (see page 132)
18H	24	2	Date stamp of file (see page 133)
1AH	26	4	File size in bytes
1EH	30	13	Filename and extension (ASCIIZ string)

Figure 10-19. *The information returned in the DTA by function 4EH.*

If this function finds a matching directory entry, it clears the carry flag and updates the DTA accordingly. If it fails to find a match, it sets the carry flag and returns error code 12H (no more files) in AX.

The usual logic for a wildcard search with functions 4EH and 4FH follows this pattern:

```
initialize DTA address with function 1AH
call function 4EH
WHILE carry flag = 0
    use current contents of DTA
    call function 4FH
```

The Drive Functions

Several MS-DOS functions, listed in Figure 10-20, are intended for disk-drive management, and do not require either an FCB or a file handle.

Function		
Hex	**Dec**	**Description**
0DH	13	Flush Disk Buffers
0EH	14	Select Disk Drive
19H	25	Get Current Disk
1AH	26	Set Disk Transfer Area
1BH	27	Get Default Drive Information
1FH	31	Get Drive Parameter Block for Default Drive
1CH	28	Get Specified Drive Information
2EH	46	Set/Clear Verify Flag

Figure 10-20. *The MS-DOS drive functions.*   *(continued)*

Figure 10-20. *continued*

| *Function* | | |
Hex	Dec	Description
2FH	47	Get Disk Transfer Area Address
32H	50	Get Drive Parameter Block for Specific Drive
36H	54	Get Disk Free Space
54H	84	Get Verify Flag

Function 0DH (decimal 13): Flush Disk Buffers

Function 0DH (decimal 13) flushes (writes to disk) all internal MS-DOS file buffers. However, this function does not update directory entries or close any open files. To ensure that the proper length of a changed file is recorded in the file directory, use the close-file function 10H (for a file opened with an FCB) or 3EH (for a file opened with a handle).

Function 0EH (decimal 14): Select Disk Drive

Function 0EH (decimal 14) selects a new current default drive. It also reports the number of logical drives that are supported. The default drive is specified in DL: 00H indicates drive A, 01H indicates drive B, and so on. The number of drives is reported in AL.

Keep a few things in mind when using this function:

- The drive IDs used by MS-DOS are consecutively numbered.

- If only one physical floppy disk drive exists, MS-DOS simulates a second drive, drive number 1 (drive B). Thus, the first hard disk drive is always drive number 2 (corresponding to drive letter C).

- If you use the value in AL to determine the number of drives in your system, beware. In MS-DOS versions 3.0 and later, the value is determined by taking the largest of the following: the number of logical drives actually installed (including RAM disks), the number of drives indicated in the LASTDRIVE command in CONFIG.SYS, or the number 5. Therefore, the minimum value returned by this function is 05H.

Function 19H (decimal 25): Get Current Disk

Function 19H (decimal 25) reports the current (default) drive number in AL, using the standard numeric code of drive A = 00H, drive B = 01H, and so on.

Function 1AH (decimal 26): Set Disk Transfer Area

Function 1AH (decimal 26) establishes the disk transfer area that MS-DOS will use for file I/O. The location of the DTA is specified by the register pair DS:DX. Normally you should specify a DTA address before you use any of the interrupt 21H functions that access a DTA. If you do not, MS-DOS uses the default 128-byte DTA at offset 80H in the program segment prefix. If you specify a DTA, ensure that the buffer does not overlap the segment boundary.

Function 1BH (decimal 27): Get Default Drive Information

Function 1BH (decimal 27) returns important information about the disk in the current (default) drive. Function 1CH performs the identical service for any drive. If unsuccessful, function 1BH returns FFH in AL.

If successful, function 1BH returns the following information:

- AL contains the number of sectors per cluster.

- CX contains the size, in bytes, of the disk sectors. (The size is 512 bytes for all standard PC formats.)

- DX contains the total number of clusters on the disk.

- DS:BX points to a byte in MS-DOS's work area that contains the MS-DOS media descriptor. Prior to MS-DOS version 2.0, the DS:BX register pair pointed to the complete disk FAT (which could be guaranteed to be in memory, complete), whose first byte would be the ID byte. In later MS-DOS versions, DS:BX points only to the single ID byte.

Beware: Function 1BH uses the DS register to return the segment portion of the address of the media descriptor byte. If your program relies on the DS register to point to data—and most high-level and assembly language programs do—you should be careful to preserve the contents of the DS register while you call function 1BH.

The following example shows how to do this:

```
push    ds          ; preserve DS
mov     ah,1Bh
int     21h         ; call function 1BH; DS:BX -> media descriptor
mov     ah,[bx]     ; get a copy of the media descriptor byte
pop     ds          ; restore DS
```

Function 1CH (decimal 28): Get Specified Drive Information

Function 1CH (decimal 28) works in the same way as function 1BH except that it reports on any drive, not only the current drive. Before calling this function, set DL to the drive ID number, where 0 = the current drive, 1 = drive A, 2 = drive B, and so forth.

Function 1FH (decimal 31): Get DPB for Current Drive

MS-DOS 5.0 documented two functions that return the drive parameter block (DPB). Function 1FH gets the DPB for the current (default) drive, and function 32H gets the DPB for a specific drive.

Function 1FH (decimal 31) requires only that the AH register contain 1FH before issuing interrupt 21. If successful, AL is set to 00H and DS:BX points to the DPB for the default drive. If the function is not successful, AL will be set to FFH. (Note that the carry flag is not set by this function.)

The format of the drive parameter block is shown in Figure 10-21.

Offset			
Hex	**Dec**	**Length**	**Description**
00H	0	1	Drive Number (00H = A, 01H = B, and so on)
01H	1	1	Unit Number (used by the driver if multiple drives are supported)
02H	2	2	Bytes per Sector
04H	4	1	Sectors per Cluster (zero-based)
05H	5	1	Cluster Shift Factor (sectors per cluster, as a power of 2)
06H	6	2	Sector Number of First Sector Containing FAT
08H	8	1	Number (Count) of FATs
09H	9	2	Number (Count) of Root Directory Entries
0BH	11	2	Sector Number of First Cluster Containing User Data
0DH	13	2	Maximum Number (Count) of Clusters, Plus 1
0FH	15	2	Number (Count) of Sectors per FAT
11H	17	2	Sector Number of First Directory Entry
13H	19	4	Address of Disk Device Driver (segment and offset)
17H	23	1	Media Descriptor Byte
18H	24	1	First Access Indicator (FFH if the drive has not been accessed)
19H	25	4	Address of Next DPB (segment and offset)
1DH	29	2	Cluster Number of Last Used Cluster
1FH	31	2	Number (Count) of Free Clusters

Figure 10-21. *Format of the drive parameter block.*

Function 2EH (decimal 46): Set/Clear Verify Flag

Function 2EH (decimal 46) controls verification of disk-write operations. You call this function with AL = 01H to set MS-DOS's internal verify flag and enable verification; you call it with AL = 00H to turn off the flag and verification. Also, in MS-DOS versions 1 and 2, you must zero DL before you call function 2EH.

The disk-verify operation requires the disk controller to perform a cyclical redundancy check (CRC) each time it writes data to the disk. This process involves reading the data just written, which significantly decreases the speed of disk writes.

With MS-DOS versions 2.0 and later, function 54H can be used to report the current setting of the verify flag. (See page 322.)

Function 2FH (decimal 47): Get Disk Transfer Area Address

Function 2FH (decimal 47) returns the address of the disk transfer area (DTA) currently used by MS-DOS. The address is returned in the register pair ES:BX. Contrast this with function 1AH, which is discussed on page 319.

Function 32H (decimal 50): Get DPB for Specific Drive

Function 32H (decimal 50) requires that DL contain a valid drive number (00H = default, 01H = A, 02H = B, and so on). If successful, AL is set to 00H and DS:BX points to the DPB for the specified drive. If the function is not successful, AL will be set to FFH. (Note that the carry flag is not set by this function.)

Function 36H (decimal 54): Get Disk Free Space

Function 36H (decimal 54) is similar to function 1CH (which gets disk information), but it also provides information about unused disk space, which function 1CH does not. Before calling this function, select the drive that you are interested in with the DL register: DL = 00H indicates the default drive, DL = 01H indicates drive A, DL = 02H indicates drive B, and so on.

If you specify an invalid drive, function 36H returns FFFFH in the AX register. Otherwise, AX contains the number of sectors per cluster, CX contains the number of bytes per sector, BX contains the number of available clusters, and DX contains the total number of clusters.

From these numbers you can perform many interesting calculations, as follows:

CX * AX = bytes per cluster
CX * AX * BX = total number of free bytes
CX * AX * DX = total storage space in bytes
(BX * 100) / DX = percentage of free space

If *S* were the size of a file in bytes, you could calculate the number of occupied clusters in this way:

$$(S + ((CX * AX) - 1)) \setminus (CX * AX)$$

Similar formulas would give you the number of sectors and the amount and proportion of space allocated to a file but not used (the *slack space*).

Function 54H (decimal 84): Get Verify Flag

Function 54H (decimal 84) reports the current state of the verify flag, which controls whether or not MS-DOS verifies disk-write operations. AL = 00H indicates that disk writes will not be verified; AL = 01H indicates that they will be verified. This function complements function 2EH, which sets or resets the verify flag.

This function brings up an annoying inconsistency in MS-DOS services: Although some get/set service pairs are integrated into one function (such as function 57H), others are split into two separate functions, such as function 54H and function 2EH.

The Network Device/Drive Functions

Although several of the interrupt 21H functions can be used with network files and devices, two functions apply only to network files and devices. These functions are listed in Figure 10-22.

Function		
Hex	*Dec*	*Description*
5EH	94	Network Machine Name and Printer Setup
5FH	95	Network Redirection

Figure 10-22. *The MS-DOS network device/drive functions.*

Function 5EH (decimal 94):
Network Machine Name and Printer Setup

Function 5EH (decimal 94) first appeared in MS-DOS version 3.1. It comprises several subfunctions that are useful only to programs running in a network. (See Figure 10-23.) You must specify a subfunction number in AL when you call function 5EH. The only error returned by function 5EH sets the carry flag and places 01H in AX, indicating that the subfunction number provided in AL is invalid.

| Subfunction | | Description |
Hex	Dec	
00H	0	Get Machine Name
02H	2	Set Printer Setup String
03H	3	Get Printer Setup String

Figure 10-23. *Subfunctions available through interrupt 21H, function 5EH.*

Subfunction 00H (decimal 0). This subfunction retrieves the network name of the computer on which the program is running. You call it with DS:DX pointing to an empty 16-byte buffer. If the function returns successfully, the carry flag is clear; the buffer contains the machine name as an ASCIIZ string; CH contains a flag that, if nonzero, indicates that the machine name is a valid network name; and CL contains the NETBIOS number associated with the machine name. If the carry flag is not set but CH = 00H, the network has not been installed.

Subfunction 02H (decimal 2). This subfunction passes a printer setup string to MS-DOS. MS-DOS adds this string to the beginning of any files that it sends to a network printer. You call this function with an assign-list index number in BX, the length of the setup string in CX, and DS:DX pointing to the string itself. The assign-list number identifies a particular printer on the network. (See function 5FH.) The maximum length of the string is 64 bytes.

Subfunction 03H (decimal 3). This subfunction complements subfunction 02H. You call it with an assign-list index number in BX and with ES:DI pointing to an empty 64-byte buffer. The subfunction places the requested printer setup string in the buffer and returns the length of the string in CX.

Function 5FH (decimal 95): Network Redirection

Like function 5EH, function 5FH (decimal 95) consists of subfunctions used by programs running in a network. (See Figure 10-24.) In a network environment, MS-DOS maintains an internal table of devices that can be shared

| Subfunction | | Description |
Hex	Dec	
02H	2	Get Assign-List Entry
03H	3	Make Network Connection
04H	4	Cancel Network Connection

Figure 10-24. *Subfunctions available through interrupt 21H, function 5FH.*

across the network; this is called an *assign list* or a *redirection list*. The table associates local logical names for such devices with their network names. The subfunctions give a program access to the table.

Subfunction 02H (decimal 2). This subfunction obtains the local name and network name for one of the devices in the assign-list table. You call this subfunction with an assign-list index number in BX, with DS:SI pointing to an empty 16-byte buffer, and with ES:DI pointing to an empty 128-byte buffer. The subfunction returns the local device name in the 16-byte buffer and the network name in the 128-byte buffer. The subfunction also indicates the device status in BH (00H = device temporarily unavailable; 01H = device is available) and the device type in BL (03H = printer; 04H = disk drive), and it updates CX with the user parameter associated with the device through subfunction 03H.

Subfunction 02H is designed to let you step through the assign-list table. The first table entry's assign-list index is 0. By incrementing the assign-list index each time you call this subfunction, you can examine each table entry in turn. When you request a table entry that is past the end of the table, subfunction 02H sets the carry flag and returns an error code of 12H (no more files) in AX. If the subfunction code provided in AL is invalid, the function returns with the carry flag set and AX = 01H.

Beware: A successful call to subfunction 02H changes DX and BP.

Subfunction 03H (decimal 3). This subfunction redirects a local device to a network device. You call this subfunction with DS:SI containing the address of a 16-byte buffer that contains an ASCIIZ local device name (for example, PRN or E:) and ES:DI pointing to a 128-byte buffer that contains an ASCIIZ network device name followed by an ASCIIZ password. You must also specify the device type in BL (03H = printer; 04H = drive) and place a user parameter in CX. (This parameter should be 00H if you are using IBM's Local Area Network software.)

If subfunction 03H successfully establishes redirection of input/output to the network device, it adds a corresponding entry to its assign-list table and clears the carry flag. If the operation fails, the carry flag is set, and AX contains an error code. The AX error codes are shown in Figure 10-25.

Subfunction 04H (decimal 4). This subfunction cancels network redirection of a device and removes the corresponding assign-list table entry. You call it with DS:SI pointing to an ASCIIZ string that specifies the local device whose redirection you want canceled. If the ASCIIZ string pointed to by DS:SI starts with two backslashes (\\), MS-DOS terminates the connection between the local computer and the network directory. If the operation is

Error Code	Description	Meaning
01H	Invalid function	Either the subfunction specified in AL is invalid or the network is not running.
03H	Path not found	
05H	Access denied	Either the password is invalid or the specified device or drive could not be found.
08H	Not enough memory	
0FH	Invalid drive	
12H	No more files	
57H	Invalid parameter	

Figure 10-25. *AX error codes for function 5FH, subfunction 03H.*

successful, subfunction 04H clears the carry flag. If the operation is unsuccessful, the carry flag is set and AX contains 01H (indicating either that the subfunction specified in AL is invalid or that the network is not running) or 0FH (indicating an invalid drive specification).

Function 5FH is supported only in MS-DOS versions 3.1 and later.

Chapter 11

BIOS and MS-DOS Video Services

In this chapter, we discuss each of the video, or *screen control,* services provided by the BIOS and by MS-DOS. Most of the useful video services are found in the BIOS, and the first and larger portion of the chapter is devoted to them. Following descriptions of the BIOS video services, the few MS-DOS video services are covered. At the end of the chapter, we include some programming hints and an assembly language routine that makes use of some of the BIOS video services. For a more general discussion of the video hardware in the PC family, see Chapter 4. For information on low-memory locations used by the BIOS for video status information, turn to page 64. All the Super VGA (SVGA) displays support VGA mode. Their support over and above VGA mode varies: Maximum resolution on many is 800×600, whereas on some it is 1024×768. A few have yet a different maximum resolution. The BIOS functions in support of these abilities exceeding VGA vary considerably by manufacturer. If you need to exploit those abilities, refer to the manufacturers' technical references.

The BIOS Video Services

The BIOS video services are requested by generating interrupt 10H (decimal 16). There are 25 principal services, used by IBM PCs and all compatibles, available under this interrupt. (See Figure 11-1.) Like all other BIOS services, the video services are numbered beginning with 00H and are selected by placing the service number in the AH register. The services usually require you to specify additional parameters in register AL, BX, CX, or DX. We cover the purpose and placement of parameters in the description of each service.

Service		Description
Hex	*Dec*	
00H	0	Set Video Mode
01H	1	Set Cursor Size
02H	2	Set Cursor Position
03H	3	Read Cursor Position
04H	4	Read Light-Pen Position
05H	5	Set Active Display Page
06H	6	Scroll Window Up
07H	7	Scroll Window Down
08H	8	Read Character and Attribute
09H	9	Write Character and Attribute

Figure 11-1. *The 25 BIOS video services.* *(continued)*

Figure 11-1. *continued*

Service		
Hex	*Dec*	*Description*
0AH	10	Write Character
0BH	11	Set 4-Color Palette
0CH	12	Write Pixel
0DH	13	Read Pixel
0EH	14	Write Character in Teletype Mode
0FH	15	Get Current Video Mode
10H	16	Color Palette Interface
11H	17	Character Generator Interface
12H	18	Alternate Select
13H	19	Write Character String
14H	20	(PC Convertible only)
15H	21	(PC Convertible only)
1AH	26	Read/Write Display Combination Code
1BH	27	Return Functionality/State Information
1CH	28	Save/Restore Video State

Service 00H (decimal 0): Set Video Mode

Service 00H (decimal 0) is used to configure your video subsystem into one of the 20 video modes listed in Figure 11-2. For details about the video modes, see page 83.

You may recall from our discussion in Chapter 4 that modes 00H through 06H apply to the Color Graphics Adapter; mode 07H applies to the Monochrome Display Adapter; modes 0DH through 10H were added for the Enhanced Graphics Adapter; and modes 11H through 13H were introduced with the Multi-Color Graphics Array and the Video Graphics Array. The manufacturers of clone video BIOS chips support additional modes, providing specific support for their products. If you have a need to support those chip sets, refer to the manufacturer's technical reference manual.

Normally the BIOS clears the screen memory buffer when the mode is set, even if it is set to the same mode again and again. In fact, resetting the same video mode can be an easy way to clear the screen. In some versions of MS-DOS, the MS-DOS command CLS clears the screen this way. Setting the video mode also sets the color palette to default color values, however, so don't rely on service 00H to clear the screen if you're working with colors; use video service 06H instead.

Mode	Type	Resolution	Colors	Video Subsystem
00H, 01H	Text	40 × 25	16	CGA, EGA, MCGA, VGA, SVGA
02H, 03H	Text	80 × 25	16	CGA, EGA, MCGA, VGA, SVGA
04H, 05H	Graphics	320 × 200	4	CGA, EGA, MCGA, VGA, SVGA
06H	Graphics	640 × 200	2	CGA, EGA, MCGA, VGA, SVGA
07H	Text	80 × 25	Mono	MDA, EGA, VGA, SVGA
08H, 09H, 0AH				(PC*jr* only)
0BH, 0CH				(Used internally by EGA BIOS)
0DH	Graphics	320 × 200	16	EGA, VGA, SVGA
0EH	Graphics	640 × 200	16	EGA, VGA, SVGA
0FH	Graphics	640 × 350	Mono	EGA, VGA, SVGA
10H	Graphics	640 × 350	16	EGA, VGA, SVGA
11H	Graphics	640 × 480	2	MCGA, VGA, SVGA
12H	Graphics	640 × 480	16	VGA, SVGA
13H	Graphics	320 × 200	256	MCGA, VGA, SVGA

Figure 11-2. *The video modes available through BIOS video service 00H.*

On the EGA, MCGA, VGA, and SVGA, you can tell the BIOS not to clear the screen when it sets up the video mode. You do this by adding 80H (decimal 128) to the video-mode number you specify in AL. For example, to change to 640 × 200, 2-color mode without clearing the screen, call service 00H with AL = 86H. Use this feature with caution, though. Displayable video data is formatted differently in different modes, so a screenful of useful data in one video mode might become unintelligible when you switch to another mode without clearing the screen. Also, some clone video BIOS manufacturers are now using video-mode numbers of 80 and higher.

See page 67, memory location 0040:0049H, for more on how a record of the mode is stored in memory. See service 0FH (decimal 15) to find out how to determine the current video mode.

Service 01H (decimal 1): Set Cursor Size

Service 01H (decimal 1) controls the form and size of the blinking cursor that appears in text modes. The default cursor appears as one or two blinking scan lines at the bottom of a character display position. You can change the default cursor size by redefining the number of lines that are displayed.

The Color Graphics Adapter (CGA) can display a cursor that has 8 scan lines, numbered from 0 at the top to 7 at the bottom. The Monochrome Display Adapter (MDA) and the Enhanced Graphics Adapter (EGA) can display a cursor that has 14 scan lines, also numbered from the top, from 0 through 13. Both the MCGA and the VGA have default text characters that are 16 scan lines high, so the maximum size of the text cursor in default MCGA and VGA text modes is 16 scan lines. You set the cursor size by specifying the starting and ending scan lines. (These are the same as the start and stop parameters of Basic's LOCATE statement.) The start line number is loaded into the CH register, and the stop line number is loaded into the CL register. Default cursor settings are CH = 6 and CL = 7 for the CGA; CH = 11 and CL = 12 for the MDA and the EGA; and CH = 13 and CL = 14 for the MCGA and the VGA.

You will notice that the default scan line numbers occupy only 4 of the bits (bits 0 through 3) placed in these registers. For future systems, bits 0 through 4 have been defined for this purpose, allowing up to 32 scan lines. If bit 5 of CH is set by specifying a value of 20H (decimal 32), the cursor disappears. This is one of two techniques that you can use to remove the cursor in the text modes. The other technique is to actually move the cursor off the screen, say to row 26, column 1. When a graphics mode is set, bit 5 is automatically set to keep the cursor from being displayed. Because there is no true cursor in the graphics modes, you must simulate a cursor with the solid-block character, DBH (decimal 219), or with a change of background attributes.

Service 02H (decimal 2): Set Cursor Position

Service 02H (decimal 2) sets the position of the cursor by using row and column coordinates. In text modes, multiple display pages can exist, each having an independently recorded cursor position. Even though the graphics modes have no visible cursor, they keep track of the logical cursor position in the same way as do the text modes. This logical cursor position is used to control character I/O.

The cursor position is specified by placing a row number in register DH, a column number in DL, and a display page number in BH. The numbering for the rows and columns begins with coordinates 0,0 in the top left corner. The graphics modes also use the character row and column coordinates, rather than pixel coordinates, to identify the cursor location. The display page number must be set to 0 in CGA-compatible graphics modes; the EGA and the VGA both support multiple display pages in 16-color graphics modes as well as in text modes.

See Figure 11-3 for a summary of register settings. See page 98 for more on display pages. See service 03H for the reverse operation, Read Cursor Position.

Service Number	Parameters
AH = 02H	DH = row number
	DL = column number
	BH = page number

Figure 11-3. *The register values for setting the cursor position by using BIOS video service 02H.*

Service 03H (decimal 3): Read Cursor Position

Service 03H (decimal 3) is the opposite of services 01H and 02H. When you specify the page number in BH, the BIOS reports the cursor size by returning the starting scan line in CH and the ending scan line in CL. In addition, it reports the cursor position by returning the row in DH and the column in DL. (See Figure 11-4.)

Service Number	Parameter	Returns
AH = 03H	BH = page number (set to 0 in graphics modes)	DH = row number
		DL = column number
		CH = starting scan line of cursor
		CL = ending scan line of cursor

Figure 11-4. *The values reported by BIOS video service 03H.*

Service 04H (decimal 4): Read Light-Pen Position

Service 04H (decimal 4) reports the light-pen status on a CGA or an EGA. Specifically, it reports whether the pen has been triggered and where it is on the screen if it has been triggered.

On return, if register AH is set, it indicates triggering: If AH = 01H, the light pen has been triggered; if AH = 00H, it has not been triggered. If the pen has been triggered, the BIOS determines the light pen's character column and pixel row (y-coordinate) from the video hardware. From these, the BIOS computes the character row and pixel column (x-coordinate). The results are returned in registers BX, CX, and DX, as shown in Figure 11-5.

Service Number	Returns
AH = 04H	AH = light-pen trigger flag
	DH = character row number
	DL = character column number
	CH = pixel line number (CGA and EGA video modes 04H, 05H, and 06H)
	CX = pixel line number (all video modes supporting >200 lines)
	BX = pixel column number

Figure 11-5. *The light-pen position values returned by BIOS video service 04H.*

Service 05H (decimal 5): Set Active Display Page

Service 05H (decimal 5) selects the active display page for text modes 0 through 3 and for 16-color EGA, MCGA, VGA, and SVGA graphics modes. You specify the page number in register AL. (See Figure 11-6.) In text modes, page numbers range from 0 through 7. Don't forget, however, that the CGA hardware can display only four 80-column pages, so CGA pages 4 through 7 overlap pages 0 through 3 when you're in 80 × 25 text mode. On the EGA, MCGA, VGA, and SVGA video subsystems, you can select among multiple display pages in 16-color graphics modes.

Service Number	Parameter
AH = 05H	AL = new display page number

Figure 11-6. *The register value used to set the active display page by using BIOS video service 05H.*

In all video modes, page 0 is used by default. Page 0 is located at the beginning of display memory; higher page numbers are in higher memory locations. See page 98 for more on display pages.

Service 06H (decimal 6): Scroll Window Up

Service 06H (decimal 6) and companion service 07H (decimal 7) are used to define a rectangular window of text on the screen and to scroll the window's contents up or down one or more lines. To accomplish the scrolling effect, blank lines are inserted at the bottom of the window area with service 06H (at the top with service 07H), and the top lines of the window (the bottom lines with service 07H) are scrolled off and disappear.

The number of lines to be scrolled is specified in AL. If AL = 00H, the entire window is blanked. (The same thing would happen if you scrolled more lines than the window size allowed.) The location or size of the window is specified in the CX and DX registers: CH is the top row, and DH is the bottom row; CL is the left column, and DL is the right column. The display attribute for the new blank lines that are inserted by the two services is taken from BH. Figure 11-7 gives the register settings for services 06H and 07H.

When you fill a window with lines of text, you'll discover that window scrolling is normally a two-stage process: When a new line is ready to be written in the window, service 06H (or service 07H) scrolls the current window contents; then the cursor-positioning and character-writing services fill the new line with text. The following example demonstrates this action:

```
DEBUG                    ; invoke DEBUG from MS-DOS utilities
A                        ; ask to assemble instructions
INT 10                   ; create interrupt 10H instruction
[Return]                 ; finish assembling
R AX                     ; ask to see and change contents of AX
0603                     ; specify service 06H (scroll up), using
                         ; 3-line window
R CX                     ; ask to see and change contents of CX
050A                     ; specify top left corner: row 5, column 10
R DX                     ; ask to see and change contents of DX
1020                     ; specify bottom right corner: row 16, column 32
D 0 L 180                ; fill screen with nonsense
G = 100 102              ; execute INT 10H, then stop
```

Service Number	Parameters
AH = 06H (scroll up)	AL = number of lines to scroll
AH = 07H (scroll down)	CH = row number of upper left corner
	CL = column number of upper left corner
	DH = row number of lower right corner
	DL = column number of lower right corner
	BH = display attribute for blank lines

Figure 11-7. *The register values for scrolling by using BIOS video services 06H and 07H.*

Service 07H (decimal 7): Scroll Window Down

Service 07H (decimal 7) is, as we've already mentioned, the mirror image of service 06H. The difference between the two services is the scrolling action. In service 07H, the new blank lines appear at the top of the window, and the old lines disappear at the bottom. The opposite scrolling action takes place in service 06H. See Figure 11-7 for the register parameter settings.

Service 08H (decimal 8): Read Character and Attribute

Service 08H (decimal 8) is used to read characters "off the screen"—that is, directly out of the display memory. This service is unusually spiffy because it works in both text and graphics modes.

In graphics modes, the same character-drawing tables used to write characters are used to recognize them by a pattern-matching operation. Even if you create your own character set in a graphics mode, this service will be able to recognize the characters. In text modes, of course, the ASCII character codes are directly available in the display memory.

Service 08H returns the ASCII character code of the character in AL. (See Figure 11-8.) In graphics modes, if the character doesn't match any characters in the graphics character set, the BIOS returns ASCII code 0. In text modes, the service also returns the character's color attributes in AH. Be sure to specify a display page number in BH when you call this service.

Service Number	Parameter	Returns
AH = 08H	BH = active display page number	AL = ASCII character read from cursor location
		AH = attribute of text character (text modes only)

Figure 11-8. *The registers used to read a character and attribute by using BIOS video service 08H.*

See page 94 for more on text characters and attribute bytes. See page 101 for more on text-mode and graphics-mode characters. See Appendix D for more on ASCII characters.

Service 09H (decimal 9): Write Character and Attribute

Service 09H (decimal 9) writes one or more copies of a single character and its color attribute. The character is specified in AL, and the text-mode attribute or graphics-mode color is specified in BL. The number of times the character is to be written (one or more times) is placed in CX, and BH contains the display page number. (See Figure 11-9.)

The BIOS writes the character and its color attribute as many times as requested, starting at the current cursor location. Although the cursor is not moved, duplicate characters are written at subsequent screen locations. In

Service Number	Parameters
AH = 09H	AL = ASCII character to write to screen
	BL = attribute value (text modes) or foreground color (graphics modes)
	BH = background color (video mode 13H only) or display page number (all other modes)
	CX = number of times to write character and attribute

Figure 11-9. *The registers used to write a text character and attribute by using BIOS video service 09H.*

text modes, the duplicated characters will successfully wrap around from line to line, which increases the usefulness of this service. In graphics modes, the characters will not wrap around.

Service 09H is quite useful for both writing individual characters and replicating a character. The repeat operation is most often used to rapidly lay out blanks or other repeated characters, such as the horizontal lines that are part of box drawings. (See Appendix D.) When you want to make a single copy of a character, be sure to set the count in CX to 1. If it's set to 0, the number of repetitions will be a lot more than you want.

Service 09H has an advantage over similar service 0EH in that you can control the color attributes. However, its one disadvantage is that the cursor is not advanced.

In graphics modes, the value specified in BL is the foreground color—the color of the pixels that make up the character drawing. Normally the BIOS displays the character with the specified foreground color on a black background. However, if you set bit 7 of the color value in BL to 1, the BIOS creates the character's new foreground color by using an exclusive OR (XOR) operation to combine each of the previous foreground pixels with the value in BL. The same feature applies to the character-writing and pixel-writing services, services 0AH and 0CH.

Here's an example of what can happen when the BIOS uses the XOR operation to display a character. Imagine that you're in 320 × 200, 4-color graphics mode and the screen is completely filled with white pixels. If you now write a white character in the usual way, with a color value of 03H (white) in register BL, the BIOS displays a white character on a black background. However, if you write the same character with a color value of 83H (bit 7 set to 1), the BIOS uses XOR to display a black character on a white background.

See page 94 for more on display attributes in text modes. See page 96 for more on color attributes in graphics modes.

Service 0AH (decimal 10): Write Character

Service 0AH (decimal 10) is the same as service 09H (Write Character and Attribute) with one exception: Service 09H lets you change the existing screen color attribute in text modes, but service 0AH does not.

However, in graphics modes you must still specify a color in BL, which makes the description of this service as only a character-writing service partly incorrect. (See Figure 11-10.) Service 0AH has the same graphics color rules as services 09H and 0CH: The color can be used directly or used with XOR and the existing color. (See service 09H for an explanation.)

See page 94 for more on display attributes in text modes. See page 96 for more on color attributes in graphics modes.

Service Number	Parameters
AH = 0AH	AL = ASCII character to write to screen
	BL = foreground color (graphics modes only)
	BH = background color (video mode 13H only) or display page number (all other modes)
	CX = number of times to write character

Figure 11-10. *The registers used to write a character by using BIOS video service 0AH.*

Service 0BH (decimal 11): Set 4-Color Palette

Service 0BH (decimal 11) actually consists of two subservices. You select either subservice 00H or subservice 01H by storing the proper value in register BH. (See Figure 11-11.) Subservice 00H lets you set the border color in CGA alphanumeric modes or the background color in CGA 320 × 200, 4-color graphics mode. You designate the border color in BL with a value from 00H through 0FH.

Subservice 01H lets you select one of the two 4-color palettes used in 320 × 200, 4-color mode. The value in BL specifies which of the two hardware palettes to use. A value of 0 designates the red-green-brown palette, and a value of 1 selects the cyan-magenta-white palette. (See page 89 for more on color palettes.)

This service was designed primarily for use with the CGA. Use service 10H to control colors in other video modes on the EGA, MCGA, VGA, and SVGA.

Service Number	Subservice Number	Parameters
AH = 0BH	BH = 00H	BL = border or background color
	BH = 01H	BL = palette number (0 or 1)

Figure 11-11. *Controlling colors in CGA-compatible video modes by using BIOS video service 0BH.*

Service 0CH (decimal 12): Write Pixel

Service 0CH (decimal 12) writes an individual pixel. You specify the pixel's location on the screen by passing its column (x-coordinate) in register CX and its row (y-coordinate) in DX. Remember that pixel rows and columns are not the same as the character rows and columns you use in other services to locate the cursor or to display a character. Pixel coordinates correspond to individual dots, not to characters.

If you're using a graphics mode that supports multiple display pages, be sure to specify the display page number in register BH. (See Figure 11-12.) Also, when you specify the pixel's color in register AL, you have the option of setting bit 7 of the color value to 1. As with service 09H, this tells the BIOS to display the pixel with an XORed color value. (See service 09H for an explanation.)

Service Number	Parameters
AH = 0CH	AL = pixel color
	BH = display page number
	DX = row number of pixel
	CX = column number of pixel

Figure 11-12. *The registers used to write a pixel by using BIOS video service 0CH.*

See page 103 for more on pixels in graphics modes.

Service 0DH (decimal 13): Read Pixel

Service 0DH (decimal 13) is the reverse of service 0CH: It reads a pixel's color value rather than writing it. A pixel has only a single color attribute, which is returned through service 0DH. (The Read Character and Attribute service, 08H, returns both a color and an ASCII character code.) The row is specified in DX, the column in CX, and the display page in BH. The pixel color value is returned in AL. (See Figure 11-13.) All high-order bits of the value returned in AL are set to 0, as you would expect.

Service Number	Parameters	Returns
AH = 0DH	BH = display page number	AL = pixel color value
	DX = row number of pixel	
	CX = column number of pixel	

Figure 11-13. *The registers used to read a pixel by using BIOS video service 0DH.*

Service 0EH (decimal 14): Write Character in Teletype Mode

Service 0EH (decimal 14) is the workhorse service of conventional character output. It writes individual characters to the screen in what is known as *teletype (TTY) mode*. This makes the screen act as the simplest and crudest form of printer—exactly what is needed for routine text output. As such, this service has no regard for such niceties as color, blinking characters, and control over the cursor location.

With this service, the character is written at the current cursor location, and the cursor is advanced one position, wrapping to new lines or scrolling the screen as needed. The character to be written is specified in register AL.

In text modes, the character is displayed as in service 0AH—that is, with the color attributes already in use at the screen location where the character is written. In graphics modes, however, you must specify the foreground color value to be used for the character. (See Figure 11-14.)

There are four characters that service 0EH reacts to according to their ASCII meaning: 07H (decimal 7), beep; 08H (decimal 8), backspace; 0AH (decimal 10), linefeed; and 0DH (decimal 13), carriage return. All other characters are displayed normally.

The primary advantage of this service over service 09H is that the cursor is moved; the advantage of service 09H is that you can control the color attribute. Now, if you could only combine the two....

Service Number	Parameters
AH = 0EH	AL = ASCII character to write
	BL = foreground color (in graphics modes only)
	BH = display page (IBM PC BIOS dated 10/19/81 or earlier)

Figure 11-14. *The registers used to write a character in teletype mode by using BIOS video service 0EH.*

Service 0FH (decimal 15): Get Current Video Mode

Service 0FH (decimal 15) returns the current video mode and two other useful pieces of information: the screen width in characters (80 or 40) and the display page number.

The video mode number, explained under service 00H, is returned in AL. The screen width is returned in AH as the number of characters per line. The display page number is returned in BH. (See Figure 11-15.)

Service Number	Returns
AH = 0FH	AL = current video mode
	AH = number of characters per line
	BH = active display page

Figure 11-15. *The information returned by BIOS video service 0FH.*

See page 83 for more on video modes. See page 67, memory location 0040:0049H, for more on how a record of the mode is kept.

Service 10H (decimal 16): Color Palette Interface

Service 10H (decimal 16) was introduced with the PC*jr* and carried forward in the EGA and the MCGA/VGA BIOS. It consists of a set of subservices that let you control palette colors, blinking, and, on the MCGA and the VGA, the video DAC. (See Figure 11-16.) Be aware that different subservices are

Subservice Number	Description
AL = 00H	Update a specified palette register.
AL = 01H	Specify the border color.
AL = 02H	Update all 16 palette registers plus border.
AL = 03H	Select background intensity or blink attribute.
AL = 07H	Read a specified palette register.
AL = 08H	Read the border color register.
AL = 09H	Read all 16 palette registers plus border.
AL = 10H	Update a specified video DAC color register.
AL = 12H	Update a block of video DAC color registers.
AL = 13H	Set video DAC color paging.
AL = 15H	Read a specified video DAC color register.
AL = 17H	Read a block of video DAC color registers.
AL = 1AH	Get video DAC color paging status.
AL = 1BH	Gray-scale a block of video DAC color registers.

Figure 11-16. *Subservices available through BIOS video service 10H.*

supported by different hardware. Before you use these subservices in a program, ensure that your program "knows" which subsystem it's running on. (Video BIOS service 1AH can provide this information to a program.)

Subservice 00H (decimal 0) updates one of the 16 palette registers on an EGA or a VGA. You specify the palette register number in BL and a new palette register value in BH when you call this subservice. The VGA BIOS supports **subservice 07H (decimal 7),** which performs the complementary operation: When you call subservice 07H with a palette register number in BL, the BIOS returns that palette register's current contents in BH. (Subservice 07H isn't available in the EGA BIOS because the EGA has write-only palette registers.)

Subservice 01H (decimal 1) sets the border color on an EGA or a VGA. You pass the color value to the BIOS in register BH when you call this subservice. The VGA BIOS supports **subservice 08H,** which returns the current border color value in BH, but again, this complementary subservice isn't available on the EGA.

Here are two tips on setting the border color on an EGA or a VGA. First, in most EGA video modes the border area is very small, and selecting any border color other than black results in a narrow, smeared border. On the VGA, the border is better. Second, if compatibility with the CGA is important, remember that you can use video service 0BH (page 337) to set the border color.

Subservice 02H (decimal 2) updates all 16 palette registers, plus the border color, with a single BIOS call. Before you call subservice 02H, you must store all 16 palette register values plus the border color value in a 17-byte table. You then pass the address of this table in segment-offset format to the BIOS in registers ES and DX when you call this subservice. The VGA provides a subservice that lets you read the palette registers back into a table: When you call **subservice 09H (decimal 9)** with ES:DX pointing to a 17-byte table, the BIOS fills the table with the 16 current palette register values and the border color.

Subservice 03H (decimal 3) lets you selectively enable or disable the blinking attribute. The BIOS uses blinking by default, but if you prefer to have a full range of 16 background colors instead of only 8, you can use subservice 03H to disable blinking. The value you pass in register BL determines whether blinking is enabled (BL = 01H) or disabled (BL = 00H).

Subservices 10H (decimal 16) and **15H (decimal 21)** are supported by only the MCGA and the VGA BIOS. These two subservices give you direct access to one of the 256 color registers in the video digital-to-analog converter (DAC). To update a video DAC color register, call subservice 10H with the color register number in BX and 6-bit red, green, and blue color values in registers DH, CH, and CL. To read a specified color register, place the color register number in BX, and use subservice 15H, which returns the RGB values in DH, CH, and CL.

The related **subservices, 12H (decimal 18)** and **17H (decimal 23),** operate on a block of video DAC color registers instead of only one. To use subservice 12H, create a table of 3-byte red-green-blue values. Then place the segment-offset address of the table in ES and DX, the first color register number to update in BX, and the number of registers to update in CX. When you call subservice 12H, the BIOS stores each red-green-blue value in turn in the block of color registers you specified in BX and CX.

The complementary subservice, 17H, requires you to pass the address of a table in ES:DX, along with a starting register number in BX and a register count in CX. The BIOS fills the table with the red-green-blue values that it reads from the block of color registers you specified.

On the VGA, which has both palette registers and video DAC color registers, you can use **subservices 13H (decimal 19)** and **1AH (decimal 26)** to switch rapidly between different palettes. By default, the BIOS configures the VGA hardware so that color decoding is the same as on the EGA: Each of the 16 palette registers contains a 6-bit value that specifies one of the first 64 video DAC registers, and these 64 color registers specify the 64 colors available in the EGA palette.

Subservice 13H lets you use the other three color pages, or groups of 64 video DAC color registers. (See Figure 11-17.) If you call subservice 13H with BH = 01H and BL = 01H, for example, the BIOS configures the VGA hardware to display colors from the second group of 64 color registers (color page 1). To use the first group (color page 0) again, you could call the same subservice with BH = 00H and BL = 01H. If, for example, you used the default, EGA-compatible colors in color page 0 and their gray-scale equivalents in color page 1, you could switch rapidly between the two with a single call to subservice 13H.

If you need to switch rapidly among more than four palettes, you can use subservice 13H with BH = 01H and BL = 00H to configure the VGA color-decoding hardware to use 4-bit palette register values instead of 6-bit values. In this case, each palette register value can specify one of only 16 different video DAC registers. This makes 16 color pages available, each comprising 16 color registers. You can select any of the 16 color pages by using subservice 13H with BL = 01H.

Parameters		Description
BL = 00H	BH = 00H	Use four 64-register pages.
	BH = 01H	Use sixteen 16-register pages.
BL = 01H	BH = *n*	Color page number. (*n* = 00H–03H if using 64-register pages; *n* = 00H–0FH if using 16-register pages)

Figure 11-17. *Video DAC color paging with BIOS video service 10H, subservice 13H.*

The VGA BIOS supplements subservice 13H with a complementary function, subservice 1AH. This subservice returns the color page status in BL (for 16-register or 64-register color pages) and BH (the current color page number).

With **subservice 1BH (decimal 27)** on the MCGA and the VGA, you can convert the color values in a block of consecutive video DAC color registers to corresponding shades of gray. You call this subservice with BX containing the number of the first video DAC register to convert and with CX containing the number of registers to update.

Service 11H (decimal 17): Character Generator Interface

Service 11H (decimal 17) first appeared in the EGA BIOS. The many subservices available in service 11H were augmented and expanded in the MCGA and the VGA BIOS to provide full support for these new video subsystems. To make sense of the many service 11H subservices, it helps to consider them in four groups (Figure 11-18):

- Subservices in the first group (subservices 00H through 04H) change the character set used in text modes.

- Subservices in the second group (subservices 10H through 14H) change the text-mode character set as well as the displayed height of text-mode characters.

- Subservices in the third group (subservices 20H through 24H) update graphics-mode character sets.

- The subservice in the fourth group (subservice 30H) returns information about the character sets currently displayed and about the character sets available to the BIOS.

Subservices 00H (decimal 0), 01H (decimal 1), 02H (decimal 2), and **04H (decimal 4)** all change the character set used to display text-mode characters on the EGA (subservice 04 does not apply to the EGA), MCGA, or VGA.

Subservices 01H, 02H, and 04H are the easiest to use. You need specify only which available tables in character generator RAM should contain the character set. Thus, for example, a call to service 11H with AL = 02H and BL = 00H instructs the BIOS to use its 8 × 8–pel characters in the first (default) table in character generator RAM.

If you want to define your own characters, you need to use subservice 00H, as follows: Place a table of the bit patterns that define the characters in a buffer; then call subservice 00H with the address of the table in ES:BP, the number of characters in CX, the ASCII code of the first character in the table in DX, and the number of bytes in each character's bit pattern in BH.

Subservice Number	Description
Load a text-mode character set:	
AL = 00H	Load a user-specified character set.
AL = 01H	Load the ROM BIOS 8 × 14 character set.
AL = 02H	Load the ROM BIOS 8 × 8 character set.
AL = 03H	Select displayed character set.
AL = 04H	Load the ROM BIOS 8 × 16 character set (MCGA and VGA only).
Load a text-mode character set and adjust the displayed character height:	
AL = 10H	Load a user-specified character set.
AL = 11H	Load the ROM BIOS 8 × 14 character set.
AL = 12H	Load the ROM BIOS 8 × 8 character set.
AL = 14H	Load the ROM BIOS 8 × 16 character set (MCGA and VGA only).
Load a graphics-mode character set:	
AL = 20H	Load a CGA-compatible, user-specified character set.
AL = 21H	Load a user-specified character set.
AL = 22H	Load the ROM BIOS 8 × 14 character set.
AL = 23H	Load the ROM BIOS 8 × 8 character set.
AL = 24H	Load the ROM BIOS 8 × 16 character set (MCGA and VGA only).
Get character generator information:	
AL = 30H	Get character generator information.

Figure 11-18. *Subservices available through BIOS video service 11H.*

Subservice 03H (decimal 3) lets you select among text-mode character sets after they are loaded into character generator RAM. The EGA and the MCGA have four such tables; the VGA has eight. The value in BL specifies which one or two of the tables is to be used to display text-mode characters. On the EGA and the MCGA, bits 0 and 1 of BL specify one table, and bits 2 and 3 specify a second table. On the VGA, bits 0, 1, and 4 specify the first table, and bits 2, 3, and 5 specify the second table. If the two bit fields specify the same table, that table will be used for all text-mode characters.

Subservices 10H (decimal 16), 11H (decimal 17), 12H (decimal 18), and 14H (decimal 20) are similar to subservices 00H, 01H, 02H, and 04H. The difference is that with these higher-numbered subservices, the BIOS not only loads a character set but also adjusts the displayed character height appropriately. This difference is obvious if you compare the effects of executing subservice 02H and subservice 12H to load the BIOS 8×8 character set. With subservice 02H, the 8×8 characters are used with no adjustment of the displayed character height, so if you're in a default BIOS text mode, you'll see 25 rows of characters. With subservice 12H, the BIOS adjusts the displayed character height so that in a default BIOS text mode you see 43 rows of characters on an EGA and 50 rows of characters on a VGA.

Subservices 20H through 24H (decimals 32 through 36) are related to subservices 00H through 04H in that they also load character sets into memory. However, this third group of subservices is designed for use only in graphics modes. Subservice 20H loads a CGA-compatible set of 8×8 characters into RAM. To use subservice 20H, place a table containing the bit patterns for ASCII characters 80H through FFH in memory, and pass the address of this table to the BIOS in registers ES:BP. Subservices 21H through 24H are similar to subservices 00H, 01H, 02H, and 04H. You call them with 00H in BL, the number of displayed character rows in DL, and, for subservice 21H, the number of bytes in each character's bit pattern in CX.

Subservice 30H (decimal 48) returns several pieces of handy information regarding the BIOS character generator. This subservice reports the height of the displayed character matrix in CL (in VGA mode, the value returned in CL is one *less* than the height of the displayed character matrix) and the number of the bottom character row in DL. For example, if you call subservice 30H in the default EGA text mode (80×25), the BIOS returns 0EH (decimal 14) in CL and 18H (decimal 24) in DL.

Subservice 30H also returns the address of any of several bit pattern tables for the default BIOS character sets. The value you pass in BH when you call this subservice determines which address the BIOS returns in ES:BP. (See Figure 11-19.)

Parameter	Returns
BH = 00H	CGA-compatible 8 × 8 graphics-mode characters (contents of interrupt 1FH vector)
BH = 01H	Current graphics-mode characters (contents of interrupt 43H vector)
BH = 02H	BIOS 8 × 14 characters
BH = 03H	BIOS 8 × 8 characters
BH = 04H	Second half of BIOS 8 × 8 character table
BH = 05H	BIOS 9 × 14 alternate characters
BH = 06H	BIOS 8 × 16 characters (MCGA and VGA only)
BH = 07H	BIOS 9 × 16 alternate characters (VGA only)

Figure 11-19. *The character bit pattern table addresses returned in ES:BP by subservice 30H of BIOS video service 11H.*

Service 12H (decimal 18): Alternate Select

Service 12H (decimal 18) made its debut along with service 11H in the EGA BIOS. It, too, is supported in the MCGA and the VGA BIOS. The name for this service is derived from the purpose of one of its subservices—namely, to select an alternate print-screen routine for the BIOS Shift-PrtSc function. The name lingers on even though service 12H has been expanded by the addition of a number of unrelated subservices. (See Figure 11-20.)

Subservice Number	Description
BL = 10H	Return video configuration information.
BL = 20H	Select alternate print-screen routine.
BL = 30H	Select scan lines for VGA text modes.
BL = 31H	Enable/disable default palette loading.
BL = 32H	Enable/disable CPU access to video RAM.
BL = 33H	Enable/disable gray-scale summing.
BL = 34H	Enable/disable BIOS cursor emulation.
BL = 35H	PS/2 display switch interface.
BL = 36H	Enable/disable video refresh.

Figure 11-20. *The subservices available through BIOS video service 12H.*

Subservice 10H (decimal 16) reports on the configuration of an EGA or other adapter in EGA mode. The value returned in BH indicates whether the current video mode is color (BH = 00H) or monochrome (BH = 01H). BL contains a number from 0 through 3 that represents the amount of RAM installed in an EGA. (The number *0* means 64 KB, *1* means 128 KB, *2* means 192 KB, and *3* means 256 KB.) The value in CH reflects the status of input from the EGA feature connector, and CL contains the settings of the EGA configuration switches.

Subservice 20H (decimal 32) is provided for the convenience of those who use an EGA or a VGA adapter. It replaces the motherboard BIOS print-screen routine with a more flexible routine in the adapter BIOS. Unlike the motherboard BIOS routine, the adapter BIOS routine can print a snapshot of a text-mode screen that has more than 25 rows of characters. In PS/2s, of course, the motherboard routine can already do this, eliminating the need for this subservice.

Subservice 30H (decimal 48) lets you specify how many scan lines to display in VGA text modes. The default BIOS text modes contain 400 scan lines. When you call subservice 30H, the value you pass in register AL can instruct the BIOS to use a different vertical resolution. If AL = 00H, BIOS text modes will display 200 scan lines, as they do on a CGA. If AL = 01H, BIOS text modes will display an EGA-compatible 350 scan lines. When AL = 02H, the BIOS uses its default resolution of 400 scan lines.

When you use subservice 30H, the vertical resolution does not change until the next time a program uses BIOS video service 00H to select a text mode. Thus, changing the vertical resolution actually requires you to make two different BIOS calls: one to specify the resolution and another to set up the text mode.

Subservice 31H (decimal 49) lets you enable or disable palette loading when the BIOS sets up a new MCGA or VGA video mode. Calling subservice 31H with AL = 01H disables palette loading so that you can subsequently change video modes without changing the colors in a previously loaded palette. A call with AL = 00H enables default palette loading.

Subservices 32H (decimal 50) and **35H (decimal 53)** are provided for programmers who want to use two different video subsystems in the same computer. In particular, these routines support the use of a VGA alongside the built-in MCGA subsystem in a PS/2 Model 30.

Subservice 32H enables or disables buffer and port addressing according to the value passed in AL. (AL = 00H means enable; AL = 01H means disable.) This feature is important if any addresses in the two video subsystems overlap: Before accessing one subsystem, you must disable addressing in the other subsystem.

Subservice 35H provides a complete switching interface that lets you selectively access both a system board video and an adapter board video in the same computer. This subservice relies on the function provided through subservice 32H to independently enable and disable each video subsystem. See Appendix A and the *IBM BIOS Interface Technical Reference Manual* for more detail.

Subservice 33H (decimal 51) tells the BIOS whether or not to average colors to gray scales when it establishes a new video mode on an MCGA or a VGA. A call to this subservice with AL = 01H disables gray scaling; a call with AL = 00H enables it. You can also use this subservice to force the BIOS to use a gray-scale palette even if you're using a color monitor.

Subservice 34H (decimal 52) enables or disables text-mode cursor emulation on the VGA. When you call this subservice with AL = 00H, the BIOS emulates CGA text-mode cursor sizing whenever you change video modes or update the cursor size. When called with AL = 01H, this subservice disables text-mode cursor emulation.

Subservice 36H (decimal 54) lets you enable or disable VGA video refresh. Calling this subservice with AL = 01H disables refresh, and a call with AL = 00H enables refresh. When you disable refresh, the screen goes blank, but reads and writes to the video buffer are somewhat faster than when refresh is enabled. If you are writing a program that needs to run as fast as possible and if you don't mind having the screen go blank while you access the video buffer, consider using subservice 36H to temporarily blank the screen while you update it.

Service 13H (decimal 19): Write Character String

Service 13H (decimal 19) allows you to write a string of characters to the display screen. Through the four subservices that make up this service, you can specify the character attributes individually or as a group. You can also move the cursor to the end of the string or leave it in place, depending on which subservice you choose.

The subservice number is placed in AL, the pointer to the string in ES:BP, the length of the string in CX, the starting screen coordinates where the string is to be written in DX (row in DH and column in DL), and the display page number in BH.

Subservices 00H (decimal 0) and **01H (decimal 1)** write a string of characters from the buffer pointed to by ES:BP to the screen by using the attribute specified in register BL. With subservice 00H, the cursor is not moved from the location specified in register DX; with subservice 01H, the cursor is moved to the location following the last character in the string.

Subservices 02H (decimal 2) and **03H (decimal 3)** write a string of characters and attributes from the buffer pointed to by ES:BP to the screen, writing first the character and then the attribute. With subservice 02H, the cursor is not moved from the location specified in register DX; with subservice 03H, the cursor is moved to the location following the last character in the string.

Service 13H is available only in the PC/AT, EGA, PS/2, and later versions of the PC/XT BIOS.

Service 1AH (decimal 26): Read/Write Display Combination Code

Service 1AH (decimal 26) was introduced in the IBM PS/2 BIOS, but it is also part of the BIOS of the VGA. This service returns a 2-byte code that indicates which combination of video subsystems and video displays is found in your computer. The display combination codes recognized by this BIOS service are listed in Figure 11-21. Service 1AH lets you select either of two subservices by using the value in register AL: subservice 00H or subservice 01H.

Subservice 00H (decimal 0) returns a 2-byte display combination code in register BX. If your computer has two different video subsystems, the value in BL indicates which is *active*—that is, which is currently being updated by the video BIOS. The value in BH indicates the inactive subsystem. If your computer has only one video subsystem, the value in BH is zero.

Code	Video Subsystem
00H	(No display)
01H	MDA
02H	CGA
03H	(Reserved)
04H	EGA with color display
05H	EGA with monochrome display
06H	Professional Graphics Controller with color display
07H	VGA with monochrome display
08H	VGA with color display
09H	(Reserved)
0AH	(Reserved)
0BH	MCGA with monochrome display
0CH	MCGA with color display
FFH	(BIOS unable to identify display type)

Figure 11-21. *The display combination codes returned by BIOS video service 1AH.*

Subservice 01H (decimal 1) performs the reverse function of subservice 00H. It lets you change the current display combination code known to the BIOS. Don't use this subservice, however, unless you know exactly what you're doing. It's a rare program indeed that requires you to change the BIOS's idea of what the video hardware is.

Service 1BH (decimal 27): Return Functionality/State Information

Service 1BH (decimal 27) is available in all IBM PS/2s as well as in the VGA. It returns a great deal of detailed information regarding the capabilities of the BIOS as well as the current BIOS and video hardware status.

Service 1BH returns this information in a 64-byte buffer whose address is passed in registers ES:DI. In addition to this address, you must specify an implementation type value of 0, indicating "return functionality and state information," in register BX. (Presumably, future video products will recognize implementation type values other than 0.)

The BIOS fills the buffer with information about the current video mode (mode number, character columns and rows, and number of colors available) as well as about the video hardware configuration (total video memory available, display combination code, and so on). Figure 11-22 describes the information returned in the buffer.

| Offset | | | |
Hex	Dec	Size	Function
00H	0	Word	Offset to static functionality info
02H	2	Word	Segment of static functionality info
04H	4	Byte	Video mode
05H	5	Word	Character columns in display
07H	7	Word	Length of regeneration buffer
09H	9	Word	Start address in regeneration buffer
0BH	11	Word	Cursor position for page 0
0DH	13	Word	Cursor position for page 1
0FH	15	Word	Cursor position for page 2
11H	17	Word	Cursor position for page 3
13H	19	Word	Cursor position for page 4
15H	21	Word	Cursor position for page 5
17H	23	Word	Cursor position for page 6
19H	25	Word	Cursor position for page 7

Figure 11-22. *The information returned by service 1BH.* (continued)

Figure 11-22. *continued*

Offset Hex	Dec	Size	Function
1BH	27	Word	Cursor type
1DH	29	Byte	Active display page
1EH	30	Word	CRT controller address
20H	32	Byte	3 x 8 register setting
21H	33	Byte	3 x 9 register setting
22H	34	Byte	Character rows in display
23H	35	Word	Character height
25H	37	Byte	Active display combination code
26H	38	Byte	Alternate display combination code
27H	39	Word	Number of colors supported in current mode
29H	41	Byte	Number of pages supported in current mode
2AH	42	Byte	Number of scan lines supported in current mode
2BH	43	Byte	Primary character block
2CH	44	Byte	Secondary character block
2DH	45	Byte	Miscellaneous information
2EH	46	3 bytes	(Reserved)
31H	49	Byte	Amount of available video memory
32H	50	Byte	Save pointer state information
33H	51	13 bytes	(Reserved)

In the first 4 bytes of the buffer, the BIOS returns a pointer to a table of "static" functionality information. This table lists nearly all the features that the BIOS and the video hardware can support: the video modes available, whether palette switching is supported, whether RAM-loadable character sets are supported, whether light pens are supported, and many other details. Figure 11-23 describes the information returned in the static functionality table.

When you write a program that runs on a PS/2 or on a system with a VGA adapter, service 1BH offers a simple and consistent way for your program to determine what the video subsystem's current and potential capabilities are. Unfortunately, you can't rely on this service if your program must be compatible with computers that don't provide VGA support. Neither the PC motherboard BIOS nor the EGA BIOS supports this service. A program can determine whether service 1BH is supported by examining the value returned by this service in AL; this value is 1BH if the service is supported.

Offset			
Hex	Dec	Size	Description
00H	0	Byte	Supported video modes
01H	1	Byte	Supported video modes
02H	2	Byte	Supported video modes
03H	3	4 bytes	(Reserved)
07H	7	Byte	Scan line modes available
08H	8	Byte	Number of char blocks available
09H	9	Byte	Maximum number of char blocks allowed
0AH	10	Byte	Miscellaneous support
0BH	11	Byte	Miscellaneous support
0CH	12	Word	(Reserved)
0EH	14	Byte	Save pointer functions
0FH	15	Byte	(Reserved)

Figure 11-23. *The information returned in the static functionality table.*

Service 1CH (decimal 28): Save/Restore Video State

Service 1CH (decimal 28) is provided by the BIOS in VGA adapters. (In other words, where you find a VGA you also find service 1CH.) This BIOS service lets you preserve all information that describes the state of the video BIOS and hardware. The BIOS can preserve three types of information: the video DAC state, the BIOS data area in RAM, and the current values in all video control registers.

You can select one of three subservices with the value you pass in register AL: subservice 00H, 01H, or 02H.

Subservice 00H (decimal 0) is designed to be called before subservice 01H or 02H. Subservice 00H requires you to specify, by setting one or more of the three low-order bits in CX, which of the three types of information you want to preserve. When this service returns, BX contains the number of 64-byte blocks you need to store the information.

Subservice 01H (decimal 1) saves the current video state information in the buffer whose address you pass in ES:BX. Then you can change video modes, reprogram the palette, or otherwise program the BIOS or video hardware.

Subservice 02H (decimal 2) lets you restore the previous video state.

> NOTE: *Several clone VGA BIOSes change the video registers when saving the video state. Therefore, it is recommended that immediately after saving the video state, you restore the state, which will correctly reload the video registers.*

The MS-DOS Video Services

As we mentioned earlier, MS-DOS does not provide much in the way of video services. About all you can do, in fact, is write single characters to the screen. In today's world of sophisticated graphical interfaces, such basic display functionality is rarely of interest. Yet these functions might occasionally be of use, so we present information on them in this section. As with most MS-DOS services, you call the screen display functions by placing the function number in register AH and invoking interrupt 21H. The MS-DOS interrupt 21H screen display functions are listed in Figure 11-24.

> NOTE: *You can also use interrupt 21H, function 40H, Write Characters to File or Device, to write characters to the screen. This is a handle-based output function that is most frequently used to write data to disk files. If you pass this function the handle 1 (standard error), it will write to the screen. If you pass it handle 0 (standard output), it will write to the screen if output has not been redirected. See Chapter 10 for details on this function.*

Function		Description
Hex	*Dec*	
02H	2	Character Output
06H	6	Direct Console Input/Output
09H	9	String Output

Figure 11-24. *The MS-DOS interrupt 21H screen display functions.*

Function 02H (decimal 2): Character Output

Function 02H (decimal 2) copies a single ASCII character from register DL to the standard output device. In MS-DOS version 1, the standard output device is always the video screen; in later MS-DOS versions, output can be redirected to a file.

In general, this function treats the ASCII control characters, such as backspace and carriage return, as commands. In the case of the backspace character, the display screen cursor is moved backward one column without causing the previous character to be erased.

Function 06H (decimal 6): Direct Console Input/Output

Function 06H (decimal 6) is a complex function that combines the operations of keyboard input and display output into one untidy package. Like other handle-related functions in MS-DOS versions 2.0 and later, the I/O is not connected to the keyboard and the display but rather to the standard input and output devices (which default to the keyboard and the display).

Here is how this function works: The AL register is used for input, and the DL register is used for output. If you call function 06H with DL = FFH (decimal 255), the function performs input:

- If a key was pressed, function 06H returns the corresponding ASCII code in AL and clears the zero flag.

- If no key was pressed, function 06H sets the zero flag.

If you call function 06H with any other value in DL, the function performs output: The character in DL is copied to the standard output device.

Function 06H does not wait for keyboard input, and it does not echo input to the display screen. In addition, function 06H does not interpret Ctrl-C as a keyboard break; instead, it returns the value 03H (the ASCII value of Ctrl-C) in AL.

Compare this function to functions 01H, 07H, and 08H. See function 0CH for a variation of this service.

Function 09H (decimal 9): String Output

Function 09H (decimal 9) sends a string of characters to the standard output device (which defaults to the display screen). The register pair DS:DX provides the address of the string. A $ character, ASCII 24H (decimal 36), marks the end of the string.

Although this function can be far more convenient than the byte-by-byte display services (functions 02H and 06H), it is flawed by the use of a real, displayable character, $, as its string delimiter. This is not a recent mistake; it's another by-product of CP/M compatibility. You should never use this function with programs that need to display dollar signs.

Comments and an Example

Now you've seen how each of the BIOS video services and the MS-DOS video services works. You might be wondering whether you should use the BIOS services or higher-level services, such as the MS-DOS services or those built into your programming language. It is usually best to use the highest-level services that will accomplish what you want to do. In this case, however, there is no specific reason for you to avoid using the BIOS video services— you can't do any harm with them. This advice differs from that offered in the previous chapter on the disk services, where we recommend that you not use the BIOS disk services because more risk is associated with them.

The video capabilities of the PC models are remarkable, and the BIOS services give you full use of them. The MS-DOS services, as you've seen, are rather weak and provide only the simplest character services. Likewise, some programming languages provide only a dressed-up version of the MS-DOS services. So if you need to use the PC's fancy screen capabilities and if you aren't using a language that provides the services you need, you should be using the BIOS services. Getting control of the display screen is one of the best reasons for using the BIOS services.

Using the BIOS services directly usually calls for an assembly language interface, so we'll give you an example of how one can be set up. For the example, we'll set up a module in a format that would be called by C. We'll make the module switch to video mode 1 (40-column text in color) and set the border color to blue.

Here is the assembly module. (See the discussion beginning on page 235 in Chapter 9 for general notes on the format.)

```
_TEXT           SEGMENT         byte public 'CODE'
                ASSUME          cs:_TEXT

                PUBLIC          _Blue40
_Blue40         PROC            near

                push            bp          ; save previous BP value
                mov             bp,sp       ; use BP to access the stack
; set video mode

                mov             ah,0        ; BIOS service number
                mov             al,1        ; video mode number
                int             10h         ; call BIOS to set 40 x 25 text mode

; set border color

                mov             ah,0bh      ; BIOS service number
                mov             bh,0        ; subservice number
                mov             bl,1        ; color value (blue)
                int             10h         ; call BIOS to set border color

                pop             bp          ; restore previous BP value
                ret
_Blue40         ENDP

_TEXT           ENDS
```

Chapter 12

BIOS and MS-DOS Keyboard Services

Both the BIOS and MS-DOS offer a variety of keyboard services that can be used to provide your programs with a flexible means of accepting and manipulating keyboard input. Although the keyboard services are not as numerous or as complicated as those for the display screen (discussed in Chapter 11) and for disk drives (discussed in Chapter 10), they are important enough to warrant their own chapter.

The BIOS Keyboard Services

The BIOS keyboard services are invoked with interrupt 16H (decimal 22). As with all other BIOS services, the keyboard services are selected according to the value in register AH. Figure 12-1 lists the BIOS keyboard services.

| Service | | |
Hex	Dec	Description
00H	0	Read Next Keyboard Character
01H	1	Report Whether Character Ready
02H	2	Get Shift Status
03H	3	Set Typematic Rate and Delay
05H	5	Keyboard Write
10H	16	Extended Keyboard Read
11H	17	Get Extended Keystroke Status
12H	18	Get Extended Shift Status

Figure 12-1. *The BIOS keyboard services.*

Service 00H (decimal 0): Read Next Keyboard Character

Service 00H (decimal 0) reports the next keyboard input character. If a character is ready in the BIOS keyboard buffer, it is reported immediately. If not, the service waits until one is ready. As described on page 152, each keyboard character is reported as a pair of bytes, called the main and auxiliary bytes. The main byte, which is returned in AL, is either 0 for special characters (such as the function keys) or an ASCII code for ASCII characters. The auxiliary byte, which is returned in AH, is either the character ID for special characters or the standard PC-keyboard scan code that identifies which key was pressed.

If no character is waiting in the keyboard buffer when service 00H is called, the service waits—essentially freezing the program that called it—until a character does appear. The service we discuss next allows a program to test for keyboard input without the risk of suspending program execution.

Contrary to what is suggested in some versions of the *IBM PC Technical Reference Manual*, service 00H applies to both ordinary ASCII characters and special characters such as function keys.

Service 01H (decimal 1): Report Whether Character Ready

Service 01H (decimal 1) reports whether a keyboard input character is ready. This is a sneak-preview or look-ahead operation: Even though the character is reported, it remains in the keyboard input buffer of the BIOS until it is removed by service 00H. The zero flag (ZF) is used as the signal: 1 indicates no input is ready; 0 indicates a character is ready. Take care not to be confused by the apparent reversal of the flag values—1 means no, and 0 means yes, in this instance. When a character is ready (ZF = 0), it is reported in AL and AH, exactly as it is with service 00H.

Service 01H is particularly useful for two commonly performed program operations. One is *test and go,* in which a program checks for keyboard action but needs to continue running if there is none. Usually this is done to allow an ongoing process to be interrupted by a keystroke. The other common operation is clearing the keyboard buffer. Programs can generally allow users to type ahead, entering commands in advance; however, in some operations (for example, at safety-check points, such as ''OK to end?'') this practice can be unwise. In these circumstances, programs need to be able to flush the keyboard buffer, clearing it of any input. Services 00H and 01H are used to flush the keyboard buffer, as the following program outline demonstrates:

```
call service 01H to test whether a character is available in the
keyboard buffer
WHILE (ZF = 0)
      BEGIN
      call service 00H to remove character from keyboard buffer
      call service 01H to test for another character
      END
```

Contrary to what some technical reference manuals suggest, service 01H applies to both ordinary ASCII characters and special characters such as function keys.

Service 02H (decimal 2): Get Shift Status

Service 02H (decimal 2) reports the shift status in register AL. The shift status is taken bit by bit from the first keyboard status byte, which is kept at memory location 0040:0017H. Figure 12-2 shows the settings of each bit.

(See page 156 for information about the other keyboard status byte, which is located at 0040:0018H.)

Bit 7 6 5 4 3 2 1 0	Meaning
X	Insert state: 1 = active
. X	Caps Lock: 1 = active
. . X	Num Lock: 1 = active
. . . X	Scroll Lock: 1 = active
. . . . X . . .	1 = Alt pressed
. . . . . X . .	1 = Ctrl pressed
. . . . . . X .	1 = Left Shift pressed
. . . . X	1 = Right Shift pressed

Figure 12-2. *The keyboard status bits returned in register AL by using BIOS keyboard service 02H.*

Generally, service 02H and the status bit information are not particularly useful. If you plan to do some fancy keyboard programming, however, they can come in handy. You'll frequently see them used in programs that do unconventional things, such as differentiating between the left and right Shift keys.

Service 03H (decimal 3): Set Typematic Rate and Delay

Service 03H (decimal 3) was introduced with the now-defunct IBM PC*jr*, but it has been supported in the PC/AT (in BIOS versions dated November 15, 1985, and later), in all PS/2s, and in all clones with 80286 or higher CPUs. Service 03H lets you adjust the rate at which the keyboard's typematic function operates—that is, the rate at which a keystroke repeats while you hold down a key. This service also allows you to adjust the *typematic delay,* which is the amount of time you can hold down a key before the typematic repeat function takes effect.

To use this service, call interrupt 16H with AH = 03H and AL = 05H. BL must contain a value from 00H through 1FH (decimal 0 through 31) that indicates the desired typematic rate. (See Figure 12-3.) The value in BH specifies the typematic delay. (See Figure 12-4.) The default typematic rate is 10 characters per second. (It is 10.9 characters per second for IBM PS/2s and most clones.) The default delay for all PCs is 500 milliseconds.

00H = 30.0	0BH = 10.9	16H = 4.3
01H = 26.7	0CH = 10.0	17H = 4.0
02H = 24.0	0DH = 9.2	18H = 3.7
03H = 21.8	0EH = 8.6	19H = 3.3
04H = 20.0	0FH = 8.0	1AH = 3.0
05H = 18.5	10H = 7.5	1BH = 2.7
06H = 17.1	11H = 6.7	1CH = 2.5
07H = 16.0	12H = 6.0	1DH = 2.3
08H = 15.0	13H = 5.5	1EH = 2.1
09H = 13.3	14H = 5.0	1FH = 2.0
0AH = 12.0	15H = 4.6	20H through FFH - Reserved

Figure 12-3. *The values for register BL in BIOS keyboard service 03H. The rates are in characters per second.*

00H = 250
01H = 500
02H = 750
03H = 1000
04H through FFH - Reserved

Figure 12-4. *The values for register BH in BIOS keyboard service 03H. The delay values are in milliseconds.*

Service 05H (decimal 5): Keyboard Write

Service 05H (decimal 5) is handy because it lets you place "keystrokes" in the keyboard buffer, exactly as if a key had been pressed. You must supply an ASCII code in register CL and a keyboard scan code in CH. The BIOS places these codes in the keyboard buffer (behind any keystroke data that is present there).

Service 05H lets a program process input as if it were typed at the keyboard. For example, if you call service 05H with the following data, the result is the same as if the keys R, U, N, and Enter were pressed:

CH = 13H, CL = 52H, call service 05H (the R key)
CH = 16H, CL = 55H, call service 05H (the U key)
CH = 31H, CL = 4EH, call service 05H (the N key)
CH = 1CH, CL = 0DH, call service 05H (the Enter key)

If your program processed this input (as shown on the previous page) when it detected that the F2 function key was pressed, the result would be the same as if you had typed the word *RUN* and pressed the Enter key. (If you use Basic, this should sound familiar.)

Beware: The keyboard buffer can hold only 15 character codes, so you can call service 05H a maximum of 15 consecutive times before the buffer overflows and the function fails.

Service 10H (decimal 16): Extended Keyboard Read

Service 10H (decimal 16) performs the same function as service 00H, but it lets you take full advantage of the 101/102-key keyboard: It returns ASCII character codes and keyboard scan codes for keys that don't exist on the 84-key keyboard. For example, the F11 and F12 keys found on the 101/102-key keyboard are ignored by service 00H but can be read with service 10H.

Here is another example. On the 101/102-key keyboard, an extra Enter key appears to the right of the numeric keypad. When this key is pressed, service 00H returns the same character code (0DH) and scan code (1CH) that it does for the standard Enter key. Service 10H lets you differentiate between the two Enter keys because it returns a different scan code (E0H) for the keypad Enter key.

Service 11H (decimal 17): Get Extended Keystroke Status

Service 11H (decimal 17) is similar to service 01H, but it lets you use the 101/102-key keyboard to full advantage. The scan codes returned in register AH by this service distinguish different keys on the 101/102-key keyboard.

Service 12H (decimal 18): Get Extended Shift Status

Like services 10H and 11H, service 12H (decimal 18) provides support for the 101/102-key keyboard. Service 12H expands the function of service 02H to provide information on the extra shift keys provided on the 101/102-key keyboard. This service returns the same value in register AL as service 02H (Figure 12-2), but it returns an additional byte of flags in register AH, as shown in Figure 12-5.

This extra byte indicates the status of each Ctrl and Alt key. It also indicates whether the Sys Req, Caps Lock, Num Lock, or Scroll Lock key is currently pressed. This information lets you detect when a user presses any combination of these keys at the same time.

Bit 7 6 5 4 3 2 1 0	Meaning
X	Sys Req pressed
. X	Caps Lock pressed
. . X	Num Lock pressed
. . . X	Scroll Lock pressed
. . . . X . . .	Right Alt pressed
. . . . . X . .	Right Ctrl pressed
. . . . . . X .	Left Alt pressed
. . . . X	Left Ctrl pressed

Figure 12-5. *The extended keyboard status bits returned in register AH by BIOS keyboard service 12H.*

The MS-DOS Keyboard Services

Like all MS-DOS services, the keyboard services are accessed via interrupt 21H, and you must first place the function number in register AH. Figure 12-6 lists the MS-DOS keyboard services.

Function		Description
Hex	Dec	
01H	1	Character Input with Echo
06H	6	Direct Console Input/Output
07H	7	Direct Console Input Without Echo
08H	8	Console Input Without Echo
0AH	10	Buffered Keyboard Input
0BH	11	Check Keyboard Status
0CH	12	Flush Keyboard Buffer, Read Keyboard

Figure 12-6. *The MS-DOS keyboard services.*

You can also read the keyboard by using a handle-based MS-DOS function—interrupt 21H, function 3FH, Read File or Device—which is described in Chapter 10. By passing this function the handle number 0, which is automatically assigned to stdin (the standard input device), you can read data from the keyboard (assuming that input has not been redirected).

Function 01H (decimal 1): Character Input with Echo

Function 01H (decimal 1) waits for character input from the standard input device; when input is available, the function returns it in the AL register in addition to sending the character to stdout (the standard output device). This function should be compared to the other keyboard function calls, particularly functions 06H, 07H, and 08H.

> NOTE: *In MS-DOS version 1, the standard input device is always the keyboard; the standard output device is always the video screen. In later MS-DOS versions, however, standard input and output can be redirected to other devices, such as files. MS-DOS processes characters from the standard input device without making a determination of whether the actual input source is the keyboard or a stream of characters redirected from a file.*

Here is how function 01H works: Keystrokes that result in an ASCII character are returned as 1 byte in AL and are immediately reported; keystrokes that result in something other than an ASCII character generate 2 bytes, which must be obtained by performing two consecutive calls to this function.

The usual way to use this function is to test whether it returns 00H in AL. If AL is not 00H, you have an ASCII character. If AL = 00H, you have a non-ASCII keystroke (which should be recorded), and this function should be repeated immediately to get the pseudo–scan code that represents the special key action. (See page 153 for a list of the actions and codes and their meanings.) None of the MS-DOS keyboard input services make the scan code for ASCII characters available, even if the corresponding BIOS keyboard services do.

The various MS-DOS keyboard service functions are distinguished primarily by three criteria: whether they wait for input and report no input when none is available; whether they echo input to stdout; and whether the standard break-key operation is active for that service. Function 01H performs all three operations: It waits for input, echoes input to stdout, and lets MS-DOS execute interrupt 23H if Ctrl-C is pressed.

Remember that function 01H always waits for the user to press a key before it returns to a program. If you don't want to wait, either use function 0BH to test whether a key was pressed, before you call function 01H, or use function 06H. See functions 07H, 08H, and 0CH for related services.

Function 06H (decimal 6): Direct Console Input/Output

Function 06H (decimal 6) is a complex function that combines the operations of keyboard input and display output. As with other services in MS-DOS versions 2.0 and later, the I/O is not connected to the keyboard and display but rather to the standard input and output devices (which default to the keyboard and display).

Here is how this function works: The AL register is used for input, and the DL register is used for output. If you call function 06H with DL = FFH (decimal 255), the function performs input:

- If a key was pressed, function 06H returns the corresponding ASCII code in AL and clears the zero flag.

- If no key was pressed, function 06H sets the zero flag.

If you call function 06H with any other value in DL, the function performs output: The character in DL is copied to the standard output device.

Function 06H does not wait for keyboard input, and it does not echo input to the display screen. In addition, function 06H does not interpret Ctrl-C as a keyboard break; instead, it returns the value 03H (the ASCII value of Ctrl-C) in AL.

Compare this function to functions 01H, 07H, and 08H. See function 0CH for a variation of this service.

Function 07H (decimal 7): Direct Console Input Without Echo

Function 07H (decimal 7) waits for character input from the standard input device; when input is available, this function returns it in the AL register. It does not echo input to the display screen, and it does not recognize Ctrl-C as a keyboard break character.

Function 07H works in the same way as function 01H: ASCII character key actions are returned as single bytes in AL and are immediately reported. Non-ASCII function keystrokes (see page 153) generate 2 bytes, which must be obtained with two consecutive calls to function 07H.

Compare this function to functions 01H, 06H, and 08H. If you want to use this function but don't want to wait when input is not ready, see function 0BH, which reports whether input is ready. See function 0CH for a variation of function 07H.

Function 08H (decimal 8): Console Input Without Echo

Function 08H (decimal 8) waits for input, does not echo, and breaks on a Ctrl-C. It is identical to function 01H except that it does not echo the input to the display screen (or standard output device).

See the discussion of function 01H for a description of function 08H. Compare this function to functions 01H, 06H, and 07H. If you want to use this function but don't want to wait when input is not ready, see function 0BH, which reports whether input is ready. See function 0CH for a variation of function 08H.

Function 0AH (decimal 10): Buffered Keyboard Input

Function 0AH (decimal 10) puts the power of the MS-DOS editing keys to work in your programs. The function gets a complete string of input, which is presented to your programs whole rather than character by character. If you assume that the input is actually from live keyboard action and is not redirected from elsewhere, the full use of the MS-DOS editing keys is available to the person who is typing the input string. When the Enter key is pressed or when a carriage return—ASCII 0DH (decimal 13)—is encountered in the input file, the input operation is complete, and the entire string is presented to your program.

This function provides many advantages, particularly to those programs needing complete, coherent strings of keyboard input rather than byte-by-byte input. The two foremost benefits are that you need not write detailed input-handling code and that your programs' users are given a familiar set of input editing tools: the MS-DOS editing conventions.

To use this function, you must provide MS-DOS with an input buffer area where the input string will be built. The register pair DS:DX points to this buffer when you call the function. The first 3 bytes of this buffer have specific purposes:

- The first byte indicates the *working size* of the buffer. The working size is the number of bytes that MS-DOS can use for input.

- The second byte is updated by MS-DOS to indicate the actual number of bytes that were input.

- The third byte is the beginning of the input string, which consists of ASCII characters. The end of the input string is signaled by the carriage-return character, ASCII 0DH. Although the carriage return is placed in the buffer, it is not included in the character count that MS-DOS returns in the second byte.

By these rules, the longest buffer you can give MS-DOS is 255 working bytes, and the longest string that MS-DOS can return is 1 byte less than the working length. Because the first 2 bytes of the buffer are used for status information, the actual working size of the buffer is 2 bytes less than the buffer's overall size. This might explain some of the mysteries of the input conventions in both MS-DOS and Basic.

If input continues beyond what MS-DOS can place in the buffer (which is 1 byte short of its working length), MS-DOS discards any further input, beeping all the while, until a carriage return is encountered.

See function 0CH for a variation of this function.

Function 0BH (decimal 11): Check Keyboard Status

Function 0BH (decimal 11) reports whether or not input is ready from the keyboard (or standard input device). If a character is ready, AL = FFH (decimal 255). If no input is ready, AL = 00H.

MS-DOS checks for Ctrl-C when you execute function 0BH, so a loop that contains a call to this function can be interrupted by a keyboard break.

Function 0CH (decimal 12): Flush Keyboard Buffer, Read Keyboard

Function 0CH (decimal 12) clears the keyboard buffer in RAM and then invokes one of four MS-DOS functions: function 01H, 06H, 07H, or 08H. The AL register is used to select which of these functions will be performed after the keyboard buffer is flushed. With the keyboard buffer clear of extraneous characters, function 0CH forces the system to wait for new input before it acts on the invoked function.

Comments and an Example

If you are in a position to choose among the keyboard services of your programming language, the BIOS keyboard services, and the MS-DOS keyboard services, you can safely and wisely use any of them. Although in some cases there are arguments against using the BIOS services directly, those arguments do not apply as strongly to the keyboard services as they do to the disk services. As always, you should fully examine the potential of the MS-DOS services before resorting to the BIOS services; you might find all you need there, and the MS-DOS services are more long-lived in the ever-changing environment of personal computers.

Most programming languages depend on the MS-DOS services for their keyboard operations, a factor that has some distinct advantages. One advantage is that the MS-DOS services allow the use of the standard MS-DOS editing operations on string input (input that is not acted on until the Enter key is pressed). Provided you do not need input control of your own, it can save you a great deal of programming effort and user education to let

MS-DOS handle the string input, either directly through the MS-DOS services or indirectly through your language's services. But if you need full control of keyboard input, you'll probably end up using the BIOS routines. The choice is yours.

Another advantage to using the MS-DOS keyboard services is that the MS-DOS services can redirect keyboard input so that characters are read from a file instead of the keyboard. If you rely on the BIOS keyboard services, you can't redirect keyboard input.

For our assembly language example of the use of keyboard services, we'll get a little fancier than we have in previous examples and show you a complete buffer flusher. This routine will utilize the action outlined under keyboard service 01H, Report Whether Character Ready.

```
_TEXT           SEGMENT byte public 'CODE'
                ASSUME  cs:_TEXT

                PUBLIC  _kbclear
_kbclear        PROC    near

                push    bp
                mov     bp,sp

L01:            mov     ah,1            ; test whether buffer is empty
                int     16h
                jz      L02             ; if so, exit

                mov     ah,0
                int     16h             ; otherwise, discard data
                jmp     L01             ; ... and loop

L02:            pop     bp
                ret

_kbclear        ENDP

_TEXT           ENDS
```

The routine works by using interrupt 16H, service 01H, to check whether the keyboard buffer is empty. If no characters exist in the buffer, service 01H sets the zero flag. Executing the instruction JZ L02 causes the routine to exit by branching to the instruction labeled L02. If the buffer still contains characters, however, service 01H clears the zero flag, and the JZ L02 instruction doesn't jump. In this case, the routine continues to the instructions that call service 00H to read a character from the buffer. Then the process repeats because the instruction JMP L01 transfers control back to label L01. Sooner or later, of course, the repeated calls to service 00H empty the buffer, service 01H sets the zero flag, and the routine terminates.

Among the new things this buffer-flusher routine illustrates is the use of labels and branching. When we discussed the generalities of assembly language interface routines in Chapter 9, we mentioned that an ASSUME CS statement is necessary in some circumstances, and you see one in action here. The ASSUME directive in this example tells the assembler that the labels in the code segment (that is, labels that would normally be addressed by using the CS register) do indeed lie in the segment whose name is _TEXT. This might seem obvious because no other segments appear in this routine. Nevertheless, it is possible to write assembly language routines in which labels in one segment are addressed relative to some other segment; in such a case, the ASSUME directive would not necessarily reference the segment within which the labels appear. In later chapters you'll see examples of this technique, but here the only segment to worry about is the _TEXT segment, and the ASSUME directive makes this fact explicit.

Chapter 13

Miscellaneous BIOS and MS-DOS Services

In this chapter, we cover the BIOS and MS-DOS services that do not belong in the disk, video, or keyboard chapters. The BIOS services include RS-232 serial communications services, system services, BIOS hooks, and printer services; the MS-DOS services include time and date services, printer and serial communications services, program loading and termination services, interrupt vector services, and memory allocation services. We also cover some BIOS and MS-DOS services that are odd enough to be considered miscellaneous even in a chapter of miscellany.

The BIOS Services

The BIOS services covered in this chapter fall into a wide range of categories. You might frequently use some of these services. For example, the serial communications services can be quite useful if you are writing a simple serial communications program. Other services are rarely used.

The RS-232 Serial Communications Services

The BIOS RS-232 asynchronous serial communications port services are invoked with interrupt 14H (decimal 20). They are summarized in Figure 13-1. To understand these services, you should be familiar with the terminology associated with the serial communications port. You might want to refer to Chapter 7 for information on serial port hardware. For more information, turn to one of the many specialty books on serial communications.

Service	Description
00H	Initialize Serial Port
01H	Send Out One Character
02H	Receive One Character
03H	Get Serial Port Status
04H	Initialize Extended Serial Port
05H	Control Extended Communications Port

Figure 13-1. *The BIOS RS-232 serial port services available through interrupt 14H.*

Service 00H (decimal 0): Initialize Serial Port

Service 00H (decimal 0) sets the various RS-232 parameters and initializes the serial port. It sets four parameters: the baud rate, the parity, the number of stop bits, and the character size (also called the *word length*). The parameters are combined into one 8-bit code, which is placed in the AL register in the format shown in Figure 13-2. The bit settings for each code are shown in

Figure 13-3. When the service is finished, the communications port status is reported in AX, just as it is for service 03H. (See service 03H for details.)

Bit 7 6 5 4 3 2 1 0	Use
X X X	Baud-rate code
. . . X X . . .	Parity code
. . . . . X . .	Stop-bit code
. . . . . . X X	Character-size code

Figure 13-2. *The bit order of the serial port parameters passed in register AL to BIOS RS-232 serial communications service 00H.*

NOTE: *Although it is painfully slow, 300 baud used to be the most commonly used baud rate for personal computers using modems. Then 1200 baud became the most common, but today many people consider that slow too. At present 2400 baud is the standard, but rates of 9600 baud and even faster are becoming common for serious applications that require faster transmission.*

BAUD RATE

Bit				
7	6	5	Value	Bits per Second
0	0	0	0	110
0	0	1	1	150
0	1	0	2	300
0	1	1	3	600
1	0	0	4	1200
1	0	1	5	2400
1	1	0	6	4800
1	1	1	7	9600

PARITY

Bit			
4	3	Value	Meaning
0	0	0	No parity
0	1	1	Odd parity
1	0	2	No parity
1	1	3	Even parity

CHARACTER SIZE

Bit			
1	0	Value	Meaning
0	0	0	Not used
0	1	1	Not used
1	0	2	7-bit*
1	1	3	8-bit

STOP BITS

Bit		
2	Value	Meaning
0	0	One
1	1	Two

*There are only 128 standard ASCII characters, so they can be transmitted as 7-bit characters, rather than as 8-bit characters.

Figure 13-3. *The bit settings for the four serial port parameters for BIOS RS-232 serial communications service 00H.*

Service 01H (decimal 1): Send Out One Character

Service 01H (decimal 1) transmits one character out the serial port specified in DX (0 = first serial port, 1 = second serial port, and so on). When you call service 01H, you place the character to be transmitted in AL. When service 01H returns, it reports the status of the communications port. If AH = 00H, the service was successful. Otherwise, bit 7 of AH indicates that an error occurred, and the other bits of AH report the type of error. These bits are outlined in the discussion of service 03H, the status service.

The error report supplied by this service has one anomaly: Because bit 7 reports that an error has occurred, it is not available to indicate a time-out error (as the details in service 03H would suggest). Consequently, when this service or service 02H reports an error, the simplest and most reliable way to check the nature of the error is to use the complete status report given by service 03H, rather than the less-complete status code returned with the error through services 01H and 02H.

Service 02H (decimal 2): Receive One Character

Service 02H (decimal 2) receives one character from the communications line specified in DX (0 = first communications line, 1 = second line, and so on) and returns it in the AL register. The service waits for a character or any signal that indicates the completion of the service, such as a time-out. AH reports the success or failure of the service in bit 7, as explained in the discussion of service 01H. Again, consider the advice under service 01H for error handling, and see service 03H for the error codes.

Service 03H (decimal 3): Get Serial Port Status

Service 03H (decimal 3) returns in the AX register the complete serial port status for the port number specified in DX. The 16 status bits in AX are divided into two groups: AH reports the line status (which is also reported

> NOTE: *One piece of information about the time-out error (AH, bit 7) is worth noting: The earliest version of the BIOS for the original IBM PC had a programming error that caused a serial port time-out to be reported as a transfer-shift-register-empty/break-detect-error combination (bits 01010000 rather than 10000000). This has been corrected in all subsequent versions of the BIOS, but it has caused many communications programs to treat these error codes skeptically. You might want to keep this in mind. See page 73 for details on identifying the BIOS version dates and machine-ID codes.*

when errors occur with services 01H and 02H), and AL reports the modem status, when applicable. Figure 13-4 contains the bit codings of the status bits. Some codes report errors, and others simply report a condition.

Bit 7 6 5 4 3 2 1 0	Meaning (When Set to 1)	Bit 7 6 5 4 3 2 1 0	Meaning (When Set to 1)
AH Register (line status)		*AL Register (modem status)*	
1	Time-out error	1	Received line signal detect
. 1	Transfer shift register empty	. 1	Ring indicator
. . 1	Transfer holding register empty	. . 1	Data-set-ready (DSR)
. . . 1	Break-detect error	. . . 1	Clear-to-send (CTS)
. . . . 1 . . .	Framing error	. . . . 1 . . .	Delta receive line signal detect
. . . . . 1 . .	Parity error	. . . . . 1 . .	Trailing-edge ring detector
. . . . . . 1 .	Overrun error	. . . . . . 1 .	Delta data-set-ready
. . . . 1	Data ready	 1	Delta clear-to-send

(handwritten annotation:) returns status of:

Figure 13-4. *The bit coding for the status bytes returned in register AX by BIOS RS-232 serial communications service 03H.*

Service 04H (decimal 4): Initialize Extended Serial Port

Service 04H (decimal 4) is available only in machines using the CBIOS introduced in the PS/2 BIOS. It expands the capabilities of service 00H to provide support for improved serial ports. If you compare service 04H to service 00H, you'll find that the four serial port initialization parameters passed in AL in service 00H are separated into four registers in service 04H. (See Figure 13-5.) Also, service 04H returns both modem and line status in register AX, exactly as service 03H does. Because service 04H has these expanded capabilities, you should generally use it instead of service 00H for CBIOS serial port initialization.

Service 05H (decimal 5): Control Extended Communications Port

(handwritten annotation:) sets DTR/RTS

Service 05H (decimal 5), which is provided only by the CBIOS (introduced in the IBM PS/2), lets you read from or write to the modem control register of a specified serial communications port. When you call service 05H with AL = 00H and a serial port number in DX, service 05H returns with register BL containing the value in the modem control register of the specified serial port. When you call service 05H with AL = 01H, the BIOS copies the value you pass in register BL into the modem control register for the specified port. In both cases, service 05H returns the modem status and line status in registers AL and AH, as does service 03H.

BREAK (Register AL)

Value	Meaning
00H	No break
01H	Break

PARITY (Register BH)

Value	Meaning
00H	No parity
01H	Odd
02H	Even
03H	Stick parity odd
04H	Stick parity even

STOP BITS (Register BL)

Value	Meaning
00H	One
01H	Two (for word length = 6, 7, or 8)
	1 ½ (for word length = 5)

WORD LENGTH (Register CH)

Value	Meaning
00H	5 bits
01H	6 bits
02H	7 bits
03H	8 bits

BAUD RATE (Register CL)

Value	Meaning	Value	Meaning
00H	110 baud	05H	2400 baud
01H	150 baud	06H	4800 baud
02H	300 baud	07H	9600 baud
03H	600 baud	08H	19,200 baud
04H	1200 baud		

Figure 13-5. *The register values for serial port initialization with BIOS RS-232 serial communications interrupt 14H, service 04H. (Register DX contains a serial port number from 0 through 3.)*

Miscellaneous System Services

The miscellaneous system services provided through interrupt 15H are indeed miscellaneous. (See Figure 13-6.) Many are intended primarily for writers of operating system software. Most applications programmers will find little use for these services in their programs because the functions provided are better carried out by calls to the operating system than they are through the BIOS. Some of these services, such as the pointing-device interface (subservice C2H), provide functionality not otherwise available in the BIOS or in MS-DOS; others are obsolete and virtually unusable.

Service	Description
21H	Read or Write CBIOS POST Error Log
4FH	Keyboard Intercept*
80H	Device Open*
81H	Device Close*
82H	Program Termination*
83H	Start or Cancel Interval Timer
84H	Read Joystick Input
85H	Sys Req Keystroke*
86H	Wait During a Specified Interval
87H	Protected-Mode Data Move
88H	Get Extended Memory Size
89H	Switch to Protected Mode
90H	Device Busy*
91H	Interrupt Complete*
C0H	Get System Configuration Parameters
C1H	Get BIOS Extended Data Segment
C2H	Pointing-Device Interface
C3H	Enable/Disable Watchdog Timer
C4H	Programmable Option Select

* This service is discussed in the following section, "The BIOS Hooks."

Figure 13-6. *Miscellaneous system services available through BIOS interrupt 15H.*

Service 21H (decimal 33): Read or Write CBIOS POST Error Log

Service 21H (decimal 33) is used internally by the BIOS Power On Self Test (POST) routines in machines using the CBIOS (introduced in the IBM PS/2) to keep track of hardware initialization errors. You will rarely, if ever, find use for this service in your own applications.

Service 83H (decimal 131): Start or Cancel Interval Timer

Service 83H (decimal 131) lets a program set a specified time interval and check a flag to determine whether the interval has expired. The program should call this service with AL = 00H, with the address of a flag byte in registers ES:BX, and with the time interval in microseconds in the register pair CX:DX. The high-order 16 bits of the interval should be in CX; the low-order 16 bits should be in DX.

Initially, the flag byte should be 00H. When the time interval elapses, the BIOS sets this byte to 80H. The program can thus inspect the flag byte at its convenience to determine when the time interval has elapsed, as below:

```
Clear the flag byte
Call service 83H to start the interval timer
WHILE   (flag byte = 00H)
        BEGIN
        (do something useful)
        END
```

The BIOS interval timer uses the system time-of-day clock, which ticks about 1024 times per second, so the timer's resolution is approximately 976 microseconds.

Service 84H (decimal 132): Read Joystick Input

Service 84H (decimal 132) provides a consistent interface for programs that use a joystick or a related input device connected to a game port that is compatible with the IBM Game Control Adapter. When you call this service with DX = 00H, the BIOS reports the adapter's four digital switch input values in bits 4 through 7 of register AL. Calling service 84H with DX = 01H instructs the BIOS to return the adapter's four resistive input values in registers AX, BX, CX, and DX. AX returns the x-coordinate for joystick 1; BX returns the y-coordinate for joystick 1; CX returns the x-coordinate for joystick 2; DX returns the y-coordinate for joystick 2.

Service 84H is not supported on the IBM PC or in the original PC/XT BIOS (dated November 8, 1982). Be sure to check the computer's model identification and BIOS revision date before you rely on this BIOS service in a program.

Service 86H (decimal 134): Wait During a Specified Interval

Like service 83H, service 86H (decimal 134) lets a program set a specified time interval to wait. Unlike service 83H, however, service 86H suspends operation of the program that calls it until the specified time interval has elapsed. Control returns to the program only when the wait is completed or if the hardware timer is unavailable. As with service 83H, the wait period is in milliseconds and is specified in the register pair CX:DX.

Service 87H (decimal 135): Protected-Mode Data Move

A program running in real mode can use service 87H (decimal 135) to transfer data to or from extended (protected-mode) memory on a system with an 80286 or higher CPU. This service is designed to be used by a protected-mode operating system. The RAMDRIVE utility uses this function to copy data to and from a virtual disk in extended memory.

Service 88H (decimal 136): Get Extended Memory Size

Service 88H (decimal 136) returns the amount of extended (protected-mode) memory installed in systems with an 80286 or higher CPU. The value, in kilobytes, is returned in register AX.

The amount of extended memory is established by the BIOS POST routines. It includes extended memory installed beyond the first megabyte—that is, memory starting at 10000:0000H. Lotus/Intel/Microsoft expanded memory is not included in the value returned by service 88H.

Service 89H (decimal 137): Switch to Protected Mode

Service 89H (decimal 137) is provided by the BIOS as an aid to configuring an 80286 or higher computer for protected-mode operation. This BIOS service is intended for operating systems that run in protected mode. To use it, you must be thoroughly acquainted with protected-mode programming techniques. See the *IBM BIOS Interface Technical Reference Manual* for details.

Service C0H (decimal 192): Get System Configuration Parameters

Service C0H (decimal 192) returns in ES:BX the address of a table of descriptive information pertaining to the hardware and BIOS configuration of a PC/AT (in BIOS versions dated June 10, 1985, and later), a PS/2, or one of the clones. Figure 13-7 shows the structure of the table. Some representative values of the model and submodel bytes are provided in Chapter 3, page 74.

Offset	*Size*	*Contents*
0	2 bytes	Size of configuration information table
2	1 byte	Model byte
3	1 byte	Submodel byte
4	1 byte	ROM BIOS revision level
5	1 byte	Feature information byte:
		Bit 7: Hard disk BIOS uses DMA Channel 3
		Bit 6: Cascaded interrupt level 2 (IRQ2)
		Bit 5: Real-time clock present
		Bit 4: BIOS keyboard intercept implemented
		Bit 3: Wait for external event supported
		Bit 2: Extended BIOS data area allocated
		Bit 1: Micro Channel bus present
		Bit 0: (Reserved)
6	2 bytes	(Reserved)
8	2 bytes	(Reserved)

Figure 13-7. *The system configuration information returned by BIOS service C0H.*

In non-IBM BIOS's, the table may be extended, and the values returned at offsets 2, 3, and 4 will be unique to the machine manufacturer.

Service C1H (decimal 193): Get BIOS Extended Data Segment

Service C1H (decimal 193) returns the segment address of the BIOS extended data area. The BIOS clears the carry flag and returns the segment value in register ES if an extended BIOS data segment is in use. Otherwise, service C1H returns with the carry flag set.

The BIOS uses the extended data area for transient storage of data. For example, when you pass the address of a pointing-device interface subroutine to the BIOS, the BIOS stores this address in its extended data area.

Service C2H (decimal 194): Pointing-Device Interface

Service C2H (decimal 194) is the BIOS interface to the built-in pointing-device controller as introduced in the IBM PS/2. This interface makes it easy to program support for a mouse attached to the interface.

To use the interface, you must write a short subroutine to which the BIOS can pass packets of status information about the pointing device. Your subroutine should examine the data in each packet and respond appropriately—for example, by moving a cursor on the screen. The subroutine must exit by using a far return without changing the contents of the stack.

To use the BIOS pointing-device interface, carry out the following sequence of steps:

1. Pass the address of your subroutine to the BIOS (subservice 07H).

2. Initialize the interface (subservice 05H).

3. Enable the pointing device (subservice 00H).

At this point, the BIOS begins sending packets of status information to your subroutine. The BIOS places each packet on the stack and calls your subroutine with a far CALL so that the stack is formatted when the subroutine gets control, as illustrated in Figure 13-8. The low-order byte of the X and Y data words contains the number of units the pointing device has moved since the previous packet of data was sent. (The Z data byte is always 0.) The status byte contains sign, overflow, and button information. (See Figure 13-9.)

When you use service C2H, the value you pass in register AL selects one of eight available subservices. (See Figure 13-10.) The register contents for each subservice are covered in Appendix A.

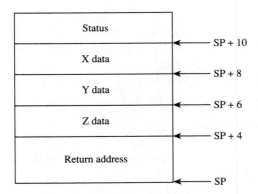

Figure 13-8. *The pointing-device data packet.*

Bit	Meaning
0	Set if left button is pressed.
1	Set if right button is pressed.
2	(Reserved; must be 0.)
3	(Reserved; must be 1.)
4	Set if X data is negative.
5	Set if Y data is negative.
6	Set if X data overflows.
7	Set if Y data overflows.

Figure 13-9. *The status byte in the pointing-device data packet.*

Subservice	Description
00H	Enable/Disable Pointing Device
01H	Reset Pointing Device
02H	Set Sample Rate
03H	Set Resolution
04H	Get Pointing-Device Type
05H	Initialize Pointing Device
06H	Extended Commands
07H	Pass Device-Driver Address to ROM BIOS

Figure 13-10. *The subservices available in the BIOS pointing-device interface (interrupt 15H, service C2H).*

Service C3H (decimal 195): Enable/Disable Watchdog Timer

Service C3H (decimal 195) provides a consistent interface with the watchdog timer in those machines that use the CBIOS. It lets an operating system enable the watchdog timer, specifying a time-out interval, or disable the timer. Because the watchdog timer is intended specifically for use in operating system software, this BIOS service will rarely be useful in your applications.

Service C4H (decimal 196): Programmable Option Select

Like many other interrupt 15H services, service C4H (decimal 196) is intended for use by operating system software. This service provides a consistent interface with the Programmable Option Select feature first introduced in certain IBM PS/2 models.

The BIOS Hooks

The BIOS in systems with 80286 or higher CPUs provides a number of hooks. These hooks are implemented as interrupt 15H "services," but to use them you must write an interrupt 15H handler that processes only these services and passes all other interrupt 15H service requests to the BIOS. (See Figure 13-11.) This arrangement lets different components of the BIOS communicate

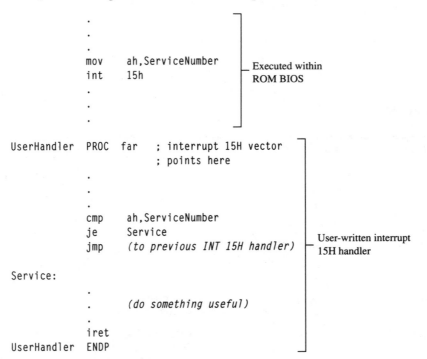

Figure 13-11. *How the BIOS hooks can be used.*

in a consistent manner with each other and with operating system or user-written programs.

The BIOS hooks are intended primarily for use in operating systems and in programs written to augment operating system or BIOS functions. However, neither MS-DOS nor OS/2 uses these BIOS hooks, and few program applications have reason to. Still, you might find it worthwhile to examine what the BIOS hooks do, if only to get an idea of how the BIOS is put together and how an operating system can interact with it.

Service 4FH (decimal 79): Keyboard Intercept

In the PC/AT BIOS (dated June 10, 1985, and later), in the PS/2 BIOS, and in the BIOS of most clones, the keyboard interrupt handler (that is, the handler for hardware interrupt 09H) executes interrupt 15H with AH = 4FH and with AL equal to the keyboard scan code. This action has little effect: The BIOS interrupt 15H, service 4FH (decimal 79) handler returns with the carry flag set, and the interrupt 09H handler continues processing the keystroke.

If you write an interrupt handler for interrupt 15H, however, you can hook service 4FH and process keystrokes yourself. You install your handler by storing its segmented address in the interrupt 15H vector. (Be sure to save the previous contents of the interrupt 15H vector.) Your interrupt 15H handler would do the following:

```
IF (AH<>4FH)
        jump to default interrupt 15H handler
ELSE
        process keyboard scan code in AL
        set or reset carry flag
        exit from interrupt handler
```

If your handler processes the scan code in AL, it must either set or reset the carry flag before it returns control to the BIOS interrupt 09H handler. Setting the carry flag indicates that the BIOS interrupt 09H handler should continue processing the scan code in AL. Clearing the carry flag causes the BIOS handler to exit without processing the scan code.

The problem with using the BIOS keyboard intercept is that other programs, including MS-DOS itself, can and do process keystrokes before the BIOS interrupt 09H handler ever has a chance to issue interrupt 15H. (The programs do this by pointing the interrupt 09H vector to their own handlers instead of to the default BIOS handler.) Because your program can't determine whether this is happening, you cannot rely on the BIOS keyboard intercept to be called for every keystroke.

Service 80H (decimal 128): Device Open

Service 80H (decimal 128) lets programs determine when a particular hardware device is available for input or output. An installable device driver can issue interrupt 15H with AH = 80H to inform an operating system that the device was opened. The operating system's interrupt 15H handler can inspect BX for an identifying value for the device, and it can inspect CX for an ID value of the program that opened the device.

Service 81H (decimal 129): Device Close

Like service 80H, service 81H (decimal 129) is provided for programs that establish input/output connections to hardware devices so they can communicate with an operating system. This service is called by such a program with a device ID value in register BX and a program ID value in CX. An operating system's interrupt 15H handler can inspect these values to determine that a particular device was closed for input/output by a particular program.

Service 82H (decimal 130): Program Termination

Service 82H (decimal 130) is provided by the BIOS so that a program can signal its own termination to an operating system. When a program executes interrupt 15H with AH = 82H and an ID value in BX, the operating system can handle the interrupt and thus be informed that the program terminated.

Service 85H (decimal 133): Sys Req Keystroke

When you press the Sys Req key on an 84-key keyboard or Alt-Sys Req on a 101/102-key keyboard, the BIOS keyboard interrupt handler executes interrupt 15H with AH = 85H (decimal 133). You can detect when this key is pressed by hooking interrupt 15H and inspecting the value in AH.

When the Sys Req key is pressed, the BIOS issues interrupt 15H with AH = 85H and AL = 00H. When the key is released, the BIOS executes interrupt 15H with AH = 85H and AL = 01H. Thus, the structure of an interrupt 15H handler that detects Sys Req keystrokes would be as follows:

```
IF (AH<>85H)
                jump to previous interrupt 15H handler
ELSE IF (AL = 00H)
                process Sys Req keystroke
    ELSE
                process Sys Req key release
    exit from interrupt handler
```

Service 90H (decimal 144): Device Busy

Service 90H (decimal 144) lets a device driver alert an operating system to the beginning of an input or output operation. For example, an operating system's interrupt 15H handler can process this information by preventing subsequent input/output to the device until the device signals, with service 91H, that it is no longer busy.

The BIOS device drivers for disks, the keyboard, and the printer all issue appropriate service 90H interrupts. Each device is identified by a value in register AL. (See Figure 13-12.) These ID values are selected according to the following guidelines:

- 00H through 7FH: Non-reentrant devices that can process only one I/O request at a time, sequentially.

- 80H through BFH: Reentrant devices that can handle multiple I/O requests at once.

- C0H through FFH: Devices that expect the operating system to wait a predetermined period of time before returning control to the device. The operating system's interrupt 15H handler must set the carry flag to indicate that the wait has been carried out.

Value	Meaning
00H	Hard disk
01H	Floppy disk
02H	Keyboard
03H	Pointing device
80H	Network
FCH	Hard disk reset
FDH	Floppy disk–drive motor start
FEH	Printer

Figure 13-12. *Device identification values for BIOS interrupt 15H, services 90H and 91H.*

Service 91H (decimal 145): Interrupt Complete

Devices that use service 90H to notify an operating system that they are busy can subsequently use service 91H (decimal 145) to signal that an input/output operation has been completed. The identification value passed in AL should be the same as the value passed in service 90H.

The Printer Services

The BIOS printer services support printer output through the parallel printer adapter. The three BIOS printer services are invoked by using interrupt 17H (decimal 23), are requested through the AH register, and are numbered 00H through 02H. (See Figure 13-13.) The PC family design generally allows more than one printer to be installed, so a printer number must be specified in register DX for all these services.

Service	Description
00H	Send 1 Byte to Printer
01H	Initialize Printer
02H	Get Printer Status

Figure 13-13. *The three BIOS printer services invoked by using interrupt 17H.*

Service 00H (decimal 0): Send 1 Byte to Printer

Service 00H (decimal 0) sends the byte you specify in AL to the printer. After the service is completed, AH is set to report the printer status, which can be used to determine the success or failure of the operation. (See service 02H.) Note the discussion of printer time-outs under service 02H.

Service 01H (decimal 1): Initialize Printer

Service 01H (decimal 1) initializes a printer. To do this, the service simply sends two control codes (08H and 0CH) to the printer control port. As with the other two printer services, the printer status is reported in AH.

Service 02H (decimal 2): Get Printer Status

Service 02H (decimal 2) reports the printer status in the AH register. The individual bit codes are shown in Figure 13-14.

Bit 7 6 5 4 3 2 1 0	Meaning (When Set to 1)
1	Printer *not* busy (0 = busy)
. 1	Acknowledgment from printer
. . 1	Out-of-paper signal
. . . 1	Printer selected
. . . . 1 . . .	I/O error
. . . . . 1 . .	Not used
. . . . . . 1 .	Not used
. . . . 1	Time-out

Figure 13-14. *The printer status bits reported in the AH register by BIOS printer services 00H, 01H, and 02H.*

The printer time-out can cause some difficulty for programmers. Any I/O driver needs to set a time limit for a response from the device being controlled. Ideally, this time limit should be short enough to ensure that an unresponsive device can be reported in a timely manner. Unfortunately, one normal printer operation, a *page eject* (''skip to the top of the next page''), can take a surprisingly long time. The time allowed varies from version to version of the BIOS. Treat a time-out signal with care.

Other BIOS Services

We now come to the grab bag of other BIOS services. (See Figure 13-15.) Some of these services are intended for use in application programs; others are more likely to be used in operating system software. The following sections describe these six service interrupts.

Interrupt		
Hex	Dec	Description
05H	5	Print-Screen Service
11H	17	Equipment-List Service
12H	18	Memory-Size Service
18H	24	ROM Basic Loader Service
19H	25	Bootstrap Loader Service
1AH	26	Time-of-Day Services

Figure 13-15. *Six miscellaneous BIOS services.*

Interrupt 05H (decimal 5): Print-Screen Service

Interrupt 05H (decimal 5) activates the print-screen service. The keyboard support routines generate interrupt 05H in response to the Shift-PrtSc combination on the 83-key and 84-key keyboards or the Print Screen key on the 101/102-key keyboard. Any other programs can safely and conveniently perform a print-screen operation by generating interrupt 05H.

In text and graphics modes, the print-screen service maintains the current cursor position on the screen and prints any printable characters from the screen. It uses both the standard video services (those that waltz the cursor around the screen and read characters from the screen buffer) and the standard printer services.

This service directs all its output to printer number 0, the default printer. There are no input or output registers for this service. However, a status code is available at low-memory location 0050:0000H. (See page 71.) If the byte at that location has a value of FFH (decimal 255), the preceding print-screen operation was not completed successfully. A value of 00H indicates that no error occurred and that the print-screen operation is available. A value of 01H indicates that a print-screen operation is currently in progress; any request for a second one will be ignored.

The BIOS print-screen routine cannot print images drawn on the screen in graphics modes. If you want to produce a printed screen snapshot in graphics modes, use the MS-DOS utility program GRAPHICS. This program installs a memory-resident, graphics-mode print-screen routine that hooks interrupt 05H. After you execute GRAPHICS, pressing Shift-PrtSc (or the Print Screen key on the 101/102-key keyboard) or executing interrupt 05H while in a graphics mode will run the routine.

Interrupt 11H (decimal 17): Equipment-List Service

Interrupt 11H (decimal 17) reports what equipment is installed in the computer. This report contains the same information that is stored at low-memory location 0040:0010H. (See Chapter 3, page 65.) The report is coded as shown in Figure 13-16, in the bits of a 16-bit word, which is placed in register AX. See interrupt 12H for a related service.

The equipment information is gathered as accurately as possible but might not be exactly correct. Different methods are used for acquiring the information in the various PC models.

The equipment list is determined only once, at power-up time, and is then left in memory. This means that you might wish to write a routine to maintain the equipment list. For example, you could take some equipment off line so that it is not used. However, modifying the equipment list is risky business—don't bet on its success. See interrupt 19H for comments on how to modify the equipment list and get reliable results.

The format of the equipment list was defined for the original IBM PC. As a result, some parts of the list vary, depending on the PC model. For example, bits 2 and 3 originally indicated the amount of RAM installed on the motherboard. (Yes, in those days you could indeed have purchased a PC with as little as 16 KB of RAM.) In other PC models, these bits have a different significance. (See Figure 13-16.)

Interrupt 12H (decimal 18): Memory-Size Service

Interrupt 12H (decimal 18) invokes the service that reports the available memory size in kilobytes—the same information stored at low-memory location 0040:0013H. (See page 66.) The memory-size value, reported in AX, reflects only the amount of base memory available. In a computer with an 80286 or higher CPU that has extended (protected-mode) memory, you must

Bit 15 14 13 12 11 10 9 8	7 6 5 4 3 2 1 0	Meaning
X X	. . . .	Number of printers installed
. . X	. . . .	(Reserved)
. . . X	. . . .	Game adapter: 1 = installed
. . . . X X X .	. . . .	Number of RS-232 serial ports
. . . . X	. . . .	(Not used)
. . . .	X X	1 less than number of floppy disk drives installed
. . . .	. . X X	Initial video mode: 11 = monochrome; 10 = 80-column color; 01 = 40-column color
. . . .	. . . . X X . .	PC with 64-KB motherboard: Amount of system board RAM (11 = 64 KB; 10 = 48 KB; 01 = 32 KB; 00 = 16 KB) PC/AT: (Not used) PS/2s and clones: Bit 3 = (unused); bit 2: 1 = pointing device installed
. . . .	. . . . . . X .	1 if math coprocessor installed
. . . .	 X	1 if any floppy disk drives exist (if so, see bits 7 and 6)

Figure 13-16. *The bit coding for the equipment list reported in register AX and invoked by BIOS interrupt 11H.*

use interrupt 15H, service 88H (Get Extended Memory Size) to determine the amount of extended memory installed.

In the standard models of the original 8088 PC, this value is taken from the setting of the physical switches inside the system unit. These switches are supposed to reflect the memory installed, although under some circumstances they are set to less memory than is actually present. In later models, the BIOS POST determines the amount of memory in the system by exploring available RAM to see what is installed. If the BIOS is using an extended data area, this data area is allocated at the highest memory address available, so the value returned by this service excludes the amount of RAM reserved for the extended data area.

Interrupt 18H (decimal 24): ROM Basic Loader Service

Interrupt 18H (decimal 24) is normally used to activate ROM Basic. ROM Basic exists only in IBM personal computers. Any program can activate Basic (or whatever has replaced it) by generating interrupt 18H. This can be done to intentionally bring up ROM Basic or to abruptly shut down, or *dead-end,* a program. However, see interrupt 19H for a better way to dead-end a program.

Interrupt 19H (decimal 25): Bootstrap Loader Service

Interrupt 19H (decimal 25) activates the standard bootstrap routine for the computer. This produces a similar result to powering on and nearly the same net result as pressing the Ctrl-Alt-Del key combination. However, interrupt 19H bypasses the lengthy memory check of the power-on routines as well as the reset operations of Ctrl-Alt-Del.

The bootstrap loader works by reading the first sector of the first track (the *boot sector*) from the floppy disk in drive A into memory at 0000:7C00H. If the BIOS cannot read from the floppy disk, it reads the boot sector from the hard disk in drive C instead. In IBM personal computers, if both attempts fail, the BIOS executes interrupt 18H to bring up ROM Basic. If the BIOS reads a sector from the disk but the sector doesn't contain an operating system boot record, the BIOS issues an error message and waits for you to reboot or replace the offending floppy disk.

We know of two uses for this interrupt service. One is to immediately shut down, or dead-end, the operation of the computer. This can be done by a program when it encounters an "illegal" situation—for example, when a copy-protected program detects an apparent violation of copy protection.

The other use for this service is to reboot the computer without going through the reset and restart operations. Such a reboot would, among other procedures, reconstruct the equipment list and memory size reported by interrupts 11H and 12H. This interrupt is particularly useful for any program that modifies either of these two items. The reasoning is simple: If you want to change the equipment list or the memory size (for example, to set aside some memory for a RAM disk), you cannot count on all programs—MS-DOS included—to check the actual memory or equipment specifications each time they are used. But a program could set aside some memory, change the memory specification, and then use this interrupt to reboot the system. When that is done and MS-DOS is activated, MS-DOS would take its own record of the available memory from the value set by your program. Neither MS-DOS nor any civilized MS-DOS program would be aware of, or interfere with, the memory area that was set aside.

To give you a brief example, here's a fragment of assembly language code that will change the BIOS's record of the memory size and then use interrupt 19H to reboot the computer:

```
mov     ax,40H                  ; get BIOS data segment of hex 40...
mov     es,ax                   ; ...into ES segment register
mov     word ptr es:[13h],256   ; set memory to 256 KB
int     19h                     ; reboot system
```

Interrupt 1AH (decimal 26): Time-of-Day Services

Interrupt 1AH (decimal 26) provides the time-of-day services. Unlike other interrupts covered in this section, but like all other BIOS services, several services can be activated by this interrupt. When you execute interrupt 1AH, you specify the service number, as usual, in register AH. (See Figure 13-17.)

Service		
Hex	*Dec*	*Description*
00H	0	Get Current Clock Count
01H	1	Set Current Clock Count
02H	2	Get Real-Time Clock Time
03H	3	Set Real-Time Clock Time
04H	4	Get Real-Time Clock Date
05H	5	Set Real-Time Clock Date
06H	6	Set Real-Time Clock Alarm
07H	7	Reset Real-Time Clock Alarm

Figure 13-17. *The time-of-day services invoked by BIOS interrupt 1AH.*

The BIOS maintains a time-of-day clock based on a count of system-clock ticks that have occurred since midnight. The system clock "ticks" by generating interrupt 08H at specific intervals. On each clock tick, the BIOS interrupt 08H service routine increments the clock count by 1. When the clock count passes 24 hours' worth of ticks, the count is reset to 0 and a record is made of the fact that midnight has been passed. This record is not in the form of a count, so you can't detect whether two midnights have passed.

The clock ticks at a rate that is almost exactly $1,193,180 \div 64$ KB, or roughly 18.2 times a second. The count is kept as a 4-byte integer at low-memory location 0040:006CH. The midnight count value, which is compared to the rising clock count, is 1800B0H, or 1,573,040; when the clock hits the midnight count value, the byte at location 0040:0070H is set to 01H and the count is reset. When MS-DOS needs to know the time, it reads the count by using the time-of-day service and then calculates the time from this raw count. If it sees that midnight has passed, it also increments the date.

You can use the following Basic formulas to calculate the current time of day from the clock count:

```
HOURS = INT(CLOCK / 65543)
CLOCK = CLOCK - (HOURS * 65543)
MINUTES = INT(CLOCK / 1092)
CLOCK = CLOCK - (MINUTES * 1092)
SECONDS = CLOCK / 18.2
```

391

In reverse, you can use the following formula to calculate a nearly correct clock count from the time:

```
COUNT = (HOURS * 65543) + (MINUTES * 1092) + (SECONDS * 18.2)
```

The BIOS services in personal computers using the 80286 or higher CPU include time-of-day and date services that perform some of these tasks automatically.

Service 00H (decimal 0): Get Current Clock Count Service 00H (decimal 0) returns the current clock count in two registers: the high-order portion in CX and the low-order portion in DX. AL = 00H if midnight has not passed since the last clock value was read or set; AL = 01H if midnight has passed. The midnight signal is always reset when the clock is read. Any program using this service must use the midnight signal to keep track of changes in the date. Application programs normally should not use this service directly. If they do, they must calculate and set a new date.

> NOTE: *It's curious that version 2.0 of MS-DOS did not consistently update the date on the midnight signal. The next version of MS-DOS (2.1) and all other versions of MS-DOS do.*

Service 01H (decimal 1): Set Current Clock Count Service 01H (decimal 1) sets the clock count in location 0040:006CH by using the values you pass in registers CX and DX. This service clears the midnight flag at 0040:0070H.

Service 02H (decimal 2): Get Real-Time Clock Time Systems with an 80286 or higher CPU have a real-time clock that maintains the current date and time in nonvolatile memory. This clock runs in parallel to the system timer referenced by services 00H and 01H. When you boot one of these systems, the BIOS initializes the system timer count by using the time indicated by the real-time clock.

You can access the real-time clock directly by using service 02H (decimal 2). This service returns the time in binary-coded decimal (BCD) format. Binary-coded decimal is a system for encoding decimal numbers in binary form to avoid rounding and conversion errors. In BCD coding, each digit of a decimal number is coded separately as a binary numeral. Each of the decimal digits 0 through 9 is coded in 4 bits, and for ease of reading, each group of 4 bits is separated by a space. This format, called 8-4-2-1 after the weights of the four bit positions, uses the following codes:

0000 = 0	0101 = 5
0001 = 1	0110 = 6
0010 = 2	0111 = 7
0011 = 3	1000 = 8
0100 = 4	1001 = 9

Thus, the decimal number 12 is 0001 0010 in BCD notation, 96 is 1001 00110, and so on. Service 02H returns the time in registers CH (hours), CL (minutes), and DH (seconds). Register DL = 01H if daylight saving time was indicated by service 03H; otherwise, DL = 00H. If the real-time clock is defective, the BIOS sets the carry flag.

Service 03H (decimal 3): Set Real-Time Clock Time Service 03H (decimal 3) complements service 02H. It lets you set the real-time clock on an 80286 or higher system by using the same register assignments as does service 02H. Again, the hours, minutes, and seconds values are in BCD format.

Service 04H (decimal 4): Get Real-Time Clock Date Service 04H (decimal 4) returns the current date, which is maintained by the real-time clock in an 80286 or higher system. The BIOS returns the century (19 or 20) in register CH, the year in CL, the month in DH, and the day in DL. Again, the values are returned in BCD format. As in service 02H, the BIOS sets the carry flag if the real-time clock is not operating.

Service 05H (decimal 5): Set Real-Time Clock Date Service 05H (decimal 5) complements service 04H. This service sets the real-time clock date by using the same registers as service 04H.

Service 06H (decimal 6): Set Real-Time Clock Alarm Service 06H (decimal 6) lets you create an alarm program that executes at a specific time. This alarm program must be memory resident at the time the alarm occurs. To use this service, make your alarm program memory resident by using the MS-DOS terminate-and-stay-resident service (see page 397), and be sure that interrupt vector 4AH (0000:0128H) points to the start of your program. Then call service 06H to set the time for the alarm to occur.

Service 06H uses the same register values as does service 03H: CH contains hours, CL contains minutes, and DH contains seconds, all in BCD format. The BIOS sets the carry flag when it returns from this service if the real-time clock is not operating or if the alarm is already in use.

When the real-time clock time matches the alarm time, the BIOS executes interrupt 4AH, which transfers control to your alarm program. Your program can then take appropriate action. (It could display a message, for example.) Because the BIOS activates your alarm program by executing an INT 4AH instruction, the program must exit by using an IRET instruction.

Service 07H (decimal 7): Reset Real-Time Clock Alarm Use service 07H (decimal 7) to disable the real-time clock alarm if it has been set by a call to service 06H.

The MS-DOS Services

As with most MS-DOS services, those in this chapter are called by placing the function number in register AH and issuing software interrupt 21H.

The Time and Date Services

The following sections cover the MS-DOS time and date services.

Function 2AH (decimal 42): Get Date

Function 2AH (decimal 42) reports MS-DOS's record of the current date. The date is reported in CX and DX. DH contains the month number (1 through 12); DL contains the day of the month (1 through 28, 29, 30, or 31, as appropriate); and CX contains the year (1980 through 2099). These values are all in hexadecimal format.

This function reports the day of the week by returning a value from 0 through 6, signifying Sunday through Saturday, in register AL. This day-of-the-week feature is something of an orphan. It has been present in MS-DOS since version 1.1, but it was not even mentioned in the manuals until version 2.0. In both the 2.0 and 2.1 manuals, it is incorrectly described as part of the get-time function and not as part of the get-date function. Starting with MS-DOS 3.0, the manual tells it as it is. Turn to the example on page 425 to see how this function can be used.

Function 2BH (decimal 43): Set Date

Function 2BH (decimal 43) sets MS-DOS's record of the current date by using the same registers as does function 2AH. The date is set in CX and DX. DH contains the month number (1 through 12); DL contains the day of the month (1 through 28, 29, 30, or 31, as appropriate); and CX contains the year (1980 through 2099). As with function 2AH, these values are in hexadecimal format. This function returns AL = 00H if the date is successfully updated or AL = FFH if you specified an invalid date.

Starting in MS-DOS version 3.3, this function also updates the real-time clock in an 80286 or higher system. In earlier versions, you must use BIOS interrupt 1AH services to change the real-time clock date.

Function 2CH (decimal 44): Get Time

Function 2CH (decimal 44) reports the time of day. The time is calculated from the BIOS timer-tick count. (See page 69.) MS-DOS responds to the BIOS's midnight-passed signal and updates the date every 24 hours.

The timer-tick count is converted into a meaningful time and placed in registers CX and DX. CH contains the hours (0 through 23, on a 24-hour clock); CL contains the minutes (0 through 59); DH contains the seconds (0 through 59); and DL contains the hundredths of a second (0 through 99). As with function 2AH, these values are in hexadecimal format.

The IBM PC timer ticks 18.2 times per second, so the time of day reported by MS-DOS is only as accurate as the timer tick—roughly 5.4 hundredths of a second. Even with this relatively low accuracy, you can use MS-DOS function 2CH to measure time intervals in many applications.

Function 2DH (decimal 45): Set Time

Function 2DH (decimal 45) sets the time of day. The time is specified in registers CX and DX. CH contains the hours (0 through 23, on a 24-hour clock); CL contains the minutes (0 through 59); DH contains the seconds (0 through 59); and DL contains the hundredths of a second (0 through 99). This function returns AL = 00H if the time is successfully updated or AL = FFH if you specified an invalid time.

Starting in MS-DOS version 3.3, this function also updates the real-time clock in an 80286 or higher system. In earlier versions, you must use BIOS interrupt 1AH services to change the real-time clock time.

The Printer and Serial Communications Services

The following sections cover the MS-DOS printer and serial communications services.

Function 03H (decimal 3): Auxiliary Input

Function 03H (decimal 3) reads one character into AL from AUX, the standard auxiliary device. The default auxiliary device is COM1, the first RS-232 serial communications port. You can, however, use the MS-DOS MODE command to assign other devices, such as COM2, to the auxiliary device.

> NOTE: *This function waits for input, but there is no buffer. If the AUX device is sending data faster than your program can process it, characters will be lost. This function does not report status information about the many miseries that a serial port can suffer. If you want to know the status of the serial port, use the BIOS communications port services.*

Function 04H (decimal 4): Auxiliary Output

Function 04H (decimal 4) writes one character from register DL to the standard auxiliary device. See the remarks under function 03H.

Function 05H (decimal 5): Printer Output

Function 05H (decimal 5) writes 1 byte from DL to the standard printer device, which is normally known as PRN or LPT1 (although printer output can be redirected to other devices by using the MS-DOS MODE command). The default standard printer is always the first parallel printer, even if a serial port is used for printer output.

The Program Loading and Termination Services

The following sections cover the MS-DOS program loading and termination services.

Function 00H (decimal 0): Terminate

Function 00H (decimal 0) ends a program and passes control back to MS-DOS. It is functionally identical to MS-DOS interrupt 20H, which is discussed on page 246. Interrupt 21H, function 00H, and interrupt 20H can be used interchangeably to exit a program.

MS-DOS versions 2.0 and later provide an enhanced terminate service through function 4CH, which allows the program to place a return code in register AL when the program ends. MS-DOS batch files can act on the return code with the MS-DOS subcommand ERRORLEVEL. Use function 4CH instead of function 00H if you want to use a return code to record errors that occur when a program ends. (See page 400.)

Like MS-DOS interrupt 20H, function 00H does not close files opened by using functions 0FH or 16H. To ensure that the proper length of such files is recorded in the file directory, use function 10H to close them before calling function 00H. Also, as with interrupt 20H, you must be sure the program segment prefix (PSP) segment address is in the CS register before exiting.

Function 26H (decimal 38): Create New Program Segment Prefix

Function 26H (decimal 38) is used within a program to prepare for loading and executing a subprogram, or overlay. When you call function 26H, DX must contain the paragraph address of the start of the memory area where you want MS-DOS to build the new PSP. MS-DOS builds a new PSP at the location you specify. You can then load an executable program from a file into the memory above the new PSP and transfer control to it.

NOTE: *Function 26H is obsolete. You should use function 4BH to load and execute a new program from within an executing program.*

Function 31H (decimal 49): Terminate and Stay Resident

Function 31H (decimal 49) terminates a program and leaves part of the program resident in memory. Except for the fact that function 31H lets you reserve memory for a memory-resident program, its function is the same as that of the program termination function (function 4CH). You call function 31H with a return code value in AL and with the number of paragraphs of memory to reserve for the program in DX.

Before you use function 31H, generally you should carry out the following steps:

1. Call function 30H or 3306H to verify that the MS-DOS version is 2.0 or later. Function 31H isn't supported in MS-DOS version 1.

2. Call function 49H to free the memory allocated to the program's environment block. (The word at offset 2CH in the program's PSP contains the paragraph address of the environment block.)

3. Determine the amount of memory to reserve for the resident program. This value must include the 16 paragraphs reserved for the program's PSP in addition to contiguous memory that is reserved for the program itself. This value does not include memory allocated dynamically by the program via function 48H.

4. Call function 31H to terminate the program.

Like function 4CH, function 31H restores the interrupt vectors for interrupts 22H (Terminate Address), 23H (Ctrl-C Handler), and 24H (Critical-Error Handler) to the MS-DOS default values; therefore, you cannot use this function to install memory-resident handlers for these interrupts.

Function 31H is more flexible than the terminate-and-stay-resident service supported by interrupt 27H. You should always use function 31H in your TSR programs unless you are concerned about maintaining compatibility with MS-DOS version 1.

Function 4BH (decimal 75): EXEC—Load and Execute a Program

Function 4BH (decimal 75) lets a parent program load a child program into memory and execute it. This function can also be used to load executable code or data into memory without executing it. In both cases, you call function 4BH with DS:DX pointing to an ASCIIZ string that contains the path and filename of the file to be loaded. The register pair ES:BX points to a parameter block that contains control information for the load operation. AL specifies whether the child program is to be executed after it is loaded.

If AL = 00H, MS-DOS allocates memory for the child program, creates a new program segment prefix at the start of the newly allocated memory, loads the child program into memory immediately above the PSP, and transfers control to it. The parent program regains control only when the child program terminates. If AL = 03H, MS-DOS does not allocate memory, create a PSP for the child program, or transfer control to the program after it is loaded. For these reasons, the AL = 03H variation is normally used to load a program overlay. It is also an effective way to load data into memory.

When AL = 00H, ES:BX points to a 14-byte block that contains the information shown in Figure 13-18. When AL = 03H, ES:BX points to a 4-byte block that contains the information shown in Figure 13-19.

| Offset | | Size | |
Hex	Dec	(Bytes)	Description
00H	0	2	Segment address of environment string
02H	2	4	Segmented pointer to command-line arguments
06H	6	4	Segmented pointer to first default FCB
0AH	10	4	Segmented pointer to second default FCB

Figure 13-18. *The information in the LOADEXEC parameter block that is pointed to by ES:BX when AL = 00H. MS-DOS builds this information into the PSP of the program that is being loaded.*

| Offset | | Size | |
Hex	Dec	(Bytes)	Description
00H	0	2	Segment address where file is to be loaded
02H	2	2	Relocation factor for program (applies only to EXE-format programs)

Figure 13-19. *The information in the LOADOVERLAY parameter block that is pointed to by ES:BX when AL = 03H.*

When AL = 01H, MS-DOS performs the same functions as when AL = 00H except that control is not transferred to the new program. For AL = 01H, ES:BX will point to a LOAD parameter block, which must contain the first 14 bytes of information shown in Figure 13-20; the last two fields are addresses that will be provided on successful execution of the function.

MS-DOS version 5.0 introduced subfunction 05H (AL = 05H), which prepares a new program for execution. Unlike the other function 4BH subfunctions, subfunction 05H expects DS:DX to point to the EXECSTATE parameter block (described in Figure 13-21), but no other input parameters are required. This subfunction does not set or clear the carry flag, and there is no associated error code.

| Offset | | Size | |
Hex	Dec	(Bytes)	Description
00H	0	2	Segment address of environment string
02H	2	4	Segmented pointer to command-line arguments
06H	6	4	Segmented pointer to first default FCB
0AH	10	4	Segmented pointer to second default FCB
0EH	14	4	SS:SP, returned starting stack address for child
12H	18	4	CS:IP, returned starting code address for child

Figure 13-20. *The LOAD parameter block.*

| Offset | | Size | |
Hex	Dec	(Bytes)	Description
00H	0	2	Reserved (00H)
02H	2	2	Type flags: Bit 0 = 1, program is an .EXE file Bit 0 = 0, program is a .COM file Bit 1 = 1, program is an overlay
04H	4	4	Segmented pointer to ASCIIZ string for filename
08H	8	2	Segment address of PSP for new program
0AH	10	4	Starting CS:IP of new program
0EH	14	4	Program size, including PSP

Figure 13-21. *The EXECSTATE parameter block.*

Except when AL = 05H (for which there is no error code), function 4BH clears the carry flag if it successfully loads a program. However, in MS-DOS version 2, this function changes all registers, including SS:SP. Therefore, you should save the current SS and SP values in the code segment before you call function 4BH.

Except when AL = 05H (for which there is no error code), if function 4BH fails, it sets the carry flag and returns one of the following error codes in AL: 01H (invalid function), 02H (file not found), 03H (path not found), 04H (too many files open), 05H (access denied), 08H (insufficient memory), 0AH (invalid environment block), or 0BH (invalid format).

When a child program is loaded and executed, it inherits any handles opened by the parent program. (The only exception, in MS-DOS versions 3.0 and later, is when a handle opened by the parent had the inheritance bit of its file-access code set to 1.) Because a child program inherits its parent's open handles, the parent program can redirect the standard I/O handles and use this technique to influence the operation of the child program. For example, a parent program might redirect the standard input and output devices to files and then use the MS-DOS SORT filter to sort the data in one file and copy it to another.

More commonly, however, a parent program uses this function to execute a copy of the MS-DOS command interpreter, COMMAND.COM. The parent program can carry out any MS-DOS command by passing the command to COMMAND.COM through the LOADEXEC parameter block. You can even get fancy by making COMMAND.COM execute a batch file—one that the parent program might well have constructed dynamically. This batch file could, in turn, invoke other programs and then perform the EXIT command, which would end the execution of the command interpreter. At that point, the parent program would be back in control. This opens up vast and complicated possibilities.

NOTE: *Strangely enough, you can't use function 4BH to load overlays created with the MS-DOS LINK program's overlay option: LINK builds all program overlays into a single executable file, not into separate files as would be needed for function 4BH.*

Function 4CH (decimal 76): Terminate with Return Code

Function 4CH (decimal 76) ends a program and passes back the return code you specify in AL. If the program was invoked as a child program, the parent program can retrieve the return code by using function 4DH. If the program was invoked as an MS-DOS command, the return code can be tested in a batch file by using the MS-DOS ERRORLEVEL option.

When this function is performed, MS-DOS does some cleanup work in case your program neglected to do so: It restores the interrupt 22H, 23H, and 24H vectors to default values, flushes the file buffers and closes all open files, and frees all memory allocated to the program.

Because function 4CH is more flexible and easier to use than interrupt 20H or interrupt 21H, function 00H, you should normally use function 4CH to terminate your programs. The only exception to this rule is if you need to maintain compatibility with MS-DOS version 1, which does not support function 4CH. In that case, you should use either interrupt 20H or function 00H of interrupt 21H.

The Interrupt Vector Services

The following sections cover the MS-DOS vector services.

Function 25H (decimal 37): Set Interrupt Vector

Function 25H (decimal 37) sets an interrupt vector. Before you call function 25H, place the segmented address of an interrupt handler in DS:DX and place an interrupt number in AL. MS-DOS stores the segment and offset of your interrupt handler in the proper interrupt vector.

When updating an interrupt vector, you should use function 25H instead of simply computing the address of the vector and updating it directly. Not only is it simpler to call this function than to do the work yourself, but this function gives the operating system the chance to detect whether an important interrupt vector has been modified.

To examine the contents of an interrupt vector, use function 35H.

Function 35H (decimal 53): Get Interrupt Vector

Function 35H (decimal 53) returns the interrupt vector for the interrupt number you specify in register AL. The vector is returned in the register pair ES:BX.

Function 35H provides a service complementary to function 25H, which sets or updates an interrupt vector.

The Memory Allocation Services

The following sections cover the MS-DOS memory allocation services.

Function 48H (decimal 72): Allocate Memory Block

Function 48H (decimal 72) dynamically allocates memory. You request in BX the number of paragraphs (16-byte units) you want allocated. On return, AX contains the segment address of the allocated memory block.

If an error occurs, the carry flag is set, and AX contains an error code: 07H (memory control blocks destroyed) or 08H (insufficient memory). If there is insufficient memory to satisfy your request, BX contains the size, in paragraphs, of the largest available block of memory.

Memory blocks allocated to a program by using function 48H are freed by MS-DOS when the program terminates by using function 00H or 4CH, but they remain allocated to a memory-resident program that terminates by using function 31H, Terminate and Stay Resident.

Function 49H (decimal 73): Free Memory Block

Function 49H (decimal 73) frees a block of memory for reuse by MS-DOS or by other programs. You call function 49H with ES containing the paragraph (segment) address of the start of the memory block. If the memory is successfully freed, the function clears the carry flag. Otherwise, the carry flag is set, and AX contains one of the following error codes: 07H (memory control blocks destroyed) or 09H (invalid memory-block address).

Although function 49H is usually used to free memory that was previously allocated by using function 48H, it will free any memory block. For example, a terminate and-stay-resident program can free its environment block by calling function 49H with ES containing the paragraph address of the environment block. (See the discussion of function 31H in this chapter.)

Function 4AH (decimal 74): Resize Memory Block

Function 4AH (decimal 74) is used to increase or decrease the size of a block of memory that was allocated by function 48H. Register ES contains the segment address of the block that will be changed. Register BX contains the desired size of the block in paragraphs (units of 16 bytes).

The function clears the carry flag if the memory block can be resized as requested. Otherwise, the carry flag is set, and AX contains an error code: 07H (memory control blocks destroyed), 08H (insufficient memory), or 09H (invalid memory-block address). If MS-DOS reported that there was insufficient memory to increase the size of a memory block, BX contains the maximum size, in paragraphs, of the memory block.

Function 58H (decimal 88): Get/Set Memory Allocation Strategy and Get/Set Upper Memory Link

Function 58H (decimal 88), subfunction 00H or 01H, gets or sets the method MS-DOS uses to allocate free memory to programs. You can choose from three memory allocation strategies and, in MS-DOS 5.0 and later, in each of three area specifications. (See Figure 13-22.) Each strategy assumes that memory resources are broken into blocks of various sizes and that each block can be randomly allocated to a program or be freed, depending on the specific requirements of MS-DOS and of each program. You might think that all free memory would be located in one large block just above where a program ends, but TSR programs and device drivers can reserve memory blocks and thereby fragment available memory into two or more smaller blocks.

When MS-DOS responds to a request for memory allocation, it searches through a list of free-memory blocks, starting at the lowest available address and working upward. With the first-fit strategy, MS-DOS allocates the first free block of memory large enough to accommodate the memory allocation request. With the last-fit strategy, MS-DOS allocates the last free block in the list that is large enough. With the best-fit strategy, MS-DOS searches the entire list and allocates the smallest block that is large enough. MS-DOS uses the first-fit strategy by default.

Bit 7 6 5 4 3 2 1 0	Strategy
1 0	Search upper memory area first. If no block is available, search conventional memory.
0 1	Search only the upper memory area for an available block.
0 0	Search only conventional memory for an available block.
. . . . . . 0 0	Search for available block having the lowest address (first-fit strategy).
. . . . . . 0 1	Search for available block closest in size to request (best-fit strategy).
. . . . . . 1 0	Search for available block having the highest address (last-fit strategy).

Figure 13-22. *Strategy values used in function 58H, subfunctions 00H and 01H.*

To obtain the allocation strategy from MS-DOS, you call function 58H with AL = 00H. MS-DOS reports the current allocation strategy (00H, 01H, 02H, 40H, 41H, 42H, 80H, 81H, or 82H) in AX. To set the allocation strategy, call this function with AL = 01H and the desired strategy (00H, 01H, 02H, 40H, 41H, 42H, 80H, 81H, or 82H) in BX. Strategy values larger than 02H are supported by MS-DOS 5.0 and later. The only error detected by subfunction 01H occurs when you call the function with an invalid strategy value in BX: The carry flag is set, and AX contains an error code of 01H (invalid function).

Miscellaneous MS-DOS Services

The following sections cover a variety of miscellaneous MS-DOS services.

Function 2EH (decimal 46): Set/Reset Verify Flag

Function 2EH (decimal 46) controls verification of disk-write operations. You call this function with AL = 01H to set MS-DOS's internal verify flag and enable verification; you call it with AL = 00H to turn off the flag and the verification. In MS-DOS versions 1 and 2, you must zero DL before you call function 2EH.

The disk-verify operation requires the disk controller to perform a cyclical redundancy check (CRC) each time it writes data to the disk. This process involves reading the data just written, which significantly decreases the effective speed of disk writes.

With MS-DOS versions 2.0 and later, function 54H can be used to report the current setting of the verify flag. (See page 322.)

Function 30H (decimal 48): Get MS-DOS Version Number

In MS-DOS versions 2 through 4, function 30H (decimal 48) returns the MS-DOS major and minor version numbers. The major version number is in AL, and the minor version number is in AH. BX and CX contain a serial number (0 in PC-DOS; other possible values in MS-DOS and other non-IBM versions of DOS). For example, if you execute function 30H in MS-DOS version 3.3, the function returns AL = 03H (the major version number), AH = 1EH (30, the minor version number), BX = 00H, and CX = 00H. In the OS/2 compatibility box, function 30H returns AL = 0AH; that is, the major version number is 10.

In MS-DOS versions 5.0 and later, the BX register is divided, with BL continuing to return the high-order byte of the 3-byte user serial number. The BH register returns either a version flag or an OEM (original equipment manufacturer) number. Control of the value returned in BH is established by the value passed in AL when function 30H is called: If AL = 00H, BH will return the OEM number; otherwise, AL = 01H, which indicates that BH will return the version flag. In MS-DOS version 5, 08H is the only value that can be returned as a version flag, and it indicates that MS-DOS resides in ROM.

Note that in MS-DOS versions 5.0 and later the version number returned by this function is the value set by the SETVER command. If the actual version identifier is required, use function 33H, subfunction 06H.

Function 30H is not supported in MS-DOS version 1. Nevertheless, you can test for MS-DOS version 1 by executing function 30H; in MS-DOS version 1, function 30H is guaranteed to return AL = 00H. Thus, a simple test of the value returned in AL is sufficient to distinguish between version 1 and later versions:

```
mov ah,30h            ; AH = 30H (interrupt 21H function number)
int 21h               ; get MS-DOS version number
cmp al,2
jl  EarlyVersion      ; jump if MS-DOS version 1
```

Any program that uses interrupt 21H functions designed for specific versions of MS-DOS can use function 30H to determine whether the appropriate version is being used.

Function 33H (decimal 51): Miscellaneous Services

Function 33H (decimal 51) performs a number of miscellaneous functions, including getting or setting the Ctrl-C flag, getting the start-up driver, and getting the MS-DOS version.

Subfunctions 00H and 01H (decimals 0 and 1). These subfunctions let you test or update MS-DOS's internal Ctrl-C flag. When you call function 33H with AL = 00H, MS-DOS reports the current state of the Ctrl-C flag in DL:

- If the flag is clear (DL = 00H), MS-DOS checks for Ctrl-C keystrokes only when transmitting a character to or from a character device (interrupt 21H, functions 00H through 0CH).

- If the flag is set (DL = 01H), MS-DOS also checks for Ctrl-C when it responds to other service requests, such as file I/O operators.

When you call function 33H with AL = 01H, MS-DOS expects DL to contain the desired value for the break flag:

- DL = 00H disables the break check.

- DL = 01H enables the break check.

Subfunction 05H (decimal 5). This subfunction is used to determine the drive from which MS-DOS was loaded. On return, DL will contain the number of the start-up drive (1 = A, 2 = B, and so on).

Subfunction 06H (decimal 6). Subfunction 06H (decimal 6) returns the actual MS-DOS version number (rather than the version number set by the SETVER command) as well as additional information about the operating system. This function was introduced with MS-DOS version 5.0. It is called by placing 33H in register AH and 06H in register AL. It returns the major MS-DOS version number in register BL and the minor MS-DOS version number in register BH. In register DL, bits 0 through 2 give the revision number. In register DH, bits 3 and 4 are flags that specify how MS-DOS is running:

- If bit 3 is set, MS-DOS is running in ROM; otherwise, it is running in RAM.

- If bit 4 is set, MS-DOS is in the high-memory area; otherwise, it is in conventional memory.

All other bits in DL and DH are reserved and are set to 0.

Function 38H (decimal 56): Get/Set Country-Dependent Information

Function 38H (decimal 56) allows MS-DOS to adjust to different international currency and date format conventions. In MS-DOS version 2, this function reports a very small set of country-dependent information. In MS-DOS versions 3.0 and later, function 38H reports a more detailed list of country-dependent items; in these versions of MS-DOS, a program can also change the country-dependent information by making a call to function 38H.

To get country-dependent information from MS-DOS, you call function 38H with DS:DX containing the address of a 32-byte buffer. (In MS-DOS versions 3.0 and later, the size of the buffer must be 34 bytes.) Register AL must be set to 00H to get the current country information. For MS-DOS versions 3.0

and later, register AL can also be set to a predefined *country code*. (This country code is the same three-digit code used as the country's international telephone access code.) To specify a country code of 255 or greater, AL can be set to FFH (decimal 255), and the country code can be put into register BX.

If the requested country code is invalid, MS-DOS sets the carry flag (CF) and places an error code in AX: 0001H = invalid function; 0002H = file not found. Otherwise, register BX contains the country code, and the buffer at DS:DX is filled with the country-specific information shown in Figure 13-23 (for MS-DOS 2) or Figure 13-24 (for MS-DOS 3.0 and later).

To set the current country code in MS-DOS versions 3 and later, set DX equal to FFFFH, and call function 38H with AL equal to the country code. (If the code is greater than 254, set AL equal to FFH and register BX equal to the country code.)

The country-dependent information is used by MS-DOS utilities like DATE and TIME. A program can call function 38H to obtain the information MS-DOS uses to configure itself for country-dependent conventions.

The *date format* is an integer word whose value specifies the display format for the date. This word has three predefined values and three corresponding date formats. (See Figure 13-25.) Room is reserved so that others can be added in the future.

The *currency symbol* is the symbol used when displaying an amount of money. In the United States, the currency symbol is a dollar sign ($); in the United Kingdom, it's the pound symbol (£); and in Japan, it's the yen symbol (¥). In MS-DOS versions 2.0 and 2.1, the currency symbol can only be a single character, but in MS-DOS versions 3.0 and later, a string that is up to four characters in length can be used. For example, a currency string that can be used in MS-DOS version 5.0 is DKR, which stands for Danish kroner.

| Offset | | Size | |
Hex	Dec	(Bytes)	Description
00H	0	2	Date format
02H	2	2	Currency symbol string (ASCIIZ format)
04H	4	2	Thousands separator string (ASCIIZ format)
06H	6	2	Decimal separator string (ASCIIZ format)
08H	8	24	(Reserved)

Figure 13-23. *The country-dependent information reported by function 38H in MS-DOS version 2.*

| Offset | | Size | |
Hex	Dec	(Bytes)	Description
00H	0	2	Date format
02H	2	5	Currency symbol string (ASCIIZ format)
07H	7	2	Thousands separator string (ASCIIZ format)
09H	9	2	Decimal separator string (ASCIIZ format)
0BH	11	2	Date separator string (ASCIIZ format)
0DH	13	2	Time separator string (ASCIIZ format)
0FH	15	1	Currency symbol location
			00H - Precede, no space
			01H - Follow, no space
			02H - Precede, one space
			03H - Follow, one space
			04H - Currency symbol replaces decimal point
10H	16	1	Currency decimal places
11H	17	1	Time format: 1 = 24-hour clock; 0 = 12-hour clock
12H	18	4	Extended ASCII map call address
16H	22	2	List separator string (ASCIIZ format)
18H	24	10	(Reserved)

Figure 13-24. *The country-dependent information returned by function 38H in MS-DOS versions 3.0 and later.*

Value	Use	Date
00H	American	month day year
01H	European	day month year
02H	Japanese	year month day

Figure 13-25. *The three predefined date formats returned by MS-DOS function 38H.*

The *thousands separator* is the symbol used to punctuate the thousands mark in numbers. The U.S. uses a comma as a thousands separator, as in the number 12,345; other countries use a period or a blank.

The *decimal separator* is the symbol used to punctuate decimal places. The U.S. uses a period as a decimal separator; other countries use a comma.

The *date separator* is the punctuation used in displaying the date (for example, a hyphen as in 7-4-1993). The *time separator* is the punctuation used in displaying the time (for example, a colon as in 12:34).

The *currency symbol location* indicates placement of the currency symbol. A value of 00H places the currency symbol immediately before the amount (¥1500); 01H places the symbol immediately after it (15¢); 02H places the symbol before the amount with an intervening space (Fr 15); 03H places the symbol after the amount with an intervening space (15 DK); and 04H replaces the decimal separator with the currency symbol.

The *currency decimal places* value specifies how many decimal places are used in the currency. For example, the value would be 02H for U.S. currency (dollars and cents) and 00H for Italian currency (lire).

The *time format* field specifies whether time appears in a 12-hour or 24-hour format. Only the low-order bit (bit 0) is currently used: If the bit is set to 0, a 12-hour clock is used; if it is set to 1, a 24-hour clock is used.

The *extended ASCII map call address* is the segmented address of a routine that maps ASCII characters 80H through FFH to characters in the range 00H through 7FH. Not all printers or plotters can display extended ASCII characters in the range 80H through FFH, so the routine at this address is called when it is necessary to map such characters into the usual range of ASCII characters (00H through 7FH).

The *list separator* indicates the symbol used to separate items in a list, such as the commas in the list A, B, C, and D.

Function 44H (decimal 68): IOCTL — I/O Control for Devices

Function 44H (decimal 68) performs input/output control operations, mostly for devices. (See Figure 13-26.) You specify one of 18 subfunctions, numbered 00H through 11F, in AL; two of these subfunctions (0CH and 0DH) have sub-subfunctions you specify with a "minor code" in CL.

The main purpose of the IOCTL function is to provide a consistent interface between MS-DOS programs and device drivers. In general, you shouldn't use IOCTL calls unless you know something about how device drivers are structured, a topic covered in Chapter 8. A few IOCTL calls, however, are useful even if you don't understand the details of device-driver operations. We point these out as we summarize the various IOCTL calls.

NOTE: *Not all IOCTL subfunctions are supported in earlier versions of MS-DOS. Likewise, not all sub-subfunctions of subfunctions 0CH and 0DH were introduced at the same time. Figure 13-26 indicates the MS-DOS versions in which the various IOCTL subfunctions were introduced.*

| Subfunction | | | MS-DOS |
Hex	Dec	Description	Version
00H	0	Get Device Data	2.0
01H	1	Set Device Data	2.0
02H	2	Receive Control Data from Character Device	2.0
03H	3	Send Control Data to Character Device	2.0
04H	4	Receive Control Data from Block Device	2.0
05H	5	Send Control Data to Block Device	2.0
06H	6	Check Input Status	2.0
07H	7	Check Output Status	2.0
08H	8	Check If Block Device Is Removable	3.0
09H	9	Check If Block Device Is Remote	3.1
0AH	10	Check If Handle Is Remote	3.1
0BH	11	Change Sharing Retry Count	3.0
0CH	12	Generic I/O Control for Character Devices	3.2*
0DH	13	Generic I/O Control for Block Devices	3.2*
0EH	14	Get Logical Drive Map	3.2
0FH	15	Set Logical Drive Map	3.2
10F	16	Query IOCTL Handle	5.0
11F	17	Query IOCTL Device	5.0

* Sub-subfunctions have been added in MS-DOS versions following the one shown here.

Figure 13-26. *Subfunctions available under interrupt 21H, function 44H (IOCTL).*

Subfunctions 00H and 01H (decimals 0 and 1). These subfunctions get and set device information formatted in DX by a complicated set of bit coding. Bit 7 is set to 1 for devices and to 0 for disk files. For devices, bits 0 through 5 are specified as shown in Figure 13-27. For disk files, bits 0 through 5 provide the disk-drive number: A value of 0 represents drive A, a value of 1 represents drive B, and so on. If bit 6 is set, the file has not been written to. Both subfunctions should be called with a file or device handle in BX. Subfunction 00H can be called for both disk files and character devices; subfunction 01H can be called only for character devices.

								Bit									Use
15	14	13	12	11	10	9	8	7	6	5	4	3	2	1	0	
															X	1 = standard input device.
														X		1 = standard output device.
													X			1 = null device.
												X				1 = clock device.
											X					1 = special device.
										X						1 = data is "raw" (without control-character checking); 0 = data is "cooked" (with control-character checking).
									X							0 = end of file; 1 = not end of file (for input).
								X								1 = device.
							R									(Reserved.)
						R										(Reserved.)
					R											(Reserved.)
				X												Specifies whether the driver supports device-drive functions 0DH, 0EH, and 0FH.
			R													(Reserved.)
		X														1 = Character device driver supports "output until busy" or block device driver requires MS-DOS to provide FAT.
	X															1 = device can process control strings transferred by IOCTL subfunctions 02H through 05H.
X																1 = character device. 0 = block device.

Figure 13-27. *The bit settings of the device data word DX for subfunctions 00H and 01H of MS-DOS interrupt 21H, function 44H.*

You can modify how MS-DOS processes I/O for the CON device (the keyboard/video display combination) by setting raw input/output mode for the device. You do this by clearing bit 5 of the device data word in DX and calling subfunction 01H:

```
    mov     ax,4400h        ; AH = 44H (interrupt 21H function number)
                            ; AL = 0 (subfunction number)
    mov     bx,0            ; BX = 0 (handle for CON device)
    int     21h             ; get device data into DX
    or      dx,0020h        ; set bit 5 (raw mode)
    and     dx,D8FFh        ; zero reserved bits 8-11, 13
    mov     ax,4401h        ; set up for subfunction 1
    mov     bx,0            ; BX = CON device handle
    int     21h             ; set device data for CON
```

After you execute this sequence of code, MS-DOS no longer recognizes Ctrl-P and Ctrl-S characters, nor does it expand tabs on output.

Subfunctions 02H through 05H (decimals 2 through 5). These subfunctions transfer control data between your program and a device driver. Subfunctions 02H and 03H get and send control data for character-oriented devices; subfunctions 04H and 05H get and send control data for block-oriented devices. In all four subfunctions, you specify the subfunction number in AL, the address of a data buffer in DS:DX, and the number of bytes to transfer in CX. For subfunctions 02H and 03H, you must specify a handle in BX; for subfunctions 04H and 05H, you must specify a drive number in BL (00H = default drive, 01H = drive A, and so on).

The control data you transfer to or from a device driver is not necessarily part of the device's input/output data stream. The control data is often used to obtain the device status or to control hardware-specific features such as printer font characteristics or tape drive rewind.

These four subfunctions can be used only if the device can process control strings. This capability is indicated by bit 14 in the device data word returned by subfunction 00H.

Subfunctions 06H and 07H (decimals 6 and 7). These subfunctions return the current input or output status of a device or file. You call them with a handle in BX: Subfunction 06H returns the current input status; subfunction 07H returns the current output status.

Both of these subfunctions use the carry flag to indicate a successful call. If the carry flag is clear, AL contains the status: AL = 00H means the device is not ready for input or output; AL = FFH means the device is ready. (For a file, input status AL = 00H means end of file; output status is always "ready" regardless of the value in AL.) If the carry flag is set, AX contains one of the following error codes: 01H (invalid function), 05H (access denied), or 06H (invalid handle).

Subfunction 08H (decimal 8). This subfunction, supported only in MS-DOS versions 3.0 and later, indicates whether a block-oriented device has removable media. (The floppy disks in a floppy disk drive are removable; the hard disk in a hard disk drive is not.) Subfunction 08H can be extremely useful because it lets a program know whether it has to check for a disk change or whether it can rely on the same disk always being there. You call subfunction 08H with a drive number in BL (00H = default drive, 01H = drive A, and so on). The subfunction clears the carry flag after a successful return, and it leaves AX = 00H if the storage medium is removable or AX = 01H if the storage medium is nonremovable. If the carry flag is set, AX contains an error code: 01H (invalid function) or 0FH (invalid drive).

Subfunction 09H (decimal 9). In a network configuration, this subfunction determines whether a particular block device is local (attached to the computer running the program) or remote (redirected to a network server). You must specify a drive number in BL when you call this subfunction.

Subfunction 09H clears the carry flag to indicate a successful call. In this case, bit 12 of the value in DX indicates whether the device is remote (bit 12 = 1) or local (bit 12 = 0). If bit 12 is 1, the remaining bits in DX will be 0. If bit 12 is 0, the remaining bits can be interpreted using Figure 13-28.

Bit	Description
1	1 = Drive accepts 32-bit sector addressing
6	1 = Drive accepts functions 440DH, 440EH, and 440FH
7	1 = Drive accepts function 4411H
9	1 = Drive is local but shared on a network
11	1 = Drive accepts function 4408H
13	1 = Drive requires media descriptor in FAT
14	1 = Drive accepts functions 4404H and 4405H
15	1 = Drive letter set by SUBST command

Figure 13-28. *Bit values for a local network device returned in DX by interrupt 21H, function 44H, subfunction 09H.*

If the carry flag is set, AX contains one of two error codes: 01H (invalid function) or 0FH (invalid drive). Subfunction 09H is available in MS-DOS versions 3.1 and later.

Subfunction 0AH (decimal 10). This subfunction is similar to subfunction 09H but is used with a file handle or a device handle instead of a drive number. You specify the handle in BX when you call this subfunction.

Like subfunction 09H, subfunction 0AH clears the carry flag and returns a value in DX that indicates whether the device is local or remote. If bit 15 of DX/1, the device is remote; if bit 15 = 0, the device is local.

If bit 7 is 1, the handle identifies a device, and the remaining bits in DX can be interpreted using Figure 13-29. If bit 7 is 0, the handle identifies a file, and the remaining bits can be interpreted using Figure 13-30.

If an error occurs, the function sets the carry flag and returns an error code in AX: 01H (invalid function) or 06H (invalid handle). Subfunction 0AH is available in MS-DOS versions 3.1 and later.

Bit	Description
0	1 = Console input device
1	1 = Console output device
2	1 = Null device
3	1 = Clock device
4	1 = Special device
5	1 = raw mode; 0 = cooked mode
6	0 = End of file, if following a read
11	1 = Network spooler
12	1 = No inherit
13	1 = Named pipe
15	1 = Remote device; 0 = local device

Figure 13-29. *Bit values for devices returned in DX by interrupt 21H, function 44H, subfunction 0AH.*

Bit	Description
0–5	Drive number (0 = A, 1 = B, and so on)
6	1 = File has not been written to
12	1 = No inherit
14	1 = Date/time not set at close
15	1 = Remote file; 0 = local file

Figure 13-30. *Bit values for files returned in DX by interrupt 21H, function 44H, subfunction 0AH.*

Subfunction 0BH (decimal 11). This subfunction, which is supported only in MS-DOS versions 3.0 and later, controls the way MS-DOS attempts to resolve file-sharing conflicts. Because some programs lock files for only brief periods, file-sharing conflicts can be transitory. MS-DOS can try more than once to gain access to a shared file before reporting a conflict, in the hope that the lock condition goes away in the meantime.

Subfunction 0BH can help you empirically tune a network in which you expect transient file-sharing conflicts to occur. You call this subfunction with DX containing the number of times you want MS-DOS to retry access to a shared file before it gives up and reports an error. CX should specify the delay value between retries. MS-DOS creates a delay by executing an empty loop 65,536 times; the value in CX indicates the number of times you want MS-DOS to execute the empty delay loop. (The MS-DOS defaults are three retries and one delay loop between retries.)

If the subfunction executes successfully, it clears the carry flag. If the carry flag is set, AX contains an error code of 01H (invalid function).

Subfunction 0CH (decimal 12). This subfunction provides miscellaneous control functions for character-oriented devices. The device handle is specified in BX. Each control function is designated by a minor code in CL and a major code (also called a category code) in CH. The various major and minor codes are listed in Figure 13-31.

Minor codes 45H and 65H were introduced in MS-DOS version 3.2. They apply only to print devices (major code 05H). They deal with the number of times MS-DOS attempts to send a character to a printer before it assumes the printer is busy. The minor codes 4AH, 4CH, 4DH, 6AH, and 6BH were introduced in MS-DOS version 3.3. They provide detailed support for defining and loading code pages for output devices that can use multiple character sets or fonts. Minor codes 5FH and 7FH, introduced in MS-DOS 4.0, provide support for setting and determining video display modes.

For details on the use of the services provided in this IOCTL subfunction, see the MS-DOS technical reference manual.

Hex	*Dec*	*Description*
Major Code (Specified in CH)		
01H	1	Serial port (COM1, COM2, COM3, COM4).
03H	3	Console (CON).
05H	5	Printer (LPT1, LPT2, LPT3).
Minor Code (Specified in CL)		
45H	69	Set iteration count.
4AH	74	Select code page.
4CH	76	Start code page preparation.
4DH	77	End code page preparation.
5FH	95	Set display mode.
65H	101	Get iteration count.
6AH	106	Query selected code page.
6BH	107	Query code page prepare list.
7FH	127	Get display mode.

Figure 13-31. *The major and minor codes for MS-DOS IOCTL subfunction 0CH (generic I/O control for handles).*

Subfunction 0DH (decimal 13). Subfunction 0DH (decimal 13) provides nine generic services for block-oriented devices. The drive ID (1 = A, 2 = B, and so on) is specified in BX. DS:DX points to a parameter block, the contents of which vary by minor code. Each service is designated by a major code in CH and a minor code in CL. (See Figure 13-32.) In general, these services are similar to services provided by the BIOS for floppy disks and hard disks, but these IOCTL services provide a consistent interface to *any* block-oriented device with a device driver that supports these IOCTL calls.

Subfunction 0DH is available in MS-DOS 3.2 and later, although minor codes 46H and 66H were not introduced until MS-DOS 4.0, and minor code 68H was not introduced until MS-DOS 5.0. See the MS-DOS technical reference manual for details on subfunction 0DH services.

Hex	Dec	Description
Major Code (Specified in CH)		
08H	8	Disk drive.
Minor Code (Specified in CL)		
40H	64	Set parameters for block device.
41H	65	Write track on logical drive.
42H	66	Format and verify track on logical drive.
46H	70	Set media ID.
60H	96	Get parameters for block device.
61H	97	Read track on logical drive.
62H	98	Verify track on logical drive.
66H	102	Get media ID.
68H	104	Sense media type.

Figure 13-32. *The major and minor codes for MS-DOS IOCTL subfunction 0DH (generic I/O control for block devices).*

Subfunctions 0EH and 0FH (decimals 14 and 15). These two subfunctions relate logical mapping of drive letter assignments to physical drives. For example, in systems with only one floppy disk drive, MS-DOS maps drive letter B to physical drive A.

You call these subfunctions with a logical drive ID in BL. (01H represents drive A, 02H represents drive B, and so on.) Subfunction 0EH returns the logical drive ID that is mapped to the drive you specified in BL. Subfunction 0FH also updates MS-DOS's internal logical map so that the drive

ID you specify becomes the new logical drive ID. Both subfunctions use AL to return the logical drive ID. If AL = 00H, only one logical drive is associated with the drive ID you specified in BL. If an error occurs, the carry flag is set, and AX contains one of two error codes: 01H (invalid function) or 0FH (invalid drive).

For example, if you execute the following instructions on a system with only one floppy disk drive, MS-DOS associates drive B with the disk drive:

```
mov bl,2           ; BL = logical drive number
mov ax,440Fh       ; set logical drive map
int 21h            ; update the logical drive ID
                   ; (MS-DOS returns AL = 02H)
```

Subfunctions 10H and 11H were added in MS-DOS 5.0 and provide information on a device driver's ability to support specific IOCTL functions. Subfunction 10H determines whether the specified IOCTL function is supported by the given character device driver, and subfunction 11H determines whether the specified IOCTL function is supported by the given block device driver. Subfunction 10H expects a handle number in BX, whereas subfunction 11H expects a drive number (0 = default, 1 = A, 2 = B, and so on) in BL. In both instances, CH is used to specify the device category (01 = serial device, 03 = display, 05 = parallel printer, 08 = block device). CL specifies the function to check. If the device driver supports the IOCTL function specified in CL, the carry flag is cleared; otherwise, the carry flag is set. If the carry flag is set, AX will contain either 0001H, indicating that the device driver has no support for IOCTL functions, or 0005H, indicating that the device driver does support IOCTL functions but not the one specified in CL. Subfunction 11H can also set the carry flag and return 000FH in AX if the drive number provided in BL is invalid.

Function 4DH (decimal 77): Get Return Code

Function 4DH (decimal 77) gets the return code of a child program invoked with function 4BH and terminated with function 31H or 4CH. The information is returned in two parts. AL reports the return code issued by the child program. AH reports how the child program ended and has four possible values, as follows:

- AH = 00H indicates a normal voluntary end.

- AH = 01H indicates termination by MS-DOS due to a keyboard break (Ctrl-C).

■ AH = 02H indicates termination by MS-DOS within a critical-error handler.

■ AH = 03H indicates a voluntary end when using a terminate-and-stay-resident service (interrupt 27H or function 31H).

You should call this function only after you call function 4BH. Function 4DH does not indicate an error if you call it when no previous child program has terminated. You can call function 4DH only once for each function 4BH call. The second time you call function 4DH, you'll get garbage in AH and AL instead of return codes.

Function 59H (decimal 89): Get Extended Error Information

Function 59H (decimal 89) is used after an error occurs. It provides detailed information about the errors that occur under these circumstances: inside a critical-error (interrupt 24H) handler; after an MS-DOS function call invoked by using interrupt 21H reports an error by setting the carry flag (CF); and after old-style FCB file operations report a return code of FFH. It will not work with other MS-DOS functions that do not report errors by setting CF, even though they might have ended in an error.

This function is called in the standard way, by placing function code 59H in register AH. You must also specify a version code in the BX register. For MS-DOS version 3.0 and later, you set the version code to 0.

Four types of information are returned on completion of this service:

■ AX contains the extended error code.

■ BH indicates the class of error.

■ BL gives the code of any suggested action that your program should take.

■ CH gives a *locus code*, which attempts to show where the error occurred.

Beware: All registers except SS:SP and CS:IP are changed by function 59H. Be sure you save these registers as necessary before you make a call to this function.

The extended error codes can be organized into three groups. Codes 01H through 12H are returned by interrupt 21H functions. Codes 13H through 1FH are used in critical-error (interrupt 24H) handlers. The remaining error codes were introduced in MS-DOS version 3.0 or later and generally report network-related errors. Figure 13-33 lists the extended error codes, Figure 13-34 lists the error classes, Figure 13-35 lists the action codes, and Figure 13-36 lists the locus codes.

Error Code		
Hex	**Dec**	**Description**
Returned by interrupt 21H functions:		
00H	0	(No error.)
01H	1	Invalid function number.
02H	2	File not found.
03H	3	Path not found.
04H	4	No more handles (too many open files).
05H	5	Access denied (e.g., attempt to write to read-only file).
06H	6	Invalid handle.
07H	7	Memory control blocks destroyed.
08H	8	Not enough memory.
09H	9	Invalid memory-block address.
0AH	10	Invalid environment block.
0BH	11	Invalid format.
0CH	12	Invalid file-access code.
0DH	13	Invalid data.
0EH	14	(Reserved.)
0FH	15	Invalid drive specification.
10H	16	Attempt to remove the current directory.
11H	17	Not the same device.
12H	18	No more files.
Used in critical-error (interrupt 24H) handlers:		
13H	19	Disk is write protected.
14H	20	Unknown disk unit ID.
15H	21	Disk drive not ready.
16H	22	Unknown disk command.
17H	23	Disk data error.
18H	24	Bad disk request structure length.
19H	25	Disk seek error.
1AH	26	Non-DOS disk.
1BH	27	Disk sector not found.
1CH	28	Printer out of paper.
1DH	29	Write error.

Figure 13-33. *The MS-DOS extended error codes.* *(continued)*

Figure 13-33. *continued*

Error Code		
Hex	**Dec**	**Description**
1EH	30	Read error.
1FH	31	General failure.

Used in MS-DOS versions 3.0 and later:

20H	32	File-sharing violation.
21H	33	File-locking violation.
22H	34	Invalid disk change.
23H	35	No FCB available.
24H	36	Sharing buffer overflow.
25H	37	Mismatched code page.
26H	38	EOF on device opened with handle.
27H	39	Disk full on device opened with handle.
28H–31H	40–49	(Reserved.)
32H	50	Network request not supported.
33H	51	Remote computer not listening.
34H	52	Duplicate name on network.
35H	53	Network name not found.
36H	54	Network busy.
37H	55	Network device no longer exists.
38H	56	Network BIOS command limit exceeded.
39H	57	Network adapter hardware error.
3AH	58	Incorrect response from network.
3BH	59	Unexpected network error.
3CH	60	Incompatible remote adapter.
3DH	61	Print queue full.
3EH	62	Not enough space for print file.
3FH	63	Print file was deleted.
40H	64	Network name was deleted.
41H	65	Access denied.
42H	66	Network device type incorrect.
43H	67	Network name not found.
44H	68	Network name limit exceeded.
45H	69	Network BIOS session limit exceeded.

(continued)

Figure 13-33. *continued*

Error Code		
Hex	**Dec**	**Description**
46H	70	Sharing temporarily paused.
47H	71	Network request not accepted.
48H	72	Print or disk redirection is paused.
49H–4FH	73–79	(Reserved.)
50H	80	File already exists.
51H	81	Duplicate FCB.
52H	82	Cannot create directory entry.
53H	83	Fail on interrupt 24H.
54H	84	Out of network structures.
55H	85	Network device already assigned.
56H	86	Invalid password.
57H	87	Invalid parameter.
58H	88	Network data fault.
59H	89	Invalid network function.
5AH	90	System component not loaded.

Code		
Hex	**Dec**	**Meaning**
01H	1	Out of resource: no more of whatever you asked for.
02H	2	Temporary situation: Try again later.
03H	3	Authorization: You aren't allowed; someone else might be.
04H	4	Internal error in MS-DOS: not your fault.
05H	5	Hardware failure.
06H	6	System software error: other MS-DOS problems.
07H	7	Applications software error: It's your fault.
08H	8	Item requested not found.
09H	9	Bad format (e.g., unrecognizable disk).
0AH	10	Item locked.
0BH	11	Media error (e.g., disk reports CRC error).
0CH	12	Already exists.
0DH	13	Error class is unknown.

Figure 13-34. *The error classes returned in register BH by MS-DOS function 59H.*

Code		Meaning
Hex	Dec	
01H	1	Try again several times, and then issue ''Abort or Ignore'' prompt.
02H	2	Try again after a pause, and then issue ''Abort or Ignore'' prompt.
03H	3	Ask the user to change incorrect information (e.g., bad filename).
04H	4	Shut down the program, but OK to clean up (e.g., close files).
05H	5	Shut down immediately; don't try to clean up.
06H	6	Ignore the error: It's for information only.
07H	7	Retry after user action (e.g., change floppy disks).

Figure 13-35. *The suggested action codes returned in register BL by MS-DOS function 59H.*

Code		Meaning
Hex	Dec	
01H	1	Unknown: sorry
02H	2	Block device (e.g., disk drive)
03H	3	Network
04H	4	Serial device (e.g., printer)
05H	5	Memory

Figure 13-36. *The locus codes returned in register CH by MS-DOS function 59H.*

Function 5DH (decimal 93): Set Extended Error Information

Function 5DH (decimal 93), introduced in MS-DOS version 4.0, is used to set the information that will be returned by the next call to function 59H (Get Extended Error Information). Normally, of course, you will not use this function because MS-DOS will set the error information based on the most recent error. In special cases, however, such as program testing and debugging, this function can be useful. To use this function, place 5D0AH in AX and the segment:offset of an ERROR structure in DS:SI. The ERROR structure contains 22 bytes and has the following form:

```
ERROR STRUCT
    errAX        dw  ?
    errBX        dw  ?
    errCX        dw  ?
```

(continued)

421

```
        errDX           dw ?
        errSI           dw ?
        errDI           dw ?
        errDS           dw ?
        errES           dw ?
        errReserved     dw ?
        errUID          dw ?
        errPID          dw ?
ERROR ENDS
```

The first eight structure items are relevant. You load them with the values that you want to be returned in the corresponding registers by a subsequent call to function 59H. For example, to see how your program's extended error–handling code would respond to a certain error, you would load the desired values into structure elements errAX, errBX, and errCX (see Figures 13-33 through 13-36) and then call function 5DH, passing it the address of the ERROR structure. A subsequent call to function 59H will return the "error" information you specified. If, however, a real MS-DOS error occurs between the call to function 5DH and the call to function 59H, function 59H will report the real error information instead of what you specified.

Function 62H (decimal 98): Get PSP Address

Function 62H (decimal 98) returns the segment (paragraph) address of the program segment prefix in BX.

When MS-DOS transfers control to a program, registers DS and ES always contain the segment address of the program's PSP. Function 62H provides an alternative method of determining this address in MS-DOS versions 3.0 and later.

Function 65H (decimal 101): Get Extended Country Information

Function 65H (decimal 101) was introduced in MS-DOS version 3.3 along with support for global code pages, which are user-configurable character sets for output devices. This function returns a superset of the country information available by using function 38H. Function 65H has subfunctions, each of which returns a different type of information. (See Figure 13-37.)

You call function 65H with a subfunction number in AL, a code page number in BX, a buffer size in CX, a country ID in DX, and the address of an empty buffer in ES:DI. Calls with BX = FFFFH refer to the active code page; calls with DX = FFFFH return information for the default country ID.

The size of the buffer you supply to this function depends on which subfunction you call. The function clears the carry flag and fills the buffer with the information you requested.

| Subfunction | | Description |
Hex	Dec	
01H	1	Get Extended Country Information
02H	2	Get Pointer to Uppercase Table
04H	4	Get Pointer to Filename Uppercase Table
05H	5	Get Pointer to Allowed-Character Table
06H	6	Get Pointer to Collating Sequence Table
07H	7	Get Pointer to Double-Byte Character Table
20H	32	Convert Character to Uppercase
21H	33	Convert String to Uppercase
22H	34	Convert ASCIIZ String to Uppercase

Figure 13-37. *The subfunctions available through MS-DOS interrupt 21H, function 65H.*

Subfunction 01H (decimal 1). This subfunction returns the same information as function 38H, but it also includes the current code page and country ID. (See Figure 13-38.)

| Offset | | Size | Description |
Hex	Dec	(Bytes)	
00H	0	1	Subfunction ID (always 01H)
01H	1	2	Size of following information (38 bytes or less)
03H	3	2	Country ID
05H	5	2	Code page
07H	7	2	Date format
09H	9	5	Currency symbol string (ASCIIZ format)
0EH	14	2	Thousands separator string (ASCIIZ format)
10H	16	2	Decimal separator string (ASCIIZ format)
12H	18	2	Date separator string (ASCIIZ format)
14H	20	2	Time separator string (ASCIIZ format)
16H	22	1	Currency symbol location
17H	23	1	Currency decimal places
18H	24	1	Time format
19H	25	4	Extended ASCII map call address
1DH	29	2	List separator string (ASCIIZ format)
1FH	31	10	(Reserved)

Figure 13-38. *The format of extended country information returned by MS-DOS function 65H, subfunction 01H. The information starting at offset 7 is the same as that returned by interrupt 21H, function 38H.*

Subfunction 02H (decimal 2). This subfunction returns 5 bytes of data in the buffer at ES:DI. The first byte always has the value 02H (the subfunction number). The 4 remaining bytes contain the segmented address of a translation table used to convert extended ASCII characters (ASCII codes 80H through FFH) to uppercase characters with ASCII codes 00H through 7FH. This table is used by the character-mapping routine whose address is returned by subfunction 01H.

Subfunction 04H (decimal 4). This subfunction also fills the buffer pointed to by ES:DI with a single subfunction ID byte followed by the 4-byte segmented address of a translation table. This table serves the same purpose as the table whose address is returned by subfunction 02H, but this table is used for filenames.

Subfunction 05H (decimal 5). This subfunction fills the buffer pointed to by ES:DI with a single subfunction ID byte followed by the 4-byte segmented address of a table of characters that must not be used for filenames.

Subfunction 06H (decimal 6). Like subfunctions 02H, 04H, and 05H, this subfunction fills the buffer pointed to by ES:DI with a subfunction ID byte followed by a segmented address. In this case, the address points to a table that specifies the collating sequence for the character set that is defined in the code page.

Subfunction 07H (decimal 7). This subfunction fills the buffer pointed to by ES:DI with a single subfunction ID byte followed by the 4-byte segmented address of a table. The table contains values that specify the valid ranges for lead bytes in the double-byte character set for the specified country.

Subfunction 20H (decimal 32). This subfunction converts the character specified in DL to uppercase, using the current uppercase table. The converted character is returned in DL.

Subfunction 21H (decimal 33). This subfunction performs the same service as subfunction 20H, except that subfunction 20H expects DS:DX to point to a string to be converted. CX must be loaded with the length of the string.

Subfunction 22H (decimal 34). This subfunction performs the same service as subfunction 21H, except that the string must be zero-terminated (an ASCIIZ string), which eliminates the need for the string length to be provided in CX.

Function 66H (decimal 102): Get/Set Global Code Page

Function 66H (decimal 102), introduced with MS-DOS version 3.3, consists of two subfunctions that provide support for code page switching within a program. You call this function with a subfunction number (01H or 02H) in AL.

Subfunction 01H (decimal 1). This subfunction returns the number of the active code page in BX. It also reports (in DX) the number of the default code page used when the system is booted.

Subfunction 02H (decimal 2). You call this subfunction with a new code page number in BX. MS-DOS copies the new code page information from the COUNTRY.SYS file and uses it to update all devices configured for code page switching. For this subfunction to operate successfully, you must include the appropriate DEVICE and COUNTRY commands in your CONFIG.SYS file, and you must execute the MODE CP PREPARE and NLSFUNC commands. (See your MS-DOS reference manual for details.)

An Example

For our assembly language example in this section, we've chosen something rather interesting. It's a routine used within The Norton Utilities programs, so you'll be seeing some actual production code.

The purpose of this routine is to calculate the day of the week for any day within MS-DOS's working range, which is stated to be from Tuesday, January 1, 1980, through Thursday, December 31, 2099. Occasionally it is valuable for a program to be able to report the day of the week, either for the current date or for any other date that may be in question. For example, MS-DOS keeps track of the date and time each file was last changed. Because people often use this information to find out when they last worked with a file, it can be handy to know the day of the week as well. In fact, the day of the week is often more immediately meaningful than the date.

Although several interesting and clever algorithms let you calculate the day of the week, the actual work of writing a day-of-the-week program is usually rather tedious. Beginning with version 1.10, MS-DOS incorporated a day-of-the-week calculation, which spared programmers the chore of writing their own. MS-DOS's routine is available only in a form that reports the current day of the week, but that is no obstacle: You can temporarily change MS-DOS's date to the date you're interested in and then have MS-DOS report the day of the week. The following assembly language routine does this.

Besides being slightly foxy, this routine is interesting because it illustrates how three MS-DOS function calls operate together to produce one result. It also illustrates the minor intricacies involved in saving and restoring pointers and values on the stack. As you will see here, stack use occasionally has to be carefully orchestrated so that different values don't get in one another's way.

This particular subroutine, named *Weekday*, is set up in the form needed for use with the Microsoft C compiler. The routine is called with three integer variables, which specify the month, day, and year you are interested in. The routine returns the day of the week in the form of an integer of the range 0 through 6 (signifying Sunday through Saturday). This conforms to the C language convention for arrays, providing an index to an array of strings that give the names of the days. Therefore, you could use this subroutine in this way:

```
DayName[ Weekday( month, day, year ) ]
```

It is important to note that this routine works blindly with the date, checking neither for a valid date nor for the range of dates accepted by MS-DOS. Here is the subroutine:

```
_TEXT           SEGMENT byte public 'CODE'
                ASSUME  cs:_TEXT

                PUBLIC  _Weekday
_Weekday        PROC    near

                push    bp              ; establish stack addressing ...
                mov     bp,sp           ; ... through BP

                mov     ah,2Ah          ; get current date
                int     21h

                push    cx              ; save current date on the stack
                push    dx

                mov     cx,[bp+8]       ; CX = year
                mov     dl,[bp+6]       ; DL = day
                mov     dh,[bp+4]       ; DH = month

                mov     ah,2Bh          ; set the date specified
                int     21h

                mov     ah,2Ah          ; get the date back from MS-DOS
                int     21h             ; (AL = day of the week)

                pop     dx              ; restore the current date ...
                pop     cx              ; ... in CX and DX
                push    ax              ; save day of week on the stack
```

```
        mov     ah,2Bh          ; set the current date
        int     21h

        pop     ax              ; AL = day of week
        mov     ah,0            ; AX = day of week

        pop     bp              ; restore BP and return
        ret

_Weekday    ENDP

_TEXT       ENDS
```

Chapter 14

Microsoft Windows and Windows NT

Microsoft Windows has become quite popular and has received a lot of publicity over the past few years. Unless you have been locked in a closet, you probably know at least something about it. Because Windows has become such a dominant factor in the PC world, anyone who programs PCs needs to know at least the fundamentals of what Windows is and how to program for it. This is a huge topic, of course, and anything approaching complete coverage is well beyond the scope of this book. In this chapter, our goal is to provide basic information about Windows and programming for Windows. You can then decide whether Windows programming is for you.

What Is Microsoft Windows?

In a nutshell, Microsoft Windows is a graphical, multitasking operating environment for IBM PC–compatible microcomputers. To see exactly what that means, let's take a look at the history of Windows and at the features it provides.

The History of Microsoft Windows

Microsoft Windows was developed, in part, to remedy the shortcomings of MS-DOS and MS-DOS programs. Most of these programs were developed independently of each other, with little or no regard for such factors as consistency and the ability to transfer data between programs. Although many of these programs were elegant and powerful, the lack of standards led to a number of problems. Among the more serious problems were the following:

- Every program had its own, sometimes unique, set of commands. For example, the keystroke used to save a file in one program might have been Alt-S; in another it might have been Alt-F7; and in another it might have been Ctrl-F. Users had to learn an entirely new set of commands for each program.

- Every program had its own printer drivers and screen drivers because MS-DOS was (and is) device dependent. Consequently, a program written for one configuration of output devices would probably not run on another system.

- There was no easy way to transfer data from one program to another. The best you could do was to save the data in a disk file and hope that the destination program would be able to read the file. Often your only recourse was to print the data from one program and then manually enter it in the other.

- You could run only one program at a time. If you were working in one program and needed another, you had to exit the first program before starting the second.

Microsoft Corporation released the first version of Windows in 1985. Although it generated a great deal of interest, relatively few people used it seriously, primarily because of a scarcity of application programs for Windows and because Windows ran slowly on the hardware available at the time, the IBM PC/XT and PC/AT.

Over the next few years, Microsoft released a couple of upgrades to Windows, and at the same time PC speed was rapidly improving. The breakthrough came in May 1990 with the release of Windows 3.0. Windows 3.0 took advantage of the capabilities of the latest Intel CPUs and fixed many shortcomings of earlier Windows releases; it was the first graphical environment for the PC to gain widespread acceptance. A flood of application programs soon followed, making it feasible for many PC users to use Windows for all their work. Windows 3.1, which is the latest upgrade at the time this book is being written, was released in April 1992 and included additional features. At present Windows is installed on a significant (and growing) proportion of PCs, and there are now more people using Windows than using Macintosh computers. It is becoming increasingly impractical for developers to ignore Windows.

The remainder of this section outlines some of the features of Windows that have made it so popular. Keep in mind that although Windows can also run MS-DOS applications, only applications written specifically for Windows can take advantage of all of Windows' features.

The User Interface

Windows is a *graphical user interface,* or GUI (pronounced "gooey"). A GUI takes advantage of the bit-mapped graphics capabilities of a video display and can control each screen pixel to display any desired shapes and patterns. Because Windows and applications for Windows are graphical, they can take full advantage of every inch of the screen, and they can display information in the clearest and most convenient manner. For example, a document can be displayed on screen with exactly the same appearance it will have when printed, a capability called WYSIWYG, which stands for "What you see is what you get." Figure 14-1 shows a Windows word processor, Microsoft Word for Windows, displaying a document in WYSIWYG mode.

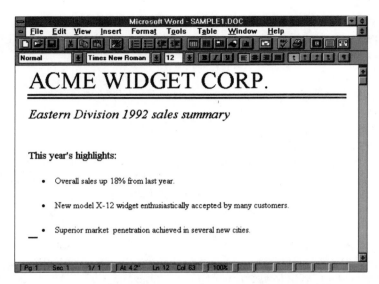

Figure 14-1. *The Windows GUI permits documents to be displayed in WYSIWYG mode.*

As its name implies, the Windows GUI makes use of screen *windows*. A window is a rectangular screen region inside which information is displayed. All windows work the same way, and they can be resized, moved, and temporarily hidden from view. This flexibility enables Windows and applications for Windows to display a wide variety of information and permits the user to arrange that information to meet his or her needs.

The Windows GUI is consistent. All applications for Windows, as well as Windows itself, must follow the same set of GUI rules. These rules standardize the design and placement of menus, the techniques for manipulating screen windows, the use of the mouse, and other factors related to the way the applications look and are used; the way information is displayed and the commands required for certain tasks are consistent. A user who is familiar with one application for Windows has a significant head start in learning another application.

Multitasking

An important feature of Windows is its ability to multitask—to do two or more tasks at the same time. These tasks can be performed by one or more open applications. Multitasking can allow you to work more efficiently. For example, you can use your word processor to write a letter while your spreadsheet program chugs along in the background printing a graph or performing a lengthy calculation. In actuality, Windows does not perform the tasks simultaneously; it manages the computer's CPU so that it works on each task for a few milliseconds at a time, rapidly switching from one to another. To the user, however, it appears that the tasks are being performed at the same time.

Windows' multitasking capability is most frequently used for task switching rather than for true multitasking. In task switching, the background programs are not actually doing anything; they are simply "idling," ready for instant access. You can have your word processor, your drawing program, and your database all open, and you can switch among them as needed. Because each program runs in its own window, you can arrange the screen so that one program takes up the entire screen, or you can make multiple programs visible. For example, Figure 14-2 shows a Windows screen with three programs visible: a word processor (Microsoft Word for Windows), a spreadsheet (Quattro Pro for Windows), and a graphics design program (Micrografx Designer).

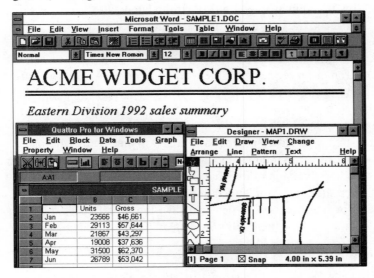

Figure 14-2. *Windows can display and run multiple programs at the same time.*

Data Transfer

As PCs are used for an increasing variety of tasks, the ability to transfer data among programs becomes more important. A financial spreadsheet might require figures from a sales database, and a word processing document might need a drawing created with a charting application. Windows provides three methods for data transfer among applications.

The first method is the *clipboard,* a temporary data storage location that is maintained by Windows. Any Windows application can copy or cut data from its active (current) window to the clipboard, and it can retrieve data from the clipboard and paste it into its active window. The clipboard can be used to move or copy data from one location to another in the same application or in different applications. For example, you could copy a column of numbers from your spreadsheet to the clipboard and then paste it into a word processing document.

The second data transfer method is called *dynamic data exchange* (DDE). When you use DDE, you establish a link between the file that needs the information, called the *client,* and the file that contains the information, called the *server.* If the data in the server changes, that change is reflected in the client. For example, if you're using a word processor to write a sales report, you could link one or more areas in the report to the cell in a spreadsheet that contains the annual sales total. If an updated sales figure is entered in the spreadsheet, the new total appears in the sales report.

The most sophisticated method of data transfer is called *object linking and embedding* (OLE). With OLE, an *object* (a piece of data, such as some text or a graph) from a server can be either linked to or embedded in a client. Object linking is similar to DDE: When the linked object changes, the change is reflected in the client. With object embedding, a link is created not only to the data object but also to the application that created it. For example, let's say that you have embedded a chart created with Microsoft PowerPoint in a Word for Windows document. While you are working on the document, the latest version of the chart is displayed in the document. If you double-click on the chart, you launch the server application and load the embedded chart for modification. When you save the modified chart, you return directly to the client, which will now display the modified chart.

Device Independence

Another advantage of Windows is *device independence.* This means that programs written for Windows do not have to be concerned with the details of the output devices (the screen and the printer) that will be used with them. Rather, Windows provides a Graphics Device Interface (GDI), which can be thought of as a graphics programming language. To display or print graphics or formatted text, all a program need do is issue the required GDI commands, and Windows takes care of all the rest. Windows converts the GDI commands to the specific commands required by the installed video system or printer. A Windows program can fully utilize any printer or video display for which a Windows device driver is available. Purchasing a new printer or video system requires only that you install the new driver once, for Windows. This is a welcome change from MS-DOS applications, in which each program has its own set of printer and video drivers.

Memory Management

Memory management is an important part of what Windows does. It is essential that a system's memory be allocated so that different programs' memory areas are kept separate and so that available memory resources are used as efficiently as possible. When in either standard mode or 386 enhanced mode, Windows 3.x runs in the CPU's protected mode, which permits Windows and applications for Windows to access as much as 16 MB of memory on 80286 machines and up to 4096 MB (4 gigabytes) on 80386 and higher machines. Now, 16 MB of memory might seem like a huge amount; relatively few systems have that much installed. Even if you have 16 MB or more available, running several large applications for Windows at the same time might fill it up. Windows uses a variety of techniques to make the best use of available memory. On machines with an 80386 or higher processor, if available memory should fill up while Windows is running in 386 enhanced mode, Windows can temporarily move data from memory to disk, storing it in a *swap file,* and then move the data back to RAM as needed.

Microsoft Windows and MS-DOS

To run Microsoft Windows, you must first load MS-DOS. Technically speaking, therefore, Windows is not an operating system but rather is an operating system enhancer that runs on top of MS-DOS. In actuality, however, Windows bypasses MS-DOS much of the time, interacting directly with the hardware rather than using the MS-DOS services. In essence, MS-DOS controls disk input/output, and Windows takes care of input from and output to all other devices: screen display, mouse, keyboard, printer, and so on. For all practical purposes, therefore, Windows should be thought of as a distinct operating system.

In addition to applications written specifically for Windows, Windows can run most regular MS-DOS applications. Microsoft refers to these as *standard applications.* When running under Windows, standard applications do not behave any differently than when running under MS-DOS; they use the same screen displays, fonts, commands, and so on. Standard applications are often run in full-screen mode under Windows. On 80386 and higher systems, Windows can run standard applications in partial-screen windows and even permits limited cut-and-paste text transfer between a standard application and an application for Windows.

Windows NT

The success of the Microsoft Windows operating system made it clear to Microsoft that future operating systems should provide a similar user interface. This conclusion was strengthened by the fact that other windowed user interfaces had been adopted for a variety of microcomputer platforms: the Apple Macintosh operating system, OS/2 for PCs, NeXTStep for NeXT systems, and X Window for UNIX systems. It was also clear to Microsoft, however, that it should design a new operating system from scratch. The user interface is only one part of an operating system—the surface layer, if you will. Underneath are the guts, the binary machinery that provides the real power of the operating system by permitting it to take advantage of the hardware. Although Windows 3.x is certainly adequate for today's systems, it was apparent that hardware advances, software innovations, and user expectations (regarding advanced networking and security, for example) would soon outpace the capabilities of Windows. Something new was needed.

That something is Windows NT. Windows NT is a totally new operating system from Microsoft. It is still under development at the time this book is being written, but it might have been released by the time you read this. In this section we provide a brief overview of the goals and structure of Windows NT. If you would like additional information, we suggest you refer to *Inside Windows NT* by Helen Custer (Microsoft Press, 1992).

The Goals of Windows NT

To the user, the Windows NT interface will not be much different from the Windows interface. Despite the apparent similarity, however, it will be a totally new operating system written from the ground up. When designing Windows NT, Microsoft had the following major objectives for the new operating system:

- **Portability.** The new operating system would be written so that it could easily be adapted to different processor architectures. This would enable Windows NT to be used not only on systems based on the Intel 80x86 processor series but also on systems based on other CPUs, including the increasingly popular reduced instruction set computing (RISC) processors.

- **Distributed computing.** It is increasingly common today for PCs to be connected to a network. A network enables individual computers to share data and, in many cases, to share hardware resources such as disk storage and processing capability. The benefits of a network are dependent on the extent to which

436

applications are able to distribute their work (data and processing) across more than one computer. To this end, distributed-processing capabilities were built into Windows NT from the start.

- **Scalable multiprocessing.** As increases in the power of single CPUs begin to be limited by basic physical constraints, multiprocessor systems have become a more practical means of obtaining increased computing horsepower. In a multiprocessor system, two or more interconnected CPUs divide the computational load among them. Multiprocessor systems have been available for some time, but the development of software to take full advantage of them has lagged behind. Windows NT is designed to be a scalable, multiprocessing operating system: It permits applications to run on both single-processor and multiprocessor systems, and it takes full advantage of the capabilities of the latter.

- **Government-certifiable security.** In any multiuser operating system, security is an important consideration. We have all read news accounts of hackers breaking into a government or commercial computer network and stealing or erasing sensitive data. Windows NT is designed to permit implementation of the different levels of security required by different customers.

The Structure of Windows NT

From the beginning, the structure of Windows NT was carefully planned to best meet the operating system's design goals. As you might imagine, this structure is complex, and it is not possible to provide a full treatment here. Yet the most basic aspects of Windows NT's structure can be described fairly easily—and that's what we do in this section.

At the most fundamental level, the structure of Windows NT consists of two parts: the *protected-mode subsystems,* or *servers,* and the *Windows NT executive.* (See Figure 14-3.) This layered structure plays an important role in the reliability and portability of Windows NT.

The servers are the highest layer of Windows NT, the part that the user interacts with most directly. Different servers can run simultaneously on Windows NT, providing broad functionality to the user. The most important job performed by a server is providing an application programming interface (API) that programs can call. Windows NT's primary API is the Win32 API, which provides support for Windows programs. Other servers include an OS/2 API for OS/2 programs and a POSIX API for POSIX programs. A server is also responsible for providing a user interface. One specialized server, the

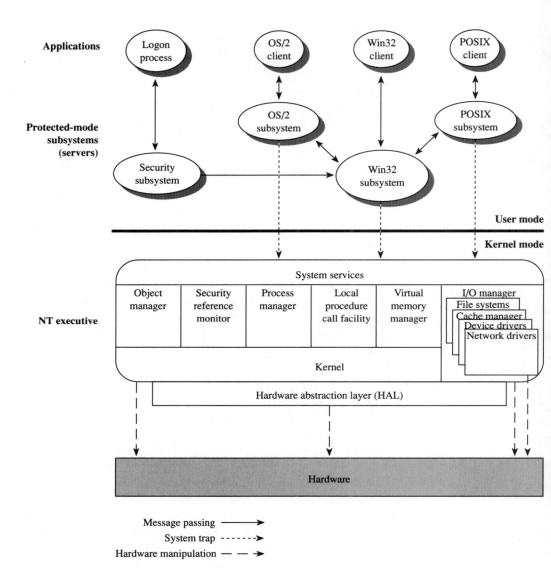

Figure 14-3. *A block diagram of the structure of Windows NT.*

security subsystem, maintains security on individual system computers. Each Windows NT server constitutes a protected subsystem whose memory areas and operations are protected from interference from other servers.

The Windows NT executive can be thought of as the heart of Windows NT. It provides the interface between the outside world (the user, the application programs, and the network) and the system hardware, and it performs a variety of essential tasks. Only the NT executive has full access to system resources, such as memory and the file system. The NT executive consists of a variety of components that work more or less independently of each other. These components have precisely defined jobs, such as memory management and file I/O. The NT executive performs the actions requested by the protected-mode servers, and it maintains the independence of the various servers running at any one time. Communication between the servers and the NT executive and among the components of the NT executive is accomplished primarily by means of a carefully defined messaging system.

Also part of the Windows NT executive is the *hardware abstraction layer* (HAL), which provides an interface between the rest of the NT executive and the system hardware. Of all the components of Windows NT, only the hardware abstraction layer is hardware specific. The job of the HAL is to translate requests from the NT executive into the CPU instructions, interrupts, and memory requests required by the host hardware. To port Windows NT to a new hardware platform requires only the creation of a new hardware abstraction layer; the protected-mode subsystems and the rest of the NT executive need not be changed.

Using Windows NT

The first step in using Windows NT is to log onto the system. During the logon process the user must satisfy whatever security requirements have been established for the system. If logon is successful, the user session is passed to the Win32 environment subsystem. This subsystem provides the user interface, which will be similar or identical to the Windows 3.1 Program Manager user interface. Thus, anyone familiar with Windows 3.1 will have no problem starting out on a Windows NT system.

The Win32 subsystem controls the screen display, the keyboard, the mouse, and any other input devices that may be in use. It is also the server for Win32 clients—that is, application programs written for the Win32 API. If the user tries to run a non-Win32 client, the Win32 subsystem takes one of two actions:

- For an MS-DOS or a Windows 3.1 client, the Win32 subsystem runs code that creates a virtual MS-DOS machine to run the application.

- For other clients (for example, OS/2 or POSIX clients), the Win32 subsystem calls another environment subsystem to run the application. Each of these subsystems supports the appropriate API for a certain type of application.

In any case, the Win32 subsystem retains control of the video display. Any virtual MS-DOS machines or non-Win32 subsystems that are running must direct their output requests, in the form of messages, to the Win32 subsystem.

Programming for Microsoft Windows

If you have guessed that programming for Microsoft Windows is more complicated than programming for MS-DOS, you are quite correct. And, if you have experience writing programs for MS-DOS, you'll find programming for Windows to be a whole new kettle of fish. It's not only more complicated, it involves some concepts and techniques that can seem strange to an experienced MS-DOS programmer. In this section, we give you a broad overview of what's involved in Windows programming. We can do no more than scratch the surface, however. If you would like more information, refer to Charles Petzold's *Programming Windows 3.1* (Microsoft Press, 1992), which provides a clear and complete treatment of the subject.

The Microsoft Windows Application Programming Interface

At the heart of Windows is the application programming interface (API). The API consists of more than 1000 functions that application programs can call to perform needed tasks, such as creating windows, displaying text, and moving data between programs. To a large extent, writing a program for Windows consists of making API calls. Anyone who programs for Windows will soon become familiar with the API!

The API is part of Windows itself. All application programs for Windows have access to the same set of API functions. Thus, if the Microsoft Word for Windows word processing program wants to create a new window, it uses the same *CreateWindow* API call that would be used by the 1-2-3 for Windows spreadsheet program, by the Micrografx Designer graphics program, or by any other program for Windows. This consistency is important. In a multitasking GUI environment such as Windows, it is essential that all programs behave in a precisely defined manner. By providing a common set of API functions that all programs use, Windows makes it easy for the needed consistency to be achieved.

The Windows API might seem complicated; with more than 1000 functions, it is indeed a formidable item. If you feel a bit overwhelmed, it might help to think of the API as a labor-saving device. From a programmer's point of view, that's exactly what it is. Just think how much time it would take you to write from scratch the code necessary to create a screen window that can be moved and sized by using either the mouse or the keyboard. The Windows API already contains this code, which is thoroughly tested and debugged. All you need to do is call the function.

Three distinct Windows APIs target different users. They are

- The Windows 3.1 API, which is sometimes called Win16 because it utilizes 16-bit instructions. This is the API that most Windows programmers are dealing with today because they are writing programs to run under the current Windows version.

- The Win32 API, which uses 32-bit instructions almost exclusively and therefore can run only on 32-bit CPUs. Win32 is a *superset* of Win16, which means that essentially every function in Win16 has a 32-bit counterpart in Win32. Win32 also includes many new functions that have no Win16 counterparts. The initial implementation of Win32 is in the Windows NT operating system.

- Win32s, which is also a 32-bit API. The *s* stands for *subset,* indicating that the Win32s API is a subset of the Win32 API. Specifically, Win32s contains only those functions that also exist in the Win16 API. This means that Win32s applications will provide all the advantages of 32-bit instructions and will be able to run on both Windows 3.x (on 80386 or higher processors) and Windows NT platforms.

You might be thinking that the Windows API functions are a lot like the library functions you call in a C program. This supposition is partly true, but it is not completely accurate. You'll see why in the next section.

Dynamic Linking

Windows API functions are located in a special kind of file called a *dynamic link library* (DLL). DLL files have either the .EXE or the .DLL extension. If you have Windows installed on your system, you'll find many .DLL files on your disk. Most of these files are application specific: They contain functions that are part of a specific application program. Most of the Windows API functions are located in four files: KRNL286.EXE and KRNL386.EXE contain functions for loading and executing programs, managing memory, and scheduling; USER.EXE contains functions for windowing and the user interface; and GDI.EXE contains graphics functions.

If you have some experience writing MS-DOS programs, the term *dynamic link library* might ring some bells. When creating an MS-DOS program, you make use of libraries, and you also perform a step called linking. However, DLLs are not really similar to these libraries.

Almost every programming language that is used to create MS-DOS programs includes one or more function libraries. As you write a program, you make calls to these library functions to perform needed tasks, such as manipulating disk files and displaying information on the screen. For example, the C language has the *open()* and *printf()* functions (among many others). So far, MS-DOS function libraries sound similar to DLLs, but there are two major differences. First, MS-DOS function libraries are provided with each programming-language compiler rather than being part of the operating system. Second, when an MS-DOS program is compiled and linked, the code for each library function that the program uses is copied from the library and made part of the program's .EXE file. Thus, if you write 10 C programs that all use the *printf()* function, there's a copy of the *printf()* library code in each program's .EXE file.

You have already learned that Windows DLLs are part of the operating system—that's one way they differ from MS-DOS function libraries. The second difference is that the code for DLL functions is not copied into every program that uses it. Rather, a single copy of the DLL is loaded into memory so that the code for all of the DLL functions is available for any program that wants to call it. Thus, a program for Windows that uses, for example, the *CreateWindow* API function does not contain the *CreateWindow* code in the program's .EXE file; it contains only the call to the function. When the program is loaded, the API function calls in the program are resolved so that they point to the location in memory where the DLL is loaded. (This is the *dynamic linking*.) No matter how many application programs are loaded, there is never more than a single copy of any API function in memory. Given the complexity of many API functions, this is a great memory saver.

Message-Driven Architecture

Another aspect of programming for Windows that will be new to MS-DOS programmers is the message-driven architecture of Windows. To see exactly what this means, let's look at what's going on in a Windows session. Windows itself is running, of course, and one or more of the programs provided with Windows, such as the Program Manager or the File Manager, are probably active as well. Other application programs, such as a word processor or a graphics program, might also be running. Programs might be transferring data here and there. A great deal of coordination among all these processes is required. The operating system needs to know what the application programs are doing and vice versa. Messages are the primary means by which the needed coordination is achieved. If a process is performing services that other processes need to know about or if it wants to request data or services from another process, it sends a message. It is the responsibility of each process to detect and respond to messages that are relevant to it.

Let's look at a concrete example. Say that a word processing program is displaying text in a full-screen window and the user changes the window size. The resizing of the window itself is handled by the Windows API, not by the application program. However, the application program must reformat the text to fit the new window size. Windows sends a message to the program, specifying the new window size; the program detects the message and responds by reformatting the text accordingly.

Practical Aspects of Programming for Microsoft Windows

Even if you find all this technical information interesting (and we hope that you do), you might be wondering how exactly you write a program for Windows and what tools you need. As we've already mentioned, programming for Windows is a complex topic. We can't cover it in detail in this book, but here are some general comments.

As you probably realize, programming for Windows is an all-or-nothing decision. That is, you cannot write a program that is part MS-DOS and part Windows; it's one or the other. Before you commit to writing an application for Windows, be sure that it's really a Windows application you need, not an MS-DOS, OS/2, or UNIX application.

A large part of programming for Windows is working with the Windows API. Knowing the capabilities of the API is essential if you are to write programs that make the best use of the Windows environment. Given that the API contains more than 1000 functions, it's unlikely that any of us will ever be able to memorize them. Therefore, a good API reference is indispensable. Both printed and online API references are available, and most of the programming tools for Windows include an API reference.

As for specific programming tools, a wide variety of excellent products is available. We will not make any specific recommendations, not only because the field changes so quickly but also because the choice of a programming tool is largely a matter of personal preferences. You'll want to consider which programming language to use. Programming tools for Windows are available in Basic, C++, Pascal, and several specialized languages. You'll also want to consider the availability of specialized programming features, such as interface design tools and customized function libraries, which can significantly speed the program creation process.

Chapter 15

OS/2

OS/2 is another major operating system for PCs. At present it has nowhere near the installed base of MS-DOS or even Microsoft Windows, but it is gaining increasing acceptance in some segments of the PC user community. As a result, OS/2 is an operating system that every PC programmer needs to know at least a little about. In this chapter, we provide an overview of OS/2 to give you a feel for what it is and how it is different from MS-DOS and Windows.

It's important to realize that a useful comparison can be made only between OS/2 and Windows NT, not between OS/2 and Windows 3.x. Because Windows NT has not been released as of this writing, it's difficult to make this comparison. In fact, the imminence of Windows NT is undoubtedly contributing to the unexpectedly slow acceptance of OS/2; users and information managers are waiting to look at Windows NT before making a decision.

The History of OS/2

The origins of the OS/2 operating system can be traced to hardware advances that occurred in 1984—specifically, to the Intel 80286 CPU and the IBM PC/AT computer that was based on it. The 80286 CPU has two operating modes, *real mode* and *protected mode*. In real mode, the 80286 is not much different from the 8088/8086 CPUs that were used in earlier PCs: It's considerably faster, but that's about all. In protected mode, however, the 80286 has significant capabilities that were lacking in earlier CPUs.

The most important of these new capabilities are related to memory. First, the 80286 can address 16 MB of memory, 16 times as much as an 8088/8086. Second, the 80286 has the ability to protect regions of memory from unauthorized access (hence the name *protected mode*). These features made the 80286 the first CPU that was suitable for multitasking (performing multiple tasks at the same time with one or more open applications). The 80286's large memory space provided the RAM that was required to load multiple applications and their data into memory at the same time, and the memory protection capability made it possible to protect each application's memory space from unauthorized access by other applications.

It was clear that implementation of multitasking would bring significant advantages to users. There was only one problem: The only operating system available for PCs, MS-DOS, was a single-user, nonmultitasking operating system. Because it had been designed for 8088/8086 CPUs, MS-DOS could run only in real mode on the 80286. Although MS-DOS programs ran faster on the 80286 and despite the development of special utilities that made some of the 80286's extra memory available for RAM disks and disk caches, the real advantages of protected mode remained unused. The discrepancy between hardware and operating system capabilities became even more pronounced in 1985 with the introduction of the 80386 CPU, which extended the power of protected mode.

To take full advantage of protected mode, a new operating system was needed. Although some attempts were made to modify MS-DOS to use protected mode, it was ultimately decided to start from scratch and create a new, protected-mode operating system. This decision marked the start of the joint project between IBM and Microsoft that produced OS/2. Creating a new operating system is a complex and time-consuming business, however, and it was to be a long time before users actually saw the product.

It was to be about 3 years, in fact. OS/2 version 1.0, released in December 1987, was pretty basic: It lacked a graphical interface and support for large hard disks, and you could not use a mouse with it. It was a start, however, and it provided developers with the platform necessary to begin writing applications for OS/2. Because it was an entirely new operating system, OS/2 required that the software to be used with it—compilers, libraries, applications, and so on—be redone from the ground up. It did provide a *DOS compatibility box* to run MS-DOS applications. However, applications run in the DOS box behaved just as if they were running under MS-DOS, with none of the advantages of OS/2. True OS/2 applications were slow in coming because of the large development effort required.

In late 1988, IBM and Microsoft released version 1.1 of OS/2. It offered a number of improvements over version 1.0, including support for large hard disks and a windowing graphical user interface called the Presentation Manager. Version 1.2 was introduced in 1989. It offered an improved Presentation Manager and an optional High Performance File System that greatly enhanced disk operations. OS/2 was available in both Standard and Extended editions. The Extended edition provided extra capabilities, including sophisticated network and database support. An increasing number of OS/2 applications became available, and the new operating system started to look like a viable alternative to MS-DOS, for high-end users.

However, several factors limited the acceptance of OS/2. For one, the hardware that was required to run OS/2 effectively was rather expensive. (Fast CPUs with a lot of RAM were not always as inexpensive as they are today.) Also, despite the introduction of more OS/2 applications, the number simply could not compare with the huge number of high-quality applications available for MS-DOS. Performance problems and incompatibility with some non-IBM hardware contributed to the wait-and-see attitude taken by most users toward OS/2.

An additional obstacle to the acceptance of OS/2 arose in 1990, when Microsoft released version 3.0 of Windows, which overcame various limitations that had kept it from widespread acceptance. Sales shot through the roof, and Windows 3.0 was soon followed by a flood of powerful applications. Users looking for a graphical, multitasking operating system flocked to Windows, and more copies of Windows 3.0 were sold in the first month after its release than copies of OS/2 had sold in 3 years. OS/2 languished as developers concentrated their resources on creating Windows applications. In 1991 Microsoft reevaluated its plans regarding operating system development. Believing that its future lay in Windows, Microsoft pulled out of the OS/2 project to concentrate on developing Windows NT (discussed in Chapter 14). OS/2 became purely an IBM effort.

Version 1.3 of OS/2 was released in 1991. It offered a faster user interface and some other enhancements. However, the real future of OS/2 was in version 2.0, which IBM announced in 1991 and released in March 1992. This version fixed many of the shortcomings that limited the acceptance of earlier releases and provided significant enhancements in functionality and compatibility. Finally OS/2 had evolved into a viable operating system.

Systems Applications Architecture

To appreciate the features of OS/2, it helps to have some understanding of a set of standards called Systems Applications Architecture, or SAA. The origins of SAA lie in IBM's past. As you might know, IBM earned its fame and fortune in the field of mainframe computers. The development of the PC was quite a change for the company, and everybody—IBM included—was surprised at the rapid growth of the PC market. IBM also markets minicomputers, which are positioned somewhere between mainframes and PCs. With three lines of computers, or platforms, IBM faced some problems. Major differences among the user interfaces presented by the platforms made it difficult for users to move from one platform to another. There were also major programming differences among platforms, which meant that a program written for one platform could not be recompiled and run on another platform; it had to be rewritten from scratch. Finally, communications incompatibilities made it difficult to establish data communications links among platforms.

To deal with these problems, which are collectively referred to as *cross-platform incompatibilities,* IBM developed a set of standards that would apply to all of its computers. This set of standards is SAA, and it consists of three main parts, which are described on the next page.

- The Common Programming Interface ensures that a program written for one platform can be recompiled and run on the other platforms.

- Common User Access governs the details of the user interface, which is similar on all the platforms.

- Common Communications Access defines communications standards so that all IBM systems can readily communicate with each other.

Clearly, OS/2's adherence to the SAA standard makes it a particularly attractive operating system when compatibility with other IBM platforms is a concern. SAA aside, OS/2 is a powerful operating system that appeals to many users who couldn't care less about IBM compatibility.

Features of OS/2

OS/2 is a large and complicated operating system that offers a wealth of tools and features to the user. The remainder of this chapter presents a brief overview of some of OS/2's features.

The Workplace Shell Graphical User Interface

Like Microsoft Windows and the Apple Macintosh, OS/2 has a graphical user interface (GUI) that provides the screen display seen by the user. A GUI displays information in screen windows; uses icons to represent programs, data, and tasks; and uses menus to offer choices to the user. A GUI is designed to be used with a mouse, and it presents a much easier and more intuitive way to use a computer than does a command-line, text-based interface.

Early versions of OS/2 had a graphical user interface called the Presentation Manager, which was similar in many ways to the Microsoft Windows GUI. The current version's GUI is called the Workplace Shell, and it is quite different from the Presentation Manager. In some ways, the Workplace Shell is more similar to the Apple Macintosh GUI.

The Workplace Shell is an object-oriented GUI. (In this context, the term *object oriented* has a different meaning than it does when applied to a programming language.) All user actions take place on a screen called the Desktop. On the Desktop, icons are used to represent the various system objects. Each part of the system—programs, data, and hardware—is treated as an object. An object can contain other objects. Activating any of these objects results in the opening of a related window on the Desktop screen. See Figure 15-1.

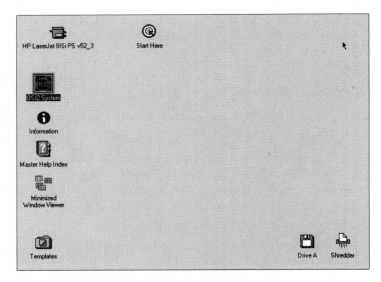

Figure 15-1. *The OS/2 2.0 Workplace Shell.*

All system-related user actions are accomplished by manipulating objects, usually by using a mouse. For example, to print a document you drag the document object's icon to the printer object's icon. To create a new document object you drag a blank form off a stack of form objects. To start a program you double-click on the program's icon. By providing a consistent and intuitive interface, the Workplace Shell hides the complexity of the operating system and the hardware from the user.

The High Performance File System

Since version 1.2, OS/2 has offered a file system called the High Performance File System, or HPFS. The HPFS is a replacement for the file allocation table (FAT) file system used by MS-DOS and Microsoft Windows 3.x.

The FAT system had its origins when the PC was introduced. Some readers might remember that the original PC had no hard disk, and floppy disks could hold only 160 KB of data. The FAT system was perfectly adequate at the time. When hard disks became available and rapidly grew in size, the disadvantages of the FAT system became evident. Clever programmers have been able to adapt the FAT system to today's larger and faster disks, but its disadvantages remain. The HPFS was designed to remedy the shortcomings of the FAT system.

■ The HPFS permits filenames to be as long as 254 characters. This gives users much greater flexibility in assigning filenames than the 11-character limit (8-character name plus 3-character extension) allowed by the FAT system.

■ The HPFS stores information about the location of a file near the file itself. This arrangement minimizes read/write head movement and maximizes disk speed. In contrast, the FAT system stores all file location information in one disk location regardless of where on the disk the file itself is stored. More read/write head movement is required, which diminishes disk access speed.

■ The HPFS automatically sorts filenames in directories alphabetically, making it much easier for a program to find a file it must access. In contrast, the FAT system does not sort filenames, so a program can find a file only by looking through a directory one file at a time. When a directory contains hundreds of files, this can slow operations considerably.

■ The HPFS permits *extended attributes* to be attached to each file. This allows descriptive information, such as the author's name, a summary, or keywords, to be associated with each file without being part of the file itself. The FAT system offers no such feature.

■ The HPFS organizes disk data in a way that permits efficient random access rather than requiring the entire file to be read in a sequential manner. This type of disk access is commonly needed by database programs. Under the FAT system, random disk access is significantly slower.

OS/2 can use either the HPFS or the FAT system. When you install OS/2, you have the option of reformatting your entire disk or one or more logical partitions on it with the HPFS. If you use MS-DOS and OS/2 on the same system, any partition on the disk formatted for the HPFS will not be accessible if the system is booted with MS-DOS. (See the section entitled "Dual Boot Capability," later in this chapter.)

MS-DOS and Windows Compatibility

The designers of OS/2 were well aware that most users already had a significant investment of both money and training in application programs for MS-DOS and Windows. They also knew that there is a relative scarcity of OS/2 applications compared to applications for MS-DOS and Windows. People would be more willing to make the switch to OS/2 if they could continue to use the application programs they already owned. For this reason, OS/2 version 2.0 includes both MS-DOS and Microsoft Windows compatibility. In other words, OS/2 can run most applications designed for MS-DOS and Windows.

Most MS-DOS applications can be run in a *DOS session,* in which the application appears in a window on the Desktop. OS/2 has the ability to run multiple DOS sessions, and each session is independent of other DOS sessions. Within each DOS session, an application appears to have an 8088/8086 CPU and associated memory to itself. This is made possible by the ability of the Intel 80386 and 80486 chips to emulate multiple 8086 CPUs. Each DOS session is referred to as a Virtual DOS Machine, or VDM. As many as 240 VDMs can exist at one time. An MS-DOS session running on a VDM can access disk areas that have been formatted with the HPFS.

Not all MS-DOS programs can run on a VDM. Some programs go beyond the 8088/8086 instruction set and use some 32-bit instructions. Such programs conform to one of two so-called *DOS extenders:* the DOS Protected Mode Interface (DPMI) or the Virtual Control Program Interface (VCPI). An OS/2 VDM supports DPMI programs but not VCPI programs. In addition, some MS-DOS programs are tied so closely to the system hardware that they cannot run under OS/2. Such programs typically include games, communications software, and disk defragmenters.

Windows compatibility was a bit more complicated to achieve than MS-DOS compatibility. As you learned in Chapter 14, programs for Windows operate by making calls to the Windows API (application programming interface) to perform the desired tasks. OS/2 also has an API, which OS/2 programs use, but the OS/2 API is different from the Windows API. One way to allow programs for Windows to run under OS/2 would have been to provide a translator, which would intercept the programs' API calls and translate them into the corresponding OS/2 API calls. However, a translation step takes time, and execution speed was a top priority. The solution was to include the Windows API as part of OS/2 so that applications for Windows could run directly, without the need for a translation step.

Note, however, that OS/2 supports the Windows 3.0 API, not the Windows 3.1 API. Although the differences between the two APIs are relatively minor, programs written specifically for Windows 3.1 cannot be executed under OS/2. Whether future versions of OS/2 will support programs for Windows 3.1 is not known at this time.

The REXX Batch Language

Anyone who has used MS-DOS has probably worked with its batch language at some time—and has probably grumbled about how difficult it is to use for any but the simplest tasks. A flexible batch language can be a powerful operating system tool, and one is provided with OS/2. Called REXX, it had its origins on IBM mainframe computers.

REXX is similar to the MS-DOS batch language in that it consists of commands that instruct the operating system to perform certain actions, such as running programs or displaying information. For example, let's say that your system is connected to a network and you need to execute three programs to complete the network logon process. Under MS-DOS, the necessary batch commands would look something like this:

```
rem Batch program for network logon
echo off
echo Commencing network logon procedure
program1
program2
program3
```

You could save these commands in a file named LOGON.BAT and then automate the entire logon process simply by running the batch file. Under REXX, you could perform the same actions. The syntax is slightly different, and the batch file extension is .CMD, but the basics are the same:

```
/* Batch program for network logon */
say "Commencing network logon procedure"
program1
program2
program3
```

So far, the two batch languages seem fairly similar. However, REXX has significantly more features than does the MS-DOS batch language. For example, REXX can prompt the user for input, as shown below. (We're assuming that the logon program *program3* can pass the user's password as a command-line parameter.)

```
/* Batch program for network logon with password */
say "Commencing network logon procedure"
say "Please enter your password"
parse pull password
program1
program2
program3 password
```

453

This last example also shows that REXX can store information in variables. Both string and numeric information can be stored, and the values can be assigned directly in the program code or by accepting input from the user. The next example illustrates this; it also shows that a REXX program can carry out mathematical operations:

```
/* Batch program to calculate half of a number */
say "Please enter a number"
parse pull x
z = x/2
say "Half of" x "is" z
```

REXX is truly a full-featured language, and it's more similar in many ways to "real" programming languages, such as C, than it is to the MS-DOS batch language. Among its other capabilities are decision making with IF...THEN...ELSE, looping with DO WHILE and DO UNTIL, useful error reporting, time functions, and debugging capabilities.

Dual Boot Capability

When you install OS/2, you can select the dual boot option. This provides the choice of booting either OS/2 or MS-DOS (version 3.2 or later). When you boot MS-DOS with this option, it is really MS-DOS, not an OS/2 VDM. You can run all MS-DOS programs without the limitations that exist when running a VDM. The only limitation is that any areas of the disk formatted with the HPFS will not be accessible. The dual boot option is ideal for users who are interested in trying OS/2 but who want to retain the ability to run MS-DOS and Microsoft Windows 3.1 on their own.

Connectivity

The term *connectivity* refers to the ability of a computer to communicate with other computers, sharing programs, data, and messages. Connectivity is becoming increasingly important these days. Whether they are connected by a Local Area Network (LAN), by a Wide Area Network (WAN), or by a micro-to-mainframe link, more PCs are being called on to communicate with other systems.

A number of functional connectivity schemes are available and in wide use for MS-DOS systems. Yet the inherent limitations of MS-DOS present significant obstacles to efficient and trouble-free networking. It's a tribute to the skills and perseverance of hardware and software designers that the MS-DOS networks function as well as they do. How much better networks would function if they used an operating system that was designed from the ground up with connectivity as an objective.

That's just the case with OS/2 (and also with Windows NT, which is covered in Chapter 14). Advanced network administration utilities, device-sharing and file-sharing capabilities, and other connectivity capabilities are built into OS/2. With the sole exception of the Apple Macintosh's AppleTalk, OS/2 supports all major connectivity platforms. The details of OS/2's connectivity capabilities are beyond the scope of this chapter, but there is plenty of published information available if you are interested.

Programming for OS/2

Writing OS/2 programs is not conceptually different from writing programs for MS-DOS or Microsoft Windows. You must choose a programming language, of course, and you must use an OS/2 compiler—one that supports the OS/2 API and translates source code into instructions that OS/2 can understand. At present, the number of compilers and other programming tools available for OS/2 cannot match the number available for MS-DOS or Windows, but that's likely to change in the near future.

PART III:

PROGRAM DEVELOPMENT

Chapter 16

Program-Development Techniques

The term *program development* refers to the process by which you create a program. Before writing a program to run on a PC, you have a lot of choices to make: which language to use, which compiler to use, and other considerations. However, no matter which choices you make, some basic concepts and procedures apply in all cases. Understanding these basics is an important first step in becoming a skilled programmer. In this chapter we cover the basics of the program-development process, and in Chapter 17 we discuss programming languages and other programming tools. In both chapters our emphasis is on programming for MS-DOS.

Source Code vs. Machine Language

A program that you write consists of *source code*—statements, equations, and other components that you create by using an editor, much like writing a document by using a word processor. The source code instructs the computer to carry out the desired actions, such as displaying information on the screen, reading data from disk, performing numeric calculations, and accepting input from the keyboard. For example, if you wanted to display the message ''Hello, world'' on the screen and you were using the Basic programming language, you would write

```
PRINT "Hello, world"
```

To perform the same task if you were using the C programming language, you would write

```
printf("Hello, world\n");
```

Don't worry now about the differences between these statements. The important point is that a computer cannot directly understand source code. Before you can run your program, the source code must be translated into the special binary instructions that the CPU can understand. These binary instructions are called *machine language,* and the job of translating source code into machine language is performed by a *compiler.* Thus, a Basic language compiler would translate the source-code statement PRINT ''Hello, world'' into the machine-language instructions required to tell the CPU to display the message ''Hello, world'' on the screen. A C language compiler would translate the source-code statement printf(''Hello, world\n''); into similar machine-language instructions.

The Edit-Compile-Link-Test Cycle

Traditional MS-DOS program development comprises a four-step cycle: edit, compile, link, and test. These steps are described in the following sections and are diagrammed in Figure 16-1.

Step 1: Writing the Source Code

To begin with, you have to write your program by using the commands and syntax of your programming language. This form of the program is the source code. For almost all MS-DOS programming languages, the source code must be in the form of an ASCII text file. By convention, source-code files have a filename extension that reflects the name of the programming language used, such as .BAS or .C.

Step 2: Translating the Source Code

The next step in creating an executable program (a program that is ready to run) is to process the source code by using a language translator, or compiler. (For assembly language, the translator is called an *assembler*.) A translator converts source code into machine-language instructions that are in a form known as *object code*. Object code contains executable machine code, and it also includes information about the structure of the executable program. The object-code format is designed so that separate object modules can be combined into a single, unified program. Object-code files, by convention, have the filename extension .OBJ.

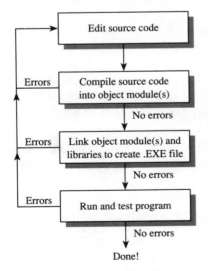

Figure 16-1. *The edit-compile-link-test cycle.*

Step 3: Linking

The next step is to link the object modules together. The *linker,* or link-editor program (known as LINK in MS-DOS) performs two main tasks: It combines separate object modules, as needed, making all the necessary connections among them. You will have multiple object modules if your source code is split among two or more files. In any case, object modules from one or more library files are linked in as well. (More information on libraries is given later in the chapter.) The linker also converts the modules from an object-code format to a loadable program in the .EXE format.

Step 4: Testing

The final step is to test your program—to run it and see whether it performs as intended. It's a rare program that works properly the first time. If the program doesn't work, you return to step 1 to modify the source code, and then you again compile, link, and test the program. That's why program development is called a cycle: In the course of developing a program you'll edit, compile, link, and test many times before you've finished.

You should note that this process is fraught with opportunities for errors. Even the most experienced programmers find it difficult to keep errors from appearing in their source code. Some errors are detected by the compiler or the linker, in which case the compile or link process is terminated and an error message is displayed. Other errors become evident only when the program is run.

Integrated Development Environments

In the traditional program-development method we have described, the various components—editor, compiler, and linker—are separate programs that you load and run as needed. These days it is more common to see *integrated development environments,* or IDEs, which combine these three functions into a single, seamless tool. Microsoft Quick C and Borland's Turbo Pascal are two popular IDEs. Many programmers prefer IDEs because they feel that IDEs are easier and faster to use than the traditional separate tools. Keep in mind, however, that behind the slick IDE interface, the same three steps are being performed: editing, compiling, and linking.

Interpreted Languages

Some languages take a different approach to translating source code into machine language. They are called *interpreted languages*. The compiled languages we have discussed so far translate, or compile, all the source code for a program in one operation. They store the resulting machine language in a disk file, where it can be read and executed by the CPU. In contrast, an interpreted language stores only the source code, and it translates, or interprets, the source code into machine language a section at a time as the program is executing. The best-known example of an interpreted language is the QBasic version of Basic that is supplied with MS-DOS versions 5.0 and later. Interpreted language programs run significantly slower than their compiled counterparts because translating the source code into machine language takes time. As a result, interpreted languages are not often used for serious program development, although they offer advantages for quick testing of short programs because loading and executing the compiler and linker are not required.

Libraries

Most high-level programming languages use dozens of prepared subroutines that support the operation of your programs. Naturally, these subroutines are in the translated, object-code form. It would be inconvenient, however, to have dozens of these object files taking up space on your disks. It would also be inconvenient to have to determine which files need to be combined with your own program's object files. To solve this problem, *object libraries* were created. Object libraries are collections of object modules contained in one file. By convention, libraries have the filename extension .LIB.

Most high-level programming languages come with a ready-to-use library of standard supporting subroutines. Some compilers have several libraries that provide different versions of standard routines. For example, a compiler might have two libraries of equivalent floating-point math routines: one with subroutines that use the 8087 coprocessor and the other with subroutines that emulate the same floating-point operations in software. You can also create libraries that contain object modules that you have written.

The MS-DOS linker can search through a library to find and use the subroutines it needs to create a complete, executable program. Without this library mechanism, you would be faced with the annoying task of telling the linker which object files were needed. If you omitted any, the link editing would fail; if you included any unnecessarily, your program could become extremely large. Libraries help you avoid these problems.

To manipulate the contents of an object library, you need a special utility program called a *library manager*. Most compilers that use object libraries provide their own library managers. The following discussion pertains to LIB, the library manager that is provided by the Microsoft Macro Assembler.

You can use LIB for three main purposes: simply to explore the contents of existing libraries (which can be an illuminating experience), to selectively replace modules in existing libraries, and to create new libraries.

The documentation for the LIB program in the Microsoft Macro Assembler manuals fully explains its operation, but to give you a taste of the ways LIB can be used, we have included a few examples. To create a new library named TESTLIB, enter this command:

```
LIB TESTLIB;
```

To list the contents of an existing library named TESTLIB and to direct the listing to the printer LPT1, enter the following command:

```
LIB TESTLIB,LPT1;
```

To add the module X.OBJ to TESTLIB, enter the following:

```
LIB TESTLIB +X;
```

To replace a module in TESTLIB named X.OBJ with a new version, enter the following:

```
LIB TESTLIB −+X;
```

To extract a module named X.OBJ from TESTLIB for disassembly or other separate use, enter the following:

```
LIB TESTLIB *X;
```

Most programs call a number of subroutines. The way you organize these subroutines determines how much value you'll obtain from LIB:

- If you prefer to combine the source code for your subroutines into one source file, which means the subroutines will all be compiled as a single input, you have little need for LIB.

- If you prefer to compile your subroutines into separate object files, LIB performs a valuable service: It gathers and organizes your object files.

We have no absolute recommendation for either style of operation, but many programmers prefer to break a large program into separate source-code files that can be compiled into separate object files and then linked.

Such a modular approach can be more convenient than maintaining one large source-code file that must be recompiled after each change.

Multiple-Language Programming

No matter which programming language you use, your programs are ultimately translated into machine language. This suggests that it should be possible to create a program by using more than one language—by doing multiple-language programming. This is, in fact, possible. If you take into account differences in data formats and parameter handling, you could, for example, write a program that's part Basic, part Pascal, and part C. You would have a separate source-code file for each language, of course, and you would use the appropriate compilers to translate the various source-code files into object files, which would then be combined by LINK into the executable program.

However, there's rarely a need to use two or more high-level languages to create a single program. It's much more common to combine a single high-level language with assembly language. (See Chapter 17.) The bulk of the program is written in the high-level language, and assembly language is used for critical subroutines that require the speed and flexibility of assembly language.

Subroutine Interfaces

A *subroutine interface* is a layer of assembly language code that lets a program written in a high-level language communicate with an assembly language subroutine. A subroutine interface consists of two parts: a control interface and a data interface.

The control interface handles the business of *calling and returning*—that is, of passing control of the computer from the calling program to a subroutine and back again. A control interface, by the way, can be tricky to program. It is remarkably simple if you program properly, but you can create incredible messes if you make even minor programming errors.

The data interface lets the calling program and a subroutine share data. To create a data interface that allows data to be shared successfully, you need to know how the calling program and the subroutine find and work with data, and you must understand how data is formatted so that the calling program and the subroutine can interpret it in the same way. We cover these topics in more detail in Chapter 17.

All three program elements—the calling program, the called subroutine, and the interface—must accomplish the tasks described in the next few paragraphs in order to work together successfully.

The program must be able to find its way to the subroutine. In the 8086-based system of the standard PC family, a subroutine is called by using a CALL instruction. There are two kinds of CALL instruction:

- The near CALL locates a subroutine that is within the current 64-KB code segment (CS); it does not require the CS register to be changed.

- The far CALL locates a subroutine that is outside the current CS. A complete segmented address is used in the CALL instruction, which changes the CS setting.

Because small-model and compact-model programs need to access only one executable code segment, they use near CALL instructions to call subroutines. Medium-model and large-model programs use far CALL instructions so that they can change the CS register and access multiple code segments.

The subroutine must know what to do when finished. A subroutine typically returns to the calling program by means of an instruction that corresponds to the way it was called (that is, by means of a near or far RET instruction). Occasionally, however, you might want a subroutine to take an unusual action when it has finished—for example, you might want it to terminate a program and return to MS-DOS.

The subroutine must know what supporting framework is provided by the caller. A typical supporting framework describes how the segment registers are set and whether a stack is available for use. In general, the segment registers are as they should be: CS has the correct code segment, DS points to the location of the calling program's data, and SS and SP are set up with the caller's stack.

The called subroutine usually can continue to use the caller's stack, but there is no practical way to know how much working space is available. If the subroutine's needs are reasonable—say, fewer than 64 bytes—the caller's stack space should be adequate. If the subroutine should need more working space, it can set up its own stack space in memory.

If the program needs to pass information (parameters) to the subroutine, both the program and the subroutine must know how many parameters exist, where they are, and what they are. Programs and subroutines typically work with a fixed number of parameters, although some languages, including C, can handle a variable number of parameters. The parameters are usually passed to the subroutine through the stack, either directly or indirectly. The direct method, known as *pass-by-value,* pushes the actual value of the parameter on the stack; the indirect method, known as *pass-by-reference,* pushes the parameter's address on the stack.

The parameter-passing method used depends primarily on the language in which the program is written; some languages place only addresses—never parameter values—on the stack. With languages that can handle both addresses and values, you can decide which method to use in each case, depending on how you want the parameters to be dealt with as they are passed from one program to another.

For example, if you want to protect a caller's parameter from being changed by the called subroutine, you'll use the pass-by-value method to pass a copy of the parameter's value on the stack. But if you want the parameter's value to be changed by the called subroutine, you must use the pass-by-reference method so that the subroutine can change the parameter's value by modifying the contents of memory at the specified address.

Parameter passing is the most complicated part of the subroutine interface, and it is made even more complicated by the different ways programming languages deal with data and stack information. Because of the complexity of parameter passing and its variability from one language to another, it is the main issue we'll discuss in our language comparisons in Chapter 17.

The subroutine must preserve certain information. Although requirements might vary in different situations, a few ground rules govern what information should be preserved and what can and cannot be done in calling a subroutine:

- Interrupts can be suspended briefly when segment registers are changed; they must be reenabled before the subroutine ends.

- The contents of any CPU registers used by both the calling program and the subroutine are preserved by being pushed on the stack.

- The BP and DS registers should usually be saved and restored if they are changed within a subroutine.

Register usage varies. One compiler might rely on the contents of ES being constant, and another compiler might require you to preserve SI and DI if you use them in a subroutine. See your compiler manual for specific information.

The stack must be cleaned up after the subroutine has finished. Four "leftovers" might clutter the stack after a subroutine has finished executing: some parameters, the return address from the CALL instruction, register values saved from before the CALL, and some working storage from the subroutine.

Three of these leftovers are not problems: Subroutines are expected to remove their own working storage from the stack, saved registers are removed by POP instructions, and the return address is removed by the RET instruction. The parameters, however, usually complicate the clean-up process because the method of removal varies in different languages. Some languages expect the subroutine to remove the parameters by specifying in the RET instruction the number of bytes to remove from the stack. Other languages expect the caller to remove them. We point out these differences as we discuss some languages in detail in Chapter 17.

With all these program design elements in mind, let's step back a bit and see how the whole process works, from creating a program or subroutine to combining it with others.

Using LINK

Although each programming language has its own compiler, all languages must undergo a linking process before a final executable program is created. In the past, most languages used LINK.EXE, the linker provided with MS-DOS, to do this. MS-DOS versions 5.0 and later no longer include LINK.EXE, however, so each programming language now provides its own linker. Microsoft languages come with LINK.EXE; Borland languages use TLINK.EXE; and so on. Despite differences in names and—in some cases—syntax, all linkers perform essentially the same function. Each product's documentation explains its operation, including options and command-line switches. Here we summarize the most common and useful linker operations, particularly as they pertain to the programming languages discussed in Chapter 17. We use LINK.EXE in these examples; other linkers are likely to have similar or identical commands.

To give you some background information, the LINK program command might be written like this:

```
LINK 1,2,3,4;
```

The first parameter lists object modules (such as PROG1 + PROG2 + PROG3); the second contains the name of the finished program; the third tells where to send the linker's display output (for example, to the printer or to the display screen); and the fourth lists libraries, if they are used.

Linking a Self-Contained Program

Now let's look at some practical examples. To start with, let's consider a completely self-contained program, one that does not access any library modules. An example is the program BEEP that is presented in Chapter 17. Before you linked BEEP, you would, of course, have to translate the program from source code to an object file. Then, to link it, you would simply type

```
LINK BEEP;
```

Linking a single program such as BEEP creates a .EXE file.

Linking a Program to a Library

Next let's consider what is surely the most common linking circumstance. Say you've compiled a program in a high-level language, such as Microsoft C. As you probably know, every compiled C program needs to be linked to one or more standard object libraries that contain all the usual C functions. Consider what happens when you compile even a simple C program, such as the following one:

```
main()
{
        printf("Hello, world");
}
```

If your source code is stored in a file called HELLO.C, the compiler generates an object file called HELLO.OBJ. This object module isn't yet ready to execute. You must use LINK to combine HELLO.OBJ with an object module that contains the *printf()* function. The *printf()* object module is in one of the C compiler's standard libraries; if you use the C compiler's small memory model, the standard subroutine library is SLIBC.LIB.

To link the two object modules and generate an executable file, you simply specify the name of the program's object module and the name of the library that contains *printf()*'s object module:

```
LINK HELLO,,,SLIBC;
```

LINK searches through SLIBC.LIB for *printf()*, links *printf()* to HELLO.OBJ, and places the resulting executable file in HELLO.EXE.

This simple example is actually more complicated than it has to be. Most modern compilers, including the Microsoft C compiler in this example, can include the names of their standard libraries in the object modules they generate. This means that LINK can do its job without being told explicitly about standard libraries:

```
LINK HELLO;
```

Of course, if you want LINK to use a nonstandard library, you need to specify its name.

Linking Object Files

You can use LINK to combine two or more object files as well as to exploit object libraries. You combine object files by listing each object filename:

```
LINK ALPHA+BETA+GAMMA;
```

You can also link several object files and one or more object libraries at the same time:

```
LINK HELLO+GOODBYE,,,MYLIB;
```

Thus, the exact method you use to link a program depends on your language translator as well as on how many object files and object libraries you need to build a complete, executable program.

The Structure of an Executable Program

As we've mentioned, the wisest approach to programming the PC family is to write nearly all your programs in a high-level language (such as Basic, Pascal, or C) and to use the MS-DOS or BIOS services for whatever your high-level language doesn't provide. On occasion you might also want to create your own assembly language routines to perform specialized tasks that can't be done by using your programming language or system services.

When creating programs within the confines of a single programming language, you really don't need to know anything more about a language than what you can find in the manuals that come with it. However, if you need to escape the confines of a single language to access MS-DOS or BIOS routines or perhaps to tie into a program that's written in a different language, you'll need to dig deeper into the technical aspects of both MS-DOS (to learn how to link programs together) and the programming languages (to learn the requirements for program interfaces, which let the different languages communicate with each other). This section describes the structure of the executable programs generated by compilers and assemblers. Every language translator imposes a certain structure on each executable program it generates. This structure is partly determined by the structure of the source code, but it also reflects the way the 80x86 addresses memory.

The Memory Map

MS-DOS loads an executable program by reading the contents of a .COM or a .EXE file directly into an area of free memory. The layout of executable code and data in memory—the *memory map*—reflects the structure of the executable file, which, in turn, is primarily determined by the language translator you use to compile or assemble your program. Language translators differ, but most produce executable programs in which logically separate portions of the program are mapped in different blocks of memory. (See Figure 16-2.)

This memory map fits comfortably into the addressing schemes that are natural to the 80x86: The CS register is used to address the executable code; the DS and ES registers are used to address the program data; and the SS register points to the stack.

Higher addresses	Stack
	Uninitialized data
	Program data
	Executable code
Lower addresses	Program segment prefix

Figure 16-2. *Memory usage in a typical MS-DOS program.*

NOTE: *This memory map is also practical because it conforms to the memory conventions for programs that run in a protected-mode environment such as Windows or OS/2. In protected mode, the 80x86 requires you to use particular segment registers to address executable code and data. When you write a program to run in protected mode, you must avoid storing data values in a code segment or branching to executable code in a data segment.*

The Use of Registers

An executable program whose code, data, and stack are mapped to distinct areas of memory can make efficient use of the 80x86 registers. This is because the 80x86's segment registers can each address a different portion of the memory map:

■ The CS and IP registers point to the currently executing instruction.

■ The DS register is used in combination with BX, SI, or DI to access program data.

■ The SS register is used in combination with the SP and BP registers to point to data in the program's stack. The SS:SP combination points to the top of the stack, and SS:BP can be used to access data above or below the top of the stack.

These aren't hard-and-fast rules for register usage. They are a natural consequence of the way the 80x86 register set is designed, and they have become the convention for most programs. If necessary, registers can be used for other purposes within a routine, but they should be restored before a program exits the routine.

Memory Models

There are various ways to produce an executable program whose memory map comprises separate code, data, and stack segments. The way a particular program addresses the different areas of its memory map is determined by the program's *memory model*.

A memory model describes exactly how executable code and data are addressed within a program. For example, with an 8086 a segment can be no larger than 64 KB, so a program with more than 64 KB of executable code must be mapped into more than one executable code segment. Similarly, a program with more than 64 KB of data must store that data in at least two data segments. Thus, the simple memory model shown in Figure 16-2 can be elaborated into four memory models. (See Figure 16-3.)

The memory model you use affects how your program uses segment registers. In a small-model program, the CS and DS registers can be initialized at the start of the program and left undisturbed for its duration. Contrast this with a large-model program, in which the CS register must be changed whenever the program branches from one code segment to another and the DS or ES register must often be updated whenever data from different segments must be accessed. (DS may point to one data segment and ES to another, requiring changes to one or the other if a third segment is addressed.)

Some high-level language compilers let you specify which memory model to use. (See your compiler documentation for more information.) If you know your program contains fewer than 64 KB of executable code and fewer than 64 KB of data, you can explicitly request such a compiler to generate a small-model executable program. (This is the memory model we have used in the assembly language examples in previous chapters.) Other compilers will use or will let you specify a compact, medium, or large model, regardless of the program size. Whatever the case, you should know which memory model your compiler uses if you want to understand how the parts of an executable program fit together.

Model	Number of Code Segments	Number of Data Segments
Small	1	1
Compact	1	More than 1
Medium	More than 1	1
Large	More than 1	More than 1

Figure 16-3. *Four common memory models.*

.EXE vs. .COM Files

You might have noticed that program files come in two varieties. Most of them, including all large programs, have the .EXE extension. Some small programs, however, have the .COM extension. A .COM program must not be larger than 64 KB, and it must follow certain rules regarding memory usage. If a .EXE program meets these requirements, it can be converted from a .EXE file to a .COM file, resulting in small improvements in program size and execution speed.

The memory model used in a .COM file must place all memory-using components—executable code, program data, uninitialized memory, the stack, and the PSP—in the same segment. Consequently, the source code for a .COM program is simpler than the source code for a .EXE program; it has only one segment, with code and data at the bottom (starting at offset 100H). A .COM program doesn't contain a stack segment; instead, MS-DOS automatically loads the .COM program into 64 KB of memory and locates the stack at the top.

If your program is constructed in .COM format, you can run the MS-DOS EXE2BIN utility to transform the .EXE file generated by LINK into a .COM file. Be forewarned, however: Few high-level language compilers use the .COM format because of its limitations. You can safely find out whether a program can be converted from a .EXE file to a .COM file simply by trying to convert it. If it works, it works. If EXE2BIN says it can't be done, however, it can't be done.

Chapter 17

Programming Languages and Other Tools

In Chapter 16, we briefly discussed the general principles of building and linking program modules. In this chapter, we discuss some of the specific program development methods and tools that are available to you. As you might expect, the material in this chapter is necessarily rather general. We cannot teach you the details of how to write a program, but we do hope to provide enough information about the various programming methods, languages, and other tools so that you can make an informed decision when selecting the approach to take in your own work.

Programming Methods

This section describes the various programming methods that you will encounter: procedural programming, object-oriented programming, and event-driven programming. Rather than being specific tools, these methods are more accurately described as approaches that are characteristic to a greater or lesser degree of various programming languages and tools. These methods are not mutually exclusive by any means; you can write a program that incorporates one, two, or all three of them. Nor are they completely distinct from each other. Object-oriented programming, for example, includes elements of procedural programming, and an event-driven program might be object oriented as well.

Procedural Programming

Procedural programming is the most fundamental of the methods. In a procedural programming language, the basic programming element is a named group of statements called a procedure, function, subroutine, or routine. Whichever name is used, the idea is the same. By placing related sections of code in their own procedures, you simplify the organization of a program. And because all program code and data in a procedure is isolated from all other program code and data, errors caused by unwanted interactions are minimized.

Consider a simple example. A mathematical analysis program might frequently need to calculate the fourth root of a number. In a procedural language, you would place the program code that performs the calculation in a procedure and then assign the procedure a name. In other parts of the program, whenever a fourth-root calculation was needed, you would activate, or call, the procedure simply by using its name in the source code. Information can be passed to and returned from a procedure, but the procedure code remains separate and independent.

Nearly every programming language is procedural, including Basic, C, Pascal, and assembly language. If you've ever written a program, no matter how simple, you have probably practiced procedural programming.

Object-Oriented Programming

Object-oriented programming (OOP) is a programming technique that is based on the use of *objects*. An object consists of data and the code that endows that data with the behaviors required by the program. To make clear how object-oriented programming works, let's look at a simple example, a program for displaying and printing graphs.

First let's see how you would accomplish these tasks by using a procedural language. You would use the language's predefined data types to define storage for the graph data, probably in an array. Then you would write one procedure to display the graph on the screen and another procedure to send the graph to the printer. To display or print a particular graph, you would call the corresponding procedure and pass it the proper data array. In a procedural language, procedures are central and data is secondary.

In an object-oriented language, the process would be quite different. You would define a graph object; this object would contain not only storage for a graph's data but also the procedures for displaying and printing the graph. In effect, the graph object would "know" how to display and print itself. To display or print a graph, you would need only to send the message "display yourself" or "print yourself" to the graph object.

A collection of predefined base objects, or classes, is provided as part of an object-oriented language package. (Classes are types of objects.) You can use these base classes as is, but you will more frequently use them as building blocks to create your own classes. This is done by using a feature of object-oriented languages called *inheritance*. By using inheritance, you can define a new class based on an existing class. The new class inherits all the components and characteristics of the original class, and it also has whatever features or restrictions you add to it.

The other fundamental features of object-oriented languages are beyond the scope of this discussion. From a conceptual point of view, the primary advantage of OOP is that it permits programmers to use the problem they need to solve, rather than the capabilities of the computer, as a starting point for program design. In other words, the program is designed around the data that needs to be manipulated.

It's important to be aware that you don't do object-oriented programming *instead* of procedural programming but rather in addition to procedural programming. Procedures are part of an object-oriented program, but they are usually subsidiary to objects.

Event-Driven Programming

Nearly every program must interact with the user in some manner. The user might enter data, make selections from menus, answer yes/no questions, and perform other tasks. He or she passes various kinds of information to a program by using the keyboard and, in some cases, a mouse. The program needs to detect and respond appropriately to these actions, or events.

With traditional programming techniques, the programmer must specifically code for every event that might occur, from a user pressing the F10 key to a user clicking the mouse at a certain screen location. Writing code for a sophisticated user interface that will detect and respond to all possible events can be a formidable task. In the traditional model, it is always the code that is in charge: The code determines which events are detected and which are ignored.

With event-driven programming, a program has the ability to detect all possible events. This ability is provided by the language compiler or by the operating system's API, and it requires no extra effort on the programmer's part. For example, if your program displays a command button on the screen, that button has the built-in ability to detect whether the user clicks the mouse on the button. Likewise, if a pull-down menu is displayed, the program can detect when the user makes a selection from that menu. The programmer's job is greatly simplified because there is no need to write code to detect events. All the programmer need do is write code to perform the various program tasks and associate various sections of code with the appropriate events. For example, the code that displays a help screen could be associated with the "press the F1 key" event, and the code that terminates the program could be associated with the "click the exit button" event.

It's important to note that event-driven capabilities are not associated with particular languages but with specific language implementations. For example, the Basic language itself is not event driven, but Microsoft's Visual Basic for MS-DOS programming system is event driven. All Windows programs are event driven; the event-driven capabilities are provided primarily by the Windows API.

Programming Languages: The Big Four

In this section we discuss some specific programming languages. We focus on those aspects of the languages that make them more or less suitable for different programming tasks and styles. We also cover details that you need to be concerned with when you link modules written in high-level languages to assembly language subroutines.

We make no attempt to cover all, or even most, of the many programming languages that are available for the PC. Instead, we limit our discussion to the "big four": assembly language, C/C++, Basic, and Pascal. We do not mean to denigrate other languages such as Modula-2, Smalltalk, FORTRAN, Ada, and LISP; they are capable languages that are used by many skilled programmers. The bulk of program development is done with the big four, however, so for practical reasons we limit the discussion to them.

If you want to create computer programs, you have to work with a specific programming language—and a programming language is much more specific than many people are led to believe.

First of all, there is no such thing as a generic programming language. You can create working programs only by using a language compiler designed for a particular machine. Although academic experts on computers would like to pretend otherwise, the general definitions of programming languages lack many of the essential features that you need to create real programs that work on real computers. So when a compiler is created for a particular programming language (such as Basic) to run on a particular computer (such as the PC), the fundamental language is altered and extended to provide support for features that are specific to the host machine. The alterations are often quite significant, and in every case they create a programming language that is related to, but distinct from, all other languages of the same name.

Because of these differences, this chapter does not and could not possibly cover every PC implementation of assembly language, C/C++, Basic, and Pascal. For pragmatic reasons we have had to select specific compilers to work with. Our discussion is at a fairly fundamental level, so most of what we say applies to other language implementations as well. For example, for C/C++ we have used the Microsoft compiler, but most of the information probably applies to the Borland, Zortech, and Watcom C/C++ compilers as well. (Please check to be sure!) The next few paragraphs list the specific implementations we have used.

Assembly language. Our discussion of assembly language is based on version 5.0 of the Microsoft Macro Assembler. A number of other versions are available from Microsoft, from IBM, and from other computer manufacturers who have licensed the use of Microsoft's basic assembler. Newer versions of the assembler have many features not implemented in earlier versions, but in our discussion we stick to the fundamental features common to most, if not all, versions of this assembler.

C/C++. For our discussion of C/C++, we use the Microsoft C/C++ compiler, version 7.0. Because we do not use any examples specific to C/C++, this information applies to all Microsoft C compilers versions 5.0 and later.

Basic. For our discussion of compiled Basic, we are guided by version 4.5 of Microsoft QuickBasic and by version 1.0 of Microsoft Visual Basic for MS-DOS. These two Basic products are essentially identical in their handling of Basic code.

Pascal. For Pascal, we use Borland's Turbo Pascal version 6.0, a popular load-and-go Pascal compiler.

Assembly Language

Assembly language can be thought of as the most fundamental of all programming languages. This is because there is a close correspondence between assembly language statements and the actual operations that can be carried out by the CPU. When you use assembly language, you have exact and almost complete control over every aspect of what the CPU does. The trade-off (yes, there's always a trade-off) is that assembly language provides you with little or no help in the form of prewritten functions that perform commonly needed tasks such as disk access and screen display.

The bottom line is that you can do nearly anything you want by using assembly language, but it is often devilishly difficult. Compared to programs written in high-level languages, assembly language programs are smaller and run faster. Although you can use assembly language to write complete stand-alone programs, it is much more common to use it to write subroutines that are called by programs written in a high-level language. In particular, programmers turn to assembly language subroutines when the speed and flexibility of assembly language are needed. Assembly language subroutines also appeal to those programmers who need to build interface routines between a high-level programming language and some of the system's BIOS or MS-DOS services.

Subroutines depend largely on the calling program to provide their structure and support, but a stand-alone assembly language program must provide its own structure and support and must cope with all the fundamental operating issues that stand-alone programs face. Assembly language subroutines are relatively easy to construct, but stand-alone assembly language programs can be quite complicated. Stand-alone programs appeal to programmers who must accomplish a task that neither conventional programming languages nor system services provide.

In this discussion of assembly language, we demonstrate techniques that will help you figure out the high-level–language interface conventions for your assembly language subroutines. We also lead you through the process of creating a stand-alone assembly language program. However, we don't try to teach you how to use assembly language—that is far too large and complex a subject.

If you are not particularly proficient at using assembly language, one way to learn about it is to study some of the readily available sources of assembly language coding. A number of excellent books have been published on the subject, and they're a good place to start. You can also look in the BIOS listings that are part of IBM's PC, PC/XT, and PC/AT technical reference manuals. Another source, available with most compilers, is the listing similar to assembly language that they can be asked to produce. This is useful both for learning how the compiler handles particular coding problems (which you can control by selecting appropriate statements in the high-level language) and for learning the subroutine interface conventions the compiler uses. A related but less useful way to learn about assembly language is to load an existing program by using the MS-DOS DEBUG program and then use DEBUG's U (Unassemble) command to look through sections of the program. Each method can help you learn different programming techniques and tricks.

Logical organization

The elements of an assembly language subroutine are easy to understand if they are laid out in the order in which they occur. The logical organization can be described as five nested parts:

    Level 1: General assembler overhead
      Level 2: Subroutine assembler overhead
        Level 3: Entry code
          Level 4: Get parameter data from caller
            Level 5: Perform desired tasks
          Level 4: Pass results back to caller
        Level 3: Exit code
      Level 2: Finish subroutine assembler overhead
    Level 1: Finish general assembler overhead

You can follow this basic organization when writing most interface routines for system services and when writing conventional assembly language subroutines, but be aware that the actual coding varies with every programming language.

Learning about interface conventions

As soon as you are comfortable with assembly language, you need to examine the assembly language conventions and interface customs that apply to your high-level programming language. Your assembly language interface has to know how to gain access to the parameters passed by the calling program, how to interpret the data format, and how to send the parameters back, among other things. Even if your high-level–language documentation doesn't provide such information, you can obtain it from the language itself.

To learn the conventions for both a calling and a called program—that is, to see both sides of the program-call interface—you can study your compiler's assembly language–style listing, as we mentioned earlier. For a somewhat different perspective, you can also study the assembly language subroutines provided with the language compiler. This technique not only provides the interface conventions for assembly language routines but also gives you specific programming examples that can serve as models.

The most accessible subroutines are often part of the libraries that accompany your compiler. Usually, it is easiest simply to choose a compiler feature that you're interested in, such as I/O, screen control, or arithmetic, and then determine which subroutines are called for that feature.

A few compiler vendors sell source code for their subroutine libraries. If source code isn't available, you have to resort to disassembling the subroutines by extracting them from your compiler's object libraries. You can locate a particular subroutine in an object library by using a library manager such as LIB to list the contents of the library. Let's assume there's a library named SLIBC.LIB on your disk. If you have installed the Microsoft Macro Assembler or other software that provides the LIB program, you can direct the library listing to a file named LISTING.TXT by using the following instruction:

```
LIB SLIBC,LISTING.TXT;
```

You can then look over the library listing to find the subroutine you're interested in and the name of the module that it's a part of. Let's say the subroutine's name is _abs and the name of the library module containing it is ABS. You can use LIB to extract ABS from the library and create a separate object file, ABS.OBJ:

```
LIB SLIBC *ABS;
```

At this point, you could try to look inside ABS.OBJ. But because this file contains extraneous link-editor information that would only get in your way, it's easier to convert the object module into an executable file, even though it's only a subroutine and not a complete program. You use the linker utility, LINK, to do this:

```
LINK ABS;
```

LINK generates an executable file, ABS.EXE. In the process, you'll probably see a few error messages because the subroutine you're linking isn't a complete program and it lacks such necessities as a stack. That's not important in this case because you really only want to examine the subroutine's executable code.

To disassemble the subroutine, you use DEBUG:

```
DEBUG ABS.EXE
```

You can now use DEBUG's U command to convert the executable code into readable assembly language instructions. First, note the size of your .EXE file, and subtract 512 bytes to determine the actual size of the subroutine. (The 512 bytes contain information that is used by MS-DOS to load an executable program but that is not part of the subroutine itself.) For example, if the size of ABS.EXE is 535 bytes, the size of the subroutine is only 23 (hexadecimal 17) bytes. The DEBUG command to use would then be

```
U 0 L17
```

These steps might seem overelaborate and cumbersome, but after you learn them, you can perform them quickly and easily, and they will give you an inside look at how your high-level programming language uses assembly language interface routines.

The next section repeats the key steps of this exercise as we demonstrate the mechanics of creating a small but complete assembly language program.

Writing and linking assembly language programs

To illustrate the process involved in writing and linking an assembly language program, we show you how to create an incredibly simple but useful program that sounds a tone on the computer's speaker. To do this on any PC-family computer or any MS-DOS computer, you write the bell character, ASCII 07H, to the screen. In this example, we do this by using MS-DOS interrupt 21H, function 02H. Then we end the program and return program control to MS-DOS by using interrupt 21H, function 4CH. Follow this example, and you'll learn quite a bit about creating self-contained assembly language programs. The source code for this little program follows.

```
; MS-DOS generic beep program

CodeSeg         SEGMENT byte
                ASSUME  cs:CodeSeg

Beep            PROC

                mov     dl,7    ; bell character
                mov     ah,2    ; interrupt 21H function number
                int     21h     ; call MS-DOS to write the character

                mov     ax,4C00h ; AH = 4CH (interrupt 21H function number)
                                 ; AL = 00H (return code)
                int     21h     ; call MS-DOS to terminate the program

Beep            ENDP

CodeSeg         ENDS

                END             Beep
```

As you see, the program is only five instructions long, and it fills only 11 bytes. If you save this program's source code in a file named BEEP.ASM, you can use the assembler to translate it into object code by using a simple command:

```
MASM BEEP;
```

The resulting object file is ready for linking. In this case, you can link the program without subroutines, libraries, or other object files, like this:

```
LINK BEEP;
```

The linker program usually expects to find a stack segment in the programs it links, but our simple program doesn't have one. The linker will complain about the missing stack, but you can ignore its complaint for now.

Linking gives you an executable program called BEEP.EXE. If you run BEEP.EXE, however, MS-DOS won't know where to locate the program's stack. You can solve this problem by converting BEEP.EXE into a .COM program by using EXE2BIN:

```
EXE2BIN BEEP BEEP.COM
```

When you run BEEP.COM, MS-DOS locates the stack for you. Now you have a finished beeper program that can be used on any computer that runs MS-DOS, and you can safely delete the intermediate files BEEP.OBJ and BEEP.EXE.

Note what happens to the size of the BEEP program as it is transformed from a source-code file to an executable .COM file. The source code for this program is approximately 400 bytes (depending on such factors as the use of spaces in the comments). When you assemble and link it, you'll discover that only 11 bytes of working machine-language instructions are created. However, the object file, which includes some standard linker information as overhead, is 71 bytes—much smaller than the source file but much larger than the 11 bytes of actual machine code. After linking, the 71-byte object file swells to a 523-byte .EXE file. (Remember that the .EXE file contains a 512-byte header that contains program-loading information.) Converting the program to .COM format eliminates the 512 bytes of overhead, and you end up with a .COM file that's only 11 bytes of pure machine code.

C and C++

We start our discussion of specific high-level languages with the C and C++ languages. We treat these together because the two languages are intimately linked and are most accurately thought of as variants of the same language. C++ is, in fact, a superset of C: It contains everything that C does plus numerous additions.

The C language was developed in the early 1970s at AT&T Bell Laboratories. It proved to be such a powerful and flexible language that its use spread rapidly, and it is now probably the most popular language used by professional programmers working on the PC and other platforms. C is a procedural language, and as program complexity increased, programmers needed to be able to use an object-oriented approach. Rather than start from scratch, it seemed a good idea to expand C to give it object-oriented capabilities. The result was C++. In this section, when we discuss the subroutine interface, we use C for examples, but the information applies to C++ also.

In previous chapters we've shown several examples of the C subroutine interface. Now let's see how to adapt that interface to different memory models and parameter-passing methods. Although the examples we give here pertain specifically to the Microsoft C compiler, you'll discover that you can use essentially the same subroutine interface design not only with other vendors' compiler implementations but also with other programming languages.

The C subroutines we presented in previous chapters used a small memory model and the pass-by-value convention. This next subroutine, which computes the absolute value of an integer, uses the same conventions.

The subroutine uses a near call-return sequence because the program uses a small memory model, with all executable code in the same segment. The parameter value is passed to the subroutine on the stack and accessed through BP in the usual way. The parameter value is found at [BP + 4] because the first 4 bytes of the stack are used by the calling program's return address (2 bytes) and the saved value of BP (2 bytes).

```
_TEXT           SEGMENT byte public 'CODE'
                ASSUME  cs:_TEXT

                PUBLIC  _AbsValue
_AbsValue       PROC    near            ; call with near CALL

                push    bp
                mov     bp,sp

                mov     ax,[bp+4]       ; AX = value of 1st parameter

                cwd
                xor     ax,dx
                sub     ax,dx           ; leave result in AX

                pop     bp
                ret                     ; near RETurn

_AbsValue       ENDP

_TEXT           ENDS
```

The subroutine uses register AX to return its result to the calling program. If the return value had been a 4-byte value, the register pair DX:AX would have been used, with the high-order word of the value in DX.

If this subroutine had used more than one parameter, the second and subsequent parameters would have been at higher addresses on the stack. For example, the second parameter would have been located at [BP + 6]. (See the *Weekday()* subroutine in Chapter 13 for an example.) In effect, the C compiler pushes parameters on the stack in the reverse of their declared order. Because of this, a subroutine always knows where to find the first parameter on the stack. A C function such as *printf()* can use a variable number of parameters as long as the first parameter specifies the actual number of parameters.

When the subroutine returns, it leaves the value of the parameter on the stack. In C, the calling program must clean up the stack after a subroutine call. For example, consider the way a C compiler generates executable code for a simple C statement that calls *AbsValue()*:

```
x = AbsValue( y );      /* x and y are integers */
```

The executable code generated by the C compiler for this statement looks something like this:

```
push Y                  ; push the value at address Y
call _AbsValue          ; call the subroutine (near CALL)
add  sp,2               ; discard the value from the stack
mov  X,ax               ; store the returned value at address X
```

Parameter passing

Let's look more closely at the difference between the pass-by-value and pass-by-reference methods of parameter passing. The pass-by-value method works by passing a copy of a parameter's current value to the subroutine. In contrast, the pass-by-reference method passes a parameter's address. This affects the subroutine interface in two ways.

First, the value of a parameter passed by reference cannot be accessed directly. Instead, you must copy the parameter's address from the stack and then obtain the parameter's value through the address. For example:

```
_TEXT           SEGMENT byte public 'CODE'
                ASSUME  cs:_TEXT

                PUBLIC  _SmallAbs
_SmallAbs       PROC    near            ; call with near CALL

                push    bp
                mov     bp,sp

                mov     bx,[bp+4]       ; BX = address of 1st parameter
                mov     ax,[bx]         ; AX = value of 1st parameter

                cwd
                xor     ax,dx
                sub     ax,dx

                mov     [bx],ax         ; leave result at parameter address
```

(continued)

```
                pop     bp
                ret                             ; near RETurn

_SmallAbs       ENDP

_TEXT           ENDS
```

SmallAbs(), which uses pass-by-reference, obtains the value of its parameter in two steps. First it copies the parameter's address from the stack (MOV BX,[BP + 4]). Then it obtains the parameter's value from that address (MOV AX,[BX]). As soon as the parameter's value is in AX, the computation of its absolute value proceeds as before.

To pass a parameter from a C program to *SmallAbs()*, you need to pass its address instead of its value:

```
SmallAbs( &x );         /* pass the address of x */
```

The corresponding executable code would look something like this:

```
mov ax,offset X         ; push the address of X
push ax
call _SmallAbs          ; call the subroutine (near CALL)
add  sp,2               ; discard the address from the stack
```

The way *SmallAbs()* returns its result points out the second way the pass-by-reference method affects the subroutine interface, which is also the key reason to use the pass-by-reference method: *SmallAbs()* actually changes the value of its parameter. Instead of simply returning a result in AX, *SmallAbs()* stores its return value at the parameter's address (MOV [BX],AX).

In high-level programming languages, both the pass-by-reference and pass-by-value methods can be used. In some languages, the method of passing parameters defaults to one method or the other. For example, Basic uses pass-by-reference by default, but C uses the pass-by-value method as the default. In many languages, the default method varies, depending on a parameter's data type. You can usually determine which method is used to call a subroutine by specifying a method in your source code (if your compiler supports such specifications) or by using a data type associated with a particular parameter-passing method.

Memory-model variations

A simple rule of thumb can help you determine how a program's memory model affects the design of its subroutines: If you have multiple segments, use far (intersegment) addressing; if you have a single segment, use near (intrasegment) addressing. Let's see how this simple rule can be applied in a pair of real subroutines.

The following variation of our absolute-value subroutine is designed for a medium-model C program. A medium-model program has multiple code segments but only one data segment. Subroutines in separate segments must be accessed with far jumps and far call-return sequences, but the single data segment can be accessed with near addresses:

```
MEDABS_TEXT     SEGMENT byte public 'CODE'
                ASSUME  cs:MEDABS_TEXT

                PUBLIC  _MedAbs
_MedAbs         PROC    far             ; call with far CALL

                push    bp
                mov     bp,sp

                mov     bx,[bp+6]       ; BX = address of 1st parameter
                mov     ax,[bx]

                cwd
                xor     ax,dx
                sub     ax,dx

                mov     [bx],ax         ; leave result at parameter address

                pop     bp
                ret                     ; far RETurn

_MedAbs         ENDP

MEDABS_TEXT     ENDS
```

MedAbs(), the medium-model version of the absolute-value subroutine, looks much like *SmallAbs()*. In *MedAbs()*, the PROC statement declares that the routine is to be called by using a far CALL and instructs the assembler to generate a far RET (return) instruction instead of a near RET. Because *MedAbs()* is called by using a far CALL, the stack contains a segmented return address (4 bytes) as well as the saved value of BP (2 bytes), so the subroutine looks for its parameter at [BP + 6] instead of [BP + 4].

A large-model program introduces one more variation in subroutine design. Because a large-model program uses multiple data segments, the addresses of subroutine parameters are far (segmented) addresses.

```
LARGEABS_TEXT    SEGMENT byte public 'CODE'
                 ASSUME  cs:LARGEABS_TEXT

                 PUBLIC  _LargeAbs
_LargeAbs        PROC    far                 ; call with far CALL

                 push    bp
                 mov     bp,sp

                 les     bx,[bp+6]           ; ES:BX = segmented address
                                             ; of first parameter
                 mov     ax,es:[bx]          ; AX = value of first parameter
                 cwd
                 xor     ax,dx
                 sub     ax,dx

                 mov     es:[bx],ax          ; leave result at parameter address

                 pop     bp
                 ret                         ; far RETurn

_LargeAbs        ENDP

LARGEABS_TEXT    ENDS
```

Because it conforms to a large memory model, *LargeAbs()* is designed to obtain both segment and offset from the stack (LES BX,[BP + 6]). The segment part of the parameter's address goes into ES; the offset goes into BX. The subroutine uses this register pair to obtain the parameter's value (MOV AX,ES:[BX]) and to return a result (MOV ES:[BX],AX).

If you call *LargeAbs()* like this:

```
LargeAbs( &x );
```

a C compiler generates executable code that looks something like this:

```
push ds                ; push the parameter's segment
mov ax,offset X
push ax                ; push the parameter's offset
call _LargeAbs         ; call the subroutine (far CALL)
add  sp,4              ; discard the address from the stack
```

Naming conventions

As we mentioned earlier, the parameter-passing and memory-model methods used in your program determine how a subroutine interface is implemented, regardless of which language or compiler you use. Unfortunately, other differences among languages and compilers can make the design of a subroutine interface tricky and somewhat tedious.

One problem is that different high-level languages and compilers use different names for the subroutines, segments, segment groups, and variables that crop up in a program. For example, the names used in Microsoft C version 7.0 (_TEXT, _DATA, DGROUP, and so on) are different not only in other vendors' C compilers but also in earlier versions of Microsoft's C compiler.

Other differences in naming appear when you compare different languages. C is case sensitive, but interpreted Basic and Pascal convert all lowercase letters to uppercase. C compilers generally prefix all the names declared in a C program with an underscore, so a name such as *printf* in C must be referenced as *_printf* in assembly language. The surest way to know exactly what naming conventions your language translator uses is to look at your compiler's manuals.

Data representation

Before we leave our discussion of C, let's look at the way C represents different data types. When you write a routine that shares data with a C program, you must know how the C compiler stores data in memory.

The data types available in C can be divided into three general categories: *integer types, floating-point types,* and *other types.*

- Integer types, including *char, int, short,* and *long,* are stored with their low-order bytes first, in the familiar "back-words" 8086 format. In 8086 C implementations, *char* is 1 byte in size, *int* and *short* are 2 bytes, and *long* is 4 bytes. The integer data types can be specified as either *signed* or *unsigned.*

- In Microsoft C, representations of floating-point data types (*float* and *double*) are based on the IEEE standard for floating-point data representation used in the 8087 math coprocessor. With this representation, a *float* value is 4 bytes long and a *double* is 8 bytes long. Despite the difference in size, a simple relationship exists between *float* and *double:* You can convert a *float* to a *double* by appending 4 bytes of zeros.

- Other C data types include *pointers* and *strings.* Pointers are address values; near pointers are 2 bytes long and far pointers are 4 bytes long. Strings are defined as arrays of type *char.* However, every string in C is stored as an ASCIIZ string—that is, as a string of bytes terminated with a single zero byte. In a C program, you must accommodate the extra byte when you declare a string. For example, you would reserve storage for 64 bytes of string data plus the terminating null byte like this:

```
char s[65];
```

In C, the value of the name *s* would be the address of the string data associated with it. A subroutine called with *s* as a parameter can obtain the value of *s* (the address of the string data) directly from the stack and access the string data by reference to this address.

Basic

Basic is an acronym for Beginner's All-purpose Symbolic Instruction Code. It was originally developed as a teaching tool, and ease of use and simplicity were emphasized over power and flexibility. As a result, Basic was seen as a toy—fine for teaching but not suitable for serious programming. Over the years, however, Basic has evolved, and Basic compilers are now available with all the power and flexibility needed for large, complex programming projects. The language remains relatively easy to learn and use, and as a result, it is becoming increasingly popular.

Two general types of Basic are available: compiled Basic and interpreted Basic. With compiled Basic, source code is compiled (translated) into machine language and then linked into an executable program that is stored on disk. Interpreted Basic, on the other hand, converts source-code statements into machine-language instructions on the fly, as the program is executing. Many early versions of Basic were interpreted, and the QBasic that is provided as part of MS-DOS is also an interpreted Basic. Although interpreted Basic is fine for some tasks, the inherent limitations of interpreted languages make interpreted Basic unsuitable for serious programming. The following discussion is therefore limited to compiled Basic.

The subroutine interface

QuickBasic's default is a medium memory model, which has multiple executable code segments and one default data segment. You must design your subroutines to use a far call-return sequence, but you can access the single default data segment by using near addresses. QuickBasic passes parameters by reference in the order in which they appear in the Basic source code.

The Basic source code used to call an assembly language subroutine is relatively simple, as you'll see when you examine the following code:

```
DEFINT A-Z                          ' default all variables to integer type
DECLARE SUB MEDABS (A%)             ' declare the assembly language subroutine

FOR X = -10 TO 10
 Y = X
 CALL MEDABS(Y)                     ' call the subroutine
 PRINT "ABS("; X; ")=";Y
 NEXT
END
```

The assembly language subroutine is as follows:

```
MEDABS_TEXT     SEGMENT byte public 'CODE'
                ASSUME  cs:MEDABS_TEXT

                PUBLIC  MEDABS
MEDABS          PROC    far             ; call with far CALL

                push    bp
                mov     bp,sp

                mov     bx,[bp+6]       ; BX = address of first parameter
                mov     ax,[bx]

                cwd
                xor     ax,dx
                sub     ax,dx

                mov     [bx],ax         ; leave result at parameter address

                pop     bp
                ret     2               ; far return, discard parameter value

MEDABS          ENDP

MEDABS_TEXT     ENDS
```

Note that the assembly language code includes a PUBLIC declaration for the name of the subroutine. When you use the linker to generate an executable program, the linker associates the PUBLIC name with the same name used in the Basic program.

NOTE: *QuickBasic provides two ways to link an assembly language subroutine to a Basic program. You can use the BC compiler to compile your Basic source code and then link the resulting object (.OBJ) file to the assembled subroutine's object file. The other technique is to use LINK and LIB to create a Quick library so that the subroutine can be accessed within the QuickBasic environment. The QuickBasic manuals describe both techniques in detail.*

Data representation

QuickBasic supports 2-byte integers and a 4-byte LONG integer data type that is represented by a variable name with a terminal ampersand (for example, *X&*). Floating-point values are 4 bytes for single-precision numbers and 8 bytes for double-precision numbers, and the floating-point representation follows the 8087-compatible IEEE standard.

QuickBasic dynamically allocates memory for strings, with each string represented by a two-part string descriptor. QuickBasic's string descriptor is 4 bytes in size, and the maximum length of a QuickBasic string is 65,535 bytes.

Pascal

We conclude this chapter with a look at Borland's widely used Turbo Pascal compiler. Pascal is a procedural language that was developed in the late 1960s. It's a capable language that has many devoted users, and it is roughly comparable to C in terms of power. Compared to C, Pascal has a fairly rigid set of rules regarding program syntax and structure. Pascal devotees argue that these rules encourage programmers to write concise, well-structured programs that tend to be relatively free of bugs. C fans respond that C's relative lack of rules permits greater flexibility. As much as anything else, it's a matter of personal preference.

Turbo Pascal's data formats and support for assembly language subroutines are different from those found in traditional Pascal compilers such as those from IBM or Microsoft. However, you can use the same principles of subroutine interface design in Turbo Pascal that you use in any other language.

NOTE: *Our description of the subroutine interface applies to versions 4.0 and later of Turbo Pascal. Versions 3.0 and earlier use a different interface that isn't compatible with the one we cover.*

The subroutine interface

Turbo Pascal uses a large memory model, which has multiple executable code segments and multiple data segments. However, Turbo Pascal compiles all the executable code in the body of a program into a single segment, so assembly language subroutines that you declare within the main body of a program should use a near call-return sequence. In contrast, Turbo Pascal uses separate segments for subroutines declared in the INTERFACE section of a Turbo Pascal UNIT. (A *UNIT* in Turbo Pascal is a collection of pre-defined subroutines and data items.) Such subroutines must be accessed by using a far call-return sequence. Data is accessed only by using far addresses. When you write an assembly language subroutine for Turbo Pascal, be sure you use the correct call-return sequence.

The following example is a Turbo Pascal variation of our absolute-value function. Because this subroutine is designed to be called from the main body of a Pascal program, it uses a near call-return sequence.

```
CODE            SEGMENT byte public
                ASSUME  cs:CODE

                PUBLIC  AbsFunc
AbsFunc         PROC    near            ; call with near CALL

                push    bp
                mov     bp,sp

                mov     ax,[bp+4]       ; AX = value of parameter
                cwd
                xor     ax,dx
                sub     ax,dx           ; AX contains the result

                pop     bp
                ret     2               ; near RETurn

AbsFunc         ENDP

CODE            ENDS
```

If you assemble this subroutine into the object file ABSFUNC.OBJ, you can link it into a Turbo Pascal program by using the $L compiler directive and declaring *AbsFunc()* as an EXTERNAL function:

```
{$L absfunc}        { object filename }
FUNCTION AbsFunc(x: INTEGER): INTEGER; EXTERNAL;
```

Because Turbo Pascal uses a large memory model, data pointers are always passed to subroutines as 32-bit addresses. You can see this if you write the same subroutine as a PROCEDURE instead of as a FUNCTION and you declare *x* as an integer variable. The VAR keyword in the parameter list instructs the Turbo Pascal compiler to pass the parameter by reference—that is, to pass the parameter's address instead of its value:

```
{$L absproc}                 { object filename }
PROCEDURE AbsProc (VAR x:INTEGER); EXTERNAL;
```

The subroutine differs from the previous one in that it must obtain the 32-bit address of *x* from the stack in order to obtain the actual value of *x*:

```
CODE            SEGMENT byte public
                ASSUME  cs:CODE

                PUBLIC  AbsProc
AbsProc         PROC    near            ; call with near CALL

                push    bp
                mov     bp,sp

                les     bx,[bp+4]       ; ES:BX = segmented addr of x
                mov     ax,es:[bx]      ; AX = value of x
                cwd
                xor     ax,dx
                sub     ax,dx

                mov     es:[bx],ax      ; leave result in x

                pop     bp
                ret     4               ; near RETurn

AbsProc         ENDP

CODE            ENDS
```

This subroutine resembles *LargeAbs()*, our large-model example for Microsoft C. The important difference is that Turbo Pascal's subroutine-calling convention requires a near subroutine call because the subroutine was declared in the body of a Pascal program. Had we declared *AbsProc()* in the INTERFACE portion of a UNIT, the subroutine would have used a far call-return sequence.

Data representation

Like the other languages discussed in this chapter, Turbo Pascal supports integer, floating-point, and string data types. Integers are stored in the familiar 2-byte format, but floating-point and string representations present some novelties.

Turbo Pascal supports five types of floating-point (real) numbers. The REAL type is a 6-byte floating-point representation designed by Borland. The other four (SINGLE, DOUBLE, EXTENDED, and COMP) are representations used by the 8087 math coprocessor.

Turbo Pascal stores strings in a simple data structure: a 1-byte count followed by the string data itself. (See Figure 17-1.) The count byte is treated as an unsigned value, so the maximum length of a string is 255 (FFH) bytes.

String length												
0CH	H	e	l	l	o	,		w	o	r	l	d

String data

Figure 17-1. *String data representation in Turbo Pascal.*

Turbo Pascal represents other Pascal data types in equally reasonable ways. For example, Boolean values are represented in a single byte (01H = true; 00H = false). Sets are represented as bit strings in which the position of each bit corresponds to the ordinal value of one member of the set. (See Figure 17-2.) The low-order bit in each byte corresponds to an ordinal value that is evenly divisible by 8. The compiler stores only as many bytes as are needed to represent the set.

```
TYPE LETTERS = 'a' .. 'z'; {ordinal values 97 through 122}
VAR X :SET OF LETTERS;

X := ['a', 'b', 'c', 'y', 'z'];
```

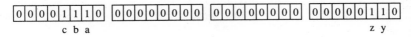

0	0	0	0	1	1	1	0	0	0	0	0	0	0	0	0	0	0	0	0	0	0	0	0	0	0	0	0	0	1	1	0

c b a   z y

Figure 17-2. *A representation of a set in Turbo Pascal. The set X is represented as a 4-byte bit string in which each bit corresponds to one of the ordinal values 'a' through 'z' (decimal 97 through 122). The bits are aligned so that ordinal values evenly divisible by 8 are represented in bit 0 of each byte.*

A Comment

In the previous sections of this chapter we examined four programming languages and covered the major design issues involved in building an executable program that calls subroutines. Figures 17-3, 17-4, and 17-5 summarize some characteristics of the language translators we discussed.

Language	Default Memory Model
QuickBasic	Medium
Microsoft C	Small
Turbo Pascal	Large

Figure 17-3. *The default memory models of three popular programming languages.*

Language	Default Parameter-Passing Method	Parameter Order
QuickBasic	Reference	Forward
Microsoft C	Value	Reverse
Turbo Pascal	(Varies)	Forward

Figure 17-4. *The parameter-passing conventions of three popular programming languages.*

Language	Registers Used by Language Translator
QuickBasic	DS, SS, BP, SI, DI
Microsoft C	DS, SS, BP, SI, DI
Turbo Pascal	DS, SS, BP

Figure 17-5. *The register usage conventions followed by three popular programming languages. Preserve these registers if you change them in a subroutine.*

Even if you never plan to write an assembly language program or link subroutines written in different languages into the same program, we hope you've found it interesting to see how these different language translators do their work.

Other Programming Tools

The following sections describe other tools that make programming easier, faster, and more reliable.

Integrated Development Environments

It is becoming increasingly common for vendors to offer an integrated development environment (IDE) as one of their programming-language products. An IDE includes the compiler, linker, and function or object library as well as all the other tools you need to create programs: source code editor, debugger, library manager, and so on.

Specialized Editors

No matter which language you use, you'll spend at least some of your programming time writing and editing source code. If you do not use an IDE, which includes a built-in editor, you'll need a text editing program. Word processors are poorly suited to program editing because most of their features are for adding fancy formatting, changing fonts, and enhancing the document in ways that are unnecessary when working on source code.

All you need is a program that can edit ASCII text files. You can use any text editor program, including the EDIT program that is provided with MS-DOS versions 5.0 and later, but editing programs that are designed specifically for programmers are available. These editors have built-in features that make the job of editing source code much easier. Examples of features found in most programming editors are automatic indenting, compilation from within the editor, and automatic location of compilation errors. Most of these editors are programmable, which means that you can write programs that run within the editor to perform complex and repetitive editing tasks.

Debuggers

A debugger is a tool that assists you in finding and fixing program bugs. As you probably know, a bug is an error in a program that prevents it from operating correctly. Some bugs are quite easy to locate and fix, but others—particularly in large and complex programs—can be very difficult to find. A debugger is almost indispensable for serious program development.

Debuggers vary widely in their capabilities. The simplest are found as part of IDEs such as Microsoft Quick C. These debuggers let you execute code one statement at a time, examine and modify variables, and control program flow. They are useful for simple debugging tasks. More sophisticated debuggers, such as Microsoft CodeView and Borland's Turbo Debugger, operate as stand-alone programs and provide many more features. The most powerful debuggers consist of both software and a special hardware board that protects operating system code and debugger code from the most unruly program. These hardware debuggers are required only for the most serious debugging tasks.

Profilers

For most programs, execution speed is a concern. There's no such thing as a program that runs too fast. To fine-tune your program's performance, you must be able to determine exactly what's happening when the program is running. You need to know which parts of the code are running quickly and which parts are running more slowly than you might expect. You need to know whether certain sections of code are slowing the program down and whether rewriting sections of code would result in significant speed gains. You can get this information by using a tool called a profiler.

A profiler is loaded into memory before you run the program you are testing. The profiler monitors the program, keeping track of the number of times each part of the program executes and how long each part takes to execute. Using this information, you can identify any bottlenecks in program execution, and then you can modify the source code and recompile and retest the program. Not all slowdowns can be fixed, of course, but many can. A profiler is a useful tool for optimizing performance.

Visual Interface Design Tools

The screen interface presented to the user is a crucial part of any program. With many programs, the bulk of the programmer's time is spent designing and coding the interface. Traditional methods of interface design involve writing source code to create the screen elements you want. This method is usually time consuming and can require many passes through the write-compile-test cycle before you get the interface code right. There's a better way, however.

Visual interface design tools let you draw the desired interface elements on the screen during program development. If you want a screen window to have a particular size and position, you simply use the mouse to draw and position it as desired; there's no coding involved. Other screen elements, such as menus, command buttons, text boxes, and option buttons can be created in the same way. The design tool puts the necessary code in the program. Microsoft Visual Basic is probably the best-known programming language that provides a visual interface design tool.

Of course, a visual interface design tool cannot write the entire program for you. You must still write the bulk of the code—the code that performs the noninterface tasks that the program must execute, such as disk access and data manipulation. However, drawing, rather than coding, your interface can save a lot of time; it's also sort of fun.

Programmable Application Programs

An application program is a program that is designed for a specific task. Some application programs, such as Lotus 1-2-3 (a spreadsheet), Borland Paradox (a relational database), and Microsoft Word (a word processor) are programmable. Programmable application programs have their own built-in programming languages that let you customize them for specific tasks. For some program-development tasks, you might be better off using a programmable application than you would be writing a program from scratch.

Let's say a client has asked you to create a financial analysis program. You could get out your trusty C++, Basic, or Pascal compiler and get to work creating the analysis program from scratch. Another approach would be to use a programmable spreadsheet, such as Microsoft Excel, to create the application. If you used Excel, you would have a head start because many of the capabilities you need, such as financial calculations, graphs, and printer output, are built in; you don't have to program these yourself. The same would be true for a database project; you might turn to the Paradox database, which has a wide range of built-in database functions.

There are shortcomings to this approach: A programmable application does not provide the same degree of flexibility that you can obtain by using a regular programming language, and some projects might simply be beyond the capabilities of a programmable application. In addition, your client must have a copy of the application as well as a copy of your program. However, in many cases, using a programmable application is a perfectly adequate approach, and the advantages in development time might offset any disadvantages.

PART IV:

REFERENCE

Appendix A

BIOS Services Summary

This appendix summarizes the BIOS service routines. You can use it to find the services you need and to determine which registers they use. Where a particular service is detailed or tricky to use, we refer you to the discussion in the chapters of this book or to the IBM technical reference manuals.

Short Summary

In Figure A-1, we briefly list all the BIOS services so that they can be seen together, at a glance.

Subject	Interrupt Hex	Interrupt Dec	Service	Description	Notes*
Print screen	05H	5	N/A	Send screen contents to printer.	
Video	10H	16	00H	Set video mode.	
Video	10H	16	01H	Set cursor size.	
Video	10H	16	02H	Set cursor position.	
Video	10H	16	03H	Read cursor position.	
Video	10H	16	04H	Read light-pen position.	
Video	10H	16	05H	Set active display page.	
Video	10H	16	06H	Scroll window up.	
Video	10H	16	07H	Scroll window down.	
Video	10H	16	08H	Read character and attribute.	
Video	10H	16	09H	Write character and attribute.	
Video	10H	16	0AH	Write character.	
Video	10H	16	0BH	Set 4-color palette.	
Video	10H	16	0CH	Write pixel.	
Video	10H	16	0DH	Read pixel.	
Video	10H	16	0EH	Write character in teletype mode.	
Video	10H	16	0FH	Get current video mode.	
Video	10H	16	10H	EGA/VGA color palette interface.	
Video	10H	16	11H	EGA/VGA character generator interface.	
Video	10H	16	12H	EGA/VGA "alternate select."	
Video	10H	16	13H	Write character string.	PC/AT, PS/2, EGA, VGA only
Video	10H	16	1AH	Get/set display combination code.	PS/2 only

* In the *Notes* column, *PC/XT* refers to the IBM PC/XT and generally to any clone that has an 8088/8086 processor and a hard disk. *PC/AT* refers to the various IBM PC/AT models and to any clone with an 80286 or higher CPU. *PS/2 only* and *PS/2 models with Micro Channel* include clones but exclude the earlier IBM machines and clones of those early machines. Any reference to *VGA* also applies to SVGA.

Figure A-1. *A short summary of the BIOS services.* (continued)

Figure A-1. *continued*

Subject	Interrupt Hex	Dec	Service	Description	Notes*
Video	10H	16	1BH	Get functionality/state information.	PS/2 only
Video	10H	16	1CH	Save/restore video state.	VGA only
Equipment	11H	17	N/A	Get list of peripheral equipment.	
Memory	12H	18	N/A	Get base memory size (in KB).	
Disk	13H	19	00H	Reset disk system.	
Disk	13H	19	01H	Get disk status.	
Disk	13H	19	02H	Read disk sectors.	
Disk	13H	19	03H	Write disk sectors.	
Disk	13H	19	04H	Verify disk sectors.	
Disk	13H	19	05H	Format disk track.	
Disk	13H	19	06H	Format disk track and set bad sector flags.	PC/XT hard disk only
Disk	13H	19	07H	Format drive starting at specified cylinder.	PC/XT hard disk only
Disk	13H	19	08H	Get current drive parameters.	
Disk	13H	19	09H	Initialize hard disk parameter tables.	
Disk	13H	19	0AH	Read long.	
Disk	13H	19	0BH	Write long.	
Disk	13H	19	0CH	Seek to cylinder.	
Disk	13H	19	0DH	Alternate hard disk reset.	
Disk	13H	19	10H	Test for drive ready.	
Disk	13H	19	11H	Recalibrate drive.	
Disk	13H	19	14H	Controller diagnostics.	
Disk	13H	19	15H	Get disk type.	
Disk	13H	19	16H	Get floppy disk change status.	
Disk	13H	19	17H	Set floppy disk type for format.	
Disk	13H	19	18H	Set media type for floppy disk format.	
Disk	13H	19	19H	Park heads.	PS/2 only
Disk	13H	19	1AH	Format ESDI unit.	PS/2 models with Micro Channel
Serial port	14H	20	00H	Initialize serial port.	
Serial port	14H	20	01H	Send out one character.	
Serial port	14H	20	02H	Receive one character.	

(continued)

Figure A-1. *continued*

Subject	Interrupt Hex	Dec	Service	Description	Notes*
Serial port	14H	20	03H	Get serial port status.	
Serial port	14H	20	04H	Extended serial port initialize.	PS/2 only
Serial port	14H	20	05H	Extended serial port control.	PS/2 only
System	15H	21	21H	Read/write POST error log.	PS/2 models with Micro Channel
System	15H	21	4FH	Keyboard intercept.	PC/AT, PS/2 only
System	15H	21	80H	Device open.	PC/AT, PS/2 only
System	15H	21	81H	Device close.	PC/AT, PS/2 only
System	15H	21	82H	Program termination.	PC/AT, PS/2 only
System	15H	21	83H	Start/stop interval timer.	PC/AT, PS/2 only
System	15H	21	84H	Get joystick input.	PC/AT, PS/2 only
System	15H	21	85H	Sys Req keystroke.	PC/AT, PS/2 only
System	15H	21	86H	Wait.	PC/AT, PS/2 only
System	15H	21	87H	Protected-mode data move.	PC/AT, PS/2 models with Micro Channel
System	15H	21	88H	Get extended memory size.	PC/AT, PS/2 models with Micro Channel
System	15H	21	89H	Switch to protected mode.	PC/AT, PS/2 models with Micro Channel
System	15H	21	90H	Device busy.	PC/AT, PS/2 only
System	15H	21	91H	Interrupt complete.	PC/AT, PS/2 only
System	15H	21	C0H	Get system configuration parameters.	
System	15H	21	C1H	Get extended BIOS data segment.	PS/2 only
System	15H	21	C2H	Pointing-device interface.	PS/2 only
System	15H	21	C3H	Enable/disable watchdog timer.	PS/2 models with Micro Channel
System	15H	21	C4H	Programmable Option Select interface.	PS/2 models with Micro Channel
Keyboard	16H	22	00H	Read next keystroke.	
Keyboard	16H	22	01H	Report whether keystroke ready.	
Keyboard	16H	22	02H	Get shift status.	
Keyboard	16H	22	03H	Set typematic rate and delay.	PC/AT, PS/2 only
Keyboard	16H	22	05H	Write to keyboard buffer.	PC/AT, PS/2 only

(continued)

Figure A-1. *continued*

Subject	Interrupt Hex	Dec	Service	Description	Notes*
Keyboard	16H	22	10H	Extended keyboard read.	PC/AT, PS/2 only
Keyboard	16H	22	11H	Get extended keyboard status.	PC/AT, PS/2 only
Keyboard	16H	22	12H	Get extended shift status.	PC/AT, PS/2 only
Printer	17H	23	00H	Send 1 byte to printer.	
Printer	17H	23	01H	Initialize printer.	
Printer	17H	23	02H	Get printer status.	
Basic	18H	24	N/A	Switch control to ROM Basic.	
Bootstrap	19H	25	N/A	Reboot computer.	
Time	1AH	26	00H	Read current clock count.	
Time	1AH	26	01H	Set current clock count.	
Time	1AH	26	02H	Read time in real-time clock.	PC/AT, PS/2 only
Time	1AH	26	03H	Set time in real-time clock.	PC/AT, PS/2 only
Time	1AH	26	04H	Read date from real-time clock.	PC/AT, PS/2 only
Time	1AH	26	05H	Set date in real-time clock.	PC/AT, PS/2 only
Time	1AH	26	06H	Set real-time clock alarm.	PC/AT, PS/2 only
Time	1AH	26	07H	Reset real-time clock alarm.	PC/AT, PS/2 only

Long Summary

In Figure A-2, we expand the previous summary table to show the register usage for input and output parameters. The preceding section is best used to quickly find *which* service you need; this section is best used to quickly find *how* to use each service.

Service	Interrupt	Register Input	Output	Notes
Print screen.	05H	N/A	N/A	Send screen contents to printer. Status and result byte at 0050:0000H.

Video Services

Service	Interrupt	Register Input	Output	Notes
Set video mode.	10H	AH = 00H AL = video mode	None	*Video modes in AL:* 00H: 40 × 25 16-color text (gray-scaled on composite monitors). 01H: 40 × 25 16-color text. 02H: 80 × 25 16-color text (gray-scaled on composite monitors). 03H: 80 × 25 16-color text. 04H: 320 × 200 4-color graphics. 05H: 320 × 200 4-color graphics (gray-scaled on composite monitors). 06H: 640 × 200 2-color graphics. 07H: 80 × 25 monochrome text (MDA, EGA, VGA). 0DH: 320 × 200 16-color graphics (EGA, VGA). 0EH: 640 × 200 16-color graphics (EGA, VGA). 0FH: 640 × 350 monochrome graphics (EGA, VGA). 10H: 640 × 350 16-color graphics (EGA, VGA). 11H: 640 × 480 2-color graphics (MCGA, VGA). 12H: 640 × 480 16-color graphics (VGA). 13H: 320 × 200 256-color graphics (MCGA, VGA).

Figure A-2. *A complete summary of the BIOS services.*

(continued)

Figure A-2. *continued*

Service	Interrupt	Register Input	Output	Notes
Set cursor size.	10H	AH = 01H CH = starting scan line CL = ending scan line	None	Useful values for CH and CL depend on video mode.
Set cursor position.	10H	AH = 02H BH = page number DH = row DL = column	None	
Read cursor position.	10H	AH = 03H BH = page number	CH = starting scan line CL = ending scan line DH = row DL = column	
Read light-pen position.	10H	AH = 04H	AH = pen trigger signal BX = pixel column CH = pixel row (CGA and EGA video modes 4, 5, and 6) CX = pixel row (EGA except modes 4, 5, and 6) DH = character row DL = character column	
Set active display page.	10H	AH = 05H AL = page number	None	
Scroll window up.	10H	AH = 06H AL = lines to scroll up BH = fill attribute CH = upper row CL = left column DH = lower row DL = right column	None	

(continued)

Figure A-2. *continued*

Service	Interrupt	Input	Output	Notes
Scroll window down.	10H	AH = 07H AL = lines to scroll down BH = fill attribute CH = upper row CL = left column DH = lower row DL = right column	None	
Read character and attribute.	10H	AH = 08H BH = page number	AH = attribute AL = character	
Write character and attribute.	10H	AH = 09H AL = character BH = page number BL = attribute CX = number of characters to repeat	None	
Write character.	10H	AH = 0AH AL = character BH = page number BL = color in graphics mode CX = number of characters to repeat	None	
Set color palette.	10H	AH = 0BH If BH = 00, BL = border color for modes 0, 1, 2, and 3; background color for modes 4 and 5; foreground color for modes 6 and 11 If BH = 01, BL = palette color ID	None	

(continued)

Figure A-2. *continued*

Service	Interrupt	Register Input	Output	Notes
Write pixel.	10H	AH = 0CH AL = color BH = page number CX = pixel column DX = pixel row	None	
Read pixel.	10H	AH = 0DH BH = page number CX = pixel column DX = pixel row	AL = pixel value	
Write character in teletype mode.	10H	AH = 0EH AL = character BH = page number BL = color in graphics mode	None	Page number required only for IBM PC BIOS dated 10/19/81 and earlier.
Get current video mode.	10H	AH = 0FH	AH = width in characters AL = video mode BH = page number	
Set one palette register.	10H	AH = 10H AL = 00H BH = palette register value BL = palette register number	None	EGA, VGA.
Set border register.	10H	AH = 10H AL = 01H BH = border color	None	EGA, VGA.
Set all palette registers.	10H	AH = 10H AL = 02H ES:DX → table of palette values	None	EGA, VGA.

(continued)

Figure A-2. *continued*

Service	Interrupt	Register Input	Output	Notes
Select background intensity or blink attribute.	10H	AH = 10H AL = 03H *To enable background intensity:* BL = 00H *To enable blinking:* BL = 01H	None	EGA, VGA.
Read one palette register.	10H	AH = 10H AL = 07H BL = palette register number	BH = palette register value	VGA only.
Read border register.	10H	AH = 10H AL = 08H	BH = border color value	VGA only.
Read all palette registers.	10H	AH = 10H AL = 09H ES:DX → table of palette register values	Table at ES:DX updated	VGA only.
Update one video DAC color register.	10H	AH = 10H AL = 10H BX = color register number DH = red value CH = green value CL = blue value	None	MCGA, VGA.
Update block of video DAC color registers.	10H	AH = 10H AL = 12H BX = first register to update CX = number of registers to update ES:DX → table of red-green-blue values	None	MCGA, VGA.

(continued)

Figure A-2. *continued*

Service	Interrupt	Register Input	Output	Notes
Set video DAC color page.	10H	AH = 10H AL = 13H *To select paging mode:* BL = 00H BH = 00H selects 4 pages of 64 registers, *or* BH = 01H selects 16 pages of 16 registers *To select page:* BL = 01H BH = page number	None	VGA only.
Read one video DAC color register.	10H	AH = 10H AL = 15H BX = color register number	DH = red value CH = green value CL = blue value	MCGA, VGA.
Read block of video DAC color registers.	10H	AH = 10H AL = 17H BX = first register number CX = number of registers ES:DX → table of red-green-blue values	Table at ES:DX updated	MCGA, VGA.
Get video DAC color page.	10H	AH = 10H AL = 1AH BH = current page BL = current paging mode	None	VGA only.
Sum video DAC color values to gray shades.	10H	AH = 10H AL = 1BH BX = first color register CX = number of color registers	None	MCGA, VGA.

(continued)

Figure A-2. *continued*

Service	Interrupt	Register Input	Output	Notes
Load user-specified alphanumeric character set.	10H	AH = 11H AL = 00H BH = bytes per character in table BL = character generator RAM block CX = number of characters DX = first character ES:BP → character definition table	None	EGA, MCGA, VGA.
Load ROM BIOS 8 × 14 alphanumeric character set.	10H	AH = 11H AL = 01H BL = character generator RAM block	None	EGA, VGA.
Load ROM BIOS 8 × 8 alphanumeric character set.	10H	AH = 11H AL = 02H BL = character generator RAM block	None	EGA, MCGA, VGA.
Select displayed alphanumeric character sets.	10H	AH = 11H AL = 03H BL = character generator RAM block	None	EGA, MCGA, VGA.
Load ROM BIOS 8 × 16 alphanumeric character set.	10H	AH = 11H AL = 04H BL = character generator RAM block	None	MCGA, VGA.
Load user-specified alphanumeric character set and adjust displayed character height.	10H	AH = 11H AL = 10H BH = bytes per character definition BL = character generator RAM block	None	EGA, MCGA, VGA.

(continued)

Figure A-2. *continued*

Service	Interrupt	Register Input	Output	Notes
Load user-specified alphanumeric character set and adjust displayed character height, *continued*		CX = number of characters DX = first character ES:BP → character definition table		
Load ROM BIOS 8 × 14 alphanumeric character set and adjust displayed character height.	10H	AH = 11H AL = 11H BL = character generator RAM block	None	EGA, VGA.
Load ROM BIOS 8 × 8 alphanumeric character set and adjust displayed character height.	10H	AH = 11H AL = 12H BL = character generator RAM block	None	EGA, VGA.
Load ROM BIOS 8 × 16 alphanumeric character set and adjust displayed character height.	10H	AH = 11H AL = 14H BL = character generator RAM block	None	VGA only.
Load user-specified 8 × 8 graphics character set.	10H	AH = 11H AL = 20H ES:BP → character definition table	None	EGA, MCGA, VGA. Copies ES:BP into the interrupt 1FH vector. Only characters 80H through FFH should be defined.
Load user-specified graphics character set.	10H	AH = 11H AL = 21H CX = bytes per character definition ES:BP → character definition table	None	EGA, MCGA, VGA.

(continued)

Figure A-2. *continued*

Service	Interrupt	Register Input	Output	Notes
Load user-speci-fied graphics character set, *continued*		*User-specified number of character rows:* BL = 00H DL = number of character rows *14 character rows:* BL = 01H *25 character rows:* BL = 02H *43 character rows:* BL = 03H		
Load ROM BIOS 8 × 14 graphics character set.	10H	AH = 11H AL = 22H BL = (as for AL = 21H) DL = (as for AL = 21H)	None	EGA, VGA.
Load ROM BIOS 8 × 8 graphics character set.	10H	AH = 11H AL = 23H BL = (as for AL = 21H) DL = (as for AL = 21H)	None	EGA, MCGA, VGA.
Load ROM BIOS 8 × 16 graphics character set.	10H	AH = 11H AL = 24H BL = (as for AL = 21H) DL = (as for AL = 21H)	None	MCGA, VGA.
Get character generator information.	10H	AH = 11H AL = 30H *Contents of interrupt 1FH vector:* BH = 00H	CX = points DL = displayed character rows − 1 ES:BP → character table	EGA, MCGA, VGA.

(continued)

Figure A-2. *continued*

Service	Interrupt	*Register* Input	Output	Notes
Get character generator information, *continued*		*Contents of inter-rupt 43H vector:* BH = 01H		
		Address of ROM 8 × 14 characters: BH = 02H		
		Address of ROM 8 × 8 characters: BH = 03H		
		Address of second half of ROM 8 × 8 table: BH = 04H		
		Address of ROM 9 × 14 alternate characters: BH = 05H		
		Address of ROM 8 × 16 characters: BH = 06H		
		Address of ROM 9 × 16 alternate characters: BH = 07H		
Return video configuration information.	10H	AH = 12H BL = 10H	BH = default BIOS video mode (00H = color, 01H = monochrome) BL = amount of video RAM (00H = 64 KB, 01H = 128 KB, 02H = 192 KB, 03H = 256 KB) CH = feature bits CL = configuration switches	EGA, VGA.
Select alternate print screen routine.	10H	AH = 12H BL = 20H	None	EGA, MCGA, VGA. Updates INT 05H vector.

(continued)

Figure A-2. *continued*

Service	Interrupt	Register Input	Output	Notes
Select scan lines for alphanumeric modes.	10H	AH = 12H BL = 30H *200 scan lines:* AL = 00H *350 scan lines:* AL = 01H *400 scan lines:* AL = 02H	AL = 12H	VGA only.
Enable/disable default palette loading.	10H	AH = 12H BL = 31H *Enable default palette loading:* AL = 00H *Disable default palette loading:* AL = 01H	AL = 12H	MCGA, VGA.
Enable/disable video addressing.	10H	AH = 12H BL = 32H *Enable video addressing:* AL = 00H *Disable video addressing:* AL = 01H	AL = 12H	MCGA, VGA.
Enable/disable gray-scale summing.	10H	AH = 12H BL = 33H *Enable gray-scale summing:* AL = 00H *Disable gray-scale summing:* AL = 01H	AL = 12H	MCGA, VGA.
Enable/disable BIOS cursor emulation.	10H	AH = 12H BL = 34H *Enable cursor emulation:* AL = 00H	AL = 12H	VGA only.

(continued)

Figure A-2. *continued*

Service	Interrupt	Register Input	Output	Notes
Enable/disable BIOS cursor emulation, *continued*		*Disable cursor emulation:* AL = 01H		
Display switch interface.	10H	AH = 12H BL = 35H *Initial adapter video off:* AL = 00H *Initial planar video on:* AL = 01H *Switch active video off:* AL = 02H *Switch inactive video on:* AL = 03H ES:DX→128-byte save area	AL = 12H	MCGA, VGA.
Enable/disable video refresh.	10H	AH = 12H BL = 36H *Enable refresh:* AL = 00H *Disable refresh:* AL = 01H	AL = 12H	VGA only.
Write string; don't move cursor.	10H	AH = 13H AL = 00H BL = attribute BH = page number DH, DL = row and column of starting cursor position CX = length of string ES:BP → start of string	None	PC/AT, EGA, MCGA, VGA.

(continued)

Figure A-2. *continued*

Service	Interrupt	Register Input	Output	Notes
Write string; move cursor after string.	10H	AH = 13H AL = 01H BL = attribute BH = page number DH, DL = row and column of starting cursor position CX = length of string ES:BP → start of string	None	PC/AT, EGA, MCGA, VGA.
Write string of alternating characters and attributes; don't move cursor.	10H	AH = 13H AL = 02H BH = page number DH, DL = row and column of starting cursor position CX = length of string ES:BP → start of string	None	PC/AT, EGA, MCGA, VGA.
Write string of alternating characters and attributes; move cursor.	10H	AH = 13H AL = 03H BH = page number DH, DL = row and column of starting cursor position CX = length of string ES:BP → start of string	None	PC/AT, EGA, MCGA, VGA.
Get display combination code.	10H	AH = 1AH AL = 00H	AL = 1AH BL = active display BH = inactive display	MCGA, VGA. *Values returned in BL and BH:* 00H: no display. 01H: MDA or compatible. 02H: CGA or compatible. 04H: EGA with color display. 05H: EGA with monochrome display.

(continued)

Figure A-2. *continued*

		Register		
Service	*Interrupt*	*Input*	*Output*	*Notes*
Get display combination code, *continued*				06H: Professional Graphics Controller. 07H: VGA with monochrome display. 08H: VGA with color display. 0BH: MCGA with mono-chrome display. 0CH: MCGA with color display. FFH: unknown display type.
Set display combination code.	10H	AH = 1AH AL = 01H BL = active display BH = inactive display	AL = 1AH	MCGA, VGA. See table above for values in BL and BH.
BIOS functionality/state information.	10H	AH = 1BH BX = 00H ES:DI → 64-byte buffer	AL = 1BH Buffer at ES:DI updated	MCGA, VGA. See the *IBM BIOS Interface Technical Reference Manual* for table format.
Return save/ restore buffer size.	10H	AH = 1CH AL = 00H *CX = requested states:* Bit 0 = video hardware state; bit 1 = video BIOS data area; bit 2 = video DAC and color registers	AL = 1CH (if function supported) BX = save/restore buffer size in 64-byte blocks	VGA only. Use this service before saving the current video state.
Save current video state.	10H	AH = 1CH AL = 01H CX = requested states ES:BX → save/ restore buffer	AL = 1CH	VGA only. May disrupt current video state, so follow a call to this service with a call to the "Restore current video state" service.

(continued)

523

Figure A-2. *continued*

Service	Interrupt	Register Input	Output	Notes
Restore current video state.	10H	AH = 1CH AL = 02H CX = requested states ES:BX → save/restore buffer	AL = 1CH	VGA only.

Equipment-List Service

Service	Interrupt	Input	Output	Notes
Get list of peripheral attached equipment.	11H	None	AX = equipment list, bit-coded	*Bit settings in AX:* 00 = floppy disk drive installed. 01 = math coprocessor installed. 02, 03 = system board RAM in 16-KB blocks (PCs with 64-KB motherboard only). 02 = pointing device installed (PS/2s only). 04, 05 = initial video mode: 00 = unused; 01 = 40 × 25 color; 10 = 80 × 25 color; 11 = 80 × 25 monochrome. 06, 07 = 1 less than number of floppy disk drives installed. 08 = (not used). 09, 10, 11 = number of RS-232 cards in system. 12 = game I/O attached (PC and PC/XT only). 13 = internal modem installed. 14, 15 = number of parallel printers attached.

Memory Service

Service	Interrupt	Input	Output	Notes
Get base memory size.	12H	None	AX = memory size (KB)	See also ''Get extended memory size'' (INT 15H, service 88H).

Disk Services

Service	Interrupt	Input	Output	Notes
Reset disk system.	13H	AH = 00H DL = drive number	CF = success/failure flag AH = status code	*Status codes in AH:* See INT 13H, service 01H.

(continued)

Figure A-2. *continued*

Service	Interrupt	Register Input	Output	Notes
Get disk status.	13H	AH = 01H DL = drive number	AH = status code *Status values (hex):* AH = 00H: no error AH = 01H: bad command AH = 02H: address mark not found AH = 03H: write attempted on write-protected disk (F) AH = 04H: sector not found AH = 05H: reset failed (H) AH = 06H: floppy disk removed (F) AH = 07H: bad parameter table (H) AH = 08H: DMA overrun AH = 09H: DMA across 64-KB boundary AH = 0AH: bad sector flag (H) AH = 0BH: bad cylinder (H) AH = 0CH: bad media type (F) AH = 0DH: invalid number of sectors on format (H) AH = 0EH: control data address mark detected (H) AH = 0FH: DMA arbitration level out of range (H)	(H) = hard disk only. (F) = floppy disk only.

(continued)

Figure A-2. *continued*

Service	Interrupt	Register Input	Output	Notes
Get disk status, *continued*			AH = 10H: bad CRC or ECC AH = 11H: ECC corrected data error (H) AH = 20H: controller failed AH = 40H: seek failed AH = 80H: time out (H) or drive not ready (F) AH = AAH: drive not ready (H) AH = BBH: undefined error (H) AH = CCH: write fault (H) AH = E0H: status error (H) AH = FFH: sense operation failed (H)	
Read disk sectors.	13H	AH = 02H AL = number of sectors CH = low-order 8 bits of track/cylinder number CL = sector number in bits 0–5; bits 6–7 are the 2 high-order bits of cylinder number DH = head number DL = drive number ES:BX → buffer	CF = success/ failure flag AH = status code AL = number of sectors read	*Status codes in AH:* See INT 13H, service 01H.
Write disk sectors.	13H	AH = 03H AL = number of sectors	CF = success/ failure flag AH = status code	*Status codes in AH:* See INT 13H, service 01H.

(continued)

Figure A-2. *continued*

Service	Interrupt	Register Input	Output	Notes
Write disk sectors, *continued*		CH = low-order 8 bits of track/ cylinder number CL = sector number in bits 0–5; bits 6–7 are the 2 high-order bits of cylinder number DH = head number DL = drive number ES:BX → buffer	AL = number of sectors written	
Verify disk sectors.	13H	AH = 04H AL = number of sectors CH = low-order 8 bits of track/ cylinder number CL = sector number in bits 0–5; bits 6–7 are the 2 high-order bits of cylinder number DH = head number DL = drive number	CF = success/ failure flag AH = status code AL = number of sectors verified	*Status codes in AH:* See INT 13H, service 01H.
Format disk track (cylinder).	13H	AH = 05H AL = interleave value (PC/XT only) CH = cylinder number (bits 0–7) CL = cylinder number (bits 8–9) DH = head number DL = drive number ES:BX → table of sector format information	CF = success/ failure flag AH = status code	*Status codes in AH:* See INT 13H, service 01H. See Chapter 10 for contents of table.

(continued)

Figure A-2. *continued*

Service	Interrupt	Register Input	Output	Notes
Format disk track and set bad sector flags.	13H	AH = 06H AL = interleave value CH = cylinder number (bits 0–7) CL = high-order cylinder number (bits 6–7); bits 0–5 = sector number DH = head number DL = drive number	CF = success/ failure flag AH = status code	PC/XT hard disk only.
Format drive starting at specified cylinder.	13H	AH = 07H AL = interleave value CH = cylinder number (bits 0–7) CL = high-order cylinder number (bits 6–7); bits 0–5 = sector number DH = head number DL = drive number	CF = success/ failure flag AH = status code	PC/XT hard disk only.
Get drive parameters.	13H	AH = 08H DL = drive number	CF = success/ failure flag AH = status code DL = number of drives DH = max. read/write head number CL (bits 6–7) = max. cylinder number (bits 8–9) CL (bits 0–5) = max. sector number CH = max. number of cylinders (bits 0–7)	*Status codes in AH:* See INT 13H, service 01H.
Initialize hard disk base tables.	13H	AH = 09H DL = drive number	CF = success/ failure flag AH = status code	Interrupt 41H points to table for drive 0. Interrupt 46H points to table for drive 1. *Status codes in AH:* See INT 13H, service 01H.

(continued)

Figure A-2. *continued*

Service	Interrupt	Register Input	Output	Notes
Read long.	13H	AH = 0AH AL = number of sectors DL = drive number DH = head number CH = low-order 8 bits of cylinder/track number CL = sector number in bits 0–5; bits 6–7 are the 2 high-order bits of cylinder number ES:BX → buffer	CF = success/failure flag AH = status code	*Status codes in AH:* See INT 13H, service 01H.
Write long.	13H	AH = 0BH AL = number of sectors DL = drive number DH = head number CH = low-order 8 bits of cylinder/track number CL = sector number in bits 0–5; bits 6–7 are the 2 high-order bits of cylinder number ES:BX → buffer	CF = success/failure flag AH = status code	*Status codes in AH:* See INT 13H, service 01H.
Seek to cylinder.	13H	AH = 0CH DL = drive number DH = head number CH = low-order 8 bits of cylinder/track number	CF = success/failure flag AH = status code	*Status codes in AH:* See INT 13H, service 01H.

(continued)

Figure A-2. *continued*

Service	Interrupt	Register Input	Output	Notes
Seek to cylinder, *continued*		CL = sector number in bits 0–5; bits 6–7 are the 2 high-order bits of cylinder number		
Alternate disk reset.	13H	AH = 0DH DL = drive number	CF = success/ failure flag AH = status code	*Status codes in AH:* See INT 13H, service 01H.
Test for drive ready.	13H	AH = 10H DL = drive number	CF = success/ failure flag AH = status code	*Status codes in AH:* See INT 13H, service 01H.
Recalibrate drive.	13H	AH = 11H DL = drive number	CF = success/ failure flag AH = status code	*Status codes in AH:* See INT 13H, service 01H.
Controller diagnostics.	13H	AH = 14H	CF = success/ failure flag AH = status code	*Status codes in AH:* See INT 13H, service 01H.
Get disk type.	13H	AH = 15H DL = drive number	CF = success/ failure flag AH = disk type CX, DX = number of 512-byte sectors (hard disk only)	*Disk types:* AH = 00H: disk not there. AH = 01H: floppy disk, no change detection present. AH = 02H: floppy disk, change detection present. AH = 03H: hard disk.
Change of floppy disk status.	13H	AH = 16H DL = drive number	AH = floppy disk change status: 00H = no floppy disk change 01H = invalid parameter 06H = floppy disk changed 80H = drive not ready	

(continued)

Figure A-2. *continued*

Service	Interrupt	Register Input	Output	Notes
Set floppy disk type for format.	13H	AH = 17H AL = floppy disk type DL = drive number	CF = success/failure flag AH = status code	*Floppy disk type set in AL:* AL = 01H: 360-KB floppy disk in 360-KB drive. AL = 02H: 360-KB floppy disk in 1.2-MB drive. AL = 03H: 1.2-MB floppy disk in 1.2-MB drive. AL = 04H: 720-KB floppy disk in 720-KB drive. For other floppy disk types, use service 18H.
Set media type for disk format.	13H	AH = 18H CH = number of tracks (bits 0–7) CL (bits 6–7) = number of tracks (bits 8–9) CL (bits 0–5) = sectors per track DL = drive number	CF = success/failure flag AH = status code ES:DI → 11-byte parameter table (disk-base table)	Only in PC/AT BIOS dated 11/15/85 and later, PC/XT BIOS dated 1/10/86 and later, and PS/2.
Park heads.	13H	AH = 19H DL = drive number	CF = success/failure flag AH = status code	PS/2 only.
Format unit.	13H	AH = 1AH AL = defect table count CL = format modifiers DL = drive ES:BX → defect table	CF = success/failure flag AH = status code	For PS/2 hard disks used with IBM Enhanced Small Device Interface (ESDI) adapter. See the *IBM BIOS Interface Technical Reference Manual*.
Serial Port Services				
Initialize serial port.	14H	AH = 00H AL = serial port parameters DX = serial port number	AX = serial port status	*Serial port parameter bit settings:* Bits 0–1 = word length: 10 = 7 bits; 11 = 8 bits. Bit 2 = stop bits: 0 = 1; 1 = 2.

(continued)

Figure A-2. *continued*

Service	Interrupt	Register Input	Output	Notes
Initialize serial port, *continued*				Bits 3–4 = parity: 00, 10 = none; 01 = odd; 11 = even. Bits 5–7 = baud rate: 000 = 110; 001 = 150; 010 = 300; 011 = 600; 100 = 1200; 101 = 2400; 110 = 4800; 111 = 9600. For PC/XT/AT family only. For PS/2, use subservice 04H, ''Extended serial port initialize.''
Send one character to serial port.	14H	AH = 01H AL = character DX = serial port number	AH = status code	*Status code bit settings:* See INT 14H, service 03H.
Receive one character from serial port.	14H	AH = 02H DX = serial port number	AH = status code AL = character	*Status code bit settings:* See INT 14H, service 03H.
Get serial port status.	14H	AH = 03H DX = serial port number	AX = status code	*Status code bit settings:* *AH bit settings:* Bit 0 = data ready. Bit 1 = overrun error. Bit 2 = parity error. Bit 3 = framing error. Bit 4 = break detected. Bit 5 = transmission buffer register empty. Bit 6 = transmission shift register empty. Bit 7 = time out.

(continued)

Figure A-2. *continued*

Service	Interrupt	Register Input	Output	Notes
Get serial port status, *continued*				*AL bit settings:* Bit 0 = delta clear-to-send. Bit 1 = delta data-set-ready. Bit 2 = trailing-edge ring detected. Bit 3 = change, receive line signal detected. Bit 4 = clear-to-send. Bit 5 = data-set-ready. Bit 6 = ring detected. Bit 7 = receive line signal detected.
Extended serial port initialize.	14H	AH = 04H AL = break status BH = parity BL = stop bits CH = word length CL = baud rate DX = serial port number (0–3)	AH = line status AL = modem status	PS/2 only. See Chapter 13 for details.
Extended serial port control.	14H	AH = 05H DX = serial port number (0, 1, 2, 3) *To read modem control register:* AL = 00H *To write modem control register:* AL = 01H BL = value for modem control register	AH = line status AL = modem status *If called with AL = 00H:* BL = modem control register value	For PS/2 only. See Chapter 13 for details.

(continued)

Figure A-2. *continued*

Service	Interrupt	Register Input	Output	Notes
System Services*				
Read/write Power On Self Test error log.	15H	AH = 21H BH = device code BL = error code *To read error log:* AL = 00H *To write error log:* AL = 01H	*AH = status:* 00H = successful 01H = log full 80H = invalid command 86H = unsupported service *If called with AL = 00H:* BX = number of POST error codes logged ES:DI → POST error log *If called with AL = 01H:* CF = success/failure flag	PS/2 models with Micro Channel.
Keyboard intercept.	15H	AH = 4FH	None	See Chapter 13 for details.
Device open.	15H	AH = 80H	None	See Chapter 13 for details.
Device close.	15H	AH = 81H	None	See Chapter 13 for details.
Program termination.	15H	AH = 82H	None	See Chapter 13 for details.
Start/stop interval timer (event wait).	15H	AH = 83H *To start interval timer:* AL = 00H CX,DX = time in microseconds ES:BX → 1-byte flag *To stop interval timer:* AL = 01H	*If called with AL = 00H:* CF = 0 (if timer started) *or* CF = 1 (if timer already running or function not supported) *If called with AL = 01H:* CF = 0 (if timer canceled) *or* CF = 1 (if function not supported)	PC/AT, PS/2 models with Micro Channel. At completion of specified interval, the high-order bit of the byte at ES:BX is set to 1.

* For interrupt 15H service numbers not supported in the ROM BIOS, the PC/XT BIOS returns AH = 80H and CF = 1; the AT or PS/2 BIOS returns AH = 86H and CF = 1.

(continued)

Figure A-2. *continued*

Service	Interrupt	Register Input	Output	Notes
Joystick support.	15H	AH = 84H *To read switches:* DX = 0000H *To read resistive inputs:* DX = 0001H	*If called with DX = 0000H:* AL = switch settings (bits 4–7) ← *4 Switches* CF = 0 (if switches successfully read) *or* CF = 1 (if unsuccessful) *If called with DX = 0001H:* AX = stick A *x*-value BX = stick A *y*-value CX = stick B *x*-value DX = stick B *y*-value ← *4 analogs*	Not supported by PC or XT BIOS prior to 01/10/86.
Sys Req keystroke.	15H	AH = 85H AL = key status	None	See Chapter 13 for details.
Wait during a specified interval.	15H	AH = 86H CX,DX = time in microseconds	CF = 0 (if successful) *or* CF = 1 (if error) AH = 00H: successful AH = 80H: invalid command AH = 83H: wait already in progress AH = 86H: function not supported	PC/AT, PS/2 only.
Protected-mode data move.	15H	AH = 87H CX = number of words to copy ES:SI → global descriptor table (GDT)	CF = 0 (if successful) CF = 1 (if error) AH = 00H: source copied successfully AH = 01H: parity error AH = 02H: interrupt error AH = 03H: address line 20 gating failed AH = 80H: invalid command AH = 86H: unsupported function	PC/AT, PS/2 models with Micro Channel. See the *IBM BIOS Technical Reference Manual* for details.

(continued)

Figure A-2. *continued*

Service	Interrupt	*Register* Input	Output	Notes
Get extended memory size.	15H	AH = 88H	If CF = 0, AX = extended memory size (KB) If CF = 1, AH = 80H: invalid command AH = 86H: unsupported function	PC/AT, PS/2 models with Micro Channel. See the *IBM BIOS Technical Reference Manual* for details.
Switch to protected mode.	15H	AH = 89H BL = interrupt number for IRQ0 BH = interrupt number for IRQ8 ES:SI → global descriptor table (GDT) CX = offset into protected-mode CS to jump to	If CF = 1, AH = FFH error enabling address line 20 If CF = 0, AH = 00H successfully switched to protected mode at specified address	PC/AT, PS/2 models with Micro Channel. See the *IBM BIOS Technical Reference Manual* for details.
Device busy.	15H	AH = 90H	None	See Chapter 13 for details.
Interrupt complete.	15H	AH = 91H	None	See Chapter 13 for details.
Get system configuration parameters.	15H	AH = C0H	If CF = 1, BIOS does not support this service If CF = 0, ES:BX → BIOS system configuration parameters	See Chapter 13 for details. Not supported in PC or XT BIOS prior to 01/10/86 or in AT prior to 06/10/85.
Get extended BIOS data segment.	15H	AH = C1H	If CF = 1, error If CF = 0, ES = extended BIOS data segment address	PS/2 only.

(continued)

536

Figure A-2. *continued*

Service	Interrupt	Register Input	Output	Notes
Enable/disable pointing device.	15H	AH = C2H AL = 00H *To enable:* BH = 00H *To disable:* BH = 01H	If CF = 0, successful If CF = 1, error *AH = status:* 00H = no error 01H = invalid function call 02H = invalid input 03H = interface error 04H = resend 05H = no device driver installed	PS/2 only.
Reset pointing device.	15H	AH = C2H AL = 01H	If CF = 0, successful If CF = 1, error AH = status (as above) BH = 00H (device ID) BL = undefined	PS/2 only.
Set pointing-device sample rate.	15H	AH = C2H AL = 02H BH = sample rate: 00H: 10/second 01H: 20/second 02H: 40/second 03H: 60/second 04H: 80/second 05H: 100/second 06H: 200/second	If CF = 0, successful If CF = 1, error AH = status (as above)	PS/2 only.
Set pointing-device resolution.	15H	AH = C2H AL = 03H *BH = resolution:* 00H = 1 count/ millimeter 01H = 2 counts/ millimeter 02H = 4 counts/ millimeter 03H = 8 counts/ millimeter	If CF = 0, successful If CF = 1, error AH = status (as above)	PS/2 only.

(continued)

Figure A-2. *continued*

Service	Interrupt	Register Input	Output	Notes
Get pointing-device type.	15H	AH = C2H AL = 04H	If CF = 0, successful If CF = 1, error BH = device ID AH = status (as above)	PS/2 only.
Initialize pointing device.	15H	AH = C2H AL = 05H BH = data packet size (1–8 bytes)	If CF = 0, successful If CF = 1, error AH = status (as above)	PS/2 only.
Extended pointing-device commands.	15H	AH = C2H AL = 06H *To get status:* BH = 00H *To set scaling to 1:1:* BH = 01H *To set scaling to 2:1:* BH = 02H	If CF = 0, successful If CF = 1, error AH = status (as above) *If called with BH = 00H:* BL = status byte 1 CL = status byte 2 DL = status byte 3	PS/2 only. See Chapter 13 for contents of status bytes.
Pass pointing-device driver address to BIOS.	15H	AH = C2H AL = 07H ES:BX → device driver	If CF = 0, successful If CF = 1, error AH = status (as above)	PS/2 only.
Enable/disable watchdog timer.	15H	AH = C3H BX = timer count (01H–FFH) *To enable:* AL = 01H *To disable:* AL = 00H	If CF = 0, successful If CF = 1, error	PS/2 models with Micro Channel.

(continued)

Figure A-2. *continued*

Service	Interrupt	Register Input	Output	Notes
Programmable Option Select (POS) interface.	15H	AH = C4H *To get POS register base address:* AL = 00H *To enable slot for POS setup:* AL = 01H BL = slot number *To enable an adapter:* AL = 02H	*If called with AL = 00H:* DX = base POS register address	PS/2 models with Micro Channel.

Keyboard Services

Service	Interrupt	Register Input	Output	Notes
Read next keystroke.	16H	AH = 00H	AH = scan code AL = ASCII character code	
Report whether keystroke ready.	16H	AH = 01H	*If no keystroke available:* ZF = 1 *If keystroke available:* ZF = 0 AH = scan code AL = ASCII character code	
Get shift status.	16H	AH = 02H	AL = shift status bits	*Shift status bits:* Bit 7 = 1: Insert state active. Bit 6 = 1: Caps Lock active. Bit 5 = 1: Num Lock active. Bit 4 = 1: Scroll Lock active. Bit 3 = 1: Alt pressed. Bit 2 = 1: Ctrl pressed. Bit 1 = 1: left Shift pressed. Bit 0 = 1: right Shift pressed.
Set typematic rate and delay.	16H	AH = 03H AL = 05H BL = typematic rate BH = delay value	None	PC/AT (BIOS dated 11/15/85 and later) and PS/2 only. See Chapter 12 for rates and values.

(continued)

539

Figure A-2. *continued*

Service	Interrupt	Register Input	Output	Notes
Write to keyboard buffer.	16H	AH = 05H CH = scan code CL = ASCII character code	AL = 00H (success); AL = 01H (keyboard buffer full)	PC/XT (BIOS dated 01/10/86 and later), PC/AT (BIOS dated 11/15/85 and later), and PS/2 only.
Extended keyboard read.	16H	AH = 10H	AH = scan code AL = ASCII character code	PC/XT (BIOS dated 01/10/86 and later), PC/AT (BIOS dated 11/15/85 and later), and PS/2 only.
Extended keyboard status.	16H	AH = 11H	*If no keystroke available:* ZF = 1 *If keystroke available:* ZF = 0 AH = scan code AL = ASCII character code	PC/XT (BIOS dated 01/10/86 and later), PC/AT (BIOS dated 11/15/85 and later), and PS/2 only.
Extended shift status.	16H	AH = 12H	AL = shift status (as above) *AH = extended shift status:* Bit 7 = Sys Req pressed Bit 6 = Caps Lock pressed Bit 5 = Num Lock pressed Bit 4 = Scroll Lock pressed Bit 3 = right Alt pressed Bit 2 = right Ctrl pressed Bit 1 = left Alt pressed Bit 0 = left Ctrl pressed	PC/XT (BIOS dated 01/10/86 and later), PC/AT (BIOS dated 11/15/85 and later), and PS/2 only.

(continued)

Figure A-2. *continued*

Service	Interrupt	Register Input	Output	Notes
Printer Services				
Send 1 byte to printer.	17H	AH = 00H AL = character DX = printer number	AH = success/ failure status code	*Status code bit settings:* Bit 7 = 1: not busy. Bit 6 = 1: acknowledge. Bit 5 = 1: out of paper. Bit 4 = 1: selected. Bit 3 = 1: I/O error. Bit 2 = (unused). Bit 1 = (unused). Bit 0 = time-out.
Initialize printer.	17H	AH = 01H DX = printer number	AH = status code	Status code bit settings as above.
Get printer status.	17H	AH = 02H DX = printer number	AH = status code	Status code bit settings as above.
Miscellaneous Services				
Switch control to ROM Basic.	18H	None	N/A	No return, so no possible output.
Reboot computer.	19H	None	N/A	No return, so no possible output.
Time-of-Day Services				
Read current clock count.	1AH	AH = 00H	AL > 00H if time of day has passed midnight CX = tick count, high word DX = tick count, low word	Timer-tick frequency is about 18.2 ticks/second, or about 65,543 ticks/hour.
Set current clock count.	1AH	AH = 01H CX = tick count, high word DX = tick count, low word	None	

(continued)

Figure A-2. *continued*

Service	Interrupt	Register Input	Output	Notes
Read real-time clock.	1AH	AH = 02H	CF = 1 if clock not operating CF = 0 if successful CH = hours (in BCD) CL = minutes (in BCD) DH = seconds (in BCD) DL = 01H if daylight savings time option set	PC/AT and PS/2 only. Daylight savings option not available in PC/AT BIOS dated 01/10/84.
Set real-time clock.	1AH	AH = 03H CH = hours (BCD) CL = minutes (BCD) DH = seconds (BCD) DL = 01H for automatic adjustment for daylight savings time		Input values in BCD. PC/AT and PS/2 only. Daylight savings option not available in PC/AT BIOS dated 01/10/84.
Read date from real-time clock.	1AH	AH = 04H	CF = 1 if clock not operating CF = 0 if successful DL = day (in BCD) DH = month (in BCD) CL = year (in BCD) CH = century (19 or 20, in BCD)	PC/AT and PS/2 only.
Set date in real-time clock.	1AH	AH = 05H DL = day (in BCD) DH = month (in BCD) CL = year (in BCD) CH = century (19 or 20, in BCD)		PC/AT and PS/2 only.

(continued)

Figure A-2. *continued*

Service	Interrupt	*Register* Input	Output	Notes
Set alarm.	1AH	AH = 06H CH = hours (in BCD) CL = minutes (in BCD) DH = seconds (in BCD)	CF = 1 if clock not operating or alarm already set CF = 0 if successful	Place address for alarm routine in interrupt 4AH vector before using this service.
Reset alarm.	1AH	AH = 07H	None	Disables alarm previously set with INT 1AH, service 06H.
Get alarm time and status.	1AH	AH = 09H	CH = hours (in BCD) CL = minutes (in BCD) DH = seconds (in BCD) *DL = alarm status:* 00H = alarm not enabled 01H = alarm enabled	PS/2 models 25, 30 only.

Appendix B

MS-DOS Functions Summary

This appendix summarizes the MS-DOS functions and is designed to be used as a quick reference guide. For details about the specific operation of each function, see Chapters 10 through 13. Once you understand the MS-DOS functions, these tables should provide you with most of the programming information you'll need.

Short Summary

Figure B-1 lists the five interrupts that can be executed to obtain various MS-DOS functions. Of these, interrupt 21H is by far the most useful: It is the function-call interrupt that provides general access to nearly all MS-DOS functions. Interrupts 25H and 26H, the absolute disk read/write interface, might occasionally be needed to bypass the usual MS-DOS file interface. The remaining interrupts, 20H and 27H, provide program-termination services in MS-DOS version 1 that were made obsolete by interrupt 21H functions introduced in MS-DOS version 2.0.

Interrupt		
Hex	Dec	Description
20H	32	Program terminate: Come to a normal ending.
21H	33	General MS-DOS functions.
25H	37	Absolute disk read.
26H	38	Absolute disk write.
27H	39	Terminate and stay resident.

Figure B-1. *The five main MS-DOS interrupts.*

Figure B-2 lists the MS-DOS interrupt 21H functions. Functions and services introduced in a given version are supported in subsequent versions but not in earlier versions.

All interrupt 21H functions are called by executing interrupt 21H with a function number in the AH register and other parameters as needed in the other 8086 registers. Most MS-DOS functions return a completion code in the AL or AX register; most of the functions introduced in MS-DOS versions 2.0 and later also use the carry flag to report the success of a function call. See Chapters 10 through 13 for several program examples of interrupt 21H calls.

Function		Description	MS-DOS Version
Hex	Dec		
00H	0	Terminate.	1.0
01H	1	Character input with echo.	1.0
02H	2	Character output.	1.0
03H	3	Auxiliary input.	1.0
04H	4	Auxiliary output.	1.0
05H	5	Printer output.	1.0
06H	6	Direct character input/output.	1.0
07H	7	Direct character input without echo.	1.0
08H	8	Character input without echo.	1.0
09H	9	String output.	1.0
0AH	10	Buffered keyboard input.	1.0
0BH	11	Check keyboard status.	1.0
0CH	12	Flush keyboard buffer, read keyboard.	1.0
0DH	13	Flush disk buffers.	1.0
0EH	14	Select disk drive.	1.0
0FH	15	Open file.	1.0
10H	16	Close file.	1.0
11H	17	Find first matching directory entry.	1.0
12H	18	Find next matching directory entry.	1.0
13H	19	Delete file.	1.0
14H	20	Sequential read.	1.0
15H	21	Sequential write.	1.0
16H	22	Create file.	1.0
17H	23	Rename file.	1.0
19H	25	Get current disk.	1.0
1AH	26	Set DTA address.	1.0
1BH	27	Get default drive information.	1.0
1CH	28	Get specified drive information.	1.0
1FH	31	Get default DPB.	5.0
21H	33	Read random record.	1.0
22H	34	Write random record.	1.0

Figure B-2. *MS-DOS interrupt 21H functions.*   *(continued)*

Figure B-2. *continued*

| Function | | | MS-DOS |
Hex	Dec	Description	Version
23H	35	Get file size.	1.0
24H	36	Set FCB random record field.	1.0
25H	37	Set interrupt vector.	1.0
26H	38	Create new PSP.	1.0
27H	39	Read random records.	1.0
28H	40	Write random records.	1.0
29H	41	Parse filename.	1.0
2AH	42	Get date.	1.0
2BH	43	Set date.	1.0
2CH	44	Get time.	1.0
2DH	45	Set time.	1.0
2EH	46	Set/reset verify flag.	1.0
2FH	47	Get DTA address.	2.0
30H	48	Get MS-DOS version number.	2.0
31H	49	Terminate and stay resident.	2.0
32H	50	Get DPB.	5.0
33H	51	Miscellaneous subfunctions.	2.0
34H	52	Get InDos flag.	5.0
35H	53	Get interrupt vector.	2.0
36H	54	Get disk free space.	2.0
38H	56	Get/set country-dependent information.	2.0
39H	57	Create directory.	2.0
3AH	58	Remove directory.	2.0
3BH	59	Change current directory.	2.0
3CH	60	Create file with handle.	2.0
3DH	61	Open file with handle.	2.0
3EH	62	Close file with handle.	2.0
3FH	63	Read from file or device.	2.0
40H	64	Write to file or device.	2.0
41H	65	Delete file.	2.0
42H	66	Move file pointer.	2.0
43H	67	Get/set file attributes.	2.0
44H	68	IOCTL — I/O control for devices.	2.0

(continued)

Figure B-2. *continued*

Function		Description	MS-DOS Version
Hex	Dec		
45H	69	Duplicate file handle.	2.0
46H	70	Force duplicate file handle.	2.0
47H	71	Get current directory.	2.0
48H	72	Allocate memory block.	2.0
49H	73	Free memory block.	2.0
4AH	74	Resize memory block.	2.0
4BH	75	Load and execute a program.	2.0
4CH	76	Terminate with return code.	2.0
4DH	77	Get return code.	2.0
4EH	78	Find first matching directory entry.	2.0
4FH	79	Find next matching directory entry.	2.0
50H	80	Set PSP address.	5.0
51H	81	Get PSP address.	5.0
54H	84	Get verify flag.	2.0
56H	86	Rename file.	2.0
57H	87	Get/set file date and time.	2.0
58H	88	Get/set memory characteristics.	3.0
59H	89	Get extended error information.	3.0
5AH	90	Create temporary file.	3.0
5BH	91	Create new file.	3.0
5CH	92	Lock/unlock file region.	3.0
5DH	93	Set extended error.	5.0
5EH	94	Network machine name and printer setup.	3.1
5FH	95	Network redirection.	3.1
62H	98	Get PSP address.	3.0
65H	101	Get extended country information.	3.3
66H	102	Get/set global code page.	3.3
67H	103	Set handle count.	3.3
68H	104	Commit file.	3.3
6CH	108	Extended file open/create.	4.0

Long Summary

In the last section, we briefly listed all the MS-DOS functions so that an individual function could be found by its function number. In this section, we have expanded the listing to show the register values passed to and returned from interrupt 21H functions.

Because most new versions of MS-DOS have introduced new functions that cannot be used with earlier versions, Figure B-3 includes the MS-DOS version number in which each function was introduced.

Also note in Figure B-3 that the use of a colon to separate two registers (as in ES:BX) indicates a segmented address. The use of a comma to separate two registers (as in DX, AX) indicates a contiguous bit string in which the high-order half of the bit string is presented in the first register and the low-order half is presented in the second register.

Service	Function (Hex)	Register Input	Output	MS-DOS Version	Notes
Program Control Functions					
Terminate: End program.	00H	AH = 00H CS = segment of PSP		1.0	Obsolete. Use function 4CH instead.
Create new PSP.	26H	AH = 26H DX = segment where new PSP starts		1.0	Obsolete. Use function 4BH instead.
Terminate and stay resident.	31H	AH = 31H AL = return code DX = # of paragraphs to keep resident		2.0	
Get/set Ctrl-C flag.	33H	AH = 33H *To set flag:* AL = 01H DL = value *To get flag:* AL = 00H	*If called with* *AL = 00H:* DL = current value of flag (00 = off, 01 = on)	2.0	
Get InDOS flag.	34H	AH = 34H	ES:BX = address of InDOS flag	5.0	The InDOS flag is nonzero while an interrupt 21H function is active.

Figure B-3. *A summary of the MS-DOS interrupt 21H functions.*

(continued)

Figure B-3. *continued*

Service	Function (Hex)	Register Input	Output	MS-DOS Version	Notes
Load and execute a program.	4BH	AH = 4BH DS:DX → ASCIIZ command line ES:BX → control block *To execute child program:* AL = 00H *To load without executing:* AL = 01 *To load an overlay:* AL = 03H	*If no error:* CF clear *If error:* CF set AX = error code	2.0	Changes all registers, including SS:SP.
Set execution state.	4BH	AH = 4BH AL = 05H DS:DX → control block		5.0	
Terminate with return code.	4CH	AH = 4CH AL = return code		2.0	
Get return code.	4DH	AH = 4DH	AL = return code AH = termination method	2.0	Call only once after calling function 4CH.
Set PSP address.	50H	AH = 50H BX = segment of new PSP		5.0	
Get PSP address.	51H	AH = 51H	BX = segment address of current PSP	5.0	Identical to function 62H.
Get PSP address.	62H	AH = 62H	BX = PSP segment	3.0	Superseded by function 51H.
Standard Input Functions					
Character input with echo.	01H	AH = 01H	AL = 8-bit character	1.0	

(continued)

Figure B-3. *continued*

Service	*Function (Hex)*	*Register* *Input*	*Output*	*MS-DOS Version*	*Notes*
Direct character input without echo.	07H	AH = 07H	AL = 8-bit character	1.0	
Character input without echo.	08H	AH = 08H	AL = 8-bit character	1.0	
Buffered keyboard input.	0AH	AH = 0AH DS:DX → input buffer	Buffer contains keyboard input.	1.0	See Chapter 12 for input buffer format.
Check keyboard status.	0BH	AH = 0BH	*If character available:* AL = FFH *If no character available:* AL = 00H	1.0	
Flush keyboard buffer, read keyboard.	0CH	AH = 0CH AL = function number (01H, 06H, 07H, or 08H)	*(Depends on function specified in AL)*	1.0	

Standard Output Functions

Character output.	02H	AH = 02H DL = 8-bit character		1.0	
String output.	09H	AH = 09H DS:DX → string terminated with '$'		1.0	

Console I/O Functions

Direct character input/output.	06H	AH = 06H *To input a character:* DL = FFH *To output a character:* DL = 8-bit character (00H–FEH)	*If called with DL = FFH:* If character is read, CH = 0 AL = 8-bit character If character is not read, CF = 1	1.0	

(continued)

Figure B-3. *continued*

Service	Function (Hex)	Register Input	Output	MS-DOS Version	Notes
Miscellaneous I/O Functions					
Auxiliary input.	03H	AH = 03H	AL = 8-bit character	1.0	
Auxiliary output.	04H	AH = 04H DL = character		1.0	
Printer output.	05H	AH = 05H DL = character		1.0	
Disk Functions					
Flush disk buffers.	0DH	AH = 0DH		1.0	See also function 68H.
Select disk drive.	0EH	AH = 0EH DL = drive ID	AL = number of drives in system	1.0	In MS-DOS 3.0 and later, AL >= 05H.
Get current disk.	19H	AH = 19H	AL = drive ID	1.0	
Set DTA address.	1AH	AH = 1AH DS:DX → DTA		1.0	
Get default drive information.	1BH	AH = 1BH	*If successful:* AL = sectors per cluster CX = bytes per sector DX = total clusters on disk DS:BX → media ID byte *If unsuccessful:* AL = FFH	1.0	Obsolete. Use function 36H instead.

(continued)

Figure B-3. *continued*

Service	Function (Hex)	Register Input	Output	MS-DOS Version	Notes
Get specified drive information.	1CH	AH = 1CH DL = drive ID	*If successful:* AL = sectors per cluster CX = bytes per sector DX = total clusters on disk DS:BX → media ID byte *If unsuccessful:* AL = FFH	1.0	Obsolete. Use function 36H instead.
Get default DPB.	1FH	AH = 1FH	*If AL = FFH:* invalid default drive or disk error *If AL = 00H:* DS:BX → DPB	5.0	
Set verify flag.	2EH	AH = 2EH AL = value for flag (0 = off, 1 = on) DL = 00H		1.0	Call with DL = 00H in MS-DOS versions prior to 3.0.
Get DTA address.	2FH	AH = 2FH	ES:BX → DTA	2.0	
Get DPB.	32H	AH = 32H DL = drive ID	*If AL = FFH:* invalid specified drive or disk error *If AL = 00H:* DS:BX → DPB	5.0	
Get boot disk.	33H	AH = 33H AL = 05H	DL = startup drive	4.0	1 = drive A, 3 = drive C.
Get disk free space.	36H	AH = 36H DL = drive ID	*If bad drive ID:* AX = FFFFH *If no error:* AX = sectors per cluster	2.0	

(continued)

Figure B-3. *continued*

Service	Function (Hex)	Register Input	Output	MS-DOS Version	Notes
Get disk free space, *continued*			BX = unused clusters CX = bytes per sector DX = total clusters on disk		
Get verify flag.	54H	AH = 54H	AL = value of flag (0 = off, 1 = on)	2.0	

File Management Functions

Service	Function (Hex)	Register Input	Output	MS-DOS Version	Notes
Delete file.	13H	AH = 13H DS:DX → FCB	*If error:* AL = FFH *If no error:* AL = 0	1.0	Obsolete. Use function 41H instead.
Create file.	16H	AH = 16H DS:DX → FCB	*If error:* AL = FFH *If no error:* AL = 00H	1.0	Obsolete. Use function 3CH, 5AH, or 5BH instead.
Rename file.	17H	AH = 17H DS:DX → modified FCB	*If error:* AL = FFH *If no error:* AL = 00H	1.0	Obsolete. Use function 56H instead.
Get file size.	23H	AH = 23H DS:DX → FCB	*If error:* AL = FFH *If no error:* AL = 00H FCB contains file size.	1.0	Obsolete. Use function 42H instead.
Parse filename.	29H	AH = 29H AL = control bits DS:SI → string to parse ES:DI → FCB	AL = 00H No wildcards in filename and extension	1.0	Cannot parse pathnames.

(continued)

Figure B-3. *continued*

Service	Function (Hex)	Register Input	Output	MS-DOS Version	Notes
Parse filename, *continued*			AL = 01H At least one wild-card in filename or extension DS:SI → byte past parsed string ES:DI → FCB		
Create file.	3CH	AH = 3CH CX = attribute DS:DX → ASCIIZ file specification	*If error:* CF set AX = error code *If no error:* CF clear AX = handle	2.0	
Delete file.	41H	AH = 41H DS:DX → ASCIIZ file specification	*If error:* CF set AX = error code *If no error:* CF clear	2.0	
Get/set file attributes.	43H	AH = 43H DS:DX → ASCIIZ file specification *To get attributes:* AL = 00H *To set attributes:* AL = 01H CX = attributes	*If error:* CF set AX = error code *If no error:* CF clear CX = attributes (if called with AL = 00H)	2.0	
Rename file.	56H	AH = 56H DS:DX → old ASCIIZ file specification ES:DI → new ASCIIZ file specification	*If error:* CF set AX = error code *If no error:* CF clear	2.0	Can be used to move a file from one directory to another.

(continued)

Figure B-3. *continued*

Service	Function (Hex)	Register Input	Output	MS-DOS Version	Notes
Get/set file date and time.	57H	AH = 57H BX = handle *To get date and time:* AL = 00H *To set date and time:* AL = 01H CX = time DX = date	*If error:* CF set AX = error code *If no error:* CF clear *If called with* *AL = 00H:* CX = time DX = date	2.0	
Create temporary file.	5AH	AH = 5AH CX = attribute DS:DX → ASCIIZ path followed by 13 empty bytes	*If error:* CF set AX = error code *If no error:* CF clear AX = handle DS:DX → ASCIIZ file specification	3.0	
Create new file.	5BH	AH = 5BH CX = attribute DS:DX → ASCIIZ file specification	*If error:* CF set AX = error code *If no error:* CF clear AX = handle	3.0	
Extended file open/create.	6CH	AH = 6CH BX = mode CX = attributes DX = action DS:SI → address of filename	*If error:* CF set AX = error code *If no error:* CF clear CX = action taken	4.0	See Chapter 10 for details.

File I/O Functions

Service	Function (Hex)	Register Input	Output	MS-DOS Version	Notes
Open file.	0FH	AH = 0FH DS:DX → FCB	AL = result code	1.0	Obsolete. Use function 3DH instead.

(continued)

Figure B-3. *continued*

Service	Function (Hex)	Register Input	Output	MS-DOS Version	Notes
Close file.	10H	AH = 10H DS:DX → FCB	AL = result code	1.0	Obsolete. Use function 3EH instead.
Sequential read.	14H	AH = 14H DS:DX → FCB	AL = result code DTA contains data read.	1.0	Obsolete. Use function 3FH instead.
Sequential write.	15H	AH = 15H DS:DX → FCB DTA contains data to write.	AL = result code	1.0	Obsolete. Use function 40H instead.
Read random record.	21H	AH = 21H DS:DX → FCB	AL = result code DTA contains data read.	1.0	Obsolete. Use function 3FH instead.
Write random record.	22H	AH = 22H DS:DX → FCB DTA contains data to write.	AL = result code	1.0	Obsolete. Use function 40H instead.
Set FCB random-record field.	24H	AH = 24H DS:DX → FCB	FCB contains updated random-record field.	1.0	Obsolete. Use function 42H instead.
Read random records.	27H	AH = 27H CX = record count DS:DX → FCB	AL = result code CX = number of records read DTA contains data read.	1.0	Obsolete. Use function 3FH instead.
Write random records.	28H	AH = 28H CX = record count DS:DX → FCB DTA contains data to write.	AL = result code CX = number of records written	1.0	Obsolete. Use function 40H instead.
Open handle.	3DH	AH = 3DH AL = file access code DS:DX → ASCIIZ file specification	*If error:* CF set AX = error code *If no error:* CF clear AX = handle	2.0	

(continued)

Figure B-3. *continued*

Service	Function (Hex)	Register Input	Output	MS-DOS Version	Notes
Close handle.	3EH	AH = 3EH BX = handle	*If error:* CF set AX = error code *If no error:* CF clear	2.0	
Read from file or device.	3FH	AH = 3FH BX = handle CX = number of bytes to read DS:DX → buffer	*If error:* CF set AX = error code *If no error:* CF clear AX = number of bytes read DS:DX → buffer	2.0	
Write to file or device.	40H	AH = 40H BX = handle CX = number of bytes to write DS:DX → buffer	*If error:* CF set AX = error code *If no error:* CF clear AX = number of bytes written	2.0	
Move file pointer.	42H	AH = 42H BX = handle CX, DX = offset to move pointer *Move relative to start of file:* AL = 00H *Move relative to current location:* AL = 01H *Move relative to end of file:* AL = 02H	*If error:* CF set AX = error code *If no error:* CF clear DX, AX = new file pointer	2.0	
Duplicate file handle.	45H	AH = 45H BX = handle	*If error:* CF set AX = error code *If no error:* CF clear AX = new handle	2.0	See Chapter 10 for details.

(continued)

Figure B-3. *continued*

Service	Function (Hex)	Register Input	Output	MS-DOS Version	Notes
Force duplicate file handle.	46H	AH = 46H BX = handle CX = handle to be forced	*If error:* CF set AX = error code *If no error:* CF clear	2.0	See Chapter 10 for details.
Lock/unlock file region.	5CH	AH = 5CH BX = handle CX, DX = start of region to lock/unlock SI, DI = size of region to lock/unlock *To lock region:* AL = 00H *To unlock region:* AL = 01H	*If error:* CF set AX = error code *If no error:* CF clear	3.0	Use with SHARE or in network environment.
Set handle count.	67H	AH = 67H BX = number of handles	*If error:* CF set AX = error code *If no error:* CF clear	3.3	
Commit file.	68H	AH = 68H BX = handle	*If error:* CF set AX = error code *If no error:* CF clear	3.3	

Directory Functions

Service	Function (Hex)	Register Input	Output	MS-DOS Version	Notes
Find first matching directory entry.	11H	AH = 11H DS:DX → FCB	*If error:* AL = FFH *If no error:* AL = 00H DTA contains directory information.	1.0	Obsolete. Use function 4EH instead.

(continued)

Figure B-3. *continued*

Service	Function (Hex)	Register Input	Output	MS-DOS Version	Notes
Find next matching directory entry.	12H	AH = 12H DS:DX → FCB	*If error:* AL = FFH *If no error:* AL = 00H DTA contains directory information.	1.0	Obsolete. Use function 4FH instead.
Create directory.	39H	AH = 39H DS:DX → ASCIIZ path	*If error:* CF set AX = error code *If no error:* CF clear	2.0	
Remove directory.	3AH	AH = 3AH DS:DX → ASCIIZ path	*If error:* CF set AX = error code *If no error:* CF clear	2.0	
Change current directory.	3BH	AH = 3BH DS:DX → ASCIIZ path	*If error:* CF set AX = error code *If no error:* CF clear	2.0	
Get current directory.	47H	AH = 47H DL = drive ID DS:SI → empty 64-byte buffer	*If error:* CF set AX = error code *If no error:* CF clear DS:SI → ASCIIZ path	2.0	
Find first matching directory entry.	4EH	AH = 4EH CX = attribute DS:DX → ASCIIZ file specification	*If error:* CF set AX = error code *If no error:* CF clear DTA contains directory information.	2.0	

(continued)

Figure B-3. *continued*

Service	*Function (Hex)*	*Register* *Input*	*Output*	*MS-DOS Version*	*Notes*
Find next matching directory entry.	4FH	AH = 4FH DTA contains information from previous call to function 4EH or 4FH.	*If error:* CF set AX = error code *If no error:* CF clear DTA contains directory information.	2.0	

Date/Time Functions

Get date.	2AH	AH = 2AH	AL = day of week CX = year DH = month DL = day	1.0	
Set date.	2BH	AH = 2BH CX = year DH = month DL = day	*If error:* AL = FFH *If no error:* AL = 00H	1.0	
Get time.	2CH	AH = 2CH	CH = hours CL = minutes DH = seconds DL = 100ths of seconds	1.0	
Set time.	2DH	AH = 2DH CH = hours CL = minutes DH = seconds DL = 100ths of seconds	*If error:* AL = FFH *If no error:* AL = 00H	1.0	

Miscellaneous Functions

Set interrupt vector.	25H	AH = 25H AL = interrupt number DS:DX → specified interrupt handler		1.0	

(continued)

Figure B-3. *continued*

Service	Function (Hex)	Register Input	Output	MS-DOS Version	Notes
Get MS-DOS version number.	30H	AH = 30H AL = 01H Return version flag	AH = minor version number AL = major version number BL, CX = serial number BH = version flag	2.0	MS-DOS version 1.0 returns AL = 00H. OS/2 compatibility box returns AL = 0AH.
		AL = 00H Return OEM number	AH = minor version number AL = major version number BL, CX = serial number BH = OEM number		
Get MS-DOS version.	33H	AH = 33H AL = 06H	BL = major version number BH = minor version number DL = revision number DH = version flags	5.0	See Chapter 13 for details.
Get interrupt vector.	35H	AH = 35H AL = interrupt number	ES:BX → specified interrupt handler	2.0	
Get/set country-dependent information.	38H	AH = 38H AL = country code *or* FFH (if AL = FFH) BX = country code *To get country information:* DS:DX → empty 34-byte buffer *To set country information:* DX = FFFFH	*If error:* CF set AX = error code *If no error:* CF clear *If called with DX <> FFFFH:* DS:DX → country information	2.0	Calls with DX = FFFFH or AL = FFH are supported only in MS-DOS versions 3.0 and later. See also function 65H.

(continued)

Figure B-3. *continued*

Service	Function (Hex)	Register Input	Output	MS-DOS Version	Notes
IOCTL—I/O control for devices.	44H	AH = 44H AL = subfunction number *(Other registers depend on subfunction.)*	*If error:* CF set AX = error code *If no error:* CF clear *(Other registers depend on subfunction.)*	2.0	See Chapter 13 for details.
Get device data.	44H	AH = 44H AL = 00H BX = handle	*If error:* CF set AX = error code *If no error:* CF clear DX = device status	2.0	
Set device data.	44H	AH = 44H AL = 01H BX = handle DX = device status	*If error:* CF set AX = error code *If no error:* CF clear	2.0	
Receive control data from character device.	44H	AH = 44H AL = 02H BX = handle CX = number of bytes to receive DS:DX → buffer	*If error:* CF set AX = error code *If no error:* CF clear Buffer contains control data.	2.0	
Send control data to character device.	44H	AH = 44H AL = 03H BX = handle CX = number of bytes to send DS:DX → buffer	*If error:* CF set AX = error code *If no error:* CF clear AX = number of bytes sent	2.0	

(continued)

Figure B-3. *continued*

Service	Function (Hex)	Register Input	Output	MS-DOS Version	Notes
Receive control data from block device.	44H	AH = 44H AL = 04H BL = drive number CX = number of bytes to receive DS:DX → buffer	*If error:* CF set AX = error code *If no error:* CF clear AX = number of bytes received Buffer contains control data.	2.0	
Send control data to block device.	44H	AH = 44H AL = 05H BL = drive number CX = number of bytes to send DS:DX → buffer	*If error:* CF set AX = error code *If no error:* CF clear AX = number of bytes sent	2.0	
Check device input status.	44H	AH = 44H AL = 06H BX = handle	*If error:* CF set AX = error code *If no error:* CF clear AL = 00H Device not ready *or* file pointer at end of file. AL = FFH Device ready *or* file ready.	2.0	
Check device output status.	44H	AH = 44H AL = 07H BX = handle	*If error:* CF set AX = error code *If no error:* CF clear AL = 00H Device not ready *or* file ready. AL = FFH Device ready *or* file ready.	2.0	For an output file, always returns 'ready'.

(continued)

Figure B-3. *continued*

Service	*Function (Hex)*	*Register* *Input*	*Output*	*MS-DOS Version*	*Notes*
Check if device uses removable media.	44H	AH = 44H AL = 08H BL = drive number	*If error:* CF set AX = error code *If no error:* CF clear AX = 0000H Removable media AX = 0001H Nonremovable media	3.0	
Check if drive is remote.	44H	AH = 44H AL = 09H BL = drive number	*If error:* CF set AX = error code *If no error:* CF clear DX = device attribute	3.1	
Check if file or device is remote.	44H	AH = 44H AL = 0AH BX = handle	*If error:* CF set AX = error code *If no error:* CF clear DX = device attribute	3.1	
Set sharing retry count.	44H	AH = 44H AL = 0BH CX = pause-loop count DX = retry count	*If error:* CF set AX = error code *If no error:* CF clear	3.0	Pause time depends on computer's clock speed.
Set iteration count.	44H	AH = 44H AL = 0CH CL = 45H BX = handle CH = device category DS:DX → buffer containing 16-bit iteration count	*If error:* CF set AX = error code *If no error:* CF clear	3.3	

(continued)

Figure B-3. *continued*

Service	Function (Hex)	Register Input	Output	MS-DOS Version	Notes
Select code page.	44H	AH = 44H AL = 0CH CL = 4AH BX = handle CH = device category DS:DX → control block	*If error:* CF set *If no error:* CF clear	3.3	
Start code page prepare.	44H	AH = 44H AL = 0CH CL = 4CH BX = handle CH = device category DS:DX → control block	*If error:* CF set *If no error:* CF clear	3.3	
End code page prepare.	44H	AH = 44H AL = 0CH CL = 4DH BX = handle CH = device category	*If error:* CF set *If no error:* CF clear	3.3	
Set display mode.	44H	AH = 44H AL = 0CH CL = 5FH BX = handle CH = 03H DS:DX → display control block	*If error:* CF set AX = error code *If no error:* CF clear	4.0	ANSI.SYS driver must be loaded prior to using this function.
Get iteration count.	44H	AH = 44H AL = 0CH CL = 65H BX = handle CH = device category DS:DX → buffer	*If error:* CF set AX = error code *If no error:* CF clear Buffer contains 16-bit iteration count.	3.3	

(continued)

Figure B-3. *continued*

Service	Function (Hex)	Register Input	Output	MS-DOS Version	Notes
Query selected code page.	44H	AH = 44H AL = 0CH CL = 6AH BX = handle CH = device category DS:DX → control block	*If error:* CF set *If no error:* CF clear	3.3	
Query code page prepare list.	44H	AH = 44H AL = 0CH CL = 6BH BX = handle CH = device category DS:DX → control block	*If error:* CF set *If no error:* CF clear	3.3	
Get display mode.	44H	AH = 44H AL = 0CH CL = 7FH BX = handle CH = 03H DS:DX → display buffer	*If error:* CF set AX = error code *If no error:* CF clear Display buffer contains display mode.	4.0	ANSI.SYS driver must be loaded prior to using this function.
Set device parameters.	44H	AH = 44H AL = 0DH CL = 40H BX = drive number CH = 08H DS:DX → control block	*If error:* CF set AX = error code *If no error:* CF clear	3.2	
Write track on logical drive.	44H	AH = 44H AL = 0DH CL = 41H BX = drive number CH = 08H DS:DX → control block	*If error:* CF set AX = error code *If no error:* CF clear	3.2	

(continued)

Figure B-3. *continued*

Service	Function (Hex)	Register Input	Output	MS-DOS Version	Notes
Format track on logical device.	44H	AH = 44H AL = 0DH CL = 42H BX = drive number CH = 08H DS:DX → control block	*If error:* CF set AX = error code *If no error:* CF clear	3.2	
Set media ID.	44H	AH = 44H AL = 0DH CL = 46H BX = drive number CH = 08H DS:DX → control block	*If error:* CF set AX = error code *If no error:* CF clear	4.0	
Get device parameters.	44H	AH = 44H AL = 0DH CL = 60H BX = drive number CH = 08H DS:DX → control block	*If error:* CF set AX = error code *If no error:* CF clear Control block filled in with device parameters.	3.2	
Read track on logical drive.	44H	AH = 44H AL = 0DH CL = 61H BX = drive number CH = 08H DS:DX → control block	*If error:* CF set AX = error code *If no error:* CF clear	3.2	Address of data area is one of the fields in the control block.
Verify track on logical drive.	44H	AH = 44H AL = 0DH CL = 62H BX = drive number CH = 08H DS:DX → control block	*If error:* CF set AX = error code *If no error:* CF clear	3.2	

(continued)

Figure B-3. *continued*

Service	Function (Hex)	Register Input	Output	MS-DOS Version	Notes
Get media ID.	44H	AH = 44H AL = 0DH CL = 66H BX = drive number CH = 08H DS:DX → buffer	*If error:* CF set AX = error code *If no error:* CF clear Buffer contains media information.	4.0	
Sense media ID.	44H	AH = 44H AL = 0DH CL = 68H BX = drive number CH = 08H DS:DX → buffer	*If error:* CF set AX = error code *If no error:* CF clear Buffer contains media information.	5.0	
Get logical drive map.	44H	AH = 44H AL = 0EH BL = drive number	*If error:* CF set AX = error code *If no error:* CF clear AL= active drive number for corresponding physical drive	3.2	
Set logical drive map.	44H	AH = 44H AL = 0FH BL = drive number	*If error:* CF set AX = error code *If no error:* CF clear AL = active drive number for corresponding physical drive	3.2	
Query IOCTL handle.	44H	AH = 44H AL = 10H BX = handle CH = category CL = function	*If error:* CF set AX = error code *If no error:* CF clear IOCTL is supported.	5.0	

(continued)

Figure B-3. *continued*

Service	Function (Hex)	Register Input	Output	MS-DOS Version	Notes
Query IOCTL device.	44H	AH = 44H AL = 11H BL = drive number CH = 08H CL = function	*If error:* CF set AX = error code *If no error:* CF clear IOCTL is supported.	5.0	
Get extended error information.	59H	AH = 59H BX = 00H	AX = extended error code BH = error class BL = suggested action CH = location of error	3.0	Alters CL, DX, SI, DI, ES, and DS. See Chapter 13 for details.
Set extended error.	5DH	AH = 5DH AL = 0AH DS:SI = address of error structure		5.0	See Chapter 13 for details.
Get machine name.	5EH	AH = 5EH AL = 00H DS:DX → buffer	*If error:* CF set AX = error code *If no error:* CF clear CX = NETBIOS number, buffer contains network name	3.1	Use in network environment only. See Chapter 10 for details.
Set network printer setup.	5EH	AH = 5EH AL = 02H BX = assign-list index CX = length of setup string DS:DX → printer setup string	*If error:* CF set AX = error code *If no error:* CF clear	3.1	Use in network environment only. See Chapter 10 for details.

(continued)

Figure B-3. *continued*

Service	Function (Hex)	Register Input	Output	MS-DOS Version	Notes
Get network printer setup.	5EH	AH = 5EH AL = 03H BX = assign-list index ES:DI → buffer for printer setup string	*If error:* CF set AX = error code *If no error:* CF clear Buffer is filled in. CX = length of setup string in buffer	3.1	Use in network environment only. See Chapter 10 for details.
Get assign-list entry.	5FH	AH = 5FH AL = 02H BX = assign-list index DS:SI → buffer for local name ES:DI → buffer for network name	*If error:* CF set AX = error code *If no error:* CF clear CX = return value specified in subfunction 03H Name buffers are filled in.	3.1	Use in network environment only. See Chapter 10 for details.
Make network connection.	5FH	AH = 5FH AL = 03H BL = device code CX = user-specified return value DS:SI → buffer for local name ES:DI → buffer for network name	*If error:* CF set AX = error code *If no error:* CF clear	3.1	Use in network environment only. See Chapter 10 for details.
Delete network connection.	5FH	AH = 5FH AL = 04H DS:SI → buffer for local name	*If error:* CF set AX = error code *If no error:* CF clear	3.1	Use in network environment only. See Chapter 10 for details.
Get extended country information.	65H	AH = 65H AL = information ID code	*If error:* CF set AX = error code	3.3	See Chapter 13 for details.

(continued)

Figure B-3. *continued*

Service	Function (Hex)	Register Input	Output	MS-DOS Version	Notes
Get extended country information, *continued*		BX = code page number CX = buffer length DX = country ID ES:DI → buffer	*If no error:* CF clear ES:DI → extended country information		
Get/set global code page.	66H	AH = 66H *To get current code page:* AL = 01H *To set code page:* AL = 02H BX = code page number	*If error:* CF set AX = error code *If no error:* CF clear *If called with AL = 01H:* BX = current code page DX = default code page	3.3	

Memory Functions

Service	Function (Hex)	Register Input	Output	MS-DOS Version	Notes
Allocate memory block.	48H	AH = 48H BX = size of block in paragraphs	*If error:* CF set AX = error code BX = size of largest available block *If no error:* CF clear AX = paragraph address of allocated block	2.0	
Free memory block.	49H	AH = 49H ES = paragraph address of memory block	*If error:* CF set AX = error code *If no error:* CF clear	2.0	

(continued)

Figure B-3. *continued*

Service	Function (Hex)	Register Input	Output	MS-DOS Version	Notes
Resize memory block.	4AH	AH = 4AH BX = new size of memory block in paragraphs ES = paragraph address of memory block	*If error:* CF set AX = error code BX = size of largest available block (if increased size was requested) *If no error:* CF clear	2.0	
Get memory allocation strategy.	58H	AH = 58H AL = 00H	*If error:* CF set AX = error code *If no error:* CF clear AX = strategy code	3.0	See Chapter 13 for details.
Set memory allocation strategy.	58H	AH = 58H AL = 01H	*If error:* CF set AX = error code *If no error:* CF clear	3.0	See Chapter 13 for details.
Get upper memory link.	58H	AH = 58H AL = 02H	*If error:* CF set AX = error code *If no error:* CF clear AL = 01H if upper memory area is linked AL = 00H if upper memory area is not linked	5.0	
Set upper memory link.	58H	AH = 58H AL = 03H BX = link flag (1 = link, 0 = unlink)	*If error:* CF set AX = error code *If no error:* CF clear	5.0	

Appendix C

Hexadecimal Arithmetic

Hexadecimal numbers crop up in computer work for the simple reason that everything a computer does is based on binary numbers, and hexadecimal notation is a convenient way to represent binary numbers.

Hexadecimal numbers are built on a base of 16, exactly as decimal numbers are built on a base of 10; the difference is that hex numbers are written by using 16 symbols whereas decimal numbers are written by using 10 symbols (0 through 9). (From here on out, we'll use the terms *hexadecimal* and *hex* interchangeably.) In hex notation, the symbols 0 through 9 represent the values 0 through 9, and the symbols A through F represent the values 10 through 15. (See Figure C-1.) The hex digits A through F are usually written with capital letters, but you might also see them with the lowercase letters *a* through *f*; the meaning is the same.

Hex numbers are built out of hex digits in the same way that decimal numbers are built. For example, when we write the decimal number 123, we mean the following:

    1 times   100   (10 times 10)
    + 2 times   10
    + 3 times   1

If we use the symbols 123 as a hex number, we mean the following:

    1 times   256   (16 times 16)
    + 2 times   16
    + 3 times   1

There does not seem to be a standard way to write hex numbers, and you might find them expressed differently in different places. Basic uses the prefix *&H* to identify hex numbers, and this notation is sometimes used elsewhere, as well. In C, hexadecimal numbers start with the characters *0x*

Hex	Dec	Hex	Dec	Hex	Dec	Hex	Dec
0	Zero	4	Four	8	Eight	C	Twelve
1	One	5	Five	9	Nine	D	Thirteen
2	Two	6	Six	A	Ten	E	Fourteen
3	Three	7	Seven	B	Eleven	F	Fifteen

Figure C-1. *The decimal values of the 16 hex digits.*

(zero followed by a lowercase *x*). Occasionally the prefix # or *16#* is used, but more often (and throughout this book) a hex number is simply followed by an uppercase or lowercase *H*. Another common way to express hex numbers, especially in reference information, is without any special notation at all. You are expected to understand from the context when a number is written in decimal notation and when it is written in hex. When you see a number in any technical reference information that seems to be a decimal number, check carefully; it might actually be in hex.

When you need to work with hex numbers, you can work with them by hand or you can use interpreted Basic as an aid. (See page 58.) Whichever method you choose, you might find the conversion and arithmetic tables located toward the end of this appendix helpful. But before we get to the tables, let's first see why hex numbers and binary numbers are so compatible and then explore one of the most common uses of hex numbers in PC programming: segmented addressing.

Bits and Hexadecimal

Hex numbers are primarily used as a shorthand for the binary numbers that computers work with. Every hex digit represents 4 bits of binary information. (See Figure C-2.) In the binary (base-2) numbering system, a 4-bit number can have 16 different combinations, so the only way to represent each of the 4-bit binary numbers by using a single digit is to use a base-16 numbering system. (See Figure C-3.)

When you're using 2-byte words, remember the reverse, or "backwords," order in which they are stored in memory. (See Chapter 2, page 34.)

Hex	Bits	Hex	Bits	Hex	Bits	Hex	Bits
0	0000	4	0100	8	1000	C	1100
1	0001	5	0101	9	1001	D	1101
2	0010	6	0110	A	1010	E	1110
3	0011	7	0111	B	1011	F	1111

Figure C-2. *The bit pattern for each of the 16 hex digits.*

			Value	
Bit	Word	Byte	Dec	Hex
0	 1	 1	1	01H
1	. . . . 1.	. . . . . . 1.	2	02H
2	. . . . 1. .	. . . . . 1. .	4	04H
3	. . . . 1. . .	. . . . 1. . .	8	08H
4	. . . . 1. . . .	. . . 1. . . .	16	10H
5	. . . . 1.	. . 1.	32	20H
6	. . . . 1.	. 1.	64	40H
7	. . . . 1.	1.	128	80H
8	. . . . . . 1.		256	100H
9	. . . . . 1.		512	200H
10	. . . . 1.		1024	400H
11	. . . 1.		2048	800H
12	. . . 1.		4096	1000H
13	. . 1.		8192	2000H
14	. 1.		16,384	4000H
15	1.		32,768	8000H

Figure C-3. *The decimal and hexadecimal equivalents of each bit in a 2-byte word and each bit in a byte.*

Segmented Addresses and Hexadecimal Notation

One of the most common uses of hex numbers is for memory addressing. You might recall from Chapters 2 and 3 that a complete 8086 address is 20 bits, or 5 hex digits, wide. Because the 8086 microprocessor can work only with 16-bit numbers, addresses are broken into two 16-bit words, called the *segment* and the *relative offset*. The two parts are written together as 1234:ABCD. The segment is always written first, and both segment and offset are given in hexadecimal form.

The 8086 treats the segment of an address as if it were multiplied by 16, which is the same as if it had an extra hex 0 written after it. The two parts, added together, yield the actual 20-bit address that they represent. For example, the segmented address 1234:ABCD converts into the complete address shown on the opposite page.

```
  1 2 3 4 0     (note the zero added on the right)
+   A B C D
-----------
  1 C F 0 D
```

If you need to calculate the actual address that a segmented address refers to, follow this formula. The addition table on page 583 might also help.

On the 8086, many different segmented addresses correspond to the same location in memory. For example, the address 00400H (where the BIOS keeps its status information) is equally well represented as 0000:0400H and as 0040:0000H. (Of course, this does not hold true in protected mode on an 80286, 80386, or 80486, as we saw in Chapter 2.)

There is no one best way to break an actual 8086 address into its segmented format. One simple way is to take the first digit of the actual 20-bit address followed by three zeros as the segment-paragraph part and the remaining four digits as the relative part. Following this rule, the address above, 1CF0D, would be separated out as 1000:CF0D. IBM's listing for the BIOS in the *IBM PC Technical Reference Manual* follows this convention, so all the relative addresses that appear there have the (unshown) segment of F000.

With real segmented addresses, the segment represents the actual contents of one of the segment registers and could point to nearly anywhere in memory. The relative offset typically varies with usage. Information in executable code and data segments generally starts at a low relative offset. For example, the first instruction of a .COM program is always located at offset 100H in its segment. In contrast, stack segments usually use high relative offsets because stacks grow toward lower addresses.

To see the sort of segmented addresses in use when a program is executed, run the MS-DOS DEBUG program. When DEBUG begins, it gives you a command prompt of –. When you enter the single-letter command D, DEBUG displays part of memory; the addresses on the left are typical segmented addresses.

Decimal-Hexadecimal Conversion

The tables in Figure C-4 show the decimal equivalent of each hex digit in the first five digit positions, which covers the complete address-space arithmetic used in the 8086. As we'll demonstrate, you can use these tables to convert between hexadecimal and decimal numbers.

	First Position				Second Position		
Hex	Dec	Hex	Dec	Hex	Dec	Hex	Dec
. . . . 0	0	 8	8	. . . 0 .	0	. . . 8 .	128
. . . . 1	1	 9	9	. . . 1 .	16	. . . 9 .	144
. . . . 2	2	. . . . A	10	. . . 2 .	32	. . . A .	160
. . . . 3	3	. . . . B	11	. . . 3 .	48	. . . B .	176
. . . . 4	4	 C	12	. . . 4 .	64	. . . C .	192
. . . . 5	5	. . . . D	13	. . . 5 .	80	. . . D .	208
. . . . 6	6	. . . . E	14	. . . 6 .	96	. . . E .	224
. . . . 7	7	. . . . F	15	. . . 7 .	112	. . . F .	240

	Third Position				Fourth Position		
Hex	Dec	Hex	Dec	Hex	Dec	Hex	Dec
. . 0 . .	0	. . 8 . .	2048	. 0 . . .	0	. 8 . . .	32,768
. . 1 . .	256	. . 9 . .	2304	. 1 . . .	4096	. 9 . . .	36,864
. . 2 . .	512	. . A . .	2560	. 2 . . .	8192	. A . . .	40,960
. . 3 . .	768	. . B . .	2816	. 3 . . .	12,288	. B . . .	45,056
. . 4 . .	1024	. . C . .	3072	. 4 . . .	16,384	. C . . .	49,152
. . 5 . .	1280	. . D . .	3328	. 5 . . .	20,480	. D . . .	53,248
. . 6 . .	1536	. . E . .	3584	. 6 . . .	24,576	. E . . .	57,344
. . 7 . .	1792	. . F . .	3840	. 7 . . .	28,672	. F . . .	61,440

	Fifth Position		
Hex	Dec	Hex	Dec
0	0	8	524,288
1	65,536	9	589,824
2	131,072	A	655,360
3	196,608	B	720,896
4	262,144	C	786,432
5	327,680	D	851,968
6	393,216	E	917,504
7	458,752	F	983,040

Figure C-4. *The decimal equivalent of each hex digit position.*

Here is how you use these tables to convert a hex number to a decimal number. Let's use number A1B2H as an example. Look up each hex digit in the table that corresponds to its position, and then add the decimal values:

2	in the first position is	2
B	in the second position is	176
1	in the third position is	256
A	in the fourth position is	40,960
	The total is	41,394

To use these tables to convert a decimal number to hex, the process is equally simple but slightly more complicated to describe. Once again, let's work through an example. We'll use the decimal number 1492.

Work from the table for the fifth position to the table for the first position. In the fifth-position table, find the biggest hex digit with a value that isn't greater than 1492; write down the hex digit; subtract its decimal value from 1492; and continue to the next table with the new value (that is, the difference after subtracting). Go from table to table until the number that remains is 0. The process is shown in Figure C-5. The result is 005D4H, or 5D4H without the leading zeros.

Position	Largest Hex Digit	Decimal Value	Remaining Decimal Number
Starting			1492
5	0	0	1492
4	0	0	1492
3	5	1280	212
2	D	208	4
1	4	4	0
Result	005D4		

Figure C-5. *Converting the decimal number 1492 into a hexadecimal number.*

Using Basic for Hex Arithmetic

One easy way to manipulate hex numbers is to let interpreted Basic do the work. To do this, activate the Basic interpreter and use the command mode (without line numbers) to enter any operations you want to perform. (In MS-DOS versions 5.0 and later, start QBasic and enter the operations you want to perform. Then choose START from the Run menu.)

To display the decimal equivalent of a hex number, such as 1234H, you can simply do this:

```
PRINT &H1234
```

Be sure to prefix any hex number with &H so that Basic knows it is a hex number. To get the best display of decimal numbers, particularly large numbers, use the PRINT USING format, like this:

```
PRINT USING "###,###,###"; &H1234
```

To display the hexadecimal equivalent of a decimal number, such as 1234, you can simply do this:

```
PRINT HEX$( 1234 )
```

The examples so far have used only decimal and hex constants. You can as easily have Basic perform some arithmetic and show the result in decimal or hexadecimal. Here are two examples:

```
PRINT USING "###,###,###"; &H1000 - &H3A2 + 16 * 3
PRINT HEX$(17766 - 1492 + &H1000)
```

By using variables to hold calculated results, you can avoid having to retype an expression or a complicated number. Variables that hold hex numbers should always be written as double-precision variables (with a # at the end of the variable name) for maximum accuracy. For example,

```
X# = 1776 - 1492 + &H100
PRINT USING "###,###,###"; X#, 2 * X#, 3 * X#
```

Hex Addition

To add hex numbers, you work digit by digit, exactly as you do with decimal numbers. To make addition easier, use Figure C-6, which shows the sum of any two hex digits. To use this table, find the row for one hex digit and the column for the other. The hex number located at the intersection of the row and the column is the sum of the two digits.

	0	1	2	3	4	5	6	7	8	9	A	B	C	D	E	F
0	0	1	2	3	4	5	6	7	8	9	A	B	C	D	E	F
1		2	3	4	5	6	7	8	9	A	B	C	D	E	F	10
2			4	5	6	7	8	9	A	B	C	D	E	F	10	11
3				6	7	8	9	A	B	C	D	E	F	10	11	12
4					8	9	A	B	C	D	E	F	10	11	12	13
5						A	B	C	D	E	F	10	11	12	13	14
6							C	D	E	F	10	11	12	13	14	15
7								E	F	10	11	12	13	14	15	16
8									10	11	12	13	14	15	16	17
9										12	13	14	15	16	17	18
A											14	15	16	17	18	19
B												16	17	18	19	1A
C													18	19	1A	1B
D														1A	1B	1C
E															1C	1D
F																1E

Figure C-6. *The addition of two hex numbers.*

Hex Multiplication

To multiply hex numbers, you work digit by digit, as you do with decimal numbers. To make multiplication easier, use Figure C-7, which shows the product of any two hex digits. To use the table, first find the column for one hex digit, and then find the row for the other. The hex number located at the intersection of the column and the row is the product of the two digits.

	0	1	2	3	4	5	6	7	8	9	A	B	C	D	E	F
0	0	0	0	0	0	0	0	0	0	0	0	0	0	0	0	0
1		1	2	3	4	5	6	7	8	9	A	B	C	D	E	F
2			4	6	8	A	C	E	10	12	14	16	18	1A	1C	1E
3				9	C	F	12	15	18	1B	1E	21	24	27	2A	2D
4					10	14	18	1C	20	24	28	2C	30	34	38	3C
5						19	1E	23	28	2D	32	37	3C	41	46	4B
6							24	2A	30	36	3C	42	48	4E	54	5A
7								31	38	3F	46	4D	54	5B	62	69
8									40	48	50	58	60	68	70	78
9										51	5A	63	6C	75	7E	87
A											64	6E	78	82	8C	96
B												79	84	8F	9A	A5
C													90	9C	A8	B4
D														A9	B6	C3
E															C4	D2
F																E1

Figure C-7. *The multiplication of two hex numbers.*

Appendix D

About Characters

PCs use 256 distinct characters. These characters have numeric byte codes with values ranging from 00H through FFH (decimals 0 through 255). The characters are of two types:

- The first 128 characters, 00H through 7FH (decimals 0 through 127), are the *standard ASCII character set.* Most computers handle the standard characters in the same way (with the exception of the first 32 characters — see page 595).

- The last 128 characters, 80H through FFH (decimals 128 through 255), are special characters that make up the *extended ASCII character set.* Each computer manufacturer decides how to use these special characters.

All models of the IBM personal computers use the same extended ASCII character set. Computers that closely mimic the IBM personal computers use this set as well, but other computers often have their own set of special characters. Be aware of this when you convert programs from other computers or when you write PC programs that you plan to convert for use on other computers.

The Standard and Extended Character Sets

The following Basic program, intended for use with GW-BASIC, Basic, or BASICA, displays all 256 characters along with their numeric codes in both decimal and hexadecimal notation. The characters are also listed in Figures D-1 and D-2.

```
1000 ' display all the PC characters
1010 '
1020 MONOCHROME = 1
1030 IF MONOCHROME THEN WW = 80 : HH = &HB000
     ELSE WW = 40 : HH = &HB800
1040 GOSUB 2000                          ' initialize DS register
1050 FOR I = 0 TO 255                     ' for all character codes
1060 GOSUB 3000                           ' display the information
1070 NEXT I
1080 PRINT "Done."
1090 GOSUB 6000
1092 COLOR 0,0,0
1095 SYSTEM
1999 '
2000 ' initialize
2010 '
```

```
2020 DEF SEG = HH                              ' set up DS register for poke
2030 KEY OFF : CLS                             ' set up the screen
2040 WIDTH WW : COLOR 14,1,1
2050 FOR I = 1 TO 25 : PRINT : NEXT I
2060 PRINT " Demonstrating all characters"
2070 GOSUB 5000                                ' periodic subheading
2080 RETURN
2099 '
3000 ' display character information
3010 '
3020 PRINT USING " ###      ";I;
3030 IF I < 16 THEN PRINT "0";
3040 PRINT HEX$(I);"          ";
3050 POKE WW * 2 * 23 + 34, I                  ' insert the character
3060 GOSUB 4000                                ' print any comments
3070 IF (I MOD 16) < 15 THEN RETURN            ' pause after each 16 characters
3080 GOSUB 6000
3090 IF I < 255 THEN GOSUB 5000
3100 RETURN
3997 '
3998 ' character comments
3999 '
4000 IF I =   0 THEN PRINT "shows blank";
4007 IF I =   7 THEN PRINT "beep (bell)";
4008 IF I =   8 THEN PRINT "backspace";
4009 IF I =   9 THEN PRINT "tab";
4010 IF I =  10 THEN PRINT "linefeed";
4012 IF I =  12 THEN PRINT "page eject";
4013 IF I =  13 THEN PRINT "carriage return";
4026 IF I =  26 THEN PRINT "end text file";
4032 IF I =  32 THEN PRINT "true blank space";
4255 IF I = 255 THEN PRINT "shows blank";
4997 PRINT                                     ' finish the line
4998 RETURN
4999 '
5000 ' periodic subheading
5010 '
5020 COLOR 15
5030 PRINT
5040 PRINT
5050 PRINT "Decimal - Hex - Char - Comments"
5060 PRINT
5070 COLOR 14
5080 RETURN
```

(continued)

```
5999 '
6000 ' pause
6010 '
6020 IF INKEY$ <> "" THEN GOTO 6020
6030 PRINT
6040 COLOR 2
6050 PRINT "Press any key to continue..."
6060 COLOR 14
6070 IF INKEY$ = "" THEN GOTO 6070
6080 PRINT
6090 RETURN
```

This Basic program is designed to adjust itself to a monochrome or color video mode based on the value shown in line 1020: 1 (as shown) indicates a monochrome mode; 0 indicates a color mode. The value in line 1020 causes the program to set two values:

■ The location in screen memory at which the POKE command inserts display information

■ The screen width (40 or 80 columns)

The POKE statement in line 3050 causes the characters to appear. This extra step is necessary because a few characters cannot be displayed by the ordinary PRINT statement. See "The First 32 ASCII Characters," page 595, for an explanation.

Each of the 256 characters is visually unique except for ASCII 00H and ASCII FFH (decimal 255), which appear the same as the blank-space character, ASCII 20H (decimal 32).

The version of the Basic program that begins on page 591 is intended for use with the QBasic program provided with MS-DOS versions 5.0 and later and should work with Basic compilers as well.

The program is designed to allow the user to modify the parameter in the statement labeled SETVIDEO by specifying 0 for a monochrome display or 1 for a color display (CGA, EGA, MCGA, VGA, or SVGA) in video mode 6 or lower. The value specified is used to determine the address in screen memory in which the POKE command inserts the characters to be displayed.

The POKE statement, at label CREATEPOKE, is used to insert one character in display memory for each print line. This extra step is necessary because, as mentioned above, a few characters cannot be displayed directly by the PRINT statement.

ASCII	Ctrl	Dec	Hex	ASCII	Dec	Hex	ASCII	Dec	Hex	ASCII	Dec	Hex
	^@	0	00	\<space\>	32	20	@	64	40	`	96	60
☺	^A	1	01	!	33	21	A	65	41	a	97	61
●	^B	2	02	"	34	22	B	66	42	b	98	62
♥	^C	3	03	#	35	23	C	67	43	c	99	63
♦	^D	4	04	$	36	24	D	68	44	d	100	64
♣	^E	5	05	%	37	25	E	69	45	e	101	65
♠	^F	6	06	&	38	26	F	70	46	f	102	66
•	^G	7	07	'	39	27	G	71	47	g	103	67
◘	^H	8	08	(	40	28	H	72	48	h	104	68
○	^I	9	09	)	41	29	I	73	49	i	105	69
◎	^J	10	0A	*	42	2A	J	74	4A	j	106	6A
♂	^K	11	0B	+	43	2B	K	75	4B	k	107	6B
♀	^L	12	0C	,	44	2C	L	76	4C	l	108	6C
♪	^M	13	0D	−	45	2D	M	77	4D	m	109	6D
♫	^N	14	0E	.	46	2E	N	78	4E	n	110	6E
☼	^O	15	0F	/	47	2F	O	79	4F	o	111	6F
►	^P	16	10	0	48	30	P	80	50	p	112	70
◄	^Q	17	11	1	49	31	Q	81	51	q	113	71
↕	^R	18	12	2	50	32	R	82	52	r	114	72
‼	^S	19	13	3	51	33	S	83	53	s	115	73
¶	^T	20	14	4	52	34	T	84	54	t	116	74
§	^U	21	15	5	53	35	U	85	55	u	117	75
▬	^V	22	16	6	54	36	V	86	56	v	118	76
↨	^W	23	17	7	55	37	W	87	57	w	119	77
↑	^X	24	18	8	56	38	X	88	58	x	120	78
↓	^Y	25	19	9	57	39	Y	89	59	y	121	79
→	^Z	26	1A	:	58	3A	Z	90	5A	z	122	7A
←	^[	27	1B	;	59	3B	[	91	5B	{	123	7B
∟	^\	28	1C	<	60	3C	\	92	5C	¦	124	7C
↔	^]	29	1D	=	61	3D	]	93	5D	}	125	7D
▲	^^	30	1E	>	62	3E	^	94	5E	~	126	7E
▼	^_	31	1F	?	63	3F	_	95	5F	△	127	7F

Figure D-1. *The standard ASCII character set.*

ASCII	Dec	Hex	ASCII	Dec	Hex	ASCII	Dec	Hex	ASCII	Dec	Hex
Ç	128	80	á	160	A0	∟	192	C0	α	224	E0
ü	129	81	í	161	A1	⊥	193	C1	β	225	E1
é	130	82	ó	162	A2	⊤	194	C2	Γ	226	E2
â	131	83	ú	163	A3	├	195	C3	π	227	E3
ä	132	84	ñ	164	A4	─	196	C4	Σ	228	E4
à	133	85	Ñ	165	A5	┼	197	C5	σ	229	E5
å	134	86	ª	166	A6	╞	198	C6	μ	230	E6
ç	135	87	º	167	A7	╟	199	C7	τ	231	E7
ê	136	88	¿	168	A8	╚	200	C8	Φ	232	E8
ë	137	89	⌐	169	A9	╔	201	C9	Θ	233	E9
è	138	8A	¬	170	AA	╩	202	CA	Ω	234	EA
ï	139	8B	½	171	AB	╦	203	CB	δ	235	EB
î	140	8C	¼	172	AC	╠	204	CC	∞	236	EC
ì	141	8D	¡	173	AD	═	205	CD	φ	237	ED
Ä	142	8E	«	174	AE	╬	206	CE	ε	238	EE
Å	143	8F	»	175	AF	╧	207	CF	∩	239	EF
É	144	90	░	176	B0	╨	208	D0	≡	240	F0
æ	145	91	▒	177	B1	╤	209	D1	±	241	F1
Æ	146	92	▓	178	B2	╥	210	D2	≥	242	F2
ô	147	93	│	179	B3	╙	211	D3	≤	243	F3
ö	148	94	┤	180	B4	╘	212	D4	⌠	244	F4
ò	149	95	╡	181	B5	╒	213	D5	⌡	245	F5
û	150	96	╢	182	B6	╓	214	D6	÷	246	F6
ù	151	97	╖	183	B7	╫	215	D7	≈	247	F7
ÿ	152	98	╕	184	B8	╪	216	D8	°	248	F8
ö	153	99	╣	185	B9	┘	217	D9	•	249	F9
Ü	154	9A	║	186	BA	┌	218	DA	·	250	FA
¢	155	9B	╗	187	BB	█	219	DB	√	251	FB
£	156	9C	╝	188	BC	▄	220	DC	η	252	FC
¥	157	9D	╜	189	BD	▌	221	DD	²	253	FD
Pt	158	9E	╛	190	BE	▐	222	DE	▪	254	FE
ƒ	159	9F	┐	191	BF	▀	223	DF		255	FF

Figure D-2. *The extended ASCII character set.*

```
' display all the PC characters
'
setvideo:
monochrome = 0
IF monochrome THEN ww = 80: hh = &HB000 ELSE ww = 80: hh = &HB800
GOSUB sub2000                            ' initialize DS register
FOR i = 0 TO 255                         ' for all character codes
GOSUB sub3000                            ' display the information
NEXT i
PRINT "Done."
GOSUB sub6000
COLOR 0, 0, 0
SYSTEM
sub2000:
'
' initialize
'
DEF SEG = hh                             ' set up DS register for POKE
KEY OFF: CLS                             ' set up the screen
WIDTH ww: COLOR 14, 1, 1
FOR i = 1 TO 25: PRINT : NEXT i
PRINT " Demonstrating all characters"
GOSUB sub5000                            ' periodic subheading
RETURN
sub3000:
'
' display character information
'
PRINT USING " ###      "; i;
IF i < 16 THEN PRINT "0";
PRINT HEX$(i); "          ";
createpoke:
POKE ww * 2 * 23 + 34, i                 ' insert the character
GOSUB sub4000                            ' print any comments
IF (i MOD 16) < 15 THEN RETURN           ' pause after each 16 characters
GOSUB sub6000
IF i < 255 THEN GOSUB sub5000
RETURN
sub4000:
'
' character comments
'
IF i = 0 THEN PRINT "shows blank";
IF i = 7 THEN PRINT "beep (bell)";
IF i = 8 THEN PRINT "backspace";
IF i = 9 THEN PRINT "tab";
```

(continued)

591

```
IF i = 10 THEN PRINT "linefeed";
IF i = 12 THEN PRINT "page eject";
IF i = 13 THEN PRINT "carriage return";
IF i = 26 THEN PRINT "end text file";
IF i = 32 THEN PRINT "true blank space";
IF i = 255 THEN PRINT "shows blank";
PRINT                                   ' finish the line
RETURN
sub5000:
'
' periodic subheading
'
COLOR 15
PRINT
PRINT
PRINT "Decimal - Hex - Char - Comments"
PRINT
COLOR 14
RETURN
sub6000:
'
' pause
'
sub6020:
IF INKEY$ <> "" THEN GOTO sub6020
PRINT
COLOR 2
PRINT "Press any key to continue..."
COLOR 14
sub6070:
IF INKEY$ = "" THEN GOTO sub6070
PRINT
RETURN
```

The Character Format

All characters that appear on the display screen are composed of dots drawn within a grid called a *character box* or *character matrix*. (See Figure D-3.) The size of the character box depends on your video hardware as well as on the video mode you're using. For example, the Monochrome Display Adapter (MDA) uses a 9 × 14–character matrix; the text modes on the Color Graphics Adapter (CGA) use 8 × 8 characters; the default 80 × 25 text mode on the Enhanced Graphics Adapter (EGA) uses an 8 × 14–character matrix;

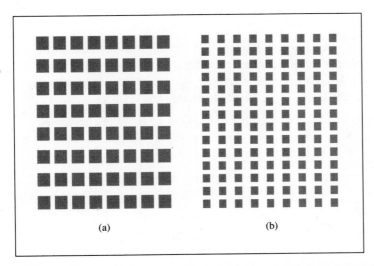

Figure D-3. *The dot-matrix pattern displayed by (a) the Color Graphics Adapter and (b) the Monochrome Display Adapter.*

and the default text modes on the Video Graphics Array (VGA) and the Super Video Graphics Array (SVGA) use 9 × 16 characters. Characters are created by filling, or lighting, the appropriate dots in the grid. The more dots in a grid, the sharper the characters appear.

Dot-matrix printers also draw characters by using a grid of dots. However, each model of printer might have its own particular way of drawing characters that might not exactly match the screen characters dot for dot.

To see how characters appear, look at the three matrices in Figure D-4. They illustrate a *Y*, a *y*, and a semicolon, all using the 8 × 8–character box.

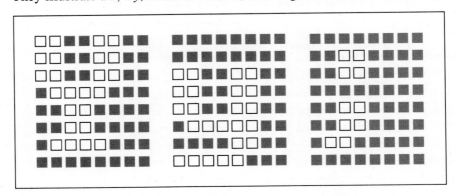

Figure D-4. *The dot pattern of three characters in an 8 × 8–character box.*

Several rules apply to the character drawings:

- For standard characters, the two right columns are unused, which provides separation between characters. These two columns are used only by characters that are supposed to fill the entire character box, such as the solid block character, ASCII DBH (decimal 219).

- The top two rows are used for *ascenders* (the parts of characters that are above the ordinary character height). The ascender space is used for capital letters and for such lowercase letters as *b*, *d*, and *k*.

- The bottom row is used for *descenders* (the parts of characters that drop below the base of ordinary characters), as in the lowercase letters *g* and *y*.

These general guidelines are occasionally compromised for overall effect. For example, the semicolon, our third example in Figure D-4, is shifted up one row from what you might expect so that it does not use the descender row.

The dots that form each character on the screen are placed there by a specialized component of the video subsystem called a *character generator*. The character generator's task is to convert ASCII codes to the corresponding patterns of dots that make up the displayed characters. The character generator accomplishes this by using ASCII codes as an index into a memory-resident bit pattern table that represents the displayed characters' dot patterns.

For example, Figure D-5 shows the table entry for an uppercase *Y* in an 8×8–character box. Note how the pattern of ones and zeros in the character definition corresponds to the pattern of dots displayed for the character.

Bit 7 6 5 4 3 2 1 0	Value (Hex)
1 1 0 0 1 1 0 0	CCH
1 1 0 0 1 1 0 0	CCH
1 1 0 0 1 1 0 0	CCH
0 1 1 1 1 0 0 0	78H
0 0 1 1 0 0 0 0	30H
0 0 1 1 0 0 0 0	30H
0 1 1 1 1 0 0 0	78H
0 0 0 0 0 0 0 0	00H

Figure D-5. *The coding of the 8 character bytes for the Y character.*

In some video modes, you have no control over the bit patterns that define the displayed characters. The MDA's character definitions, for instance, are stored in special ROM chips that can be accessed only by the adapter's character generator circuitry. In many video modes, however, the character definition table resides in RAM, which allows you to redefine the bit patterns used by the character generator and create your own fonts or character sets. (See Chapter 11 for more about RAM-based character definitions.)

The First 32 ASCII Characters

The first 32 ASCII characters, 00H through 1FH (decimals 0 through 31), have two important uses that just happen to conflict with each other. On one hand, these characters have standard ASCII meanings; they are used for both printer control—for example, ASCII 0CH (decimal 12) is the formfeed character—and communications control. On the other hand, PCs also use them for some of the most interesting and useful display characters, such as the card-suit characters (hearts, diamonds, clubs and spades)—ASCII 03H through 06H (decimals 3 through 6)—and the arrow characters (↑, ↓, →, and ←)—ASCII 18H through 1BH (decimals 24 through 27).

When MS-DOS transmits characters to the video screen or to a printer, it acts on the ASCII meaning of the characters instead of showing each character's picture. For example, the beep/bell character, ASCII 07H, has a dot for a picture. However, if you use MS-DOS (or a programming language such as Basic that relies on MS-DOS for output), nothing happens on screen when you try to display this character: Instead, the speaker beeps. But if you put the character directly on the screen by using the POKE command, like this:

```
DEF SEG = &HB800 : POKE 0, 7
```

the character's picture appears. You can always make characters appear on the screen by poking them into the screen buffer. However, it's much easier to use the PRINT statement to display characters. Poke characters directly into the video buffer only if you can't display them by using PRINT.

Most of these 32 characters can be written to the screen, but the display characters might vary, depending upon which language is used. Figure D-6 shows some of these differences. The characters not shown, ASCII 00H through 06H (decimals 0 through 6) and ASCII 0EH through 1BH (decimals 14 through 27), can always be written to the screen with predictable results.

ASCII Character		Result	
Hex	Dec	In Basic	In Most Other Languages
07H	7	Beeps	Beeps
08H	8	Character appears	Backspace action
09H	9	Tab action	Tab action
0AH	10	Linefeed and carriage-return action	Linefeed action
0BH	11	Cursor to top left	Character appears
0CH	12	Screen clears	Character appears
0DH	13	Carriage-return action	Carriage-return action
1CH	28	Cursor moves right a space	Character appears
1DH	29	Cursor moves left a space	Character appears
1EH	30	Cursor moves up a line	Character appears
1FH	31	Cursor moves down a line	Character appears

Figure D-6. *The results obtained when certain characters are written to the screen by using different languages.*

The Box-Drawing Characters

Among the most useful of the extended ASCII characters are the characters designed for drawing single-line and double-line boxes: characters B3H through DAH (decimals 179 through 218). Because they are difficult to combine properly, you might find the information in Figure D-7 helpful.

The Graph and Block Characters

In addition to the box-drawing characters, two series of characters are designed for graphs and block drawings. (See Figure D-8.) One series consists of four characters that fill the entire character box but are shaded in different densities (that is, some of each character's dots are on, or set to the foreground color, and the remaining dots are off, or set to the background color). The other series consists of four block characters that provide a solid color covering half the character box. The solid character, ASCII DBH (decimal 219), is also used with these half-characters.

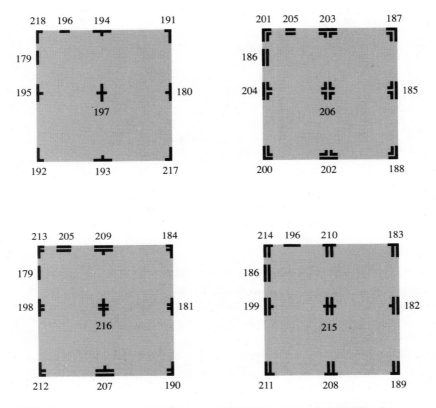

Figure D-7. *The box-drawing characters and their corresponding ASCII codes.*

ASCII 176		ASCII 220	
ASCII 177		ASCII 221	
ASCII 178		ASCII 222	
ASCII 219		ASCII 223	

Figure D-8. *The two sets of graph and block characters.*

Text File Formatting Conventions

Many programs work with files of text. As a result, most programmers have adopted text file formatting conventions that make it easier for text files to be used by different programs. The formats are defined by embedded characters that perform such functions as carriage returns, linefeeds, and backspaces.

When you write a program that reads text files, you can make it more flexible by having it recognize a variety of different text file formats. Conversely, when you design a program to write files with a simple text format, other programs can more easily share your program's output. In this section, we describe the ordinary text format that is recognized by most text-processing programs, and then go on to discuss some of the text formats used in word-processor files.

Ordinary Text File Formats

Ordinary text files are made up of only the standard ASCII characters; they do not use the extended ASCII characters. In the ASCII coding scheme, the first 32 characters, ASCII 00H through 1FH (decimals 0 through 31), have special meanings: Some are used for formatting text, and others are generally used for communications control. These control characters are rarely displayed or printed.

Only a handful of formatting characters are widely used in ordinary text files. They were originally developed as commands to tell a printer how to format a printed page and how to recognize the end of a file. Now their use extends to all output devices. We'll discuss each of the main formatting characters in turn.

ASCII 1AH (decimal 26) marks the true end of a text file. This character might come before the end of the file indicated by the file size in the directory entry. This is because some text-processing programs read and write files not byte by byte but in larger chunks — 128 bytes at a time. When they transfer data in this way, MS-DOS sees only the end of the 128-byte block and does not recognize the actual end of the file delimited by the end-of-file character.

ASCII 0DH (decimal 13) and ASCII 0AH (decimal 10) normally divide a text file into lines by marking the end of each line with a carriage return (ASCII 0DH) and a linefeed (ASCII 0AH), usually in that order. Many text-processing programs have difficulty with lines of more than 255 characters, and some are limited to 80 character lines.

A carriage return can be used by itself. Unfortunately, such usage can be interpreted as either of two things: the end of a line with a linefeed that is implied and automatically provided by some printers; or a return to the beginning of the current print line, which causes the entire line to be overprinted. (The backspace character, ASCII 08H, is also sometimes used to make a printer overstrike a character.)

ASCII 09H (decimal 9), the *tab character,* is sometimes used to represent one or more spaces, up to the tab location. Unfortunately, as yet, there is no universal convention for tab settings, which makes the use of the tab character uncertain. However, one of the most common tab settings is every eight spaces.

ASCII 0CH (decimal 12), the *formfeed* or *page eject character,* is another format character. It tells a printer to skip to the top of the next page.

Other formatting characters, such as the vertical tab (ASCII 0BH, decimal 11), are available but are not widely used with personal computers.

You can avoid many difficulties by having programs create text files with simple formats. The simplest formats allow lines no longer than 255 characters and use only the linefeed (ASCII 0AH, decimal 10), carriage-return (ASCII 0DH, decimal 13), and end-of-file (ASCII 1AH, decimal 26) formatting characters. Many programming languages, including Basic and Pascal, can automatically generate these formatting characters when creating text output.

Most compilers and assemblers expect to read source code in this ordinary, plain format. Rarely can a language translator work with the more complex formats created by some word processors.

Word-Processor Text Formats

Word-processing programs have special needs for formatting text files. The files that these programs create are rarely simple and typically have many exotic additions to the simplest ASCII format. Generally, each word processor has unique formatting rules; luckily, there are some common features.

Many of the special format codes used by word processors are created by using an extended ASCII code that is 128 higher than a normal ASCII code. This is equivalent to setting the high-order bit of an otherwise ordinary byte. For example, a "soft" carriage return, ASCII 8DH (decimal 141), is coded by adding 128 to an ordinary carriage return, ASCII 0DH (decimal 13). A soft carriage return indicates a tentative end of line, which can be changed when a paragraph is reformatted. An ordinary carriage return, on the other hand, marks the end of a paragraph that isn't changed by reformatting. This kind of coding in word-processing text can cause some programs to treat an entire paragraph as a single line.

"Soft" hyphens (ASCII ADH, decimal 173), whose ASCII value is 128 greater than ordinary hyphens (ASCII 2DH, decimal 45), are sometimes used to indicate where a word may be split into syllables at the end of a line. Ordinary "hard" hyphens are treated as regular characters and cannot be used or removed by the word-processing program in the way that soft hyphens can.

Even ordinary alphabetic text can have 128 added to its character code. Some programs do this to mark the last letter in a word. For example, a lowercase *a* is ASCII 61H (decimal 97); but when it appears at the end of a word, as in *America*, it may be stored as ASCII E1H (decimal 225), because 225 is the sum of 97 + 128.

Programs intended to work with a variety of text and word-processing data should be prepared, as much as possible, to cope with the variety of text formats that these examples suggest.

Index

Numbers in *italics* refer to figures or tables.

Peter Norton

Peter Norton was reared in Seattle, Washington, and was educated at Reed College in Portland, Oregon. Before discovering microcomputers, he spent a dozen years working on mainframes and minicomputers for companies including Boeing and Jet Propulsion Laboratories. When the IBM PC made its debut, Norton was among the first to buy one. Now recognized as a principal authority on IBM personal computer technology, he is the founder of Peter Norton Computing and the creator of the Norton Utilities. Norton is also the author of *Inside the IBM PC, Peter Norton's DOS Guide,* and several other programming titles from Brady Books.

Peter Aitken

Peter Aitken is a member of the faculty at Duke University Medical Center, where he uses personal computers in his research. He has written extensively about computer hardware and software, with more than 60 articles and 14 books to his credit. Aitken's books include *The Essential Guide to MS-DOS 5 Programming* and *Microsoft Guide to Visual Basic for MS-DOS,* both published by Microsoft Press.

Richard Wilton

Richard Wilton has been programming computers since the late 1960s. He has written systems software and graphics application programs in FORTRAN, Pascal, C, Forth, and assembly language. His articles and reviews have appeared in several computer publications, including *BYTE* and *Computer Language.* Currently an assistant professor of pediatrics at the University of California, Los Angeles, he earned an M.D. from UCLA and completed his residency in pediatrics at the Childrens Hospital of Los Angeles. He uses Windows and DDE in a patient-tracking database system in the pediatrics clinics at UCLA. Wilton is the author of *Programmer's Guide to PC & PS/2 Video Systems* and *Microsoft Windows 3 Developer's Workshop,* both published by Microsoft Press.

The manuscript for this book was prepared and submitted to Microsoft Press in electronic form. Text files were prepared using Microsoft Word for Windows 2.0.

Principal editorial compositor: Barb Runyan
Principal proofreader/copy editor: Deborah Long
Principal typographer: Carolyn M. Davids
Interior text designer: Kim Eggleston
Principal illustrator: Lisa Sandburg
Photographer: Brian Parks Photography
Cover designer: Rebecca Geisler
Cover color separator: Color Service
Indexer: Shane-Armstrong Information Systems

Text composition by Microsoft Press in Times Roman with display type in Times Roman Bold, using the Magna composition system and the Linotronic 300 laser imagesetter.

Printed on recycled paper stock.

In-Depth References
for Windows™

Programming Windows™ 3.1, 3rd ed.
Charles Petzold

*"If you're going to program for Windows, buy this book.
It will pay for itself in a matter of hours."* **Computer Language**

The programming classic for both new Windows 3.1 programmers
and owners of previous editions. *Programming Windows* is packed with
indispensable reference data, tested programming advice, keen insight,
and page after page of sample programs. This new edition includes two
disks that contain the source code and associated files from the book.
1008 pages, softcover with one 1.44-MB 3.5-inch disk
$49.95 ($67.95 Canada) ISBN 1-55615-395-3

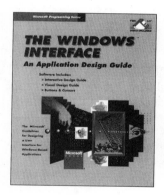

The Windows™ Interface: An Application Design Guide
Microsoft Corporation

Here is the book the developer community has been talking
about, bundled with three eagerly awaited interactive reference tools.
These are the Microsoft guidelines for creating well-designed visually and
functionally consistent user interfaces—an essential reference for all
programmers and designers working in Windows. Software includes a Visual
Design Guide, an Interactive Style Guide, and Cursors and Buttons.
248 pages, softcover with two 1.44-MB 3.5-inch disks
$39.95 ($54.95 Canada) ISBN 1-55615-439-9

Inside Windows NT™
Helen Custer
Foreword by David N. Cutler

Inside Windows NT is the definitive guide to the Microsoft
Windows NT operating system—Microsoft's highly portable, next-generation,
32-bit Windows operating system. It explains the philosophy and design goals
behind the creation of Windows NT, details the architectural models on which
Windows NT is based, and explains the result: what the operating system is,
how it works, and what it offers. Written by a member of the Windows NT design
team, this is the official look at the Windows NT system and a must-buy
book for all system software designers and computer professionals.
416 pages, softcover $24.95 ($32.95 Canada) ISBN 1-55615-481-X